USAMARU
FURUYA

This is the final volume! The kids that appear in *Picasso* are my alter egos. I passed through adolescence with similar worries, so I feel like drawing this story was therapeutic for me.

From *Jump SQ*,
February to September 2009,
plus *Jump SQ II*, volume 3.

**USAMARU FURUYA** made a splash with his 1994 manga debut in the legendary "underground" manga magazine *Garo* with his innovative four–panel series *Palepoli*, which was excerpted in the English–language anthology *Secret Comics Japan*. He also created a gag series called *Short Cuts* for *Young Sunday* magazine, which was later serialized in the English–language manga magazine *Pulp* and then published by VIZ. His other works include *Jisatsu Circle*, a manga adaptation of the film *Suicide Club*; *The Chronicles of the Clueless Age*, a collaboration with the writer Otsuichi; and *Happiness*, a series of shorts that ran in *IKKI* magazine. *Genkaku Picasso* is Furuya's first series for *Jump SQ*.

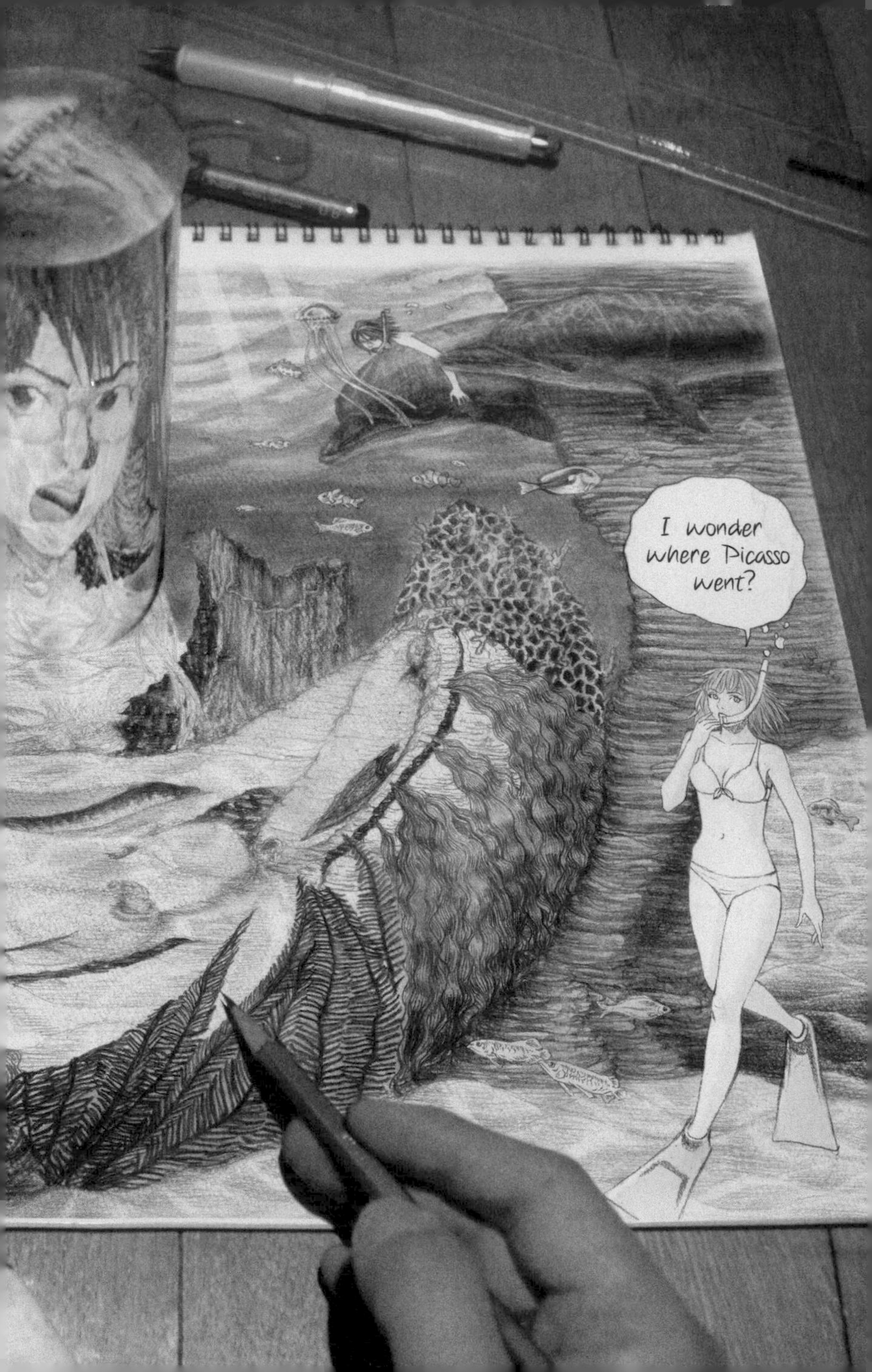
I wonder where Picasso went?

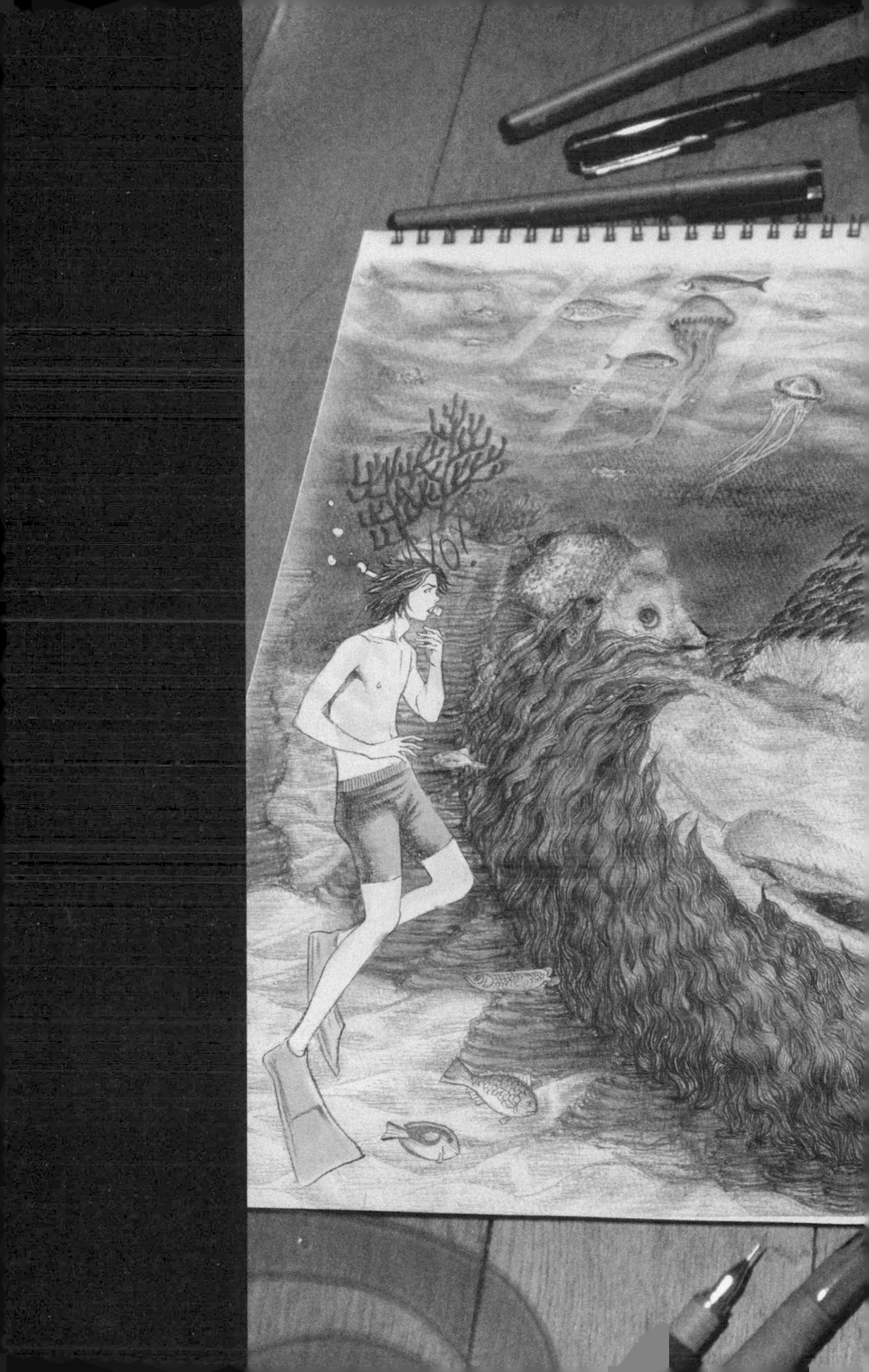

# GENKAKU PICASSO

## VOL. 3

SHONEN JUMP Manga Edition

STORY AND ART BY **USAMARU FURUYA**

Translation – John Werry
Lettering – Bill Schuch
Design – Fawn Lau
Editor – Daniel Gillespie

GENKAKU PICASSO © 2008 by Usamaru Furuya
All rights reserved.
First published in Japan in 2008 by SHUEISHA Inc., Tokyo.
English translation rights arranged by SHUEISHA Inc.

The stories, characters and incidents mentioned in this
publication are entirely fictional.

Printed in the U.S.A.

Published by VIZ Media, LLC
P.O. Box 77010
San Francisco, CA 94107

10 9 8 7 6 5 4 3 2 1
First printing, May 2011

www.viz.com

www.shonenjump.com

SHONEN JUMP MANGA

# GENKAKU PICASSO

USAMARU FURUYA

3

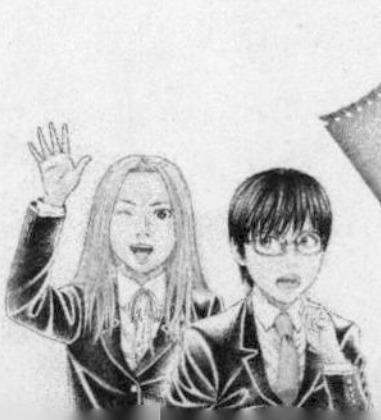

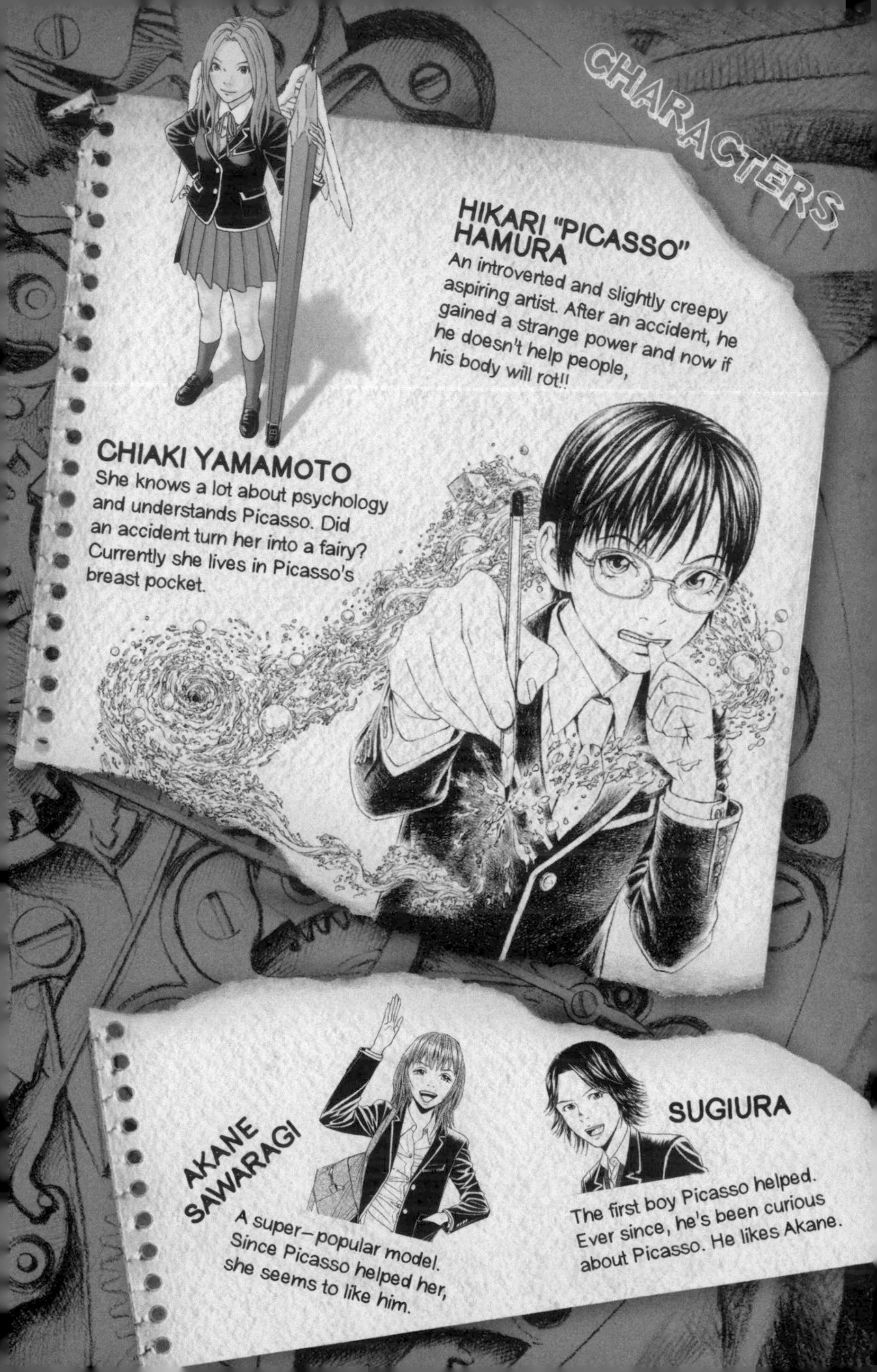
CHARACTERS
HIKARI "PICASSO" HAMURA
An introverted and slightly creepy aspiring artist. After an accident, he gained a strange power and now if he doesn't help people, his body will rot!!
CHIAKI YAMAMOTO
She knows a lot about psychology and understands Picasso. Did an accident turn her into a fairy? Currently she lives in Picasso's breast pocket.
SUGIURA
The first boy Picasso helped. Ever since, he's been curious about Picasso. He likes Akane.
AKANE SAWARAGI
A super-popular model. Since Picasso helped her, she seems to like him.

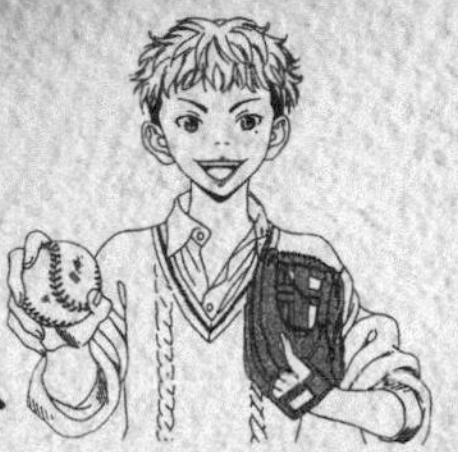

**OTA**

On the baseball team. He's friends with Sugiura, but he's had a rivalry with him ever since they were little.

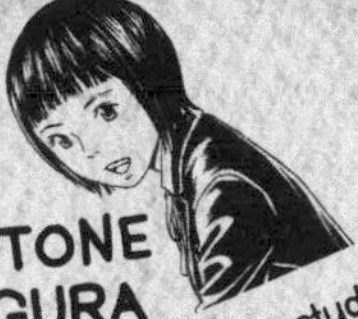

**KOTONE OGURA**

She's an honor student. She likes *Arengurion*. Her father is a famous photographer.

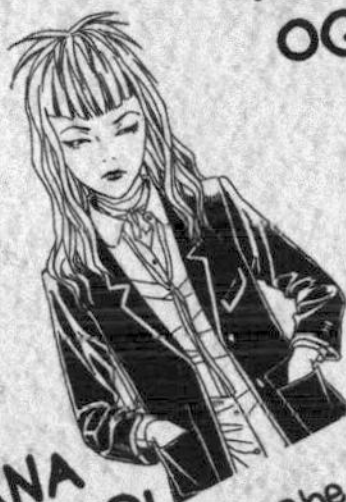

**KANA SAWARAGI**

Akane's little sister. She used to be jealous of Akane. She awakened to music under the influence of a popular Goth singer.

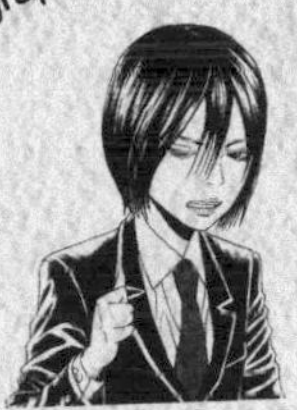

**MANBA**

A boy Picasso helped. He reads *Arengurion* a lot. He likes Kotone.

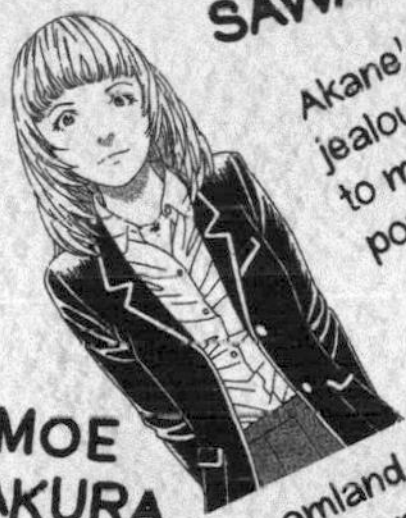

**MOE SAKURA**

A girl whose dreamland is Borise World. She wants to become an teen idol, so she's taking lessons.

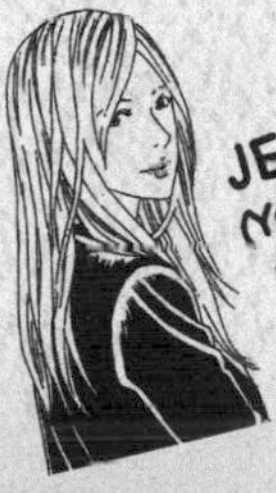

**JEANNE (YOSUKE HISHIDA)**

Born with a boy's body, but a girl inside. His classmates accept that and call him Jeanne.

# THE STORY SO FAR

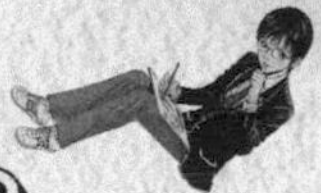

Hikari Hamura, aka Picasso, loves to draw. One day he suffers an accident together with his classmate Chiaki!! He miraculously survives, but afterward, Chiaki, who's supposed to be dead, shows up and tells him that if he doesn't help people he will rot and die. Having gained the mysterious ability to draw what's in people's hearts and to dive into the illustrations, Picasso is confused. But, seeing his arm rot, he reluctantly starts helping people together with Chiaki! The people he helps don't remember it, but they gather around him... Who will he help next?

**GENKAKU PICASSO**

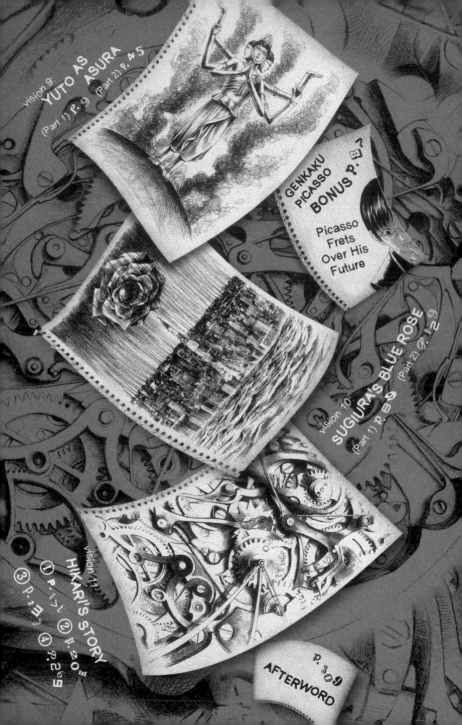

vision 9:
YUTO AS ASURA
(Part 1) P. 9    (Part 2) P. 45

GENKAKU PICASSO BONUS P. 87
Picasso Frets Over His Future

vision 10:
SUGIURA'S BLUE ROSE
(Part 1) P. 89    (Part 2) P. 129

vision 11:
HIKARI'S STORY
① P. 171  ② P. 203
③ P. 237  ④ P. 269

AFTERWORD    P. 309

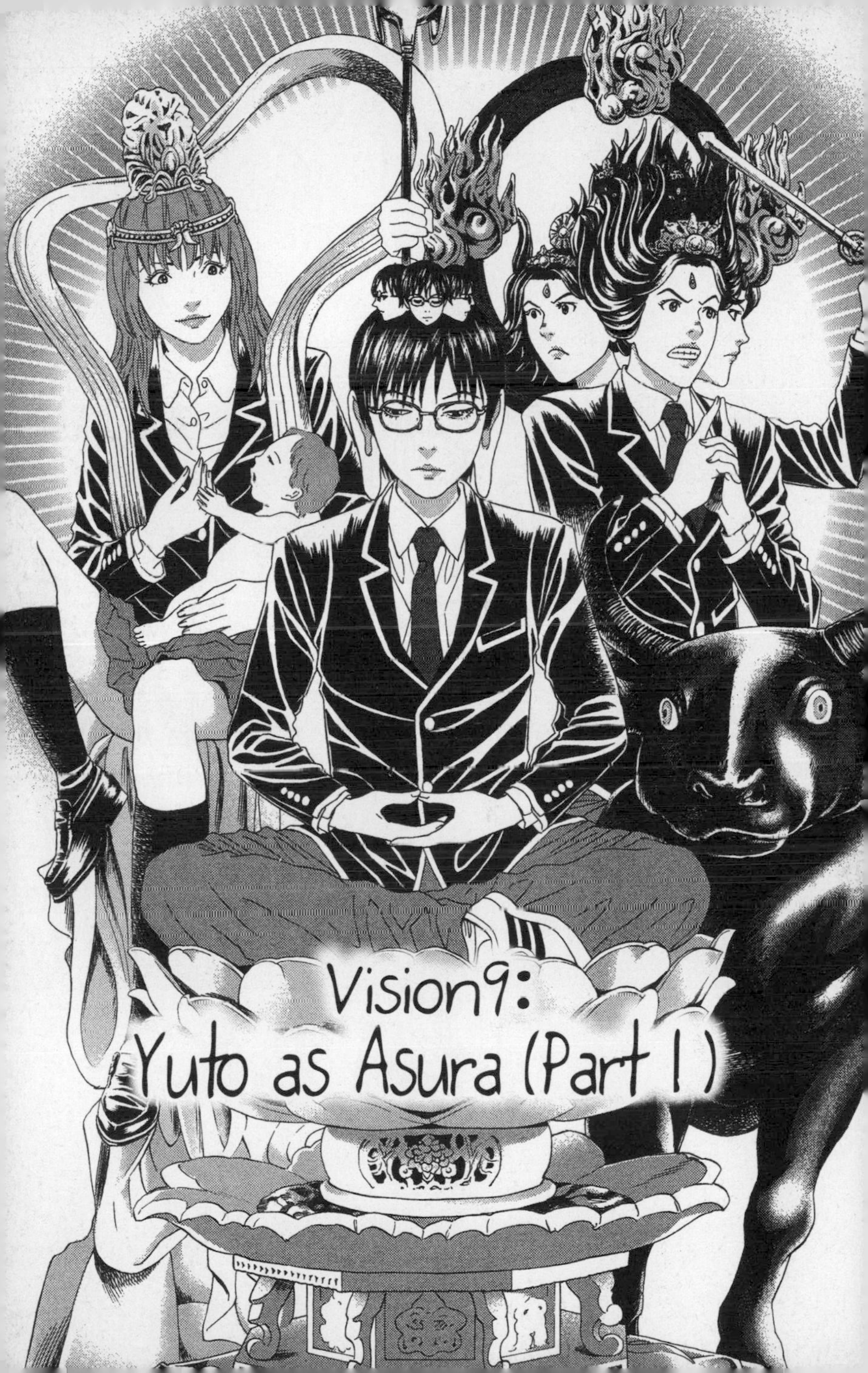
Vision9:
Yuto as Asura (Part 1)

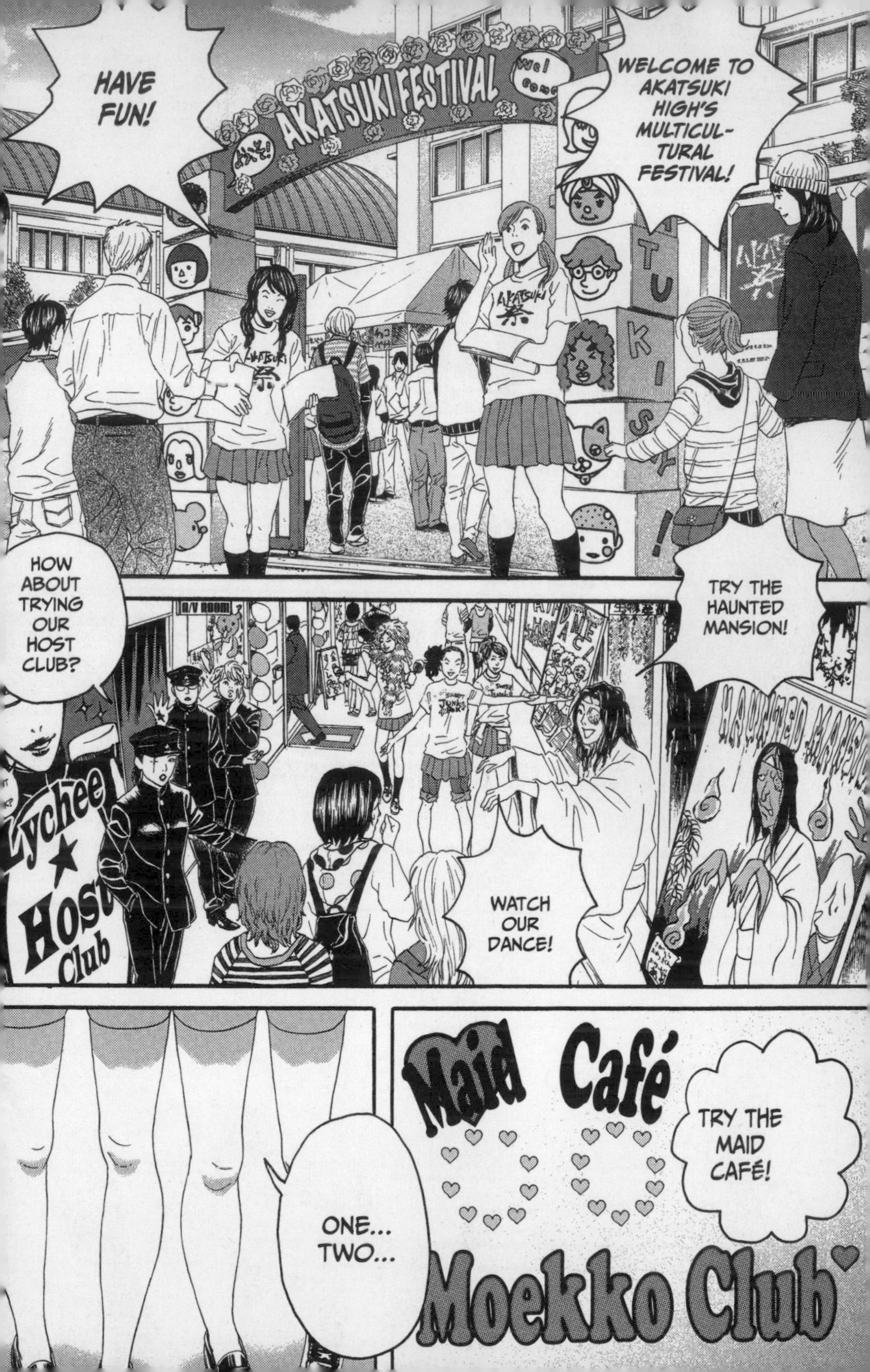
AKATSUKI FESTIVAL
WELCOME TO AKATSUKI HIGH'S MULTICULTURAL FESTIVAL!
HAVE FUN!
TRY THE HAUNTED MANSION!
WATCH OUR DANCE!
HOW ABOUT TRYING OUR HOST CLUB?
Lychee ★ Host Club
Maid Café
TRY THE MAID CAFÉ!
Moekko Club
ONE... TWO...

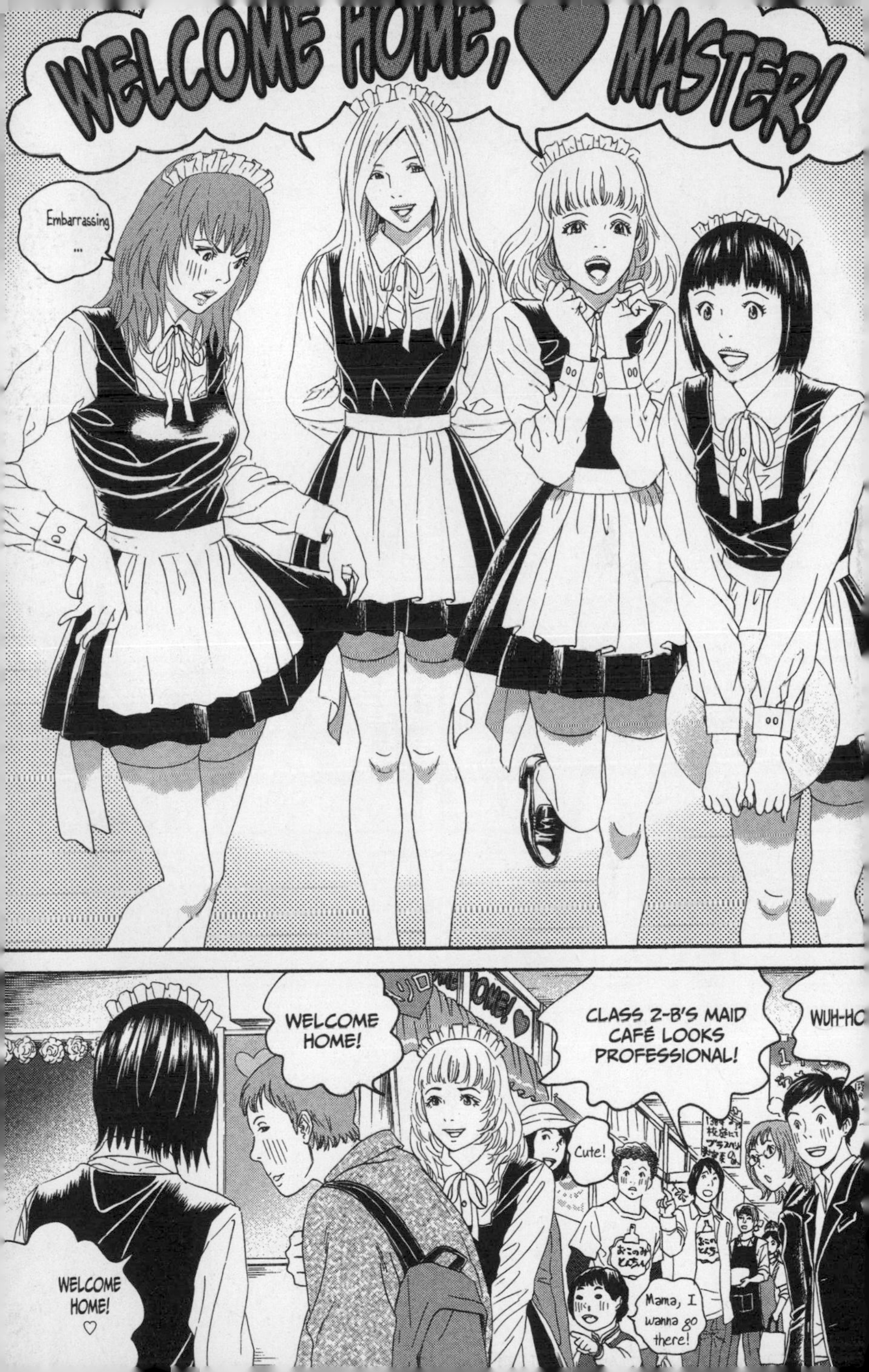
WELCOME HOME, ♥ MASTER!
Embarrassing ...
WUH-HO
CLASS 2-B'S MAID CAFÉ LOOKS PROFESSIONAL!
WELCOME HOME!
Cute!
Mama, I wanna go there!
WELCOME HOME! ♡

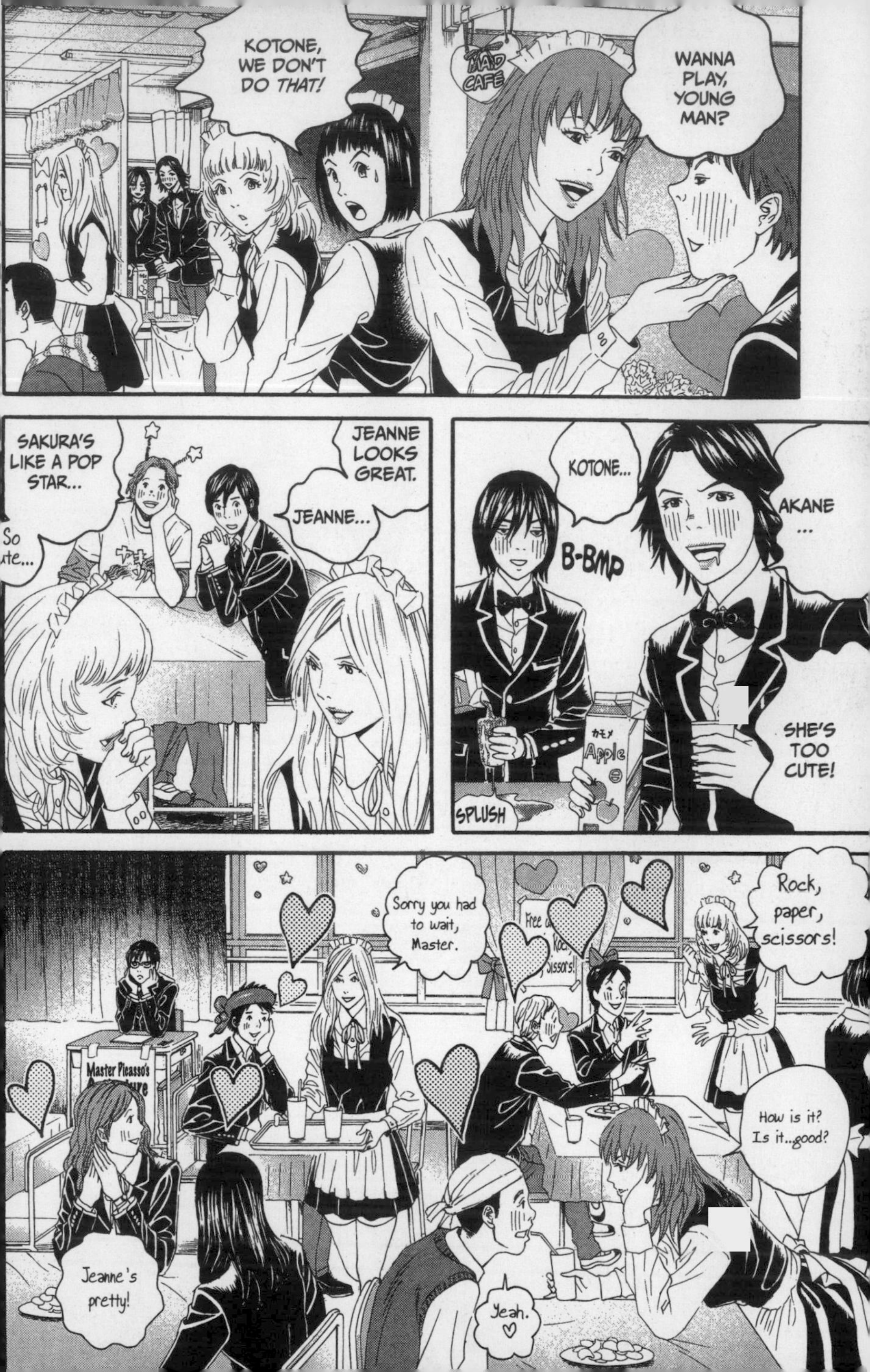
MAID CAFE
WANNA PLAY, YOUNG MAN?
KOTONE, WE DON'T DO THAT!
AKANE ...
KOTONE...
B-BMP
SHE'S TOO CUTE!
カモメ Apple
SPLUSH
JEANNE LOOKS GREAT.
JEANNE...
SAKURA'S LIKE A POP STAR...
Rock, paper, scissors!
How is it? Is it...good?
Sorry you had to wait, Master.
Master Picasso's
Yeah. ♡
Jeanne's pretty!

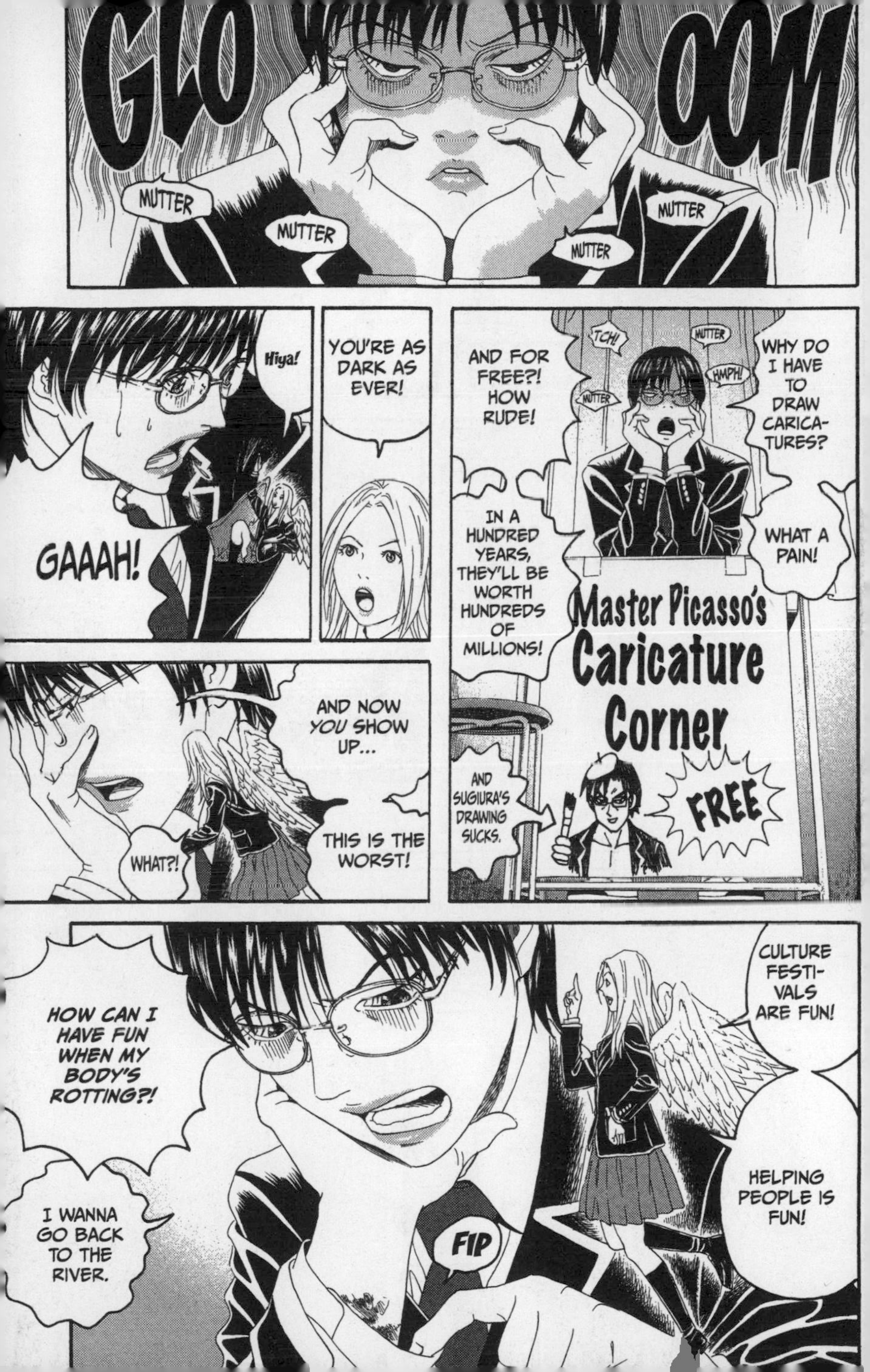
GLO OOM
MUTTER
MUTTER
MUTTER
MUTTER
WHY DO I HAVE TO DRAW CARICA-TURES?
TCH!
MUTTER
HMPH!
MUTTER
AND FOR FREE?! HOW RUDE!
WHAT A PAIN!
IN A HUNDRED YEARS, THEY'LL BE WORTH HUNDREDS OF MILLIONS!
Master Picasso's Caricature Corner
FREE
AND SUGIURA'S DRAWING SUCKS.
YOU'RE AS DARK AS EVER!
Hiya!
GAAAH!
AND NOW YOU SHOW UP...
THIS IS THE WORST!
WHAT?!
CULTURE FESTI-VALS ARE FUN!
HELPING PEOPLE IS FUN!
HOW CAN I HAVE FUN WHEN MY BODY'S ROTTING?!
FIP
I WANNA GO BACK TO THE RIVER.

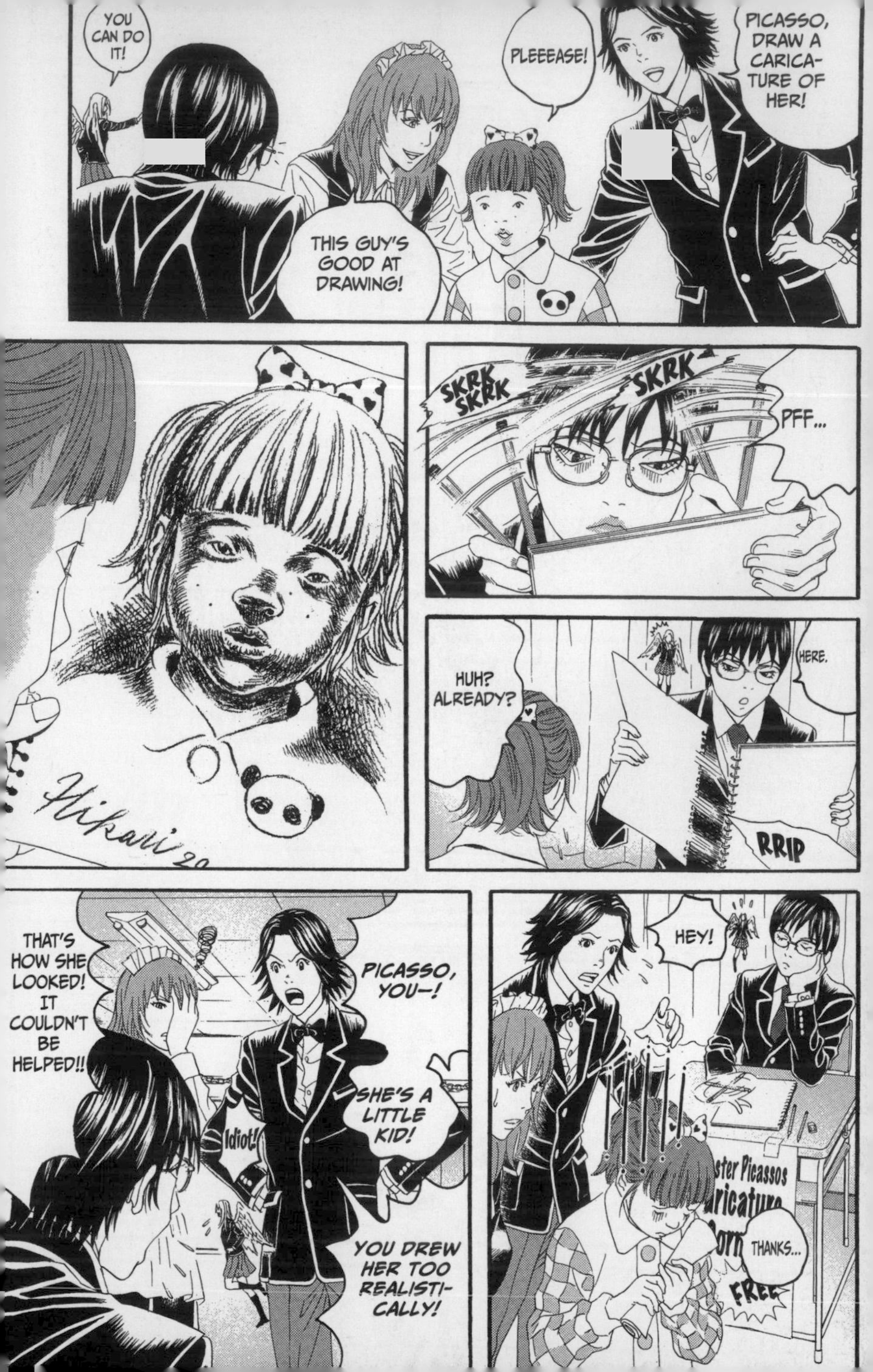
PICASSO, DRAW A CARICATURE OF HER!
PLEEEASE!
YOU CAN DO IT!
THIS GUY'S GOOD AT DRAWING!
SKRK SKRK
SKRK
PFF...
HERE.
HUH? ALREADY?
RRIP
Hikari
HEY!
THANKS...
PICASSO, YOU–!
SHE'S A LITTLE KID!
YOU DREW HER TOO REALISTICALLY!
THAT'S HOW SHE LOOKED! IT COULDN'T BE HELPED!!
Idiot!

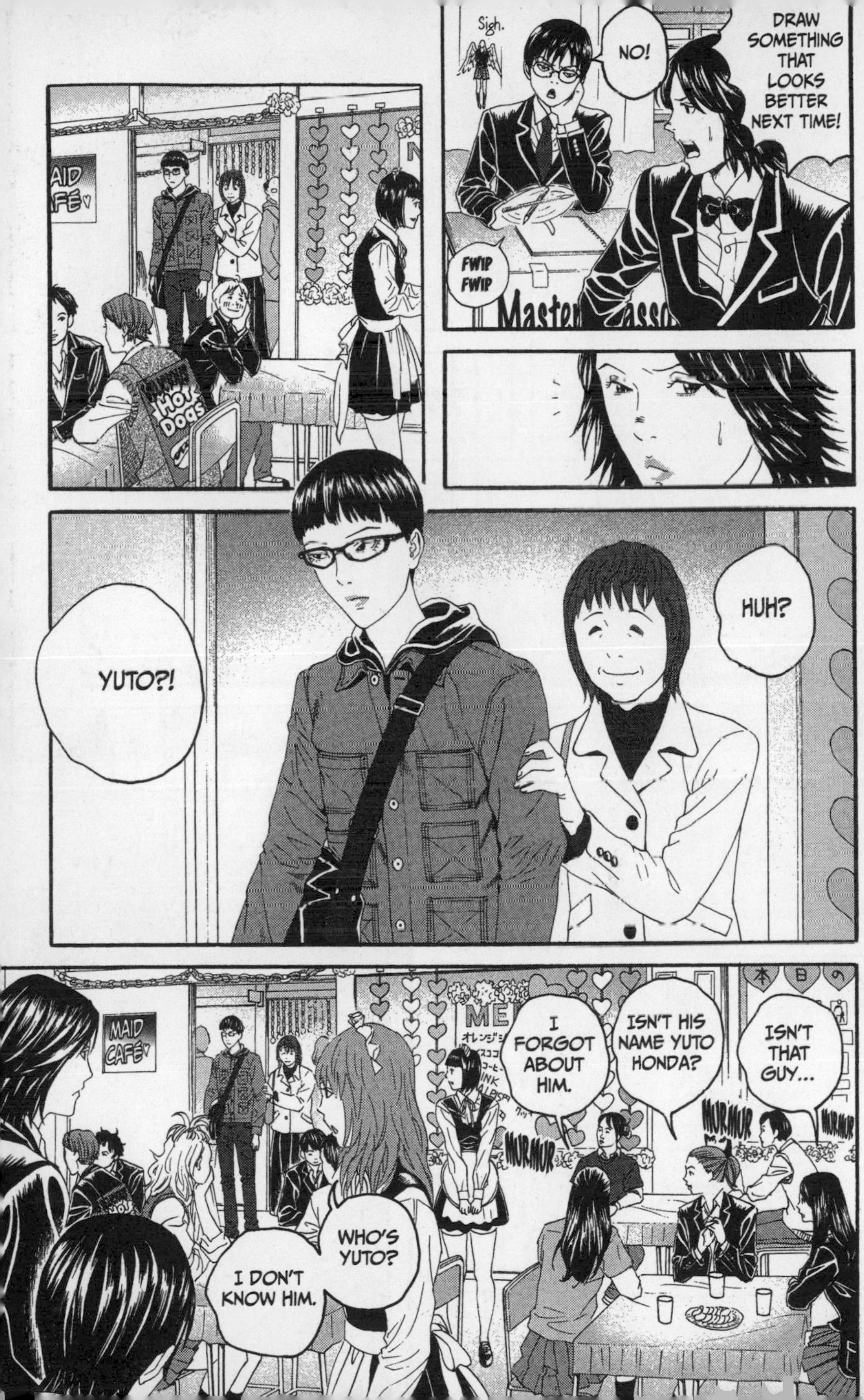
DRAW SOMETHING THAT LOOKS BETTER NEXT TIME!
NO!
Sigh.
FWIP FWIP
MAID CAFÉ
Hot Dogs
HUH?
YUTO?!
ISN'T THAT GUY...
MURMUR
ISN'T HIS NAME YUTO HONDA?
I FORGOT ABOUT HIM.
MURMUR
MURMUR
MAID CAFÉ
WHO'S YUTO?
I DON'T KNOW HIM.

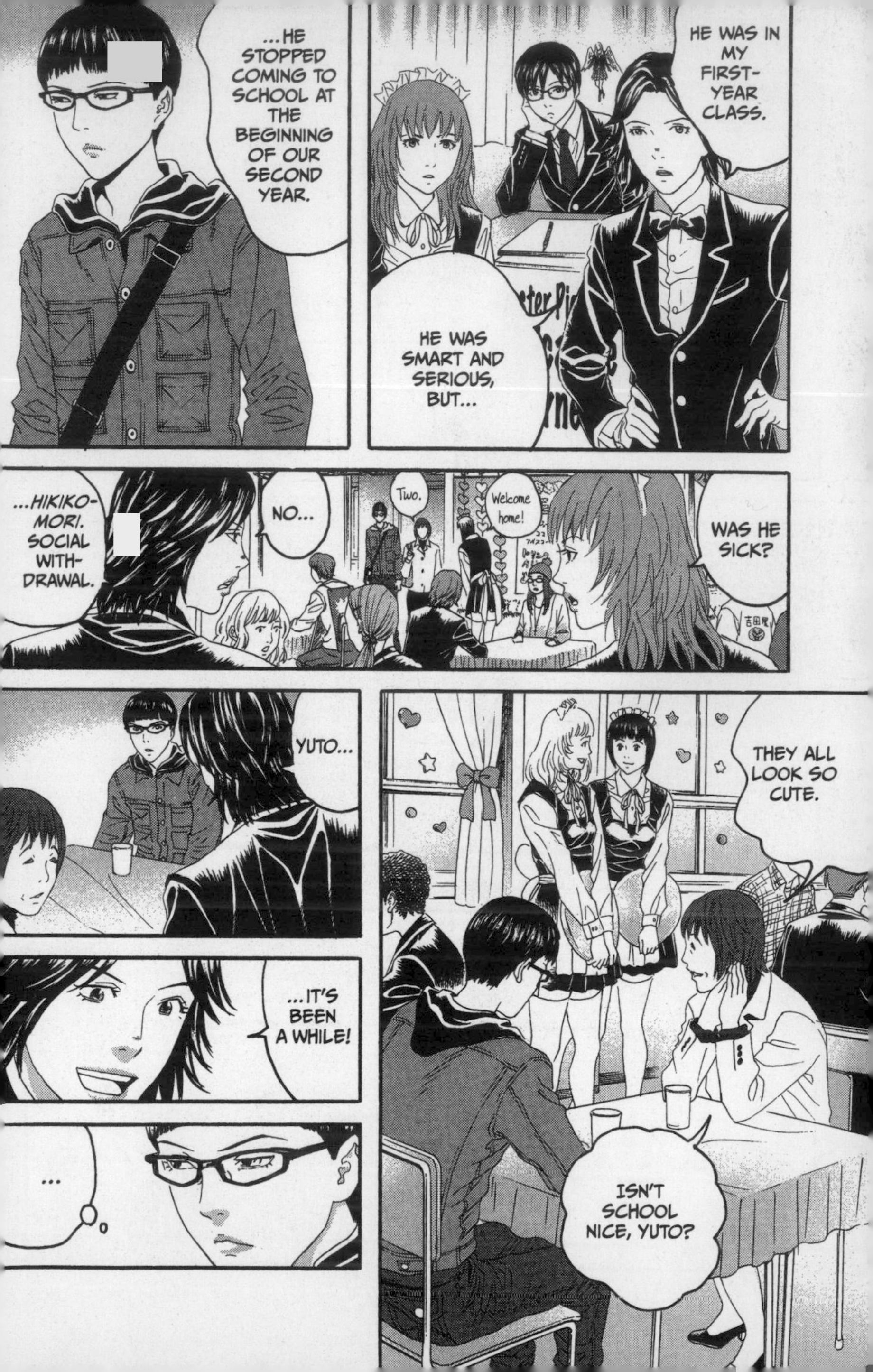
HE WAS IN MY FIRST-YEAR CLASS.
HE WAS SMART AND SERIOUS, BUT...
...HE STOPPED COMING TO SCHOOL AT THE BEGINNING OF OUR SECOND YEAR.
WAS HE SICK?
Welcome home!
Two.
NO...
...HIKIKOMORI. SOCIAL WITHDRAWAL.
THEY ALL LOOK SO CUTE.
ISN'T SCHOOL NICE, YUTO?
YUTO...
...IT'S BEEN A WHILE!
...

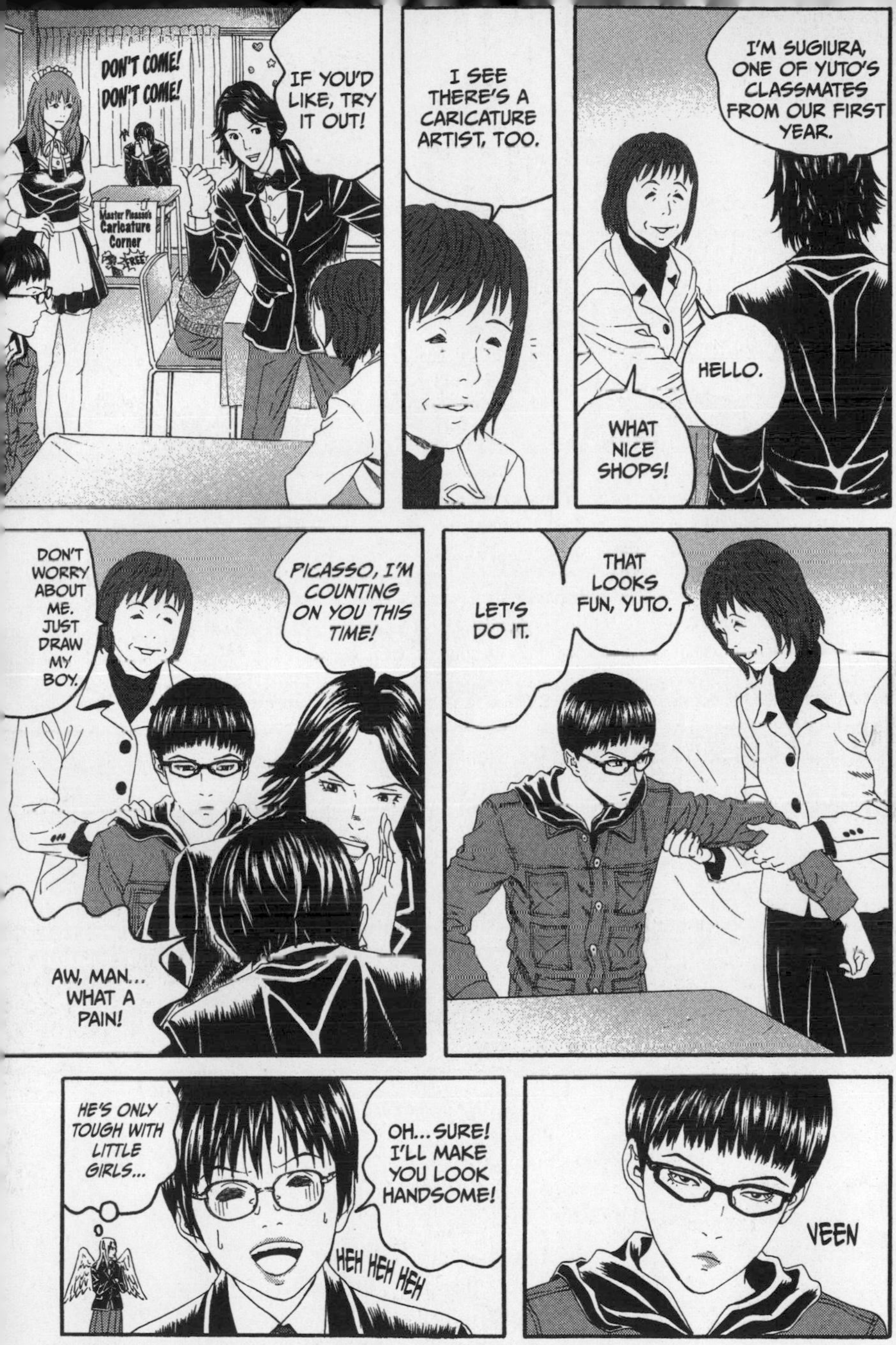
I'M SUGIURA, ONE OF YUTO'S CLASSMATES FROM OUR FIRST YEAR.
HELLO.
WHAT NICE SHOPS!
I SEE THERE'S A CARICATURE ARTIST, TOO.
IF YOU'D LIKE, TRY IT OUT!
DON'T COME! DON'T COME!
Master Picasso's Caricature Corner
FREE
THAT LOOKS FUN, YUTO.
LET'S DO IT.
PICASSO, I'M COUNTING ON YOU THIS TIME!
DON'T WORRY ABOUT ME. JUST DRAW MY BOY.
AW, MAN... WHAT A PAIN!
VEEN
OH...SURE! I'LL MAKE YOU LOOK HANDSOME!
HE'S ONLY TOUGH WITH LITTLE GIRLS...
HEH HEH HEH

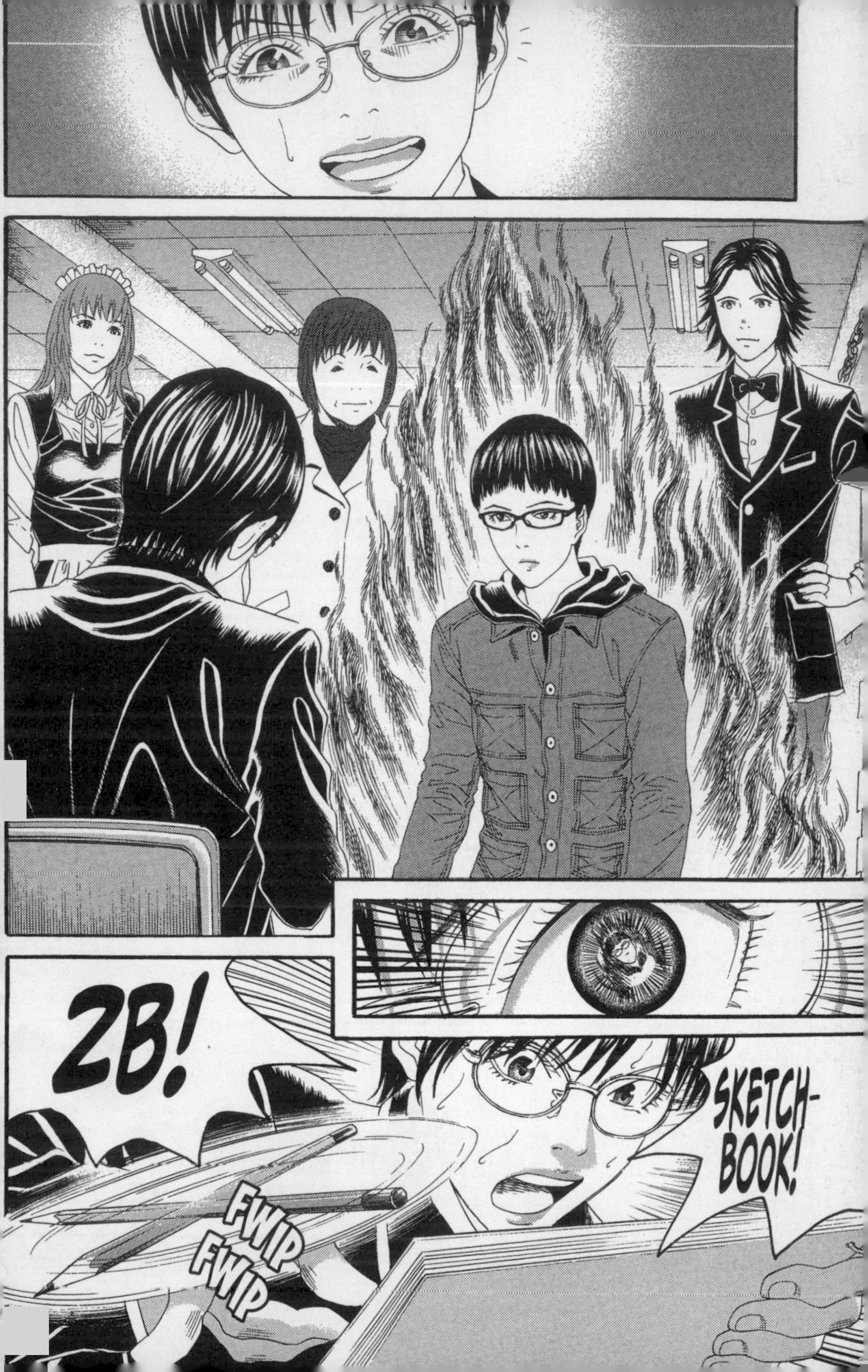

SKETCH-BOOK!
2B!
FWIP FWIP

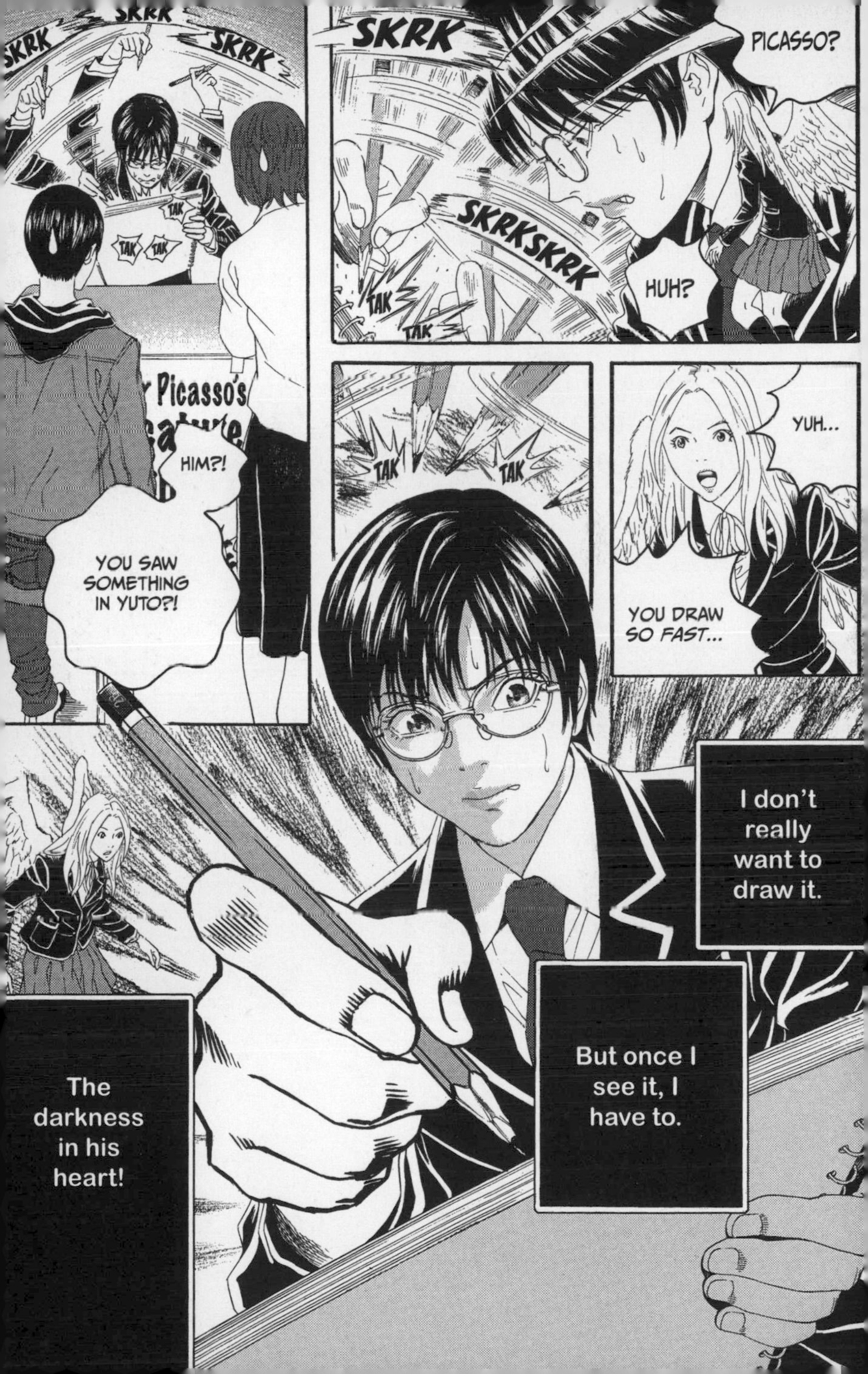

SKRK
PICASSO?
SKRKSKRK
TAK
TAK
HUH?
YUH...
YOU DRAW SO FAST...
TAK
TAK
SKRK
SKRK
SKRK
TAK
TAK
TAK
Picasso's
HIM?!
YOU SAW SOMETHING IN YUTO?!
I don't really want to draw it.
But once I see it, I have to.
The darkness in his heart!

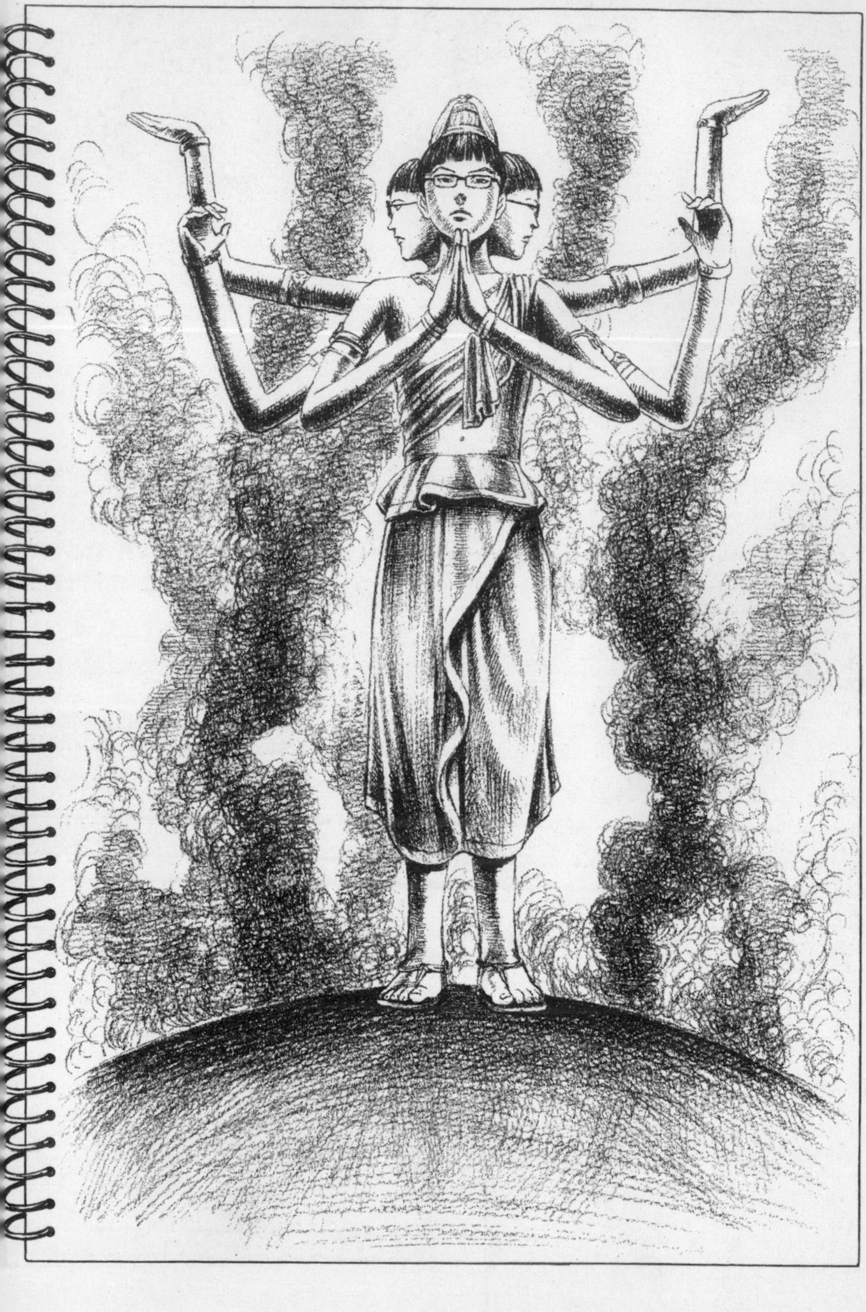

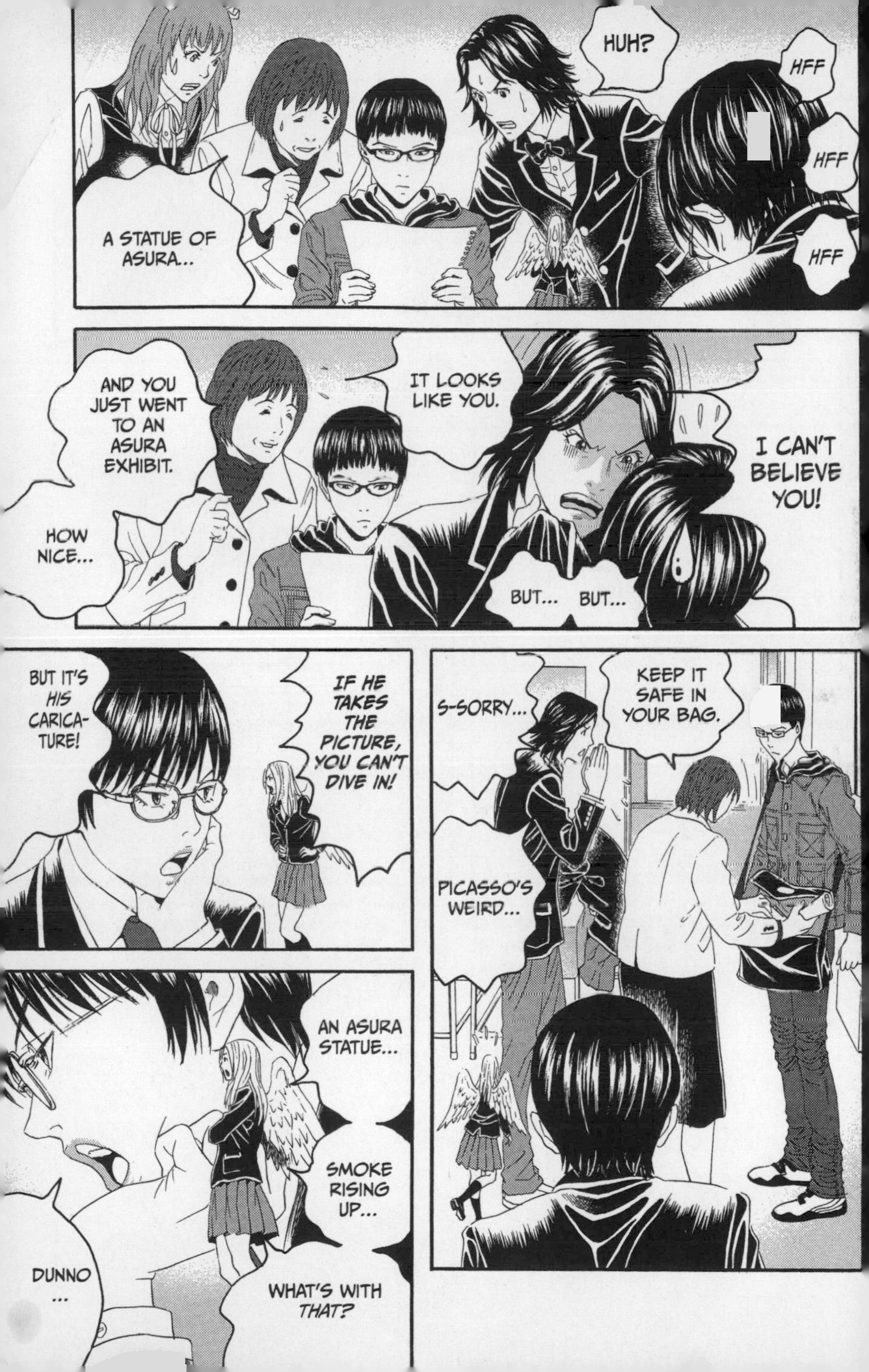
HFF
HFF
HFF
HUH?
A STATUE OF ASURA...
I CAN'T BELIEVE YOU!
BUT... BUT...
IT LOOKS LIKE YOU.
AND YOU JUST WENT TO AN ASURA EXHIBIT.
HOW NICE...
KEEP IT SAFE IN YOUR BAG.
S-SORRY...
PICASSO'S WEIRD...
*IF HE TAKES THE PICTURE, YOU CAN'T DIVE IN!*
BUT IT'S *HIS* CARICATURE!
AN ASURA STATUE...
SMOKE RISING UP...
WHAT'S WITH *THAT?*
DUNNO...

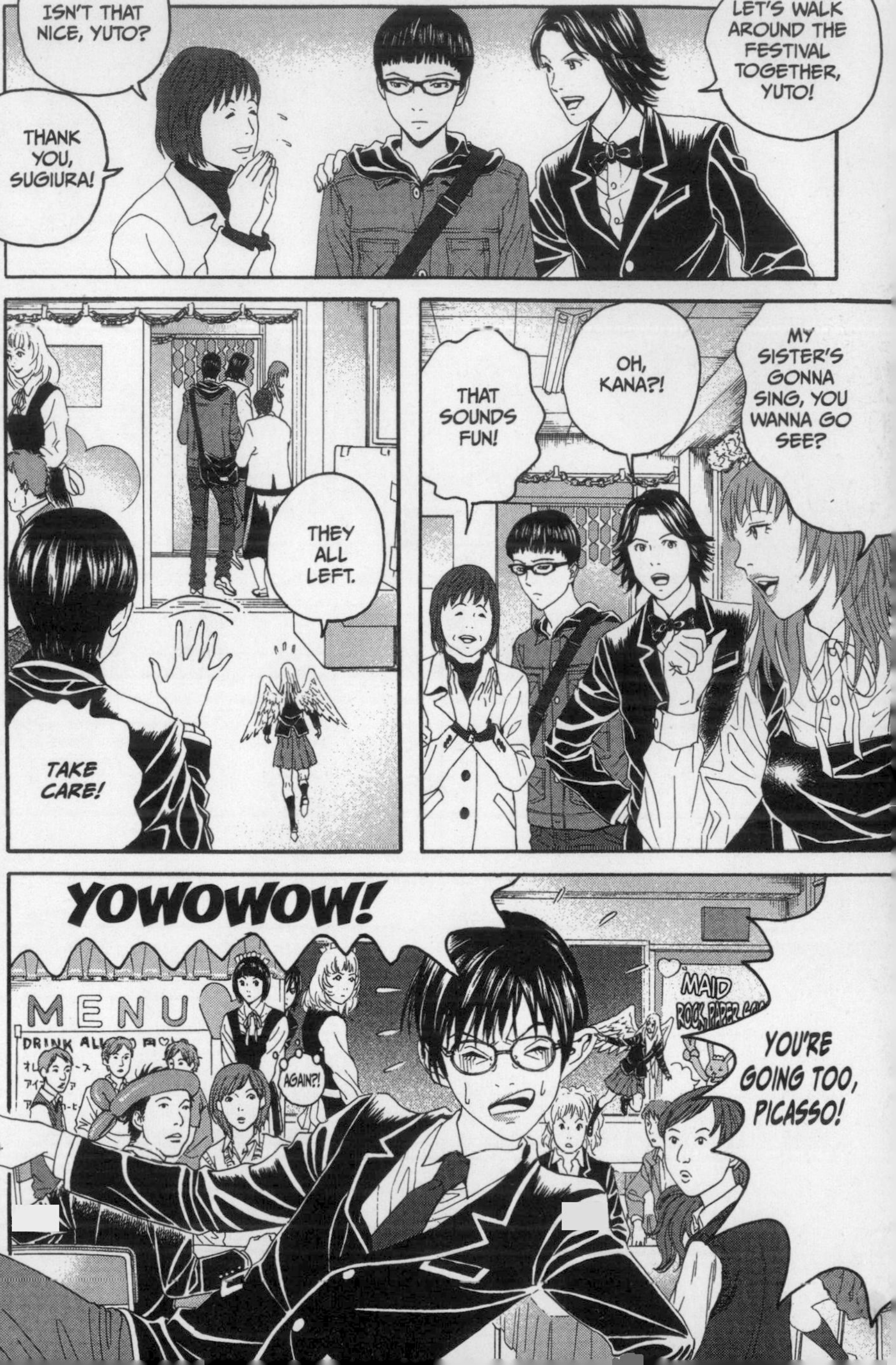
LET'S WALK AROUND THE FESTIVAL TOGETHER, YUTO!
ISN'T THAT NICE, YUTO?
THANK YOU, SUGIURA!
MY SISTER'S GONNA SING, YOU WANNA GO SEE?
OH, KANA?!
THAT SOUNDS FUN!
THEY ALL LEFT.
TAKE CARE!
YOU'RE GOING TOO, PICASSO!
MAID
AGAIN?!
MENU
YOWOWOW!

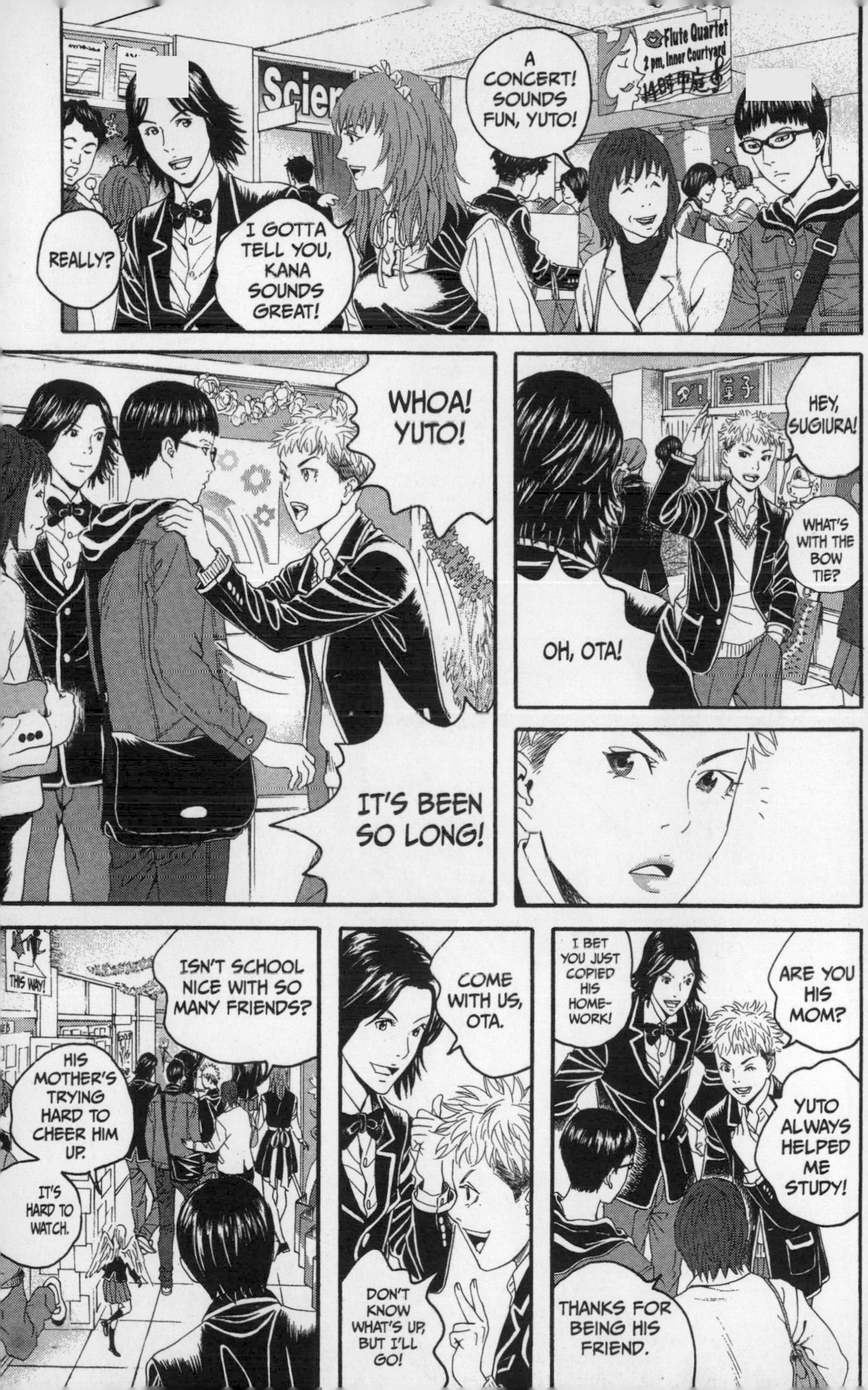
Flute Quartet
2 pm, Inner Courtyard
A CONCERT! SOUNDS FUN, YUTO!
I GOTTA TELL YOU, KANA SOUNDS GREAT!
REALLY?
HEY, SUGIURA!
WHAT'S WITH THE BOW TIE?
OH, OTA!
WHOA! YUTO!
IT'S BEEN SO LONG!
ARE YOU HIS MOM?
I BET YOU JUST COPIED HIS HOME-WORK!
YUTO ALWAYS HELPED ME STUDY!
THANKS FOR BEING HIS FRIEND.
COME WITH US, OTA.
DON'T KNOW WHAT'S UP, BUT I'LL GO!
ISN'T SCHOOL NICE WITH SO MANY FRIENDS?
THIS WAY!
HIS MOTHER'S TRYING HARD TO CHEER HIM UP.
IT'S HARD TO WATCH.

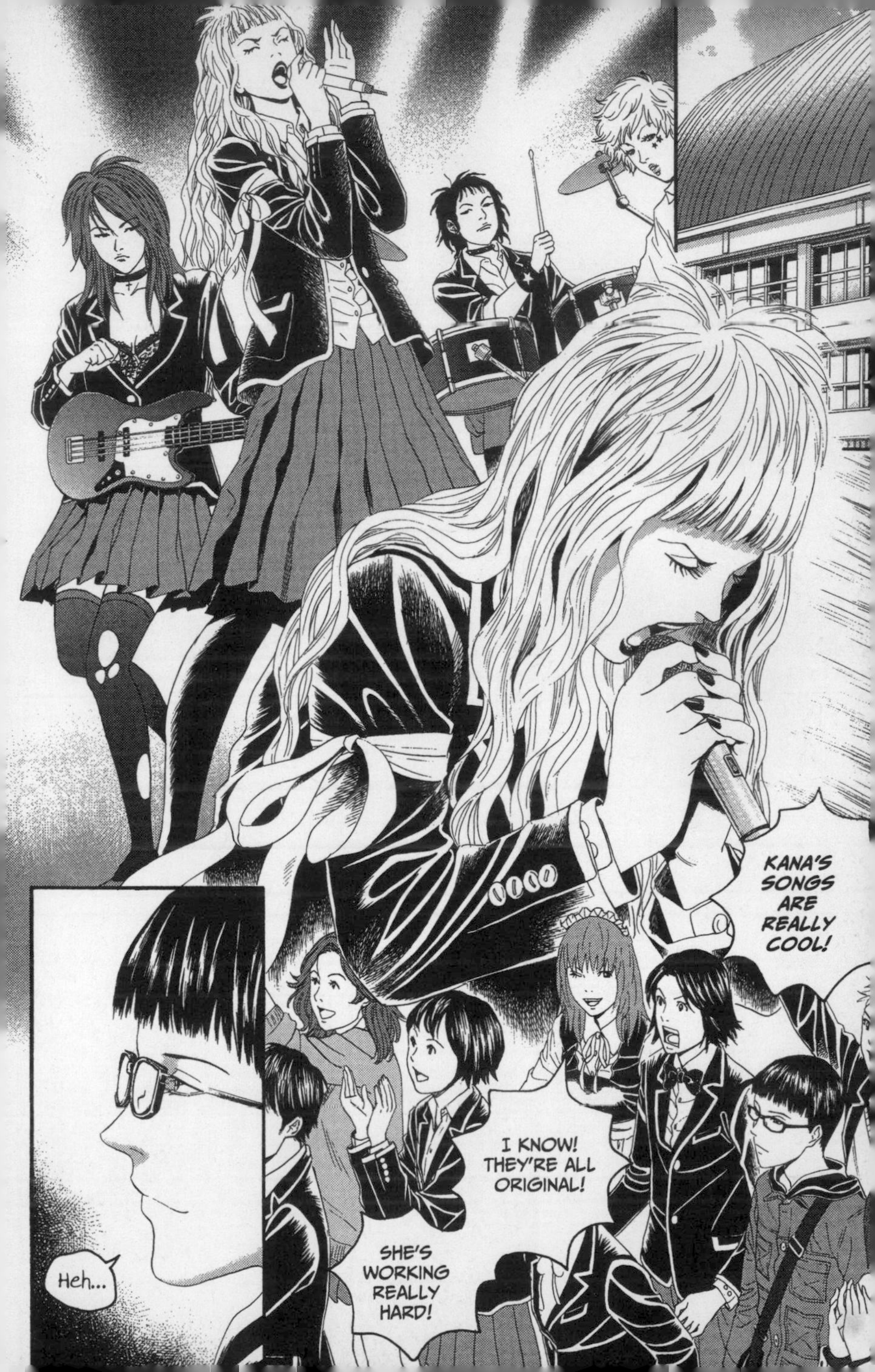
KANA'S SONGS ARE REALLY COOL!
I KNOW! THEY'RE ALL ORIGINAL!
SHE'S WORKING REALLY HARD!
Heh...

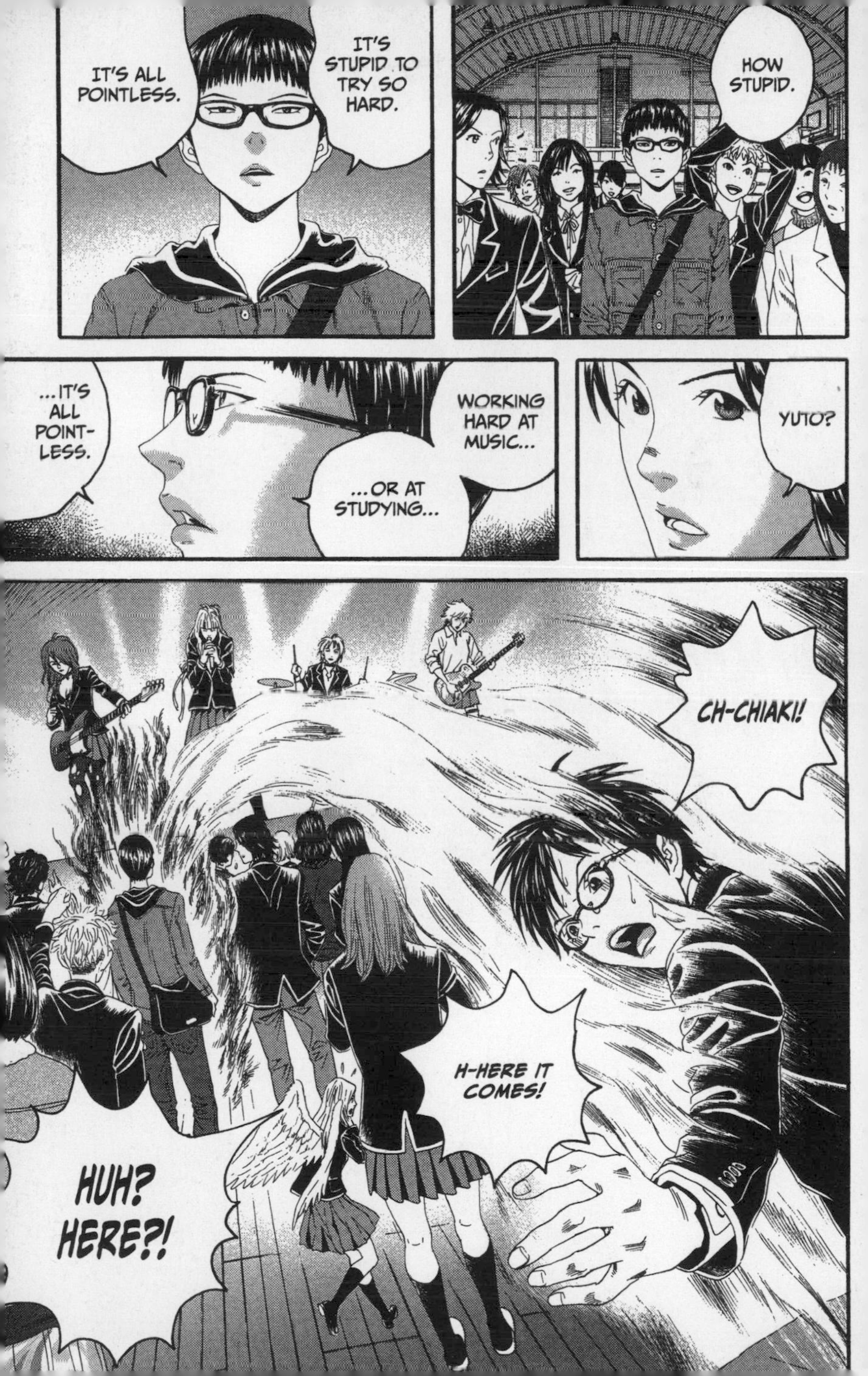
HOW STUPID.
IT'S STUPID TO TRY SO HARD.
IT'S ALL POINTLESS.
YUTO?
WORKING HARD AT MUSIC...
...OR AT STUDYING...
...IT'S ALL POINTLESS.
CH-CHIAKI!
H-HERE IT COMES!
HUH? HERE?!

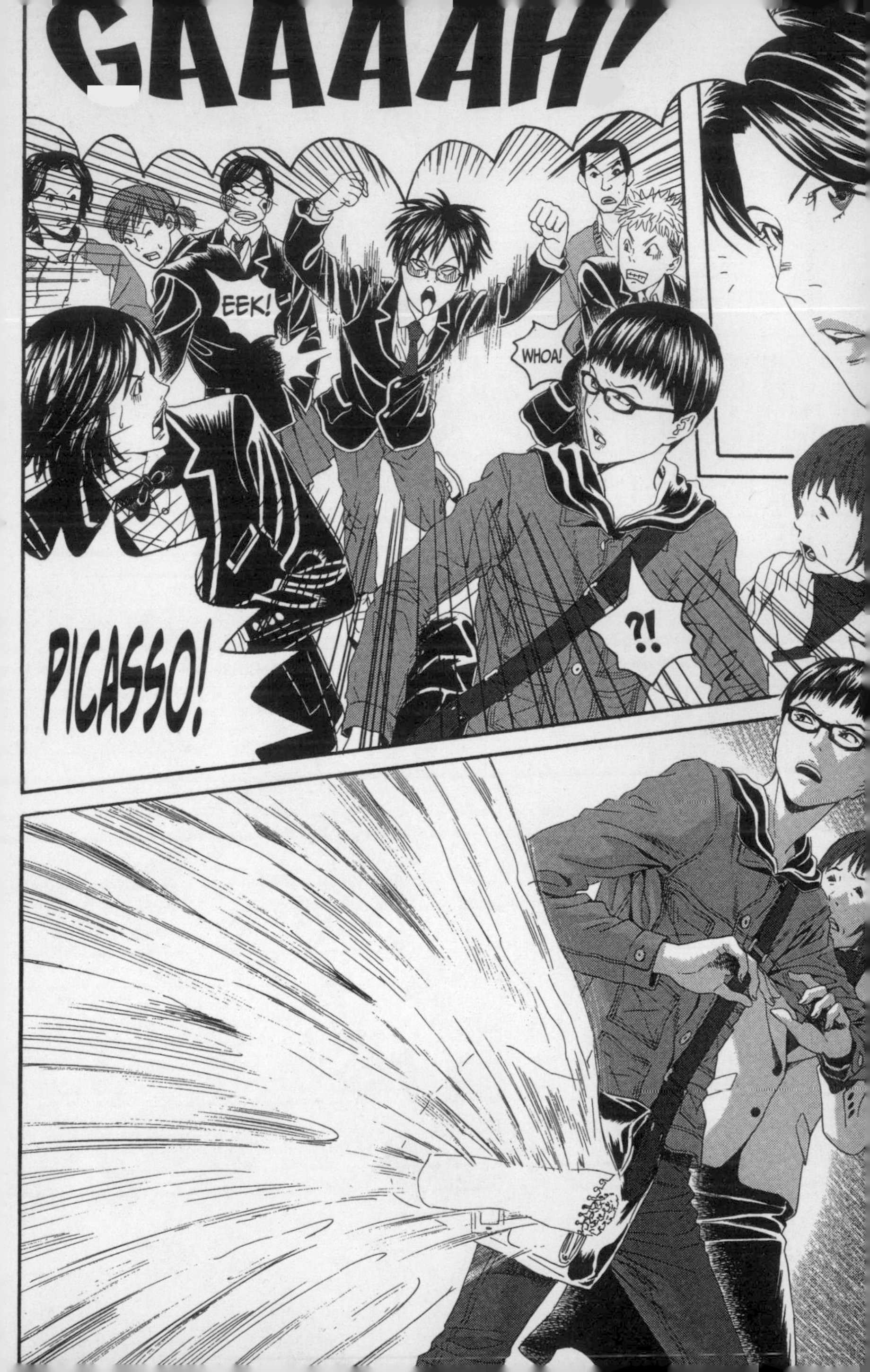
GAAAAH!
EEK!
WHOA!
?!
PICASSO!

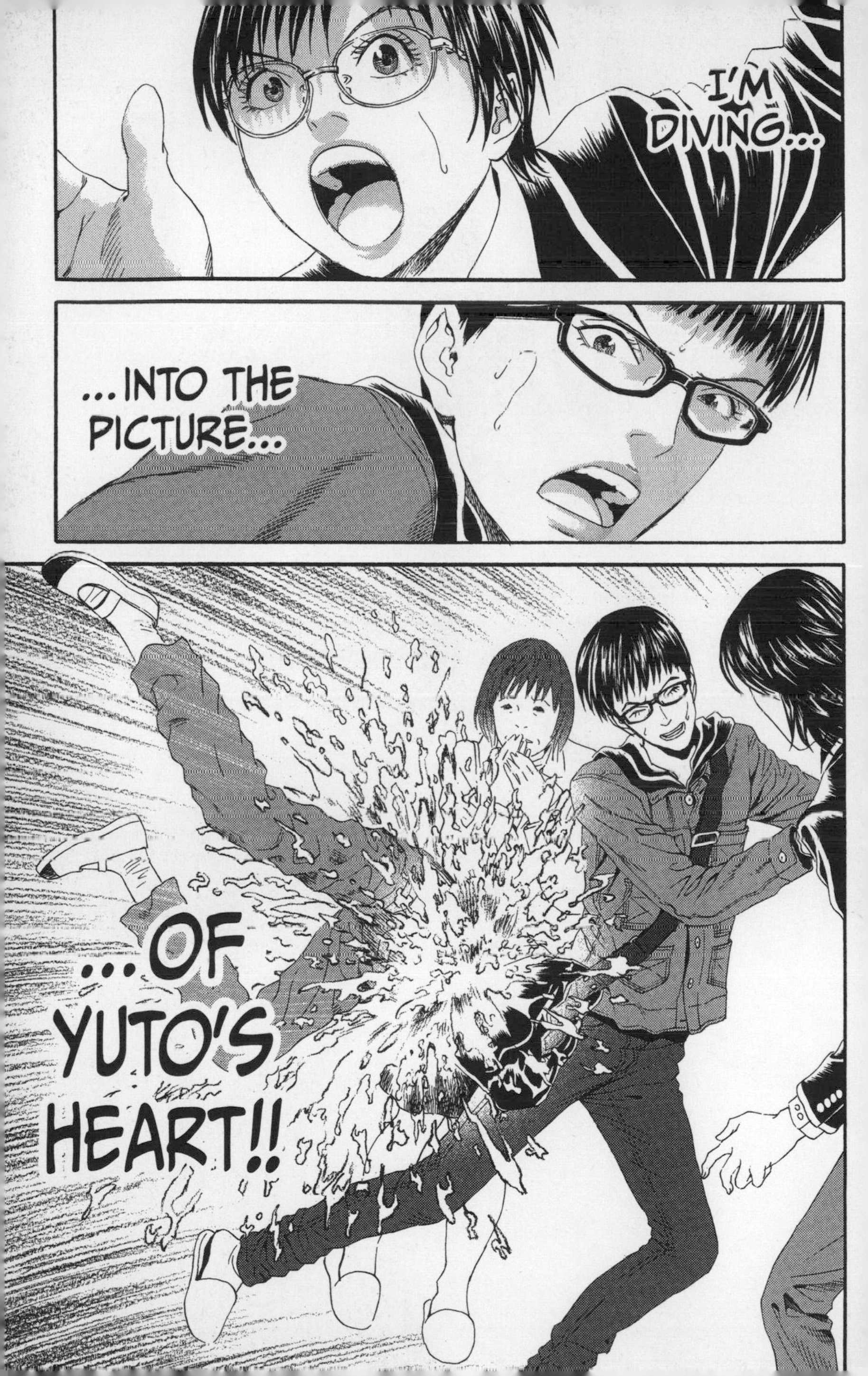
I'M DIVING...
...INTO THE PICTURE...
...OF YUTO'S HEART!!

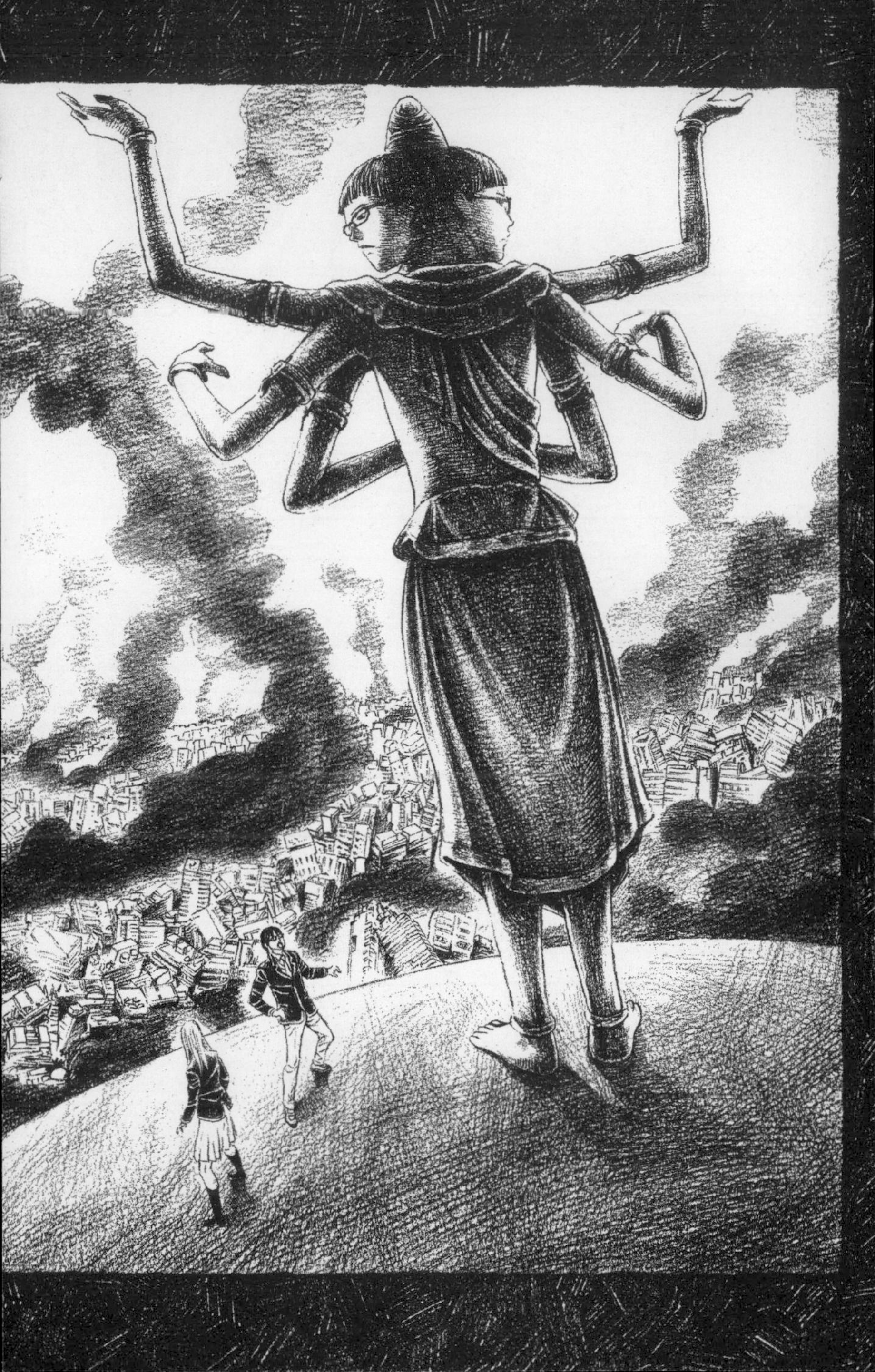

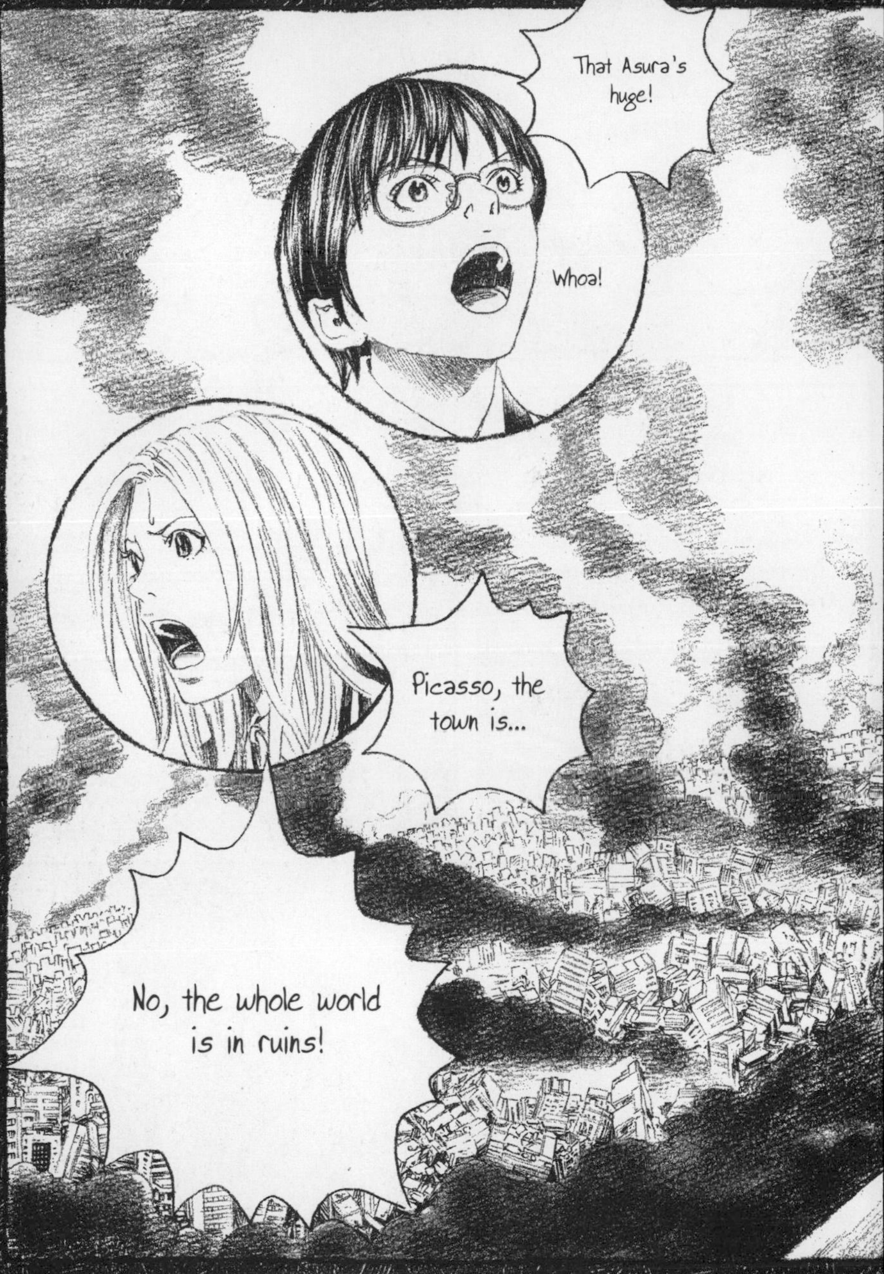
That Asura's huge!
Whoa!
Picasso, the town is...
No, the whole world is in ruins!

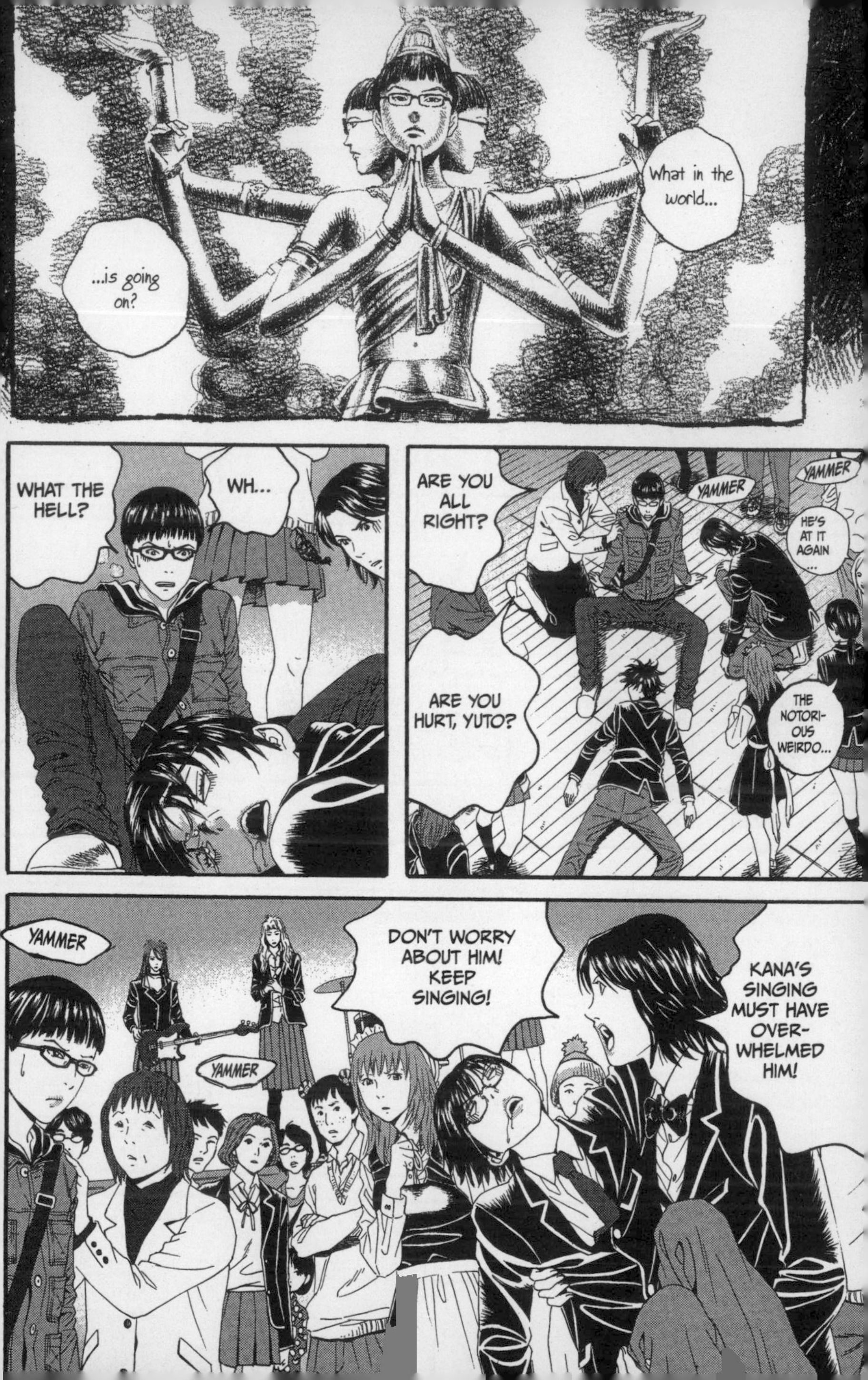
What in the world...
...is going on?
YAMMER
YAMMER
HE'S AT IT AGAIN...
ARE YOU ALL RIGHT?
THE NOTORI-OUS WEIRDO...
ARE YOU HURT, YUTO?
WH...
WHAT THE HELL?
KANA'S SINGING MUST HAVE OVER-WHELMED HIM!
DON'T WORRY ABOUT HIM! KEEP SINGING!
YAMMER
YAMMER

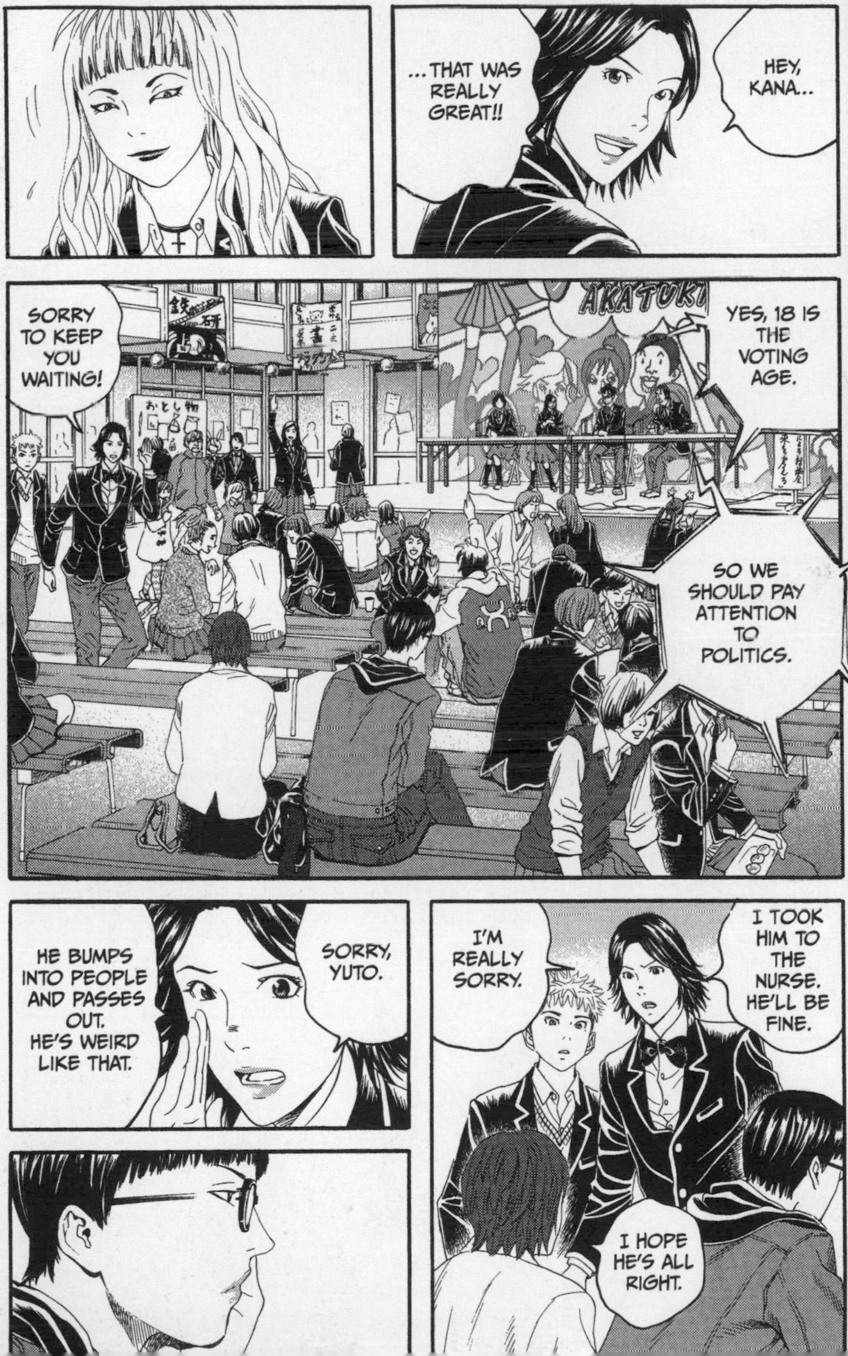
HEY, KANA...
...THAT WAS REALLY GREAT!!
AKATUKI
YES, 18 IS THE VOTING AGE.
SO WE SHOULD PAY ATTENTION TO POLITICS.
SORRY TO KEEP YOU WAITING!
I TOOK HIM TO THE NURSE. HE'LL BE FINE.
I'M REALLY SORRY.
I HOPE HE'S ALL RIGHT.
SORRY, YUTO.
HE BUMPS INTO PEOPLE AND PASSES OUT. HE'S WEIRD LIKE THAT.

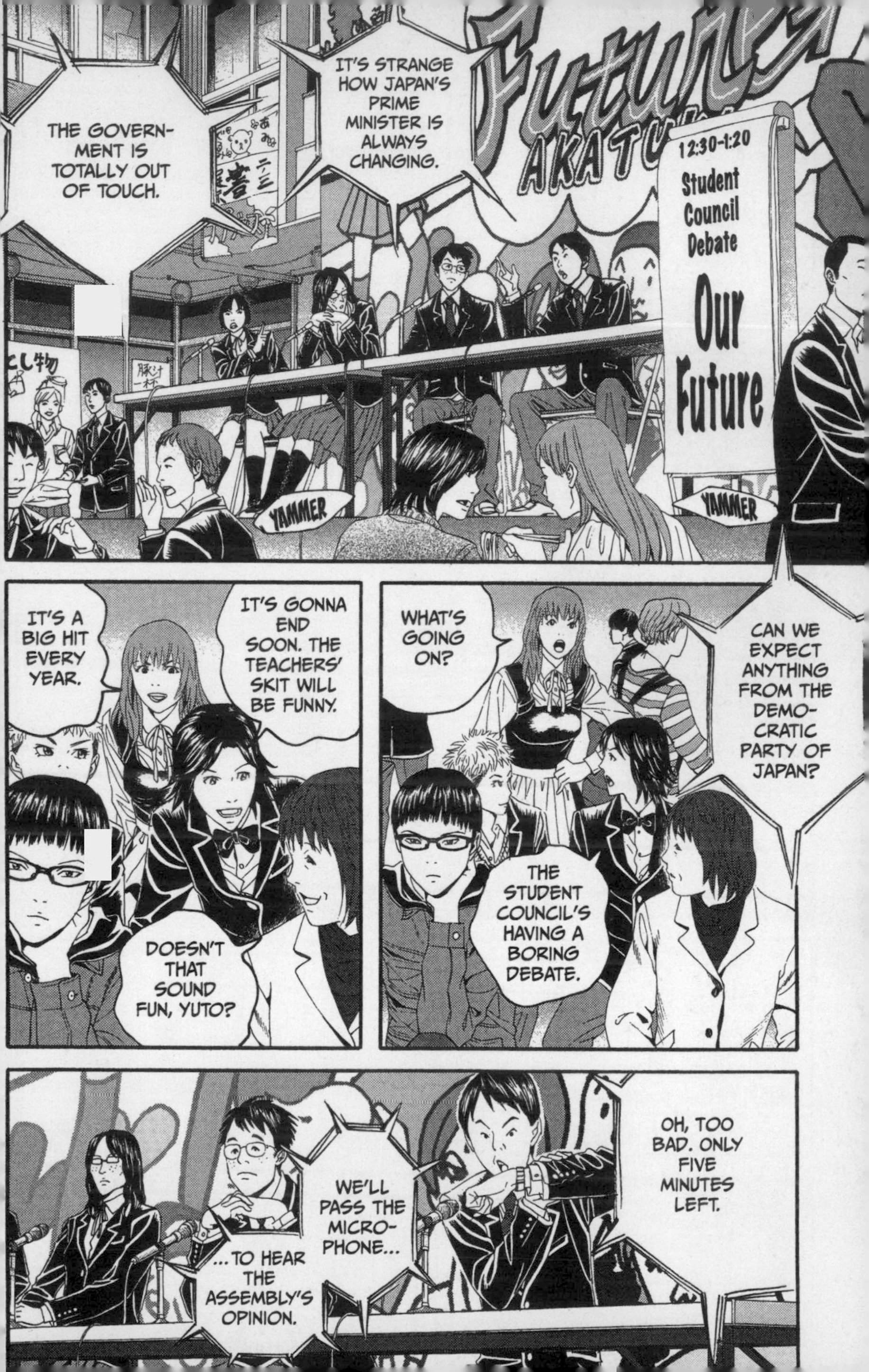
12:30-1:20
Student Council Debate
Our Future
IT'S STRANGE HOW JAPAN'S PRIME MINISTER IS ALWAYS CHANGING.
THE GOVERN-MENT IS TOTALLY OUT OF TOUCH.
YAMMER
YAMMER
CAN WE EXPECT ANYTHING FROM THE DEMO-CRATIC PARTY OF JAPAN?
WHAT'S GOING ON?
THE STUDENT COUNCIL'S HAVING A BORING DEBATE.
IT'S GONNA END SOON. THE TEACHERS' SKIT WILL BE FUNNY.
IT'S A BIG HIT EVERY YEAR.
DOESN'T THAT SOUND FUN, YUTO?
OH, TOO BAD. ONLY FIVE MINUTES LEFT.
WE'LL PASS THE MICRO-PHONE...
...TO HEAR THE ASSEMBLY'S OPINION.

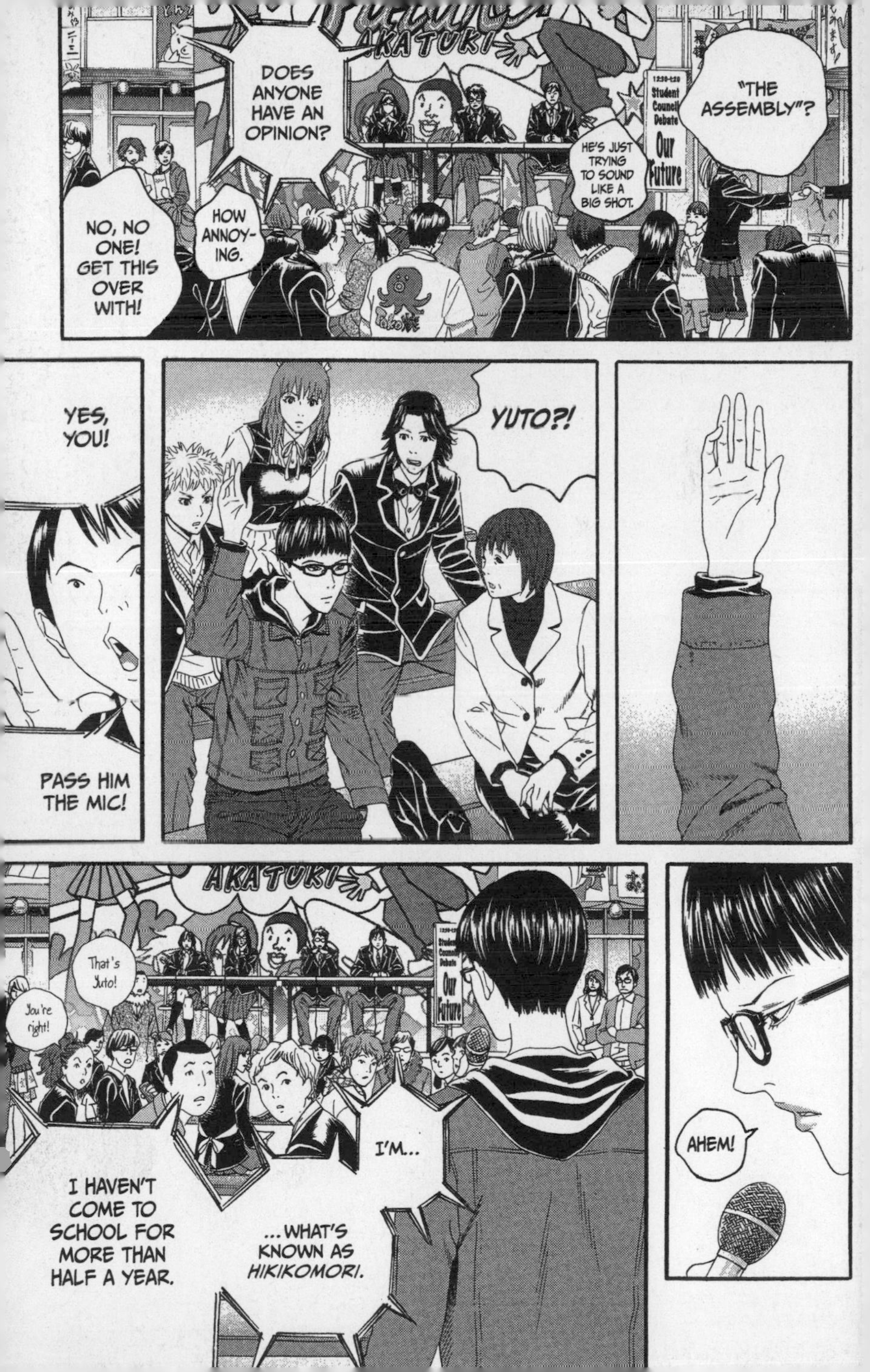
AKATUKI
Student Council Debate
Our Future
"THE ASSEMBLY"?
HE'S JUST TRYING TO SOUND LIKE A BIG SHOT.
DOES ANYONE HAVE AN OPINION?
HOW ANNOY-ING.
NO, NO ONE! GET THIS OVER WITH!
YUTO?!
YES, YOU!
PASS HIM THE MIC!
AHEM!
AKATUKI
Student Council Debate
Our Future
That's Yuto!
You're right!
I'M...
...WHAT'S KNOWN AS *HIKIKOMORI*.
I HAVEN'T COME TO SCHOOL FOR MORE THAN HALF A YEAR.

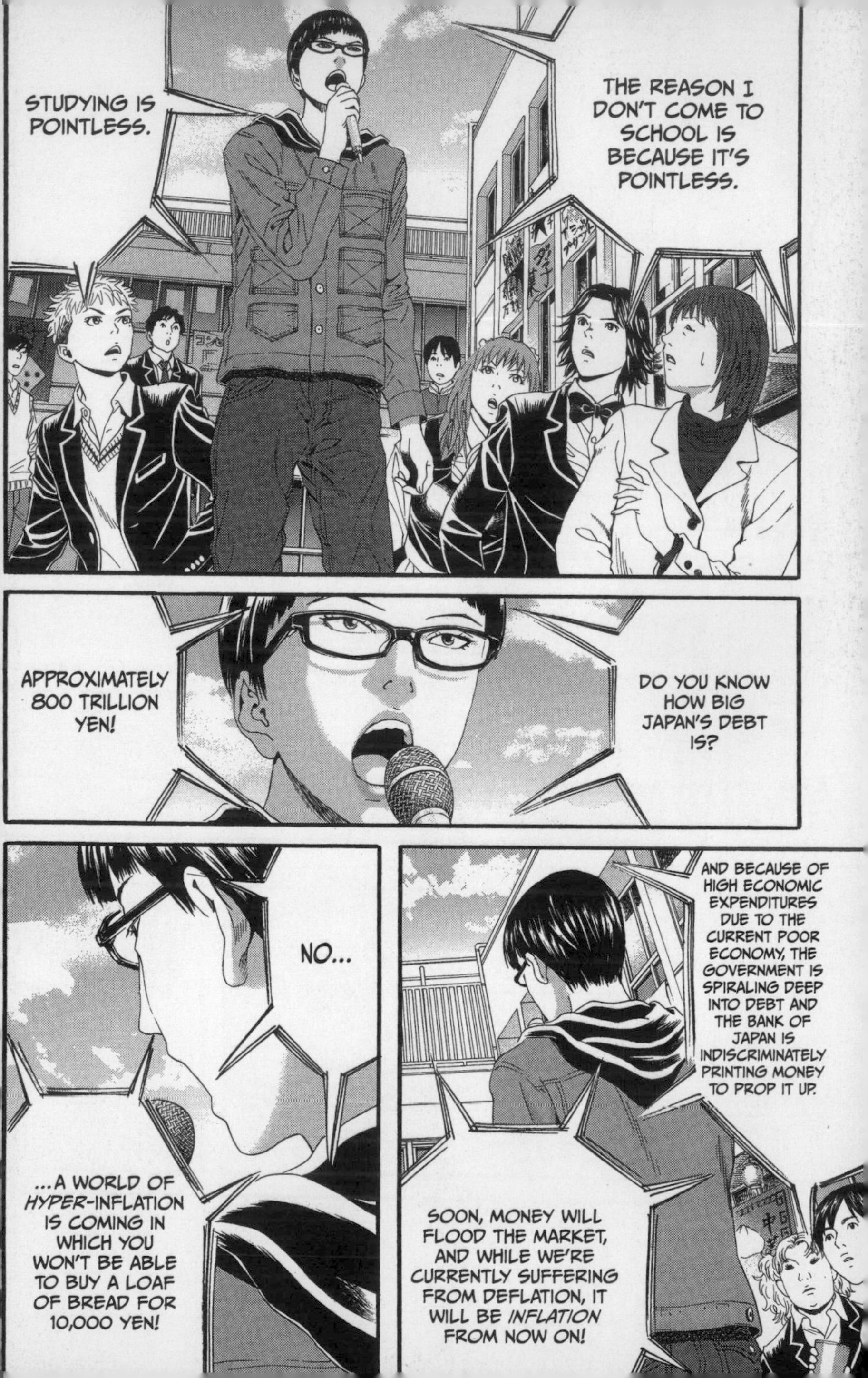
THE REASON I DON'T COME TO SCHOOL IS BECAUSE IT'S POINTLESS.
STUDYING IS POINTLESS.
DO YOU KNOW HOW BIG JAPAN'S DEBT IS?
APPROXIMATELY 800 TRILLION YEN!
AND BECAUSE OF HIGH ECONOMIC EXPENDITURES DUE TO THE CURRENT POOR ECONOMY, THE GOVERNMENT IS SPIRALING DEEP INTO DEBT AND THE BANK OF JAPAN IS INDISCRIMINATELY PRINTING MONEY TO PROP IT UP.
SOON, MONEY WILL FLOOD THE MARKET, AND WHILE WE'RE CURRENTLY SUFFERING FROM DEFLATION, IT WILL BE *INFLATION* FROM NOW ON!
NO...
...A WORLD OF *HYPER*-INFLATION IS COMING IN WHICH YOU WON'T BE ABLE TO BUY A LOAF OF BREAD FOR 10,000 YEN!

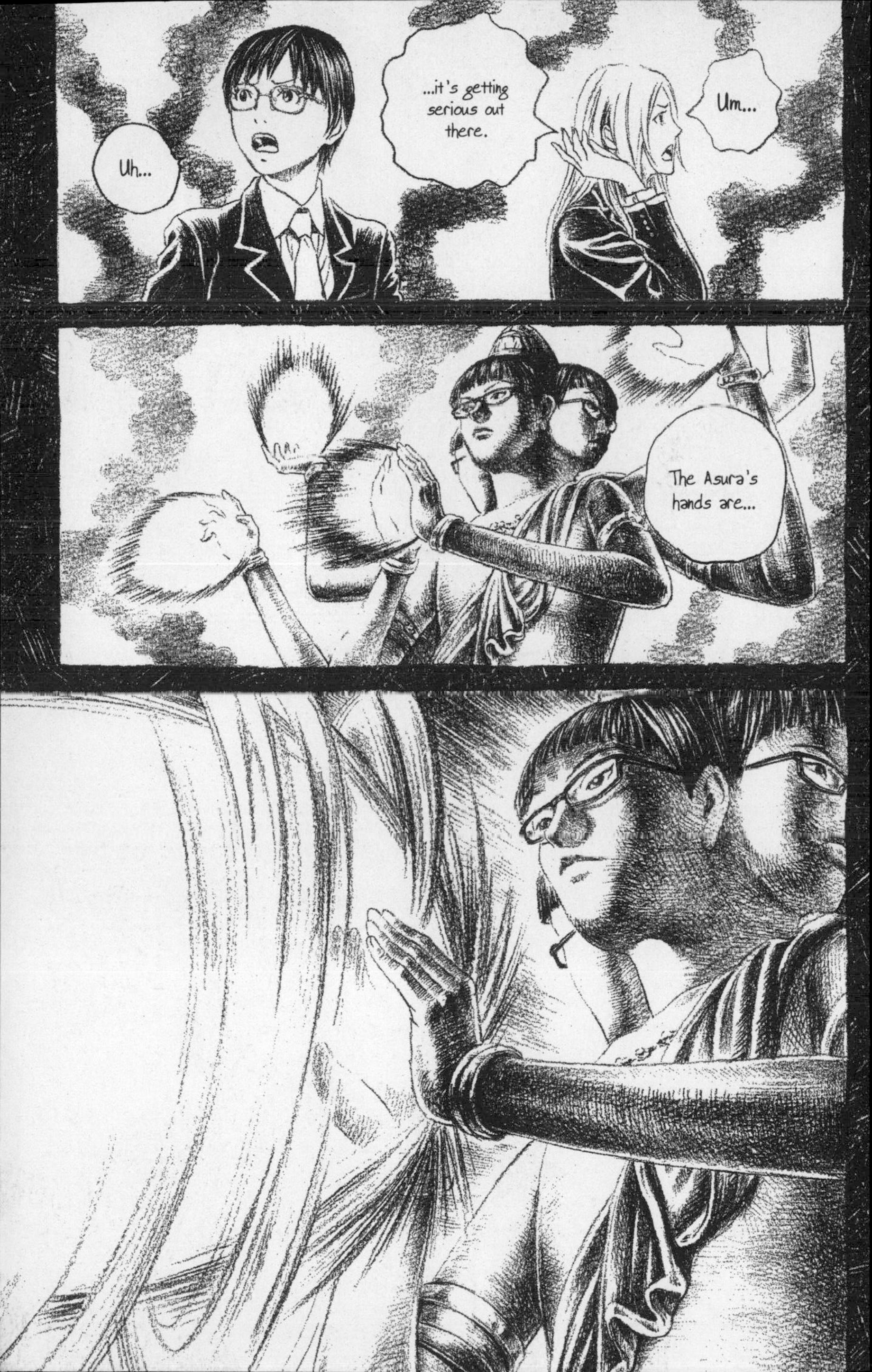
Um...
...it's getting serious out there.
Uh...
The Asura's hands are...

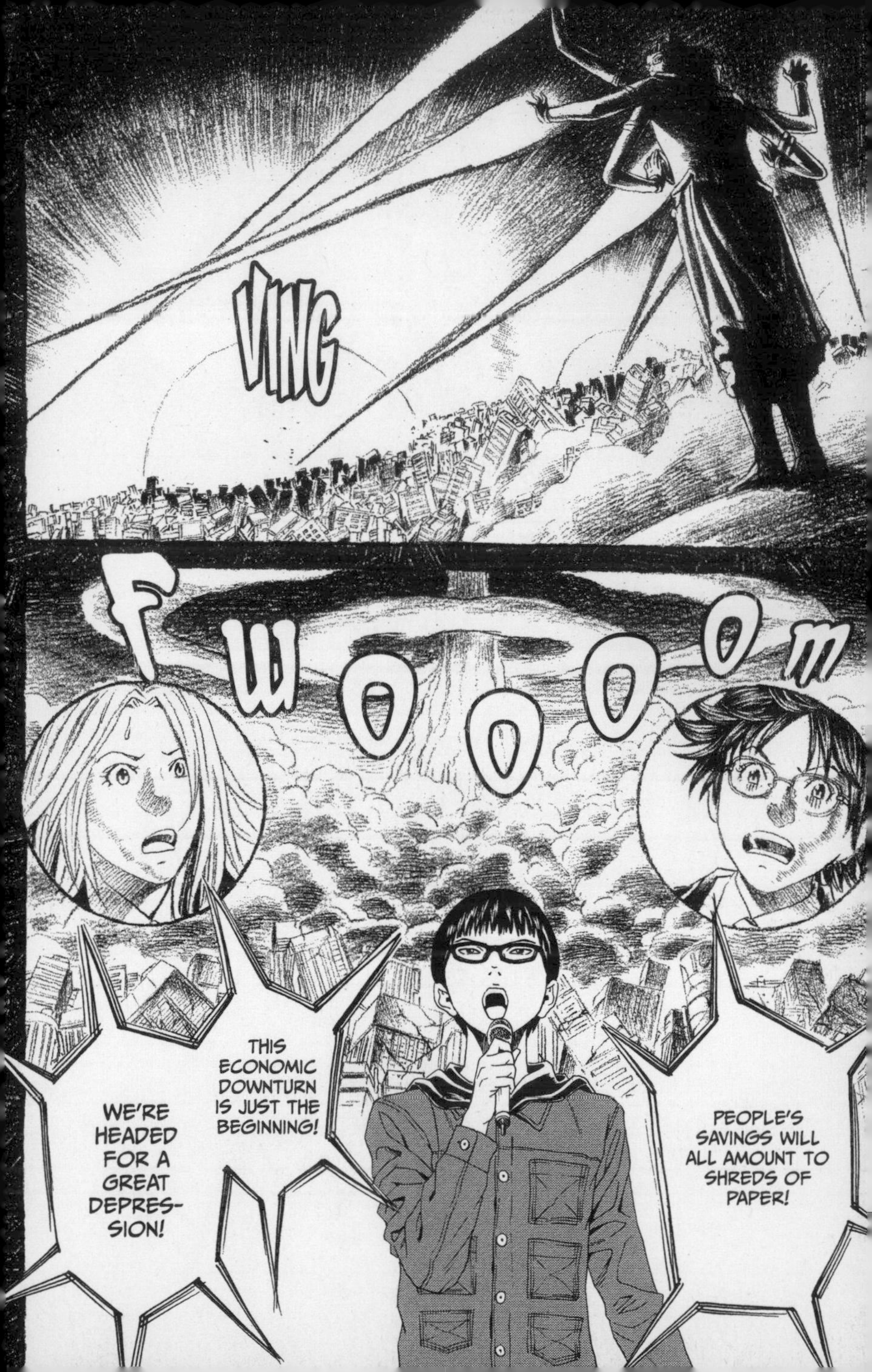
VING
FWOOOOOM
PEOPLE'S SAVINGS WILL ALL AMOUNT TO SHREDS OF PAPER!
THIS ECONOMIC DOWNTURN IS JUST THE BEGINNING!
WE'RE HEADED FOR A GREAT DEPRES-SION!

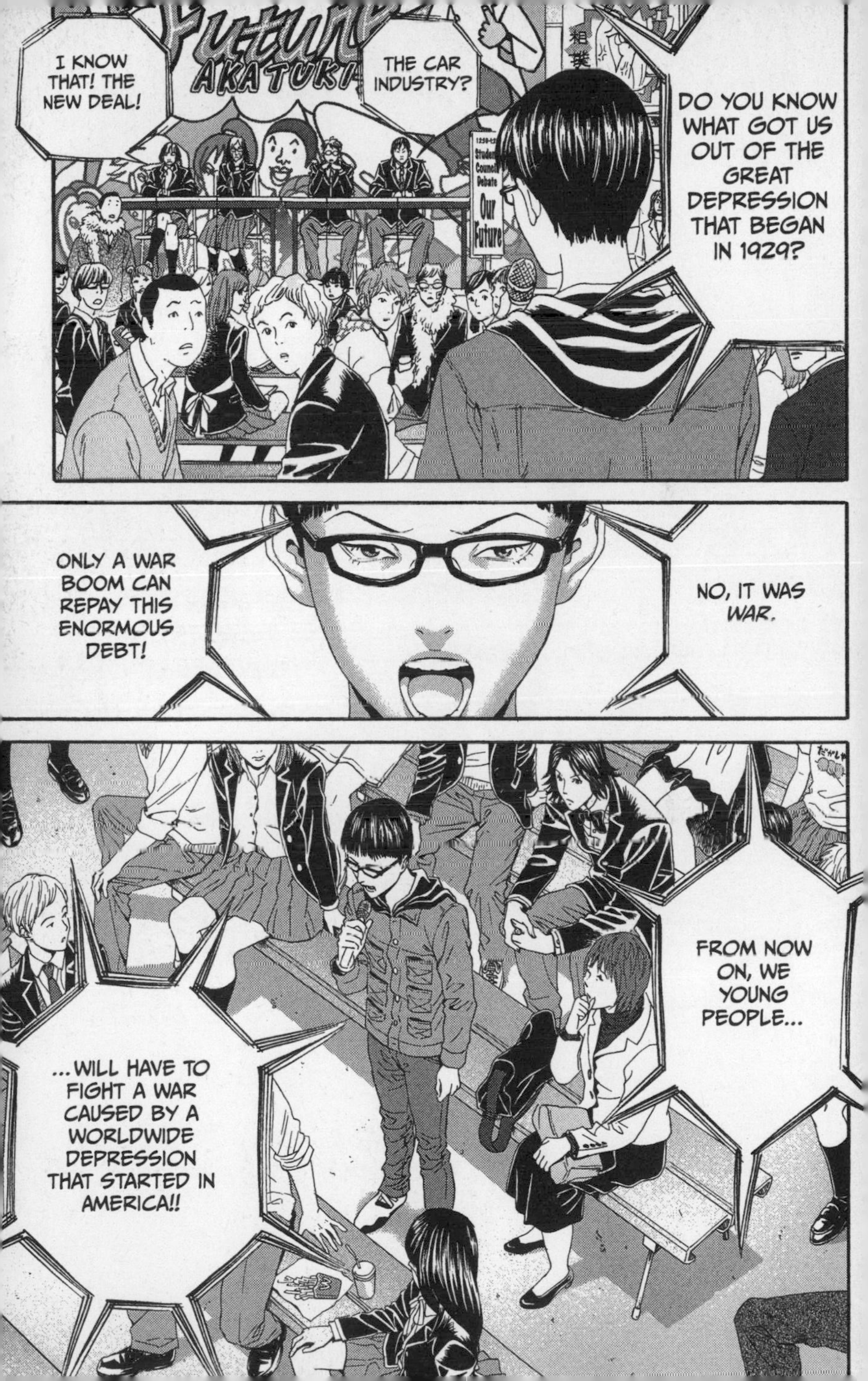
DO YOU KNOW WHAT GOT US OUT OF THE GREAT DEPRESSION THAT BEGAN IN 1929?
THE CAR INDUSTRY?
I KNOW THAT! THE NEW DEAL!
AKATUKI
Student Council Debate
Our Future
NO, IT WAS *WAR*.
ONLY A WAR BOOM CAN REPAY THIS ENORMOUS DEBT!
FROM NOW ON, WE YOUNG PEOPLE...
...WILL HAVE TO FIGHT A WAR CAUSED BY A WORLDWIDE DEPRESSION THAT STARTED IN AMERICA!!

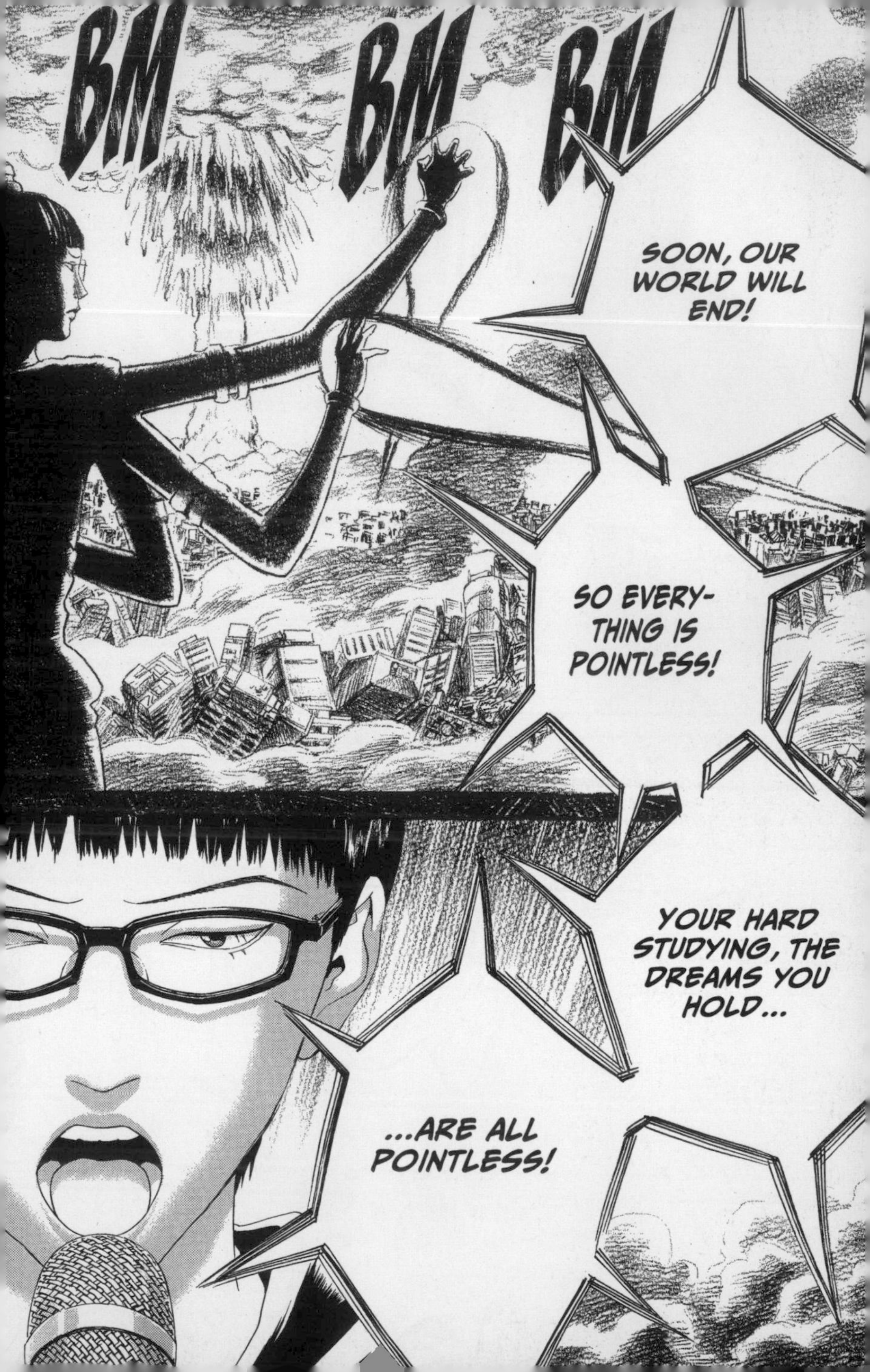
BM BM BM
SOON, OUR WORLD WILL END!
SO EVERY-THING IS POINTLESS!
YOUR HARD STUDYING, THE DREAMS YOU HOLD...
...ARE ALL POINTLESS!

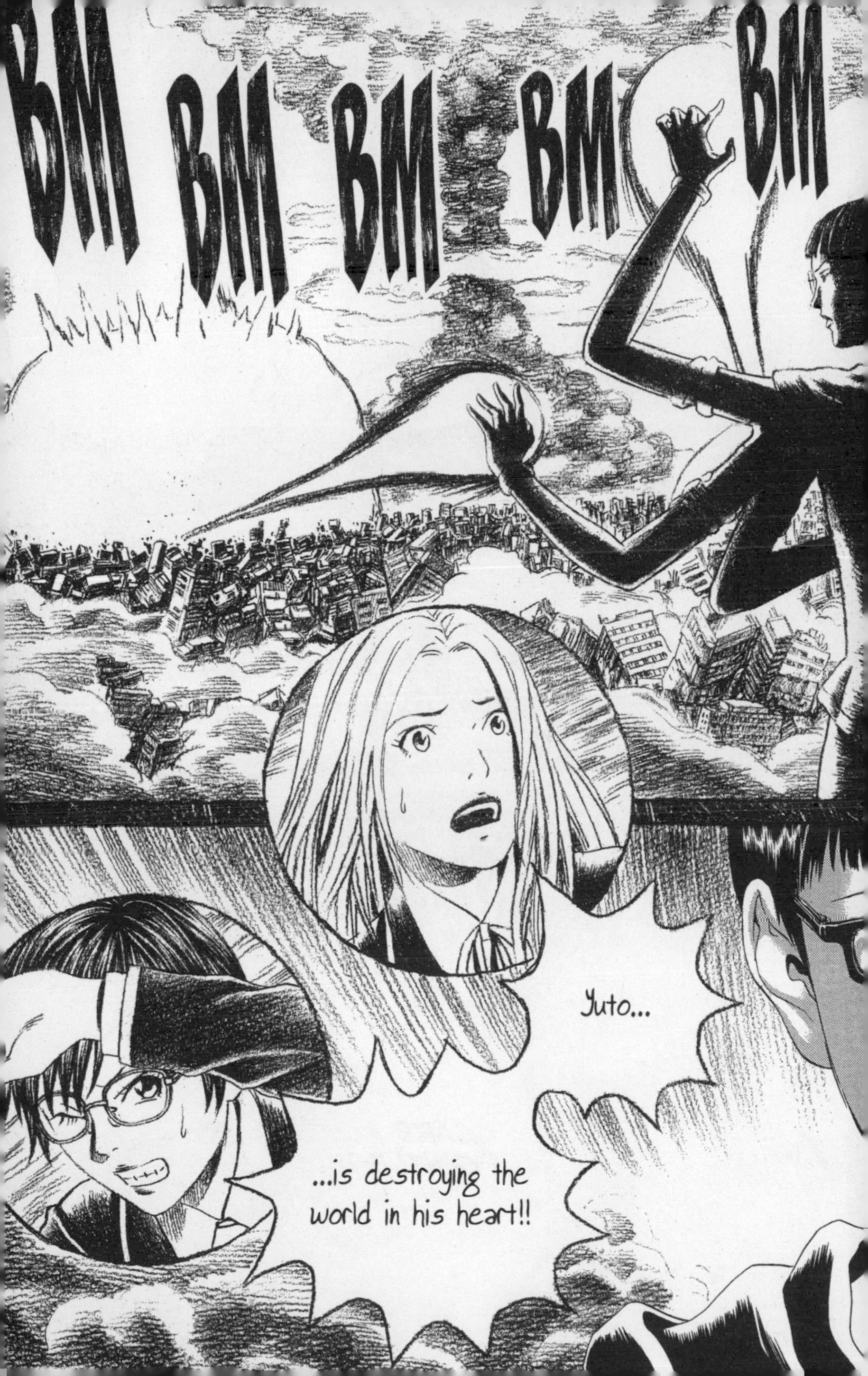
BM BM BM BM BM
Yuto...
...is destroying the world in his heart!!

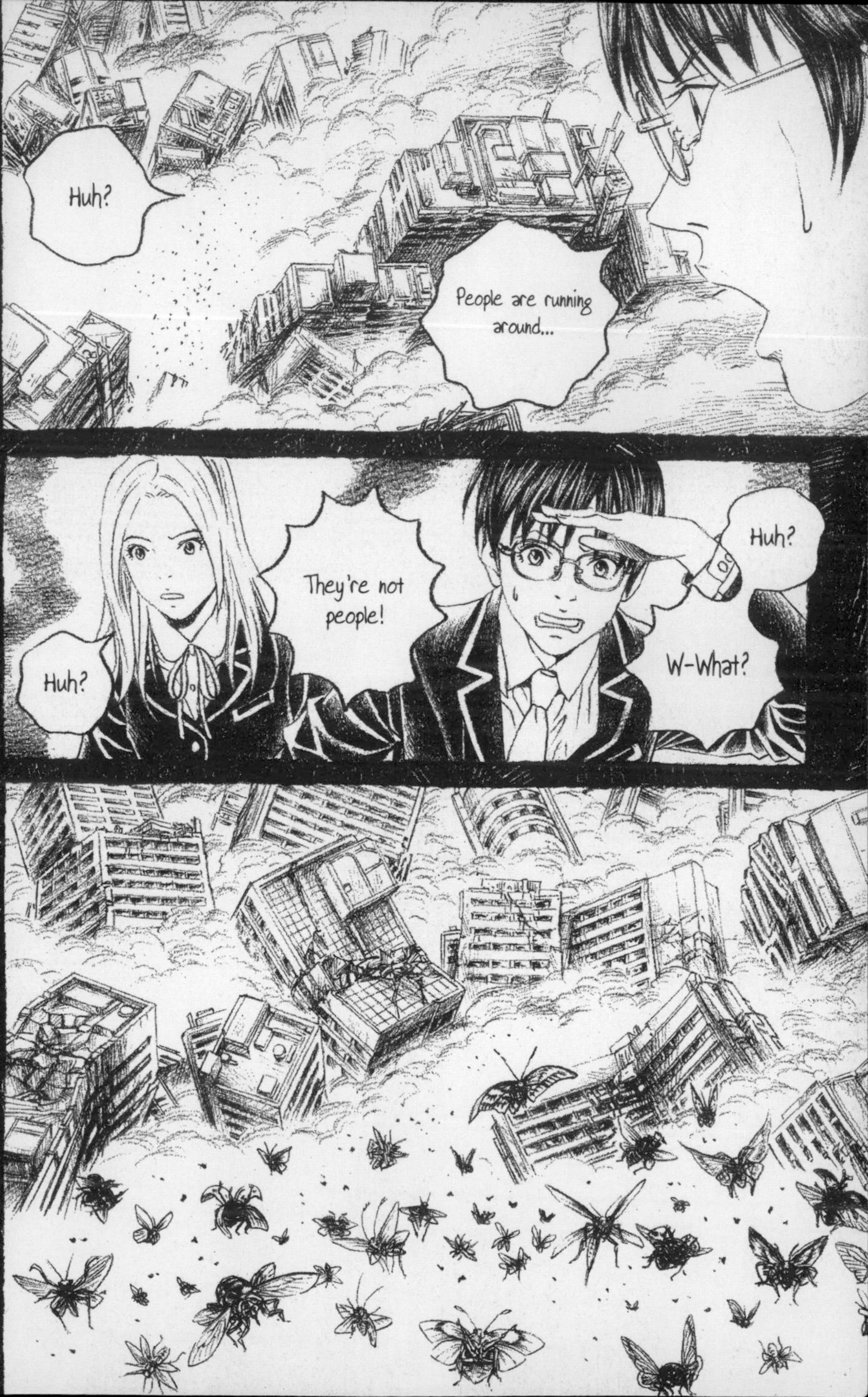
People are running around...
Huh?
Huh?
They're not people!
W-What?
Huh?

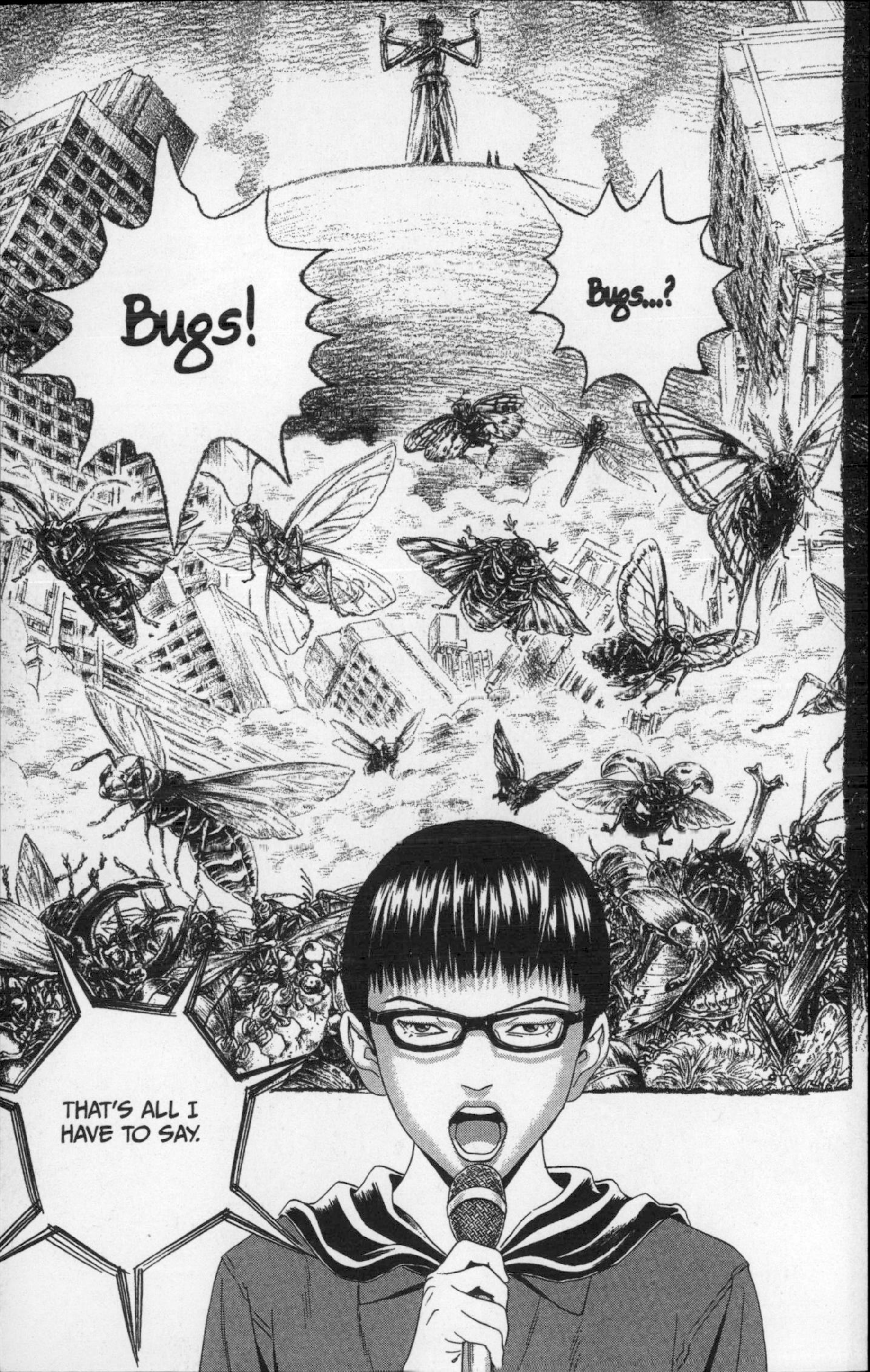
Bugs...?
Bugs!
THAT'S ALL I HAVE TO SAY.

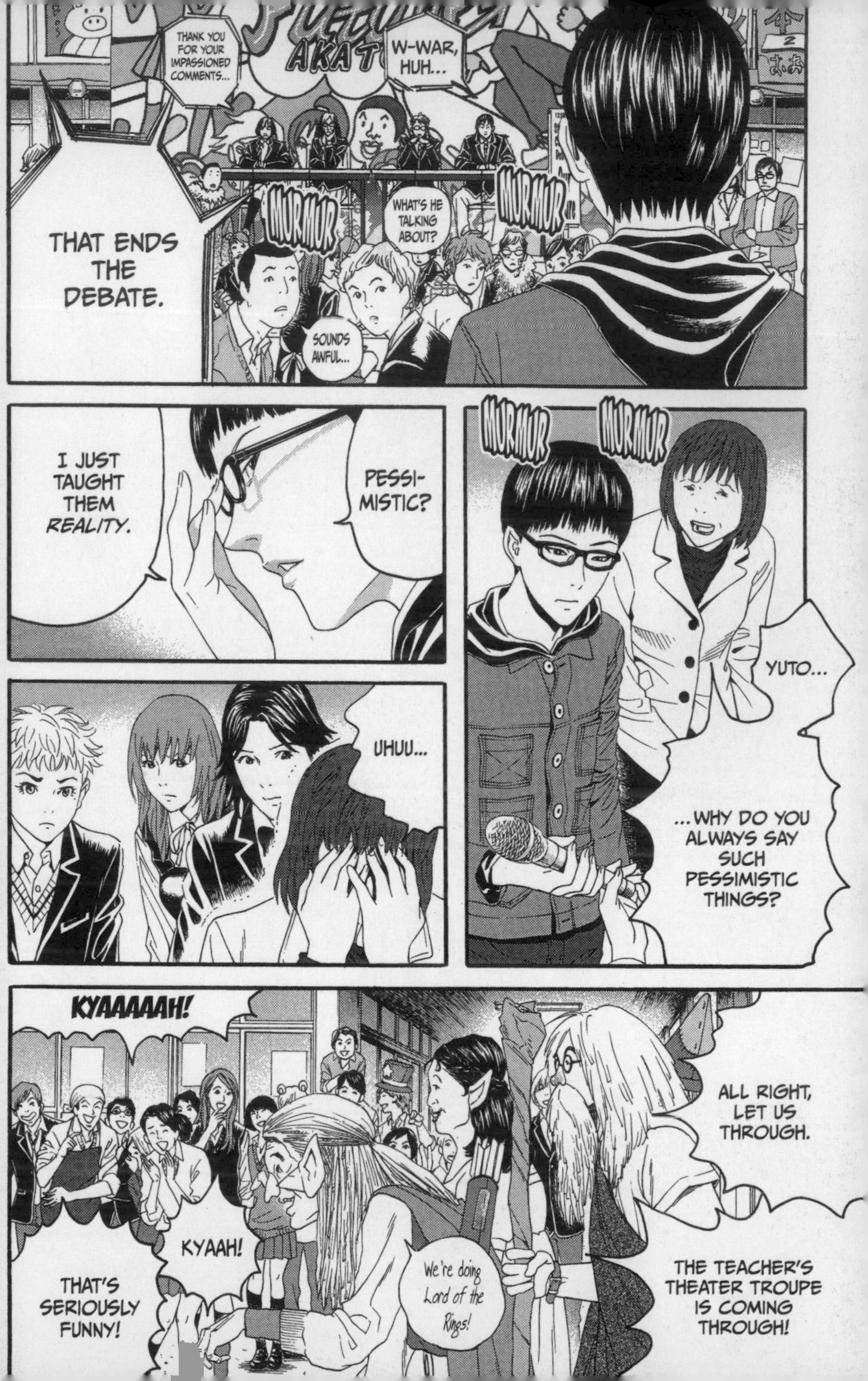
W-WAR, HUH...
THANK YOU FOR YOUR IMPASSIONED COMMENTS...
MURMUR
WHAT'S HE TALKING ABOUT?
MURMUR
THAT ENDS THE DEBATE.
SOUNDS AWFUL...
MURMUR
MURMUR
YUTO...
...WHY DO YOU ALWAYS SAY SUCH PESSIMISTIC THINGS?
PESSI-MISTIC?
I JUST TAUGHT THEM *REALITY*.
UHUU...
KYAAAAAH!
ALL RIGHT, LET US THROUGH.
THE TEACHER'S THEATER TROUPE IS COMING THROUGH!
We're doing Lord of the Rings!
KYAAH!
THAT'S SERIOUSLY FUNNY!

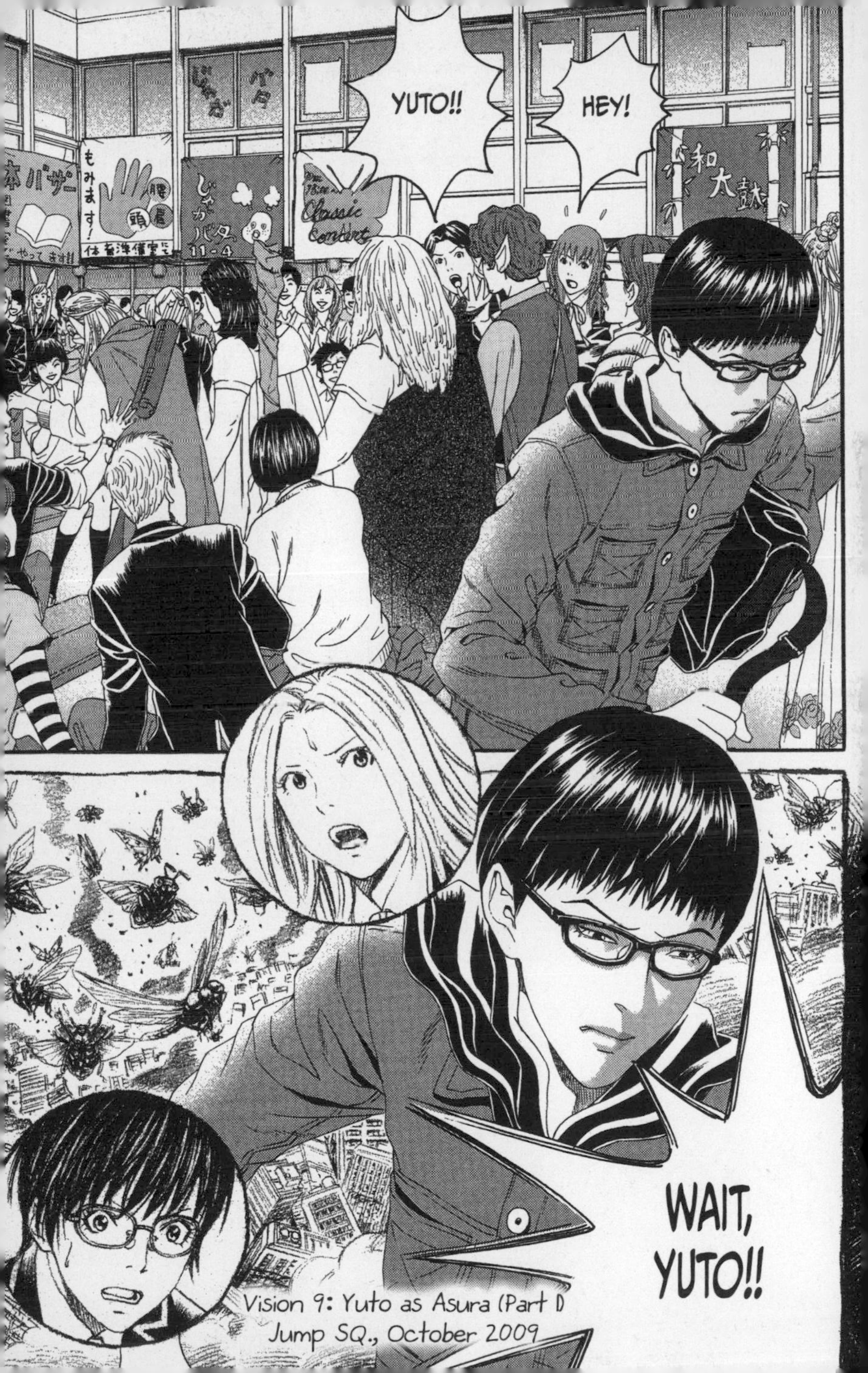
HEY!
YUTO!!
WAIT, YUTO!!

Vision 9: Yuto as Asura (Part I)
Jump SQ., October 2009

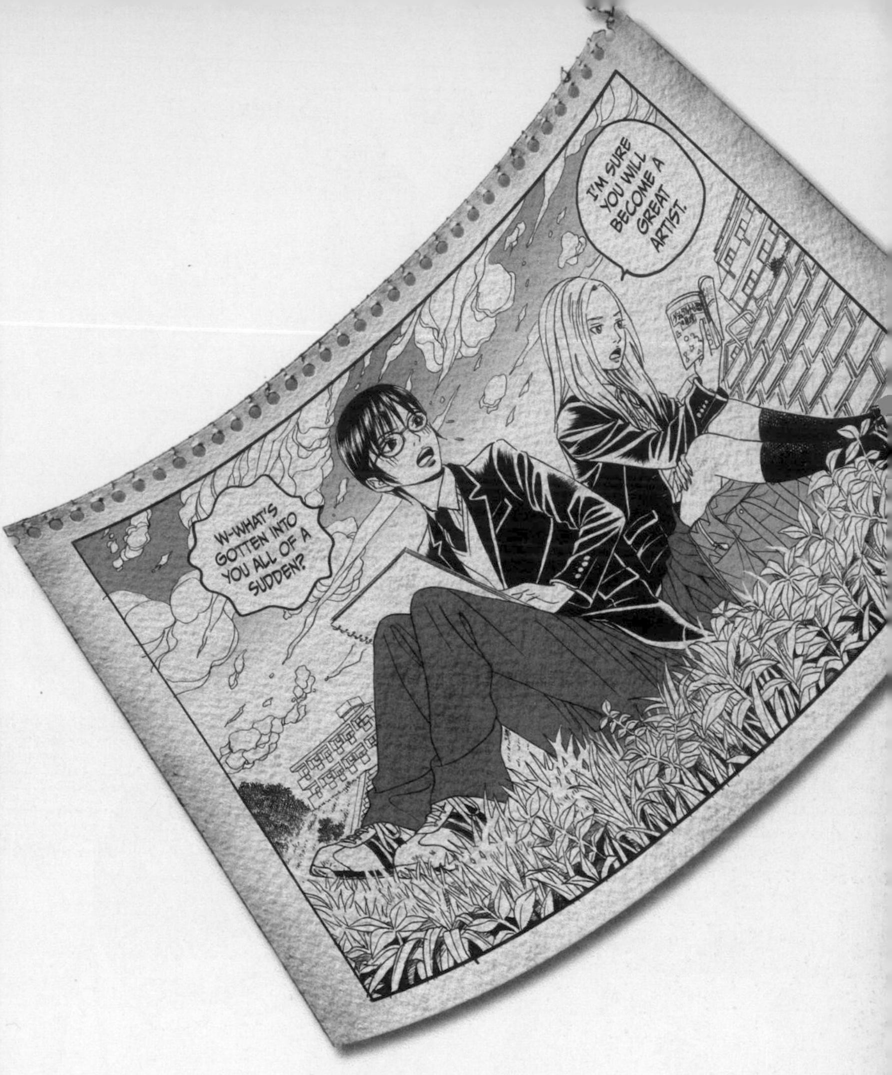
I'M SURE YOU WILL BECOME A GREAT ARTIST.
W-WHAT'S GOTTEN INTO YOU ALL OF A SUDDEN?

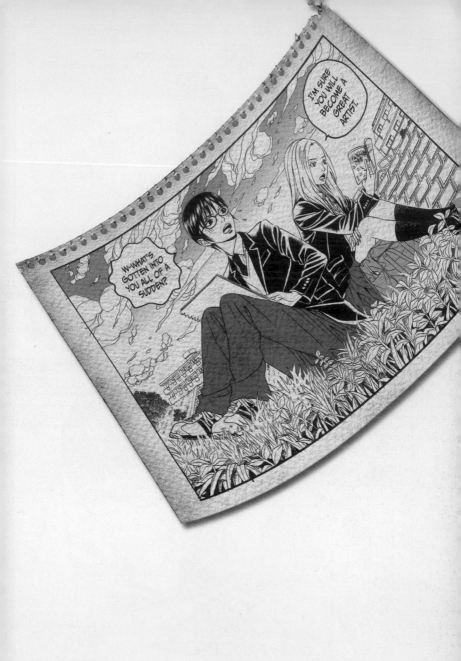

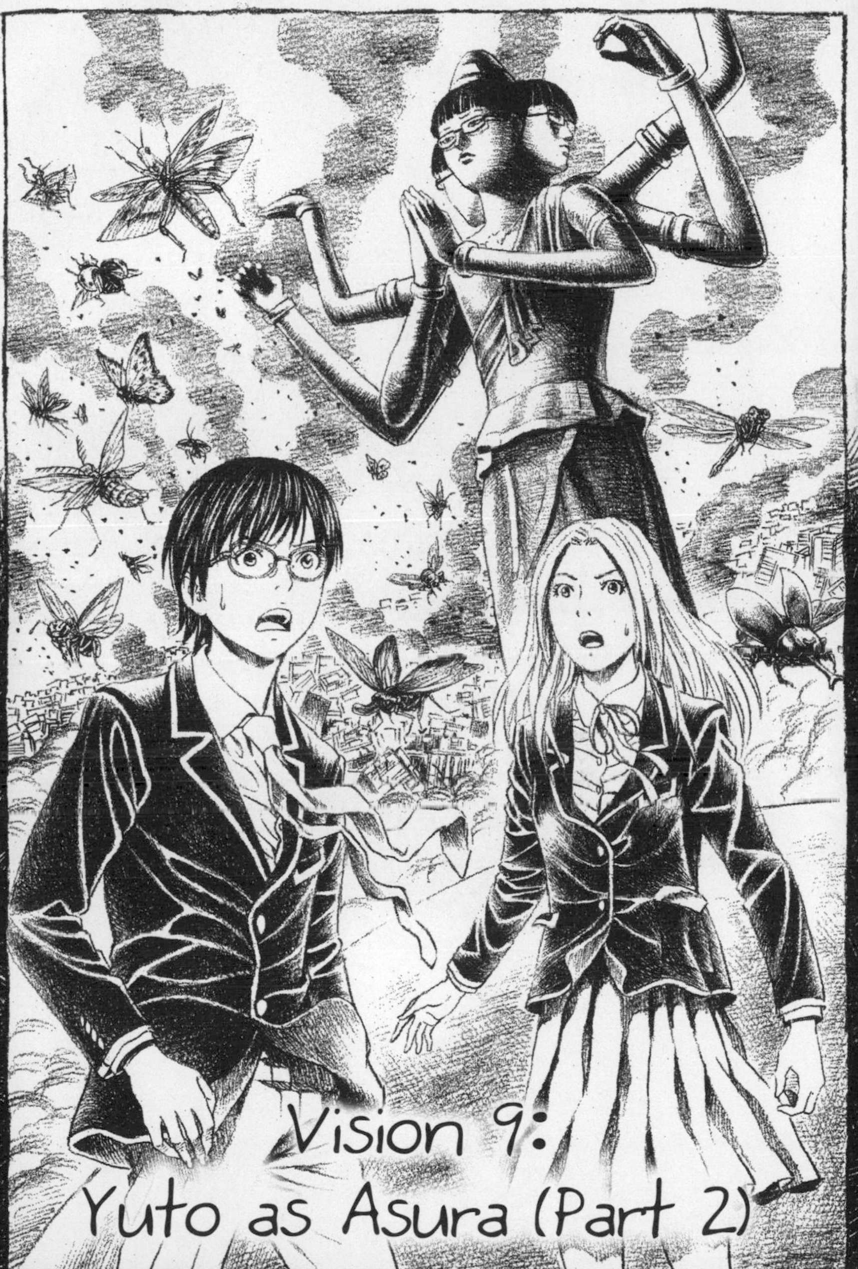
Vision 9:
Yuto as Asura (Part 2)

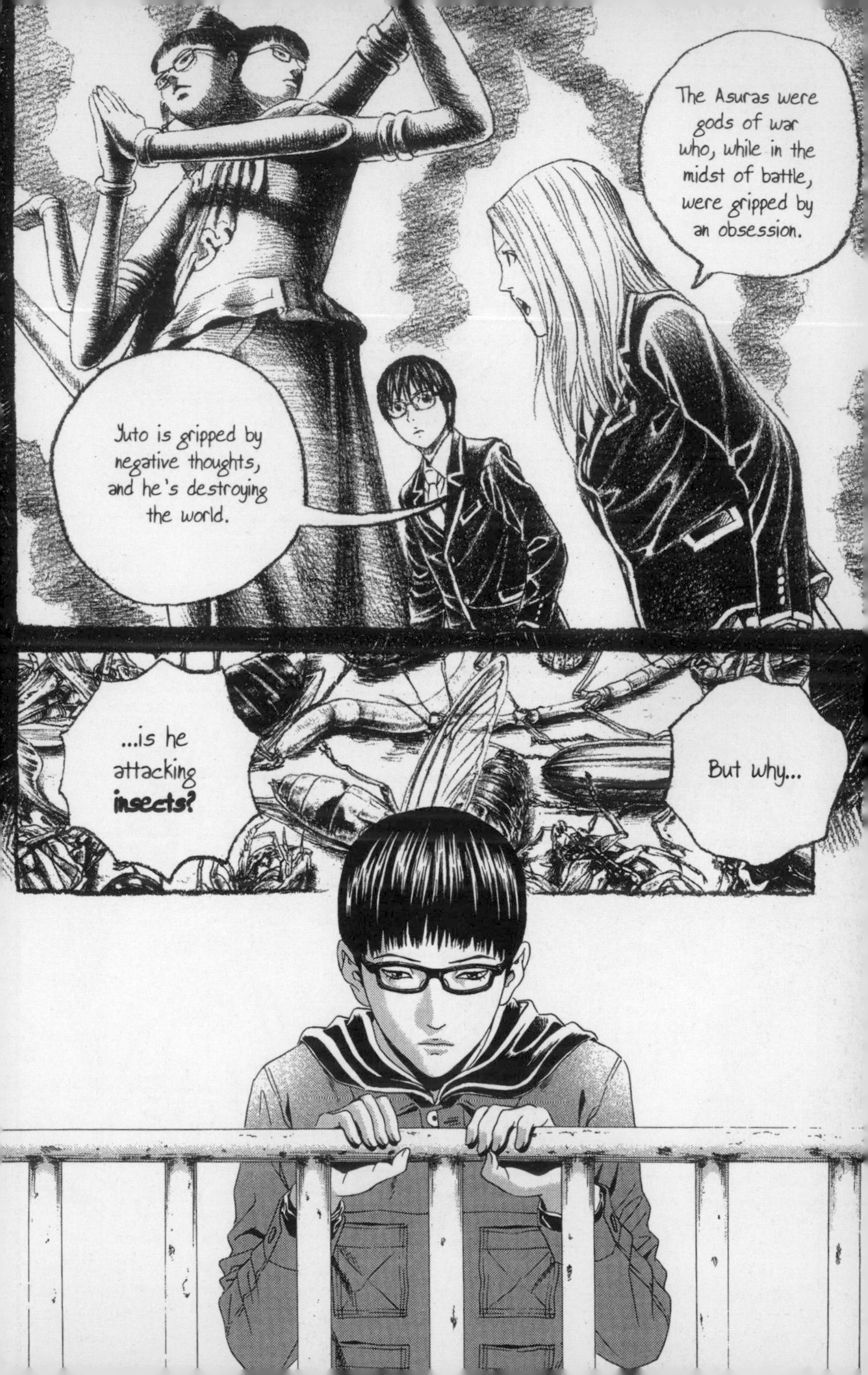
The Asuras were gods of war who, while in the midst of battle, were gripped by an obsession.
Yuto is gripped by negative thoughts, and he's destroying the world.
But why...
...is he attacking **insects?**

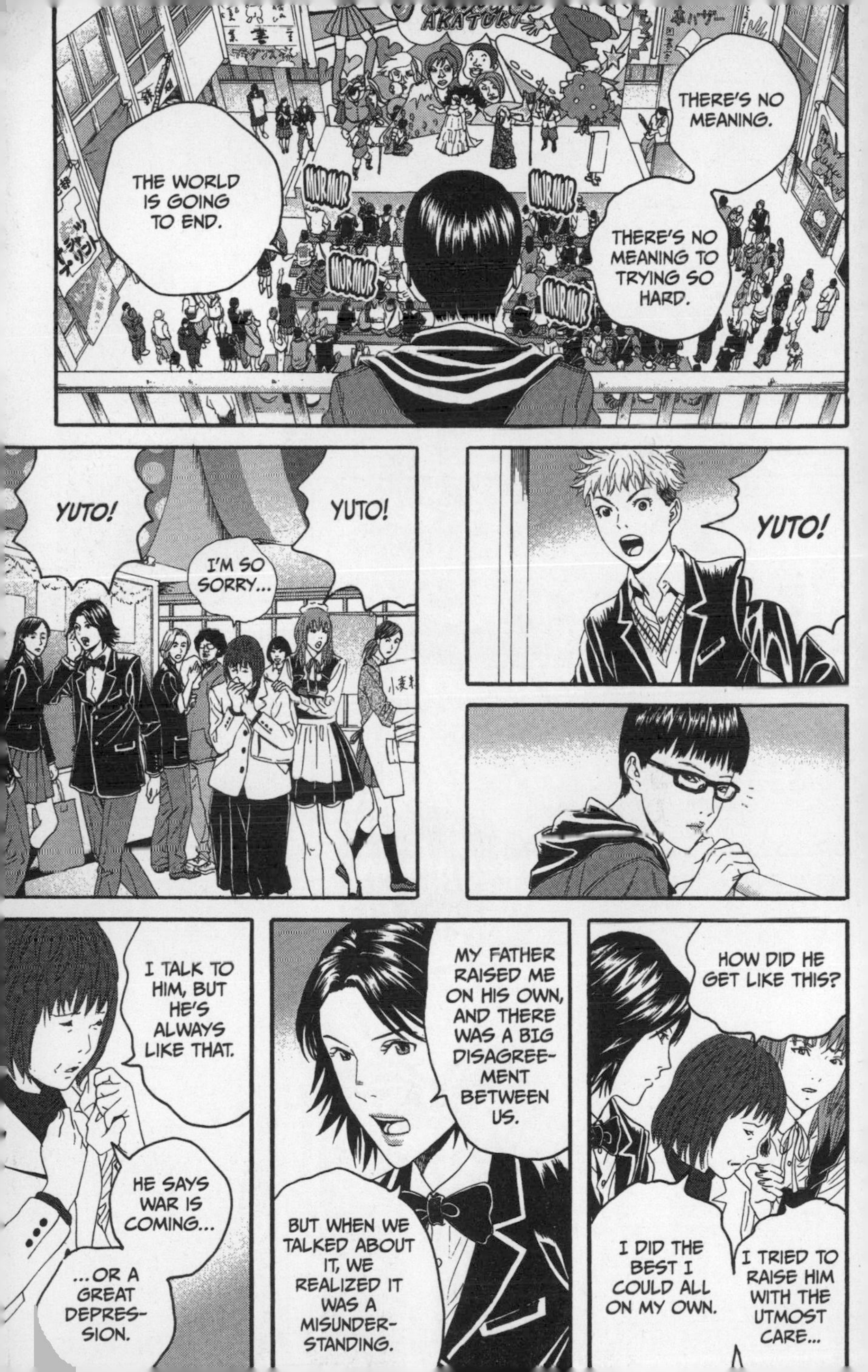
AKATURI
THERE'S NO MEANING.
THERE'S NO MEANING TO TRYING SO HARD.
MURMUR
MURMUR
MURMUR
MURMUR
THE WORLD IS GOING TO END.
YUTO!
YUTO!
YUTO!
I'M SO SORRY...
HOW DID HE GET LIKE THIS?
I TRIED TO RAISE HIM WITH THE UTMOST CARE...
I DID THE BEST I COULD ALL ON MY OWN.
MY FATHER RAISED ME ON HIS OWN, AND THERE WAS A BIG DISAGREE-MENT BETWEEN US.
BUT WHEN WE TALKED ABOUT IT, WE REALIZED IT WAS A MISUNDER-STANDING.
I TALK TO HIM, BUT HE'S ALWAYS LIKE THAT.
HE SAYS WAR IS COMING...
...OR A GREAT DEPRES-SION.

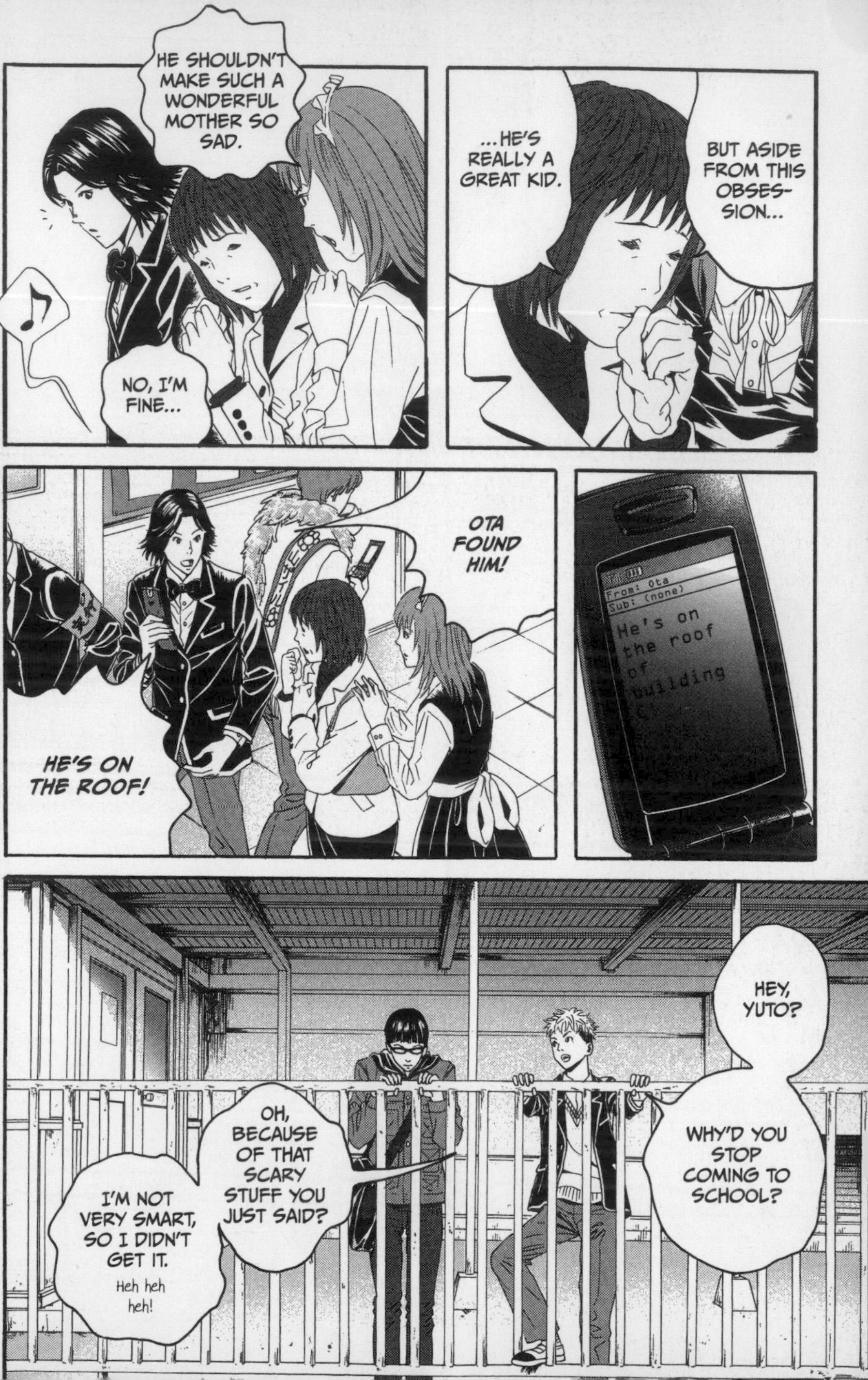
BUT ASIDE FROM THIS OBSES-SION...
...HE'S REALLY A GREAT KID.
HE SHOULDN'T MAKE SUCH A WONDERFUL MOTHER SO SAD.
NO, I'M FINE...
From: Ota
Sub: (none)
He's on the roof of building
OTA FOUND HIM!
HE'S ON THE ROOF!
HEY, YUTO?
WHY'D YOU STOP COMING TO SCHOOL?
OH, BECAUSE OF THAT SCARY STUFF YOU JUST SAID?
I'M NOT VERY SMART, SO I DIDN'T GET IT. Heh heh heh!

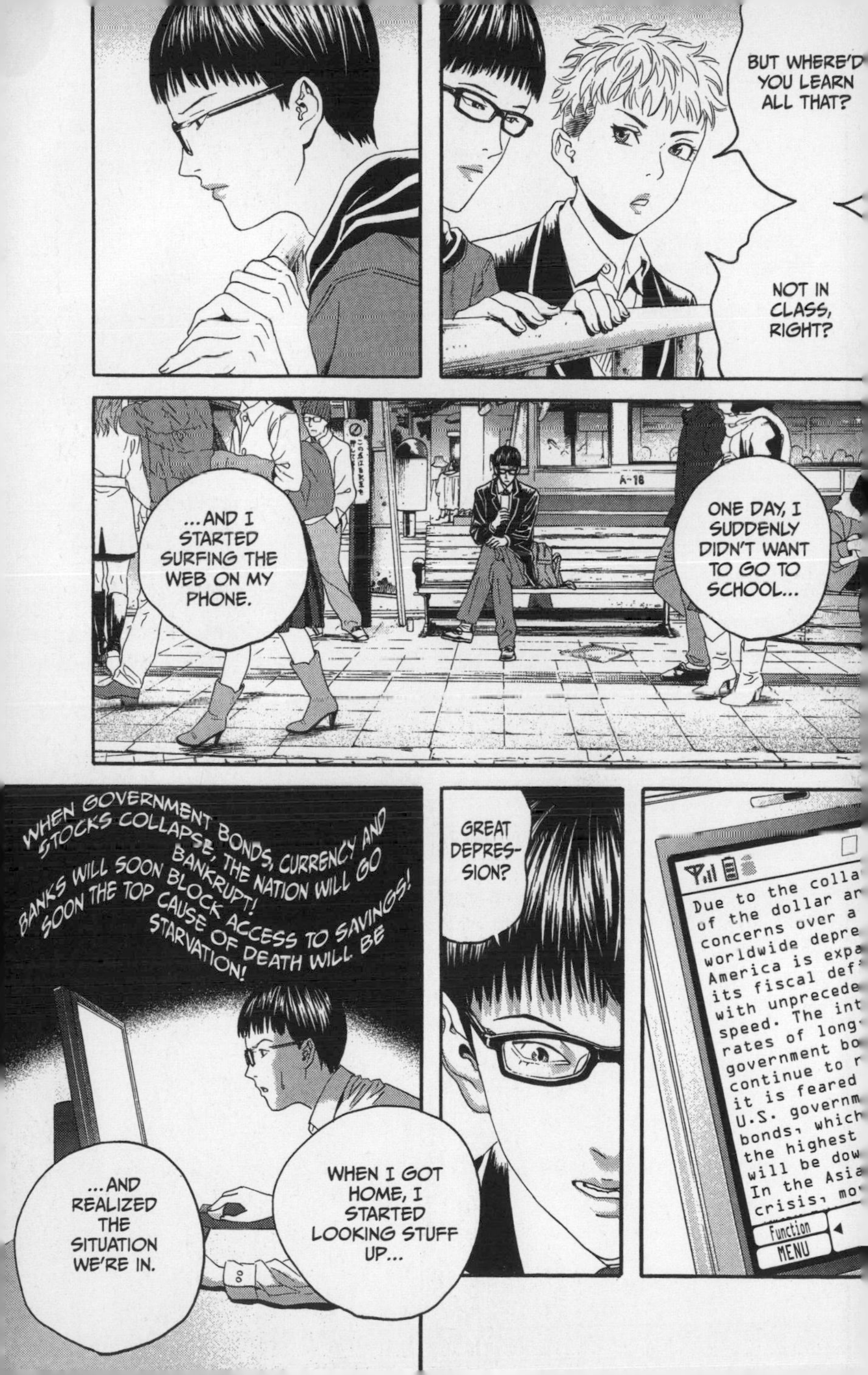
BUT WHERE'D YOU LEARN ALL THAT?
NOT IN CLASS, RIGHT?
ONE DAY, I SUDDENLY DIDN'T WANT TO GO TO SCHOOL...
A-18
...AND I STARTED SURFING THE WEB ON MY PHONE.
Due to the colla
of the dollar ar
concerns over a
worldwide depre
America is expa
its fiscal def
with unprecede
speed. The int
rates of long
government bo
continue to r
it is feared
U.S. governm
bonds, which
the highest
will be dow
In the Asia
crisis, mo
Function
MENU
GREAT DEPRES-SION?
WHEN GOVERNMENT BONDS, CURRENCY AND STOCKS COLLAPSE, THE NATION WILL GO BANKRUPT! BANKS WILL SOON BLOCK ACCESS TO SAVINGS! SOON THE TOP CAUSE OF DEATH WILL BE STARVATION!
WHEN I GOT HOME, I STARTED LOOKING STUFF UP...
...AND REALIZED THE SITUATION WE'RE IN.

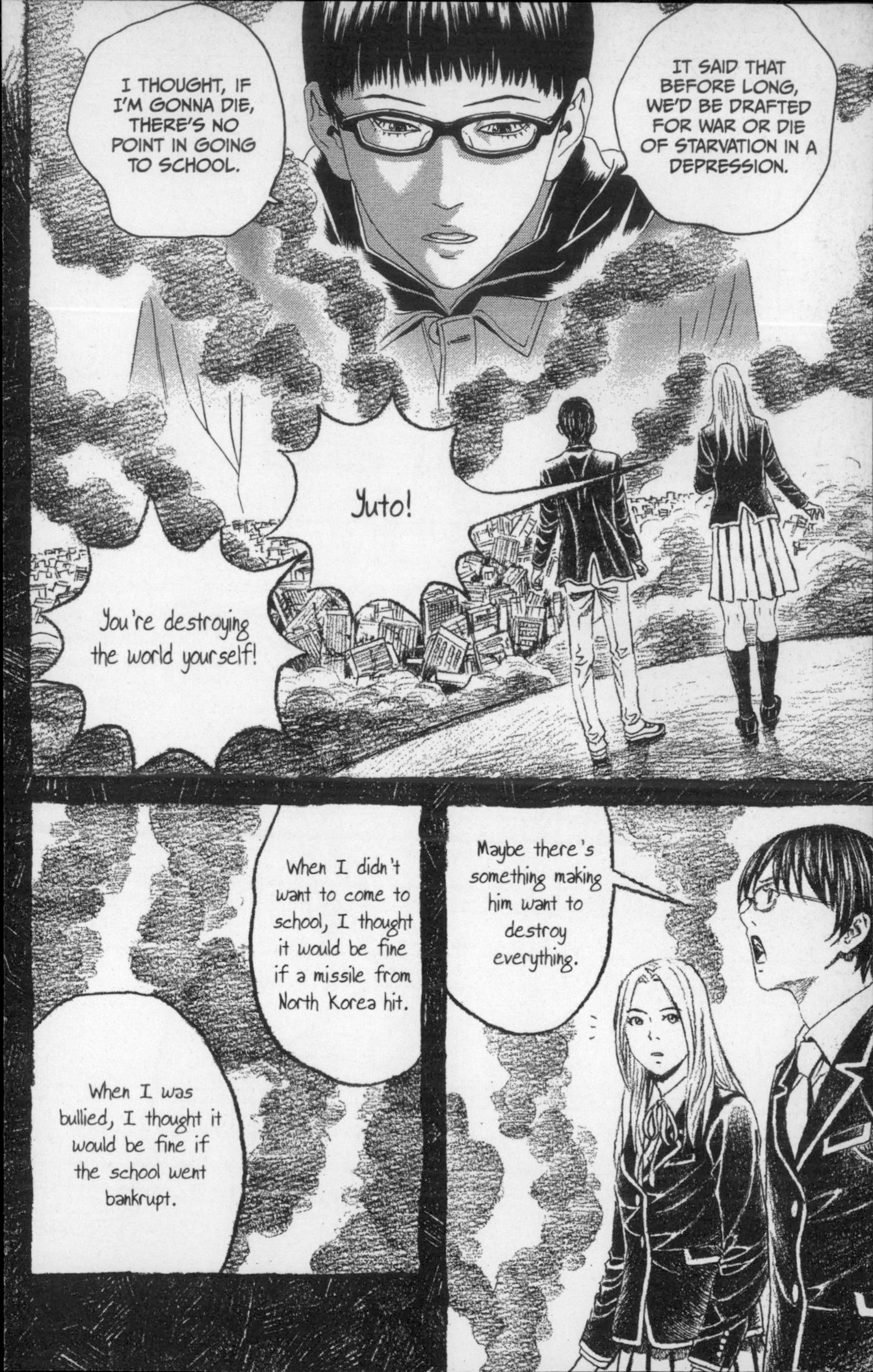
IT SAID THAT BEFORE LONG, WE'D BE DRAFTED FOR WAR OR DIE OF STARVATION IN A DEPRESSION.
I THOUGHT, IF I'M GONNA DIE, THERE'S NO POINT IN GOING TO SCHOOL.
Yuto!
You're destroying the world yourself!
Maybe there's something making him want to destroy everything.
When I didn't want to come to school, I thought it would be fine if a missile from North Korea hit.
When I was bullied, I thought it would be fine if the school went bankrupt.

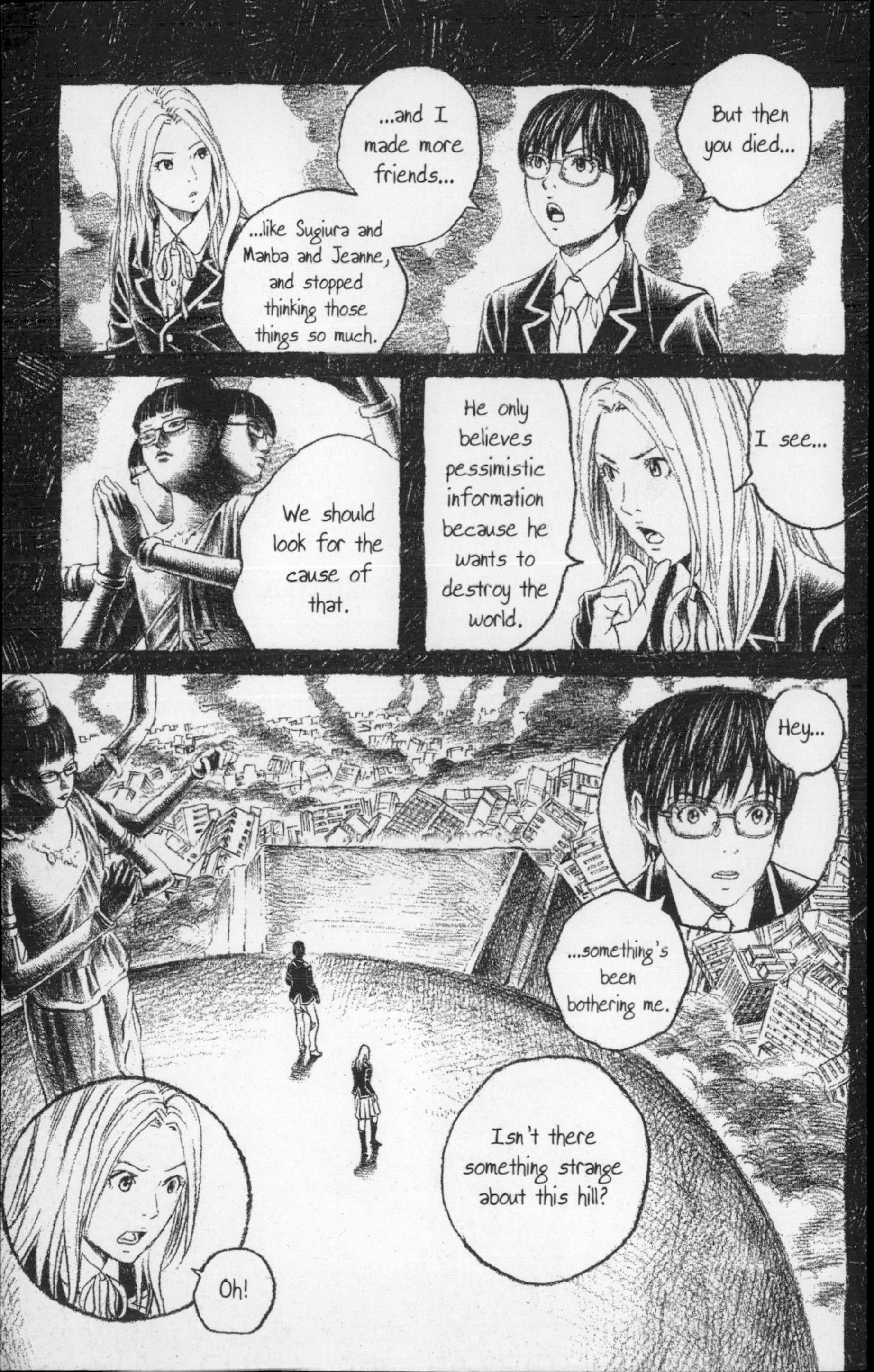
But then you died...
...and I made more friends...
...like Sugiura and Manba and Jeanne, and stopped thinking those things so much.
I see...
He only believes pessimistic information because he wants to destroy the world.
We should look for the cause of that.
Hey...
...something's been bothering me.
Isn't there something strange about this hill?
Oh!

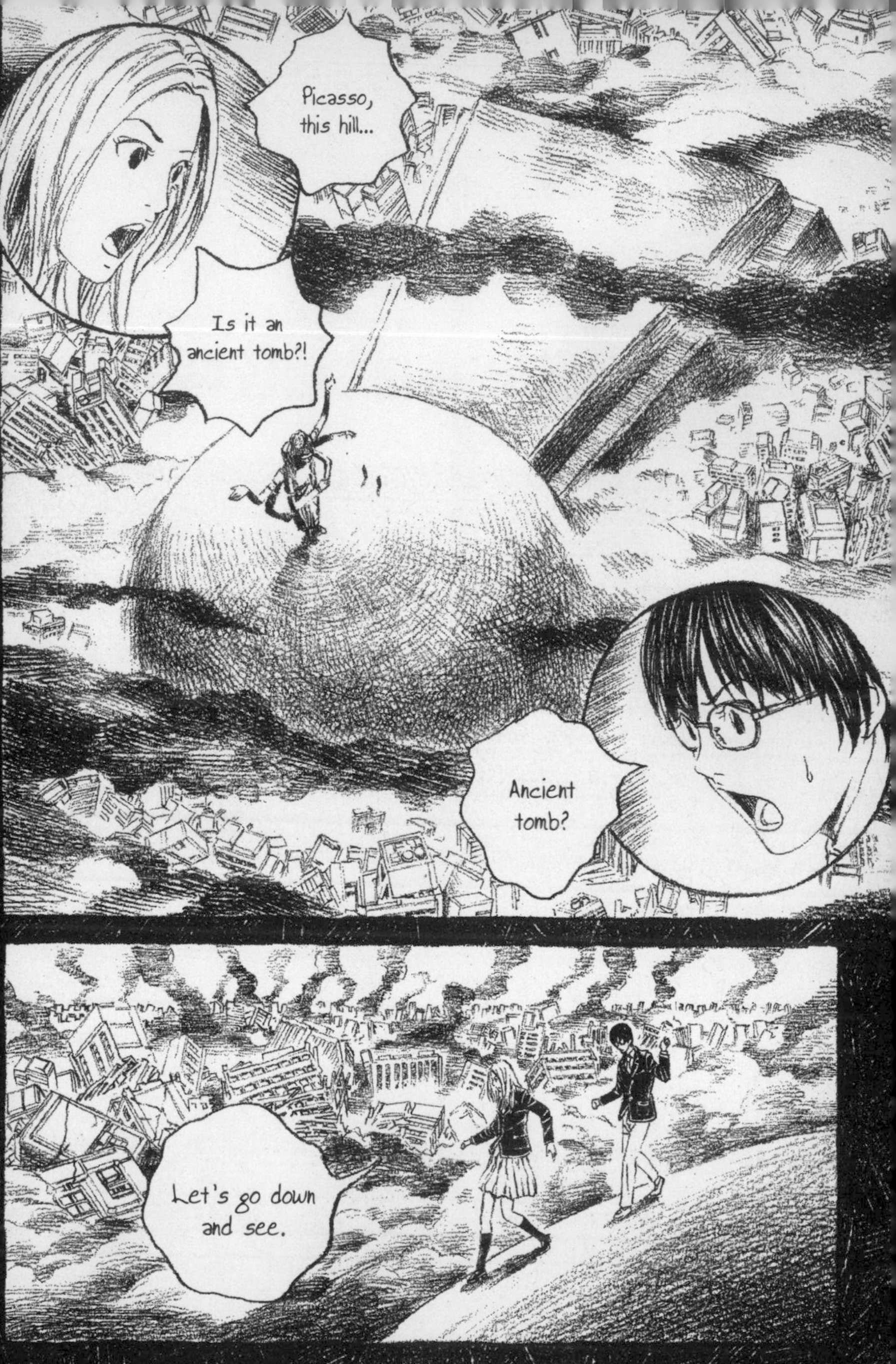
Picasso, this hill...
Is it an ancient tomb?!
Ancient tomb?
Let's go down and see.

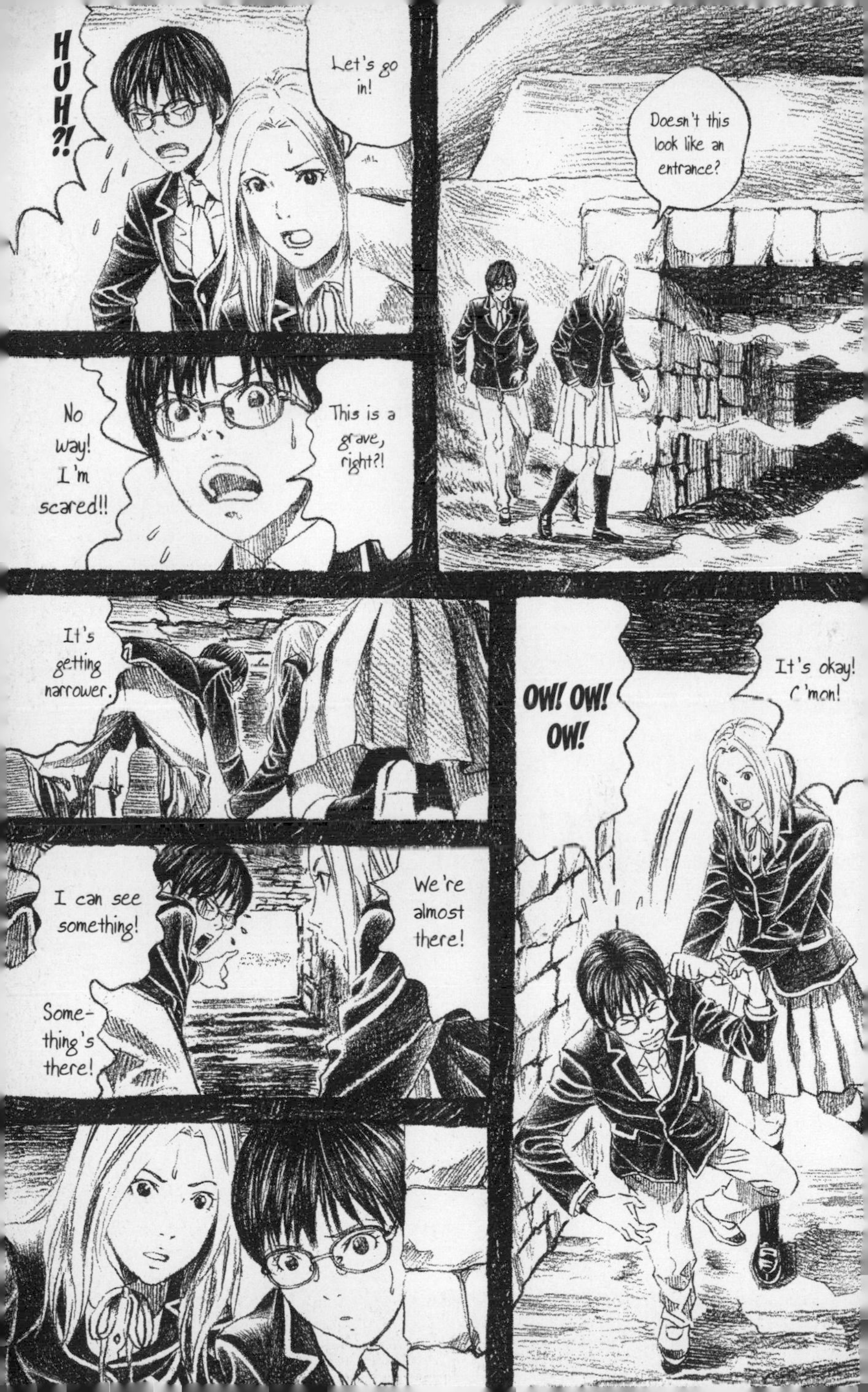
Doesn't this look like an entrance?
Let's go in!
HUH?!
This is a grave, right?!
No way! I'm scared!!
It's okay! C'mon!
OW! OW! OW!
It's getting narrower.
We're almost there!
I can see something!
Some-thing's there!

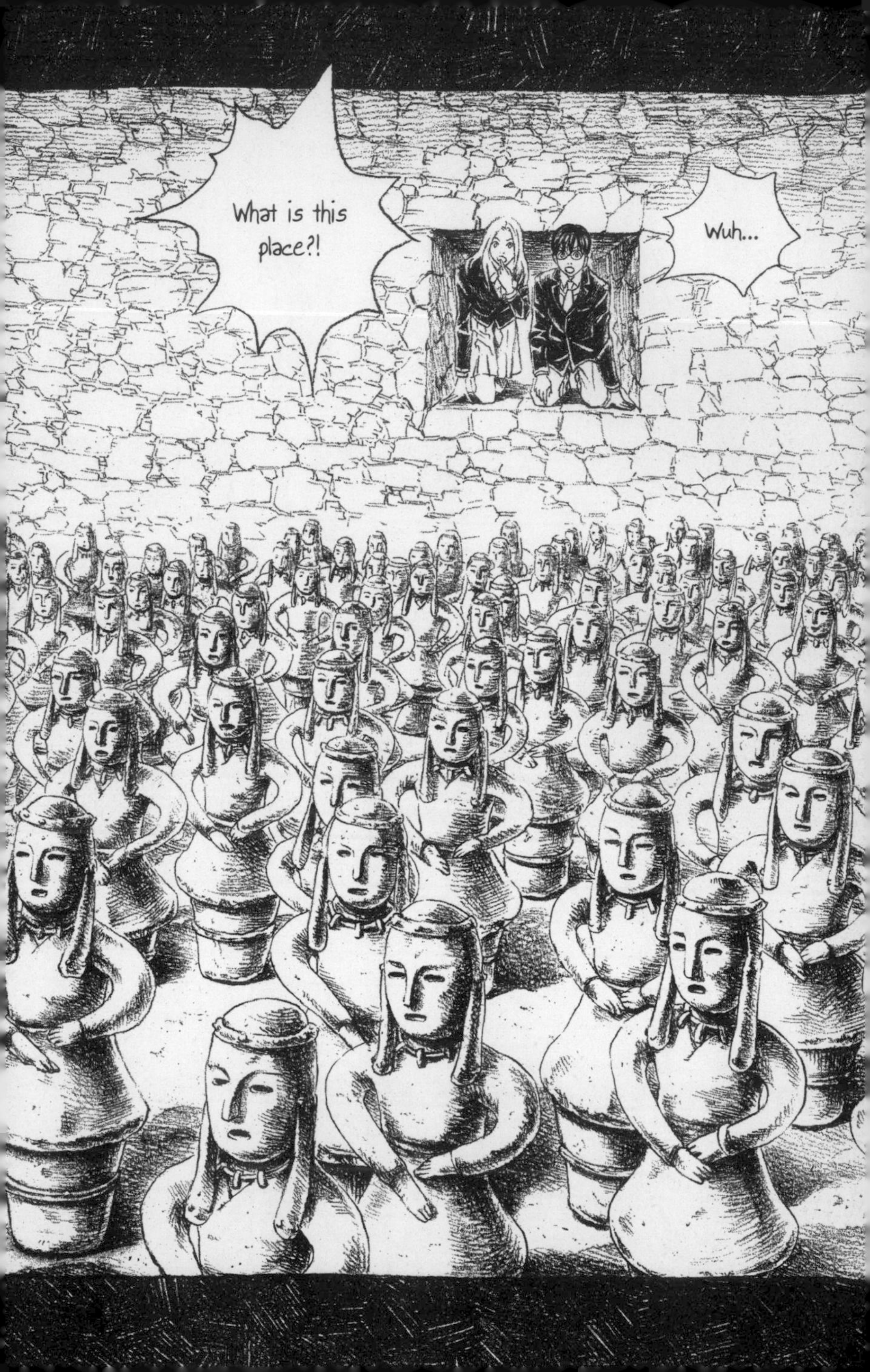
Wuh...
What is this place?!

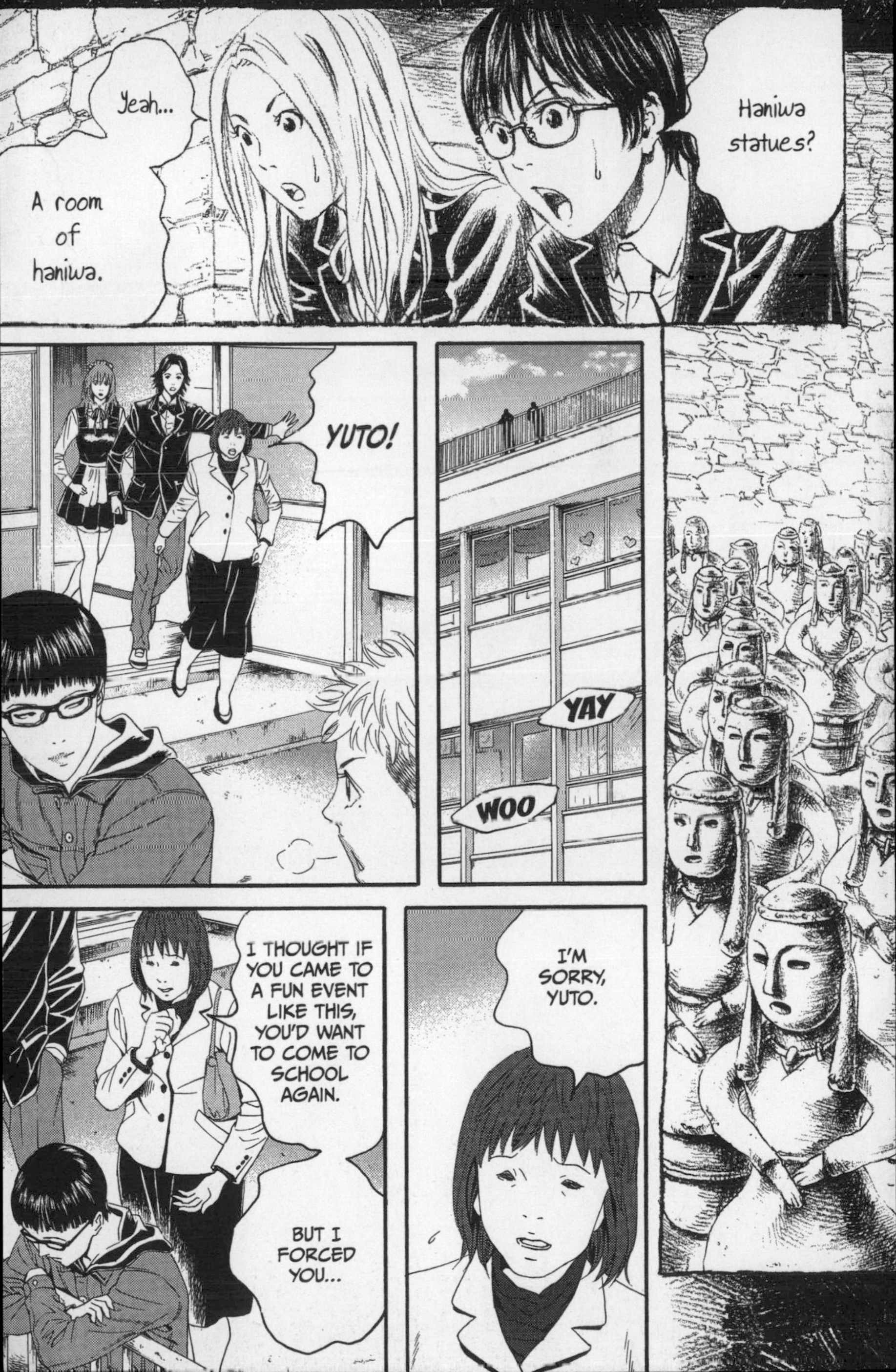
Haniwa statues?
Yeah...
A room of haniwa.
YAY
WOO
YUTO!
I'M SORRY, YUTO.
I THOUGHT IF YOU CAME TO A FUN EVENT LIKE THIS, YOU'D WANT TO COME TO SCHOOL AGAIN.
BUT I FORCED YOU...

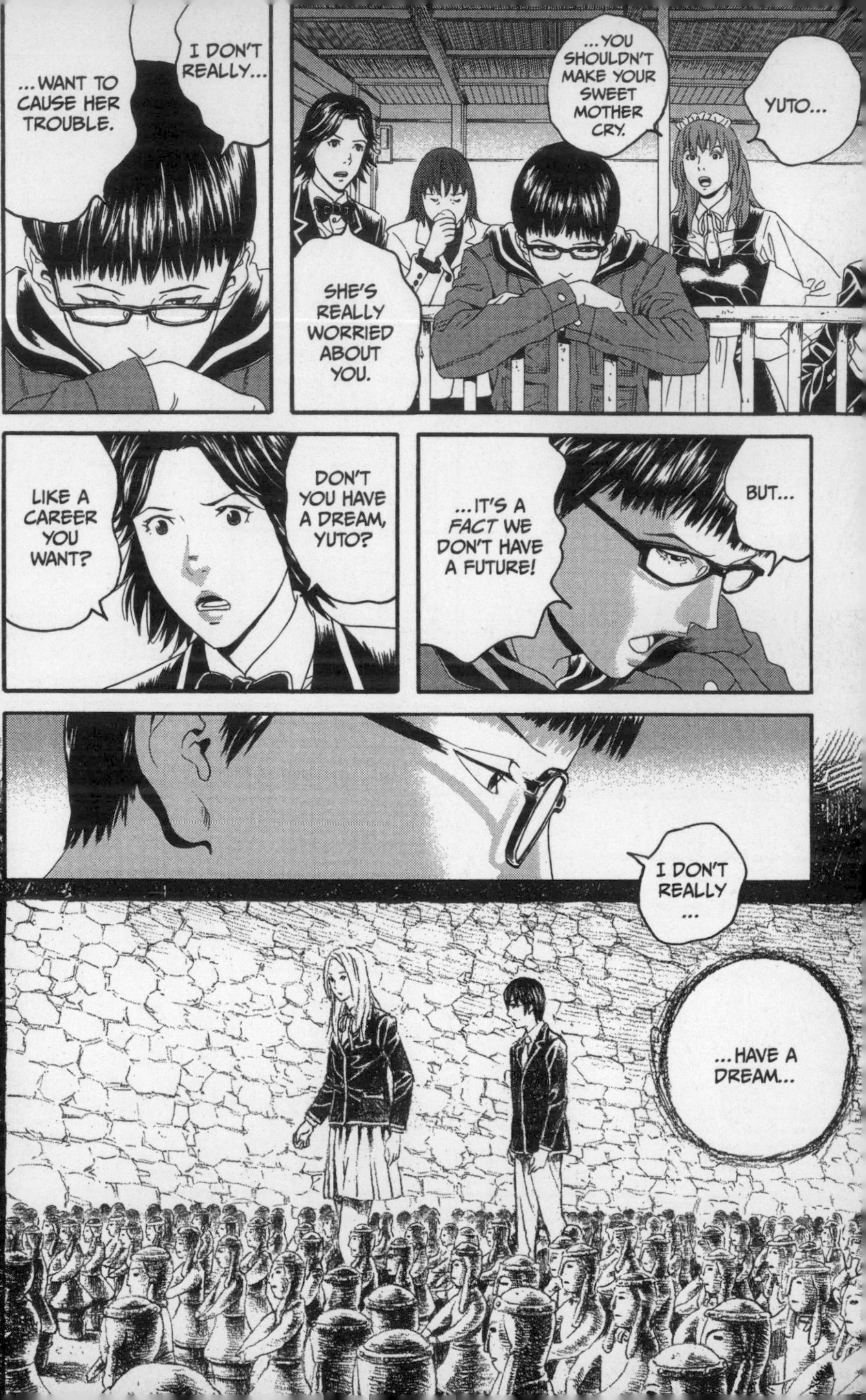
YUTO...
...YOU SHOULDN'T MAKE YOUR SWEET MOTHER CRY.
SHE'S REALLY WORRIED ABOUT YOU.
I DON'T REALLY...
...WANT TO CAUSE HER TROUBLE.
BUT...
...IT'S A *FACT* WE DON'T HAVE A FUTURE!
DON'T YOU HAVE A DREAM, YUTO?
LIKE A CAREER YOU WANT?
I DON'T REALLY ...
...HAVE A DREAM...

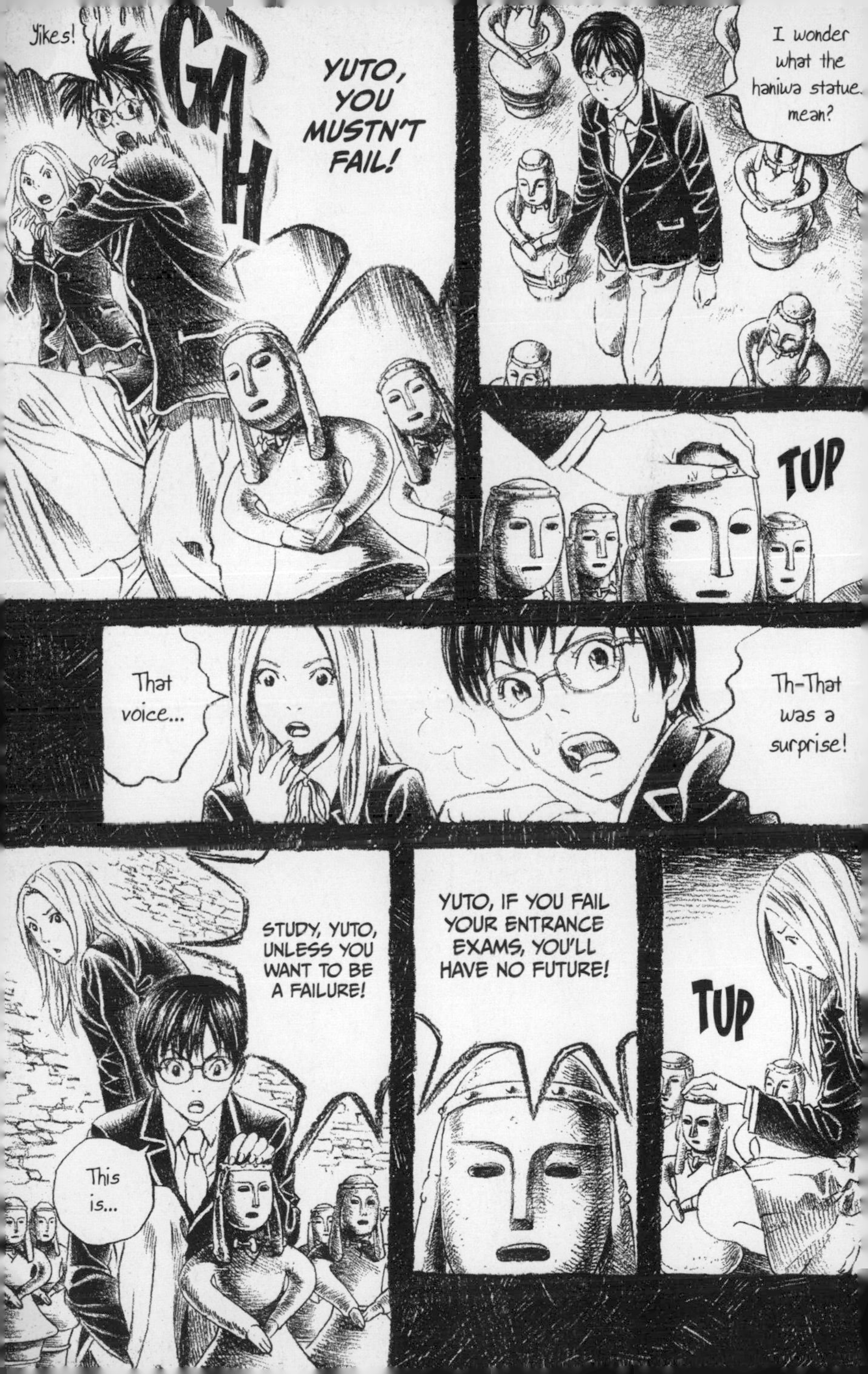
I wonder what the haniwa statue. mean?
TUP
YUTO, YOU MUSTN'T FAIL!
GAH
Yikes!
Th-That was a surprise!
That voice...
TUP
YUTO, IF YOU FAIL YOUR ENTRANCE EXAMS, YOU'LL HAVE NO FUTURE!
STUDY, YUTO, UNLESS YOU WANT TO BE A FAILURE!
This is...

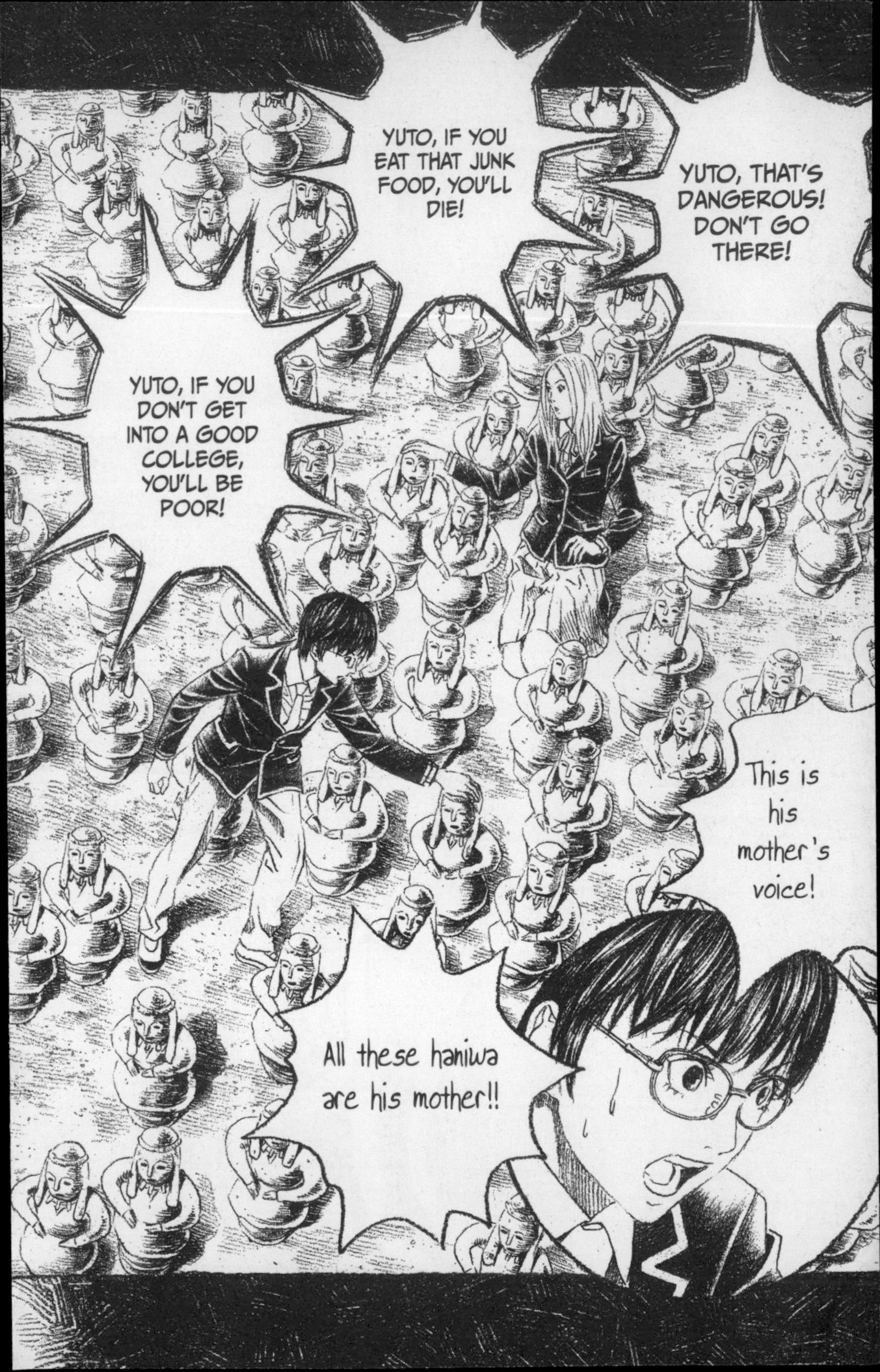
YUTO, THAT'S DANGEROUS! DON'T GO THERE!
YUTO, IF YOU EAT THAT JUNK FOOD, YOU'LL DIE!
YUTO, IF YOU DON'T GET INTO A GOOD COLLEGE, YOU'LL BE POOR!
This is his mother's voice!
All these haniwa are his mother!!

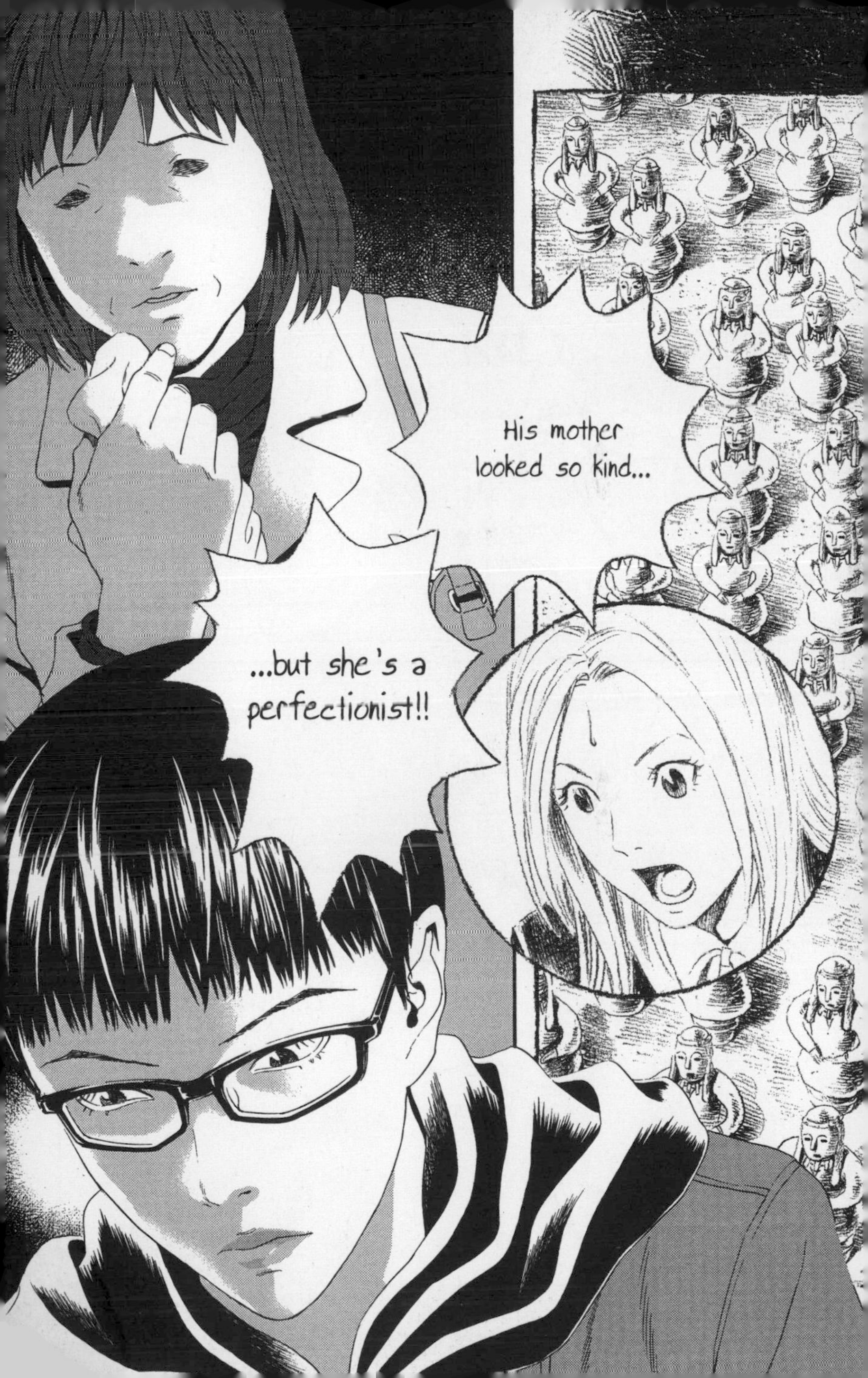
His mother looked so kind...
...but she's a perfectionist!!

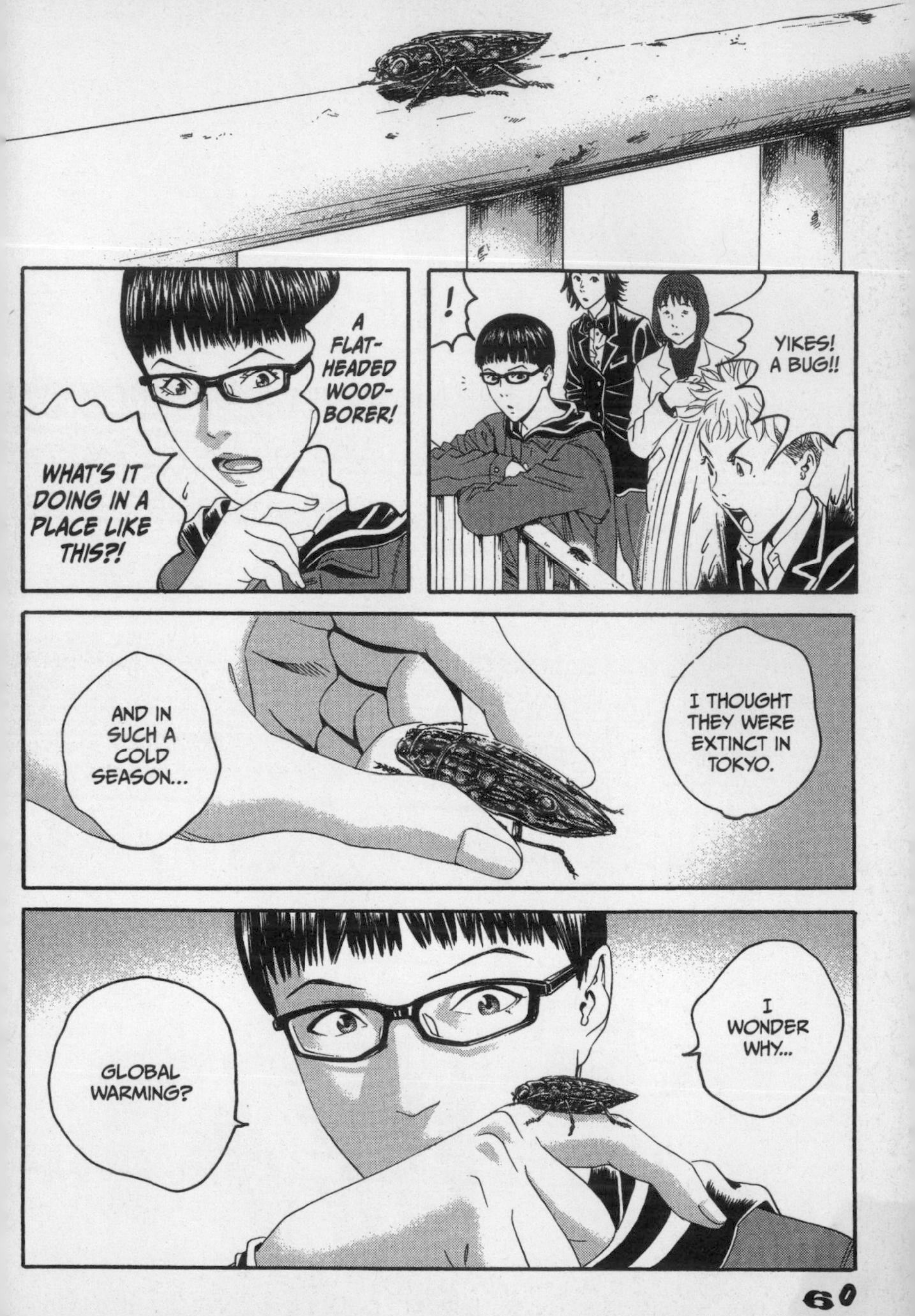
!
YIKES! A BUG!!
A FLAT-HEADED WOOD-BORER!
WHAT'S IT DOING IN A PLACE LIKE THIS?!
I THOUGHT THEY WERE EXTINCT IN TOKYO.
AND IN SUCH A COLD SEASON...
I WONDER WHY...
GLOBAL WARMING?

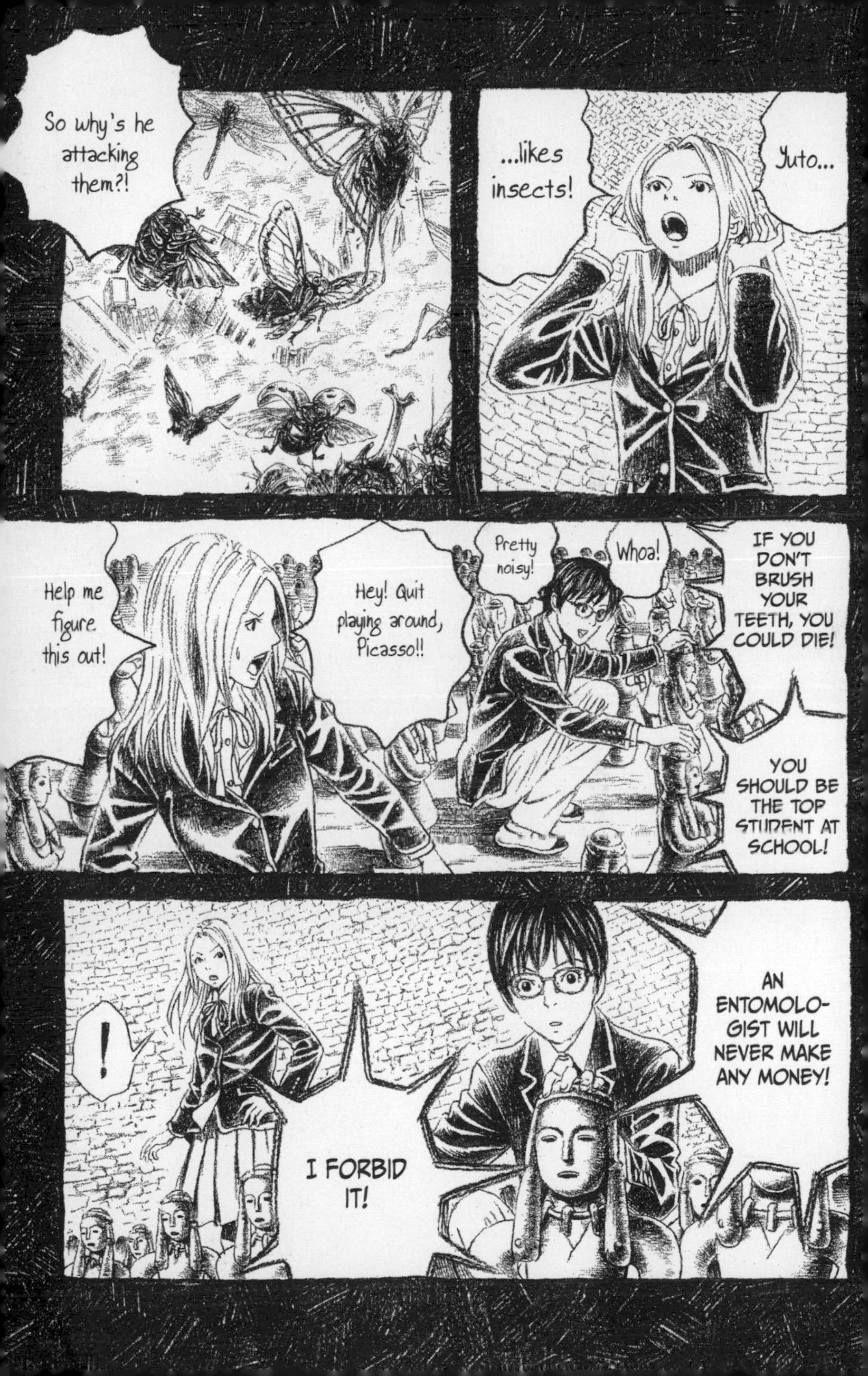
Yuto...
...likes insects!
So why's he attacking them?!
IF YOU DON'T BRUSH YOUR TEETH, YOU COULD DIE!
YOU SHOULD BE THE TOP STUDENT AT SCHOOL!
Whoa!
Pretty noisy!
Hey! Quit playing around, Picasso!!
Help me figure this out!
AN ENTOMOLO-GIST WILL NEVER MAKE ANY MONEY!
I FORBID IT!
!

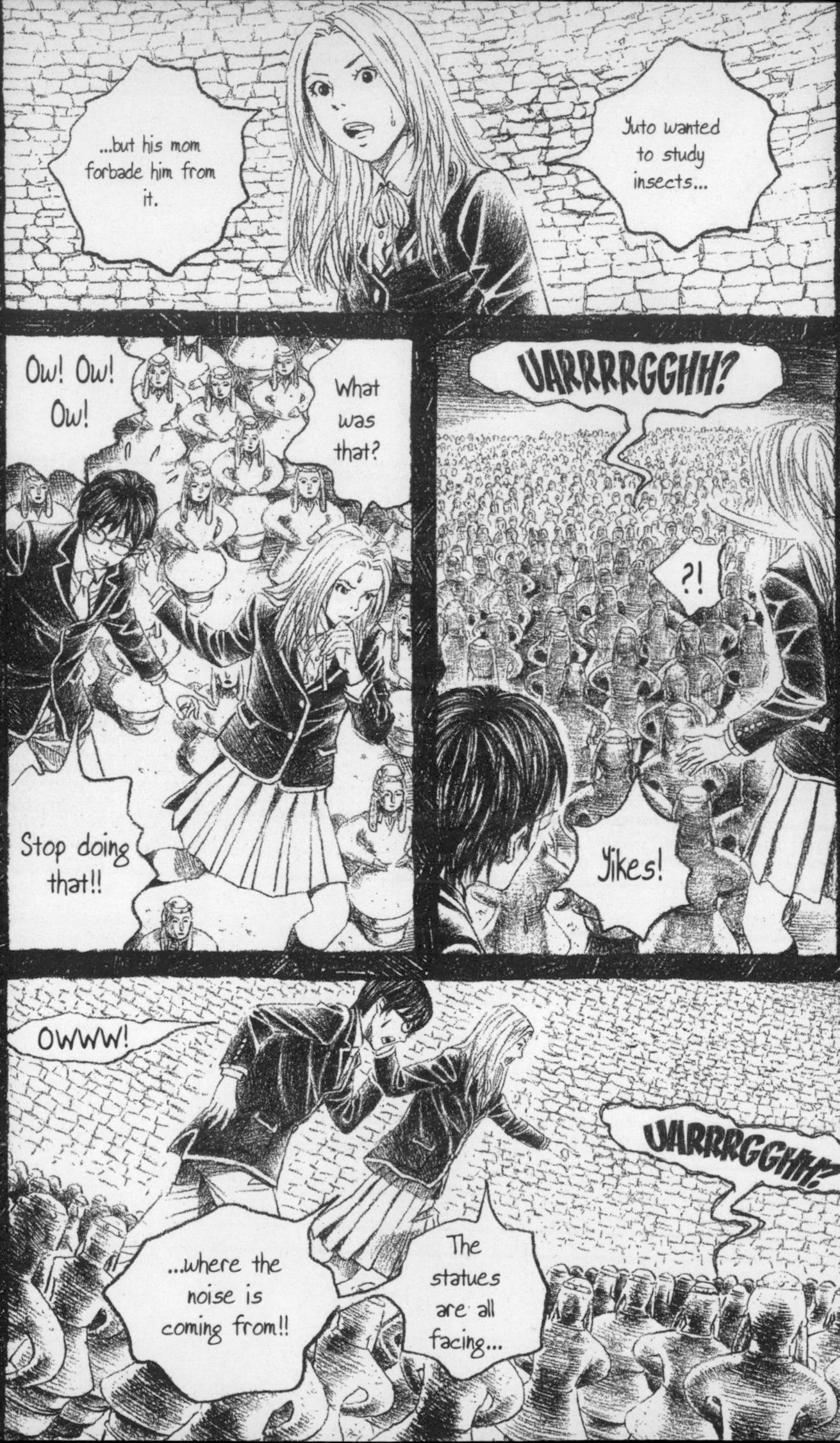
Yuto wanted to study insects...
...but his mom forbade him from it.
UARRRRGGHH?
?!
Yikes!
What was that?
Ow! Ow! Ow!
Stop doing that!!
OWWW!
UARRRGGHH?
The statues are all facing...
...where the noise is coming from!!

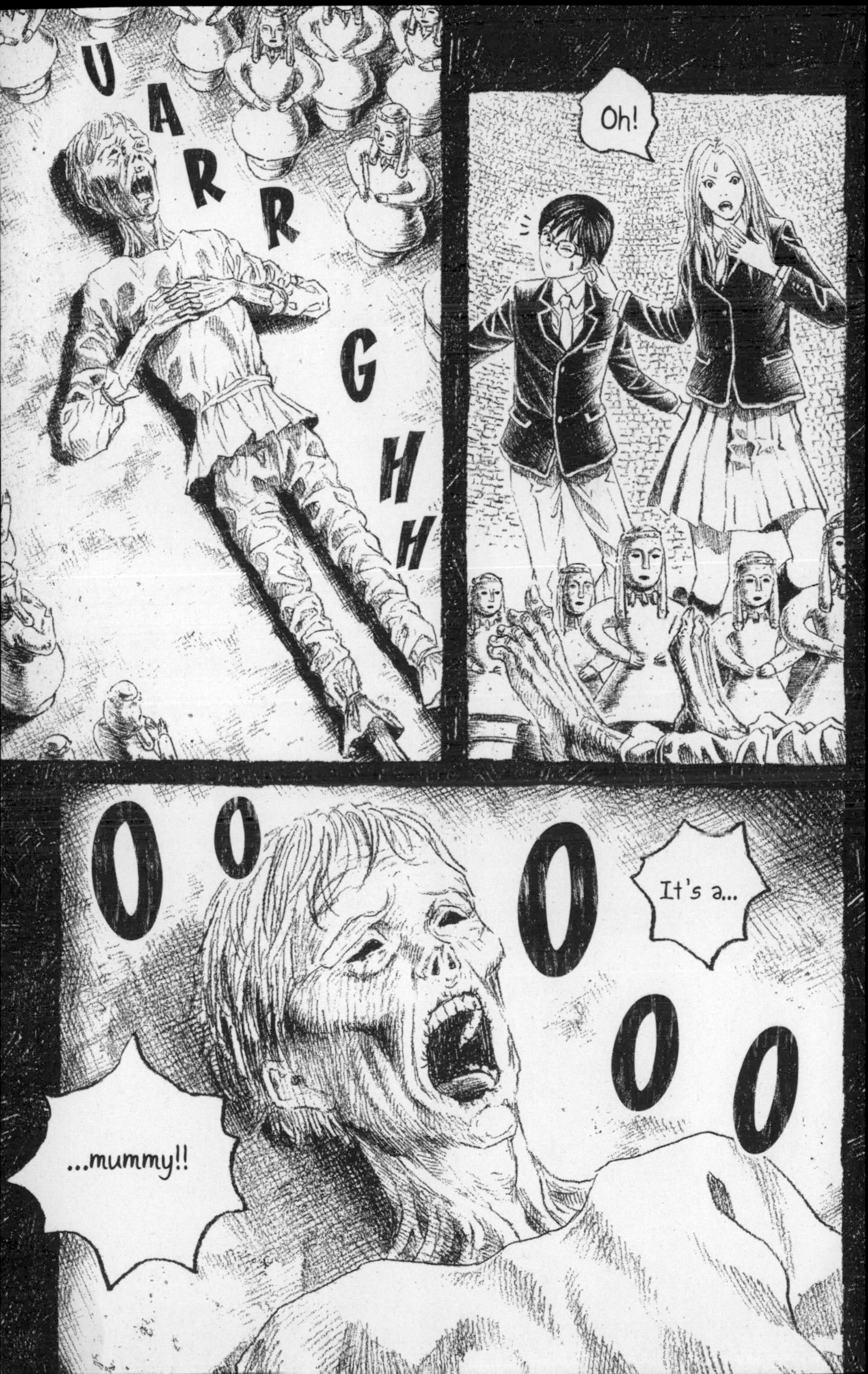
Oh!
UARRGHH
It's a...
OOOOO
...mummy!!

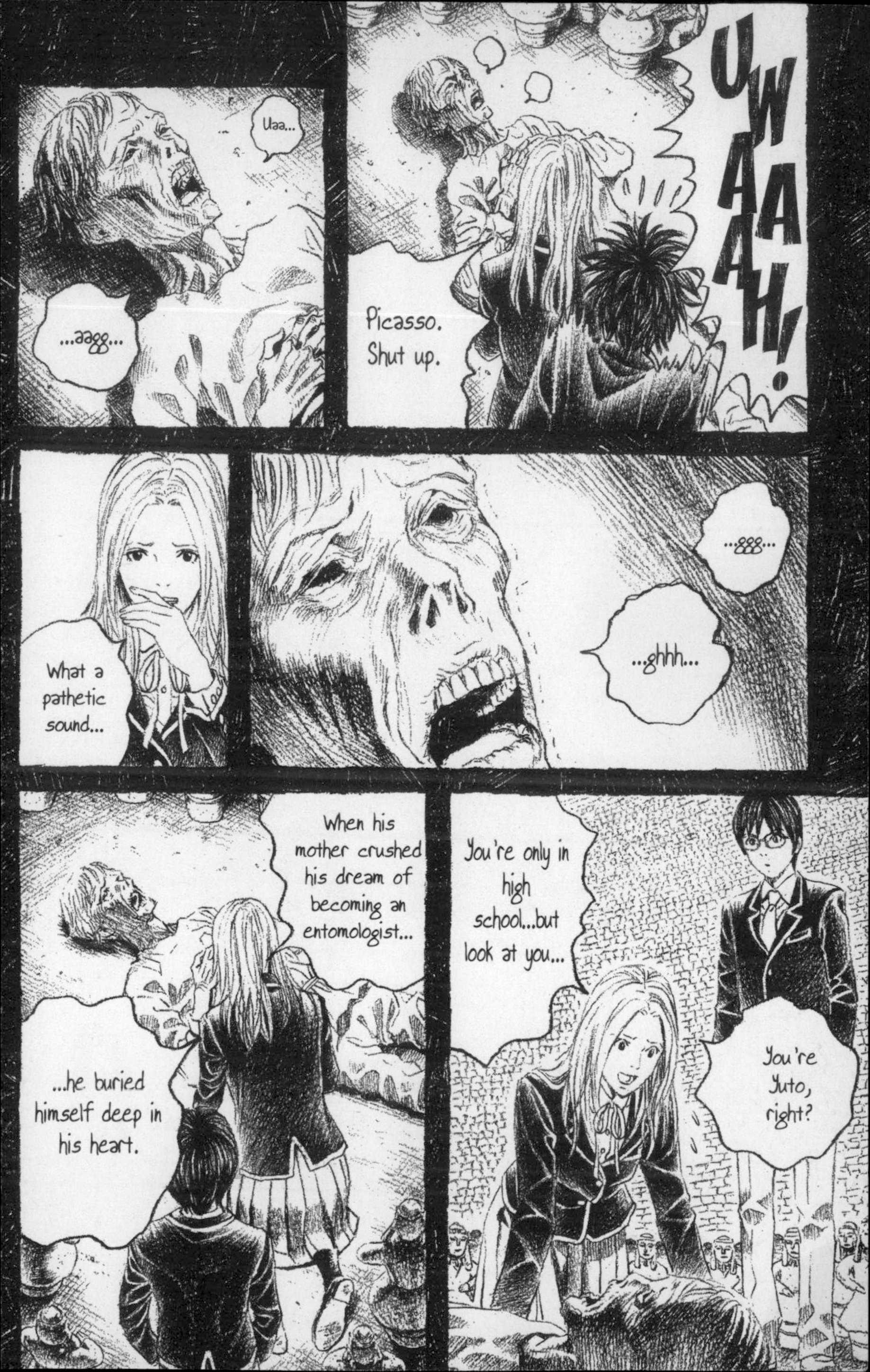
UWAAAH!
Picasso. Shut up.
Uaa...
...aagg...
...ggg...
...ghhh...
What a pathetic sound...
You're only in high school...but look at you...
You're Yuto, right?
When his mother crushed his dream of becoming an entomologist...
...he buried himself deep in his heart.

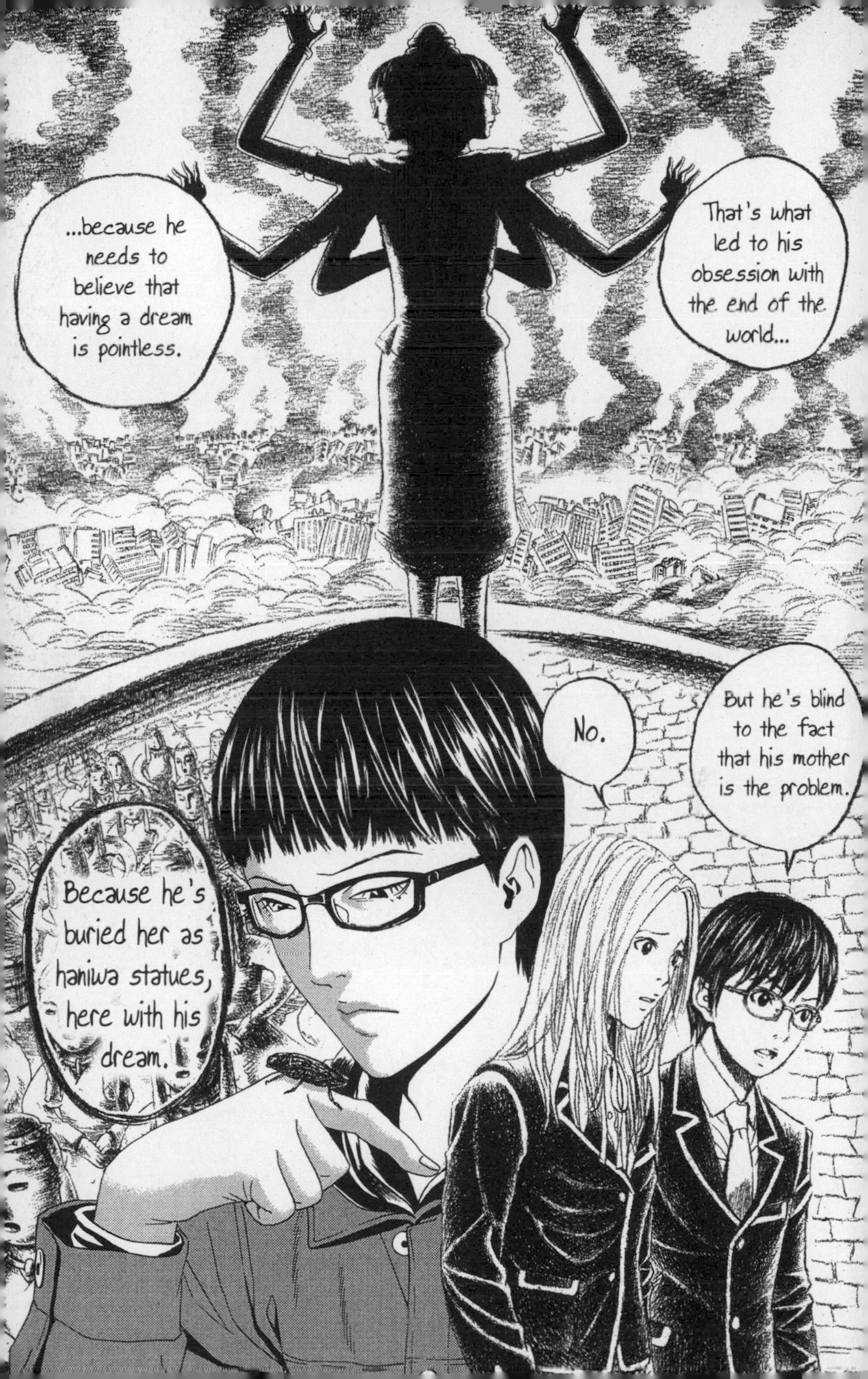
That's what led to his obsession with the end of the world...
...because he needs to believe that having a dream is pointless.
But he's blind to the fact that his mother is the problem.
No.
Because he's buried her as haniwa statues, here with his dream.

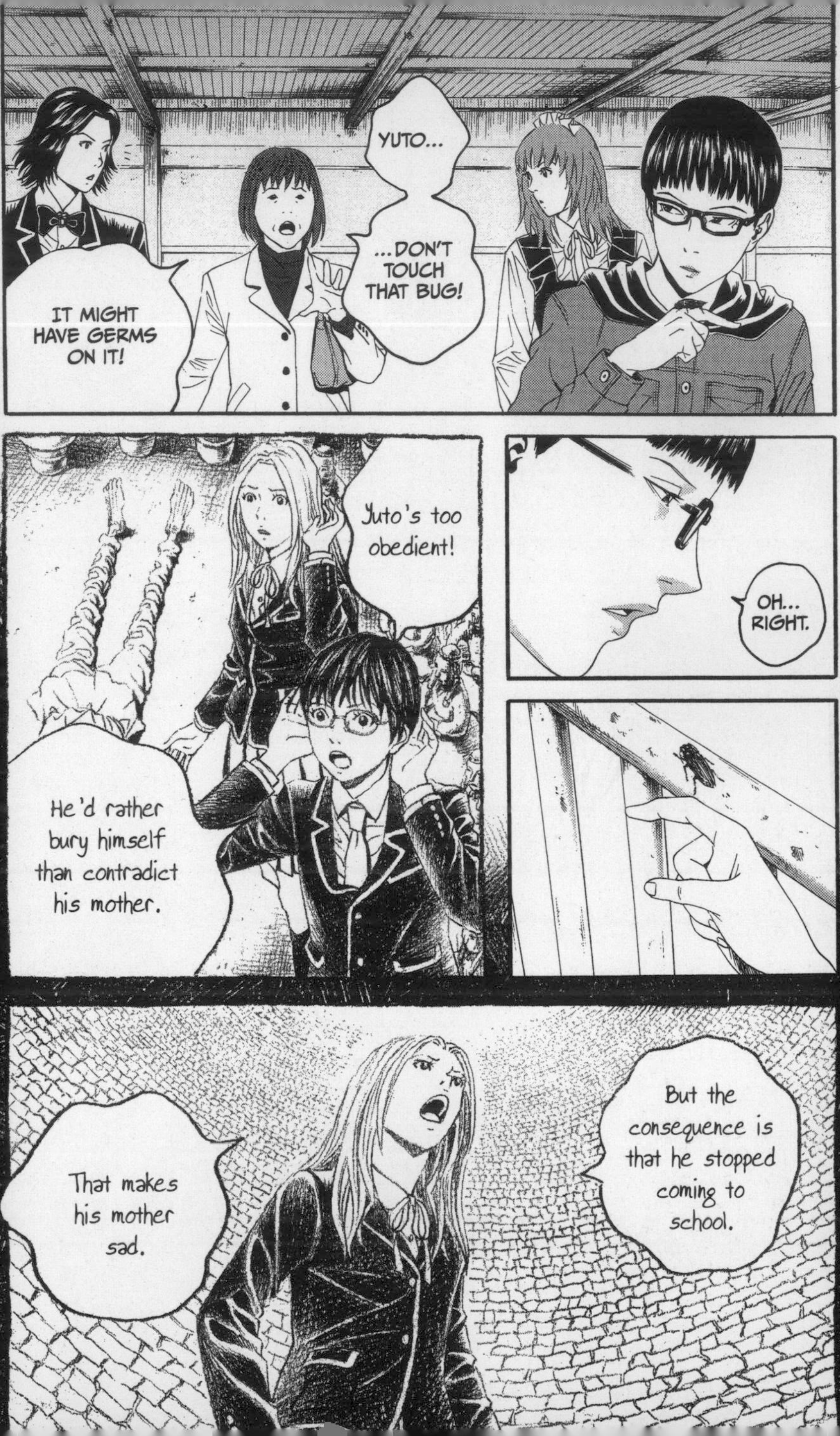
YUTO...
...DON'T TOUCH THAT BUG!
IT MIGHT HAVE GERMS ON IT!
OH... RIGHT.
Yuto's too obedient!
He'd rather bury himself than contradict his mother.
But the consequence is that he stopped coming to school.
That makes his mother sad.

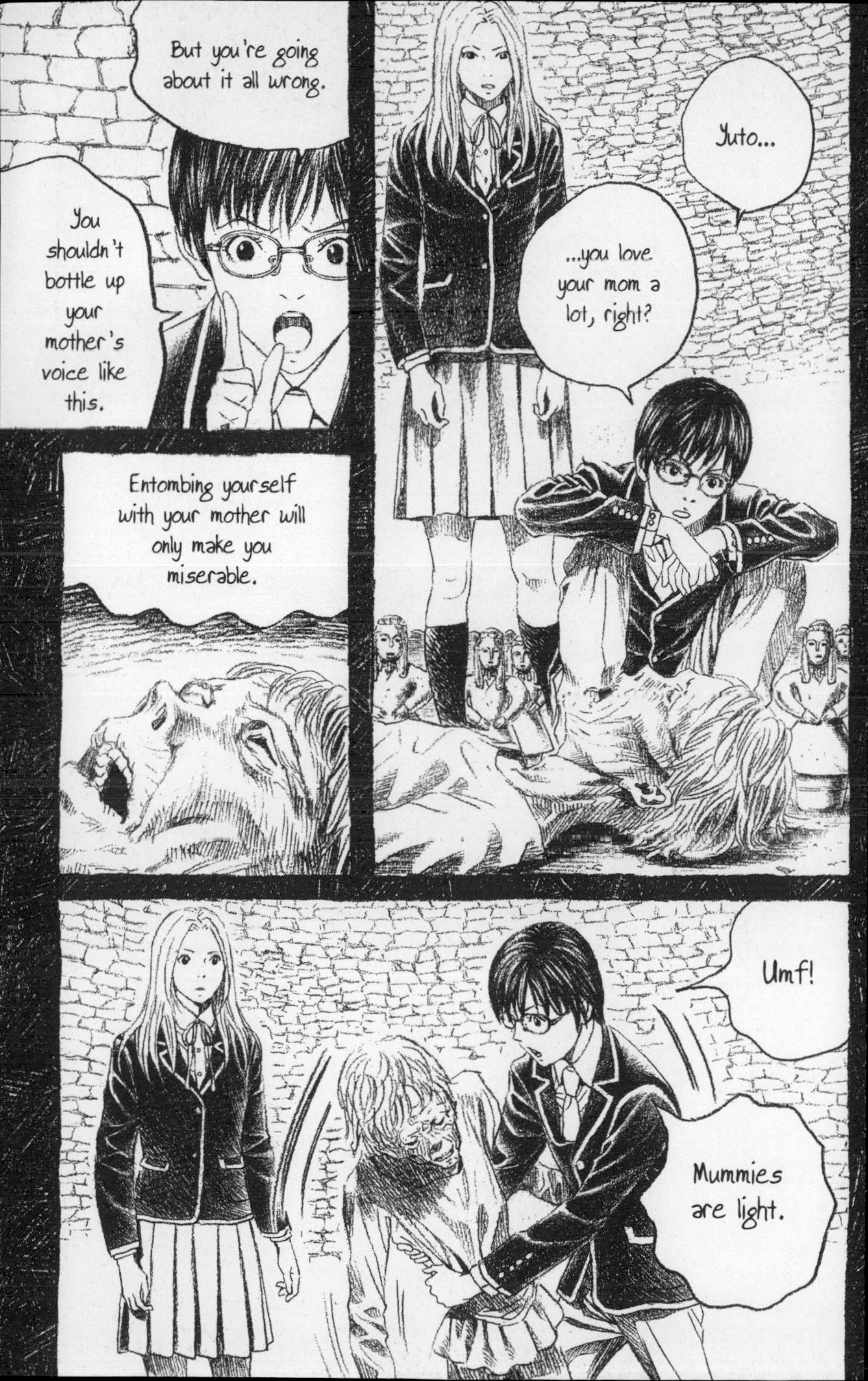
Yuto...
...you love your mom a lot, right?
But you're going about it all wrong.
You shouldn't bottle up your mother's voice like this.
Entombing yourself with your mother will only make you miserable.
Umf!
Mummies are light.

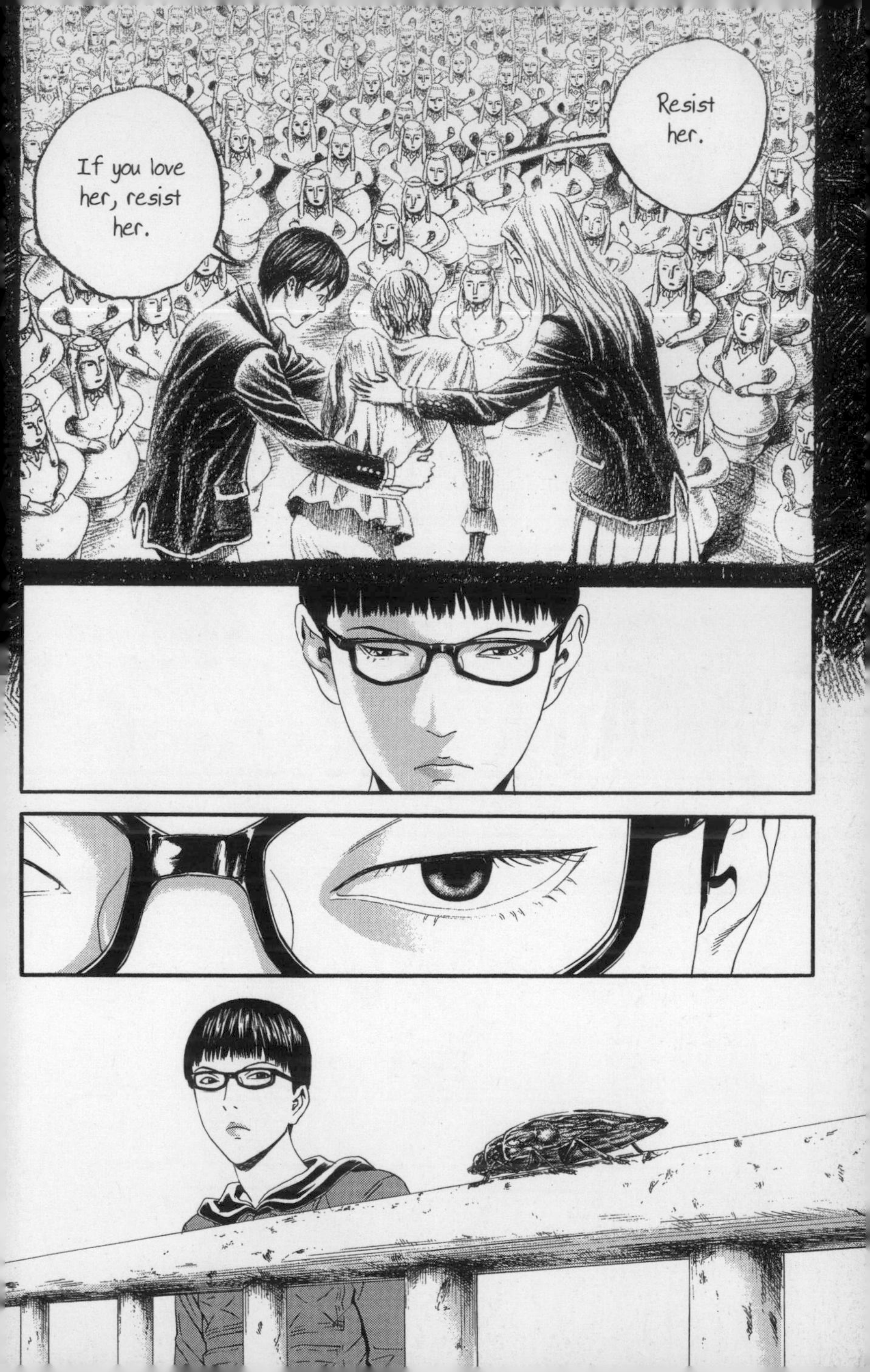
Resist her.
If you love her, resist her.

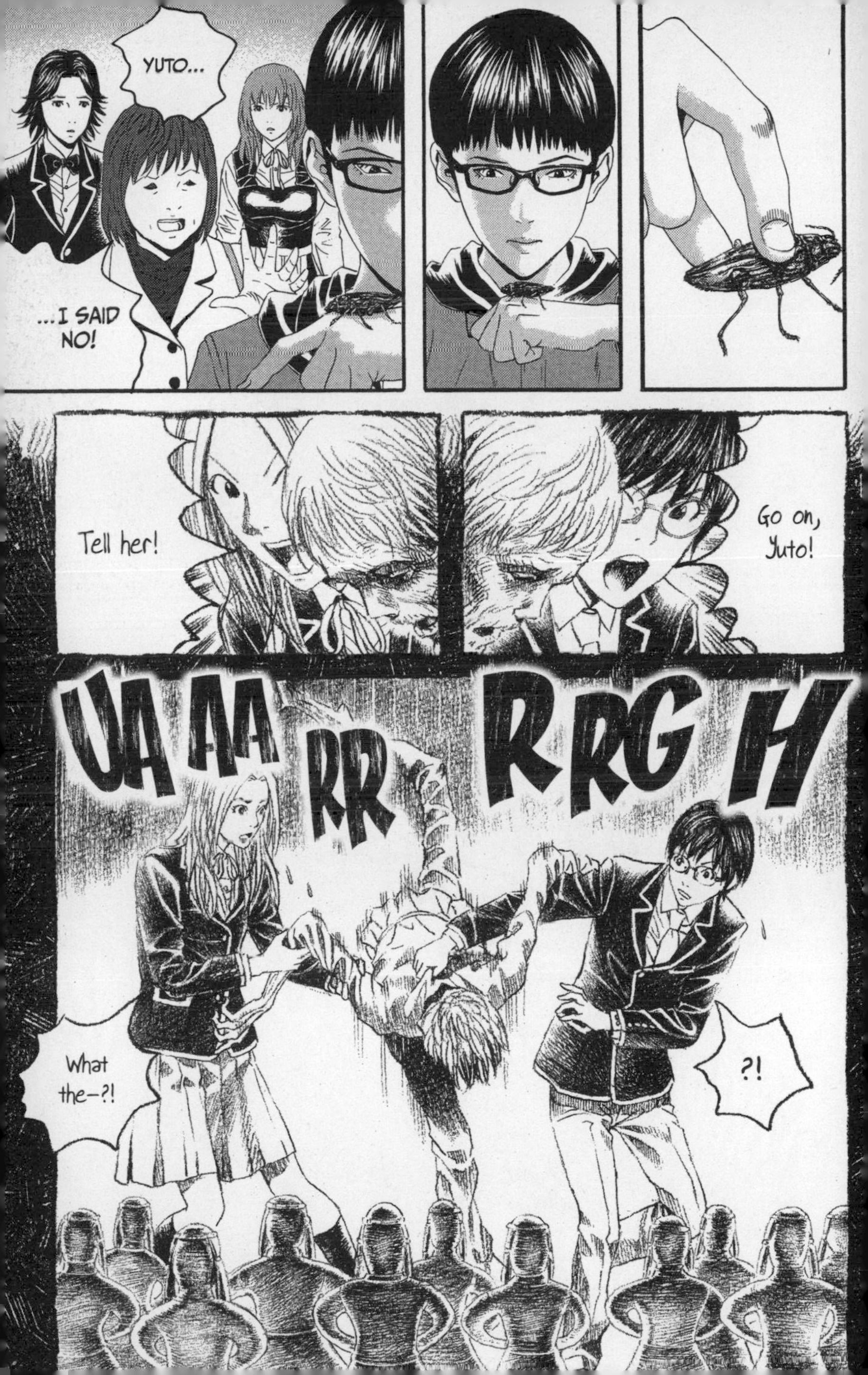
YUTO...
...I SAID NO!
Go on, Yuto!
Tell her!
UAAARRRRGH
?!
What the-?!

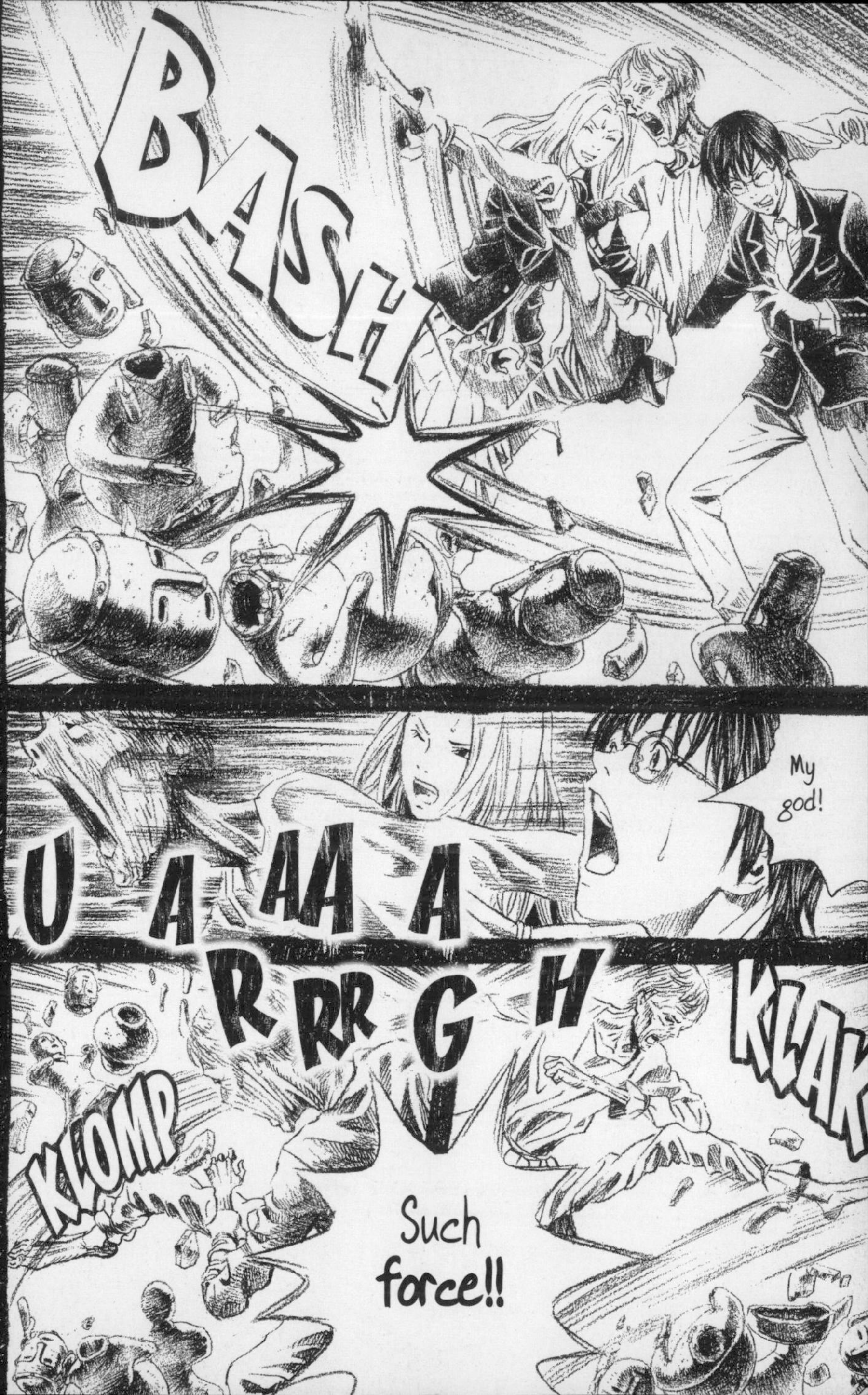
BASH
My god!
UAAAA ARRRGH
KLAK
Such force!!
KLOMP

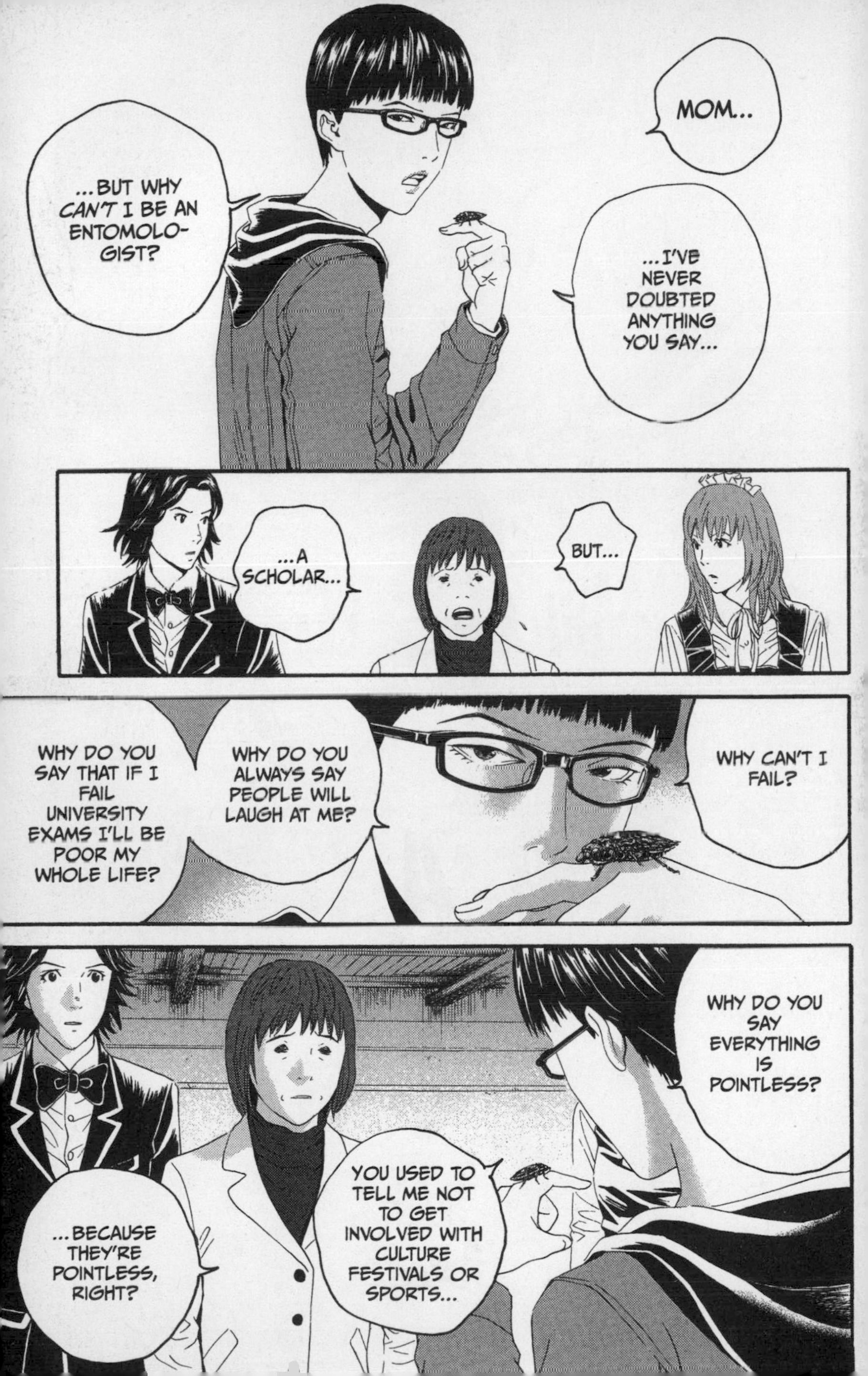
MOM...
...I'VE NEVER DOUBTED ANYTHING YOU SAY...
...BUT WHY CAN'T I BE AN ENTOMOLOGIST?
BUT...
...A SCHOLAR...
WHY CAN'T I FAIL?
WHY DO YOU ALWAYS SAY PEOPLE WILL LAUGH AT ME?
WHY DO YOU SAY THAT IF I FAIL UNIVERSITY EXAMS I'LL BE POOR MY WHOLE LIFE?
WHY DO YOU SAY EVERYTHING IS POINTLESS?
YOU USED TO TELL ME NOT TO GET INVOLVED WITH CULTURE FESTIVALS OR SPORTS...
...BECAUSE THEY'RE POINTLESS, RIGHT?

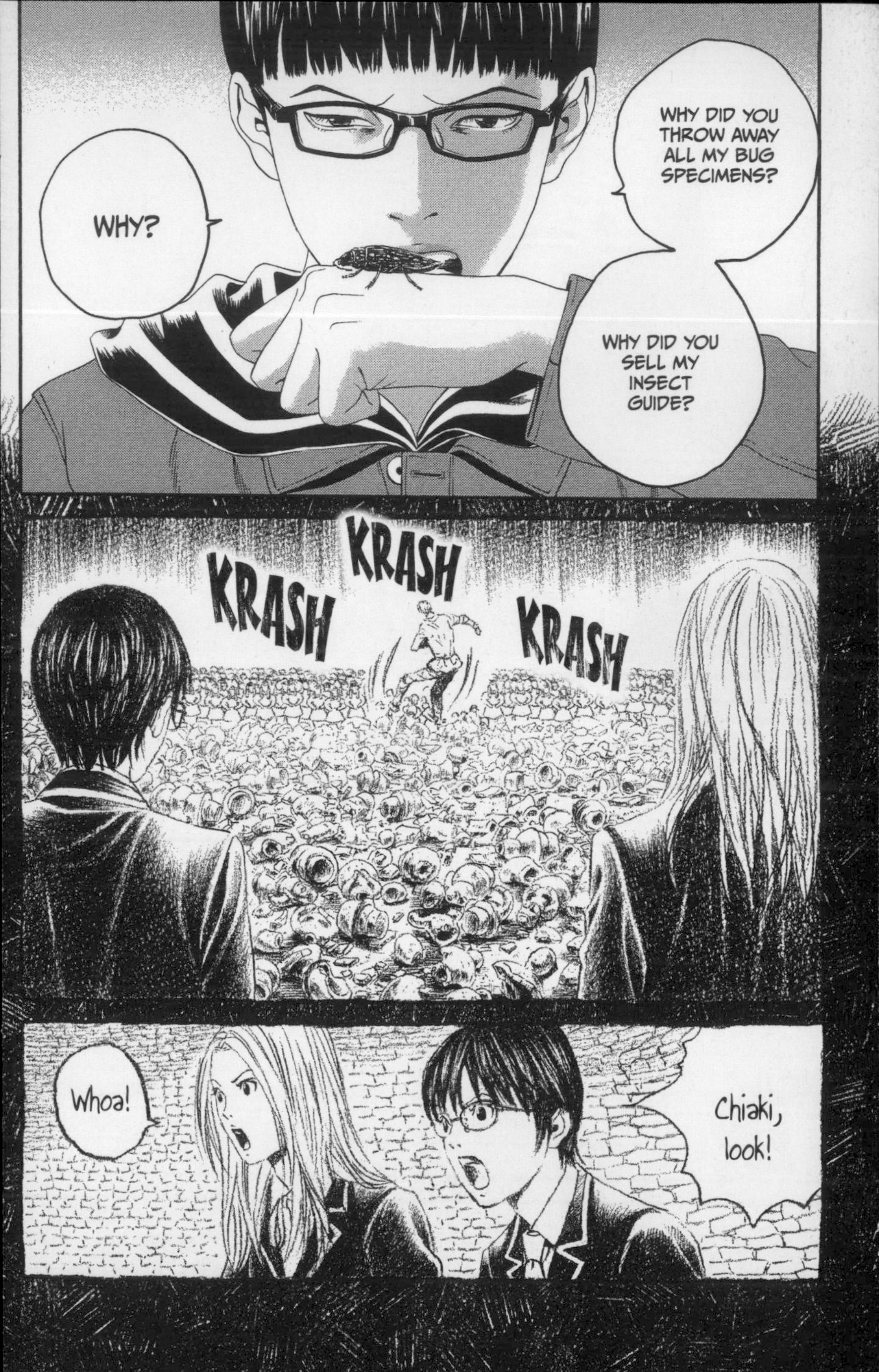
WHY DID YOU THROW AWAY ALL MY BUG SPECIMENS?
WHY DID YOU SELL MY INSECT GUIDE?
WHY?
KRASH
KRASH
KRASH
Chiaki, look!
Whoa!

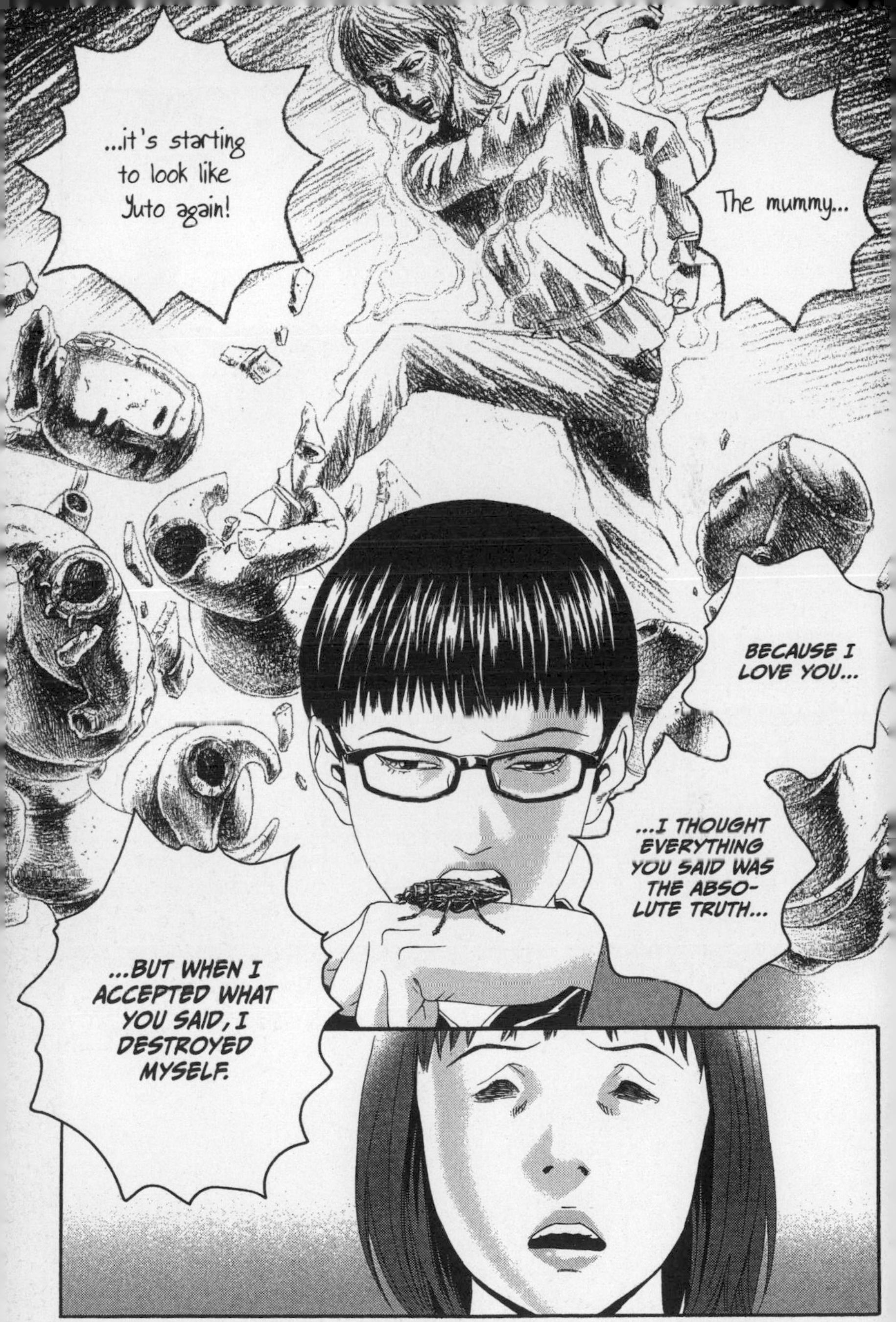
The mummy...
...it's starting to look like Yuto again!
BECAUSE I LOVE YOU...
...I THOUGHT EVERYTHING YOU SAID WAS THE ABSO-LUTE TRUTH...
...BUT WHEN I ACCEPTED WHAT YOU SAID, I DESTROYED MYSELF.

...BUT I THINK ABOUT DAD A LOT.

I'M SORRY, MOM...

HA HA...

I WONDER...

WHY ARE YOU ALWAYS READING HISTORY BOOKS, DAD?

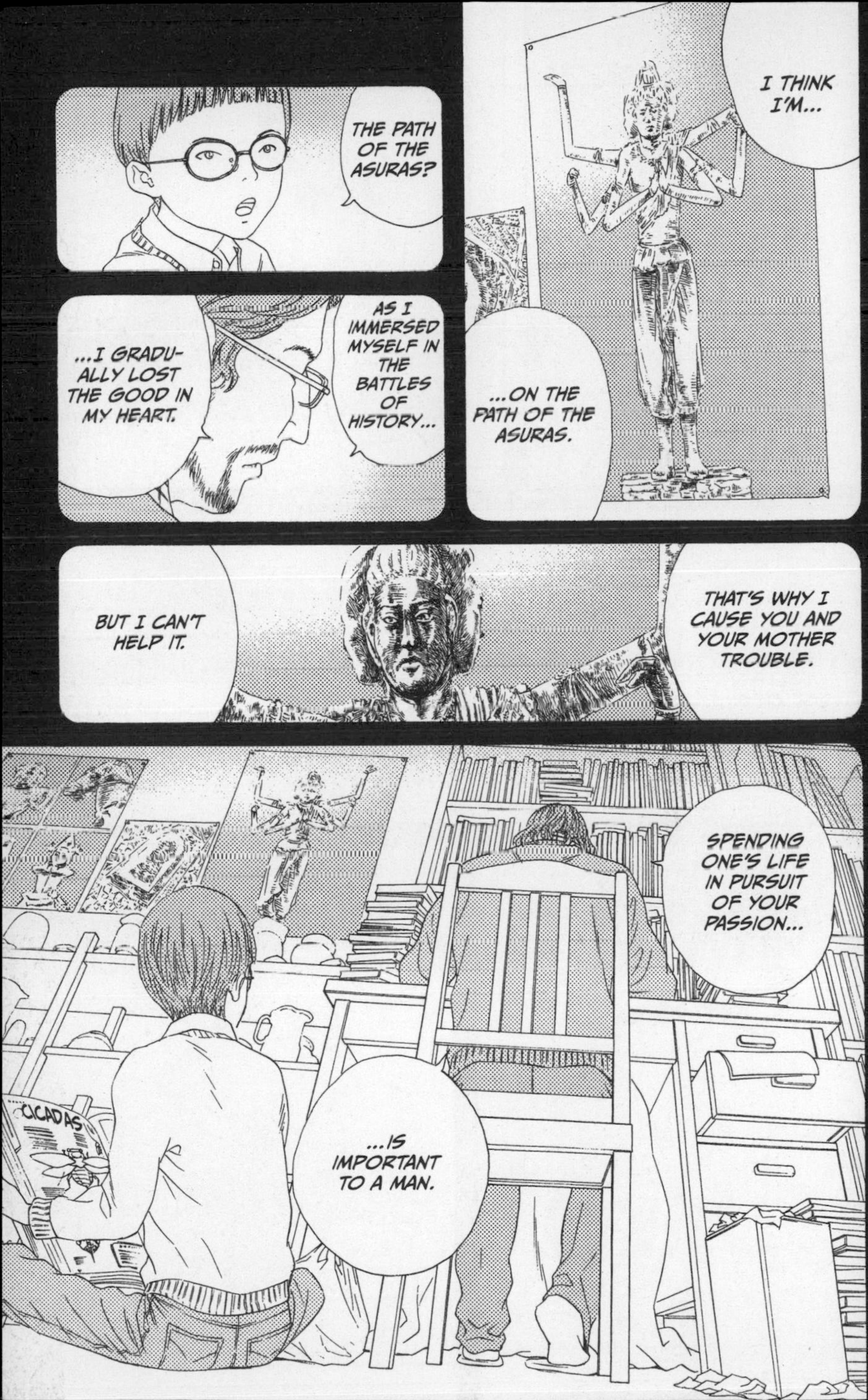
I THINK I'M...
...ON THE PATH OF THE ASURAS.
THE PATH OF THE ASURAS?
AS I IMMERSED MYSELF IN THE BATTLES OF HISTORY...
...I GRADU-ALLY LOST THE GOOD IN MY HEART.
THAT'S WHY I CAUSE YOU AND YOUR MOTHER TROUBLE.
BUT I CAN'T HELP IT.
SPENDING ONE'S LIFE IN PURSUIT OF YOUR PASSION...
CICADAS
...IS IMPORTANT TO A MAN.

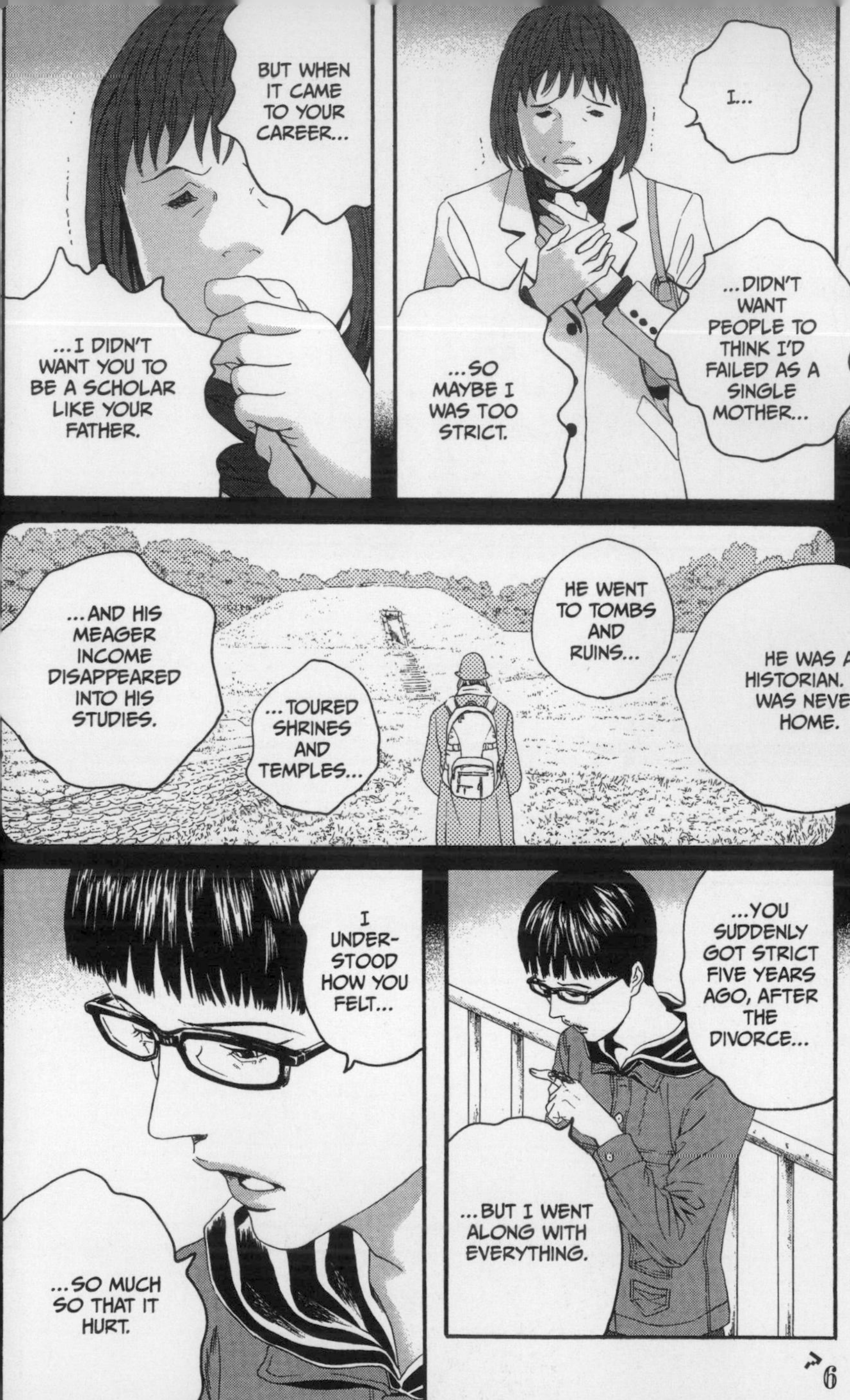
I...
...DIDN'T WANT PEOPLE TO THINK I'D FAILED AS A SINGLE MOTHER...
...SO MAYBE I WAS TOO STRICT.
BUT WHEN IT CAME TO YOUR CAREER...
...I DIDN'T WANT YOU TO BE A SCHOLAR LIKE YOUR FATHER.
HE WAS A HISTORIAN. HE WAS NEVER HOME.
HE WENT TO TOMBS AND RUINS...
...TOURED SHRINES AND TEMPLES...
...AND HIS MEAGER INCOME DISAPPEARED INTO HIS STUDIES.
...YOU SUDDENLY GOT STRICT FIVE YEARS AGO, AFTER THE DIVORCE...
...BUT I WENT ALONG WITH EVERYTHING.
I UNDER-STOOD HOW YOU FELT...
...SO MUCH SO THAT IT HURT.

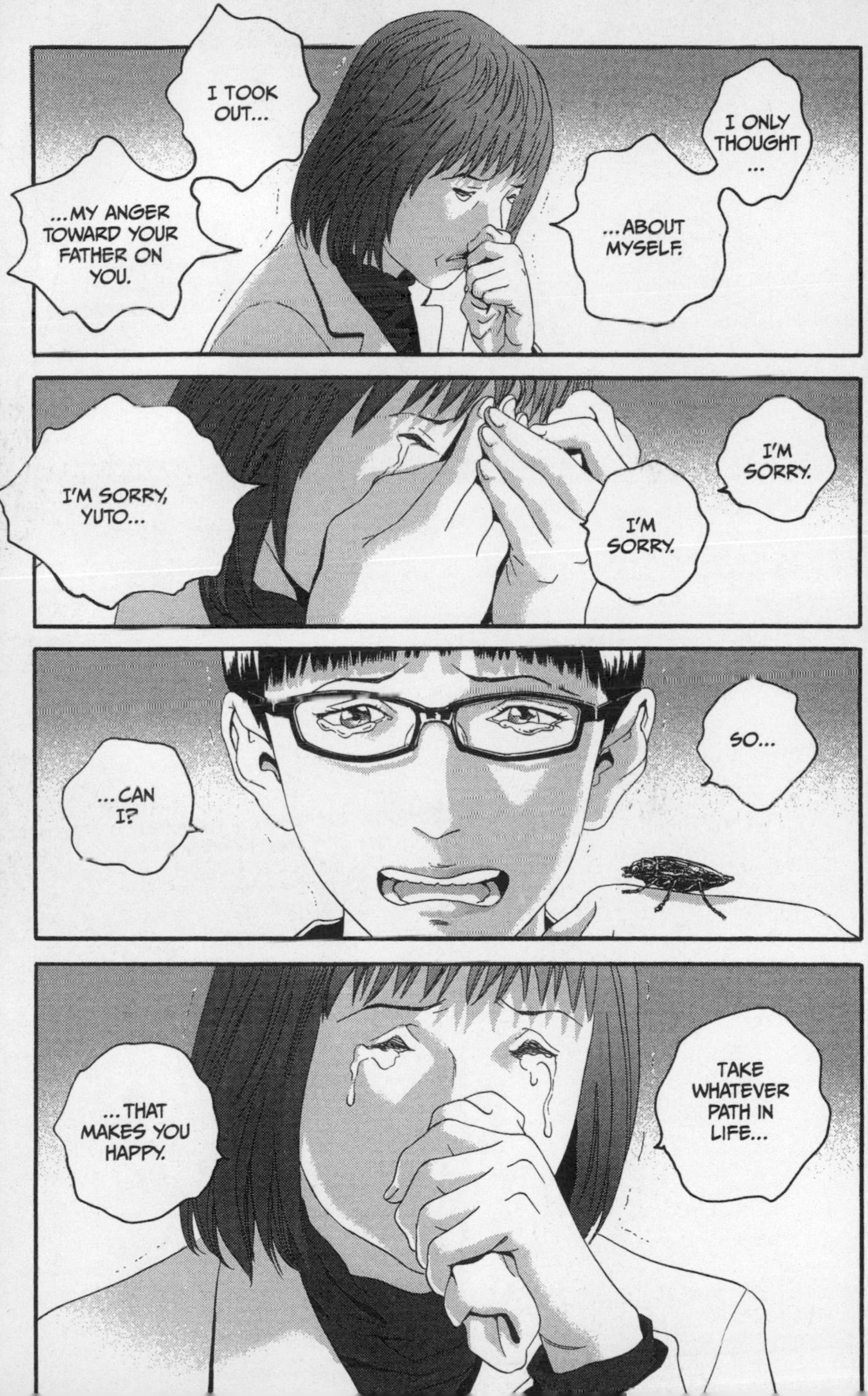
I ONLY THOUGHT ...
...ABOUT MYSELF.
I TOOK OUT...
...MY ANGER TOWARD YOUR FATHER ON YOU.
I'M SORRY.
I'M SORRY.
I'M SORRY, YUTO...
SO...
...CAN I?
TAKE WHATEVER PATH IN LIFE...
...THAT MAKES YOU HAPPY.

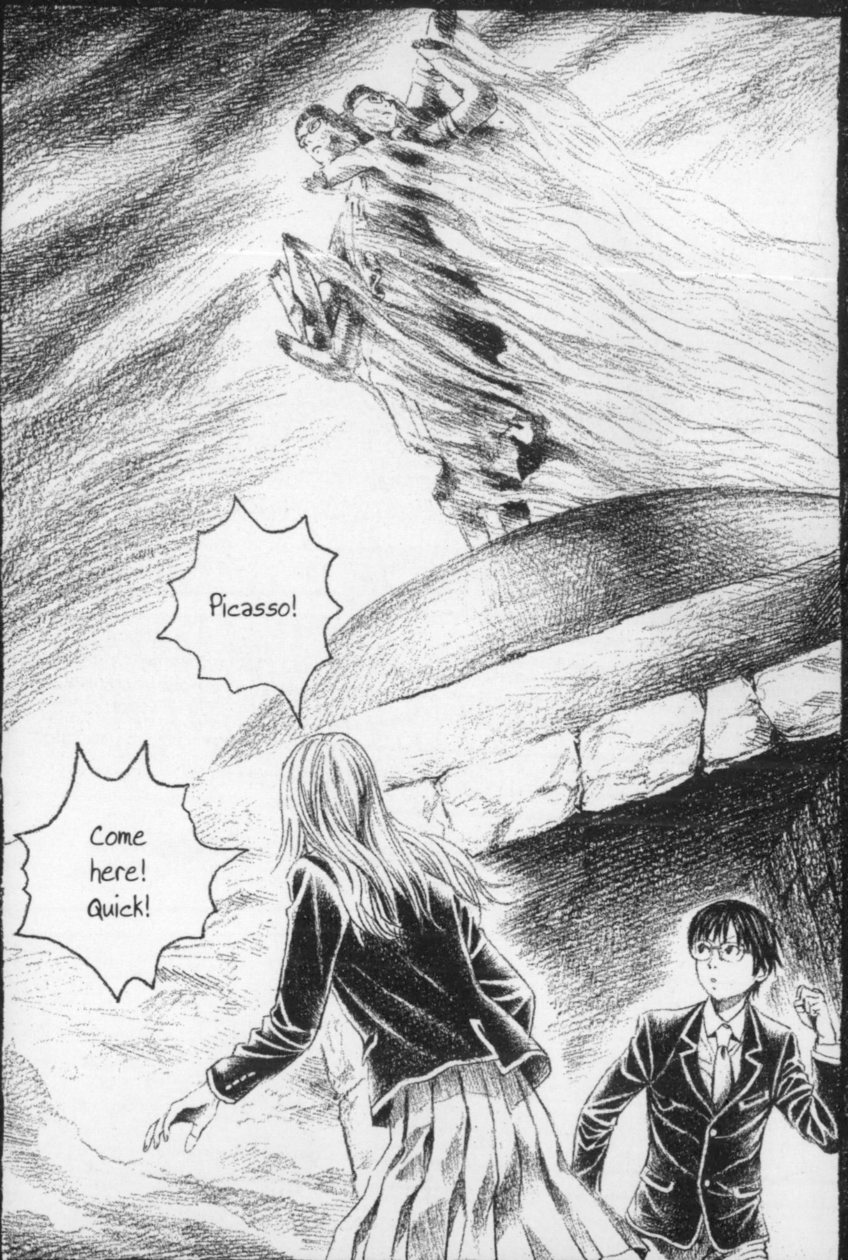
Picasso!
Come here! Quick!

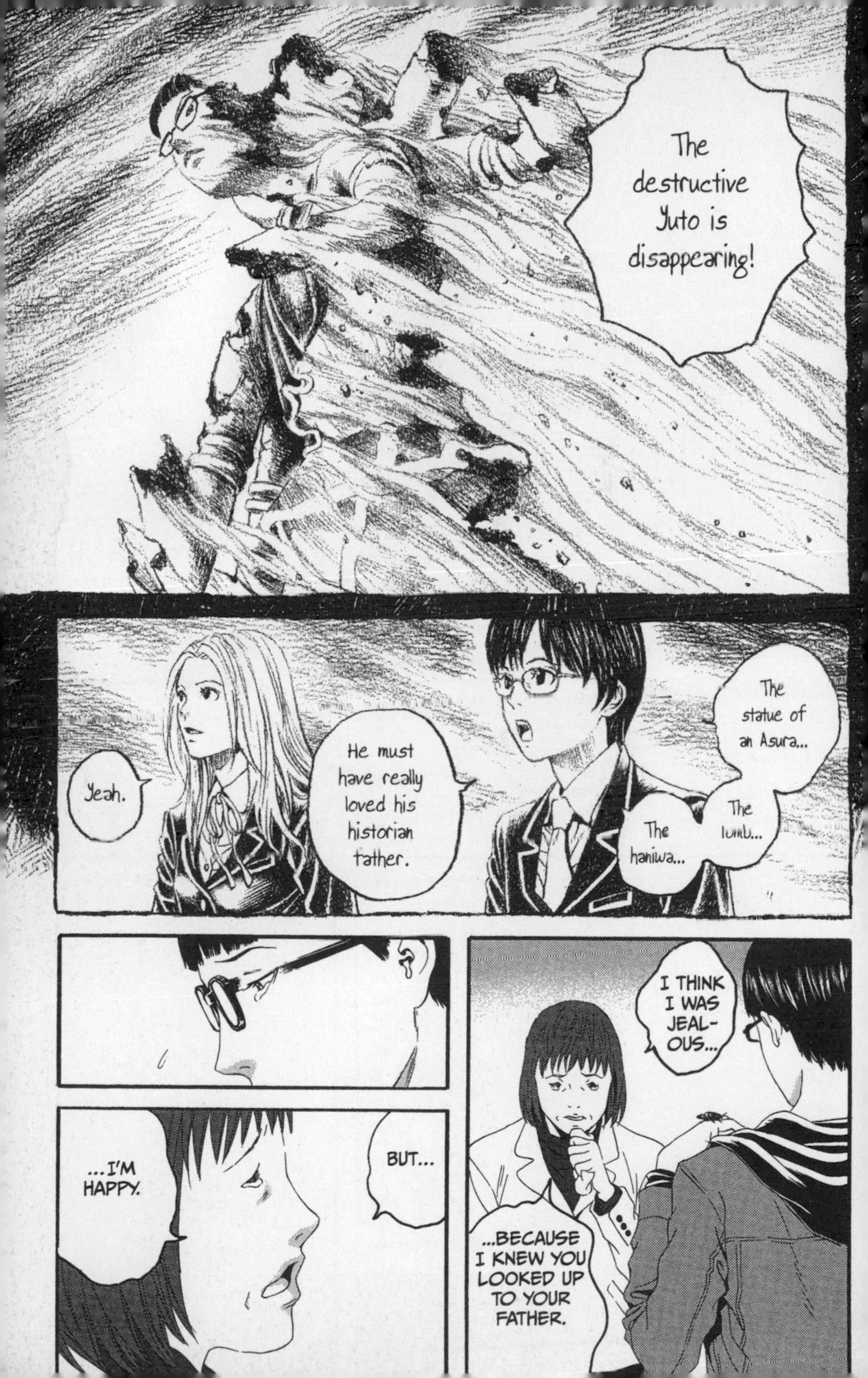
The destructive Yuto is disappearing!
The statue of an Asura...
The tomb...
The haniwa...
He must have really loved his historian father.
Yeah.
I THINK I WAS JEAL-OUS...
...BECAUSE I KNEW YOU LOOKED UP TO YOUR FATHER.
BUT...
...I'M HAPPY.

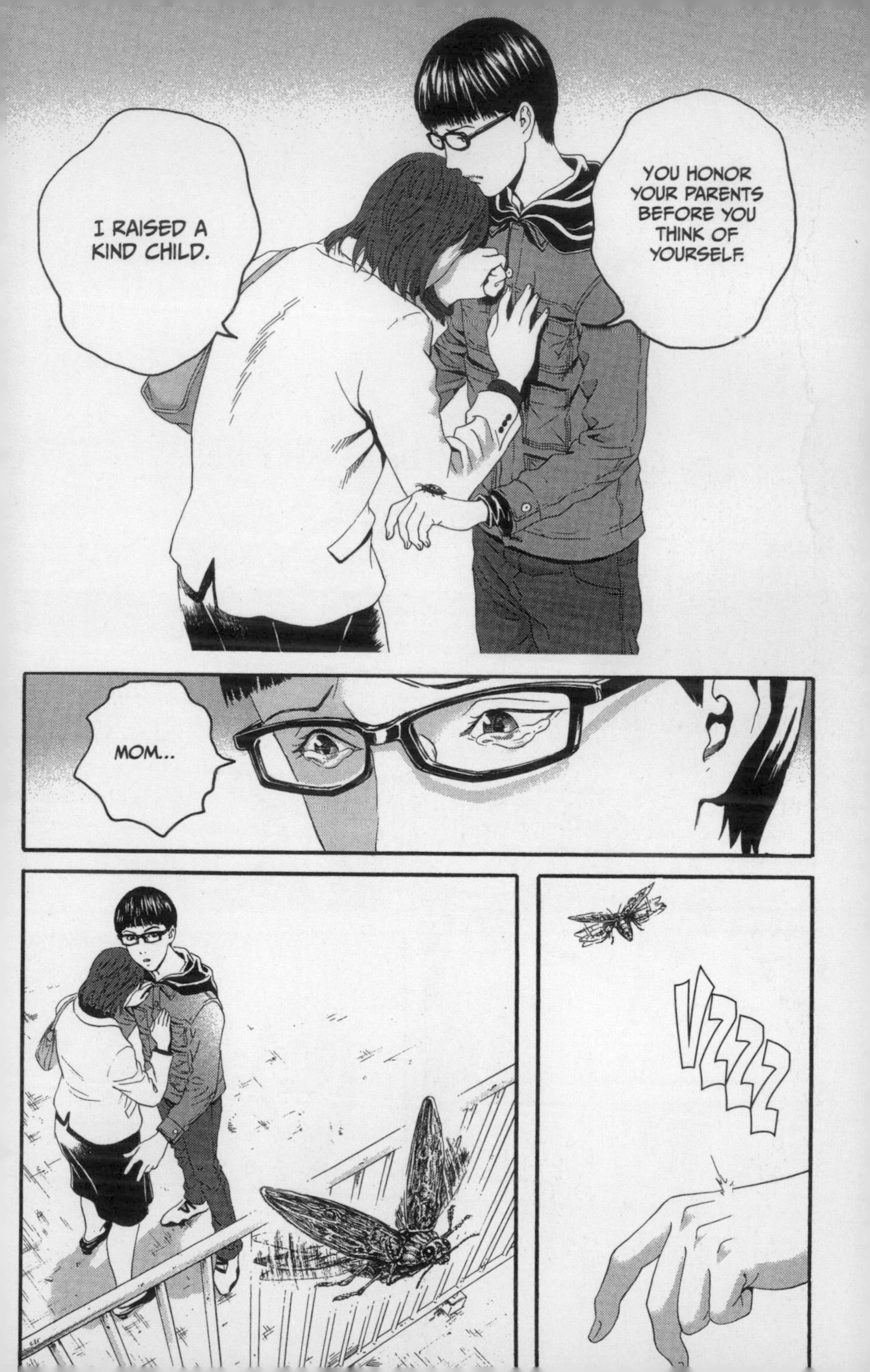
YOU HONOR YOUR PARENTS BEFORE YOU THINK OF YOURSELF.
I RAISED A KIND CHILD.
MOM...
VZZZZ

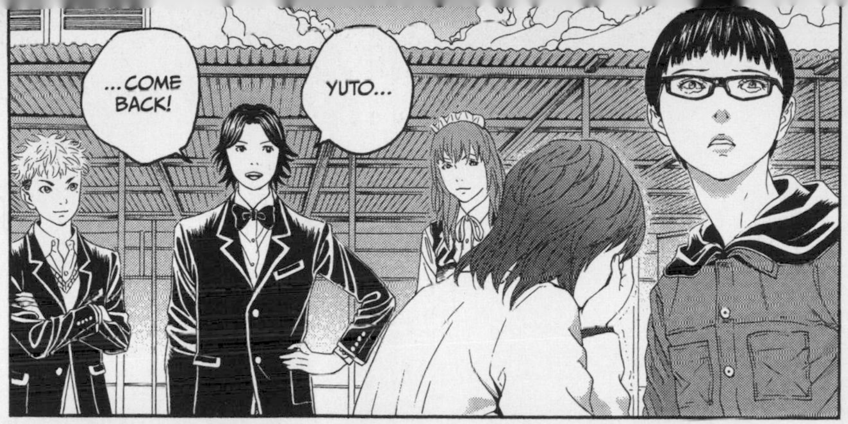
YUTO...
...COME BACK!

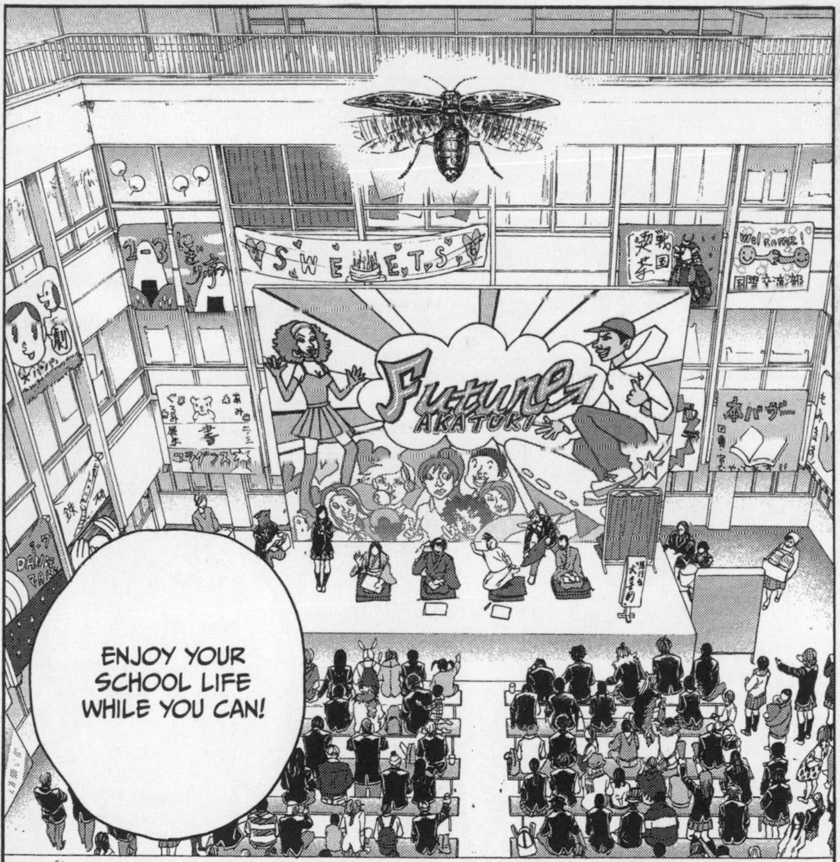
SWEETS
Future
AKATUKI
ENJOY YOUR SCHOOL LIFE WHILE YOU CAN!

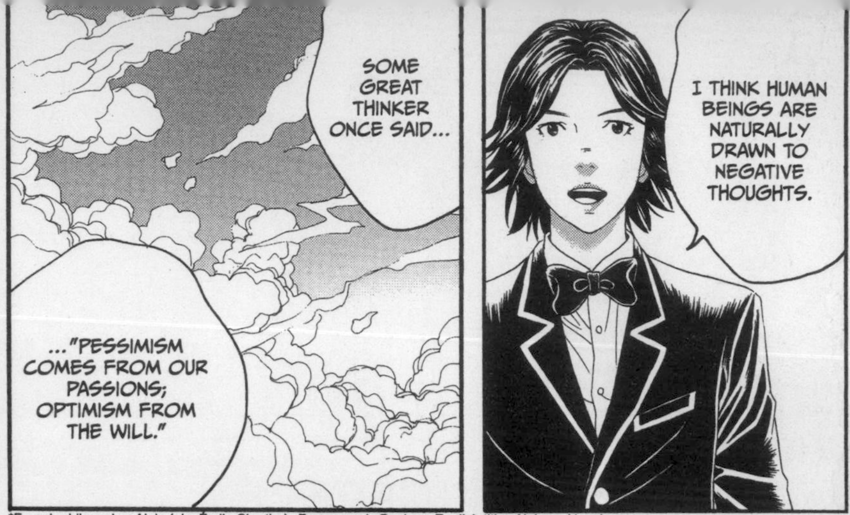
I THINK HUMAN BEINGS ARE NATURALLY DRAWN TO NEGATIVE THOUGHTS.
SOME GREAT THINKER ONCE SAID...
..."PESSIMISM COMES FROM OUR PASSIONS; OPTIMISM FROM THE WILL."

*French philosopher Alain (aka Émile Chartier), *Propos sur le Bonheur*. English title: *Alain on Happiness*.

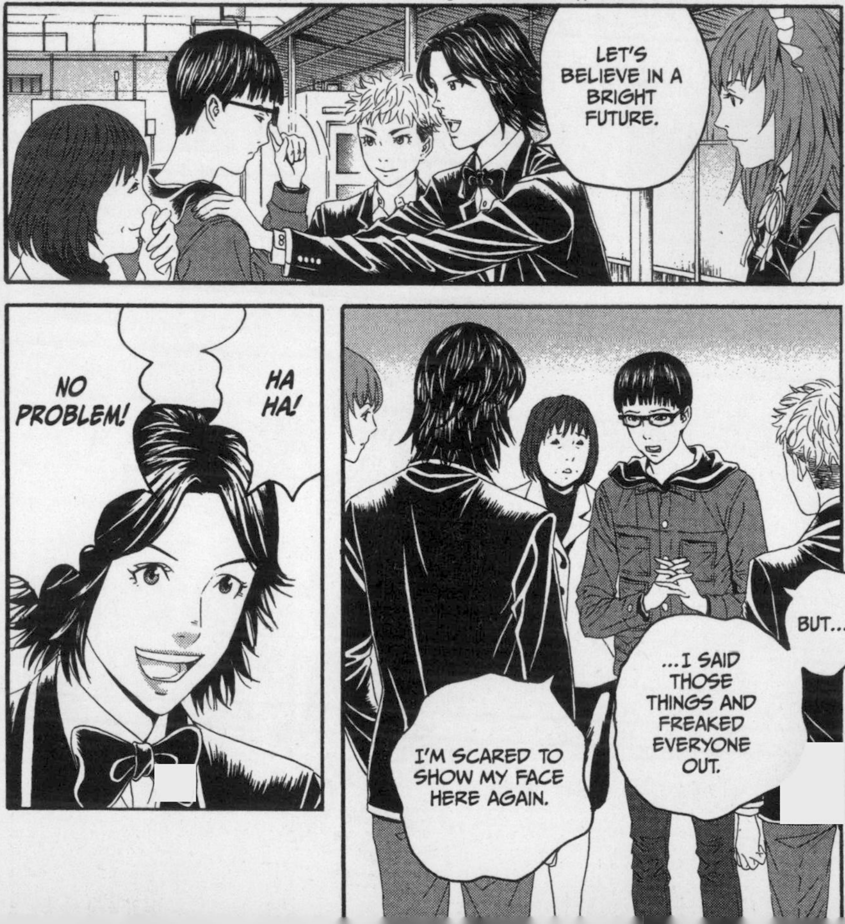
LET'S BELIEVE IN A BRIGHT FUTURE.
BUT...
...I SAID THOSE THINGS AND FREAKED EVERYONE OUT.
I'M SCARED TO SHOW MY FACE HERE AGAIN.
HA HA!
NO PROBLEM!

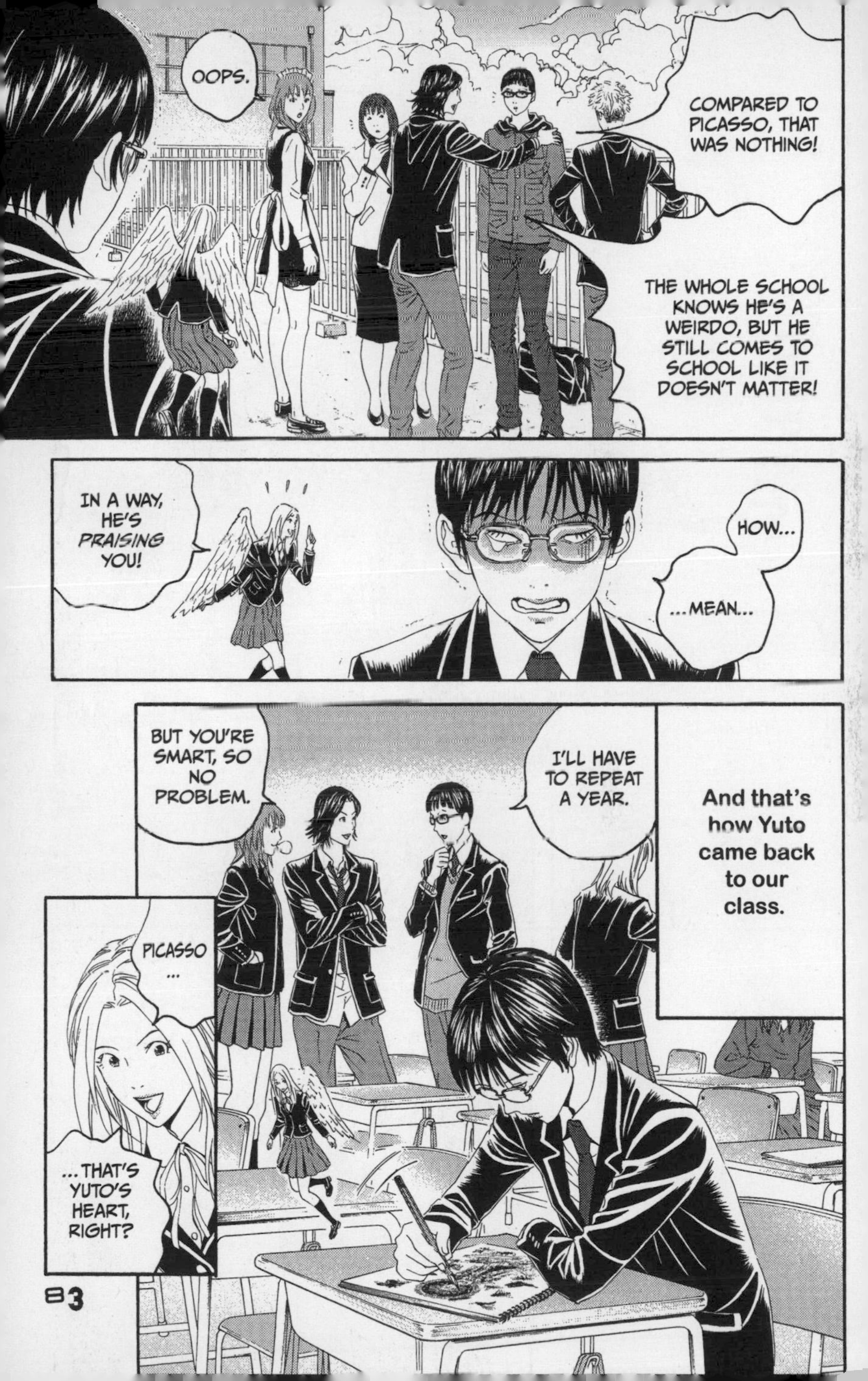
COMPARED TO PICASSO, THAT WAS NOTHING!
THE WHOLE SCHOOL KNOWS HE'S A WEIRDO, BUT HE STILL COMES TO SCHOOL LIKE IT DOESN'T MATTER!
OOPS.
HOW...
...MEAN...
IN A WAY, HE'S *PRAISING* YOU!
And that's how Yuto came back to our class.
I'LL HAVE TO REPEAT A YEAR.
BUT YOU'RE SMART, SO NO PROBLEM.
PICASSO ...
...THAT'S YUTO'S HEART, RIGHT?

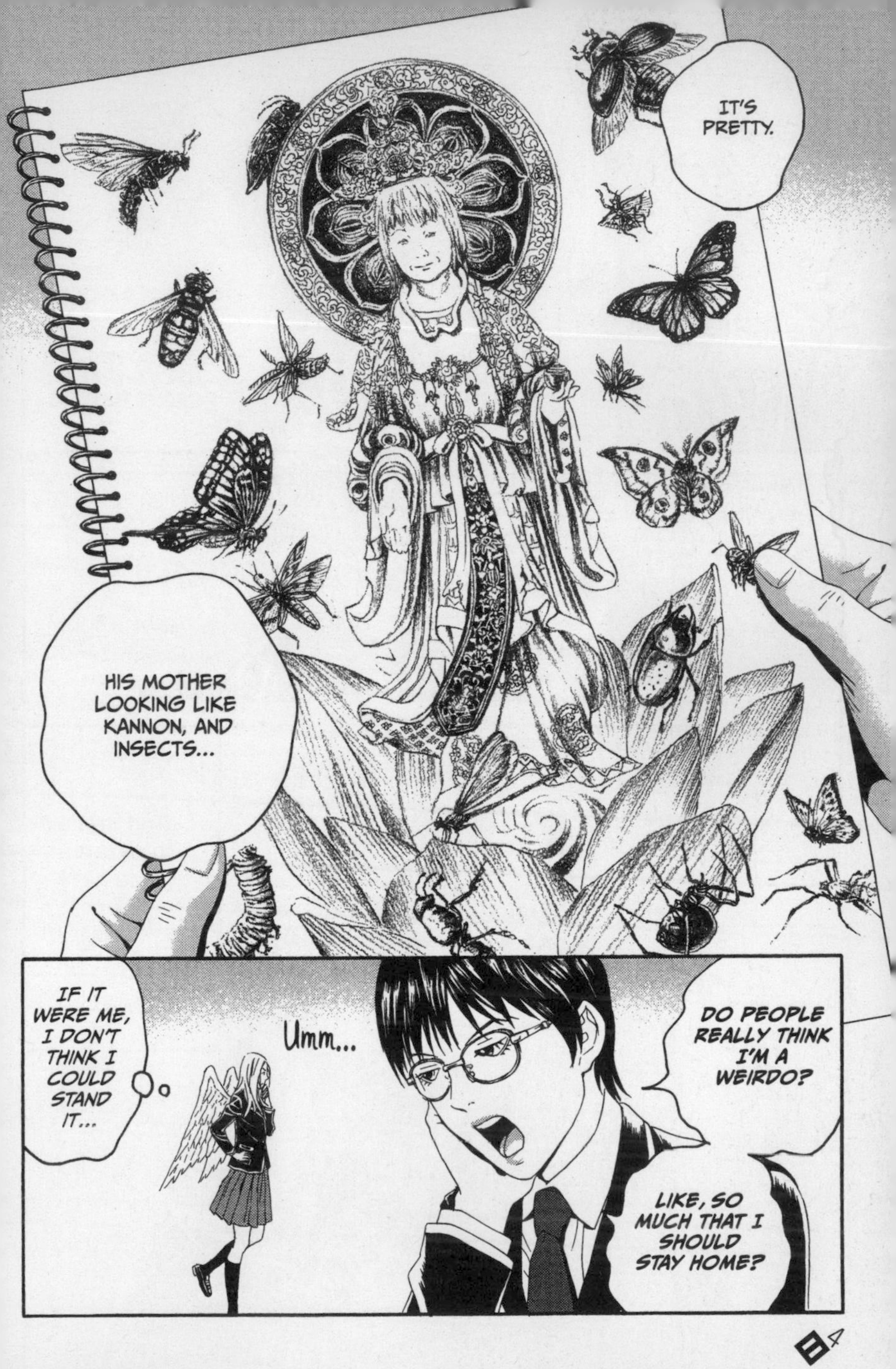
IT'S PRETTY.
HIS MOTHER LOOKING LIKE KANNON, AND INSECTS...
DO PEOPLE REALLY THINK I'M A WEIRDO?
LIKE, SO MUCH THAT I SHOULD STAY HOME?
Umm...
IF IT WERE ME, I DON'T THINK I COULD STAND IT...

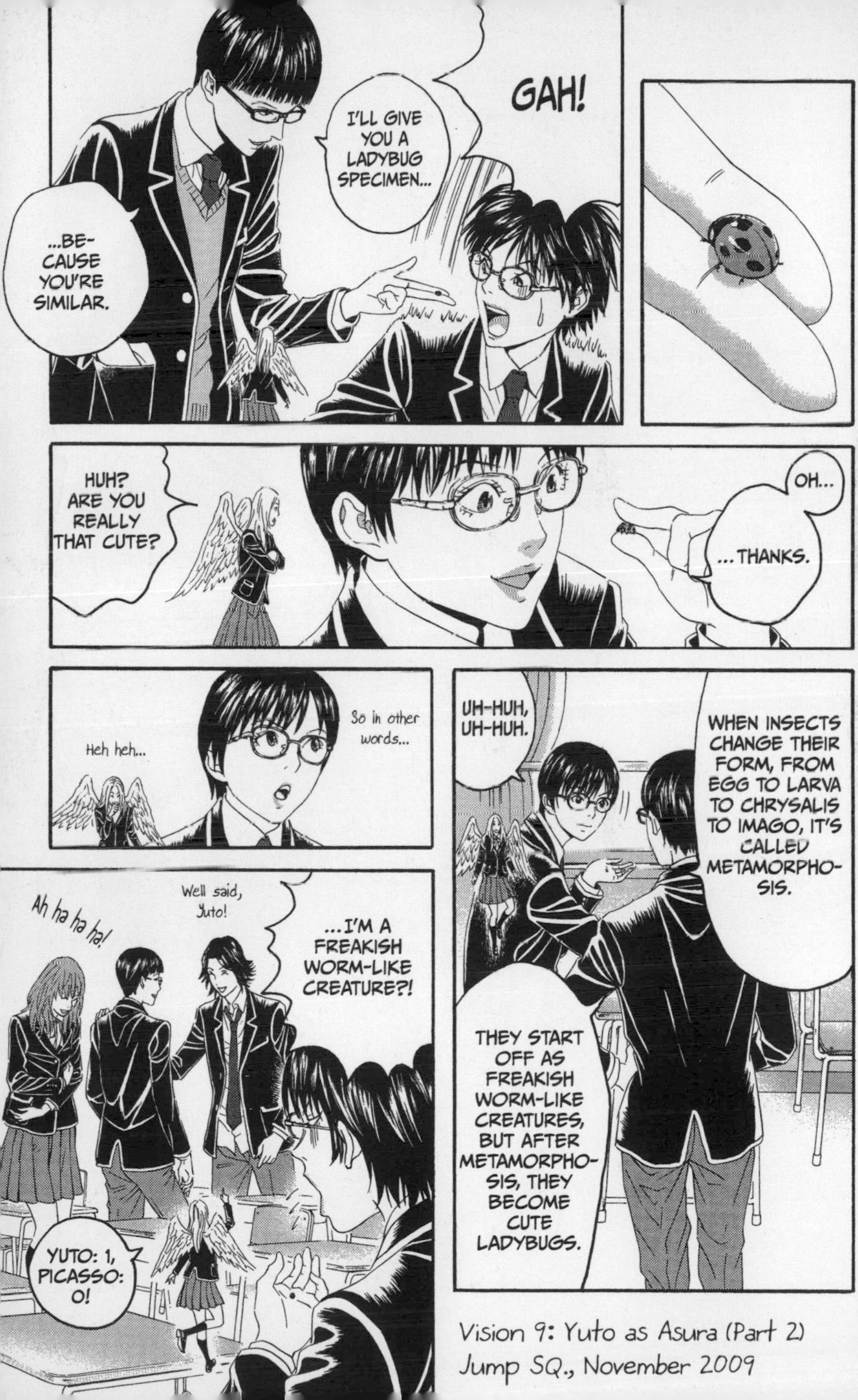
GAH!
I'LL GIVE YOU A LADYBUG SPECIMEN...
...BE-CAUSE YOU'RE SIMILAR.
OH...
...THANKS.
HUH? ARE YOU REALLY THAT CUTE?
WHEN INSECTS CHANGE THEIR FORM, FROM EGG TO LARVA TO CHRYSALIS TO IMAGO, IT'S CALLED METAMORPHO-SIS.
UH-HUH, UH-HUH.
THEY START OFF AS FREAKISH WORM-LIKE CREATURES, BUT AFTER METAMORPHO-SIS, THEY BECOME CUTE LADYBUGS.
So in other words...
Heh heh...
...I'M A FREAKISH WORM-LIKE CREATURE?!
Well said, Yuto!
Ah ha ha ha!
YUTO: 1, PICASSO: 0!

Vision 9: Yuto as Asura (Part 2)
Jump SQ., November 2009

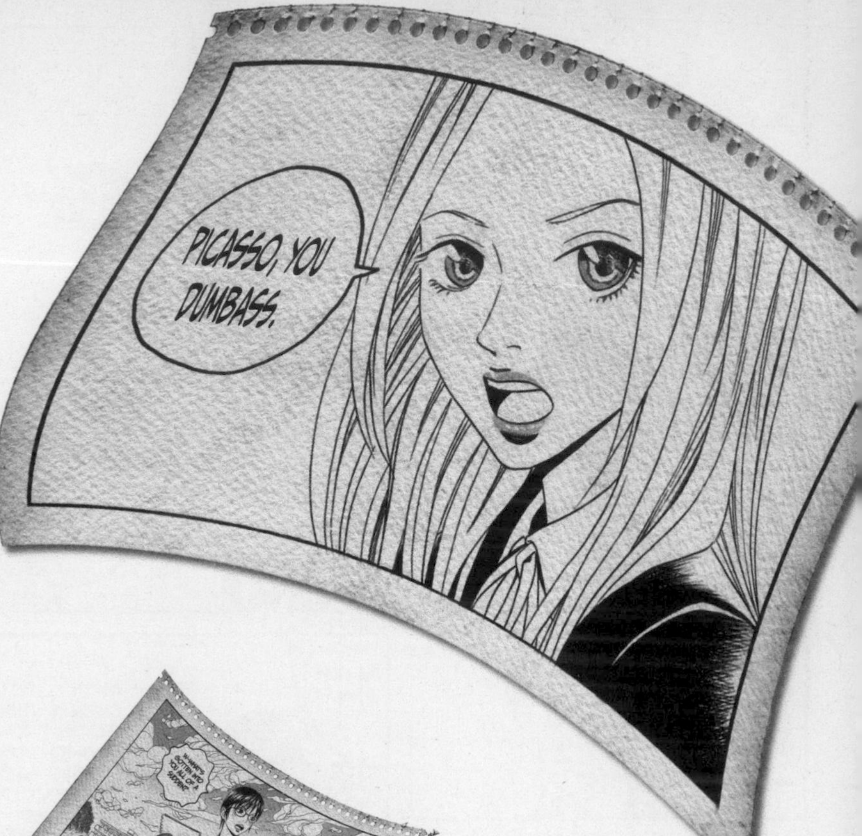
PICASSO, YOU DUMBASS.

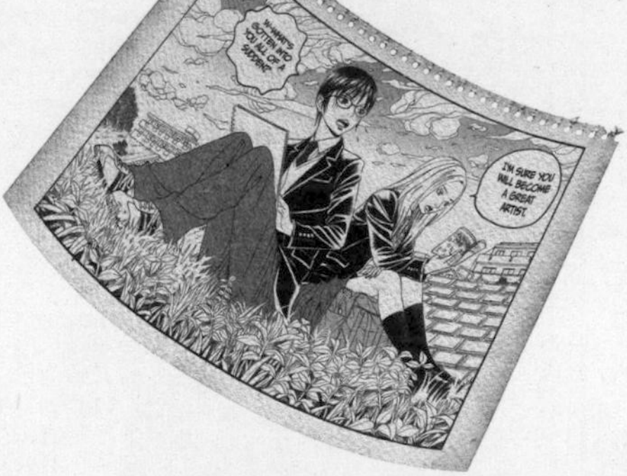
I'M SURE YOU WILL BECOME A GREAT ARTIST.
W-WHAT'S GOTTEN INTO YOU ALL OF A SUDDEN?

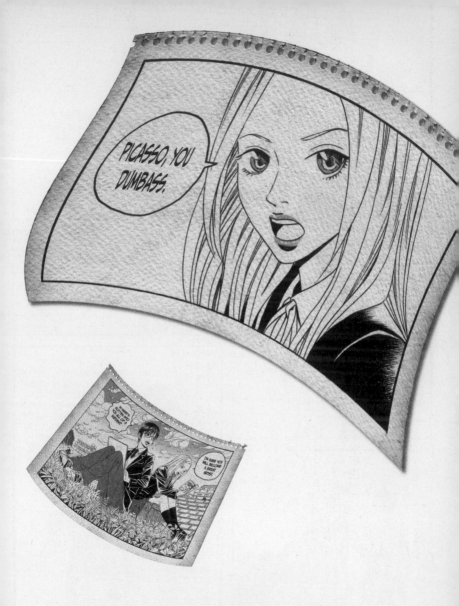

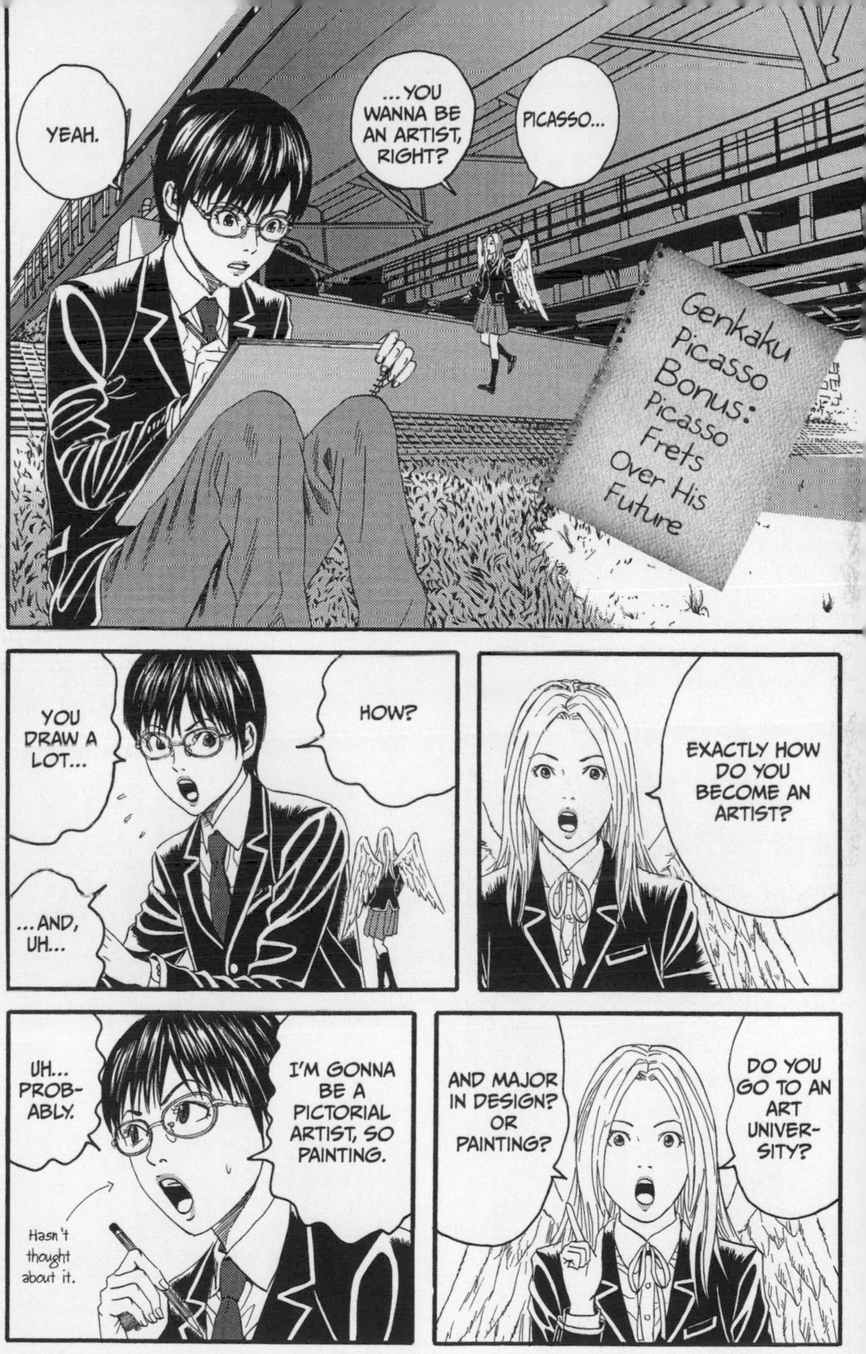
PICASSO...
...YOU WANNA BE AN ARTIST, RIGHT?
YEAH.
Genkaku Picasso Bonus: Picasso Frets Over His Future
EXACTLY HOW DO YOU BECOME AN ARTIST?
HOW?
YOU DRAW A LOT...
...AND, UH...
DO YOU GO TO AN ART UNIVER-SITY?
AND MAJOR IN DESIGN? OR PAINTING?
I'M GONNA BE A PICTORIAL ARTIST, SO PAINTING.
UH... PROB-ABLY.
Hasn't thought about it.

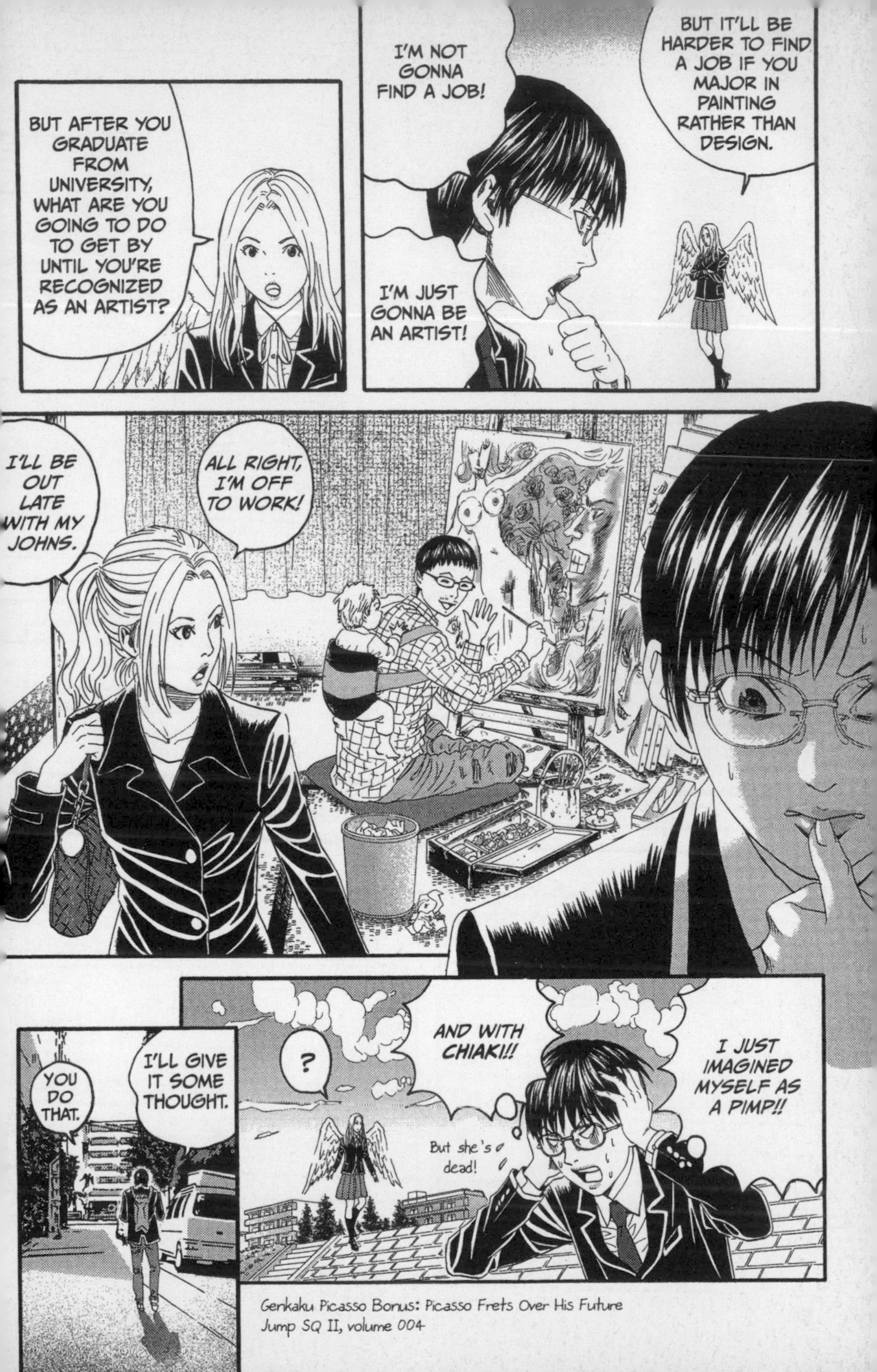
BUT IT'LL BE HARDER TO FIND A JOB IF YOU MAJOR IN PAINTING RATHER THAN DESIGN.
I'M NOT GONNA FIND A JOB!
I'M JUST GONNA BE AN ARTIST!
BUT AFTER YOU GRADUATE FROM UNIVERSITY, WHAT ARE YOU GOING TO DO TO GET BY UNTIL YOU'RE RECOGNIZED AS AN ARTIST?
ALL RIGHT, I'M OFF TO WORK!
I'LL BE OUT LATE WITH MY JOHNS.
I JUST IMAGINED MYSELF AS A PIMP!!
AND WITH CHIAKI!!
But she's dead!
?
I'LL GIVE IT SOME THOUGHT.
YOU DO THAT.

Genkaku Picasso Bonus: Picasso Frets Over His Future
Jump SQ II, volume 004

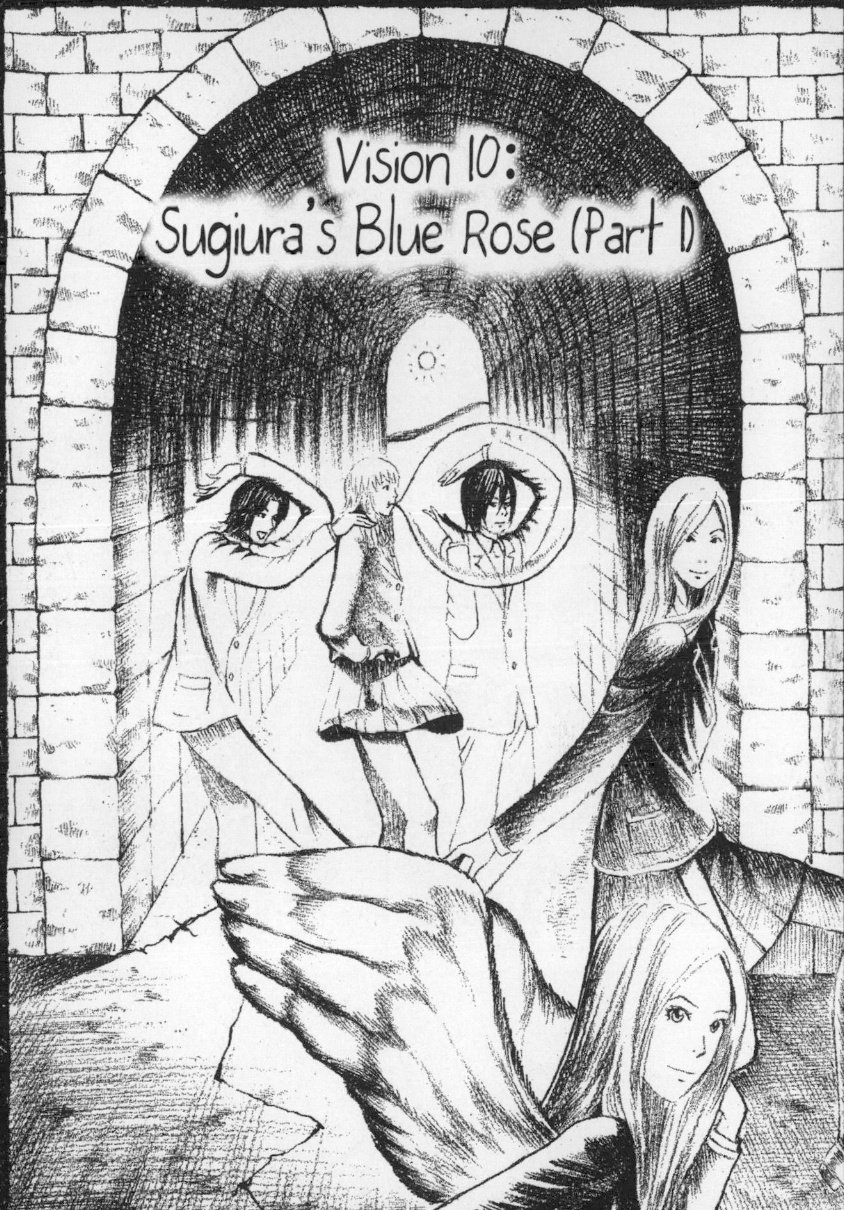
Vision 10:
Sugiura's Blue Rose (Part 1)

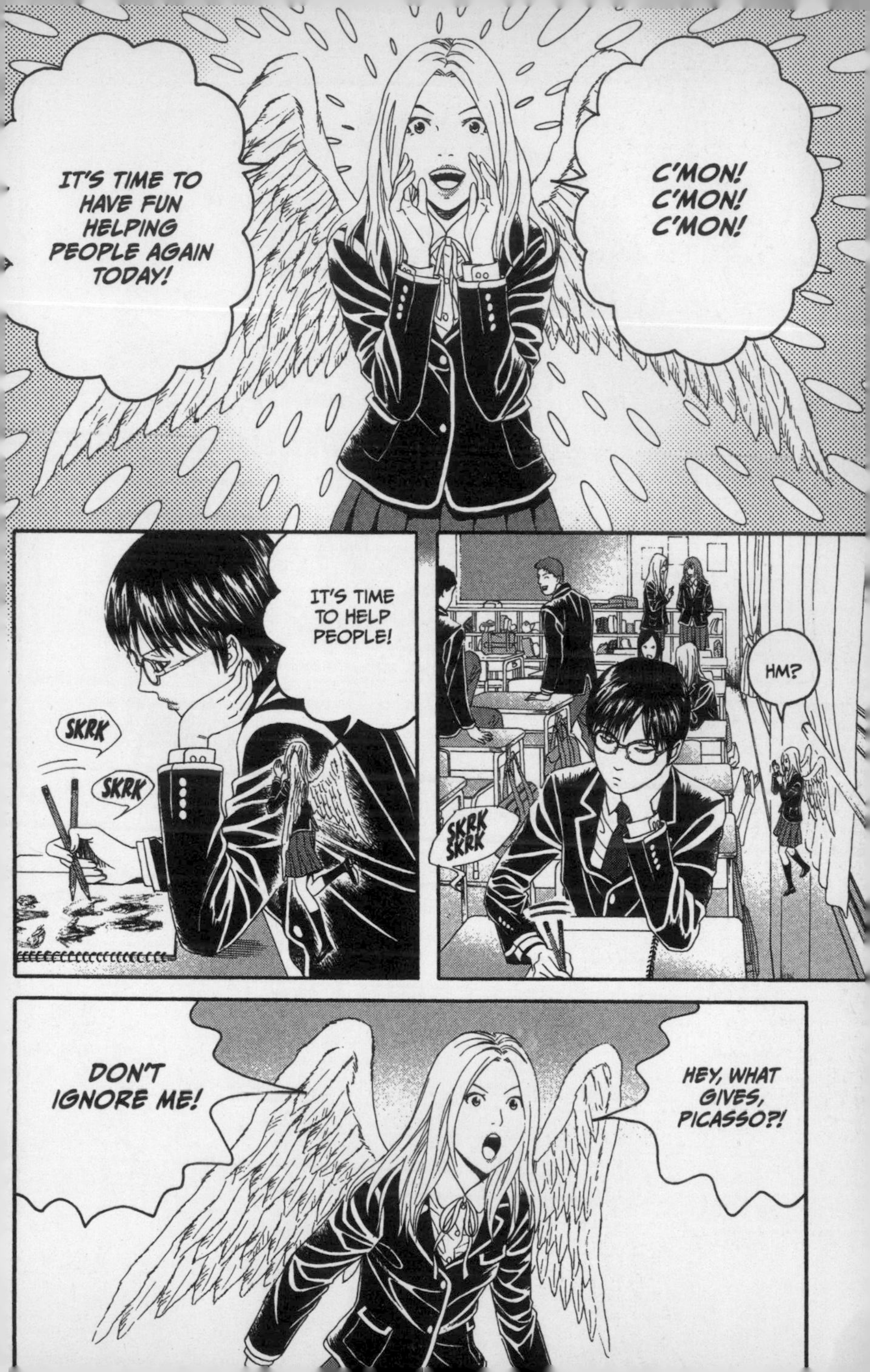
C'MON! C'MON! C'MON!
IT'S TIME TO HAVE FUN HELPING PEOPLE AGAIN TODAY!
HM?
SKRK SKRK
IT'S TIME TO HELP PEOPLE!
SKRK
SKRK
HEY, WHAT GIVES, PICASSO?!
DON'T IGNORE ME!

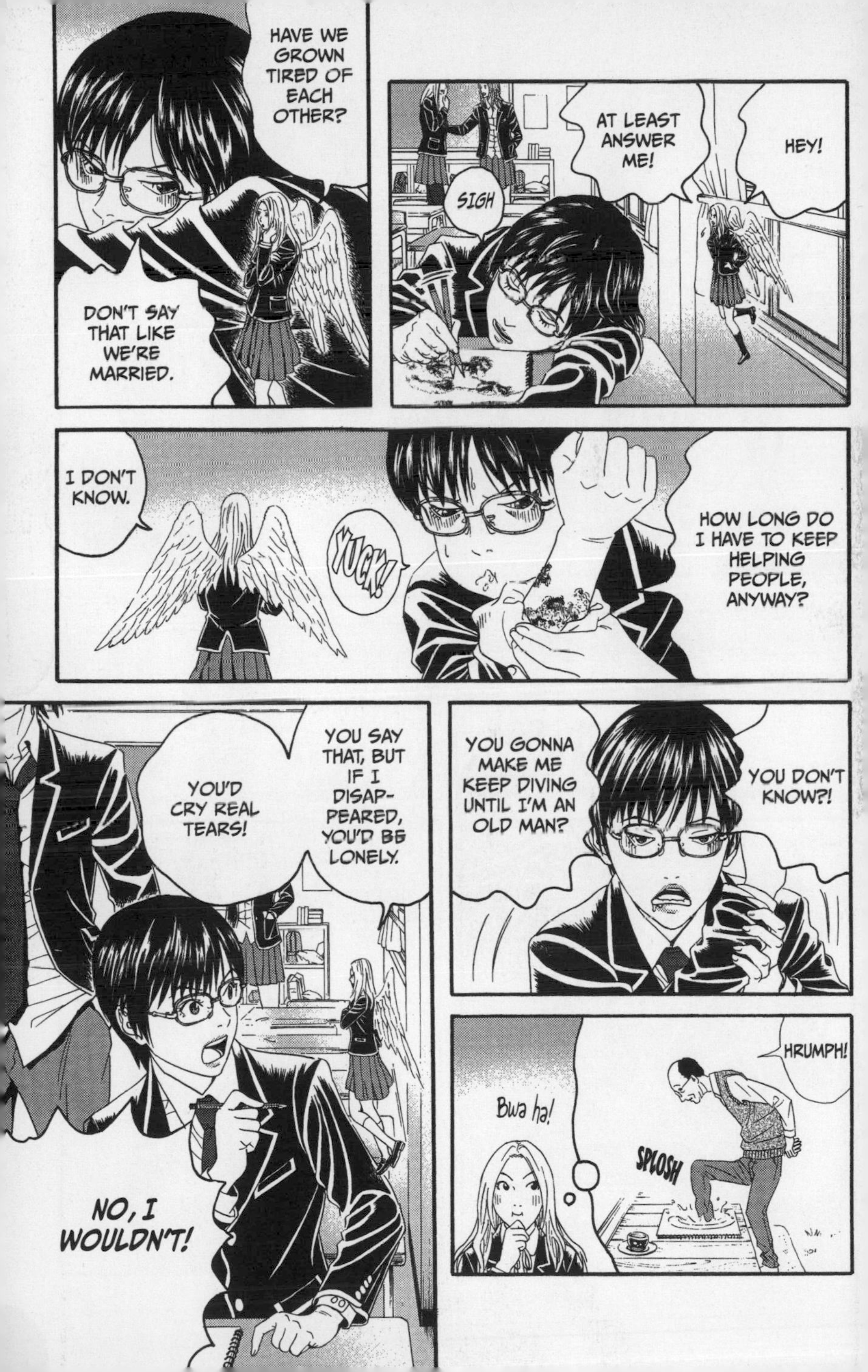
HEY!
AT LEAST ANSWER ME!
SIGH
HAVE WE GROWN TIRED OF EACH OTHER?
DON'T SAY THAT LIKE WE'RE MARRIED.
HOW LONG DO I HAVE TO KEEP HELPING PEOPLE, ANYWAY?
YUCK!
I DON'T KNOW.
YOU DON'T KNOW?!
YOU GONNA MAKE ME KEEP DIVING UNTIL I'M AN OLD MAN?
HRUMPH!
SPLOSH
Bwa ha!
YOU SAY THAT, BUT IF I DISAP-PEARED, YOU'D BE LONELY.
YOU'D CRY REAL TEARS!
NO, I WOULDN'T!

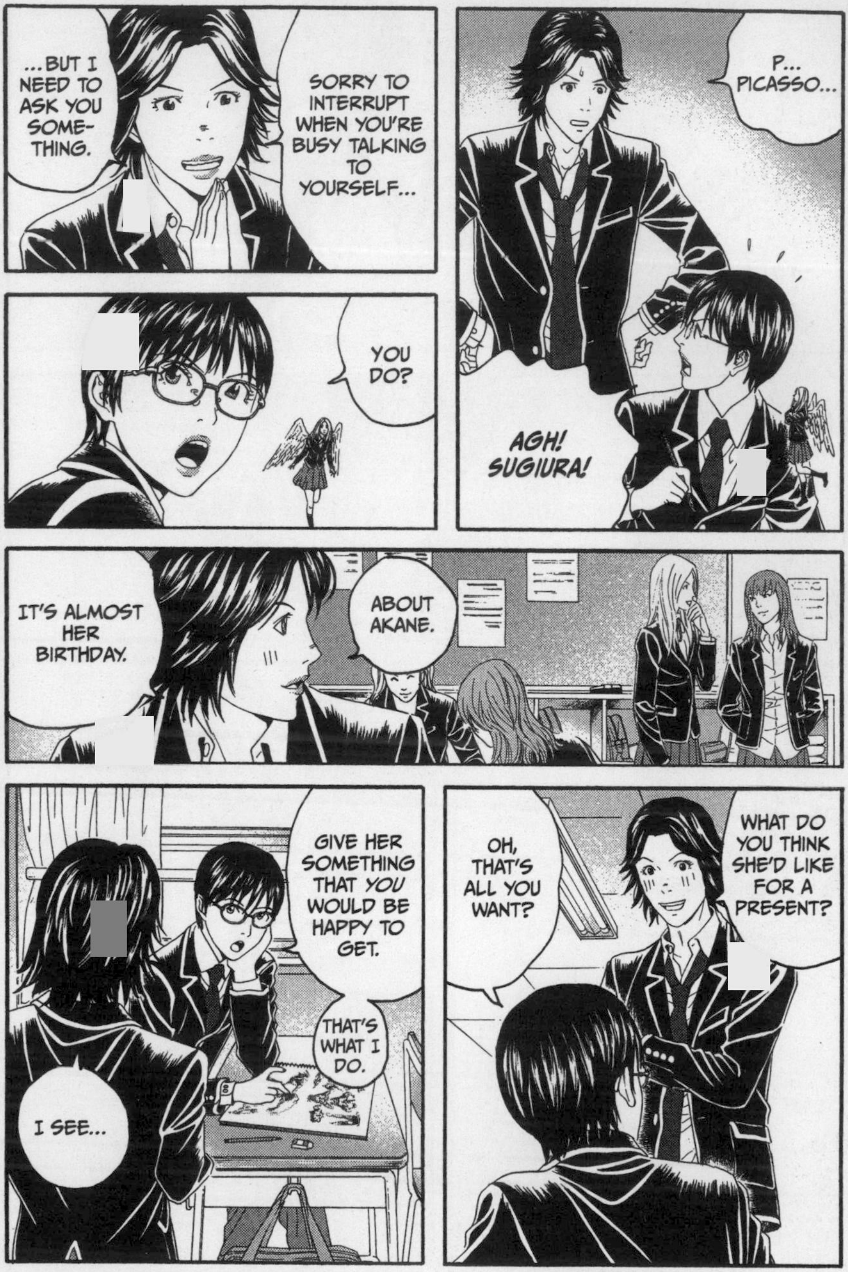
P... PICASSO...
AGH! SUGIURA!
SORRY TO INTERRUPT WHEN YOU'RE BUSY TALKING TO YOURSELF...
...BUT I NEED TO ASK YOU SOME-THING.
YOU DO?
ABOUT AKANE.
IT'S ALMOST HER BIRTHDAY.
WHAT DO YOU THINK SHE'D LIKE FOR A PRESENT?
OH, THAT'S ALL YOU WANT?
GIVE HER SOMETHING THAT *YOU* WOULD BE HAPPY TO GET.
THAT'S WHAT I DO.
I SEE...

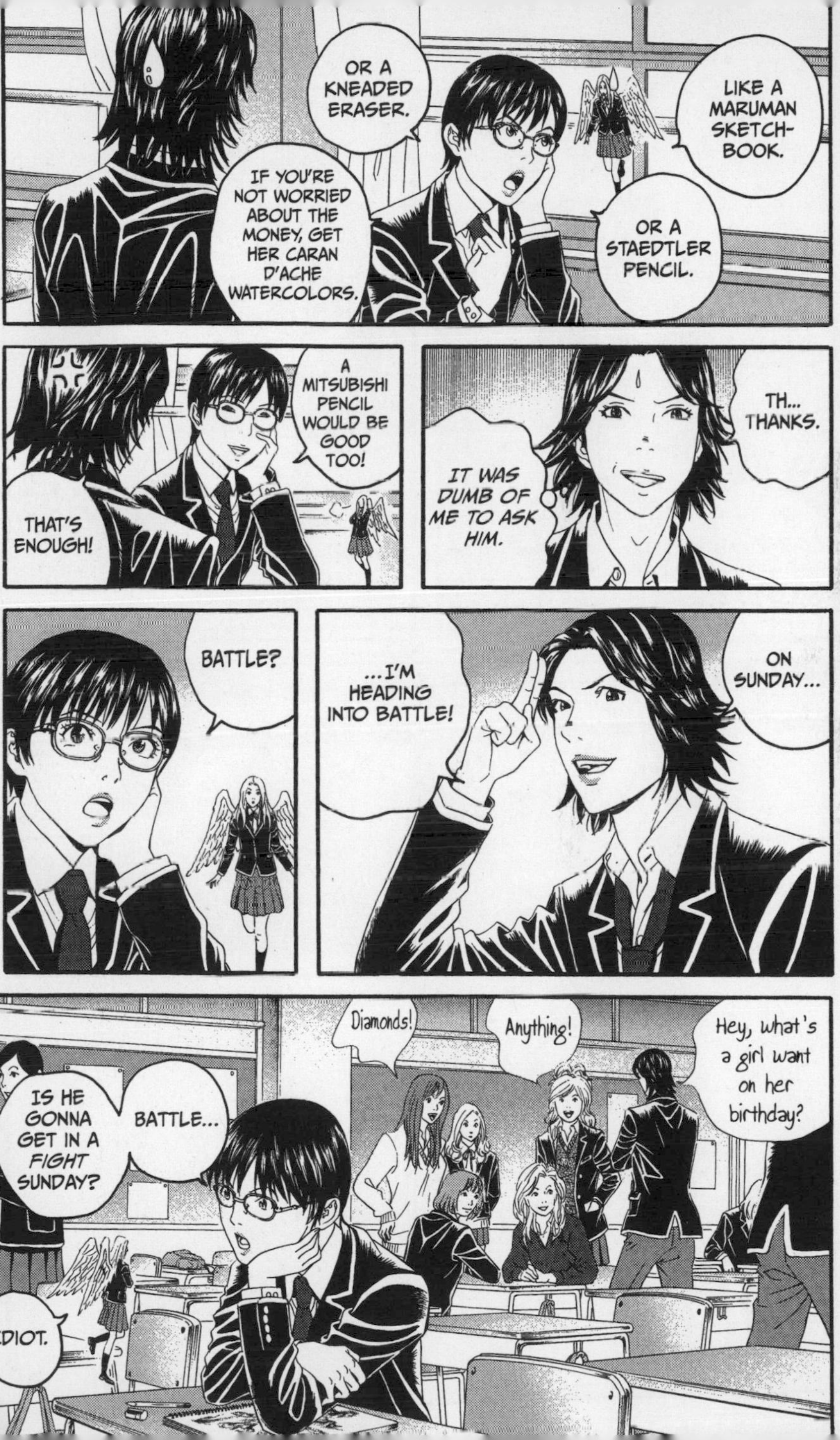
LIKE A MARUMAN SKETCH-BOOK.
OR A STAEDTLER PENCIL.
OR A KNEADED ERASER.
IF YOU'RE NOT WORRIED ABOUT THE MONEY, GET HER CARAN D'ACHE WATERCOLORS.
TH... THANKS.
IT WAS DUMB OF ME TO ASK HIM.
A MITSUBISHI PENCIL WOULD BE GOOD TOO!
THAT'S ENOUGH!
ON SUNDAY...
...I'M HEADING INTO BATTLE!
BATTLE?
Hey, what's a girl want on her birthday?
Anything!
Diamonds!
BATTLE...
IS HE GONNA GET IN A FIGHT SUNDAY?
IDIOT.

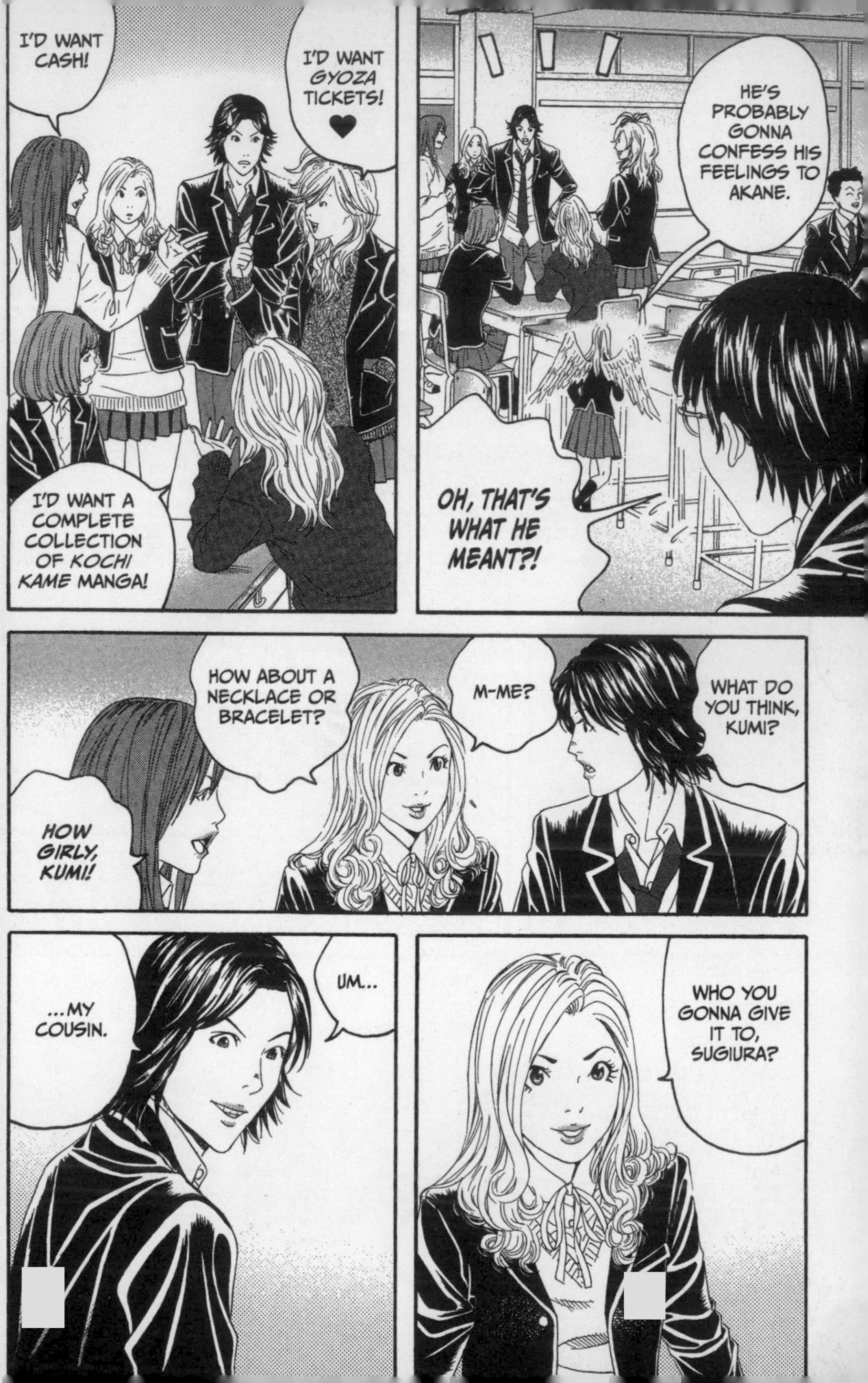
HE'S PROBABLY GONNA CONFESS HIS FEELINGS TO AKANE.
OH, THAT'S WHAT HE MEANT?!
I'D WANT *GYOZA* TICKETS! ♥
I'D WANT CASH!
I'D WANT A COMPLETE COLLECTION OF *KOCHI KAME* MANGA!
WHAT DO YOU THINK, KUMI?
M-ME?
HOW ABOUT A NECKLACE OR BRACELET?
HOW GIRLY, KUMI!
WHO YOU GONNA GIVE IT TO, SUGIURA?
UM...
...MY COUSIN.

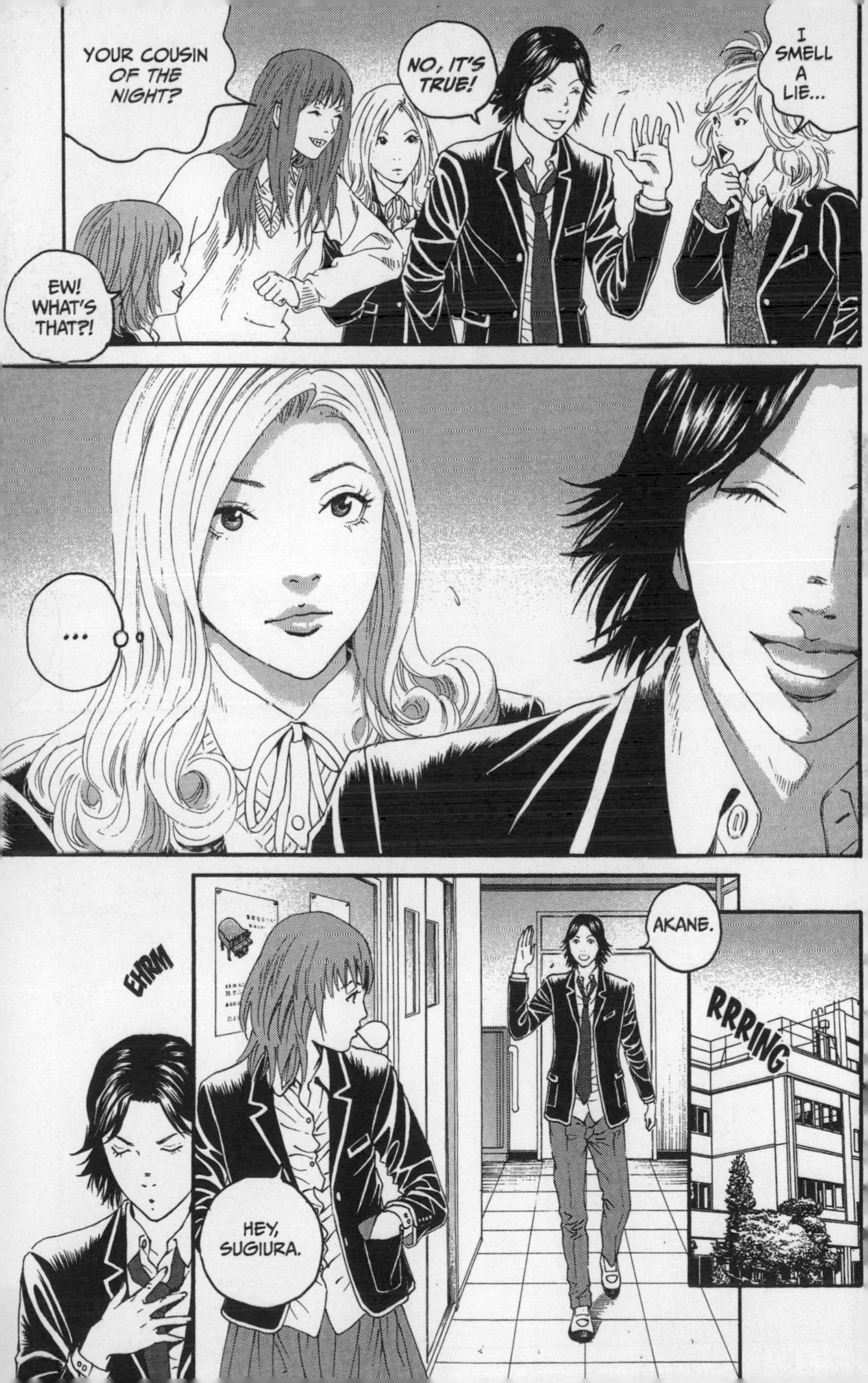
I SMELL A LIE...
NO, IT'S TRUE!
YOUR COUSIN OF THE NIGHT?
EW! WHAT'S THAT?!
...
RRRING
AKANE.
EHRM
HEY, SUGIURA.

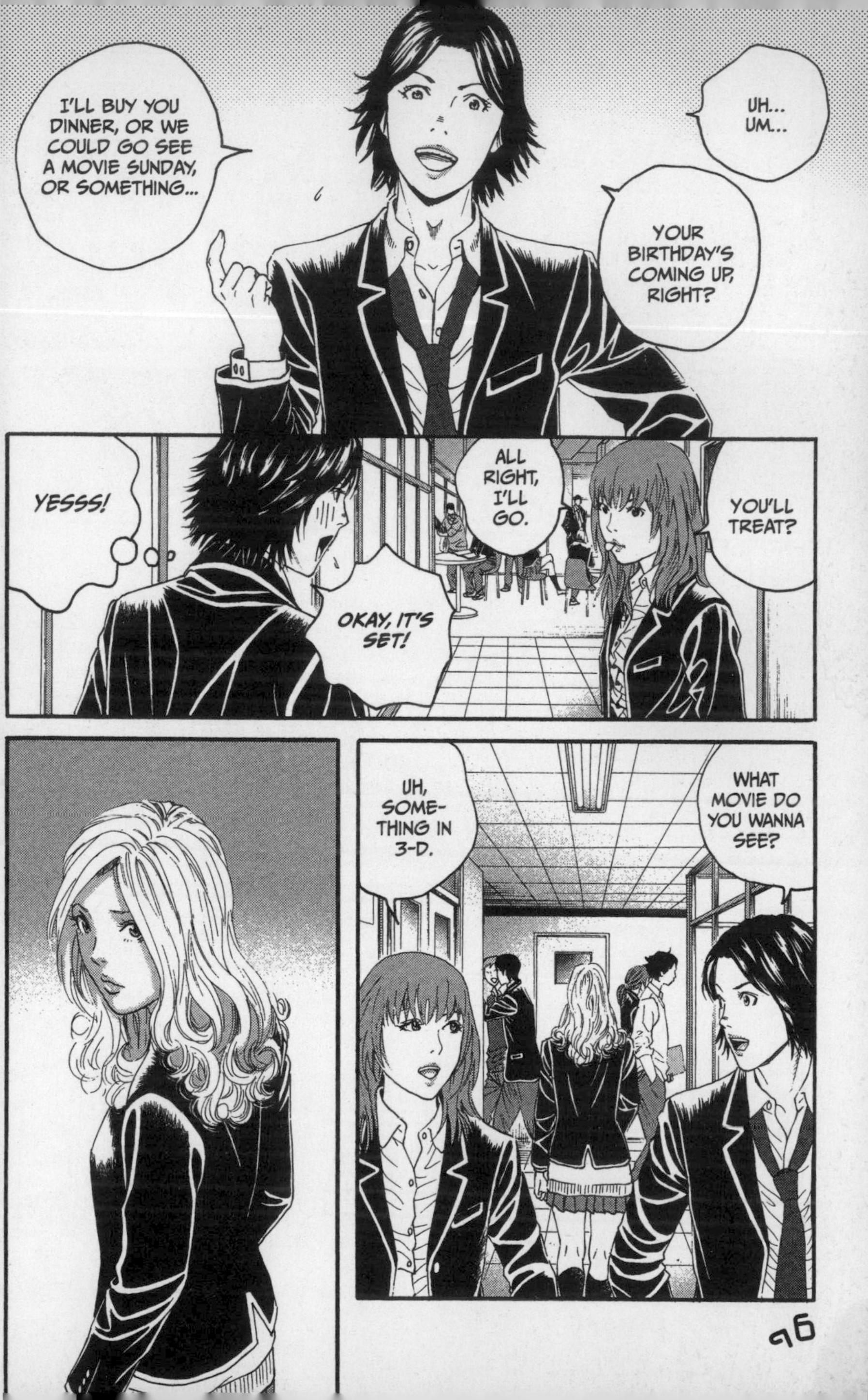
UH... UM...
YOUR BIRTHDAY'S COMING UP, RIGHT?
I'LL BUY YOU DINNER, OR WE COULD GO SEE A MOVIE SUNDAY, OR SOMETHING...
YOU'LL TREAT?
ALL RIGHT, I'LL GO.
OKAY, IT'S SET!
YESSS!
WHAT MOVIE DO YOU WANNA SEE?
UH, SOMETHING IN 3-D.

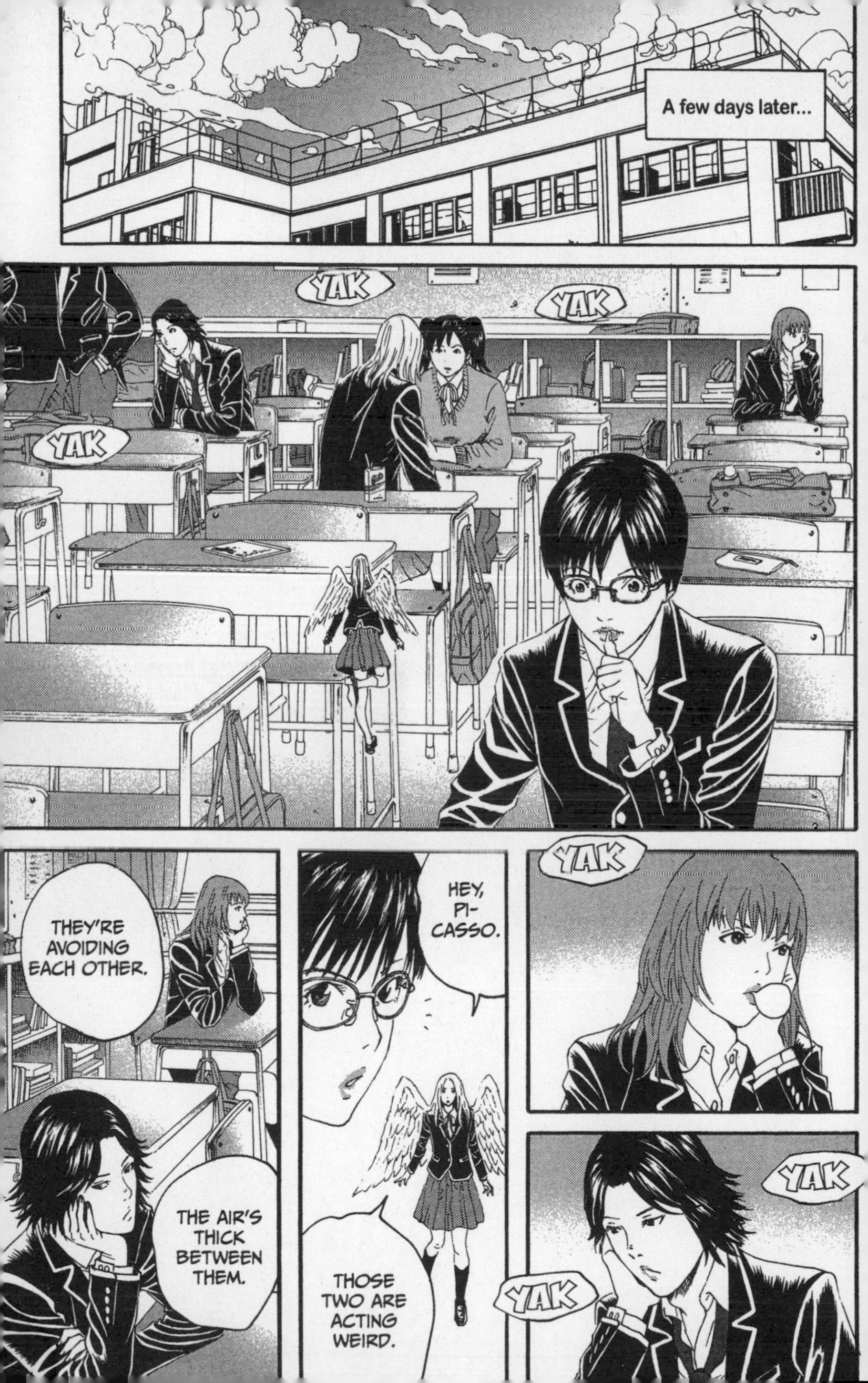
A few days later...
YAK
YAK
YAK
YAK
YAK
YAK
HEY, PI-CASSO.
THOSE TWO ARE ACTING WEIRD.
THEY'RE AVOIDING EACH OTHER.
THE AIR'S THICK BETWEEN THEM.

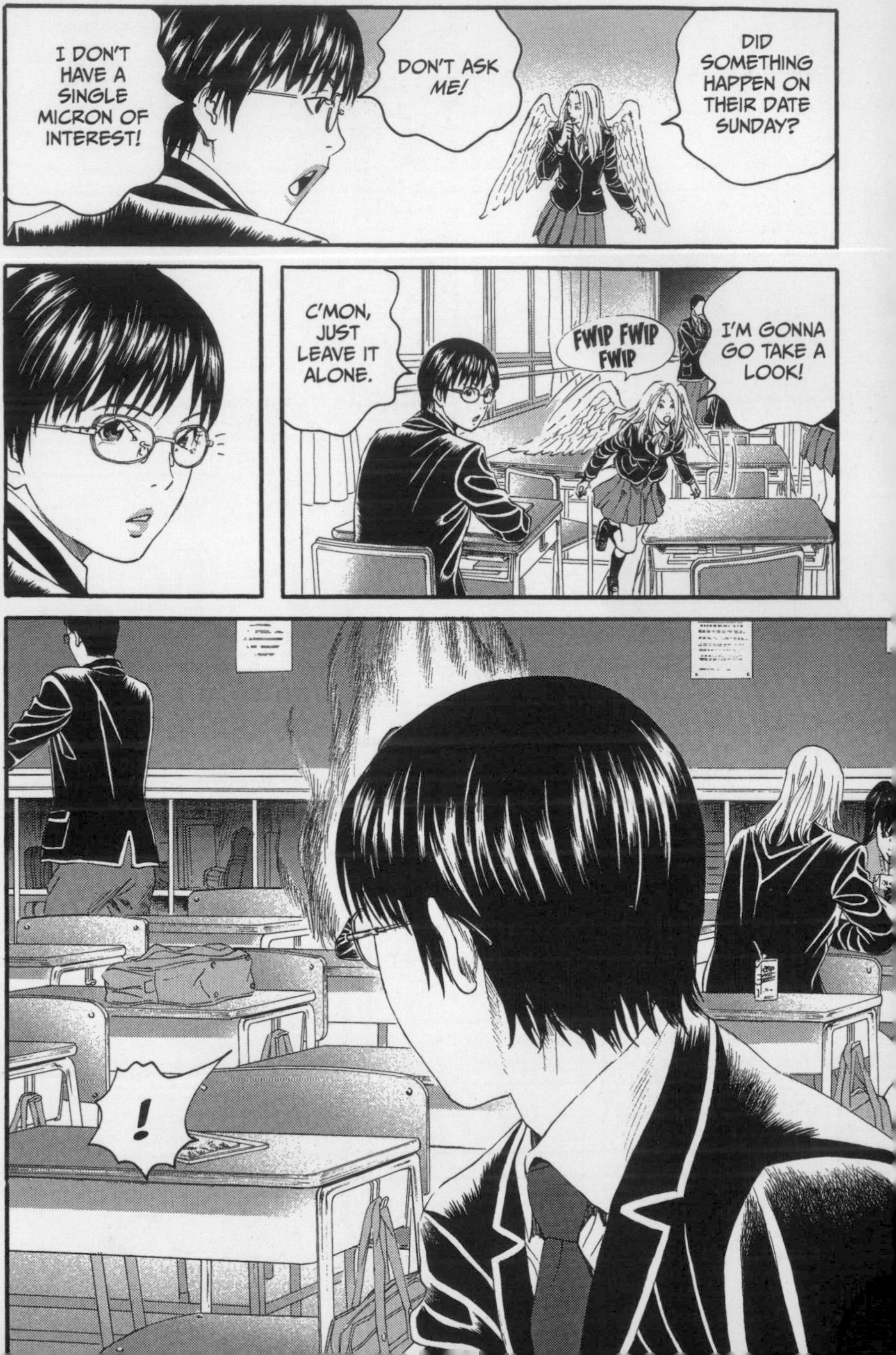
DID SOMETHING HAPPEN ON THEIR DATE SUNDAY?
DON'T ASK ME!
I DON'T HAVE A SINGLE MICRON OF INTEREST!
I'M GONNA GO TAKE A LOOK!
FWIP FWIP FWIP
C'MON, JUST LEAVE IT ALONE.
!

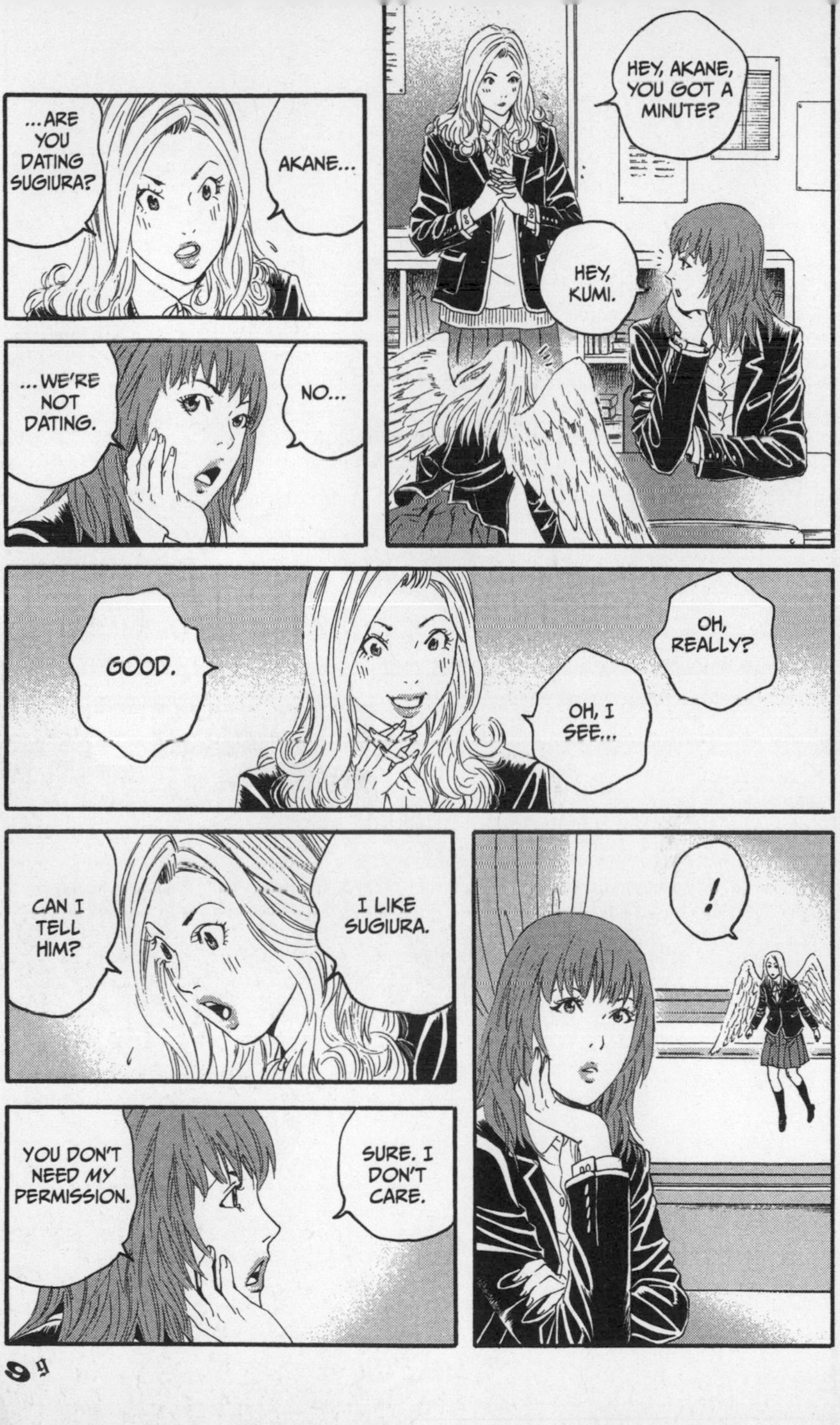
HEY, AKANE, YOU GOT A MINUTE?
HEY, KUMI.
AKANE...
...ARE YOU DATING SUGIURA?
NO...
...WE'RE NOT DATING.
OH, REALLY?
OH, I SEE...
GOOD.
!
I LIKE SUGIURA.
CAN I TELL HIM?
SURE. I DON'T CARE.
YOU DON'T NEED MY PERMISSION.

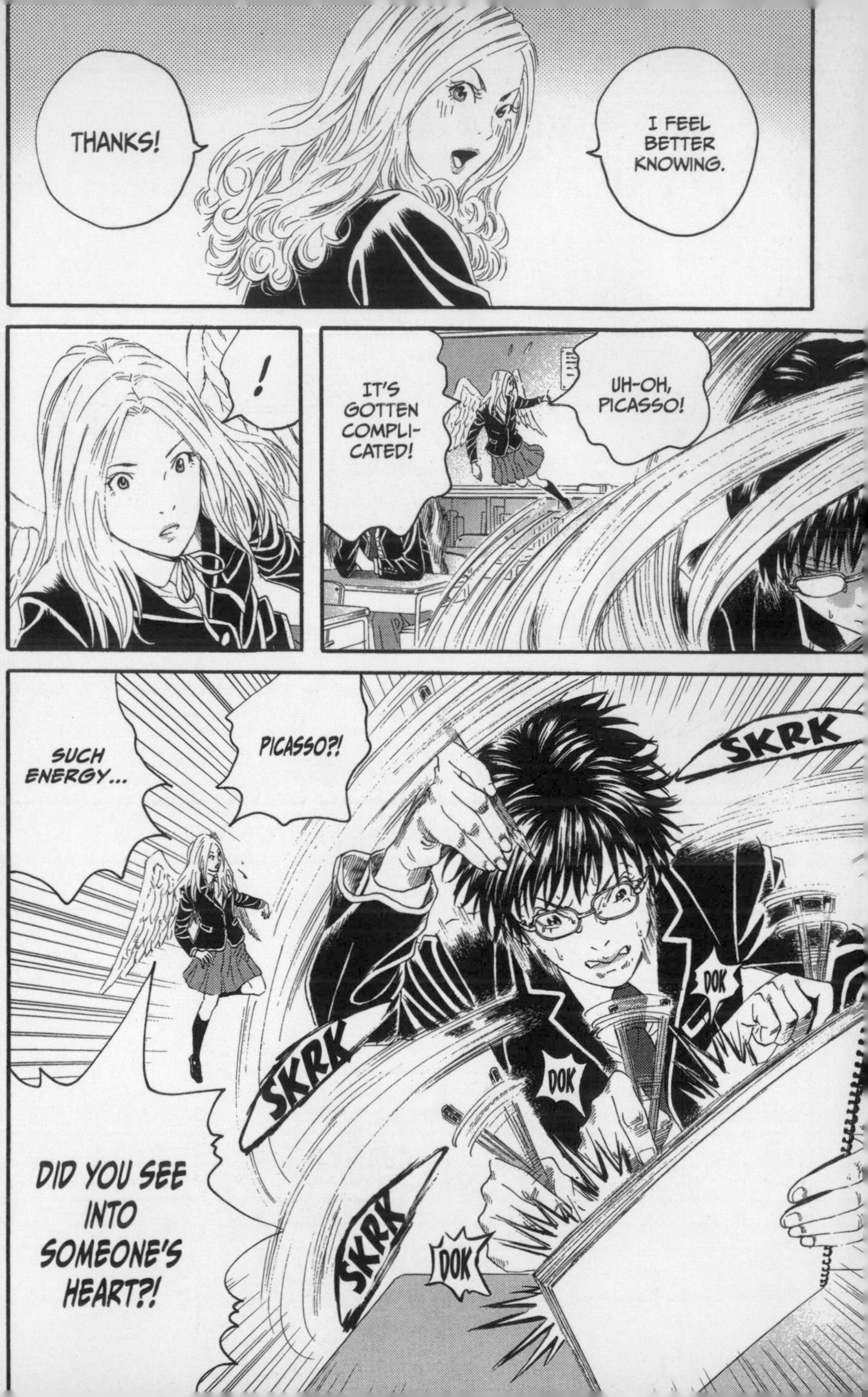
I FEEL BETTER KNOWING.
THANKS!
UH-OH, PICASSO!
IT'S GOTTEN COMPLICATED!
!
SKRK
PICASSO?!
SUCH ENERGY...
DOK
SKRK
DOK
DID YOU SEE INTO SOMEONE'S HEART?!
SKRK
DOK

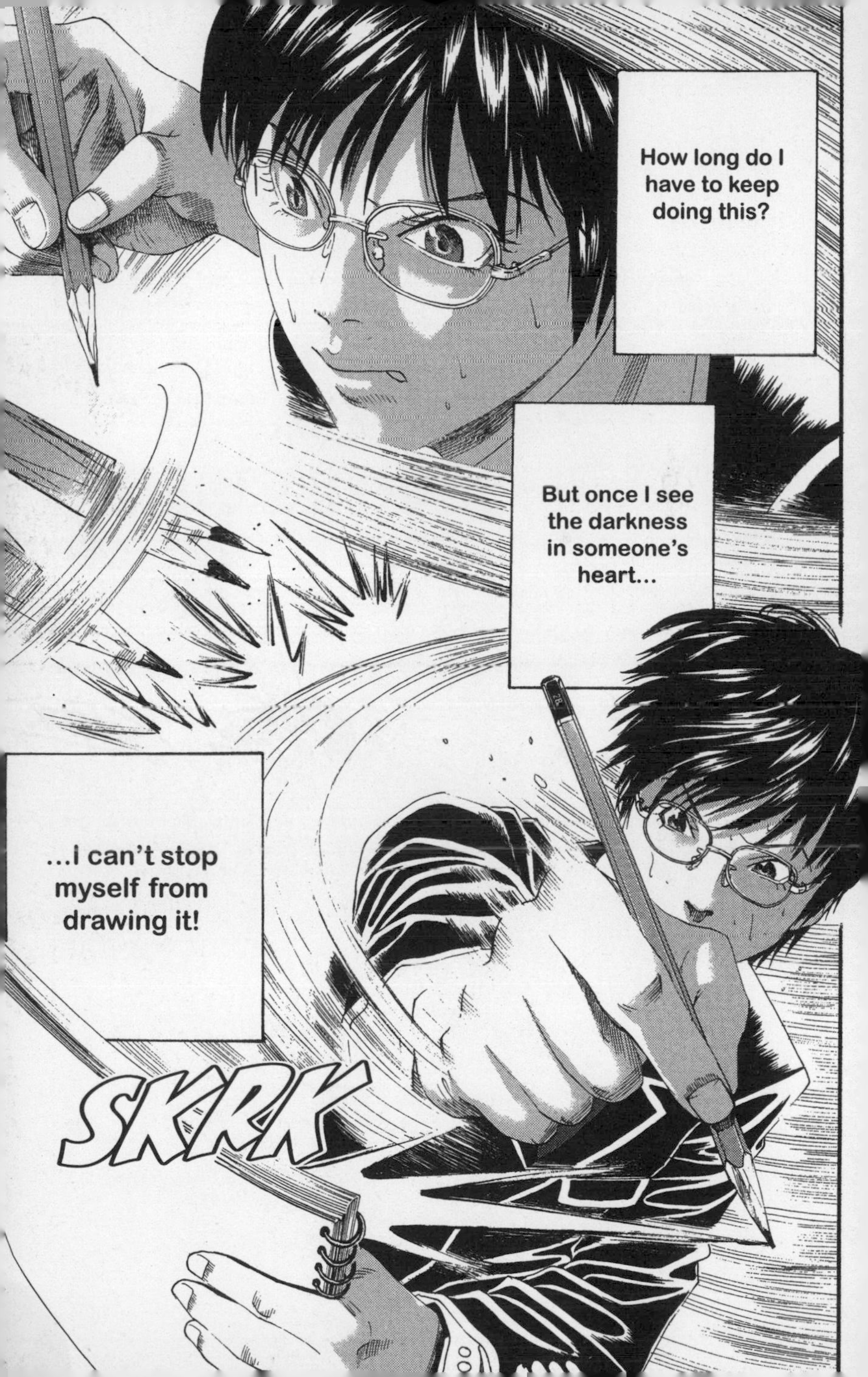
How long do I have to keep doing this?
But once I see the darkness in someone's heart...
...I can't stop myself from drawing it!
SKRK

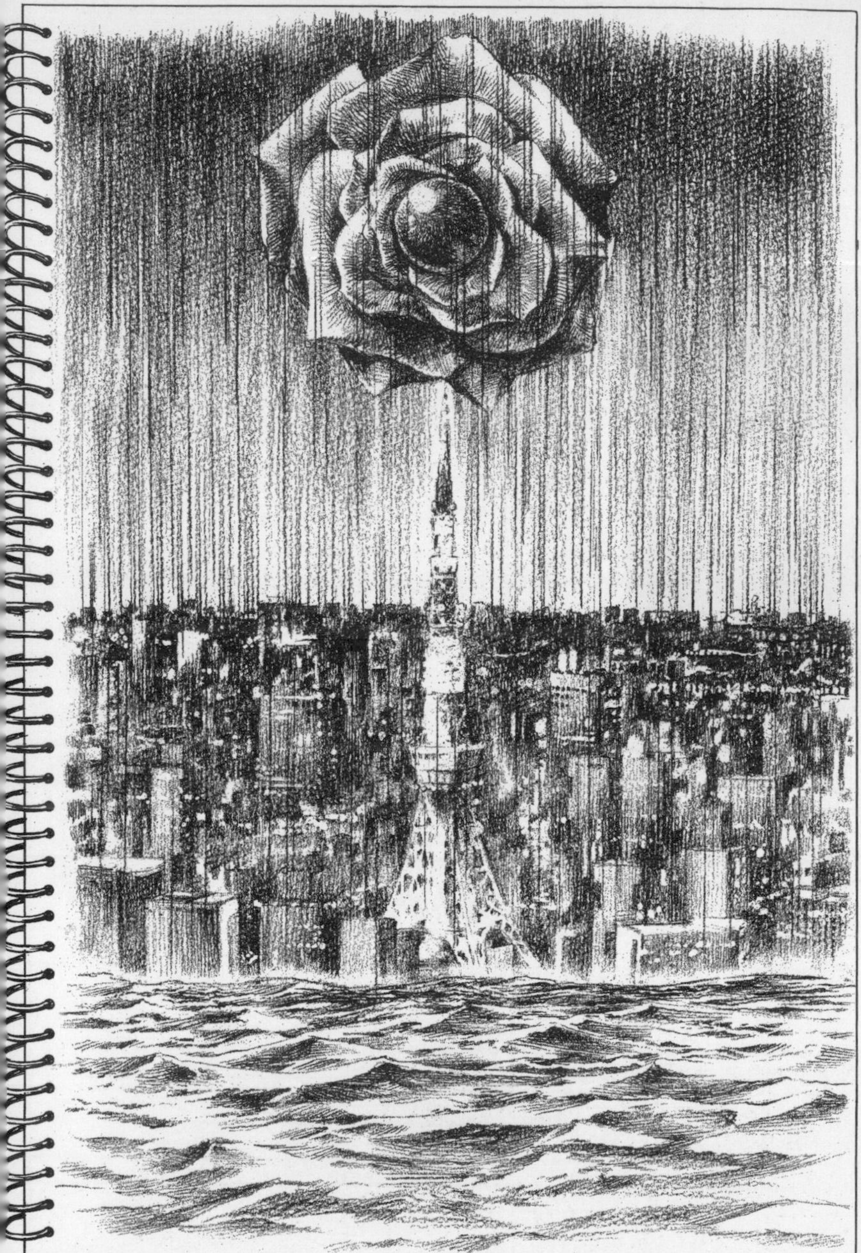

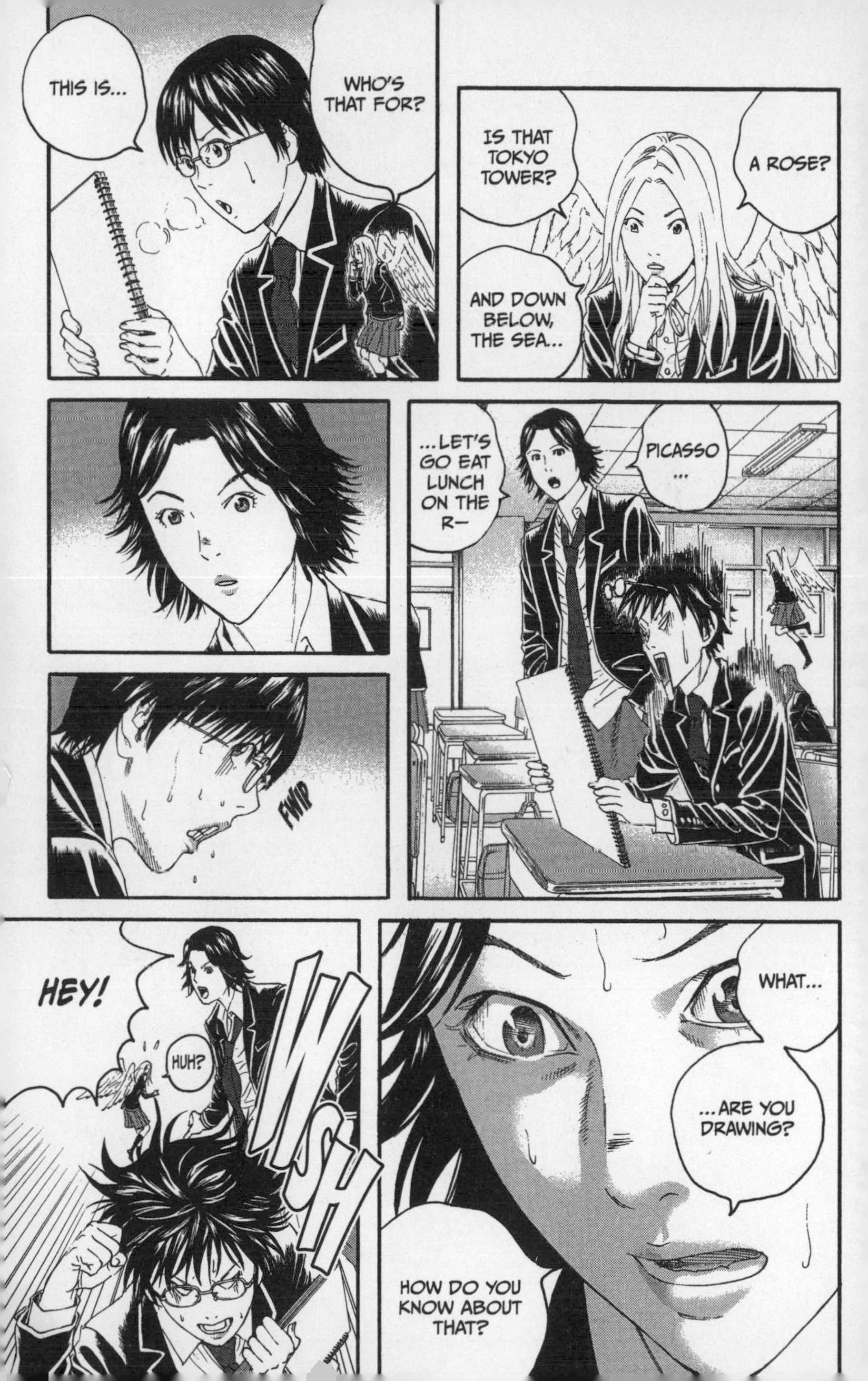
A ROSE?
IS THAT TOKYO TOWER?
AND DOWN BELOW, THE SEA...
WHO'S THAT FOR?
THIS IS...
PICASSO ...
...LET'S GO EAT LUNCH ON THE R—
FWIP
WHAT...
...ARE YOU DRAWING?
HOW DO YOU KNOW ABOUT THAT?
WHSH
HEY!
HUH?

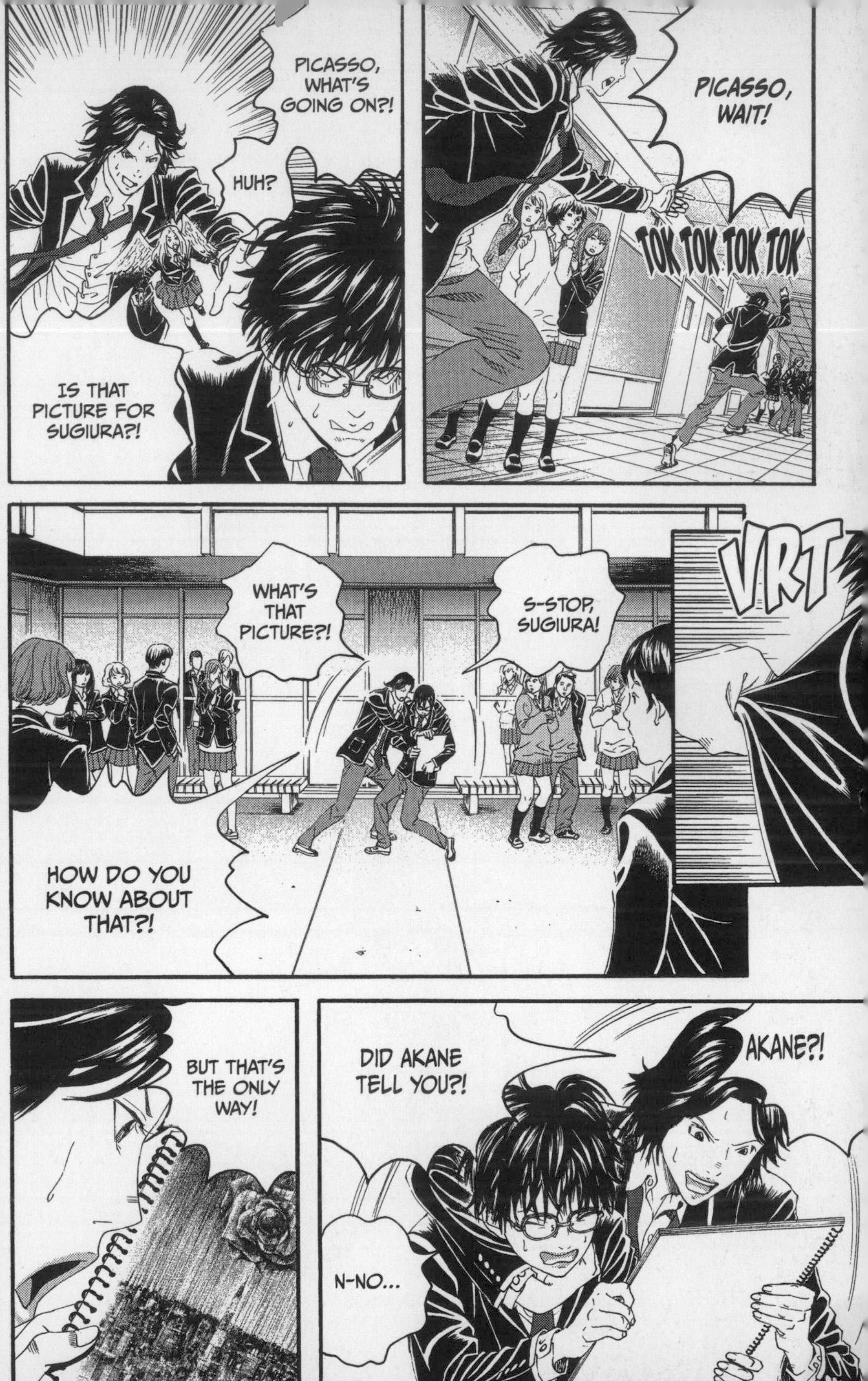
PICASSO, WAIT!
TOK TOK TOK TOK
PICASSO, WHAT'S GOING ON?!
HUH?
IS THAT PICTURE FOR SUGIURA?!
VRT
S-STOP, SUGIURA!
WHAT'S THAT PICTURE?!
HOW DO YOU KNOW ABOUT THAT?!
AKANE?!
DID AKANE TELL YOU?!
N-NO...
BUT THAT'S THE ONLY WAY!

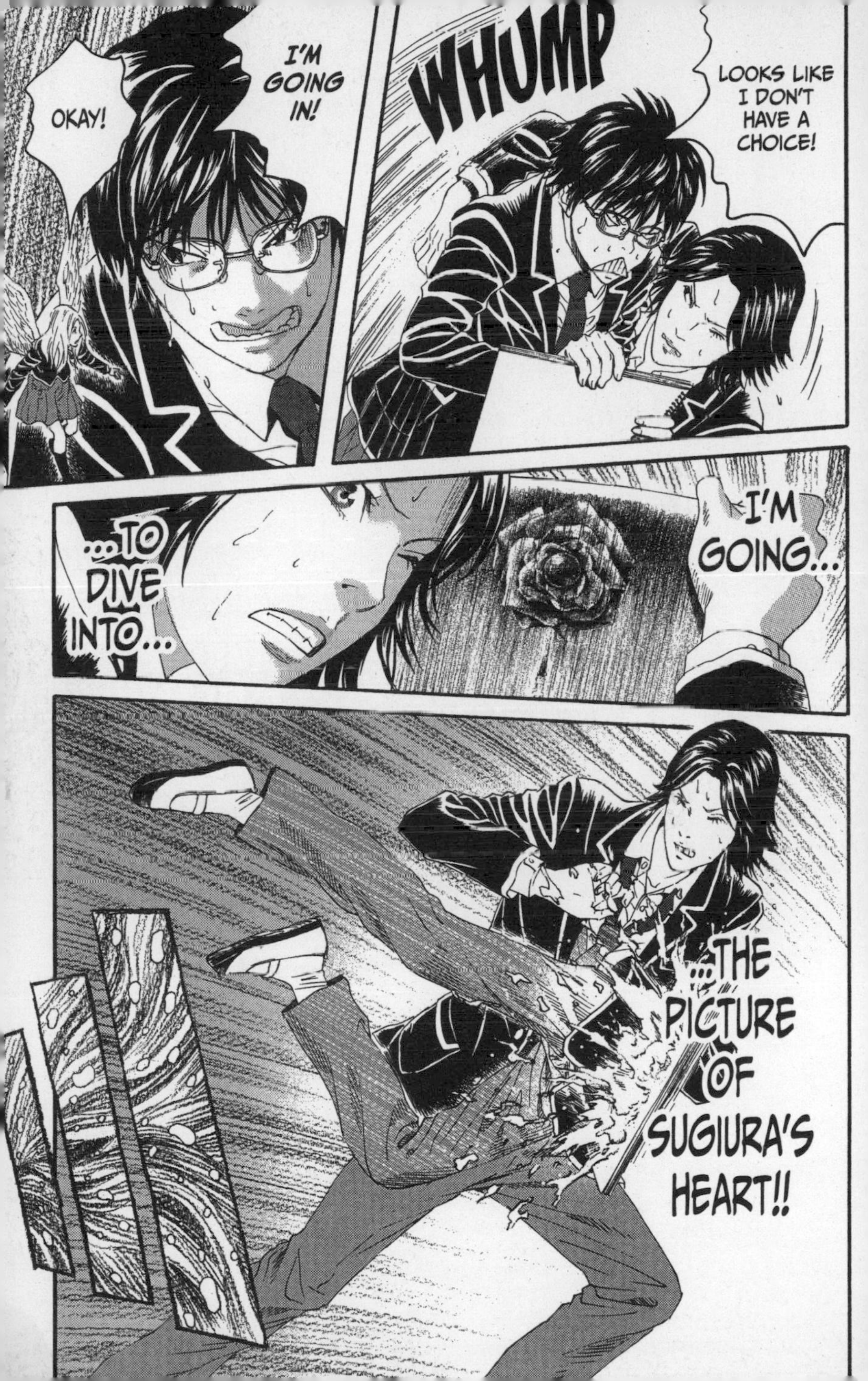
WHUMP
LOOKS LIKE I DON'T HAVE A CHOICE!
I'M GOING IN!
OKAY!
I'M GOING...
...TO DIVE INTO...
...THE PICTURE OF SUGIURA'S HEART!!

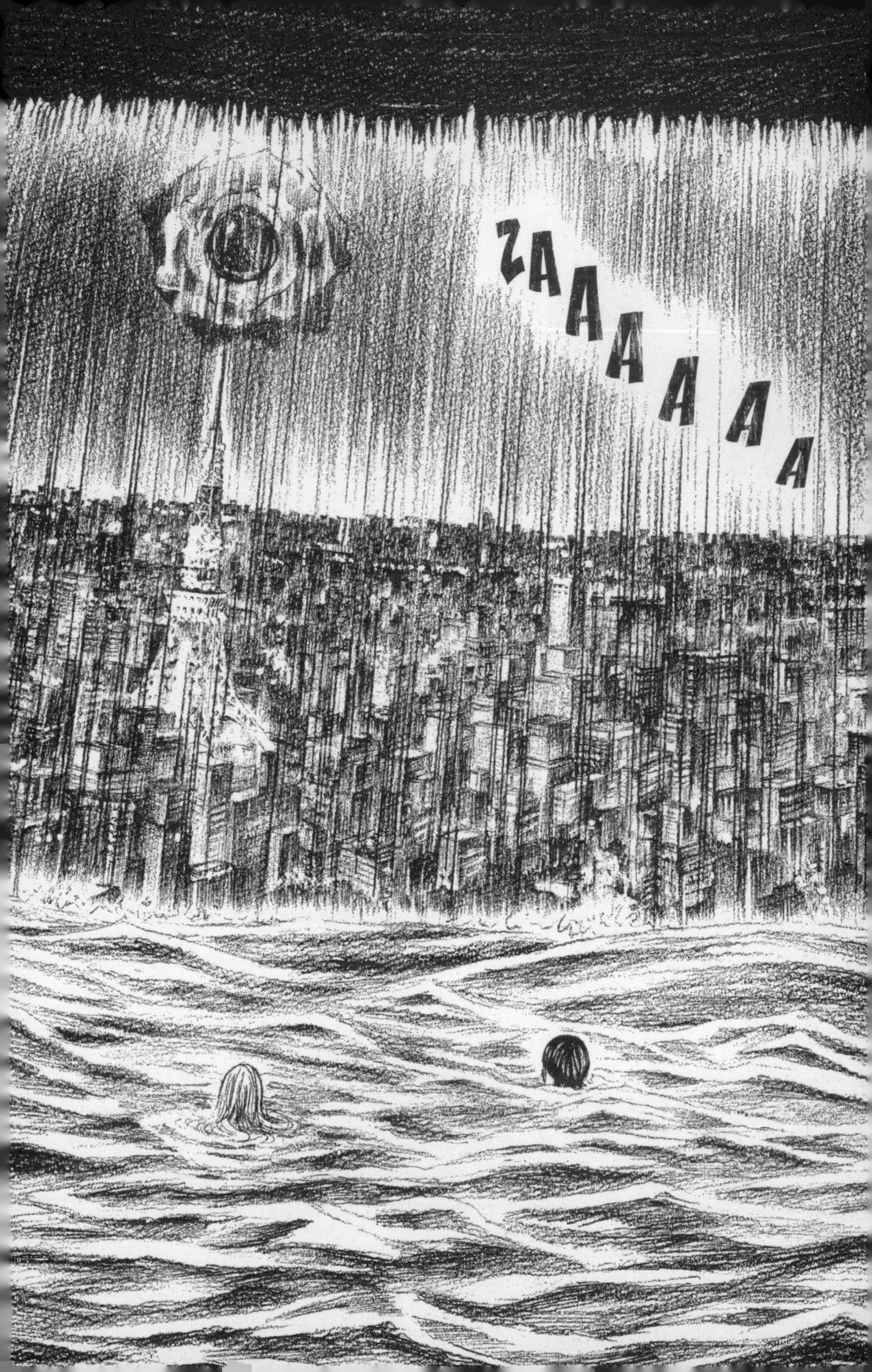
ZAAAAAA

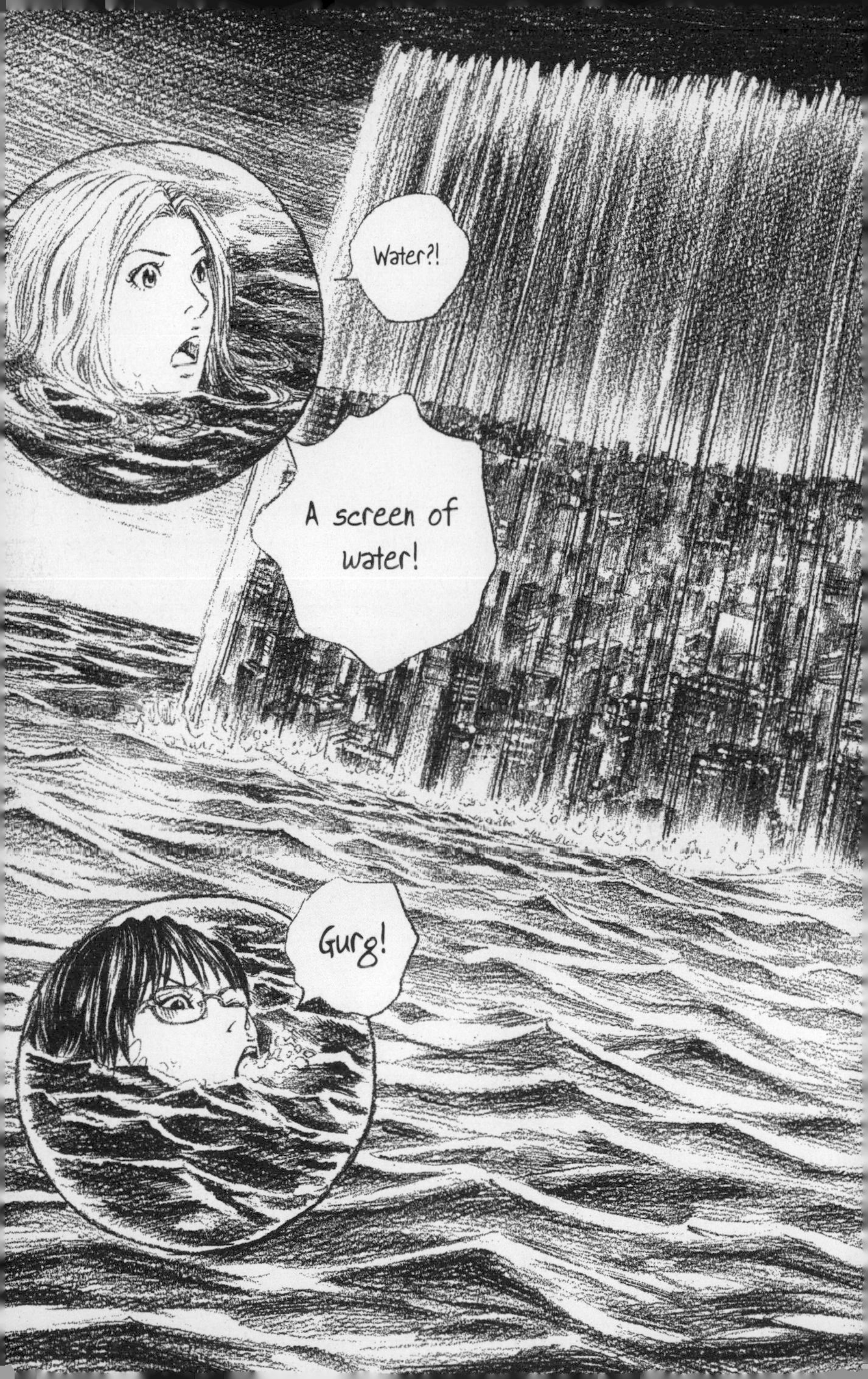
Water?!
A screen of water!
Gurg!

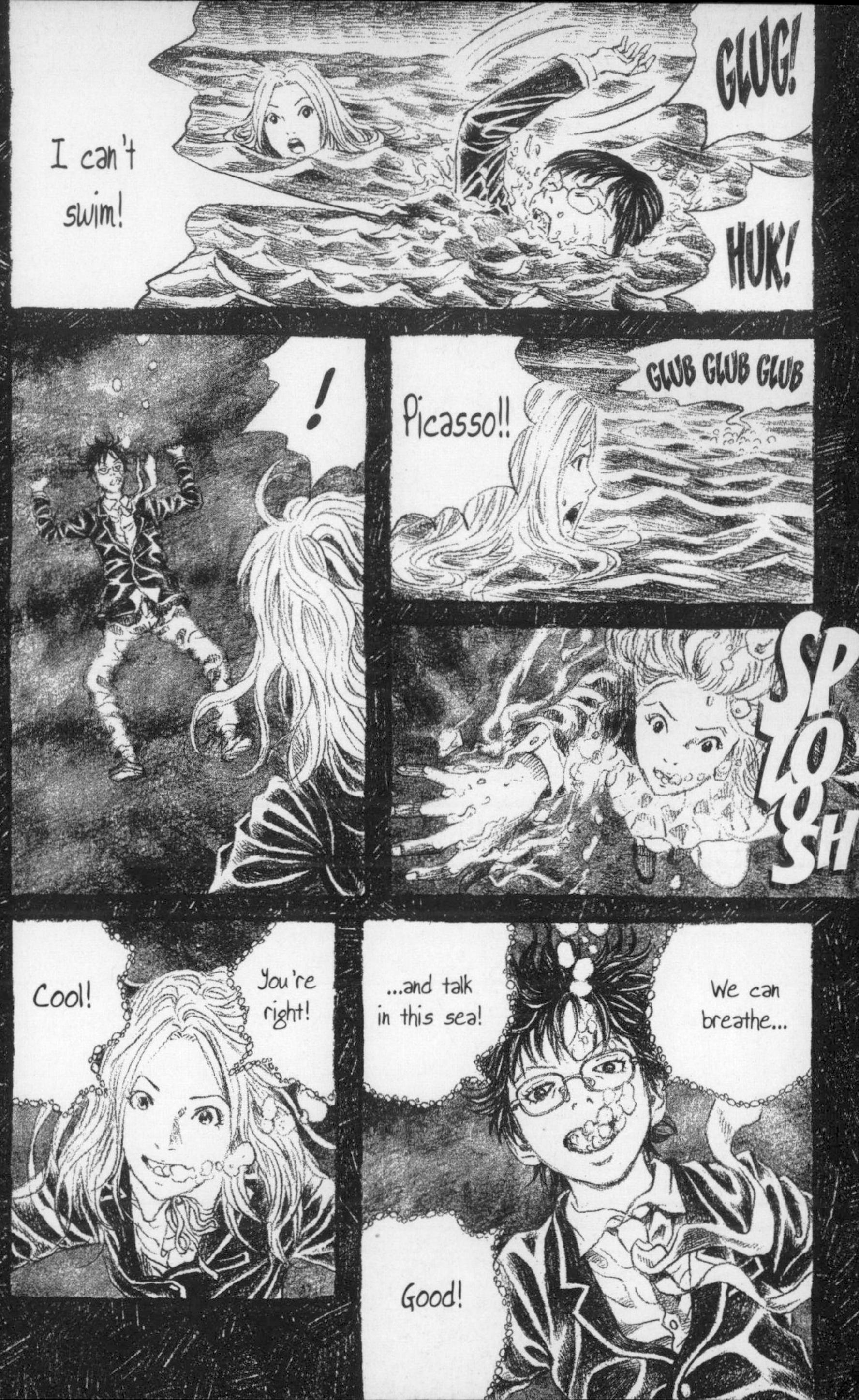
GLUG!
HUK!
I can't swim!
GLUB GLUB GLUB
Picasso!!
SPLOSH
!
We can breathe...
...and talk in this sea!
Good!
You're right!
Cool!

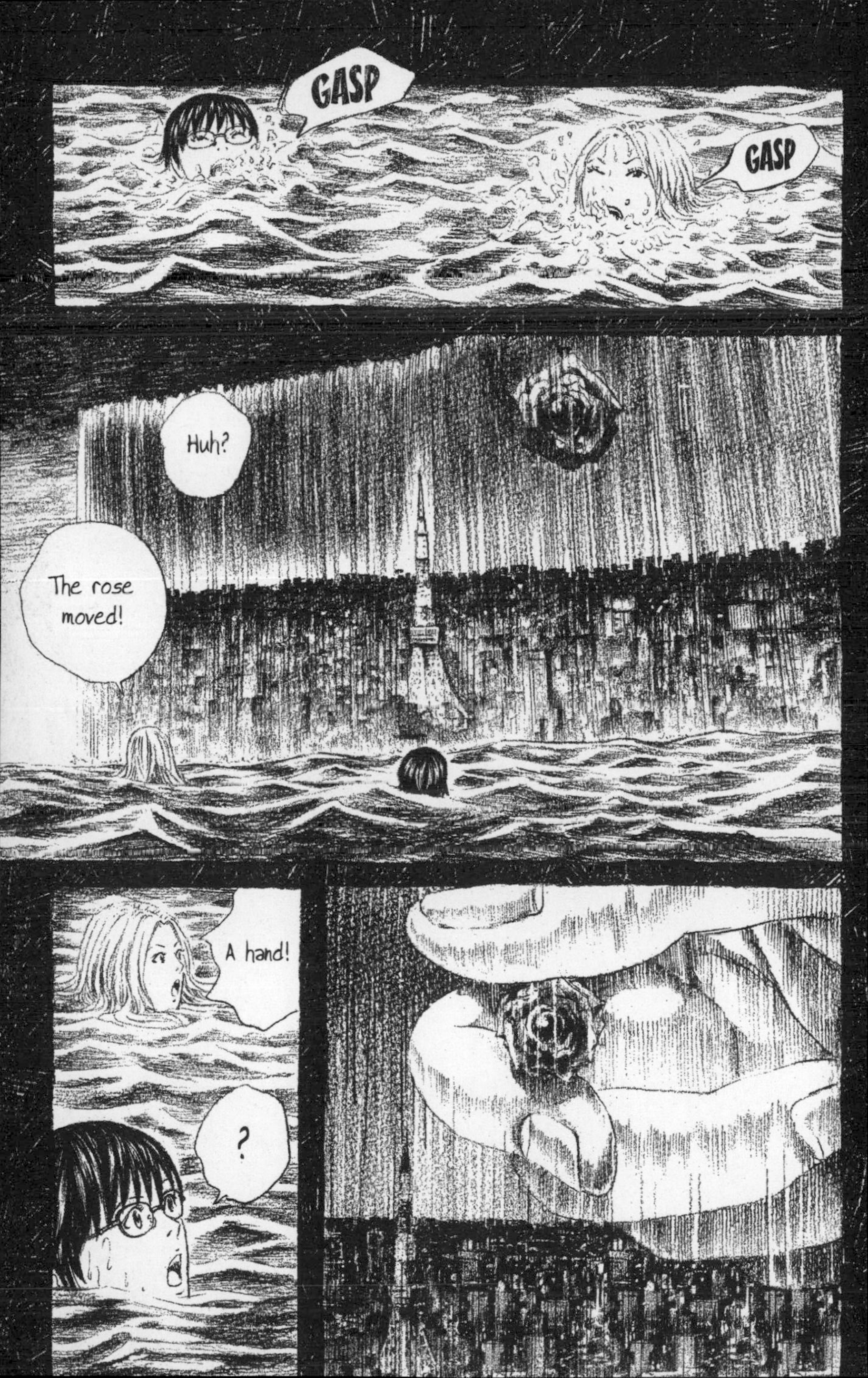
GASP
GASP
Huh?
The rose moved!
A hand!
?

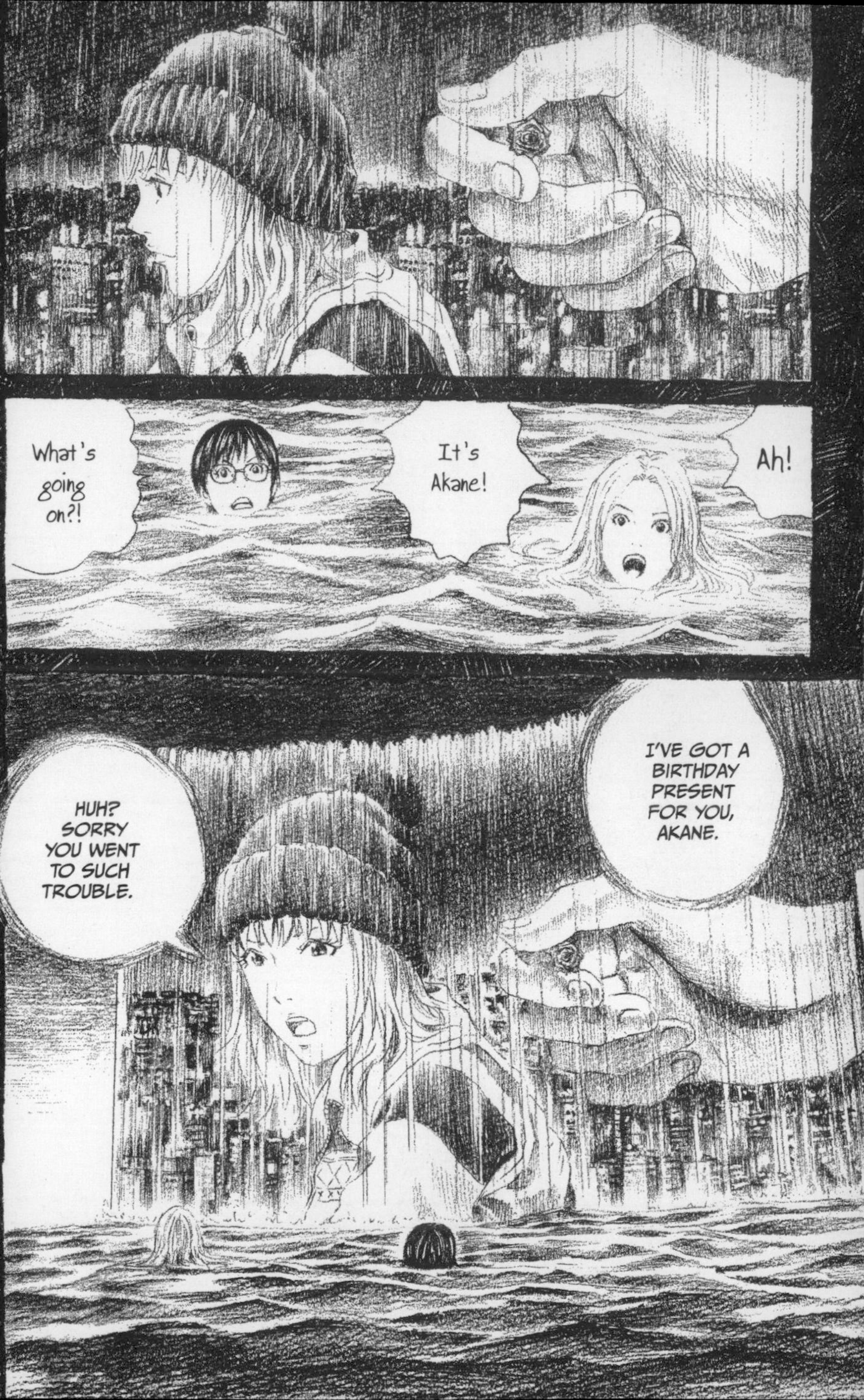
Ah!
It's Akane!
What's going on?!
I'VE GOT A BIRTHDAY PRESENT FOR YOU, AKANE.
HUH? SORRY YOU WENT TO SUCH TROUBLE.

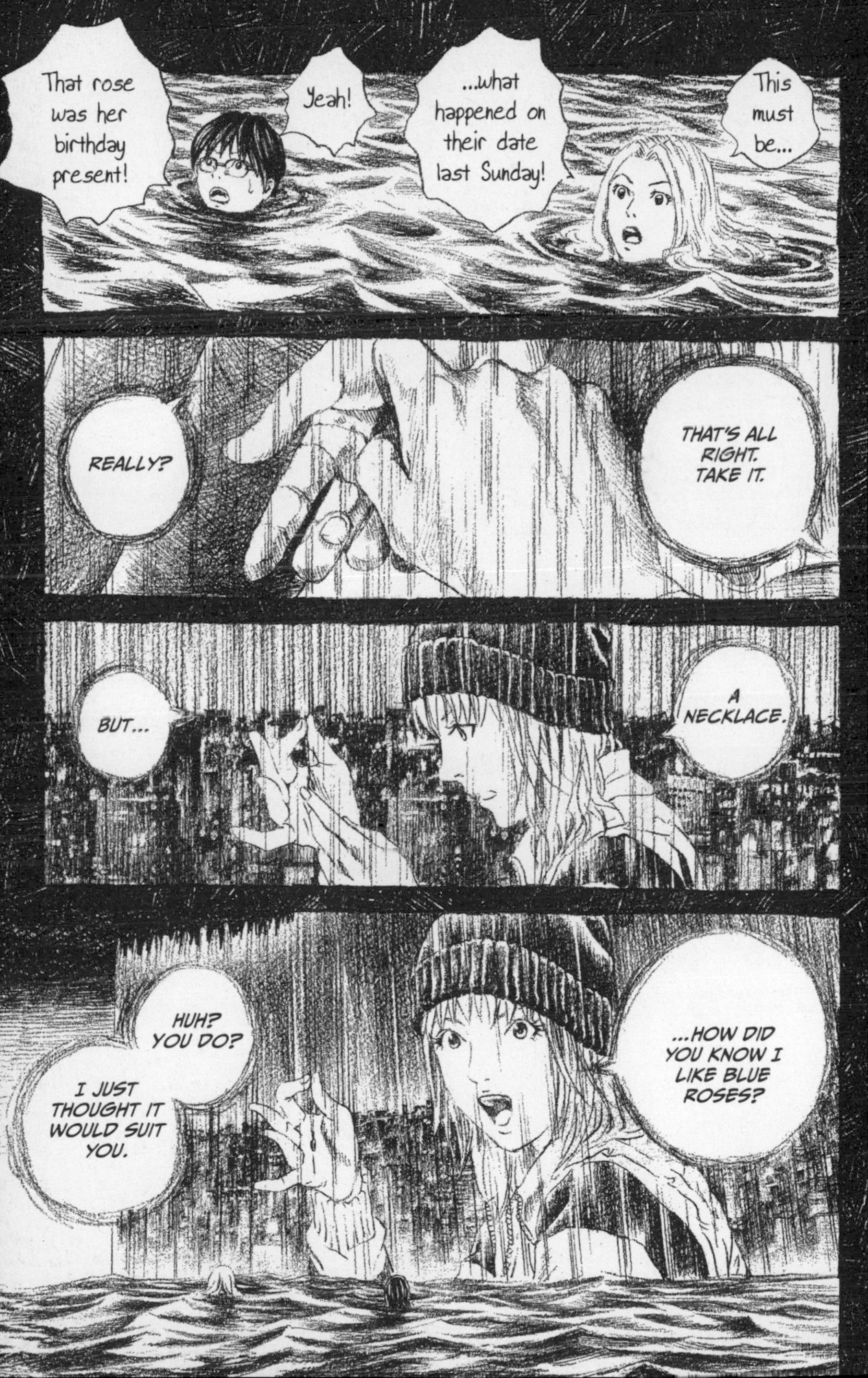
This must be...
...what happened on their date last Sunday!
Yeah!
That rose was her birthday present!
THAT'S ALL RIGHT. TAKE IT.
REALLY?
A NECKLACE.
BUT...
...HOW DID YOU KNOW I LIKE BLUE ROSES?
HUH? YOU DO?
I JUST THOUGHT IT WOULD SUIT YOU.

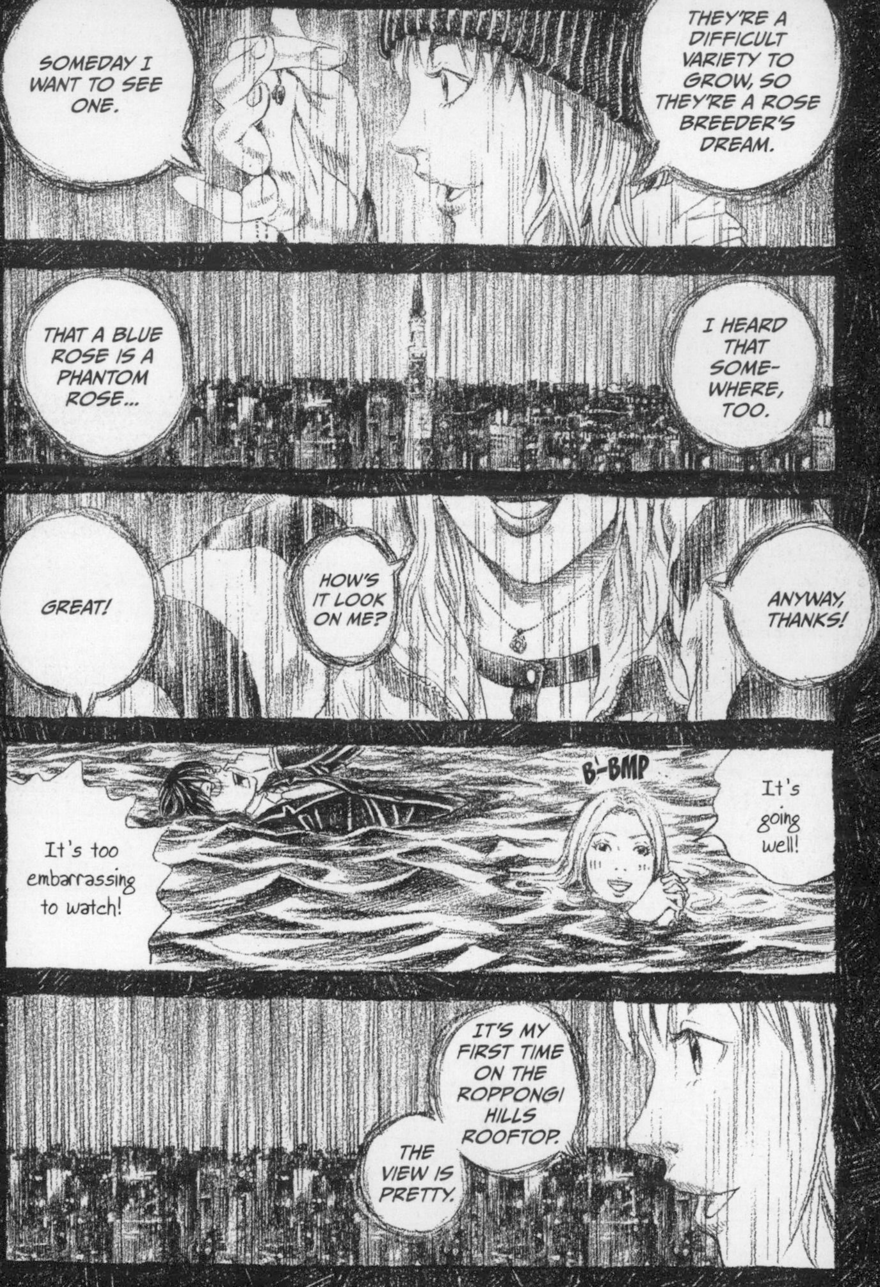
THEY'RE A DIFFICULT VARIETY TO GROW, SO THEY'RE A ROSE BREEDER'S DREAM.
SOMEDAY I WANT TO SEE ONE.
I HEARD THAT SOME-WHERE, TOO.
THAT A BLUE ROSE IS A PHANTOM ROSE...
ANYWAY, THANKS!
HOW'S IT LOOK ON ME?
GREAT!
It's going well!
B-BMP
It's too embarrassing to watch!
IT'S MY FIRST TIME ON THE ROPPONGI HILLS ROOFTOP.
THE VIEW IS PRETTY.

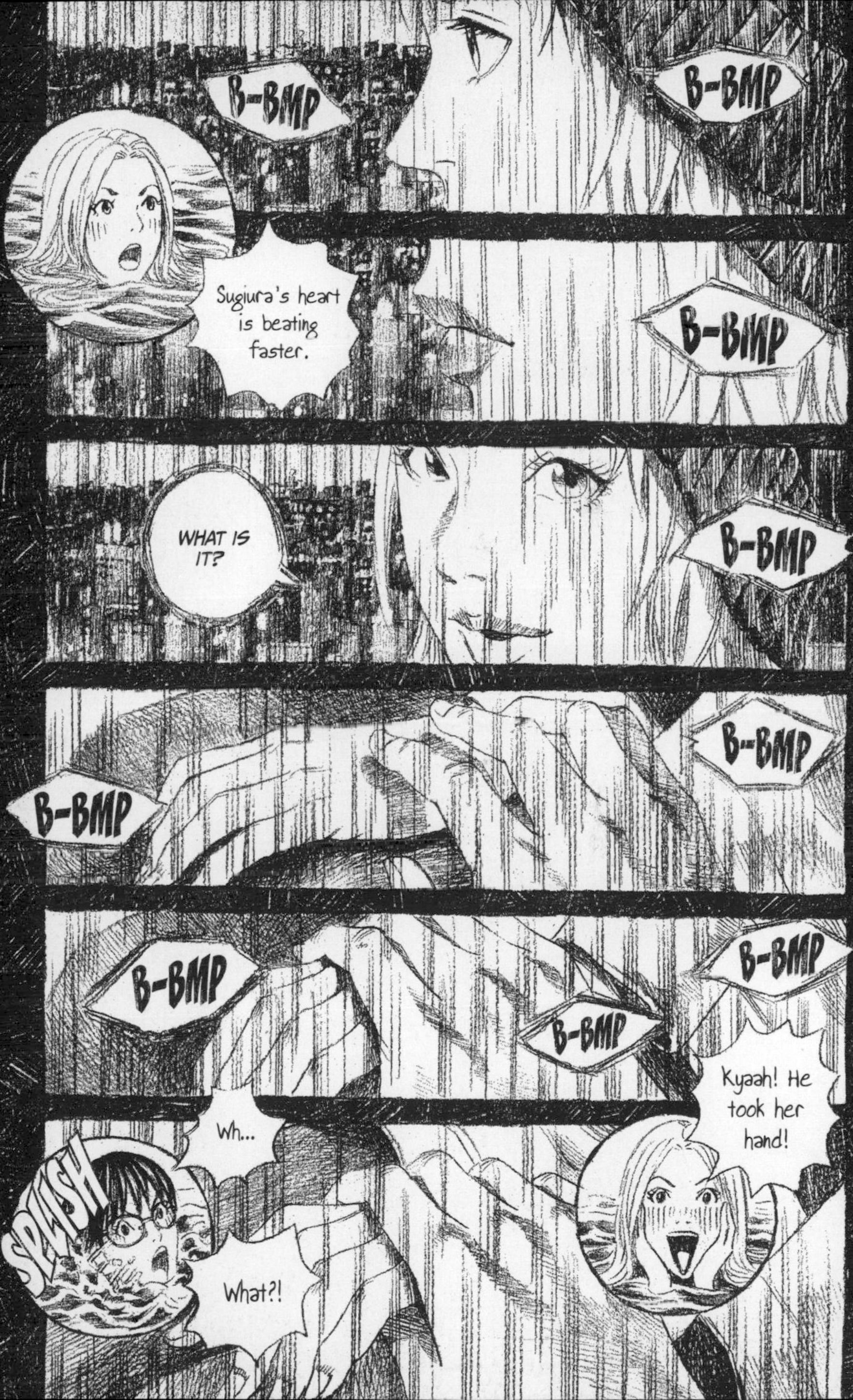

B-BMP
B-BMP
B-BMP
Sugiura's heart is beating faster.
B-BMP
WHAT IS IT?
B-BMP
B-BMP
B-BMP
B-BMP
B-BMP
Kyaah! He took her hand!
Wh...
SPLISH
What?!

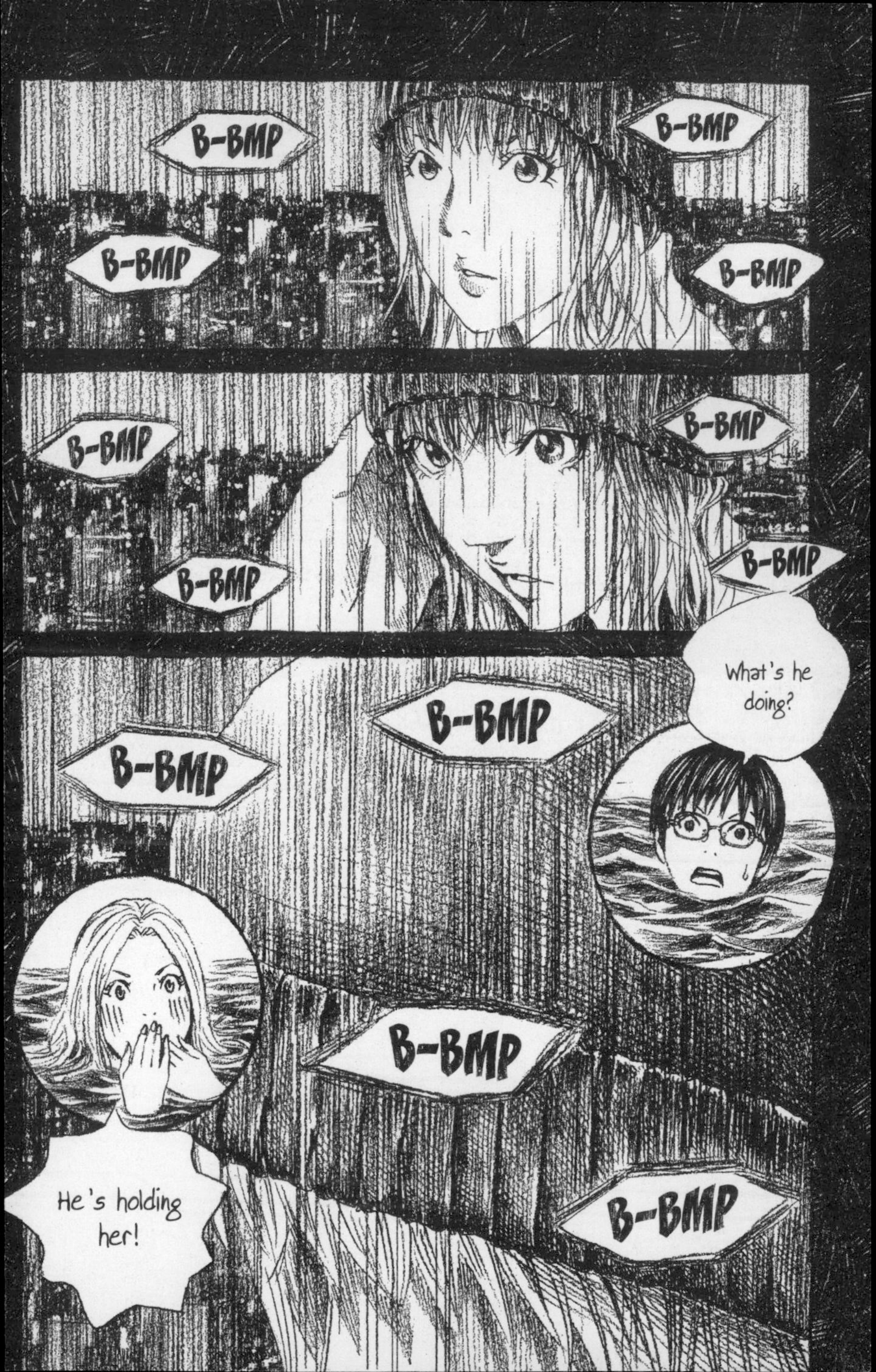
B-BMP
B-BMP
B-BMP
B-BMP
B-BMP
B-BMP
B-BMP
B-BMP
What's he doing?
B-BMP
B-BMP
B-BMP
He's holding her!
B-BMP

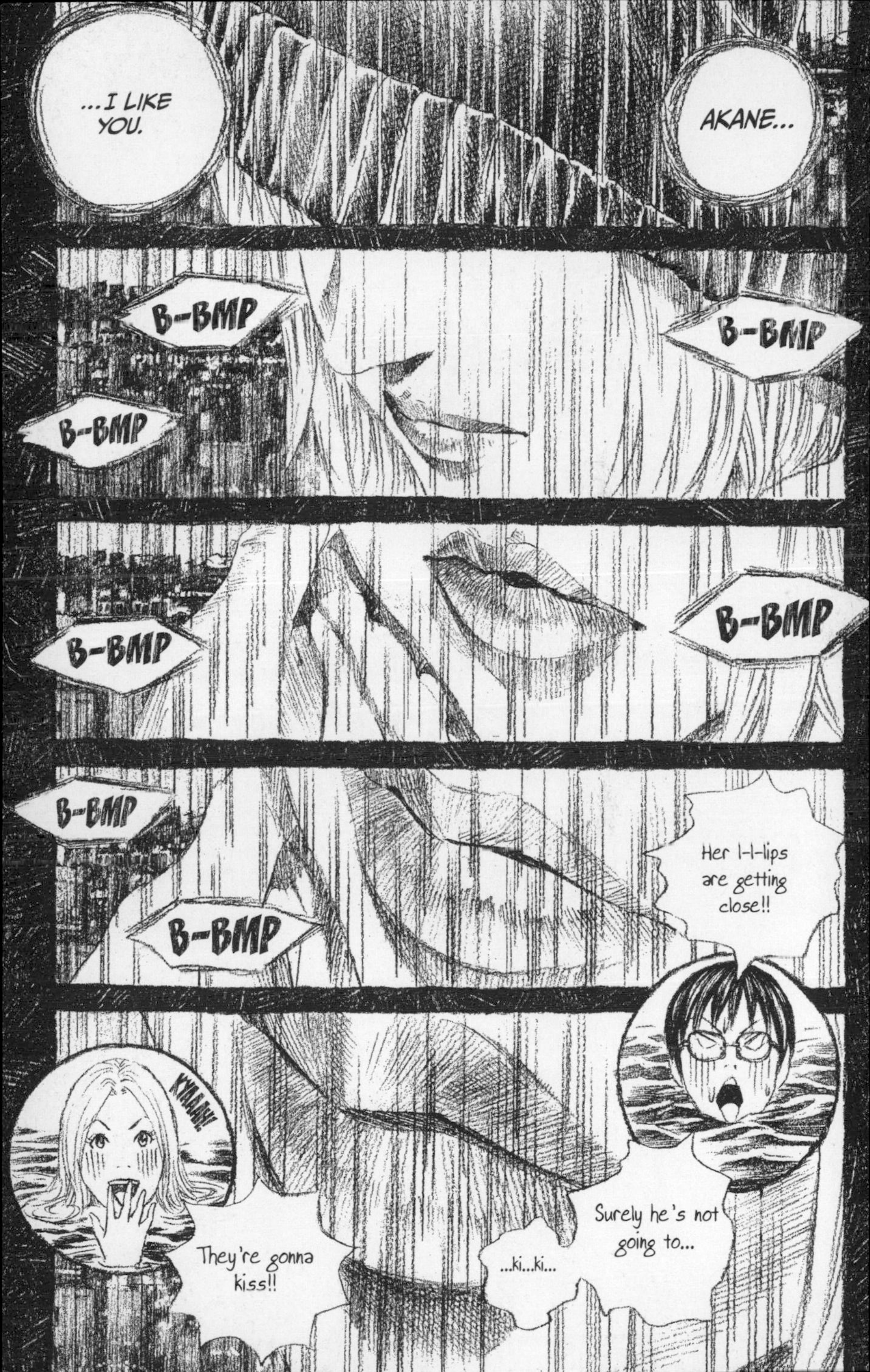
AKANE...
...I LIKE YOU.
B-BMP
B-BMP
B-BMP
B-BMP
B-BMP
Her l-l-lips are getting close!!
B-BMP
B-BMP
Surely he's not going to...
...ki...ki...
KYAAAH!
They're gonna kiss!!

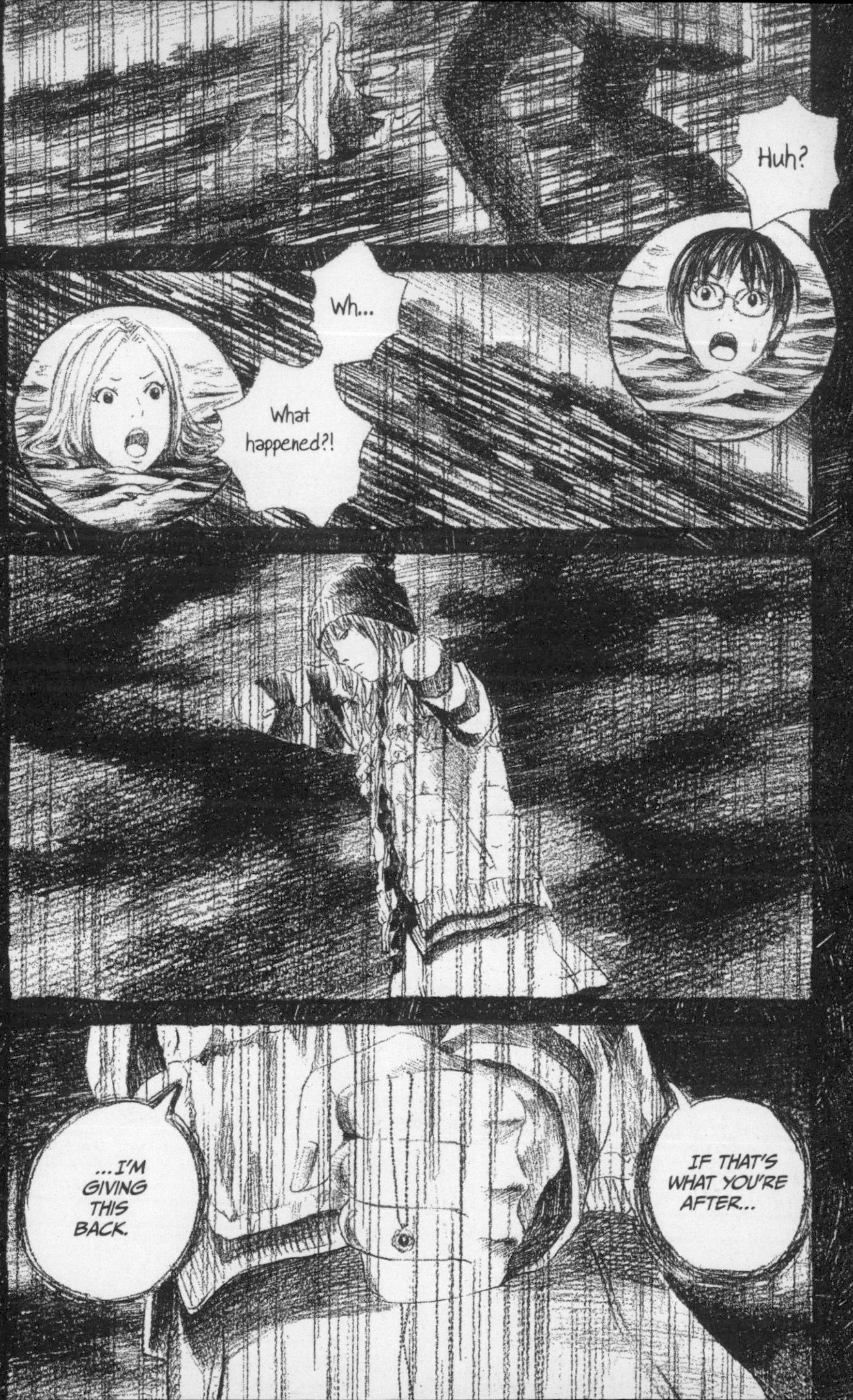
Huh?
Wh...
What happened?!
IF THAT'S WHAT YOU'RE AFTER...
...I'M GIVING THIS BACK.

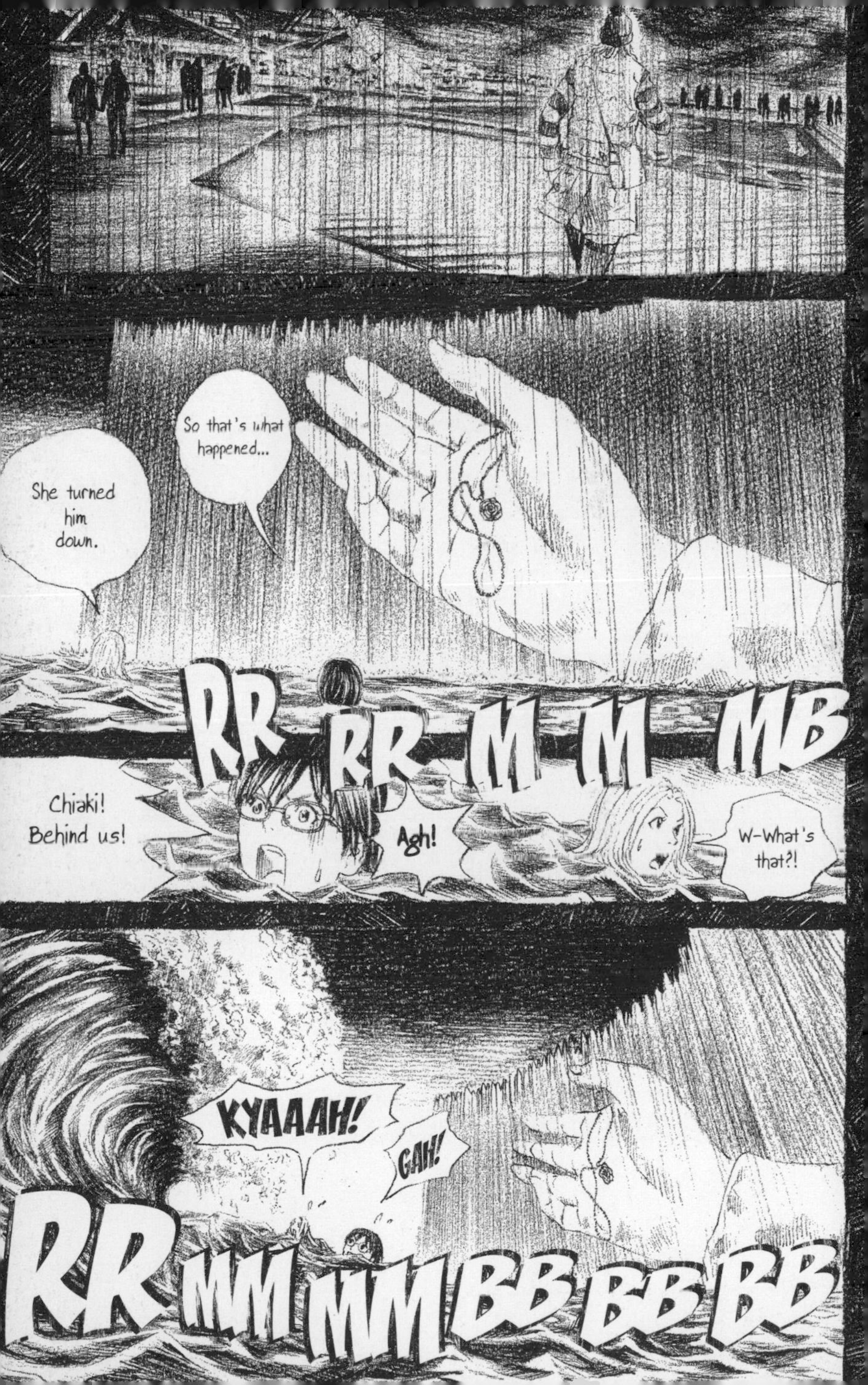
So that's what happened...
She turned him down.
RRRRMMMMB
W-What's that?!
Agh!
Chiaki! Behind us!
GAH!
KYAAAH!
RRMMMMBBBBBB

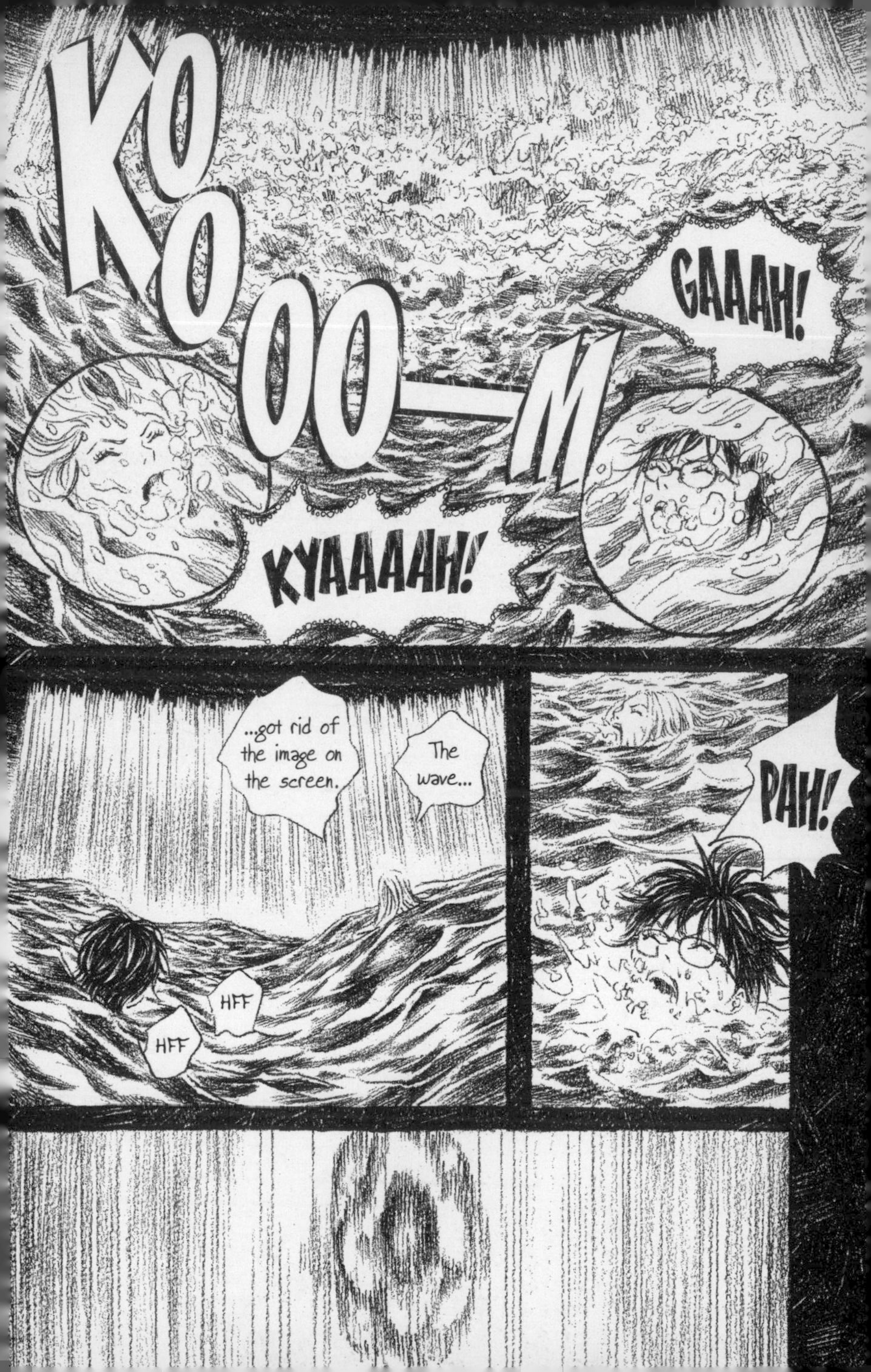

KOOOO—M
GAAAH!
KYAAAAH!
PAH!
The wave...
...got rid of the image on the screen.
HFF
HFF

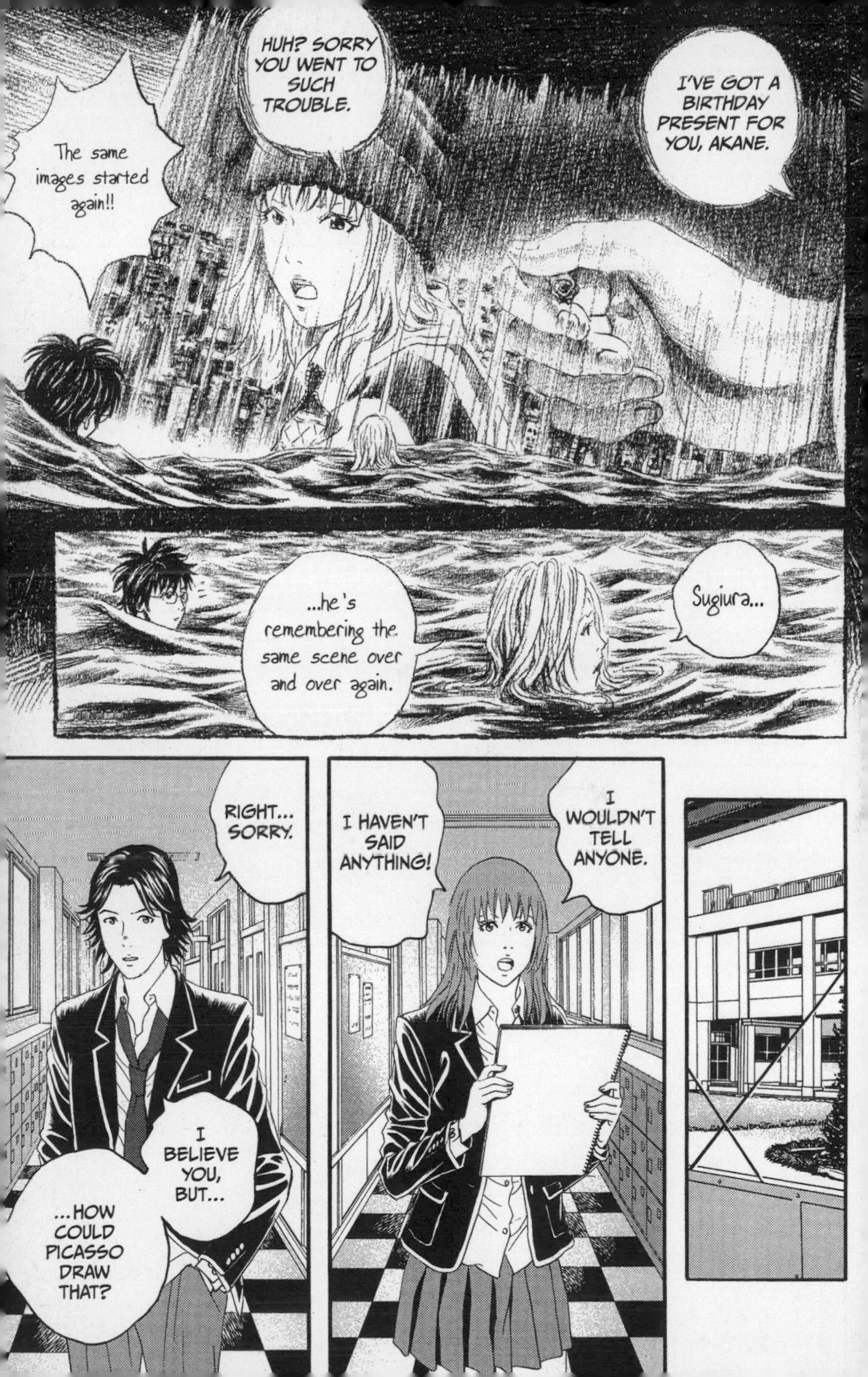
I'VE GOT A BIRTHDAY PRESENT FOR YOU, AKANE.
HUH? SORRY YOU WENT TO SUCH TROUBLE.
The same images started again!!
Sugiura...
...he's remembering the same scene over and over again.
I WOULDN'T TELL ANYONE.
I HAVEN'T SAID ANYTHING!
RIGHT... SORRY.
I BELIEVE YOU, BUT...
...HOW COULD PICASSO DRAW THAT?

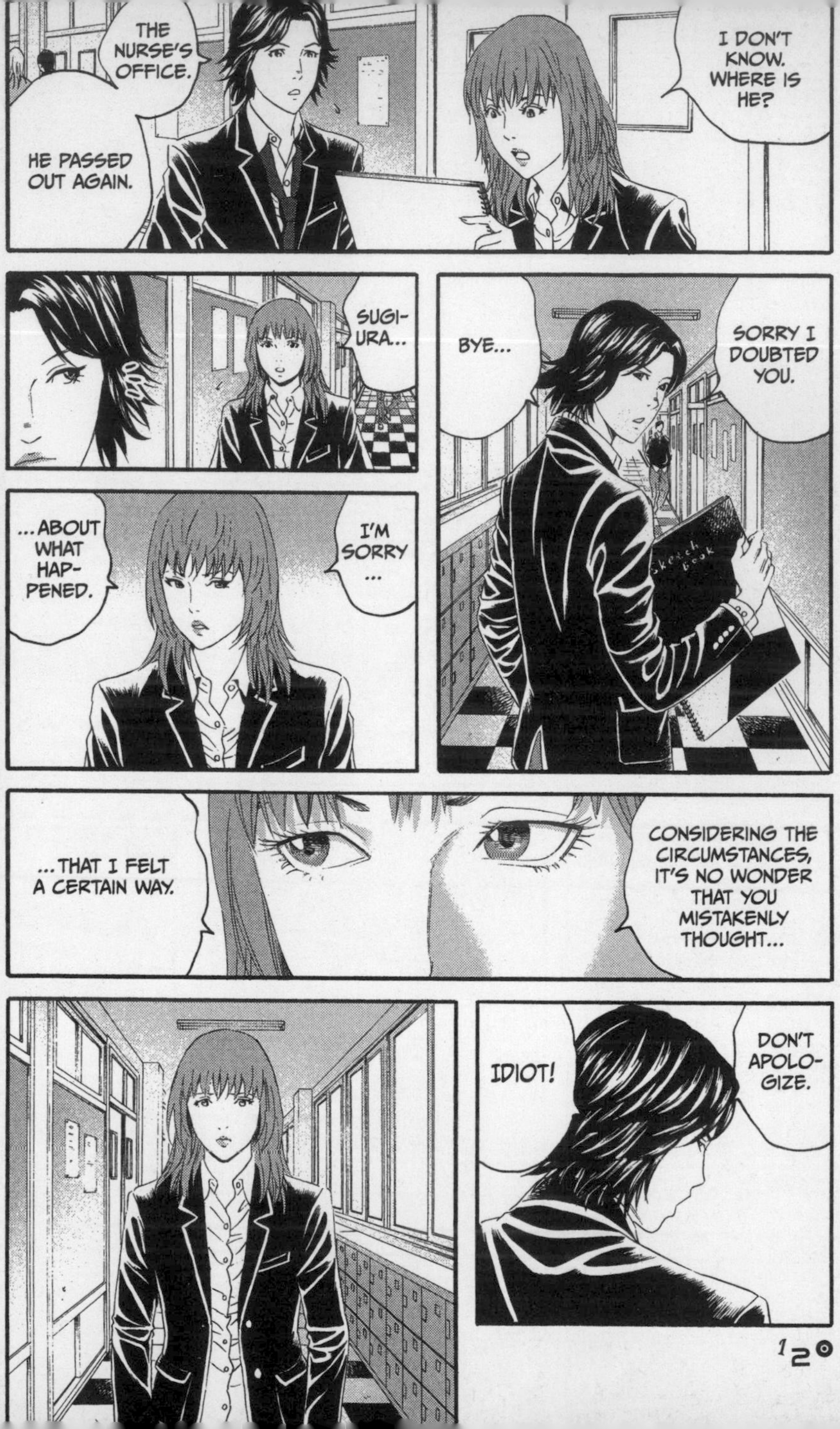
I DON'T KNOW. WHERE IS HE?
THE NURSE'S OFFICE.
HE PASSED OUT AGAIN.
SORRY I DOUBTED YOU.
BYE...
SUGI-URA...
I'M SORRY ...
...ABOUT WHAT HAP-PENED.
CONSIDERING THE CIRCUMSTANCES, IT'S NO WONDER THAT YOU MISTAKENLY THOUGHT...
...THAT I FELT A CERTAIN WAY.
DON'T APOLO-GIZE.
IDIOT!

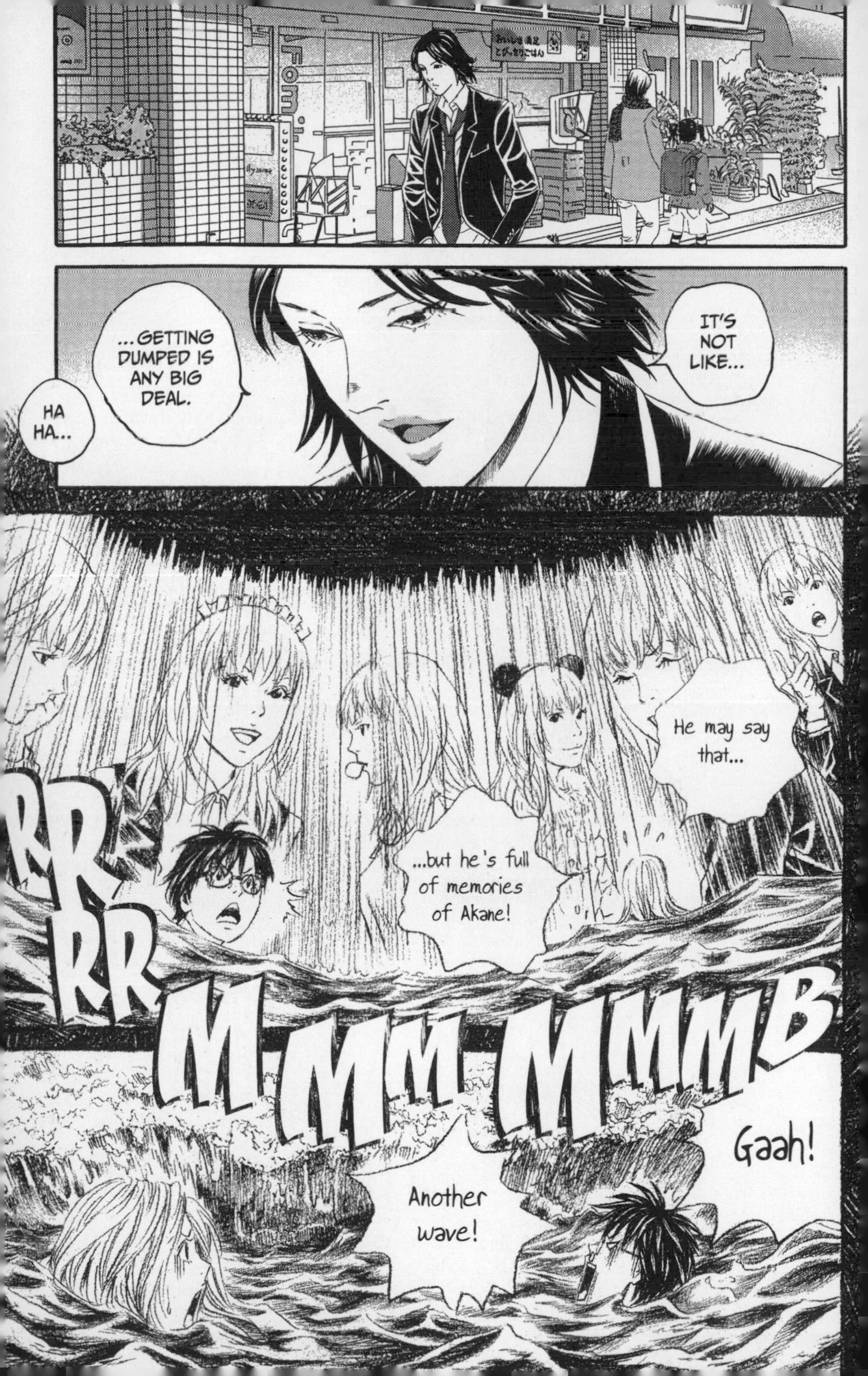
IT'S NOT LIKE...
...GETTING DUMPED IS ANY BIG DEAL.
HA HA...
He may say that...
...but he's full of memories of Akane!
RRRR
MMMMMMMB
Gaah!
Another wave!

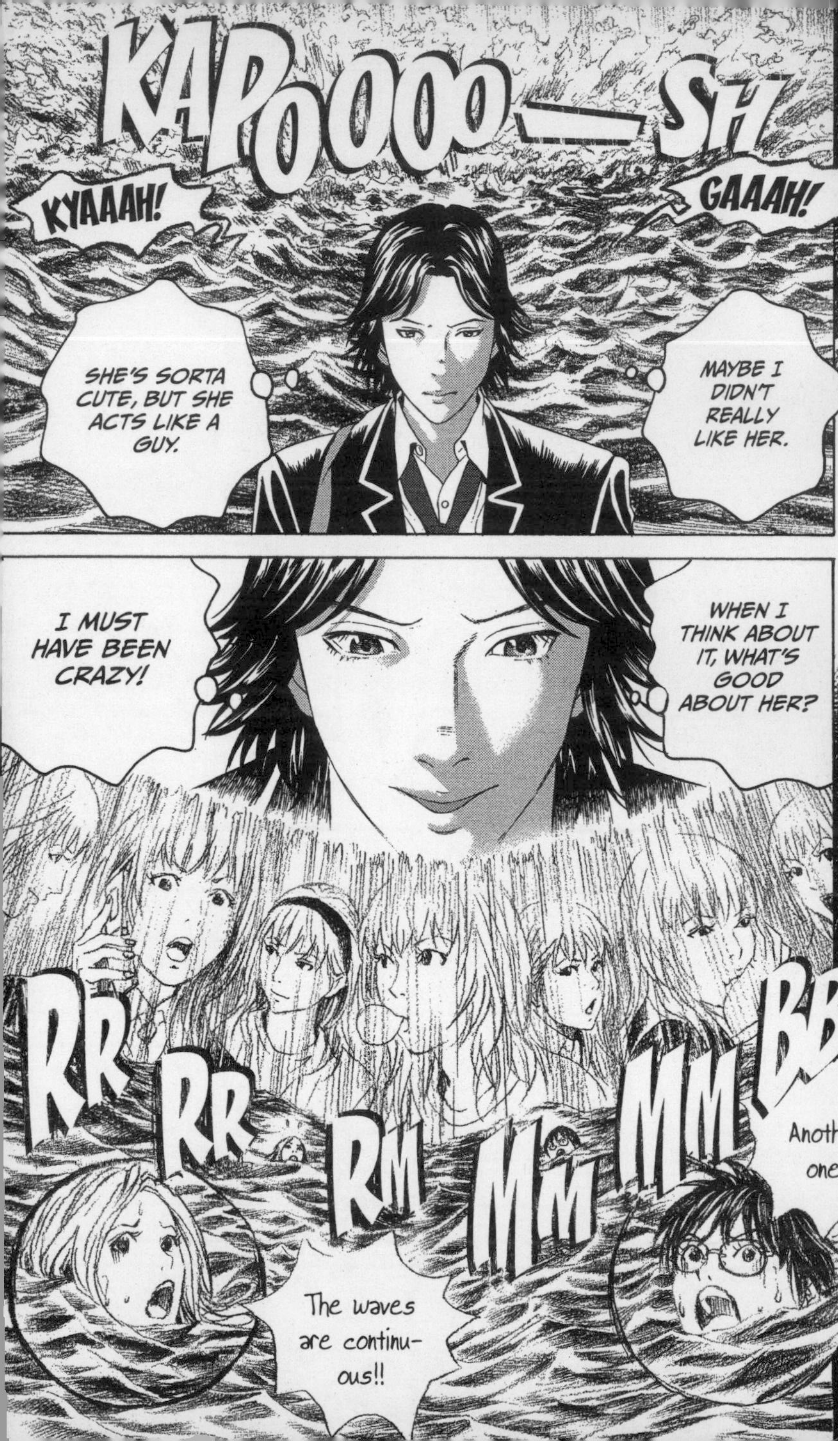
KAPOOOO—SH
GAAAH!
KYAAAH!
MAYBE I DIDN'T REALLY LIKE HER.
SHE'S SORTA CUTE, BUT SHE ACTS LIKE A GUY.
WHEN I THINK ABOUT IT, WHAT'S GOOD ABOUT HER?
I MUST HAVE BEEN CRAZY!
RRRRRMMMMMBB
Another one!
The waves are continu-ous!!

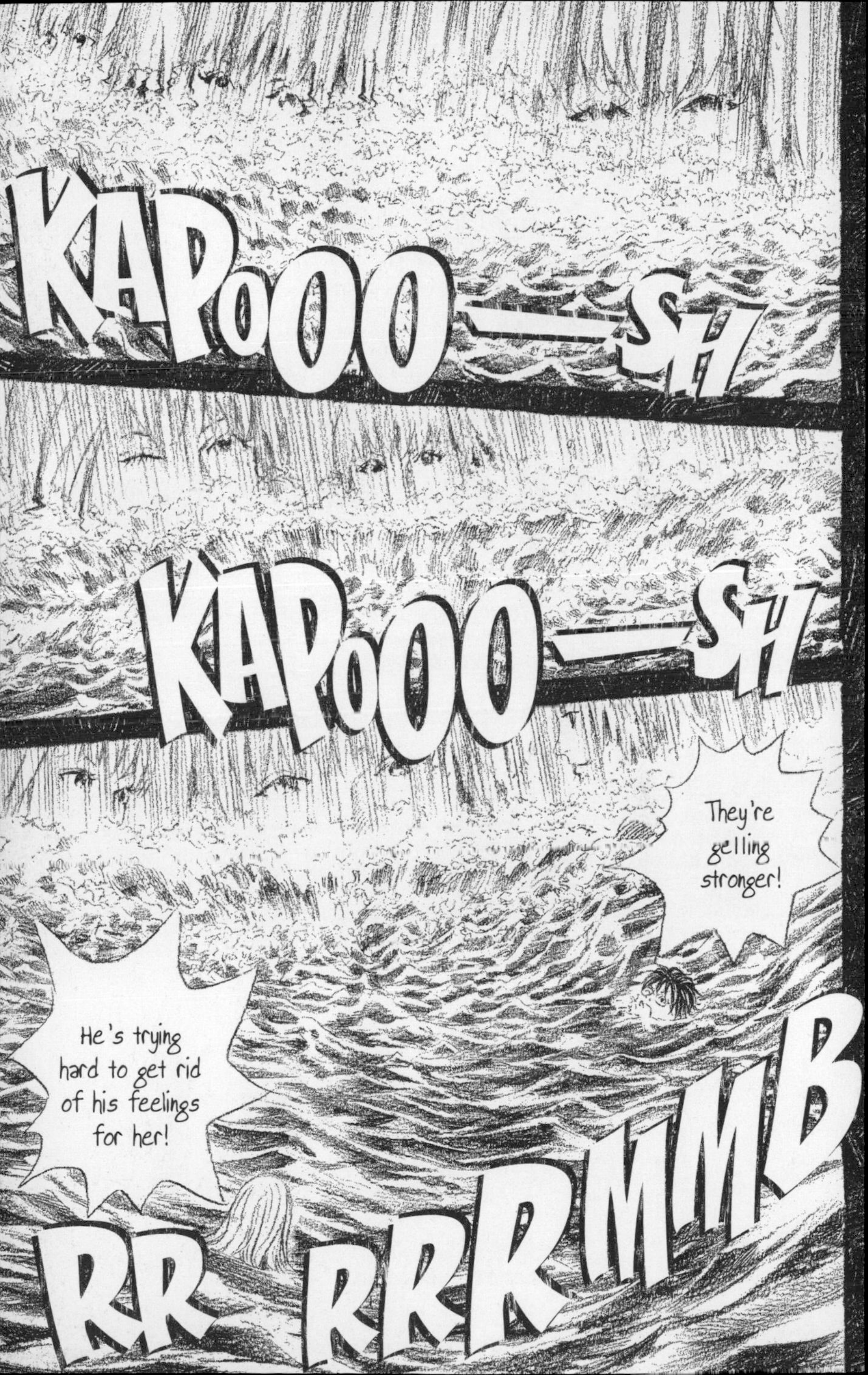
KAPOOOO—SH
KAPOOO—SH
They're getting stronger!
He's trying hard to get rid of his feelings for her!
RR RRRRMMMB

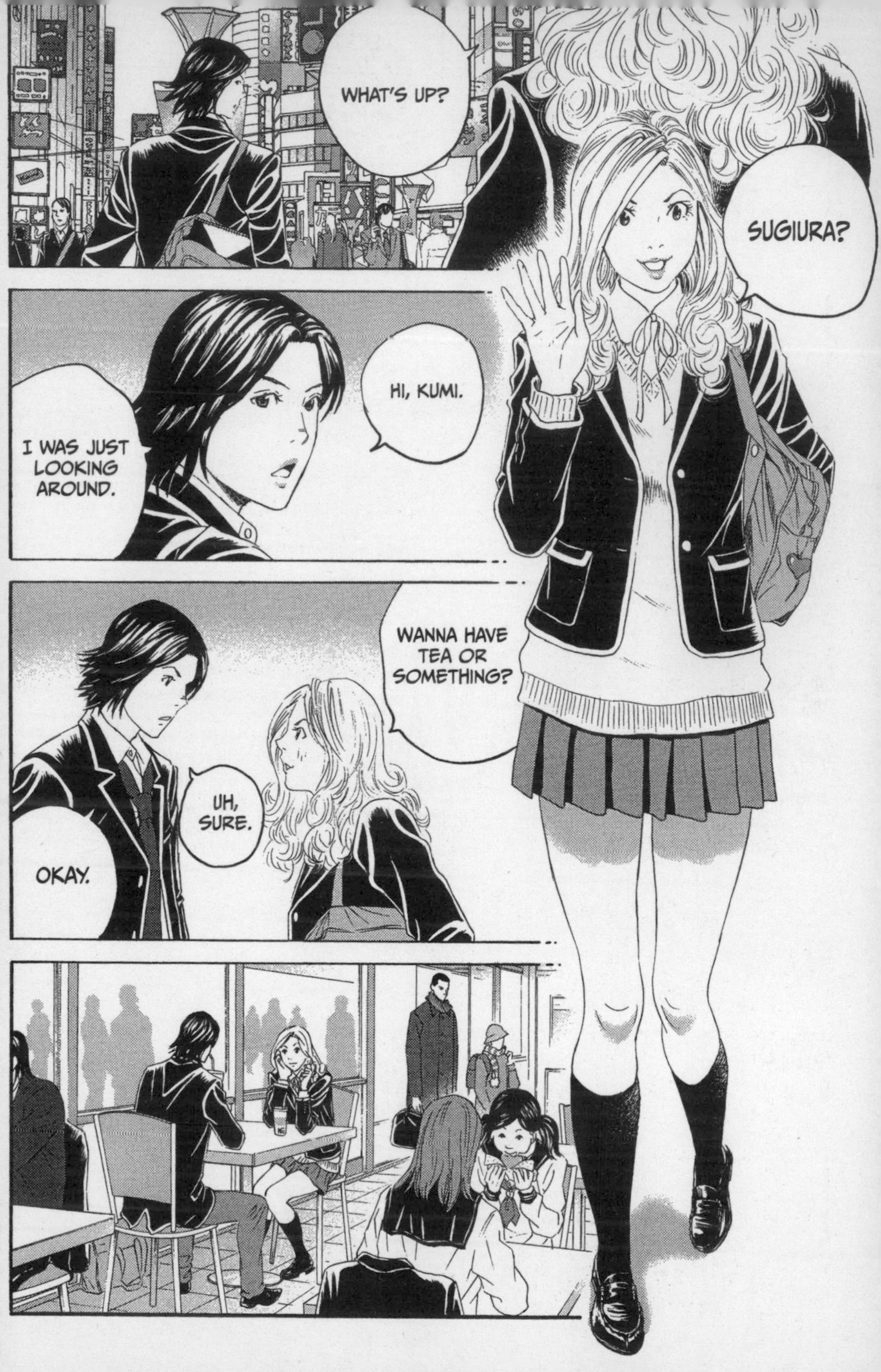
SUGIURA?
WHAT'S UP?
WANNA HAVE TEA OR SOMETHING?
HI, KUMI.
I WAS JUST LOOKING AROUND.
UH, SURE.
OKAY.

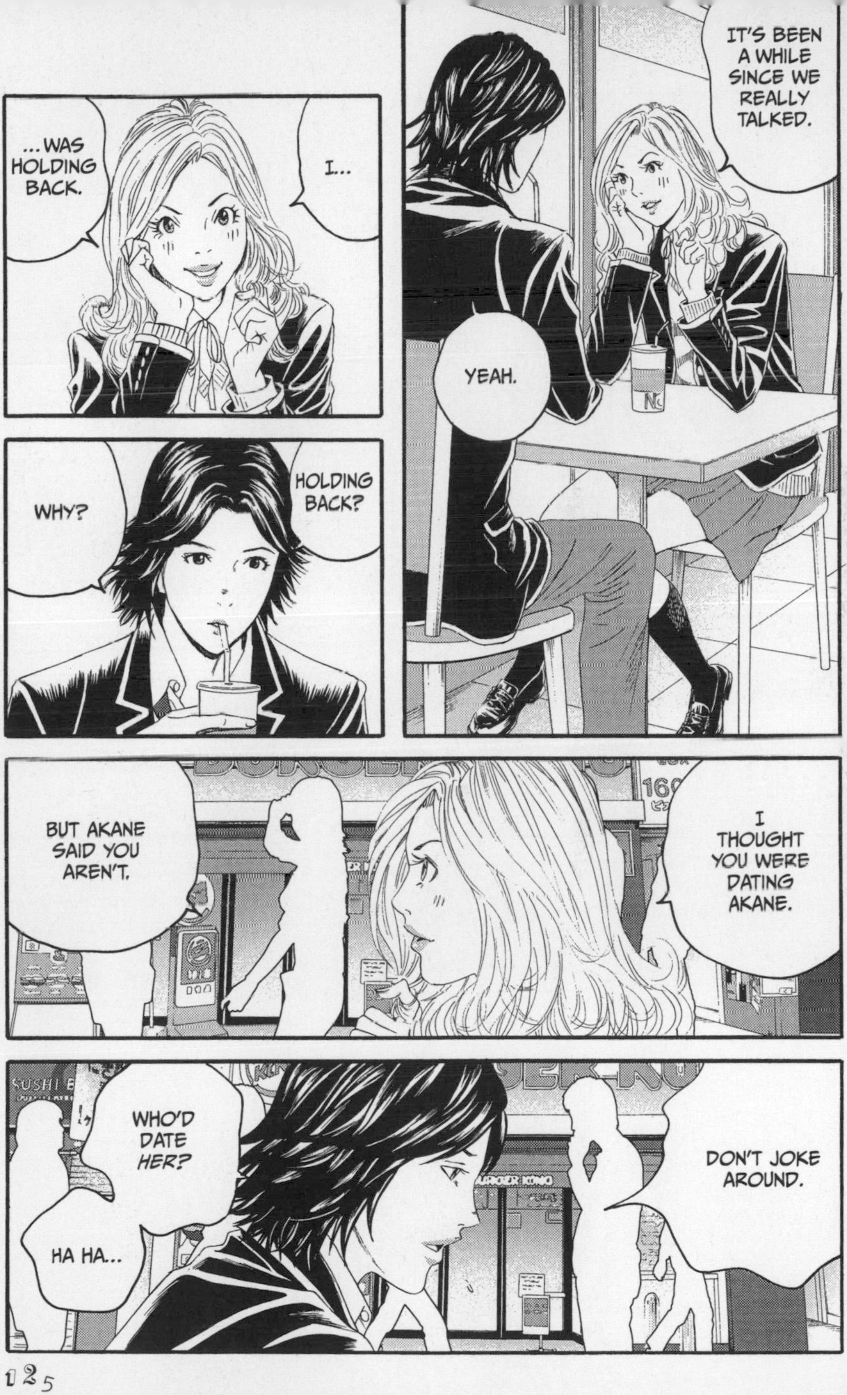
IT'S BEEN A WHILE SINCE WE REALLY TALKED.
YEAH.
I...
...WAS HOLDING BACK.
HOLDING BACK?
WHY?
I THOUGHT YOU WERE DATING AKANE.
BUT AKANE SAID YOU AREN'T.
DON'T JOKE AROUND.
WHO'D DATE HER?
HA HA...

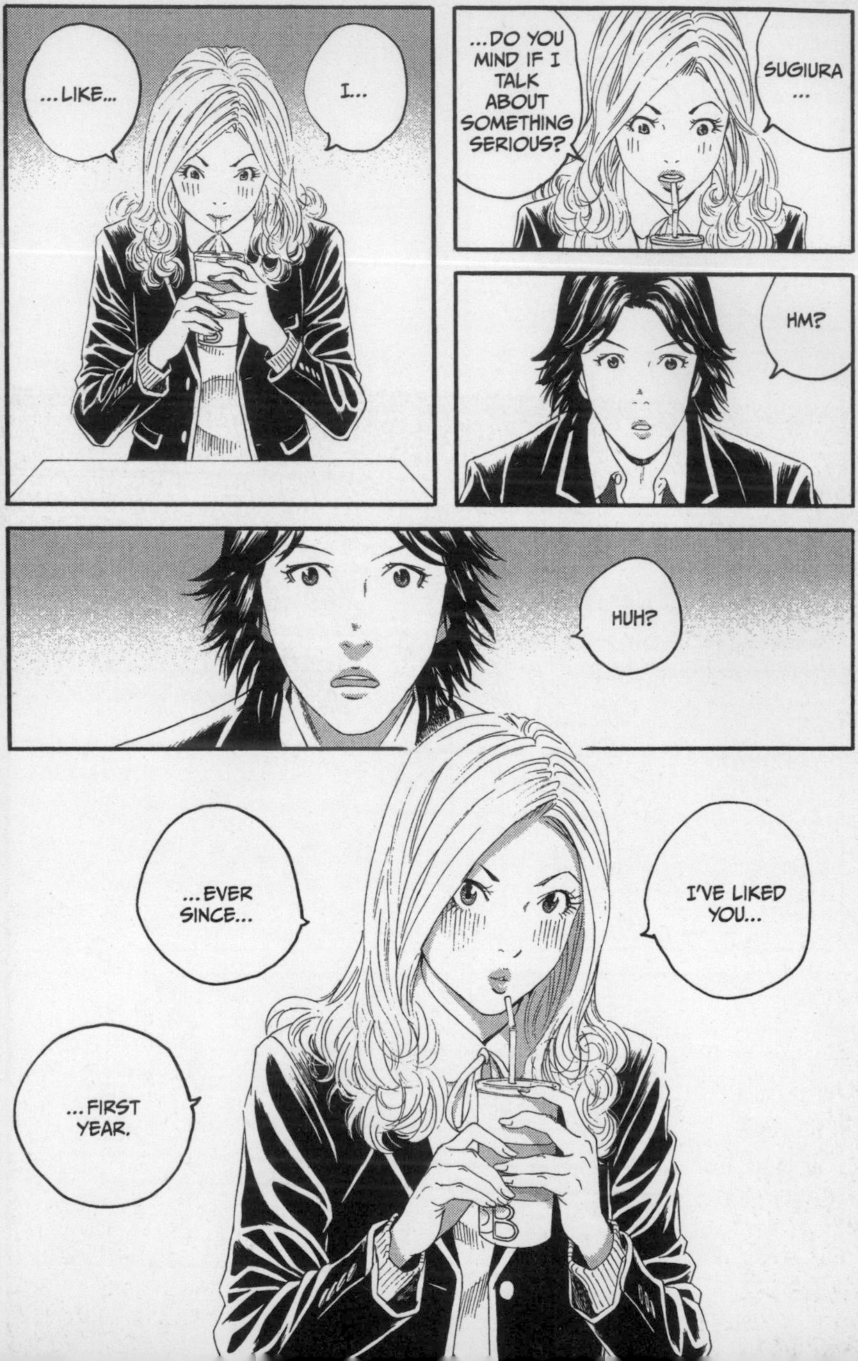
SUGIURA ...
...DO YOU MIND IF I TALK ABOUT SOMETHING SERIOUS?
HM?
I...
...LIKE...
HUH?
I'VE LIKED YOU...
...EVER SINCE...
...FIRST YEAR.

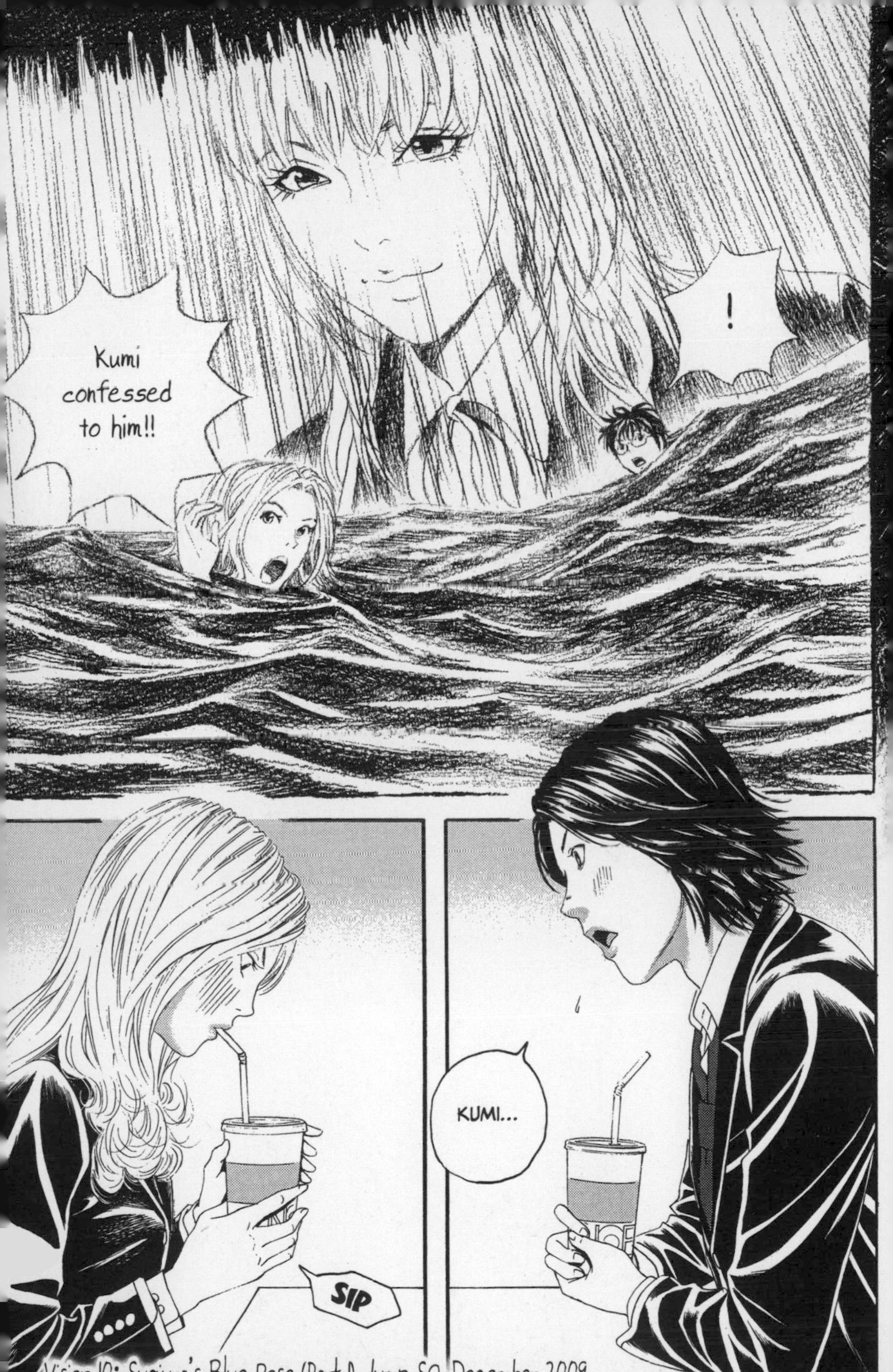
!
Kumi confessed to him!!
KUMI...
SIP

Vision 10: Sugiura's Blue Rose (Part 1)_Jump SQ, December 2009

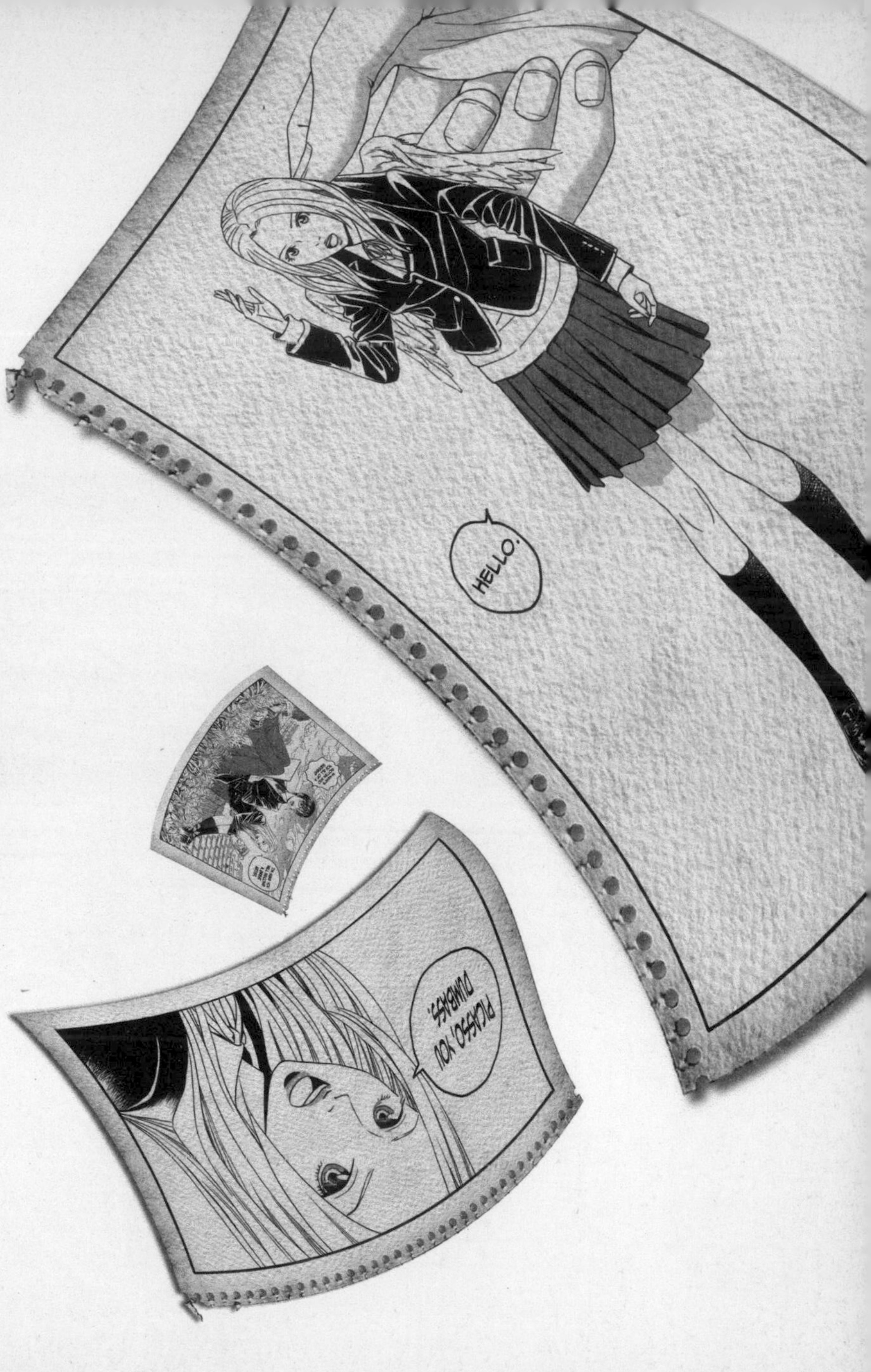
HELLO.
PICASSO, YOU DUMBASS.

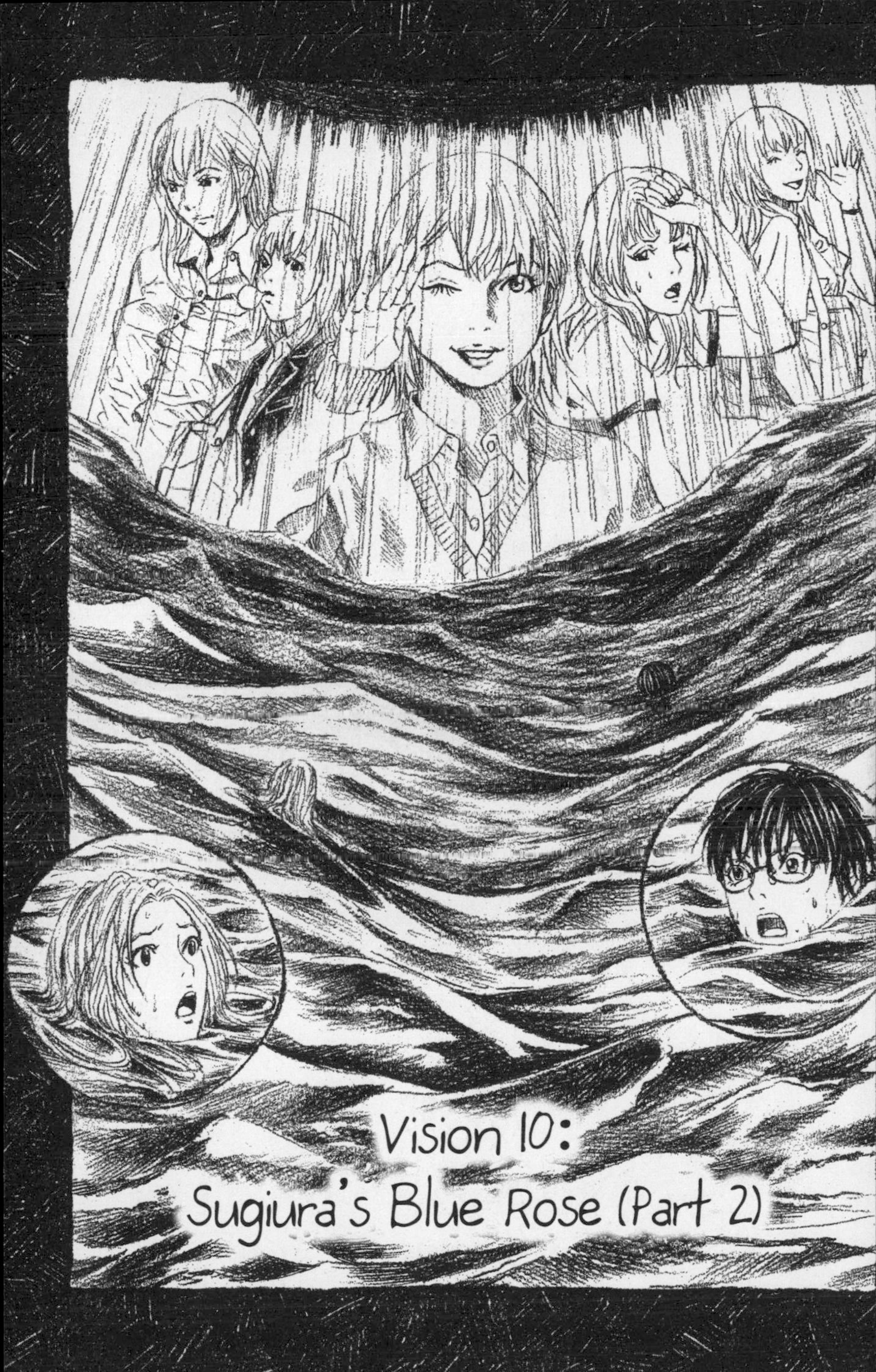
Vision 10:
Sugiura's Blue Rose (Part 2)

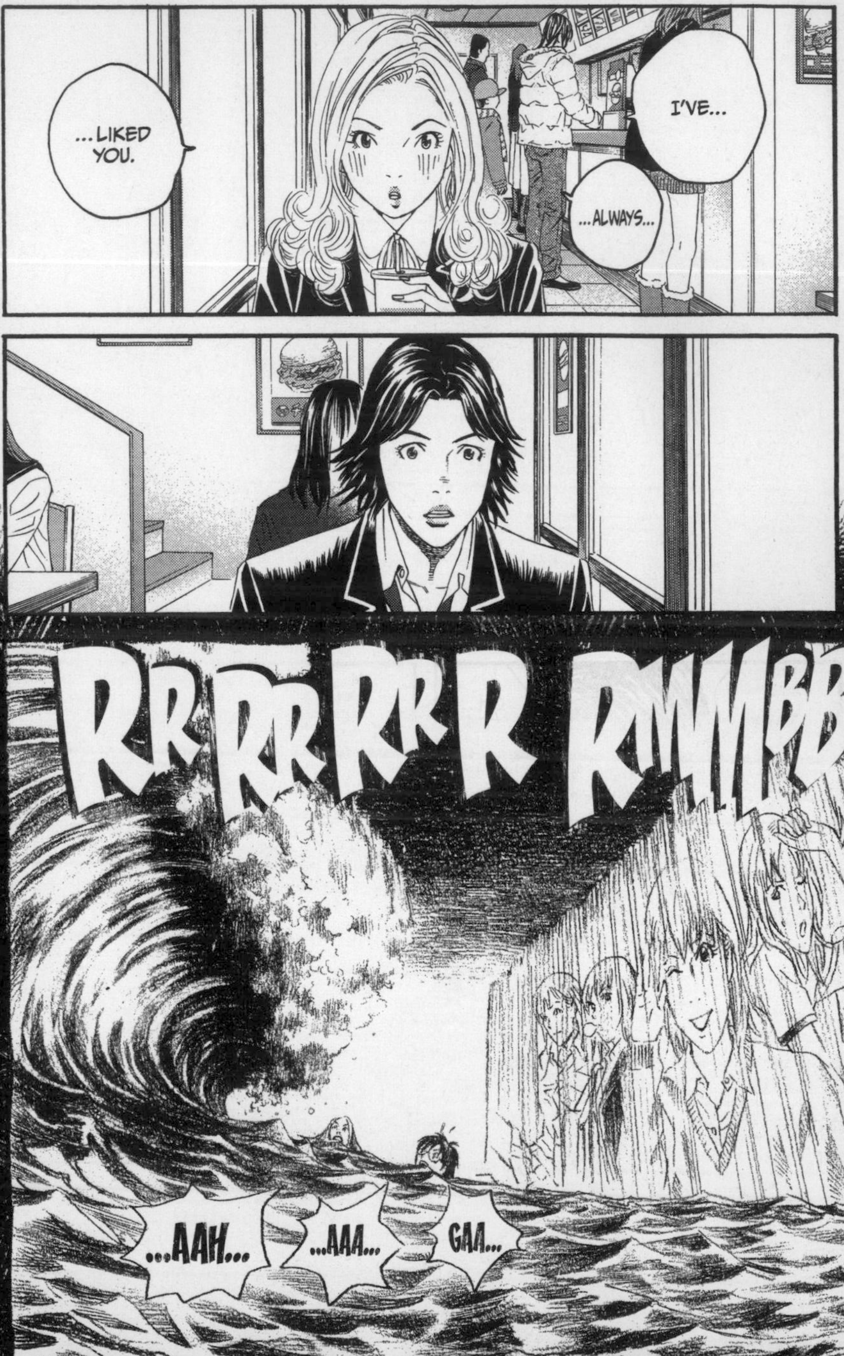

I'VE...
...ALWAYS...
...LIKED YOU.
RR RR RR R RMMBB
GAA...
...AAA...
...AAH...

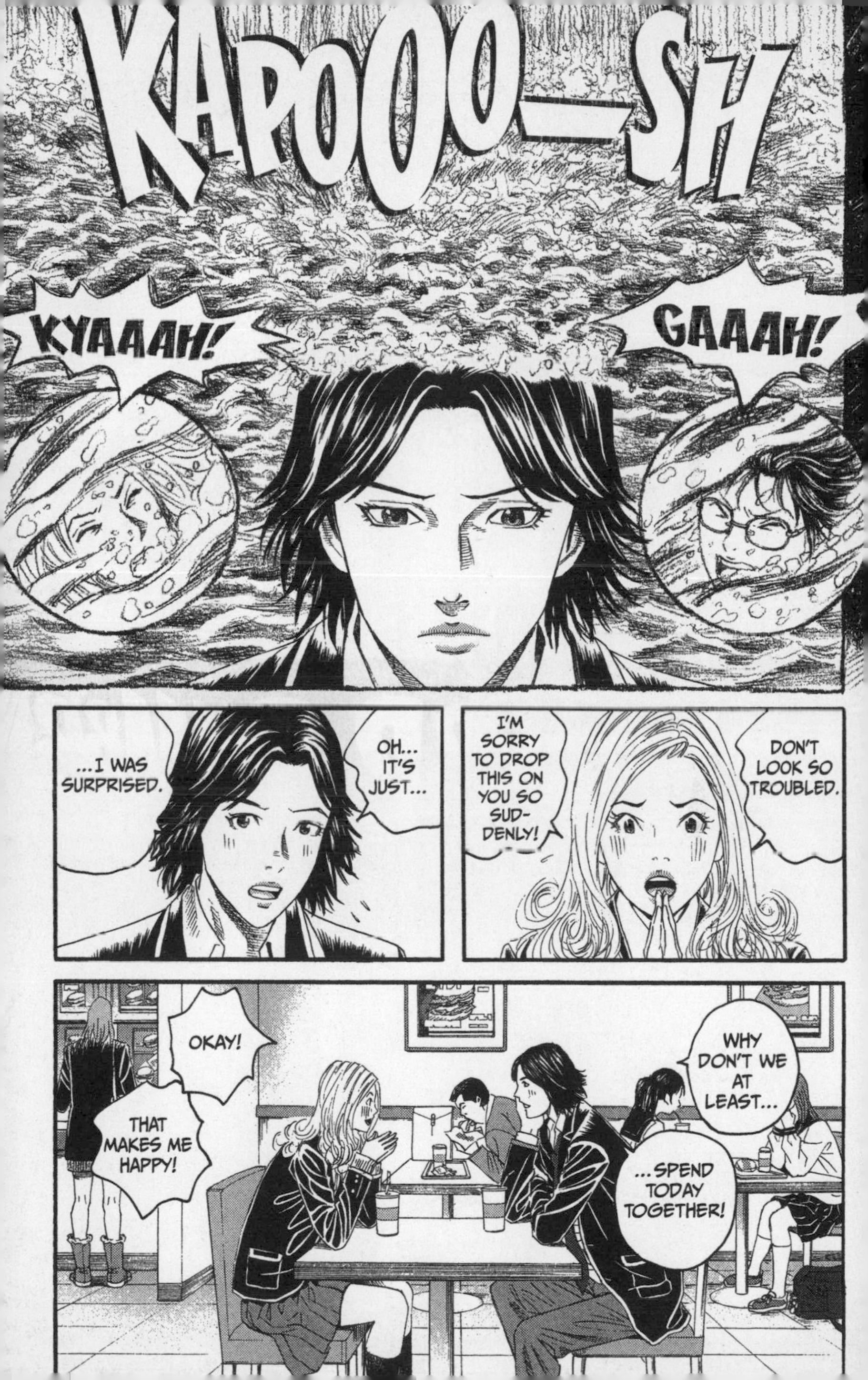
KAPOOO—SH
GAAAH!
KYAAAH!
DON'T LOOK SO TROUBLED.
I'M SORRY TO DROP THIS ON YOU SO SUD-DENLY!
OH... IT'S JUST...
...I WAS SURPRISED.
WHY DON'T WE AT LEAST...
...SPEND TODAY TOGETHER!
OKAY!
THAT MAKES ME HAPPY!

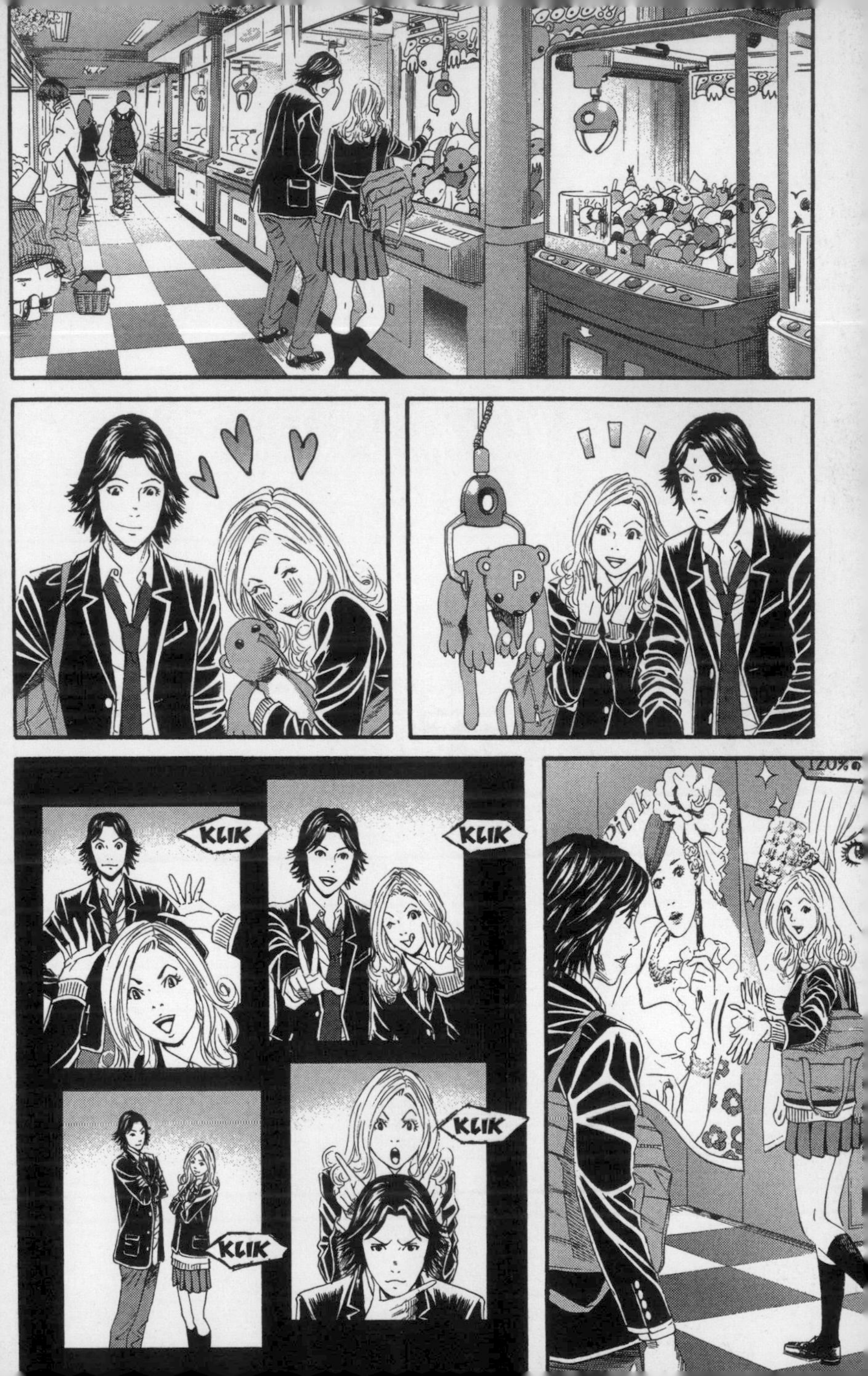
Pink
KLIK
KLIK
KLIK
KLIK

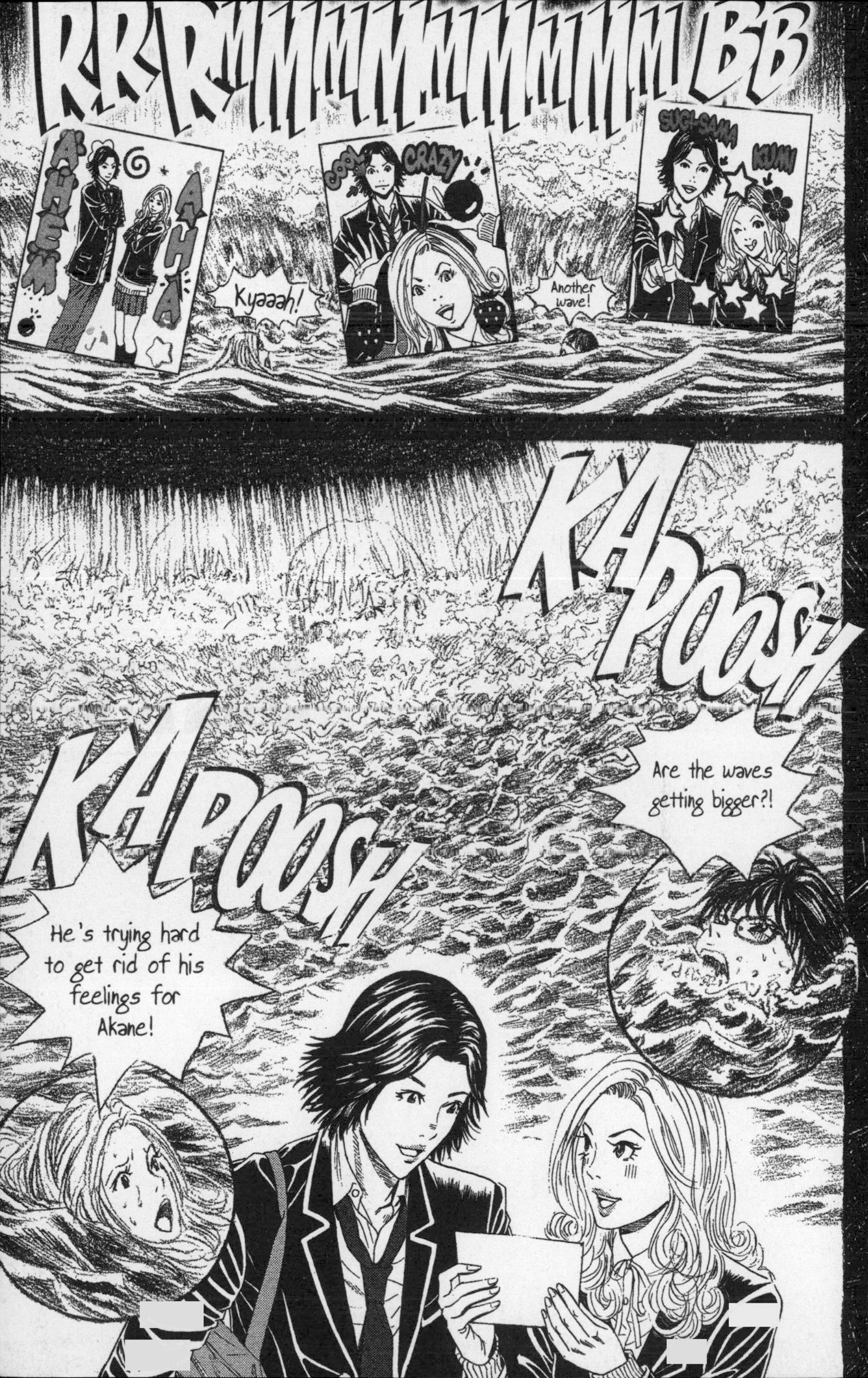
RRRMMMMMMMMMMMMBB
SUGI-SAMA
KUMI
Another wave!
CRAZY
Kyaaah!
KAPOOSH
Are the waves getting bigger?!
KAPOOSH
He's trying hard to get rid of his feelings for Akane!

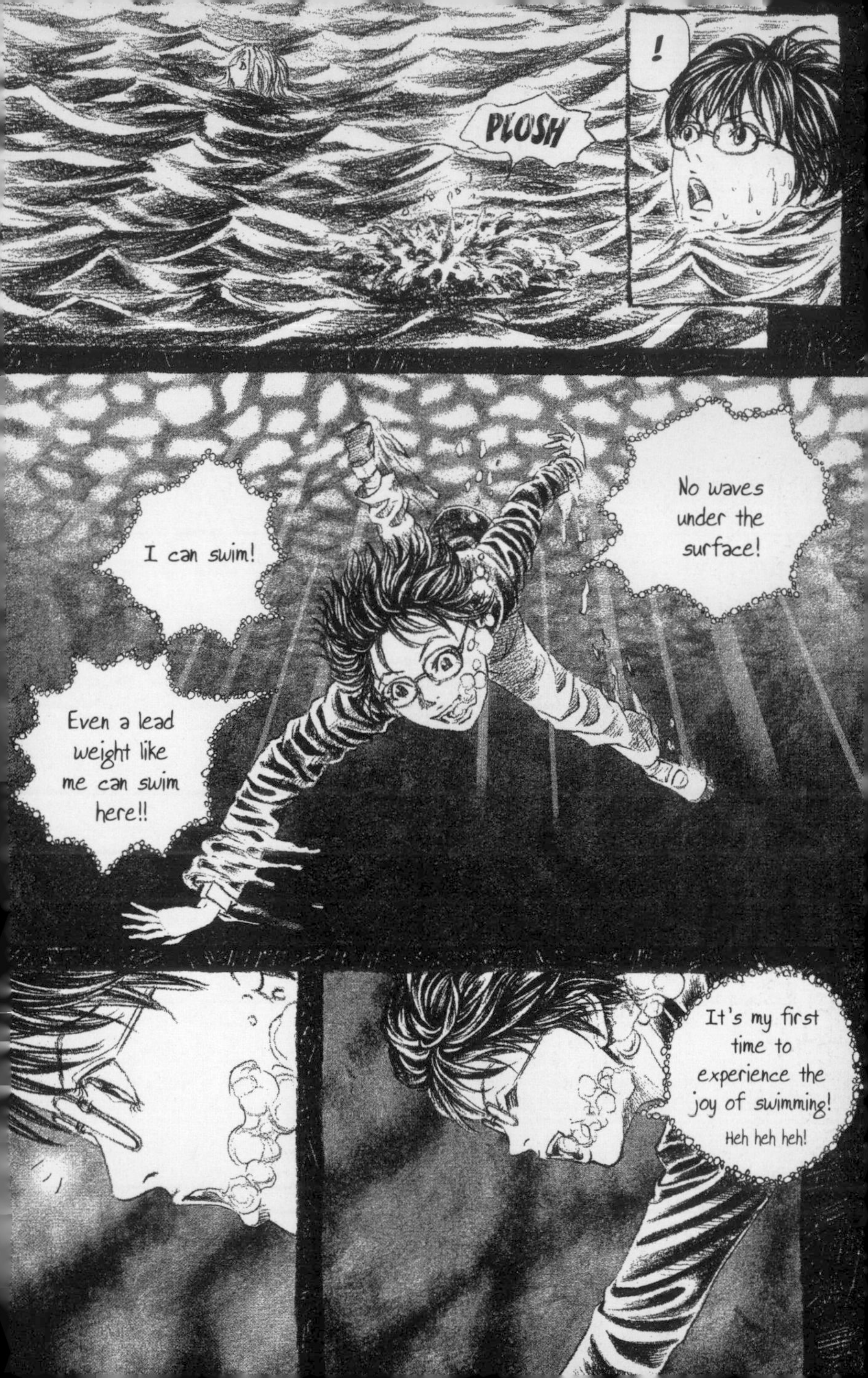
!
PLOSH
No waves under the surface!
I can swim!
Even a lead weight like me can swim here!!
It's my first time to experience the joy of swimming!
Heh heh heh!

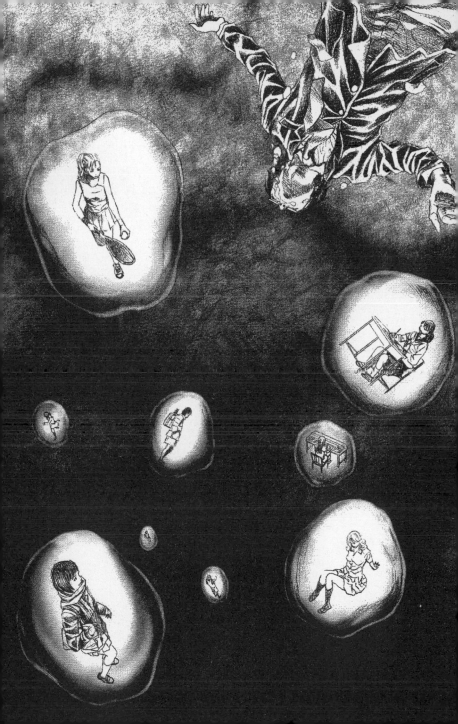

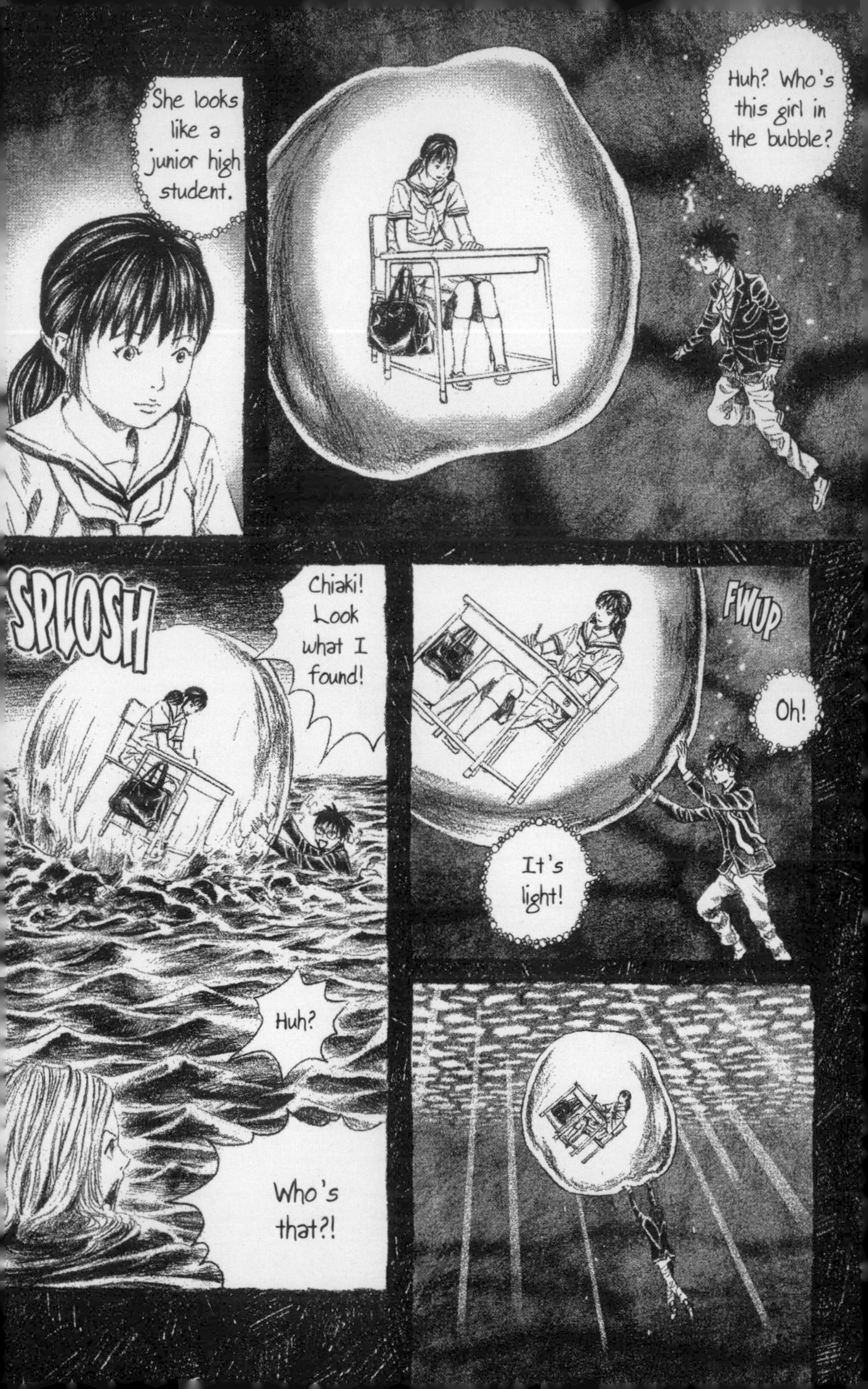

Huh? Who's this girl in the bubble?
She looks like a junior high student.
FWUP
Oh!
It's light!
SPLOSH
Chiaki! Look what I found!
Huh?
Who's that?!

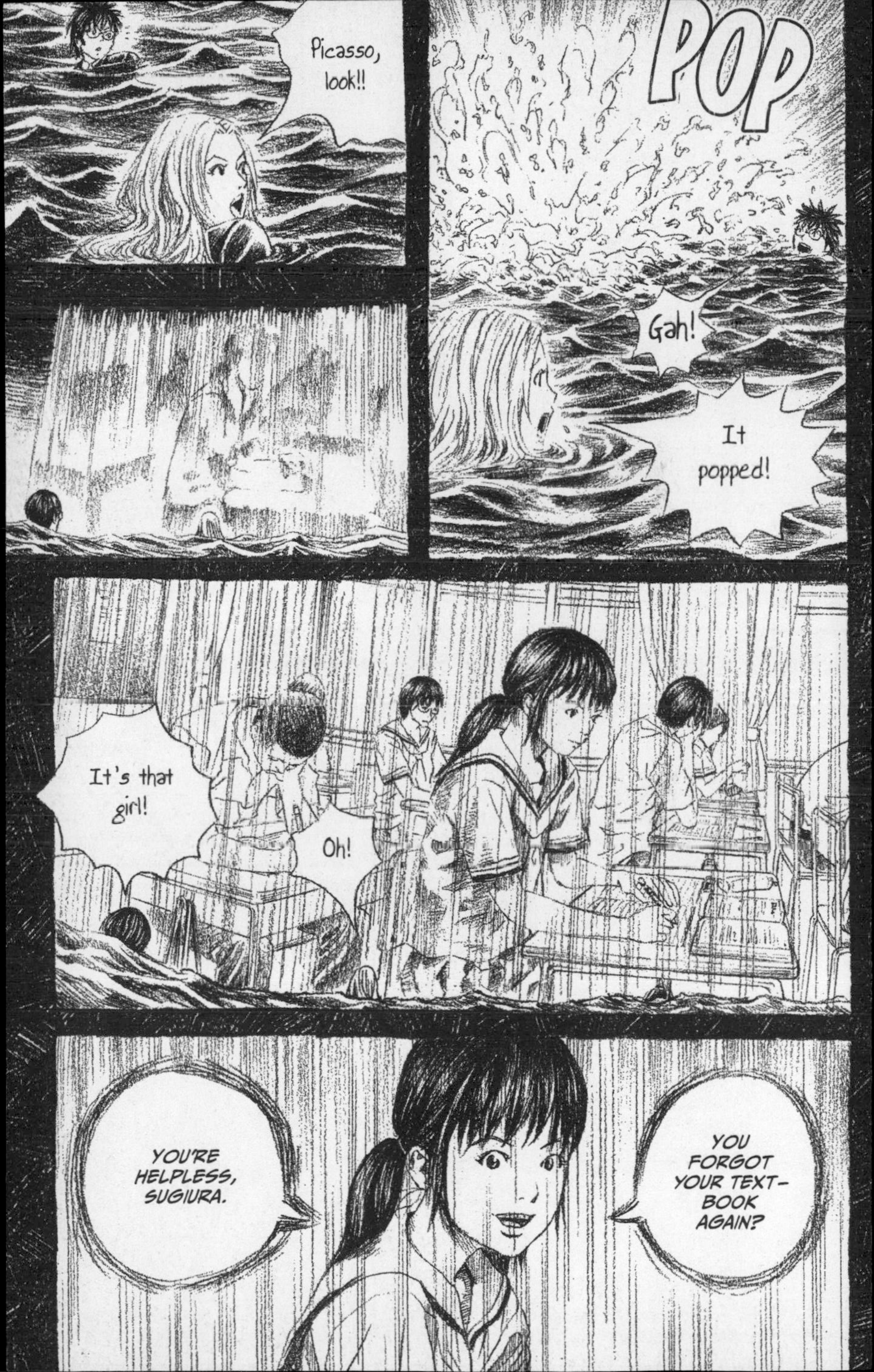
POP
Gah!
It popped!
Picasso, look!!
It's that girl!
Oh!
YOU FORGOT YOUR TEXT-BOOK AGAIN?
YOU'RE HELPLESS, SUGIURA.

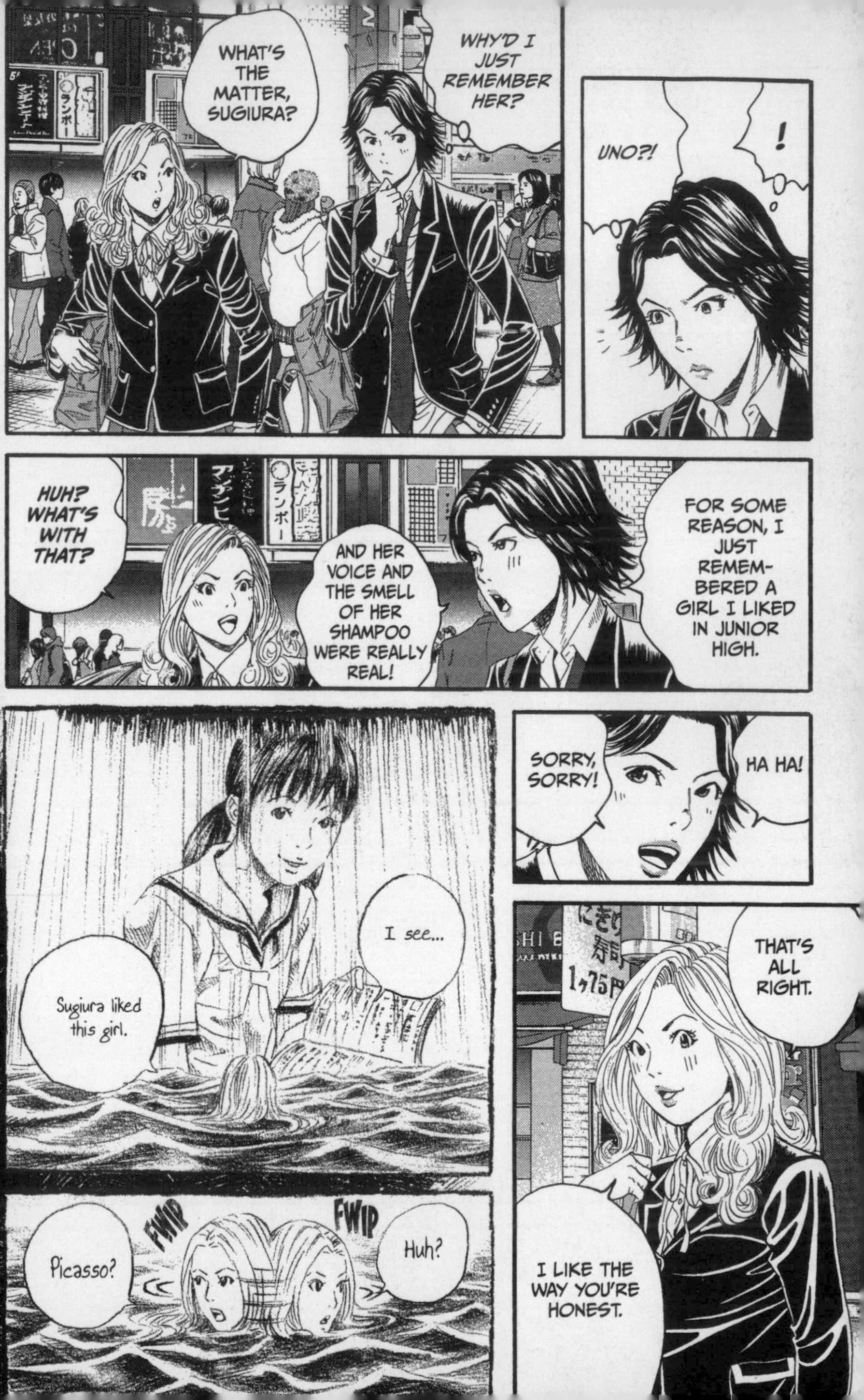
UNO?!
!
WHY'D I JUST REMEMBER HER?
WHAT'S THE MATTER, SUGIURA?
FOR SOME REASON, I JUST REMEMBERED A GIRL I LIKED IN JUNIOR HIGH.
AND HER VOICE AND THE SMELL OF HER SHAMPOO WERE REALLY REAL!
HUH? WHAT'S WITH THAT?
HA HA!
SORRY, SORRY!
THAT'S ALL RIGHT.
I LIKE THE WAY YOU'RE HONEST.
I see...
Sugiura liked this girl.
FWIP
Huh?
FWIP
Picasso?

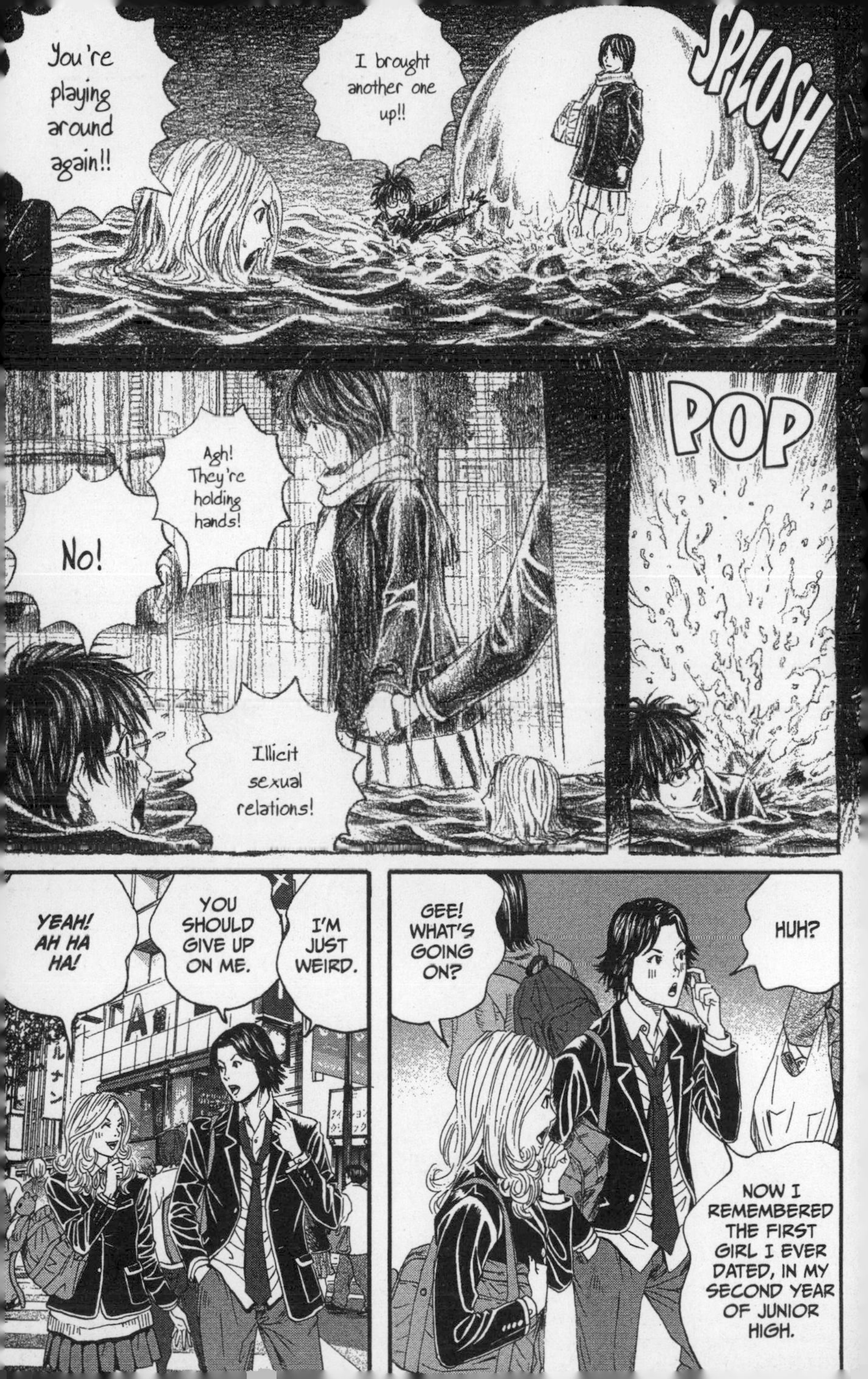
SPLOSH
I brought another one up!!
You're playing around again!!
POP
Agh! They're holding hands!
No!
Illicit sexual relations!
HUH?
GEE! WHAT'S GOING ON?
NOW I REMEMBERED THE FIRST GIRL I EVER DATED, IN MY SECOND YEAR OF JUNIOR HIGH.
I'M JUST WEIRD.
YOU SHOULD GIVE UP ON ME.
YEAH! AH HA HA!

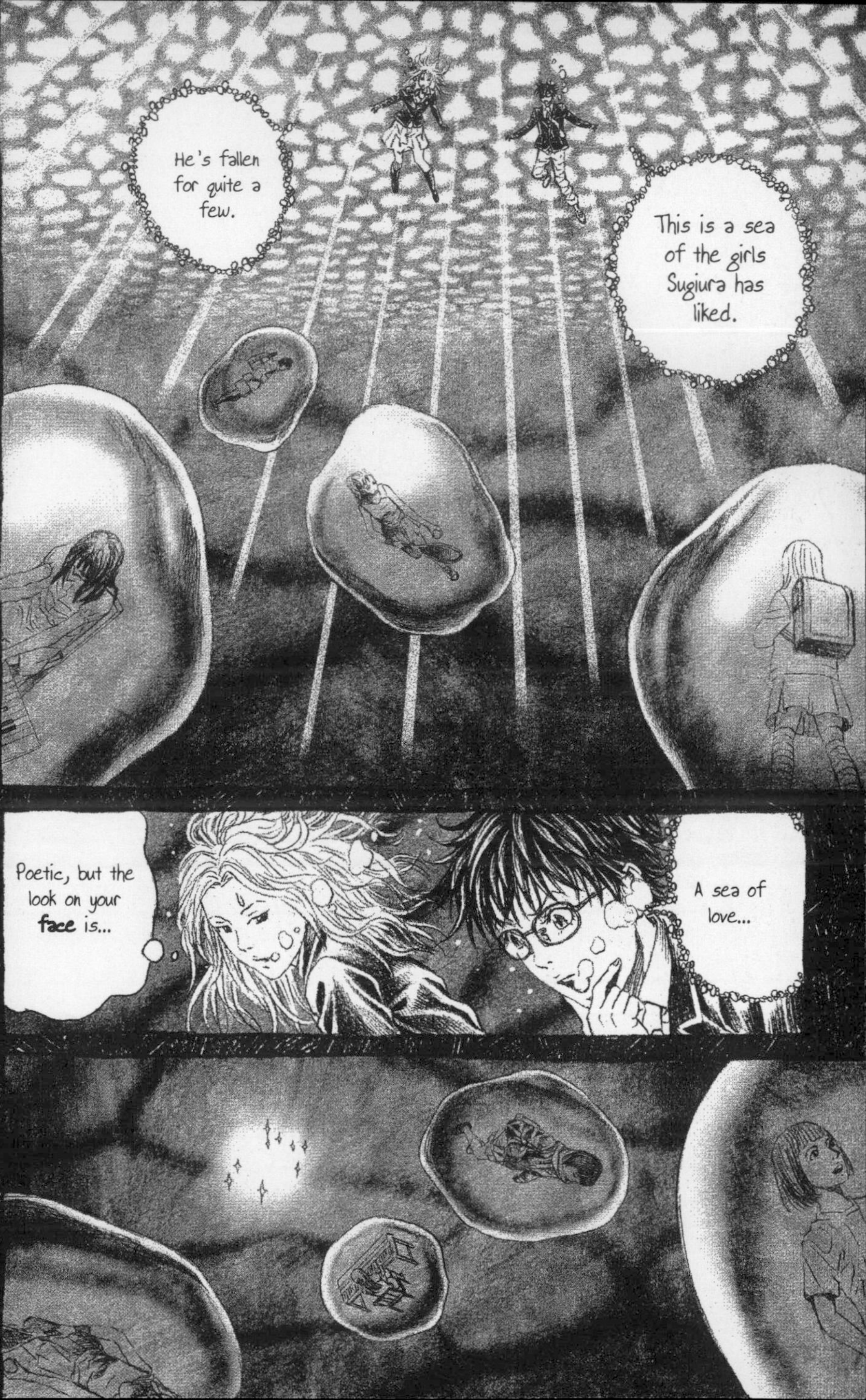
This is a sea of the girls Sugiura has liked.
He's fallen for quite a few.
A sea of love...
Poetic, but the look on your **face** is...

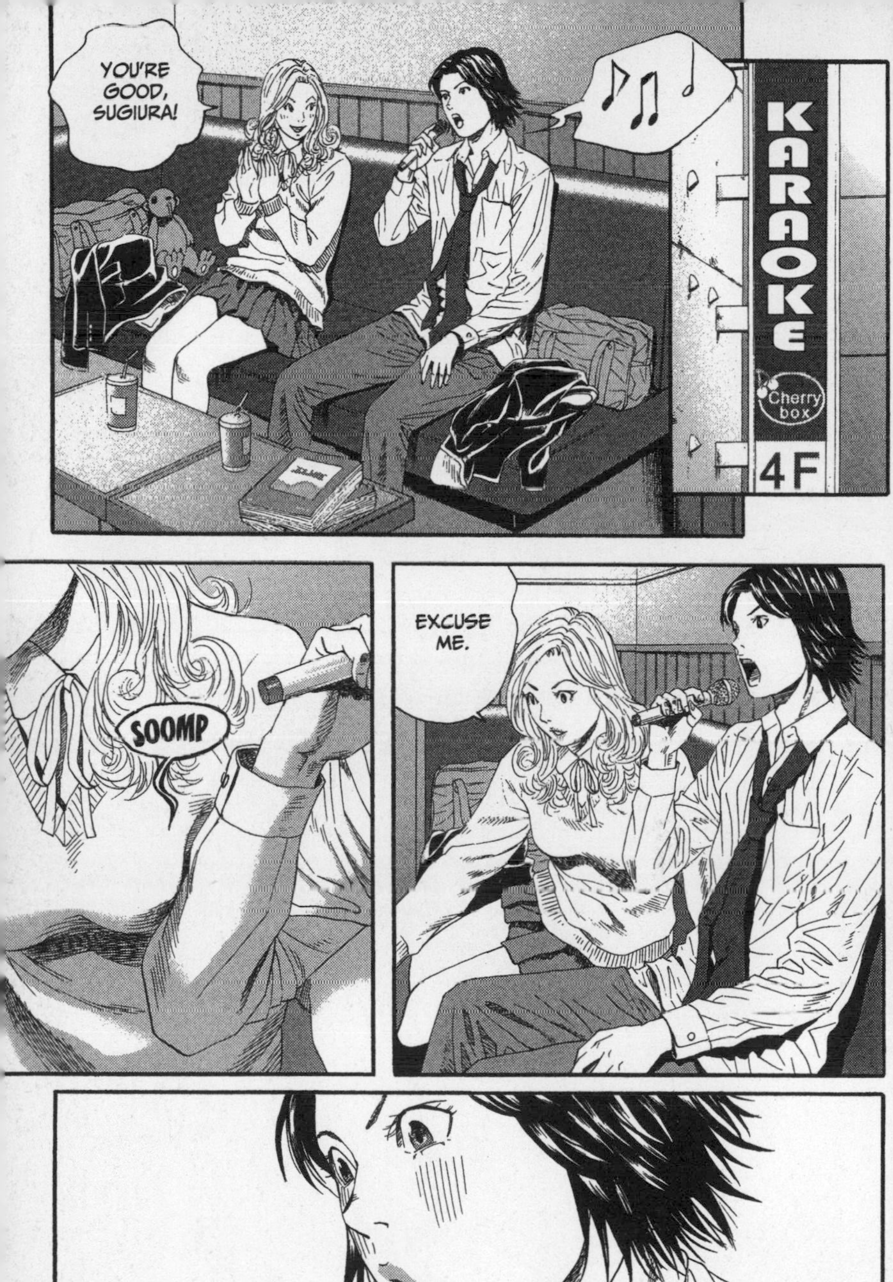
KARAOKE
Cherry box
4F
YOU'RE GOOD, SUGIURA!
EXCUSE ME.
SOOMP

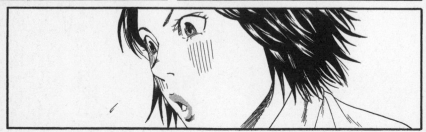

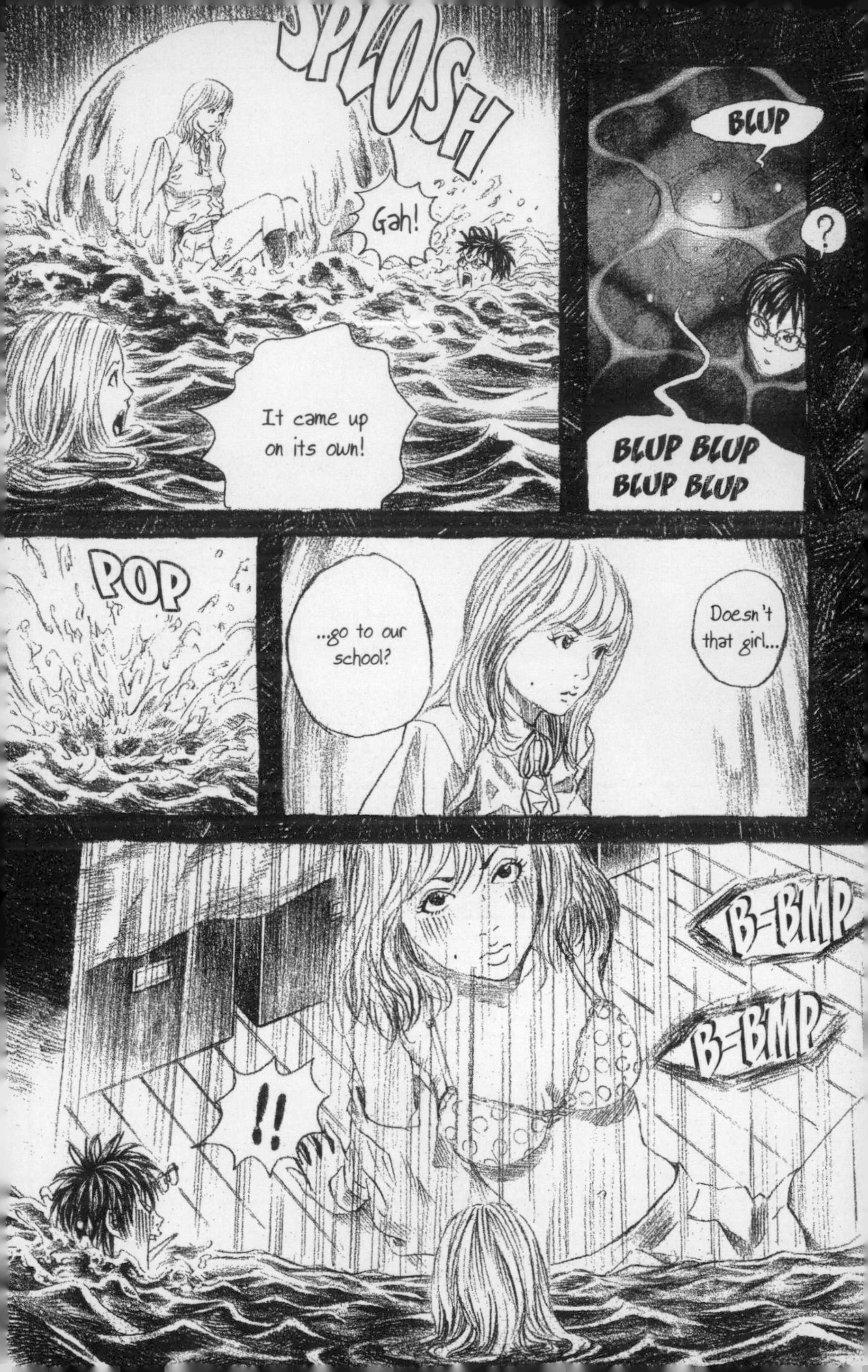
BLUP
?
BLUP BLUP
BLUP BLUP
SPLOSH
Gah!
It came up on its own!
Doesn't that girl...
...go to our school?
POP
B-BMP
B-BMP
!!

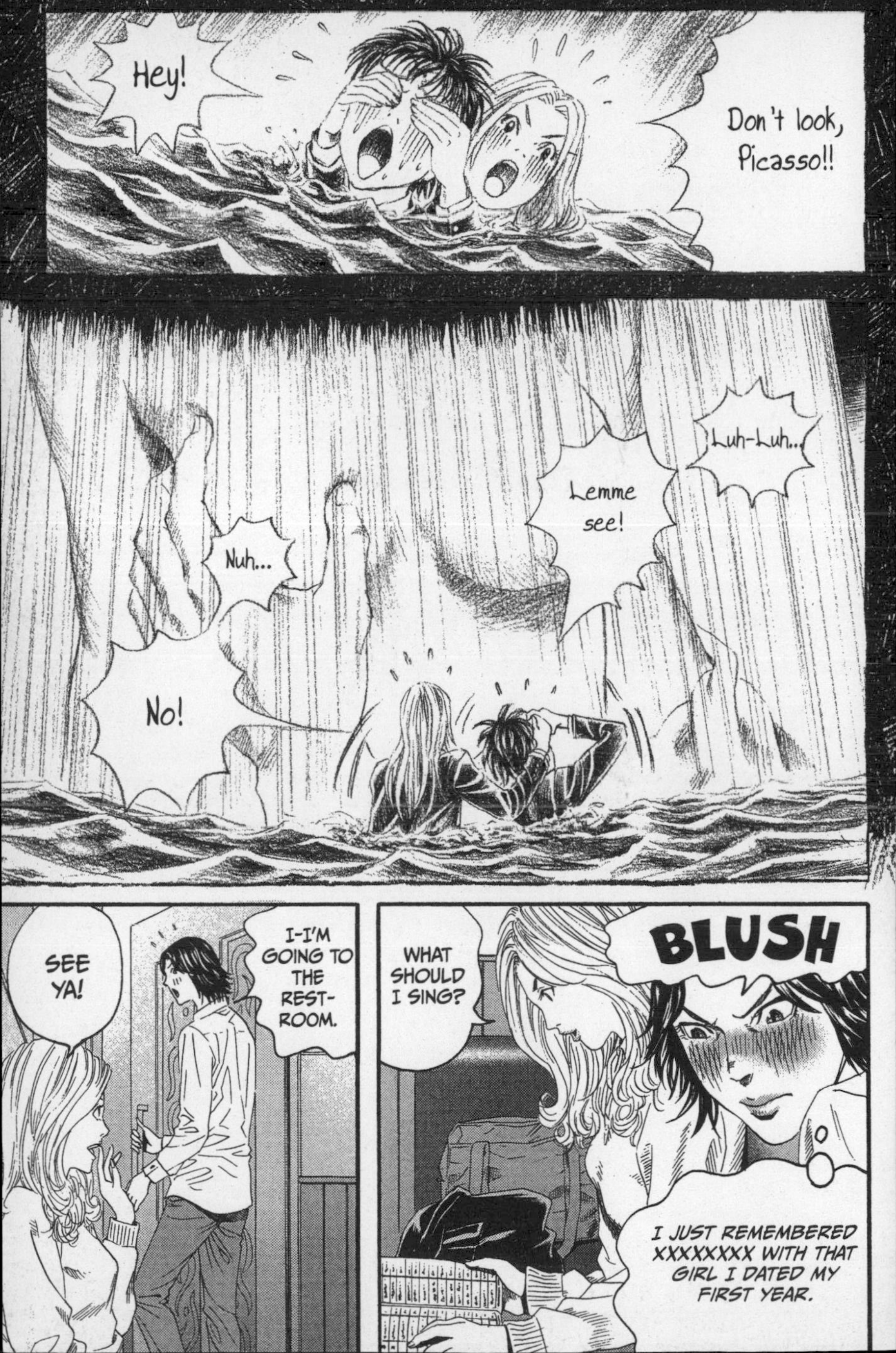

Don't look, Picasso!!
Hey!
Luh-Luh...
Lemme see!
Nuh...
No!
BLUSH
WHAT SHOULD I SING?
I JUST REMEMBERED XXXXXXX WITH THAT GIRL I DATED MY FIRST YEAR.
I-I'M GOING TO THE REST-ROOM.
SEE YA!

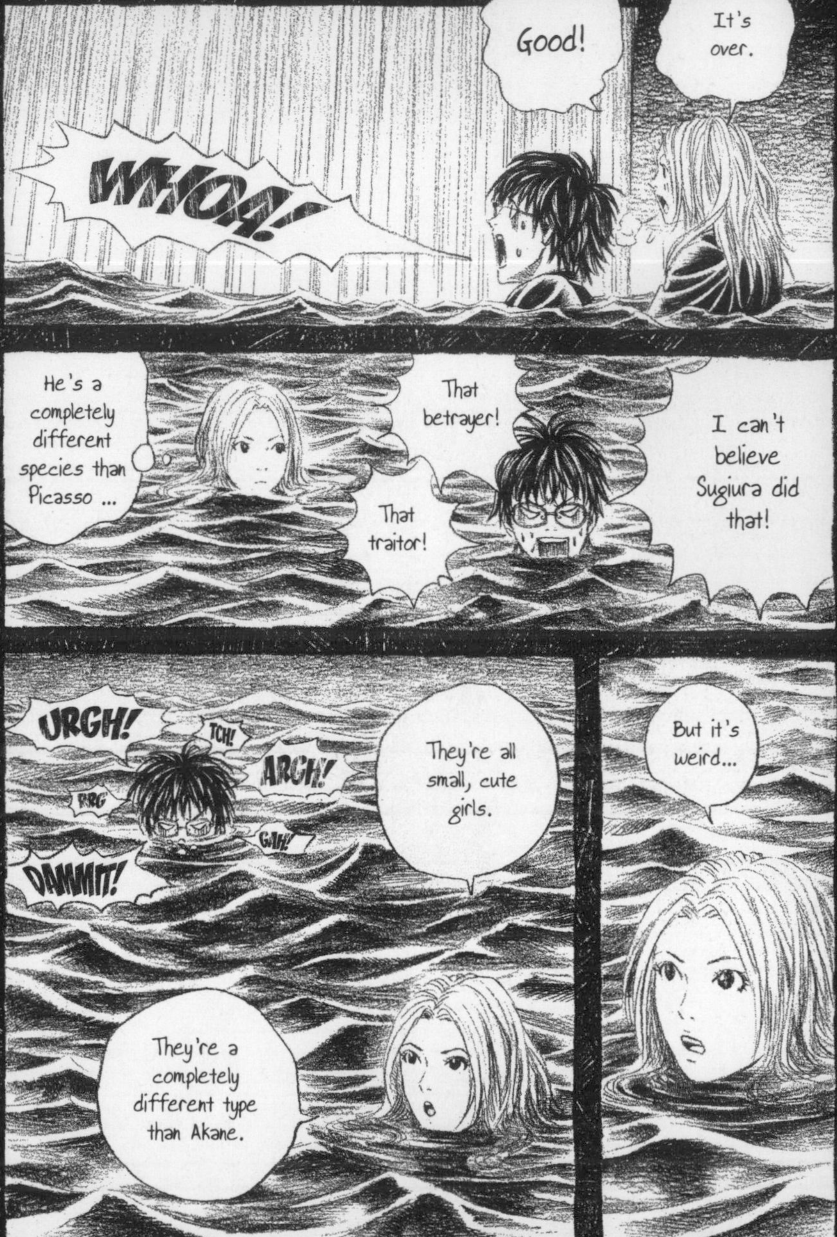
It's over.
Good!
WHOA!
I can't believe Sugiura did that!
That betrayer!
That traitor!
He's a completely different species than Picasso ...
But it's weird...
They're all small, cute girls.
ARCH!
TCH!
URGH!
RRG
GAH!
DAMMIT!
They're a completely different type than Akane.

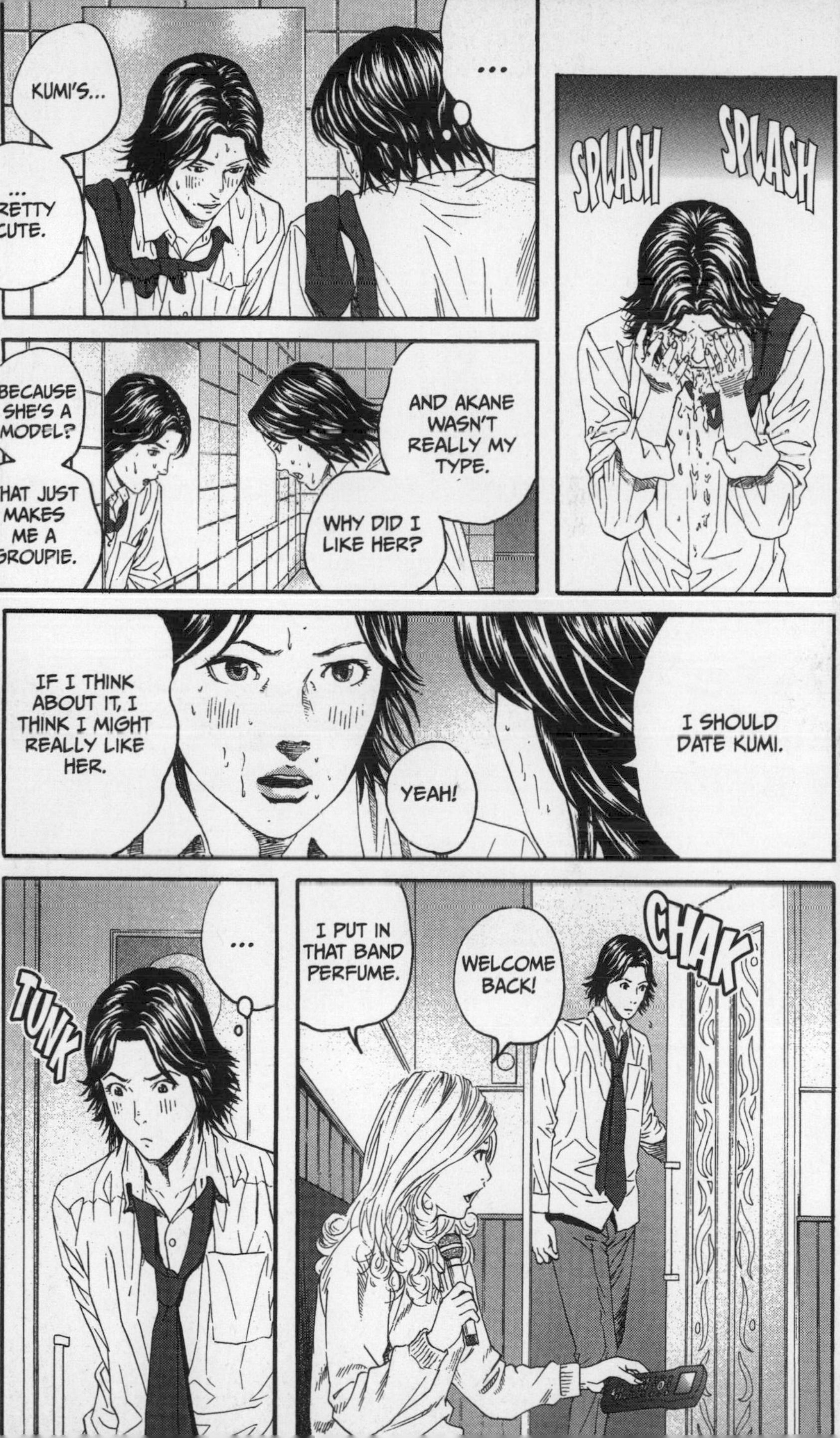
SPLASH SPLASH
...
KUMI'S...
... PRETTY CUTE.
AND AKANE WASN'T REALLY MY TYPE.
WHY DID I LIKE HER?
BECAUSE SHE'S A MODEL?
THAT JUST MAKES ME A GROUPIE.
I SHOULD DATE KUMI.
IF I THINK ABOUT IT, I THINK I MIGHT REALLY LIKE HER.
YEAH!
CHAK
WELCOME BACK!
I PUT IN THAT BAND PERFUME.
...
TUNK

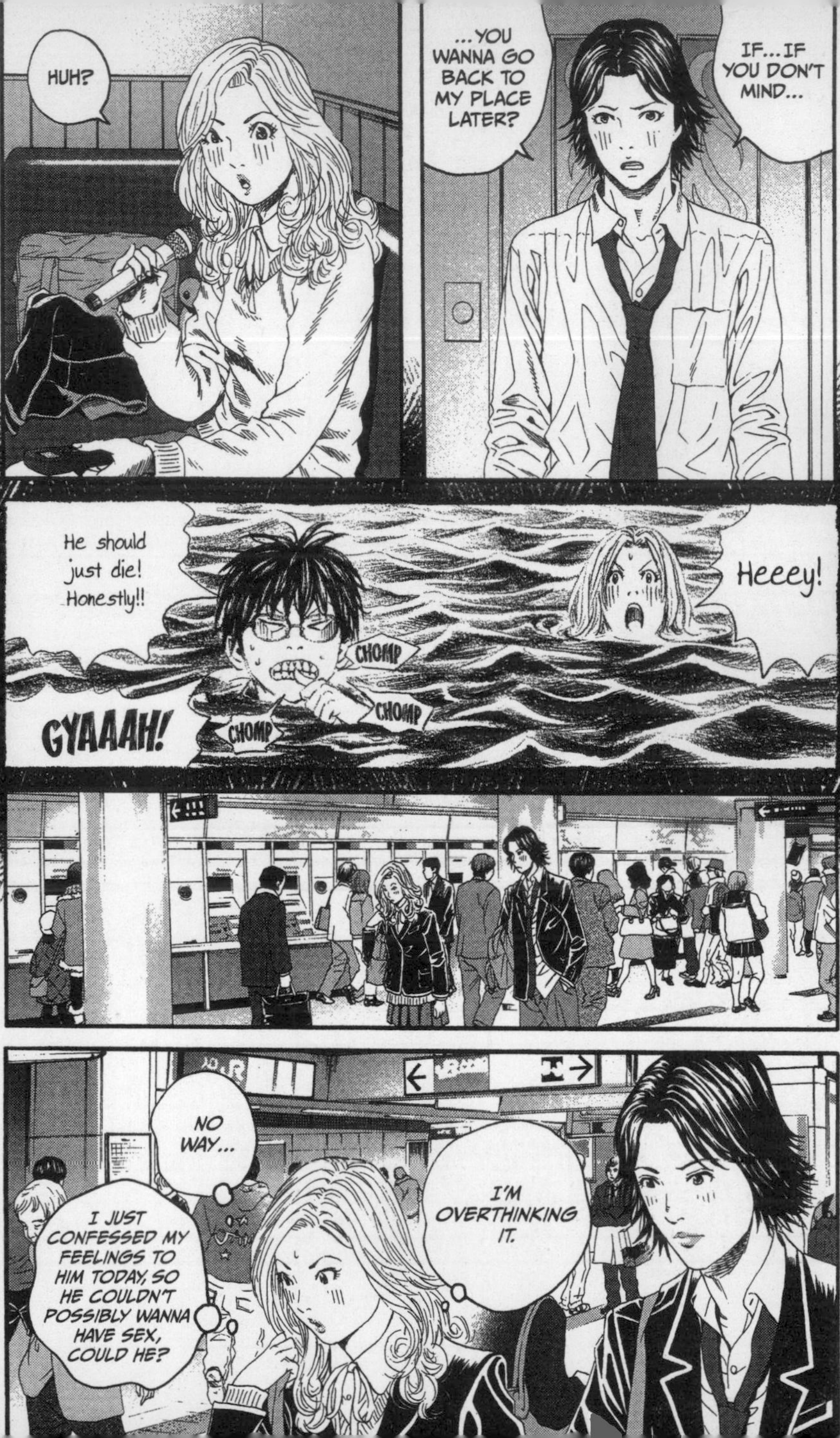
IF...IF YOU DON'T MIND...
...YOU WANNA GO BACK TO MY PLACE LATER?
HUH?
Heeey!
He should just die! Honestly!!
CHOMP
CHOMP
CHOMP
GYAAAH!
NO WAY...
I JUST CONFESSED MY FEELINGS TO HIM TODAY, SO HE COULDN'T POSSIBLY WANNA HAVE SEX, COULD HE?
I'M OVERTHINKING IT.

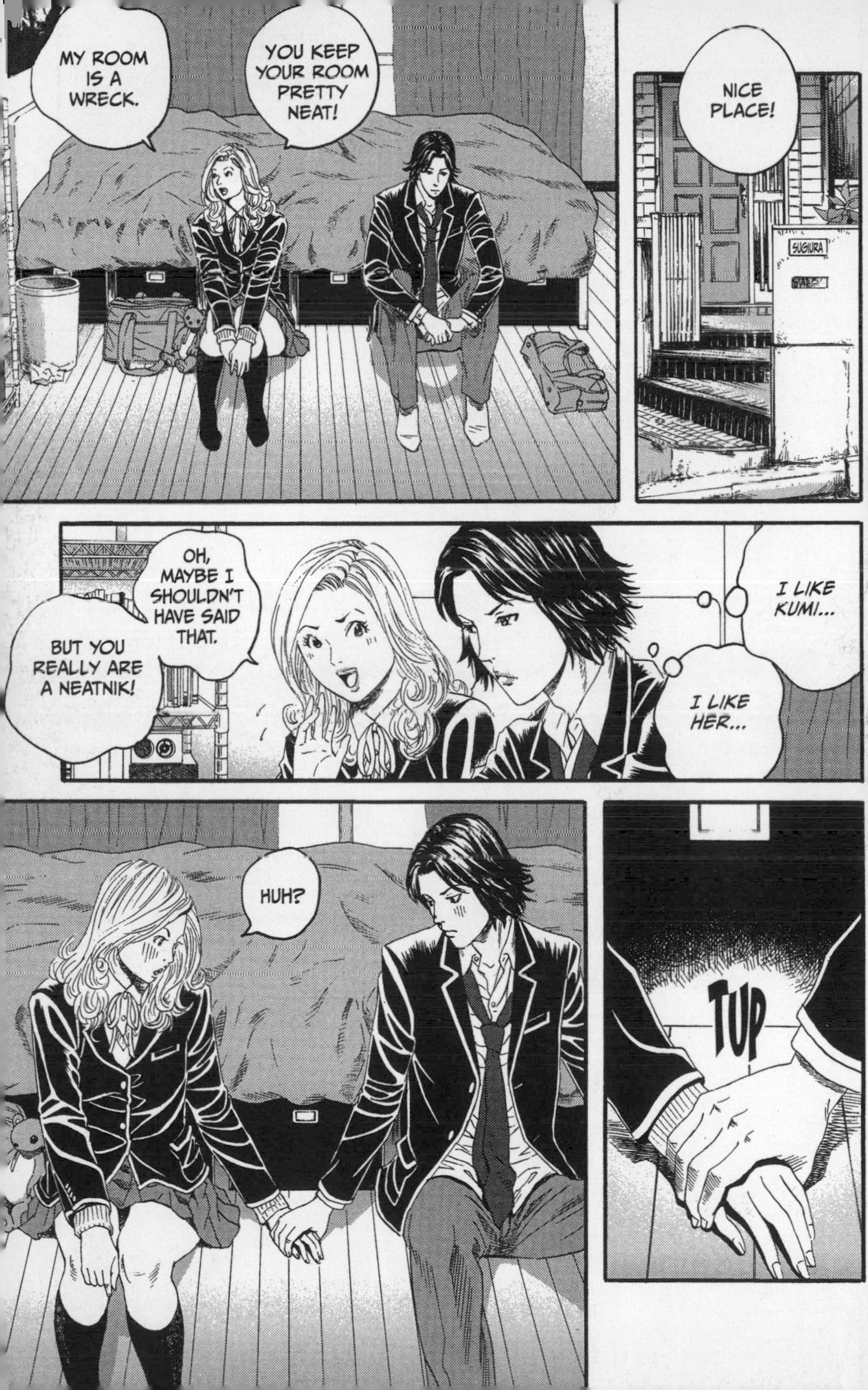
NICE PLACE!
SUGIURA
YOU KEEP YOUR ROOM PRETTY NEAT!
MY ROOM IS A WRECK.
I LIKE KUMI...
I LIKE HER...
OH, MAYBE I SHOULDN'T HAVE SAID THAT.
BUT YOU REALLY ARE A NEATNIK!
TUP
HUH?

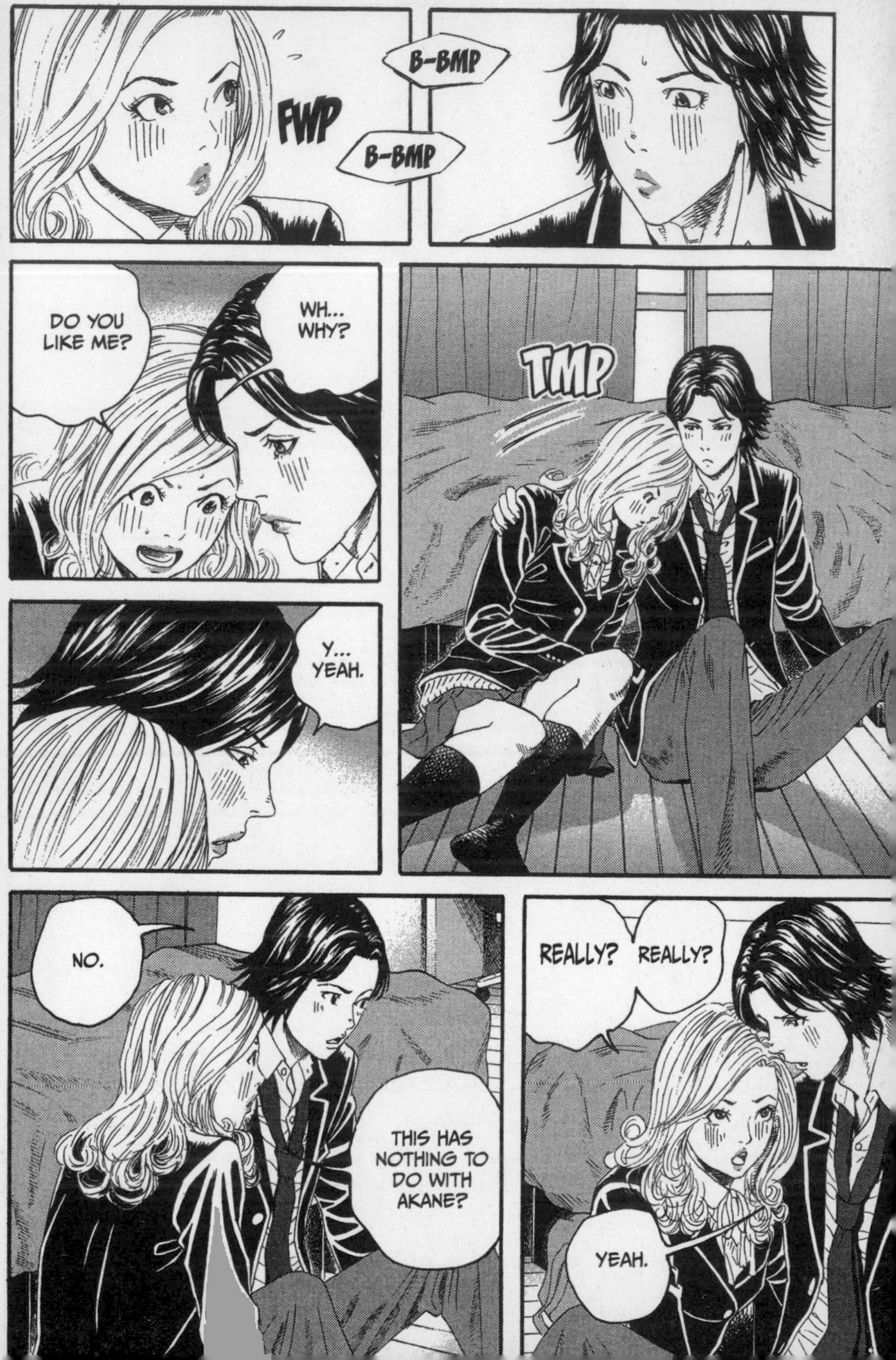
B-BMP
FWP
B-BMP
TMP
WH... WHY?
DO YOU LIKE ME?
Y... YEAH.
REALLY?
REALLY?
YEAH.
NO.
THIS HAS NOTHING TO DO WITH AKANE?

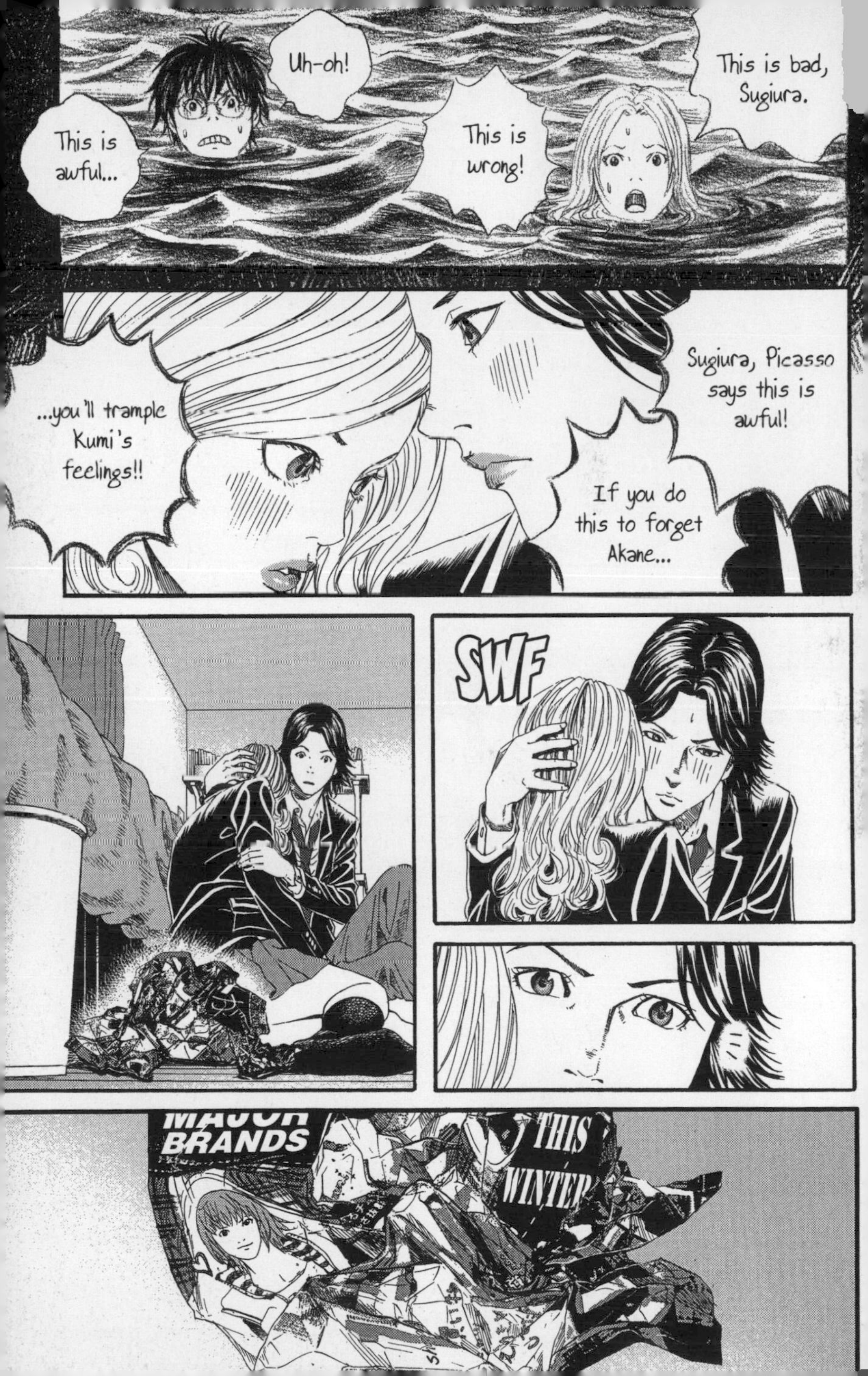
This is bad, Sugiura.
This is wrong!
Uh-oh!
This is awful...
Sugiura, Picasso says this is awful!
If you do this to forget Akane...
...you'll trample Kumi's feelings!!
SWF
THIS WINTER
BRANDS

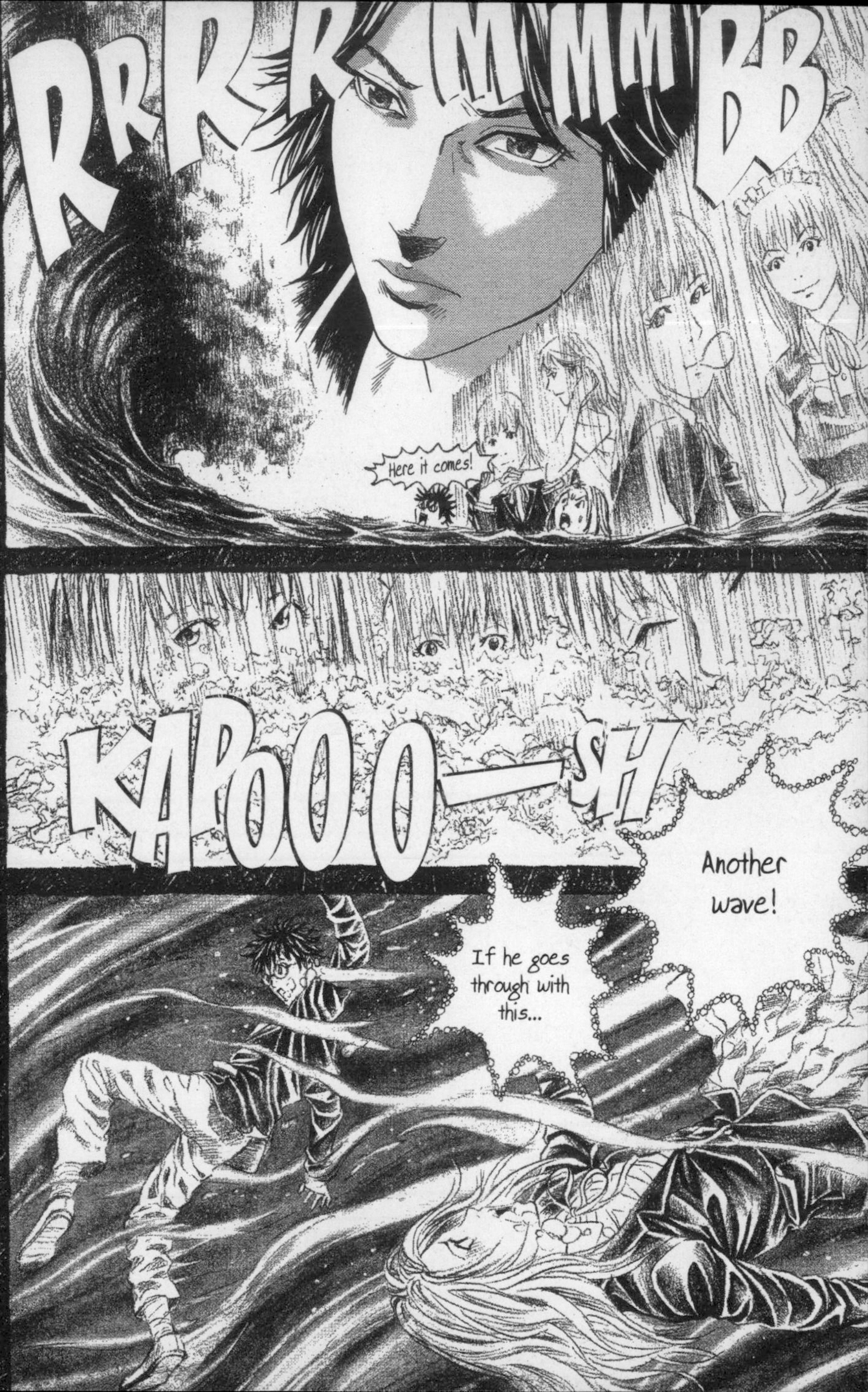
RRRRMMMMBB
Here it comes!
KAPOOOO—SH
Another wave!
If he goes through with this...

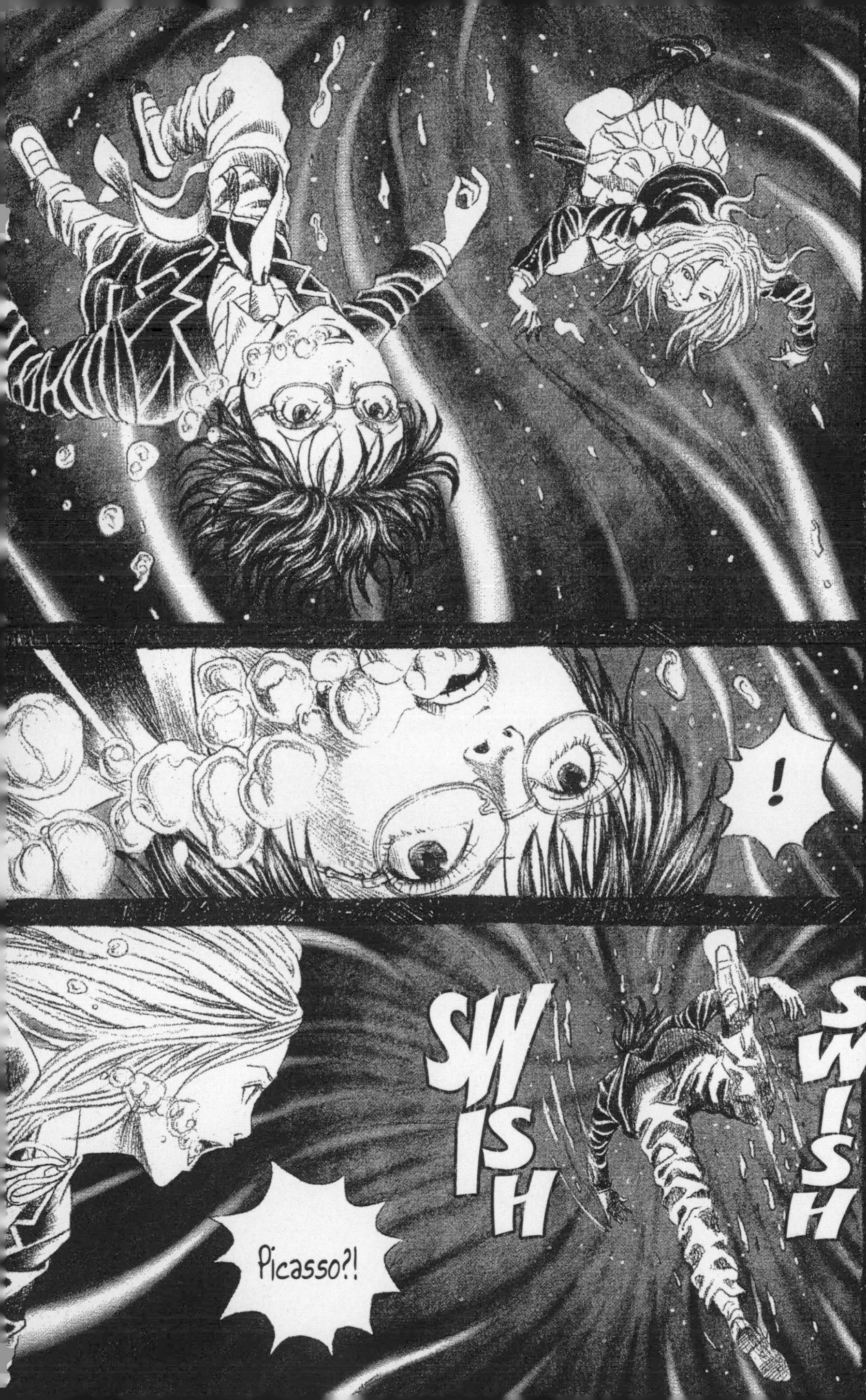
!
SWISH
SWISH
Picasso?!

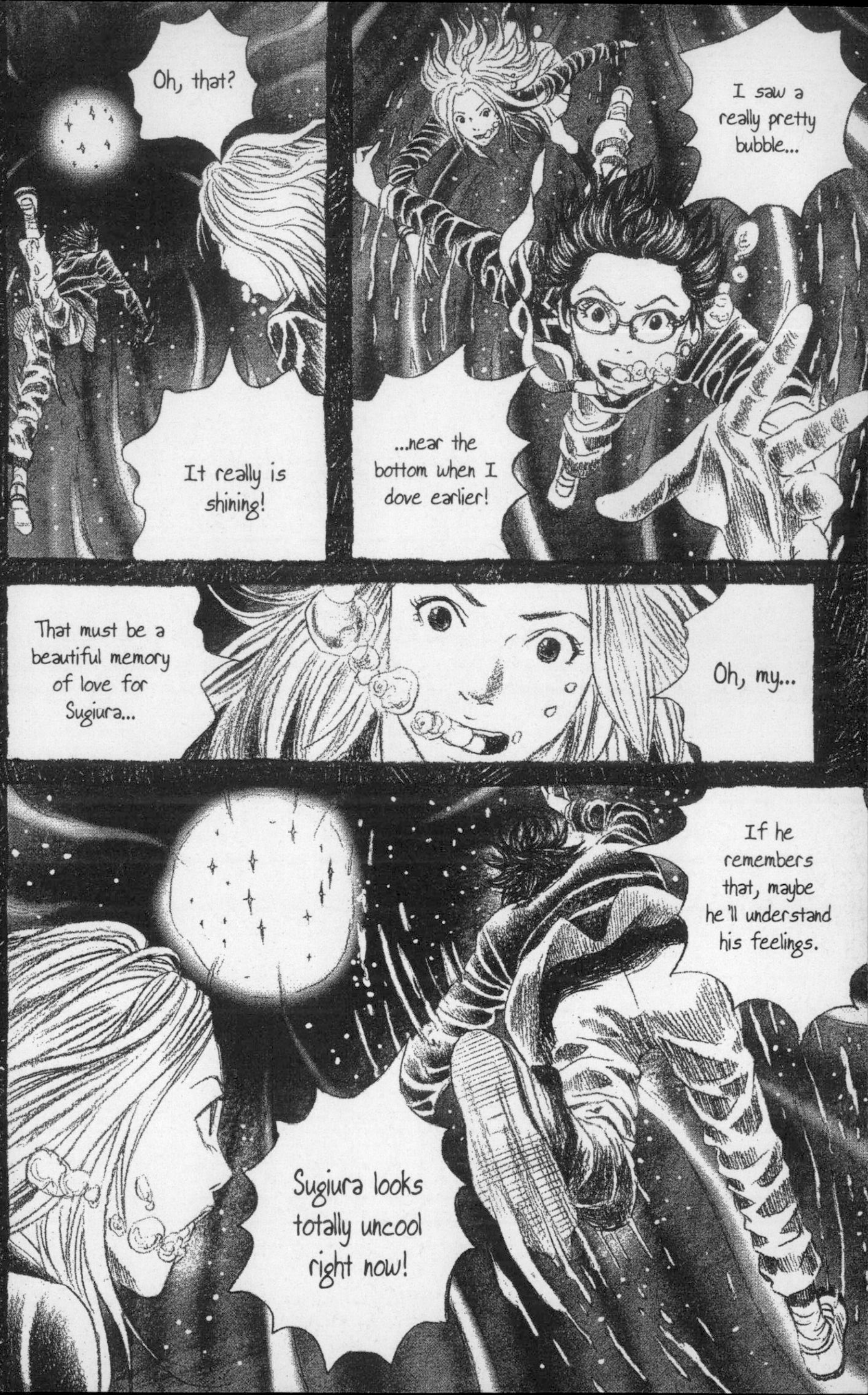
I saw a really pretty bubble...
...near the bottom when I dove earlier!
Oh, that?
It really is shining!
Oh, my...
That must be a beautiful memory of love for Sugiura...
If he remembers that, maybe he'll understand his feelings.
Sugiura looks totally uncool right now!

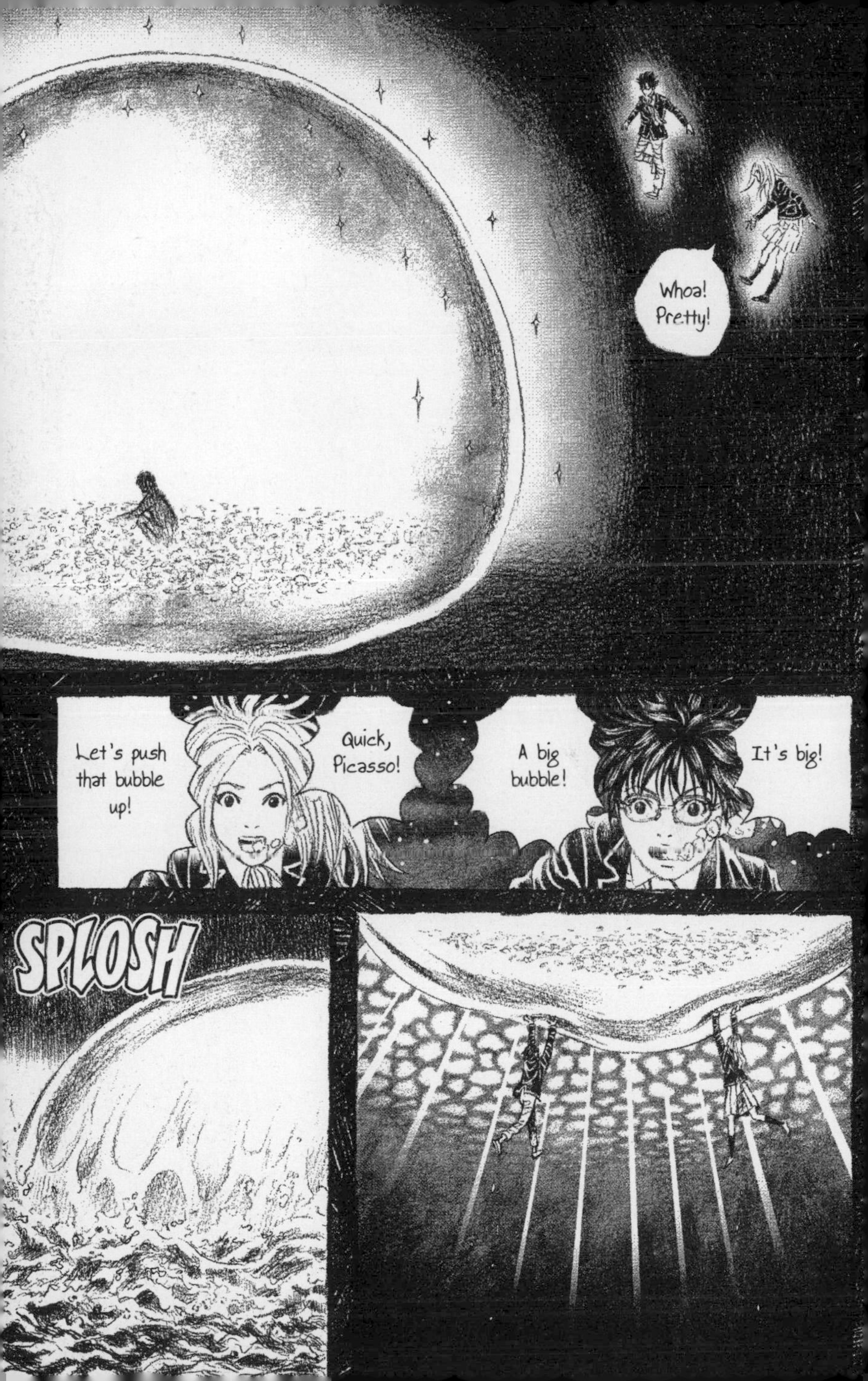
Whoa! Pretty!
It's big!
A big bubble!
Quick, Picasso!
Let's push that bubble up!
SPLOSH

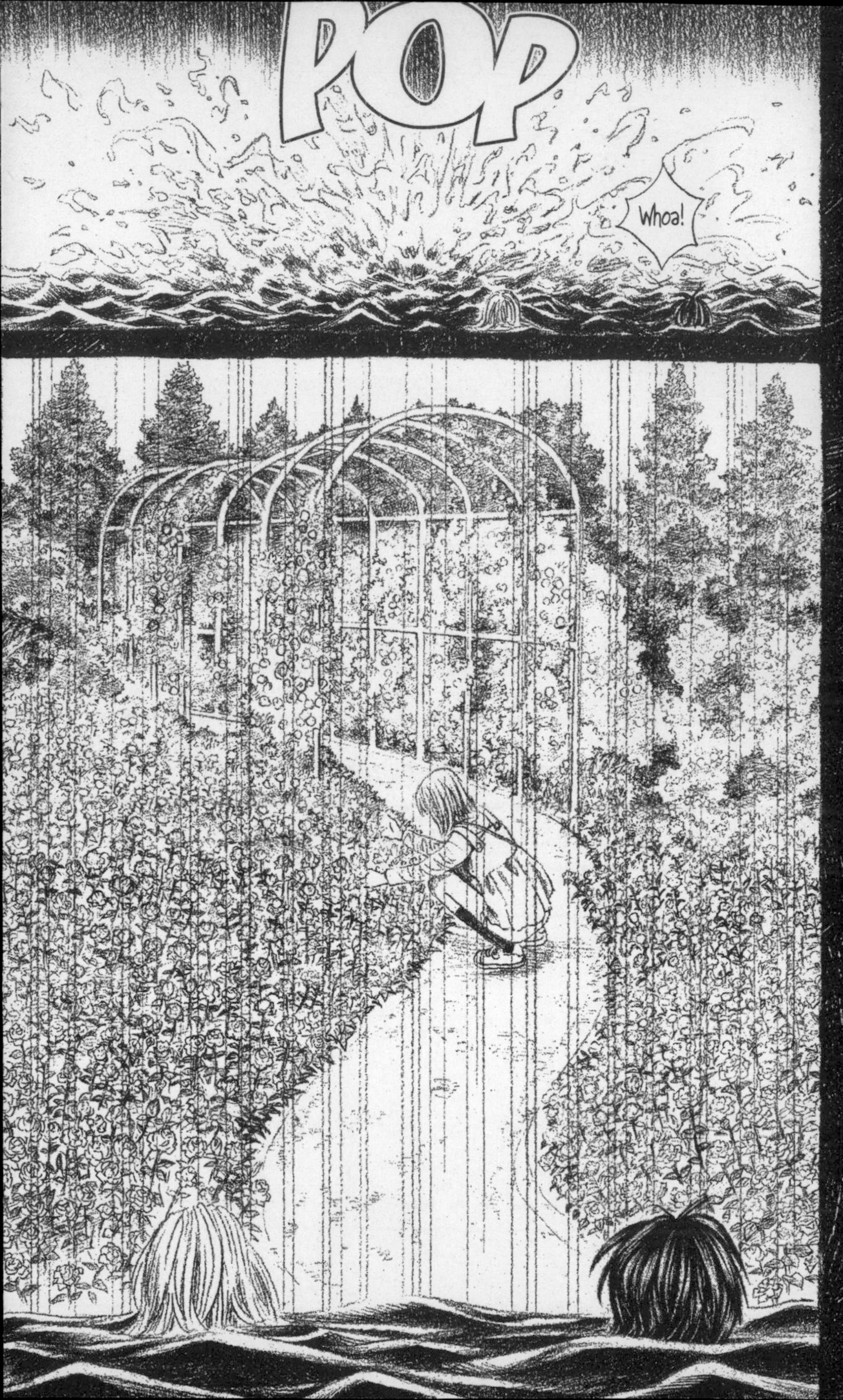
POP
Whoa!

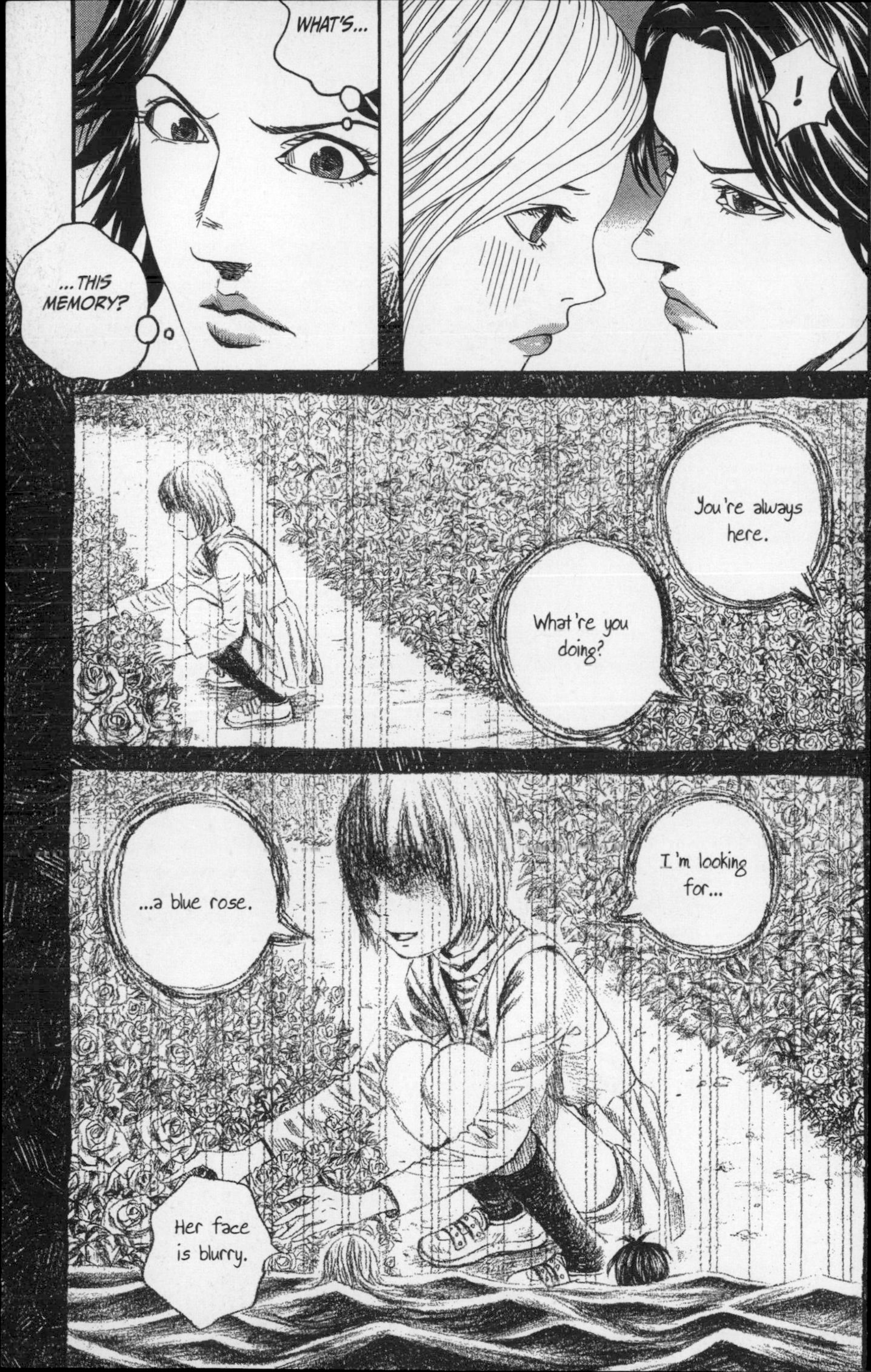
!
WHAT'S...
...THIS MEMORY?
You're always here.
What're you doing?
I'm looking for...
...a blue rose.
Her face is blurry.

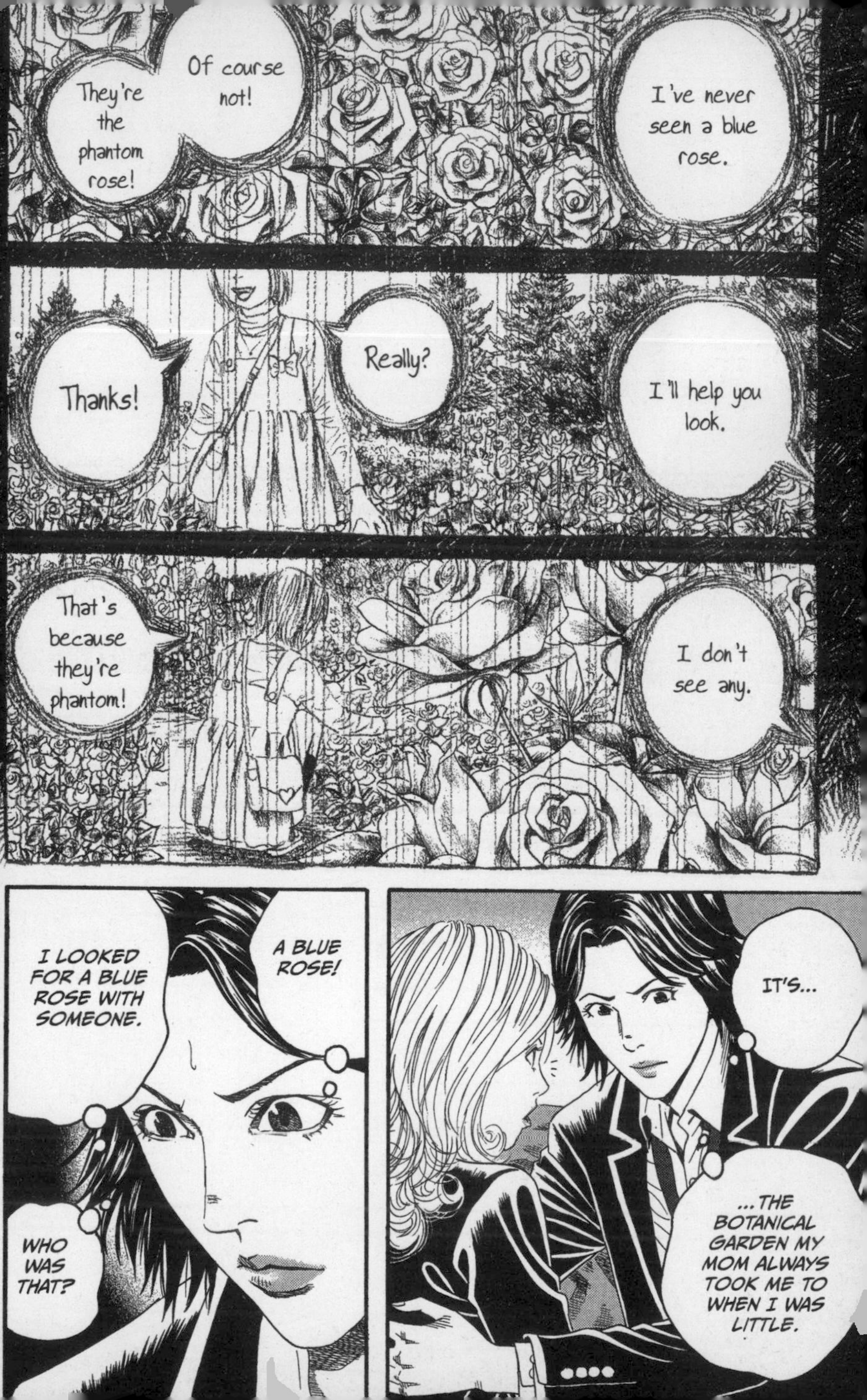
I've never seen a blue rose.
Of course not!
They're the phantom rose!
I'll help you look.
Really?
Thanks!
I don't see any.
That's because they're phantom!
IT'S...
...THE BOTANICAL GARDEN MY MOM ALWAYS TOOK ME TO WHEN I WAS LITTLE.
A BLUE ROSE!
I LOOKED FOR A BLUE ROSE WITH SOMEONE.
WHO WAS THAT?

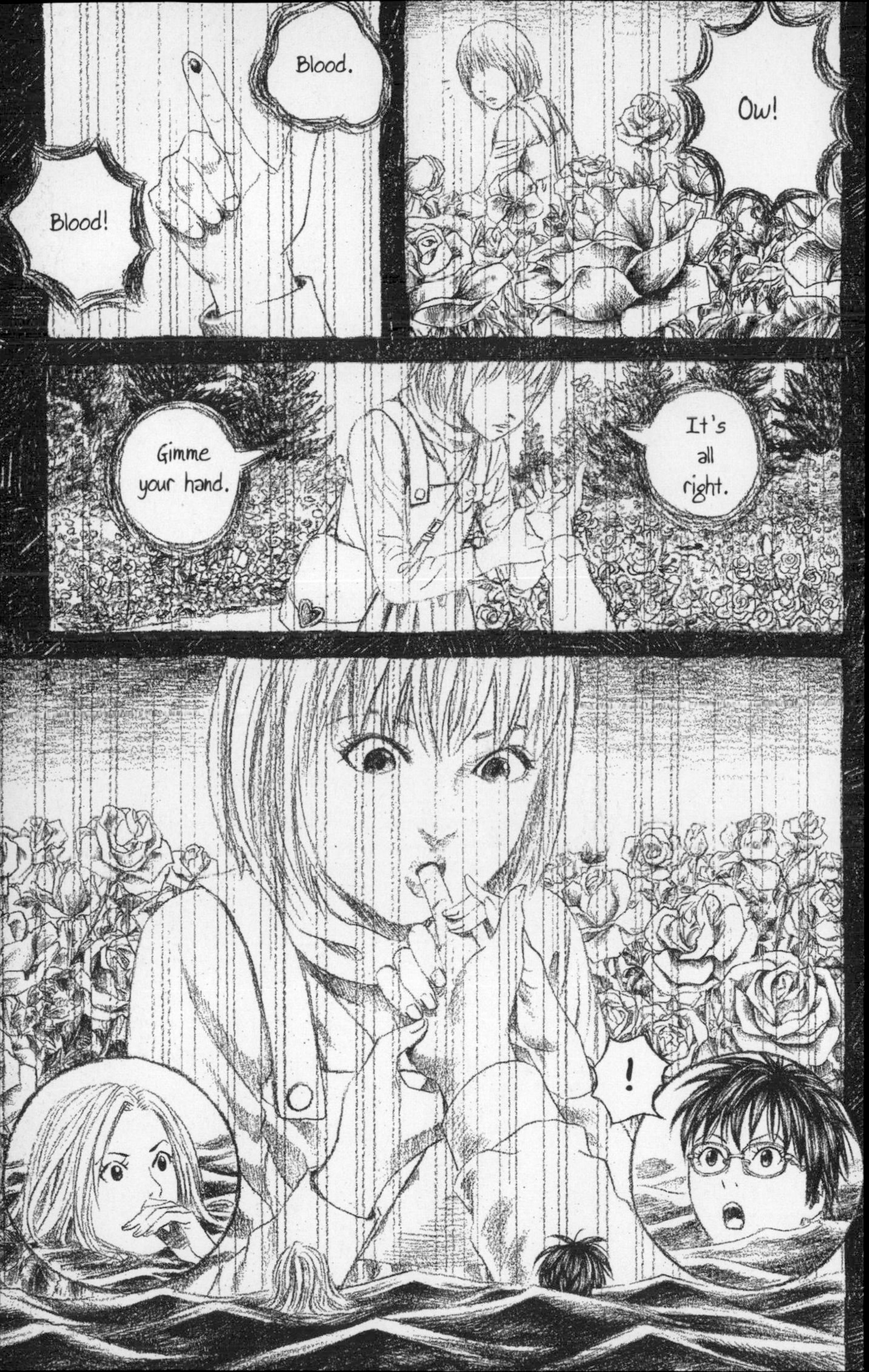
Ow!
Blood.
Blood!
It's all right.
Gimme your hand.
!

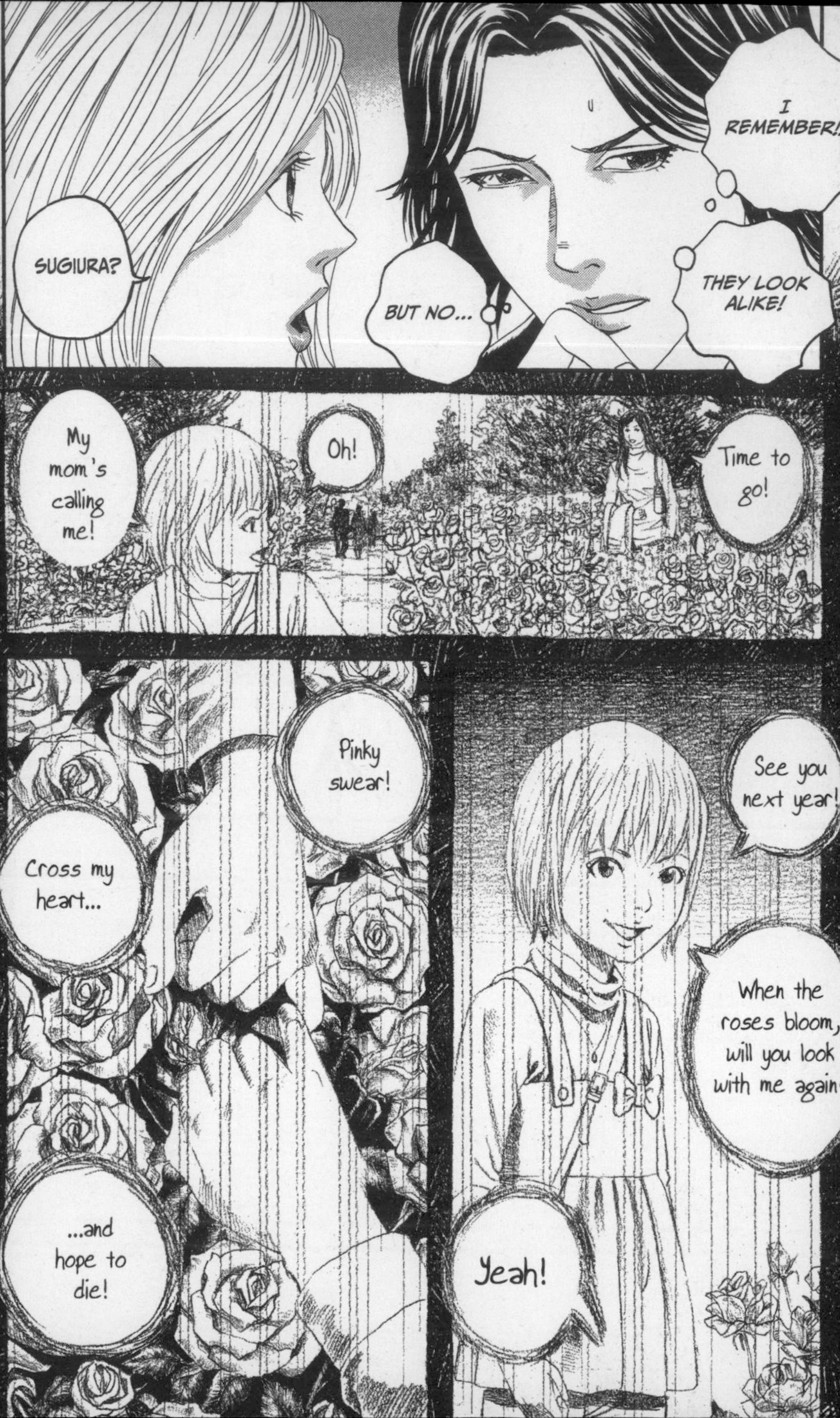
I REMEMBER!!
THEY LOOK ALIKE!
BUT NO...
SUGIURA?
Time to go!
Oh!
My mom's calling me!
See you next year!
When the roses bloom, will you look with me again?
Yeah!
Pinky swear!
Cross my heart...
...and hope to die!

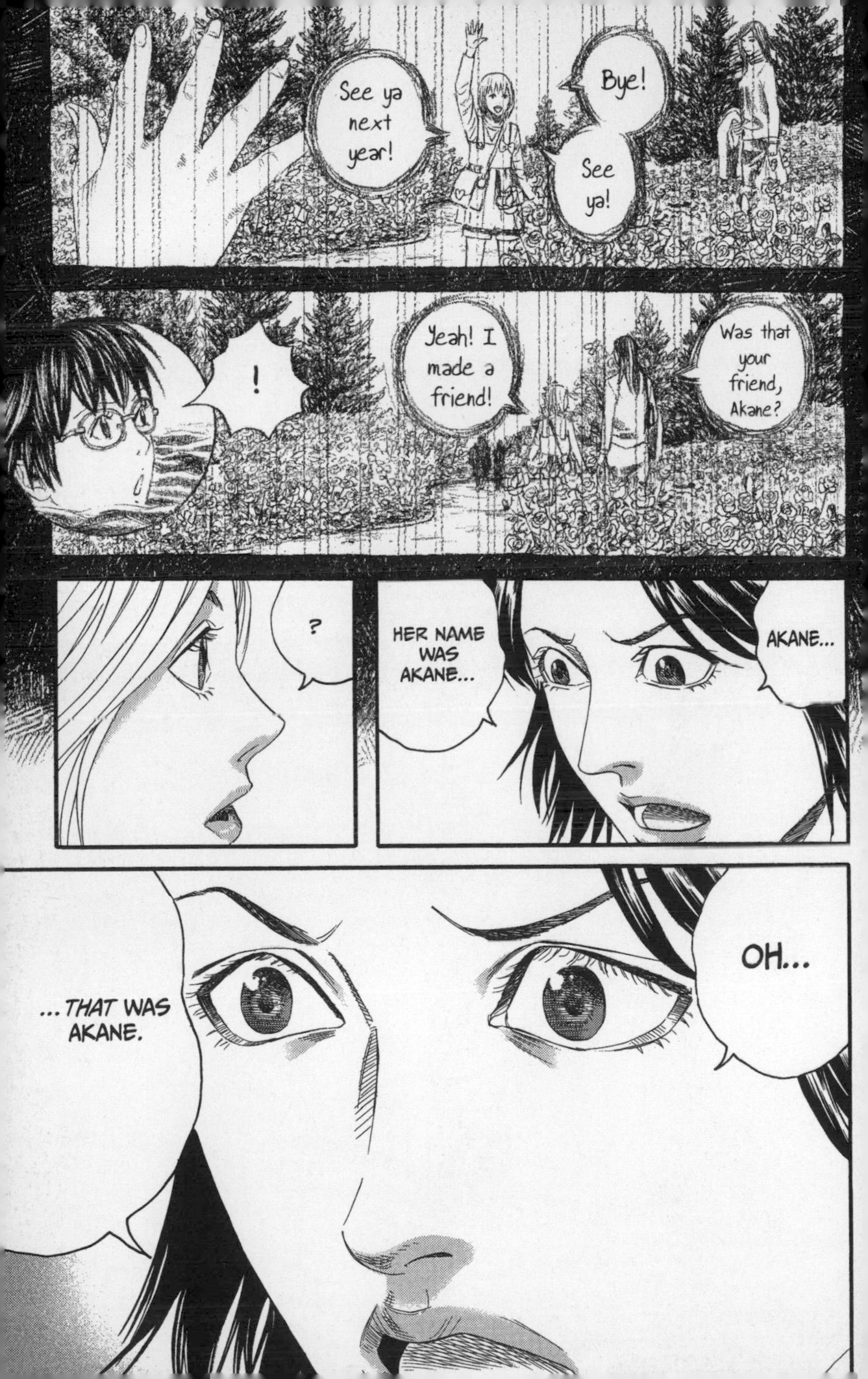
Bye!
See ya!
See ya next year!
Was that your friend, Akane?
Yeah! I made a friend!
!
AKANE...
HER NAME WAS AKANE...
?
OH...
...THAT WAS AKANE.

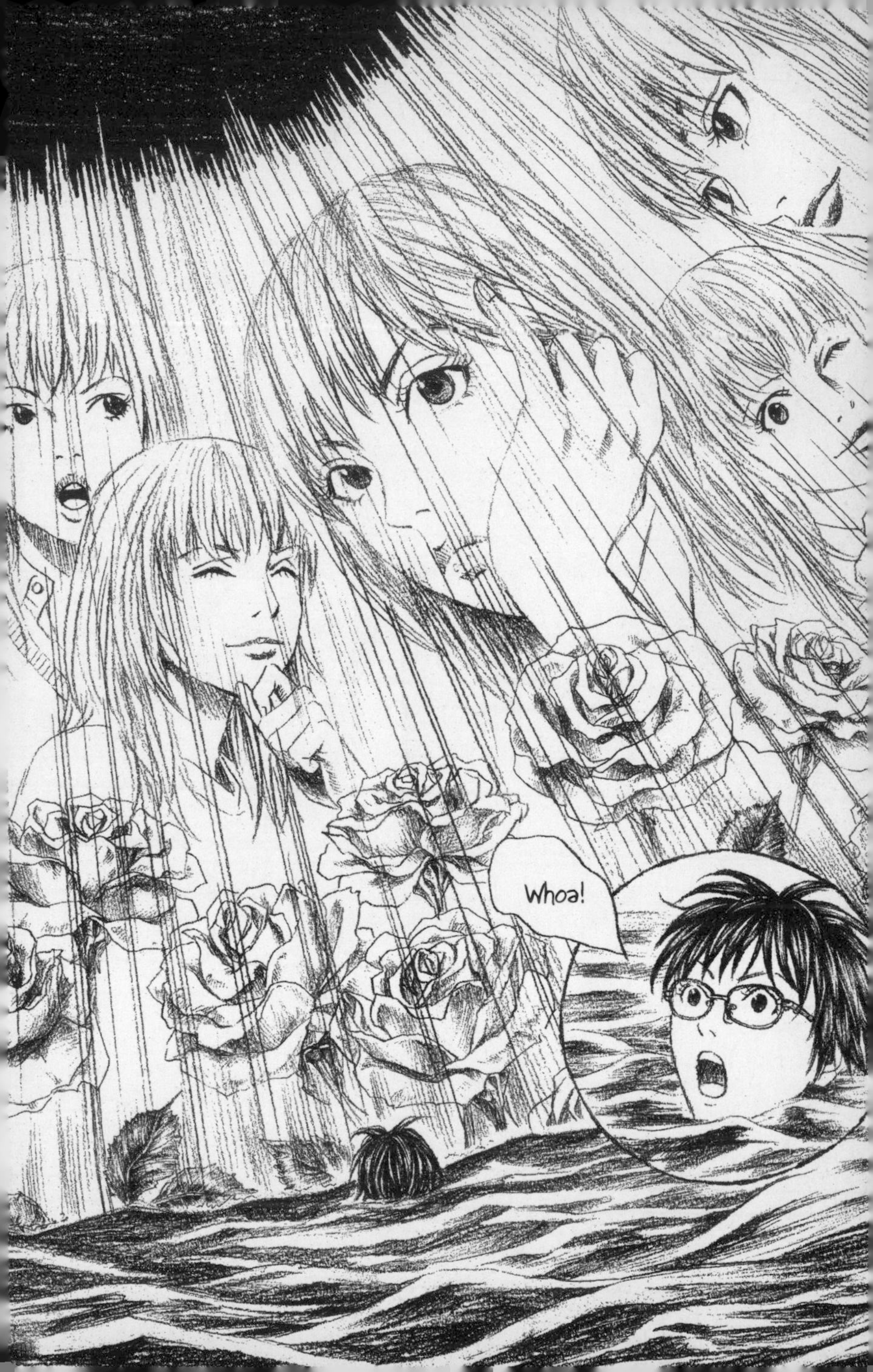
Whoa!

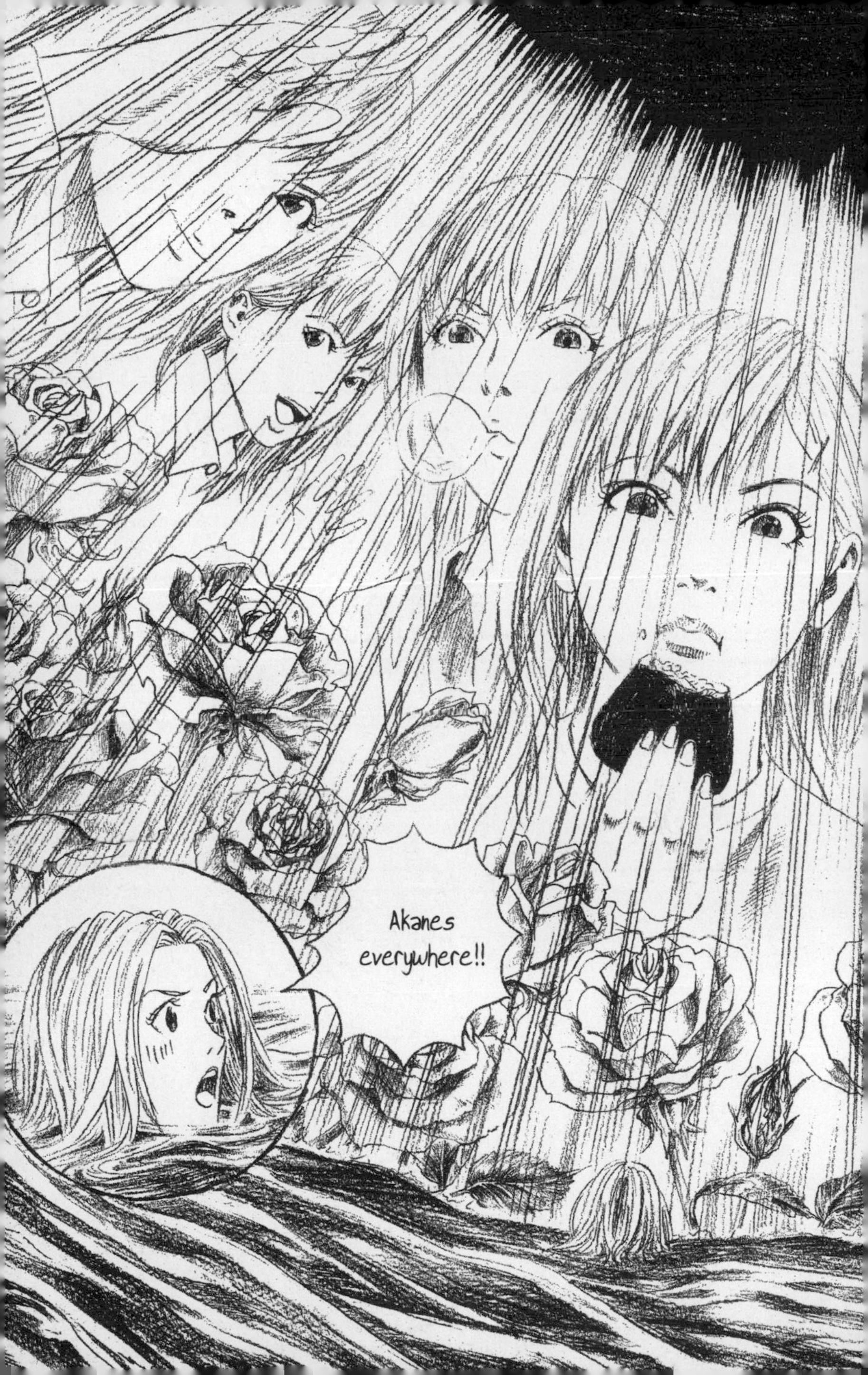
Akanes everywhere!!

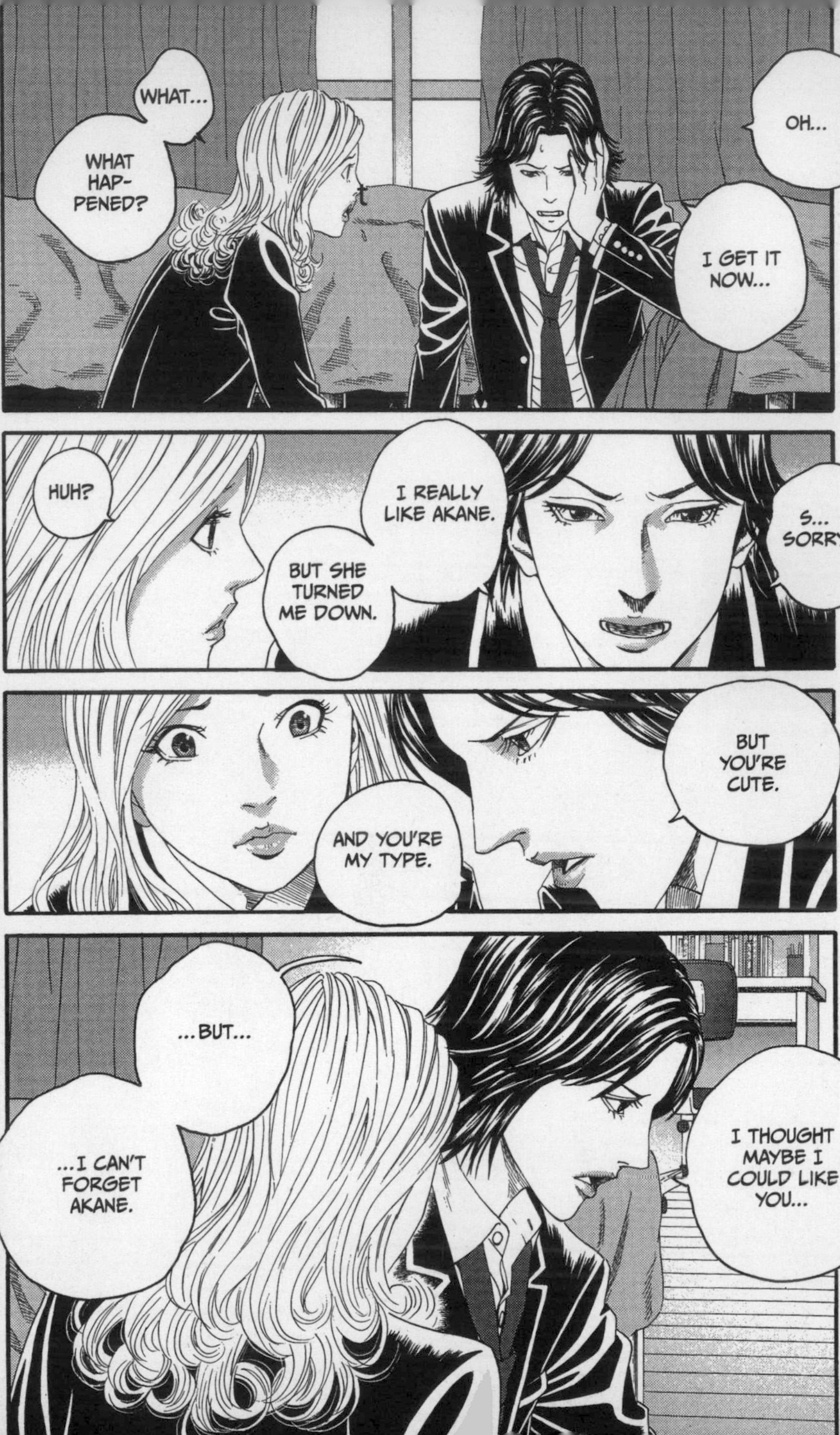
WHAT...
WHAT HAP-PENED?
OH...
I GET IT NOW...
S... SORRY.
I REALLY LIKE AKANE.
BUT SHE TURNED ME DOWN.
HUH?
BUT YOU'RE CUTE.
AND YOU'RE MY TYPE.
I THOUGHT MAYBE I COULD LIKE YOU...
...BUT...
...I CAN'T FORGET AKANE.

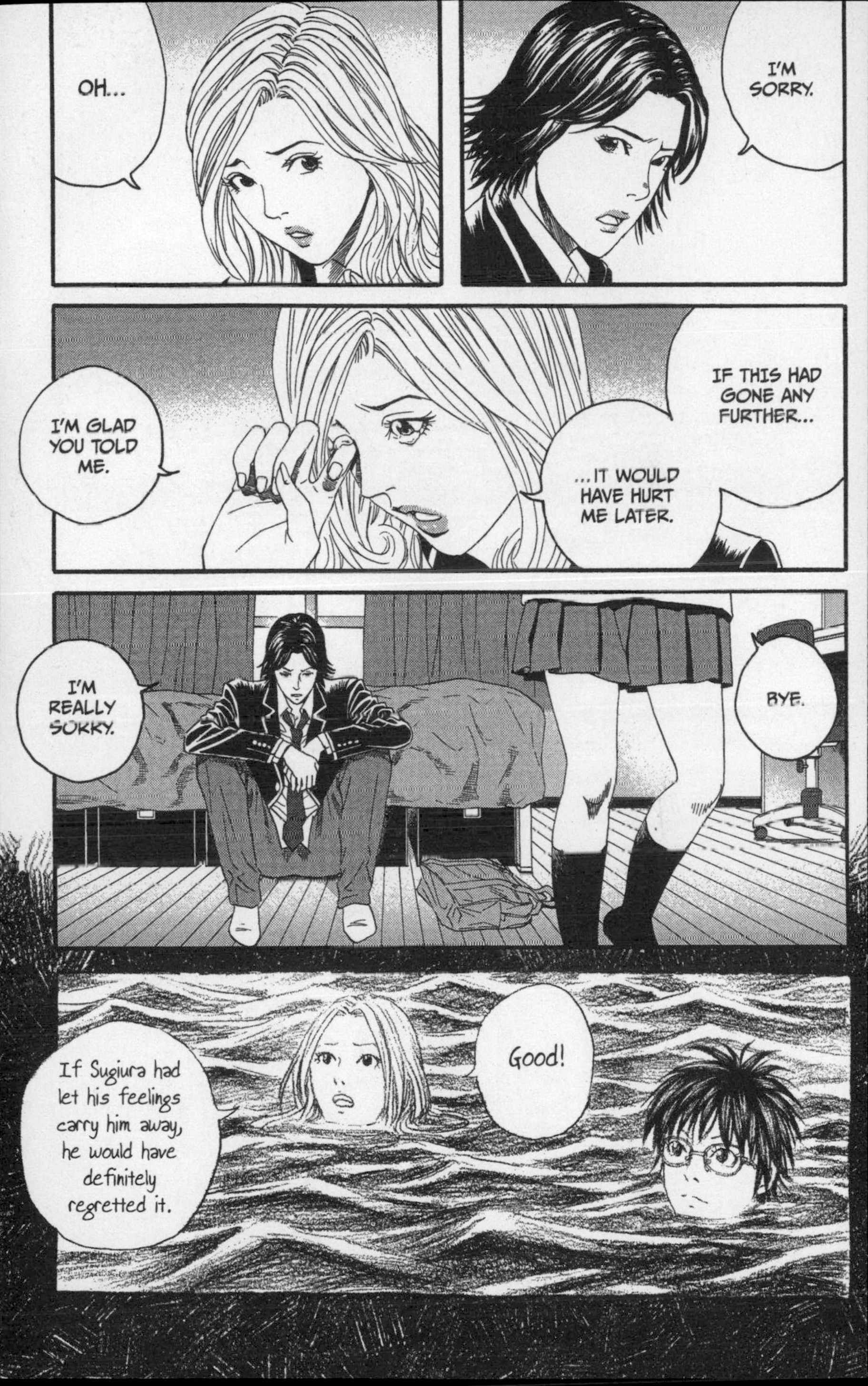

I'M SORRY.
OH...
IF THIS HAD GONE ANY FURTHER...
...IT WOULD HAVE HURT ME LATER.
I'M GLAD YOU TOLD ME.
BYE.
I'M REALLY SORRY.
Good!
If Sugiura had let his feelings carry him away, he would have definitely regretted it.

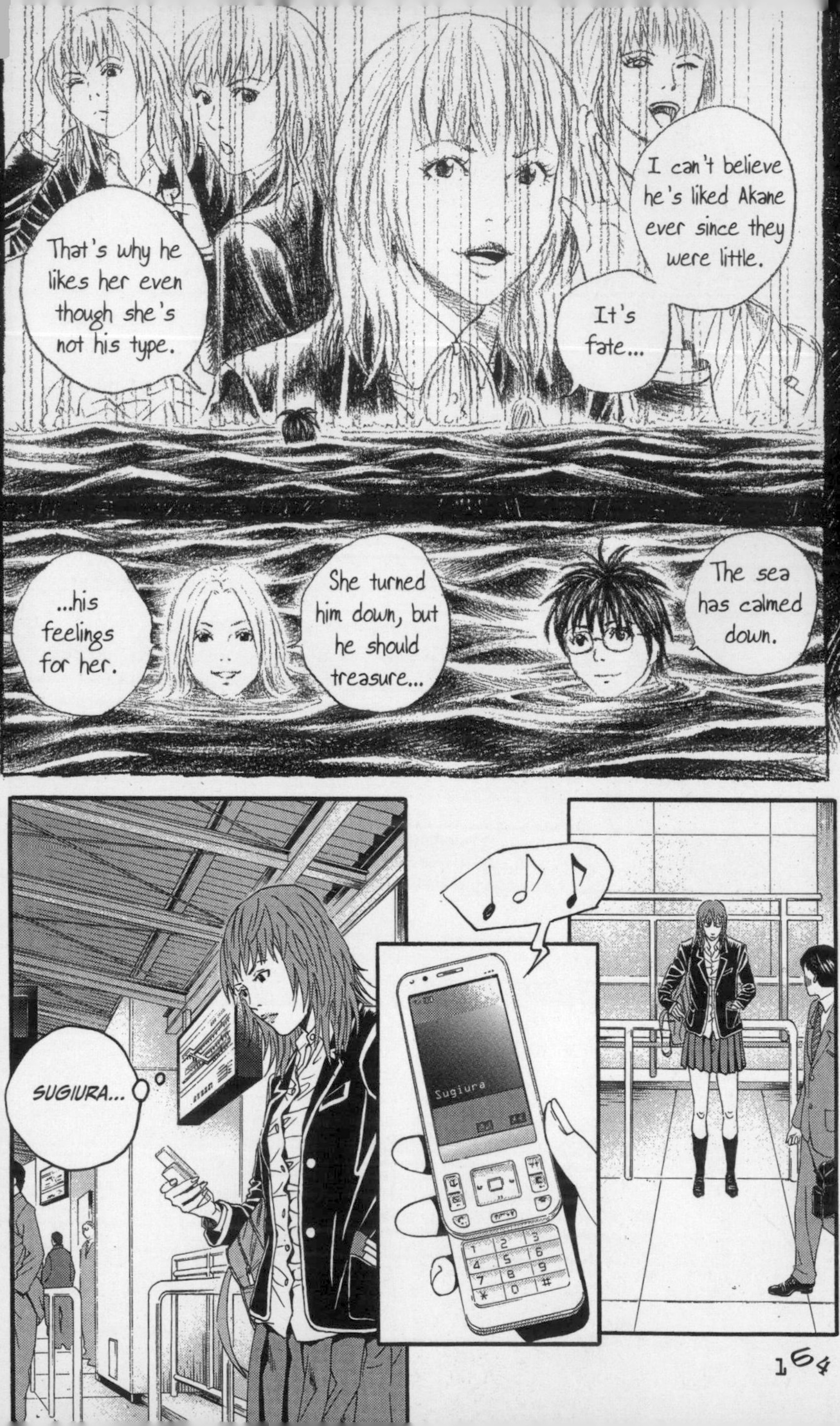
I can't believe he's liked Akane ever since they were little.
It's fate...
That's why he likes her even though she's not his type.
The sea has calmed down.
She turned him down, but he should treasure...
...his feelings for her.
Sugiura
SUGIURA...

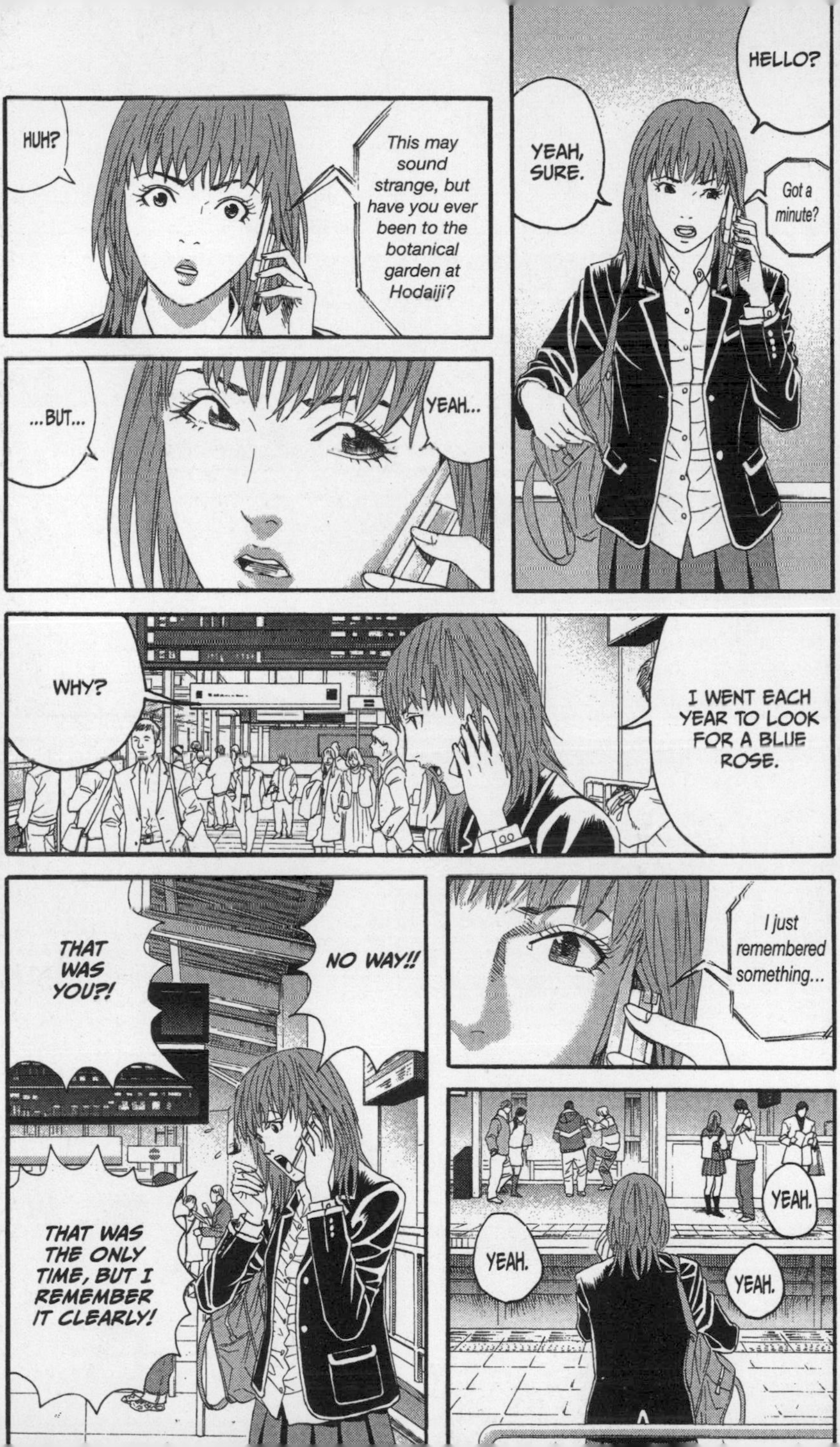
HELLO?
Got a minute?
YEAH, SURE.
This may sound strange, but have you ever been to the botanical garden at Hodaiji?
HUH?
YEAH...
...BUT...
I WENT EACH YEAR TO LOOK FOR A BLUE ROSE.
WHY?
I just remembered something...
YEAH.
YEAH.
YEAH.
NO WAY!!
THAT WAS YOU?!
THAT WAS THE ONLY TIME, BUT I REMEMBER IT CLEARLY!

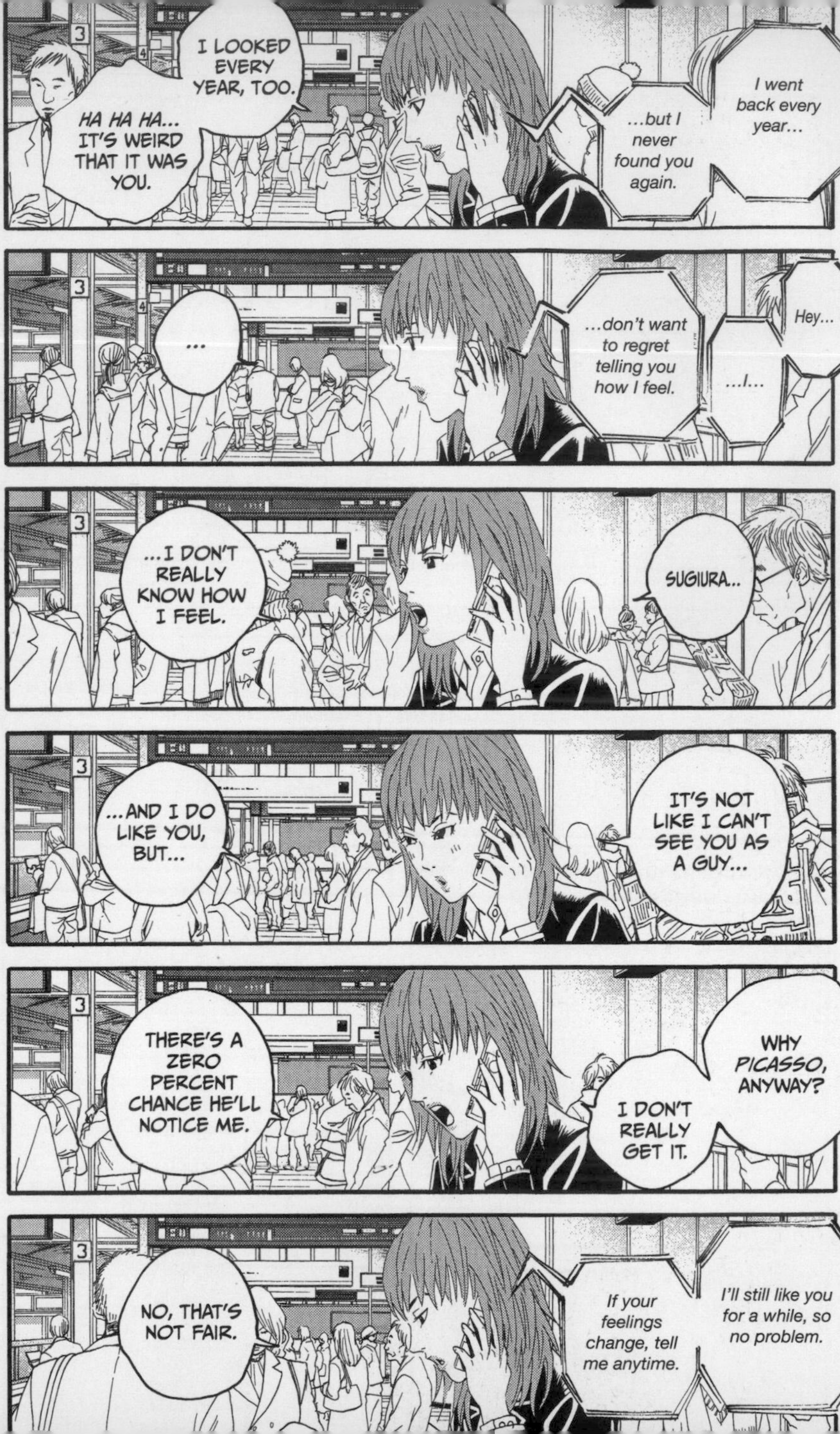
I went back every year...
...but I never found you again.
I LOOKED EVERY YEAR, TOO.
HA HA HA... IT'S WEIRD THAT IT WAS YOU.
Hey...
...I...
...don't want to regret telling you how I feel.
...
SUGIURA...
...I DON'T REALLY KNOW HOW I FEEL.
IT'S NOT LIKE I CAN'T SEE YOU AS A GUY...
...AND I DO LIKE YOU, BUT...
WHY PICASSO, ANYWAY?
I DON'T REALLY GET IT.
THERE'S A ZERO PERCENT CHANCE HE'LL NOTICE ME.
I'll still like you for a while, so no problem.
If your feelings change, tell me anytime.
NO, THAT'S NOT FAIR.

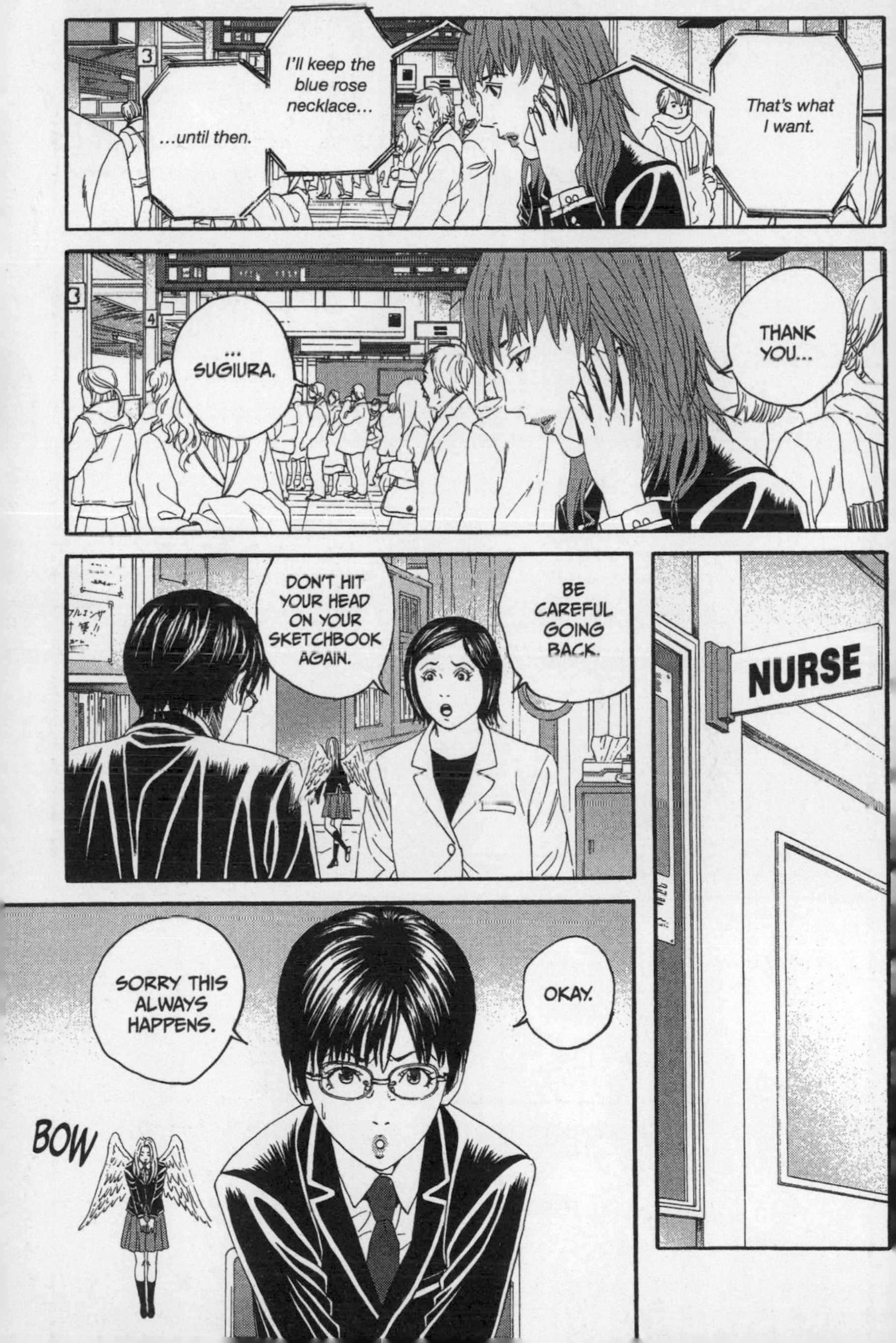
That's what I want.
I'll keep the blue rose necklace...
...until then.
THANK YOU...
... SUGIURA.
NURSE
BE CAREFUL GOING BACK.
DON'T HIT YOUR HEAD ON YOUR SKETCHBOOK AGAIN.
OKAY.
SORRY THIS ALWAYS HAPPENS.
BOW

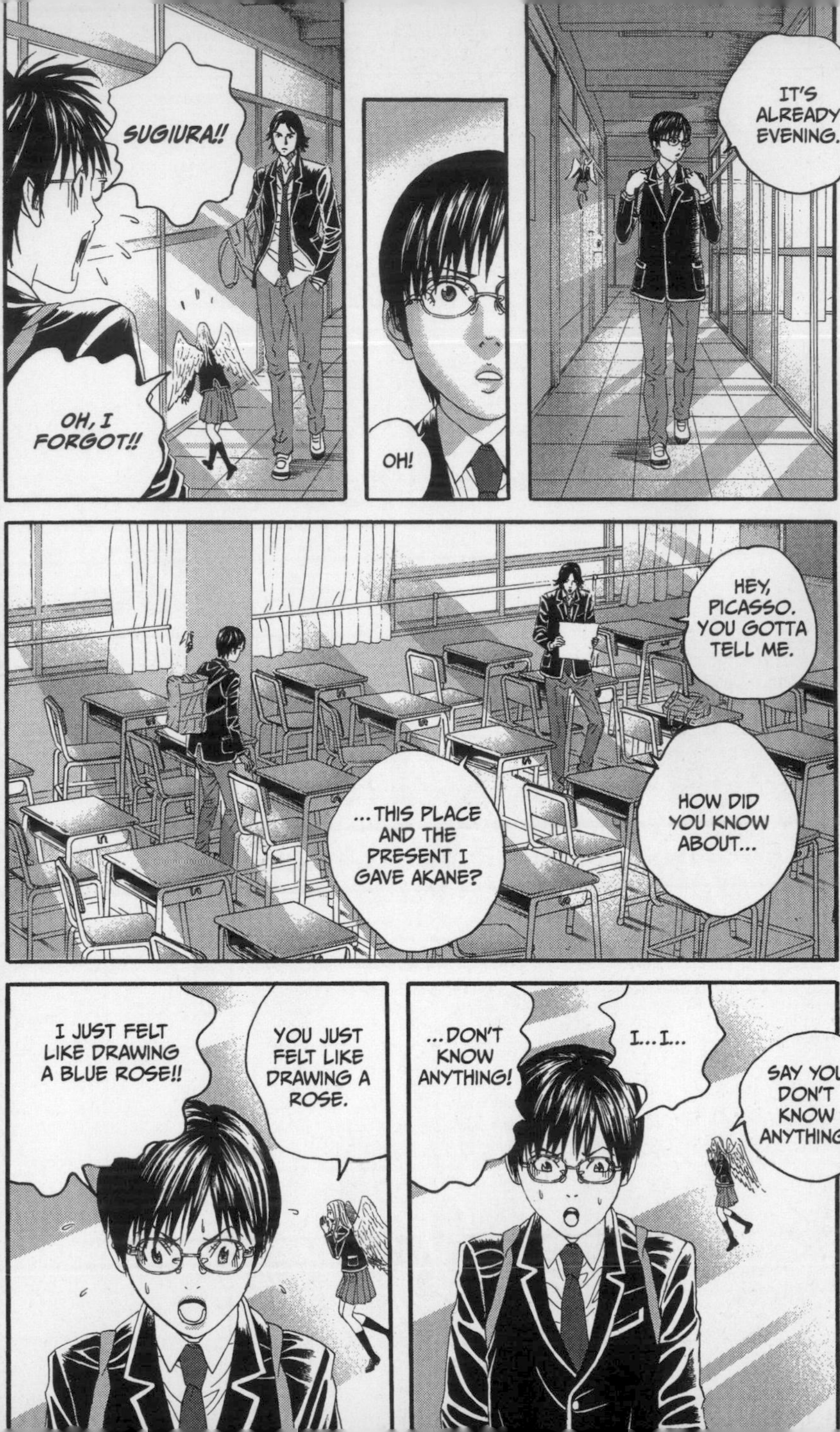
IT'S ALREADY EVENING.
OH!
SUGIURA!!
OH, I FORGOT!!
HEY, PICASSO. YOU GOTTA TELL ME.
HOW DID YOU KNOW ABOUT...
...THIS PLACE AND THE PRESENT I GAVE AKANE?
I... I...
SAY YOU DON'T KNOW ANYTHING.
...DON'T KNOW ANYTHING!
YOU JUST FELT LIKE DRAWING A ROSE.
I JUST FELT LIKE DRAWING A BLUE ROSE!!

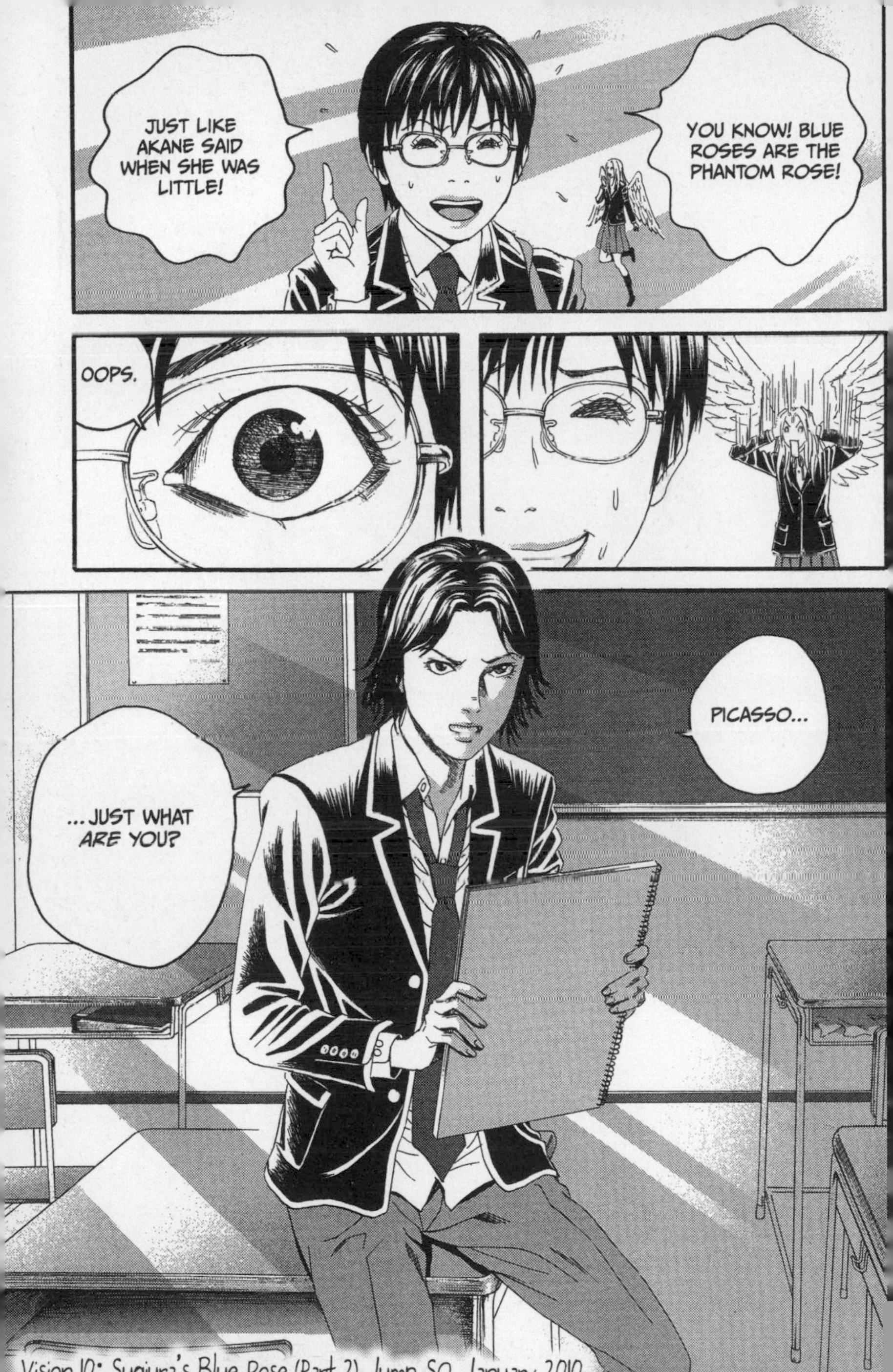
YOU KNOW! BLUE ROSES ARE THE PHANTOM ROSE!
JUST LIKE AKANE SAID WHEN SHE WAS LITTLE!
OOPS.
PICASSO...
...JUST WHAT ARE YOU?
Vision 10: Sugiura's Blue Rose (Part 2)_Jump SQ, January 2010

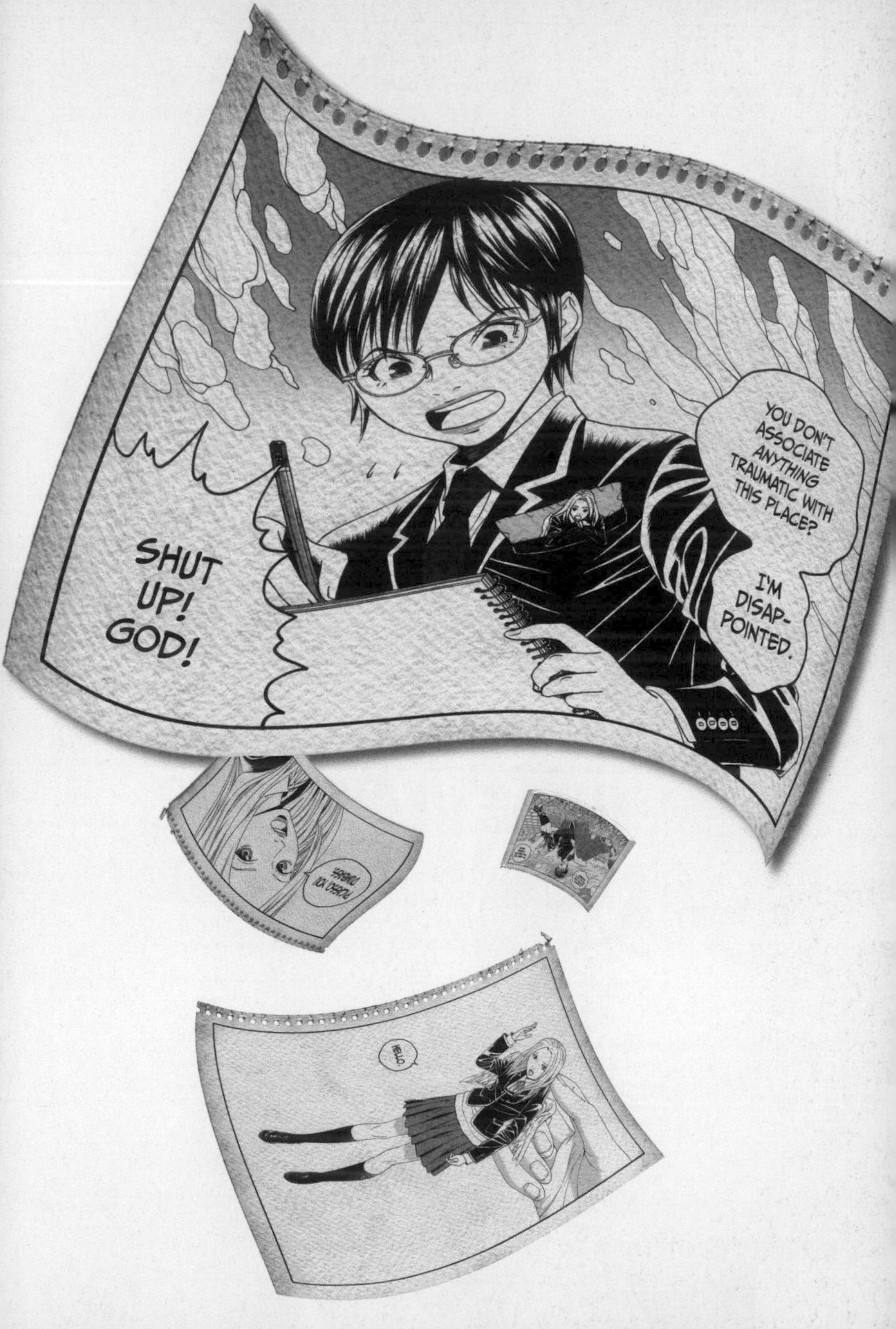
YOU DON'T ASSOCIATE ANYTHING TRAUMATIC WITH THIS PLACE?
I'M DISAP-POINTED.
SHUT UP! GOD!
HELLO.

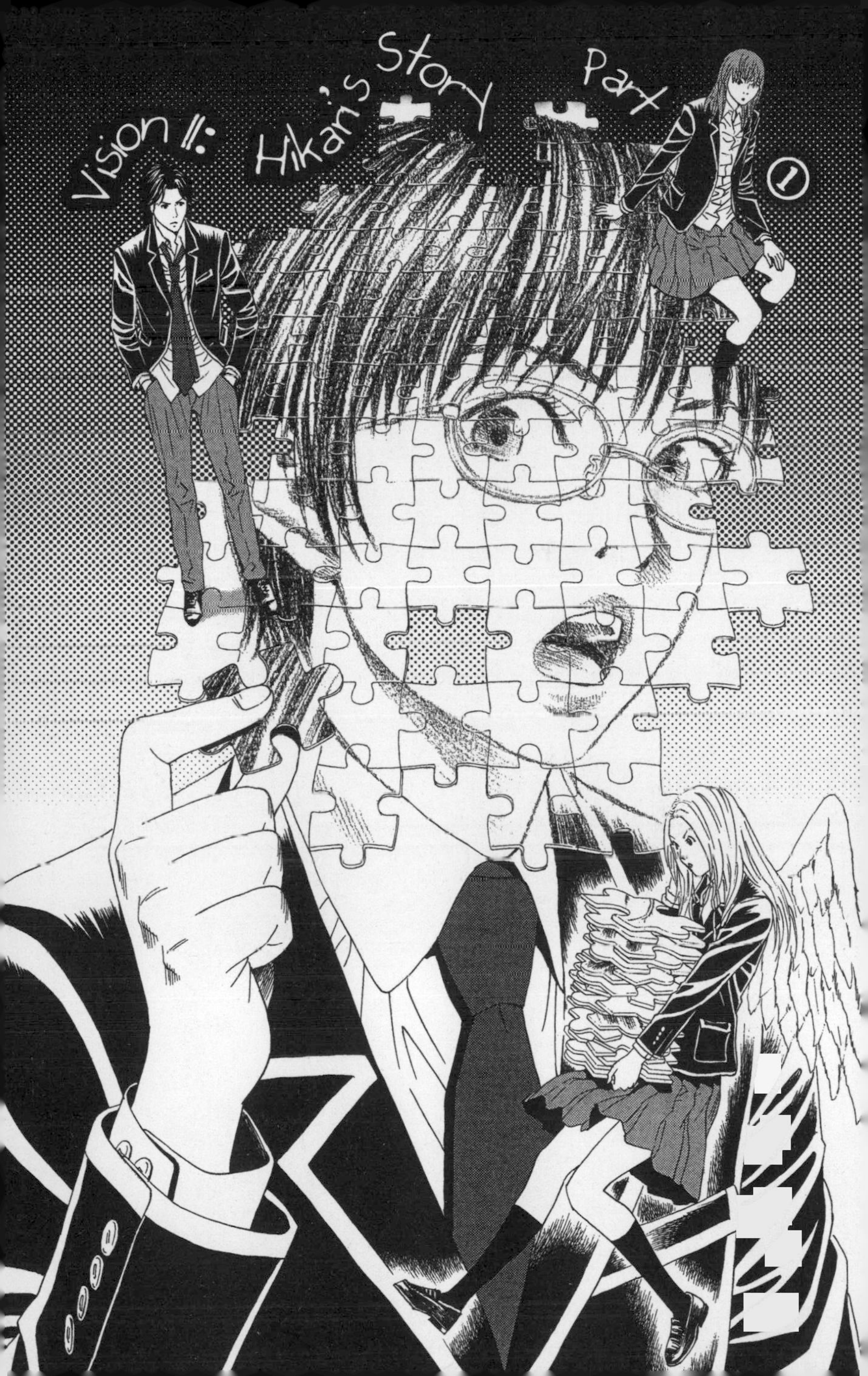
Vision 11: Hikari's Story Part 1

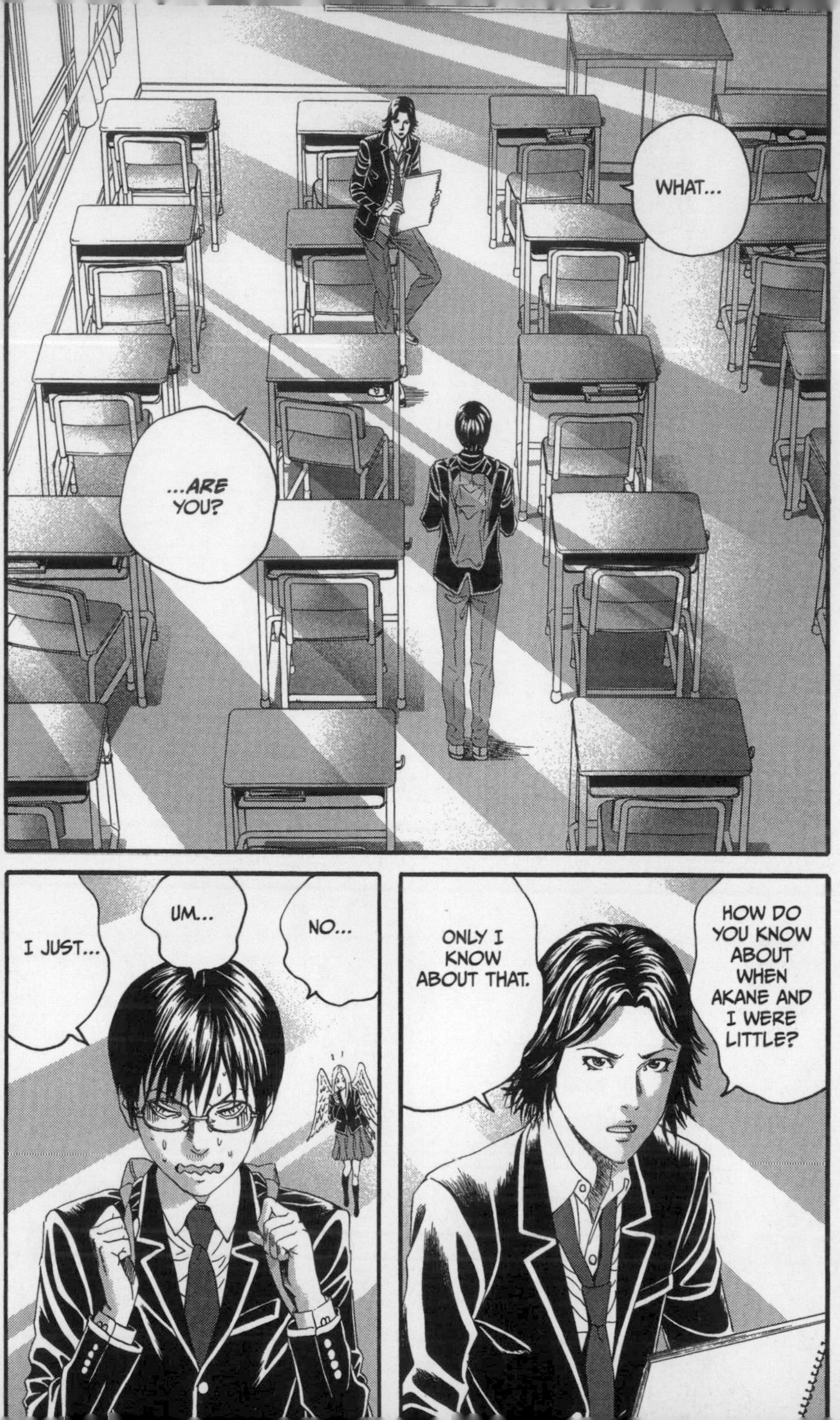
WHAT...
...ARE YOU?
HOW DO YOU KNOW ABOUT WHEN AKANE AND I WERE LITTLE?
ONLY I KNOW ABOUT THAT.
NO...
UM...
I JUST...

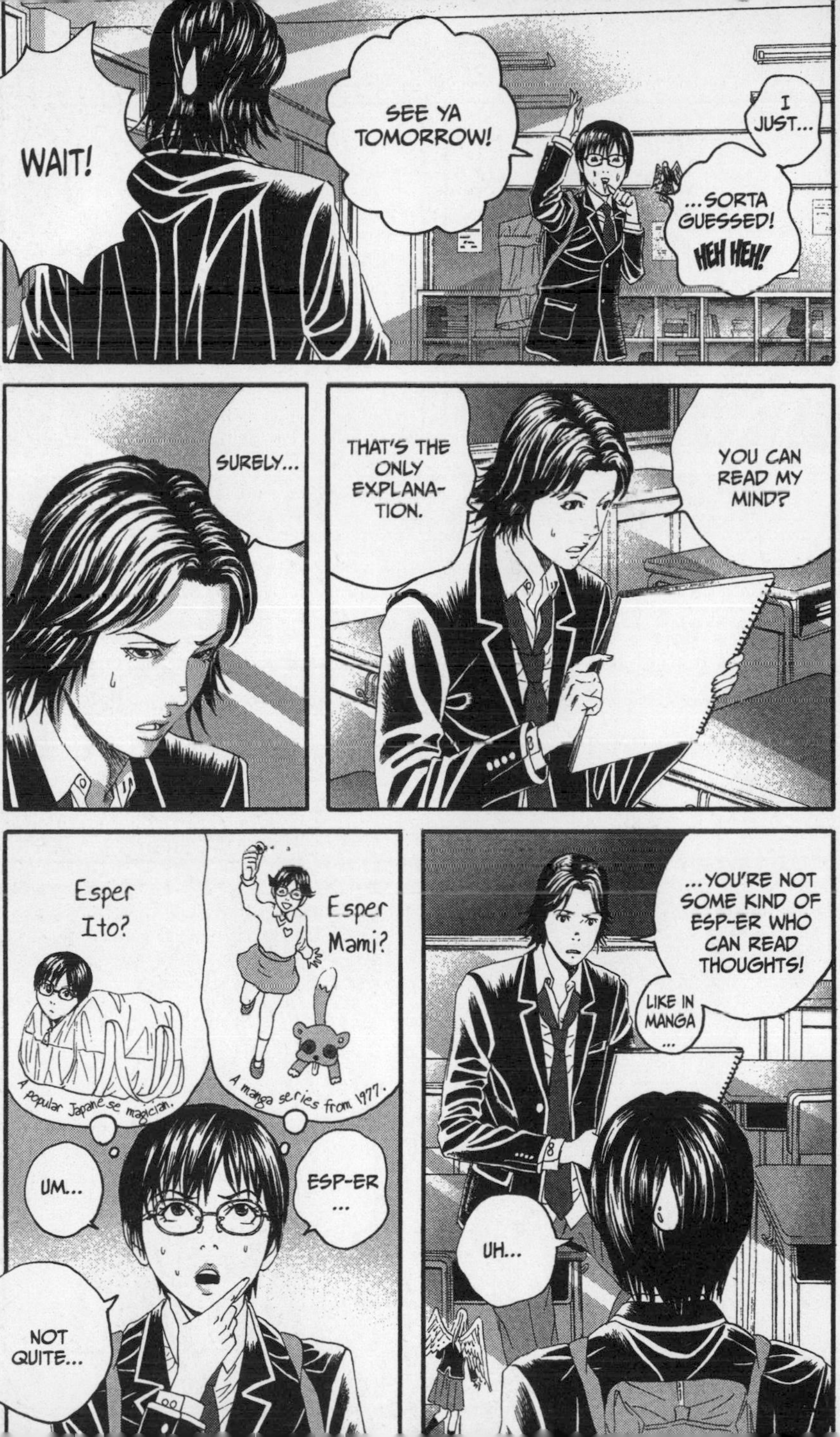
I JUST...
...SORTA GUESSED! HEH HEH!
SEE YA TOMORROW!
WAIT!
YOU CAN READ MY MIND?
THAT'S THE ONLY EXPLANATION.
SURELY...
...YOU'RE NOT SOME KIND OF ESP-ER WHO CAN READ THOUGHTS!
LIKE IN MANGA...
UH...
Esper Mami?
A manga series from 1977.
Esper Ito?
A popular Japanese magician.
ESP-ER...
UM...
NOT QUITE...

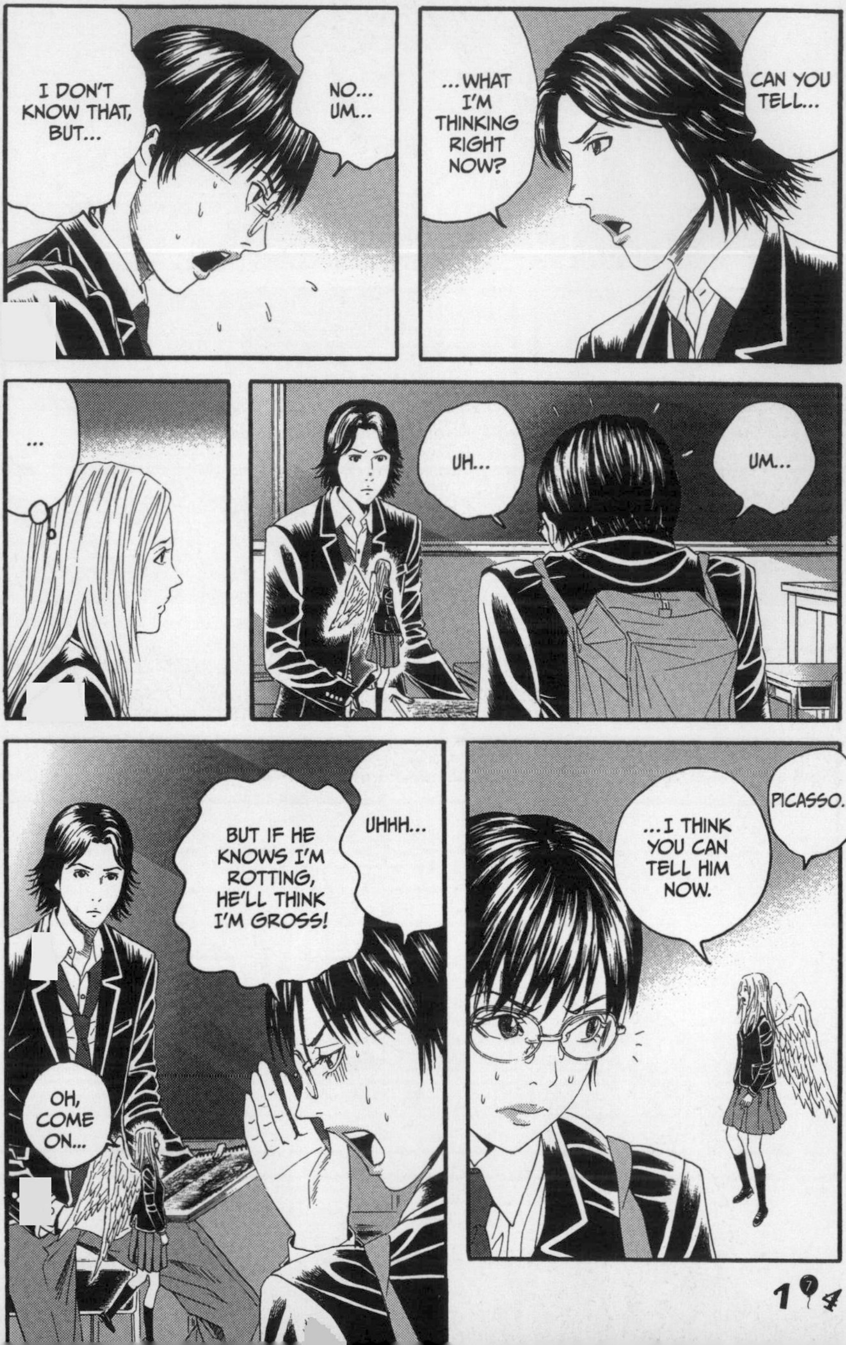
CAN YOU TELL...
...WHAT I'M THINKING RIGHT NOW?
NO... UM...
I DON'T KNOW THAT, BUT...
UM...
UH...
...
PICASSO...
...I THINK YOU CAN TELL HIM NOW.
UHHH...
BUT IF HE KNOWS I'M ROTTING, HE'LL THINK I'M GROSS!
OH, COME ON...

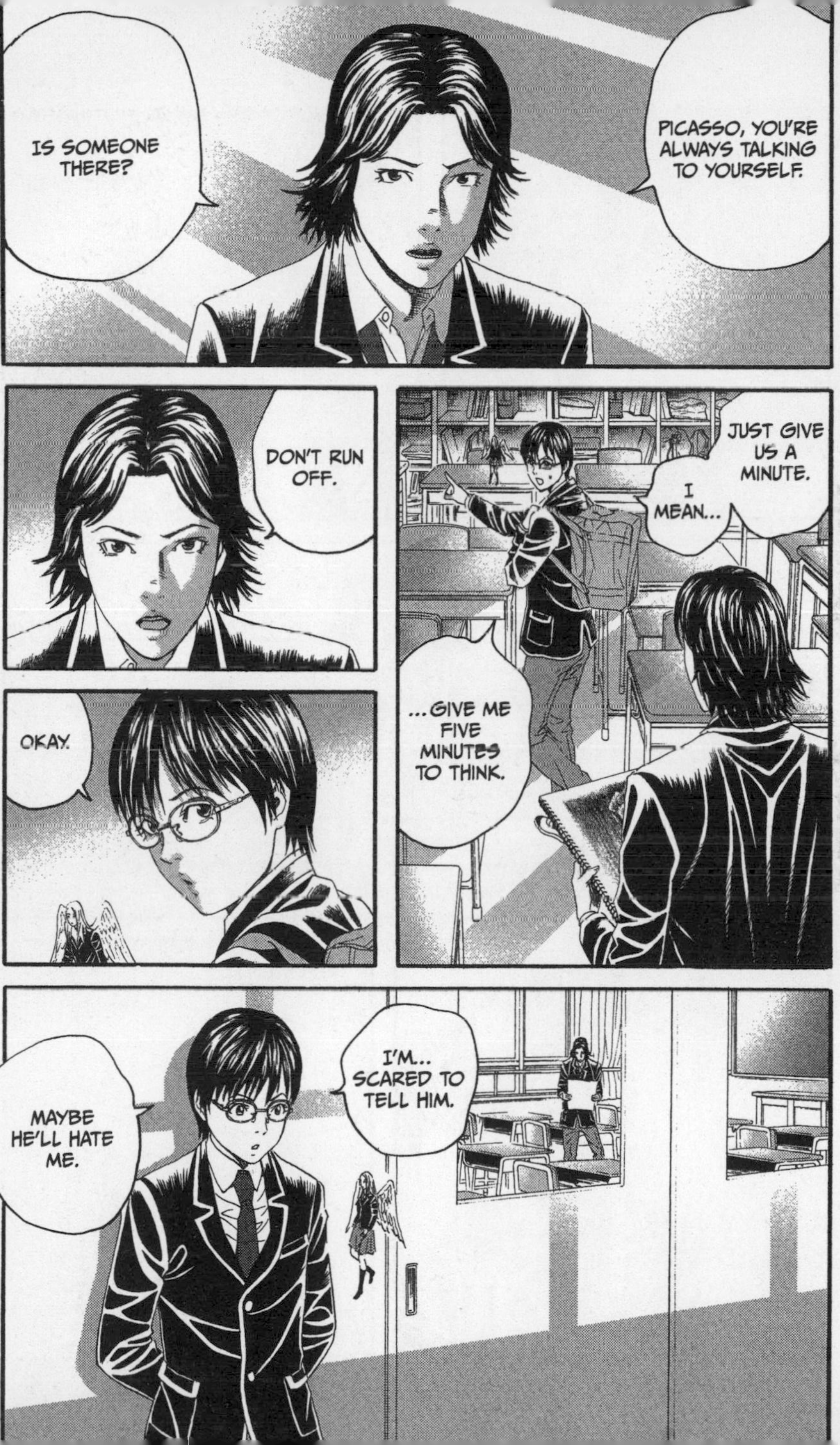
PICASSO, YOU'RE ALWAYS TALKING TO YOURSELF.
IS SOMEONE THERE?
JUST GIVE US A MINUTE.
I MEAN...
...GIVE ME FIVE MINUTES TO THINK.
DON'T RUN OFF.
OKAY.
I'M... SCARED TO TELL HIM.
MAYBE HE'LL HATE ME.

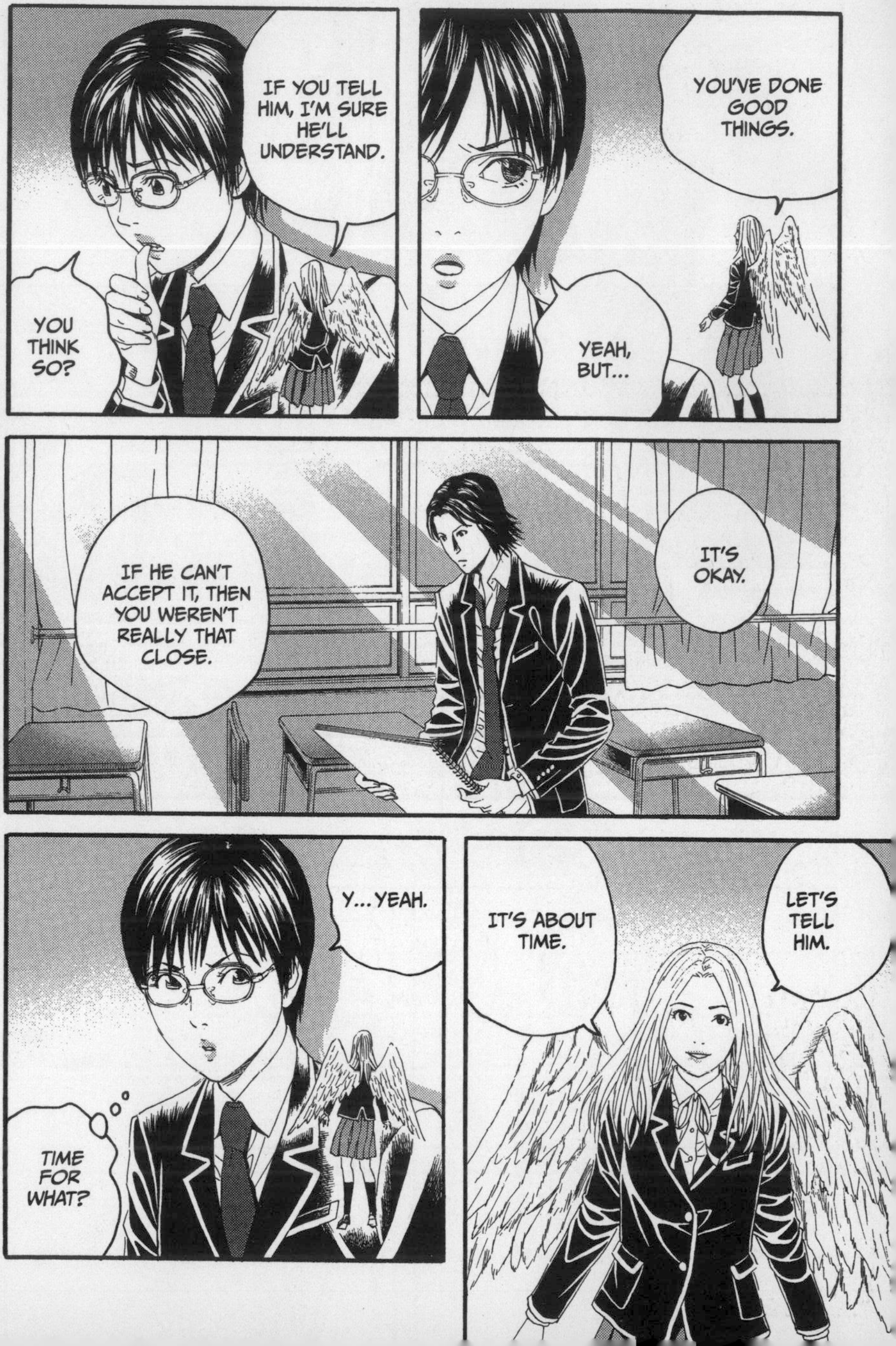
YOU'VE DONE GOOD THINGS.
YEAH, BUT...
IF YOU TELL HIM, I'M SURE HE'LL UNDERSTAND.
YOU THINK SO?
IT'S OKAY.
IF HE CAN'T ACCEPT IT, THEN YOU WEREN'T REALLY THAT CLOSE.
LET'S TELL HIM.
IT'S ABOUT TIME.
Y...YEAH.
TIME FOR WHAT?

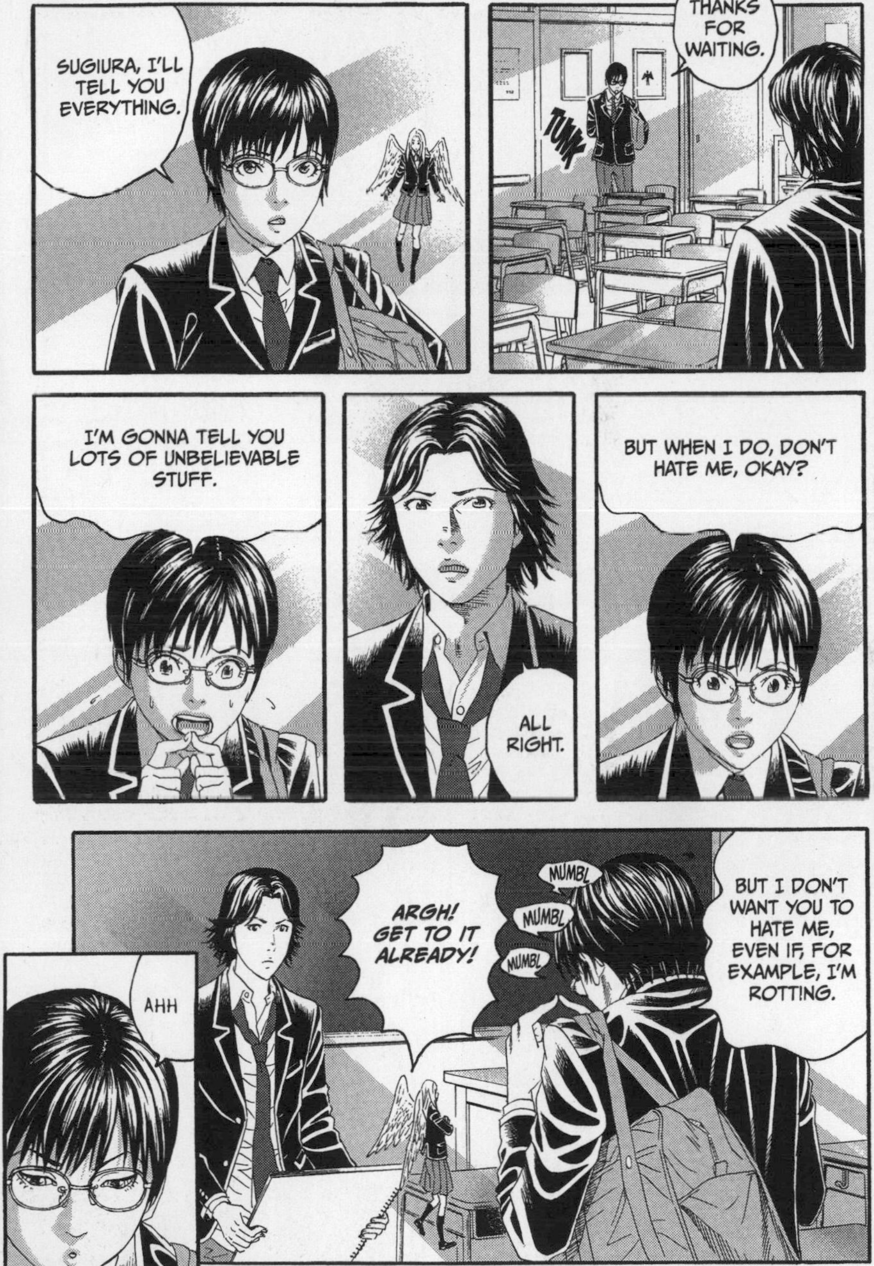
THANKS FOR WAITING.
TUNK
SUGIURA, I'LL TELL YOU EVERYTHING.
I'M GONNA TELL YOU LOTS OF UNBELIEVABLE STUFF.
ALL RIGHT.
BUT WHEN I DO, DON'T HATE ME, OKAY?
BUT I DON'T WANT YOU TO HATE ME, EVEN IF, FOR EXAMPLE, I'M ROTTING.
MUMBL
MUMBL
MUMBL
ARGH! GET TO IT ALREADY!
AHH

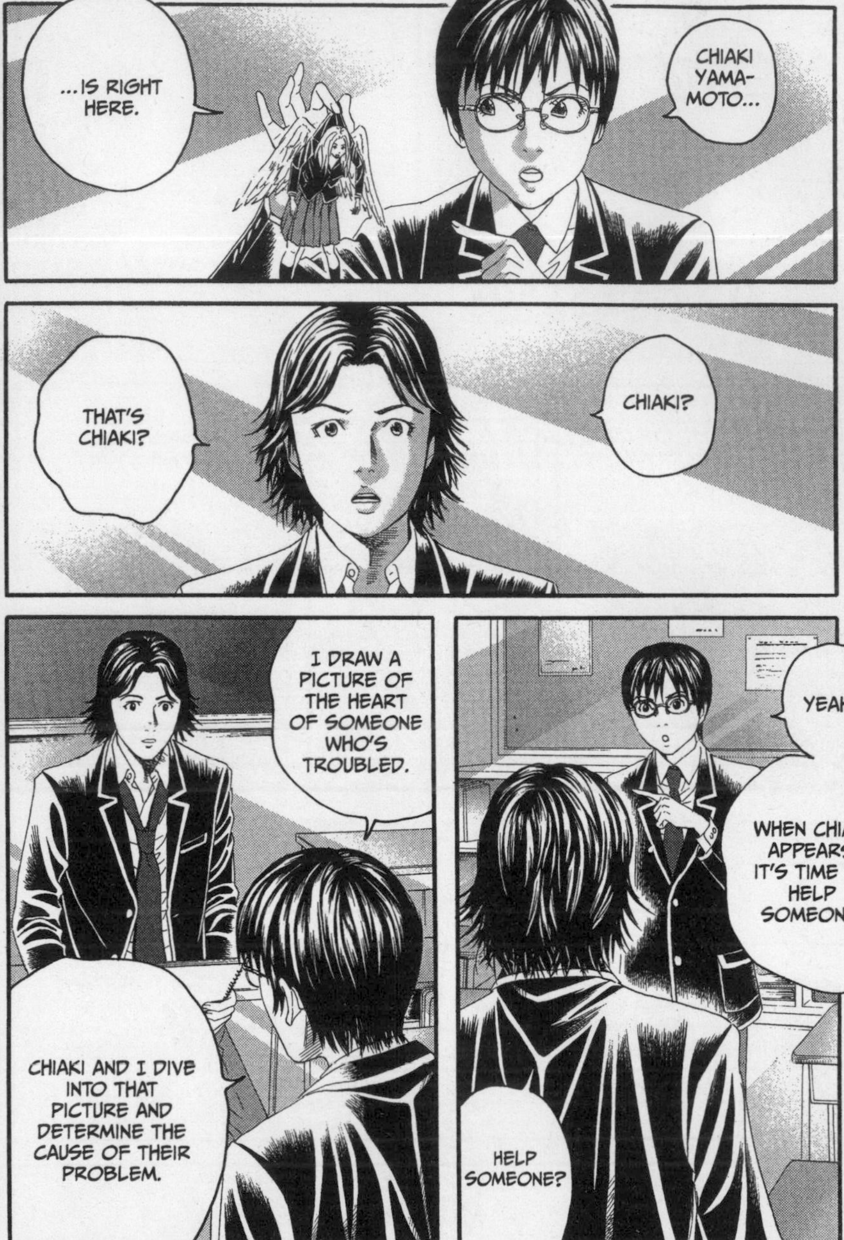
CHIAKI YAMAMOTO...
...IS RIGHT HERE.
CHIAKI?
THAT'S CHIAKI?
YEAH.
WHEN CHIAKI APPEARS, IT'S TIME TO HELP SOMEONE.
HELP SOMEONE?
I DRAW A PICTURE OF THE HEART OF SOMEONE WHO'S TROUBLED.
CHIAKI AND I DIVE INTO THAT PICTURE AND DETERMINE THE CAUSE OF THEIR PROBLEM.

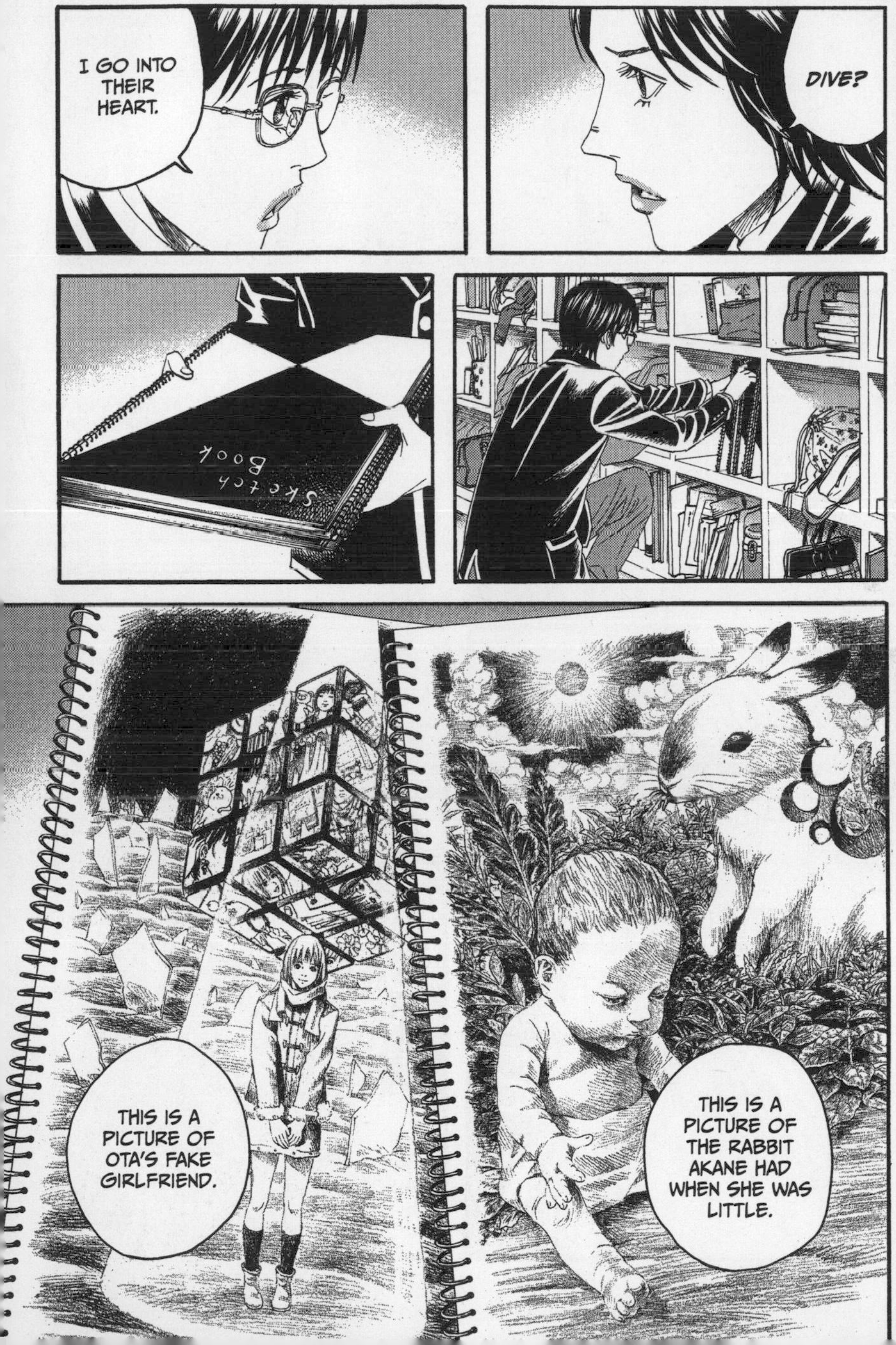
DIVE?
I GO INTO THEIR HEART.
Sketch Book
THIS IS A PICTURE OF THE RABBIT AKANE HAD WHEN SHE WAS LITTLE.
THIS IS A PICTURE OF OTA'S FAKE GIRLFRIEND.

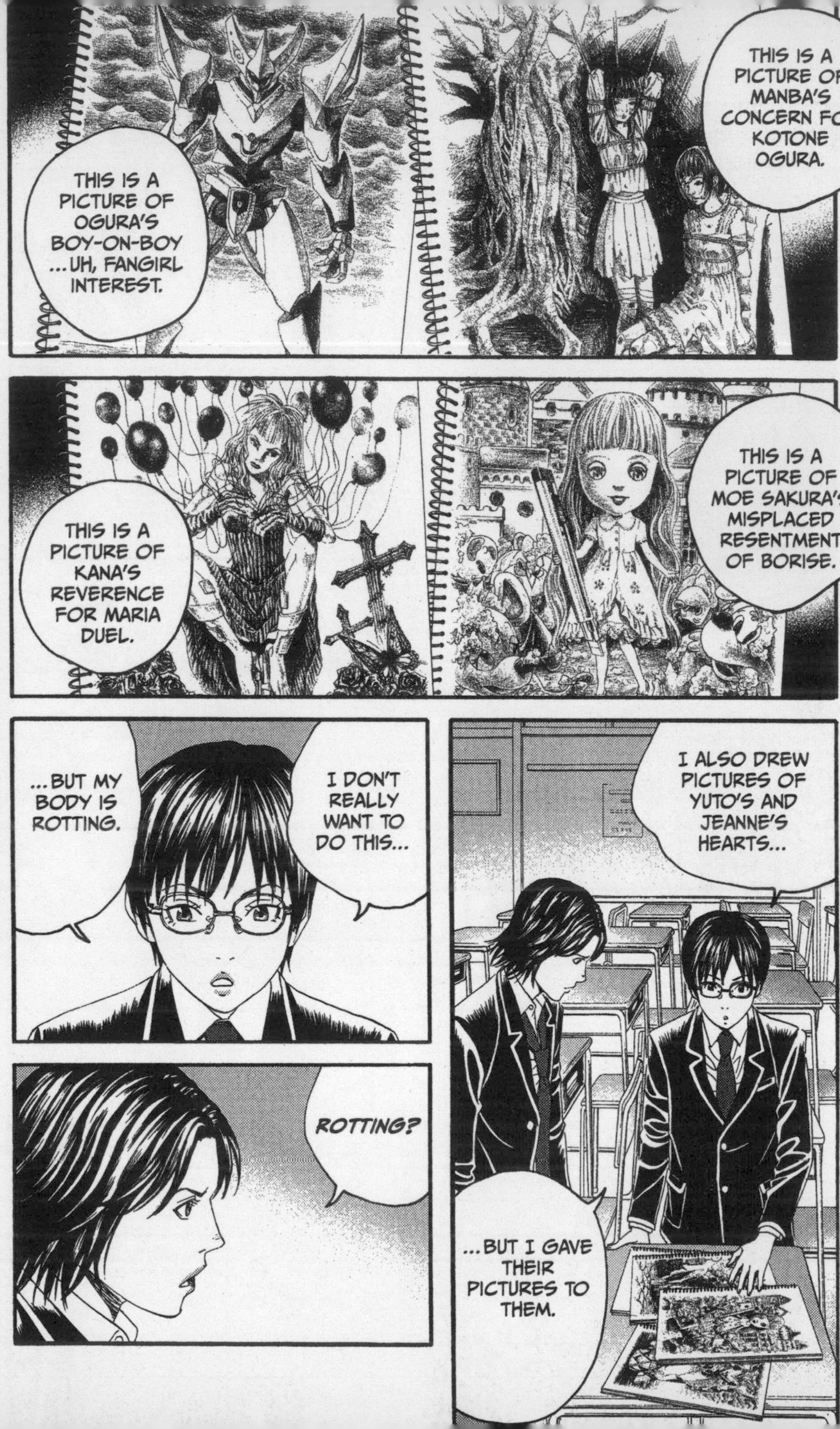
THIS IS A PICTURE OF MANBA'S CONCERN FOR KOTONE OGURA.
THIS IS A PICTURE OF OGURA'S BOY-ON-BOY ...UH, FANGIRL INTEREST.
THIS IS A PICTURE OF MOE SAKURA'S MISPLACED RESENTMENT OF BORISE.
THIS IS A PICTURE OF KANA'S REVERENCE FOR MARIA DUEL.
I ALSO DREW PICTURES OF YUTO'S AND JEANNE'S HEARTS...
...BUT I GAVE THEIR PICTURES TO THEM.
I DON'T REALLY WANT TO DO THIS...
...BUT MY BODY IS ROTTING.
ROTTING?

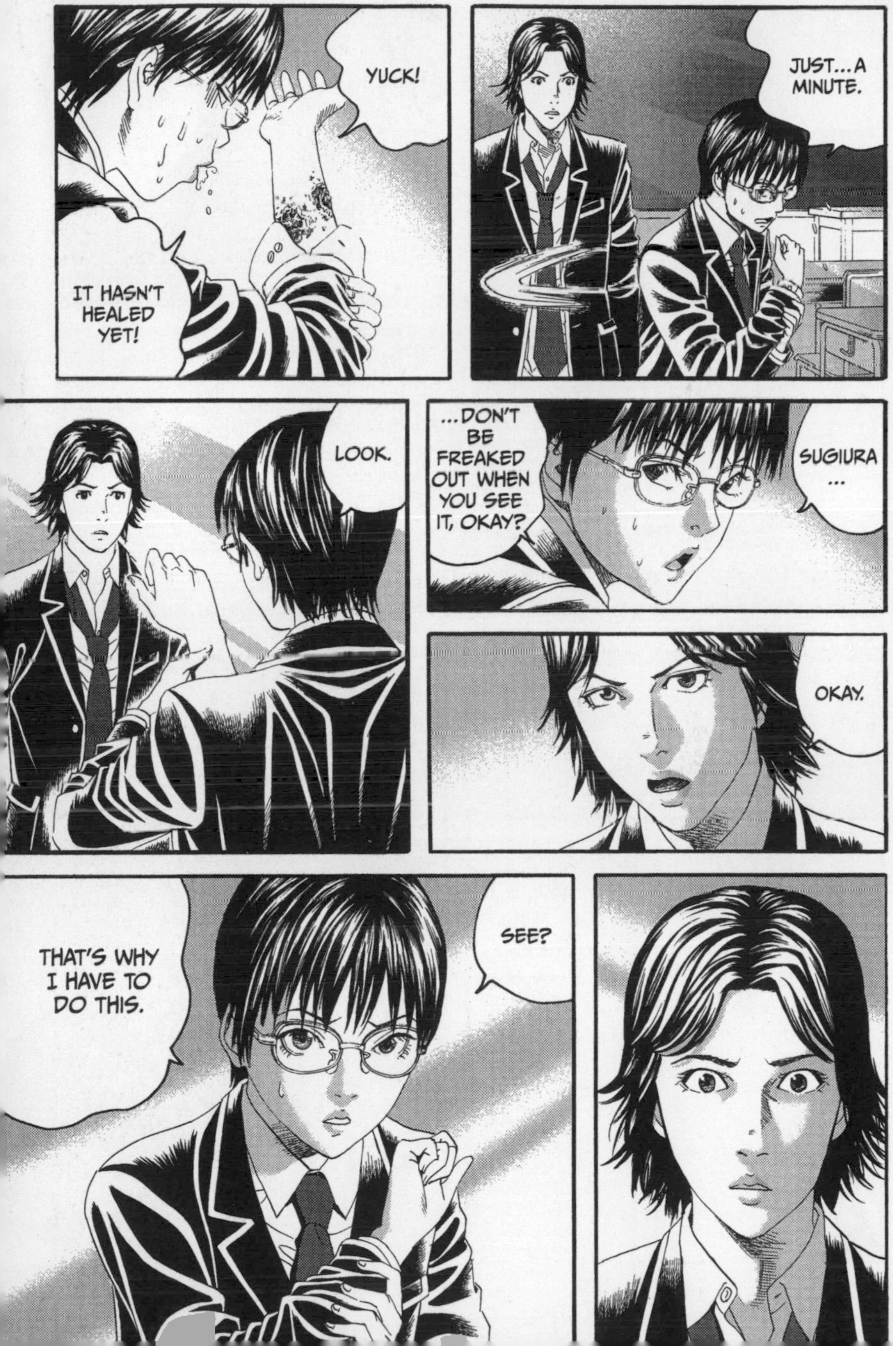
JUST... A MINUTE.
YUCK!
IT HASN'T HEALED YET!
SUGIURA ...
...DON'T BE FREAKED OUT WHEN YOU SEE IT, OKAY?
OKAY.
LOOK.
SEE?
THAT'S WHY I HAVE TO DO THIS.

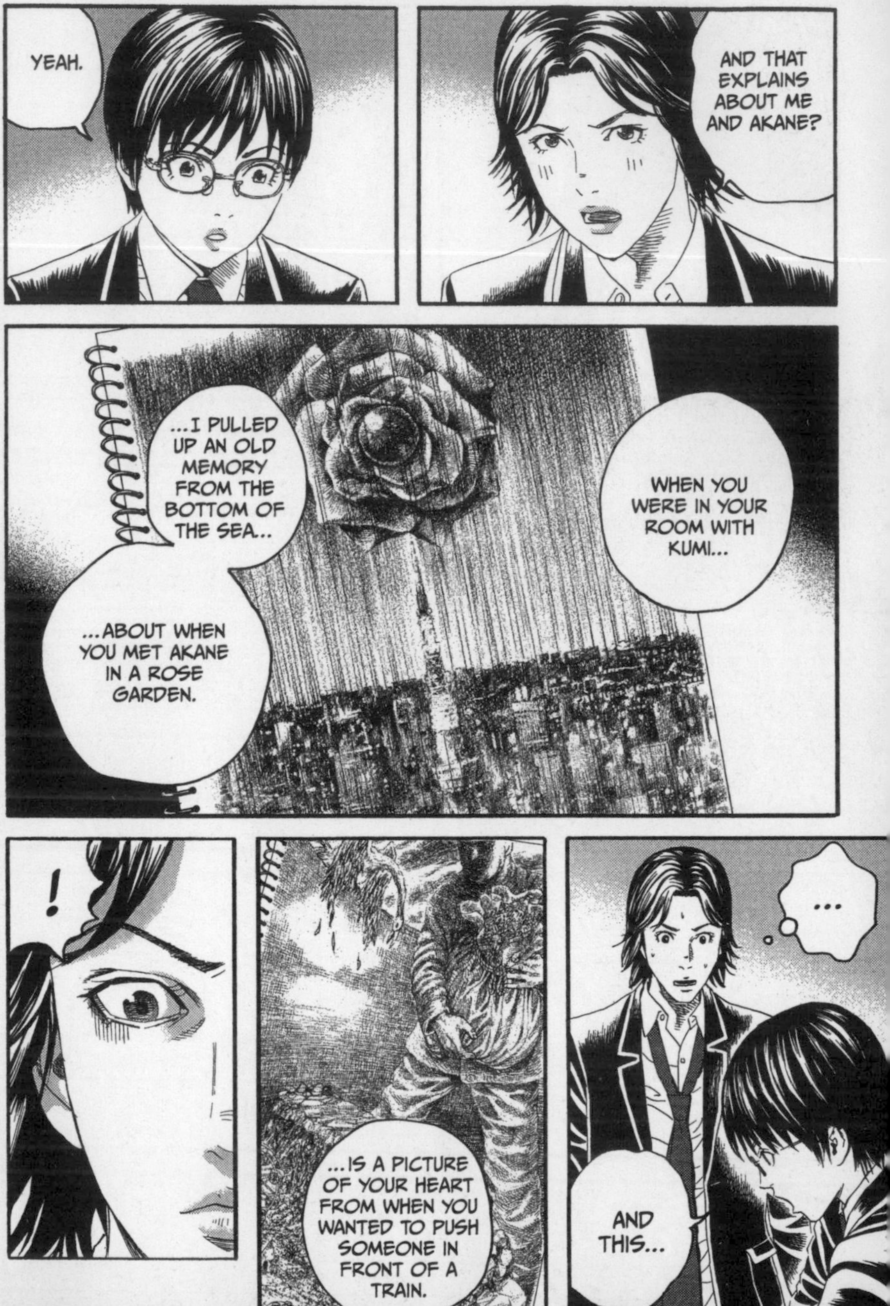
AND THAT EXPLAINS ABOUT ME AND AKANE?
YEAH.
WHEN YOU WERE IN YOUR ROOM WITH KUMI...
...I PULLED UP AN OLD MEMORY FROM THE BOTTOM OF THE SEA...
...ABOUT WHEN YOU MET AKANE IN A ROSE GARDEN.
...
AND THIS...
...IS A PICTURE OF YOUR HEART FROM WHEN YOU WANTED TO PUSH SOMEONE IN FRONT OF A TRAIN.
!

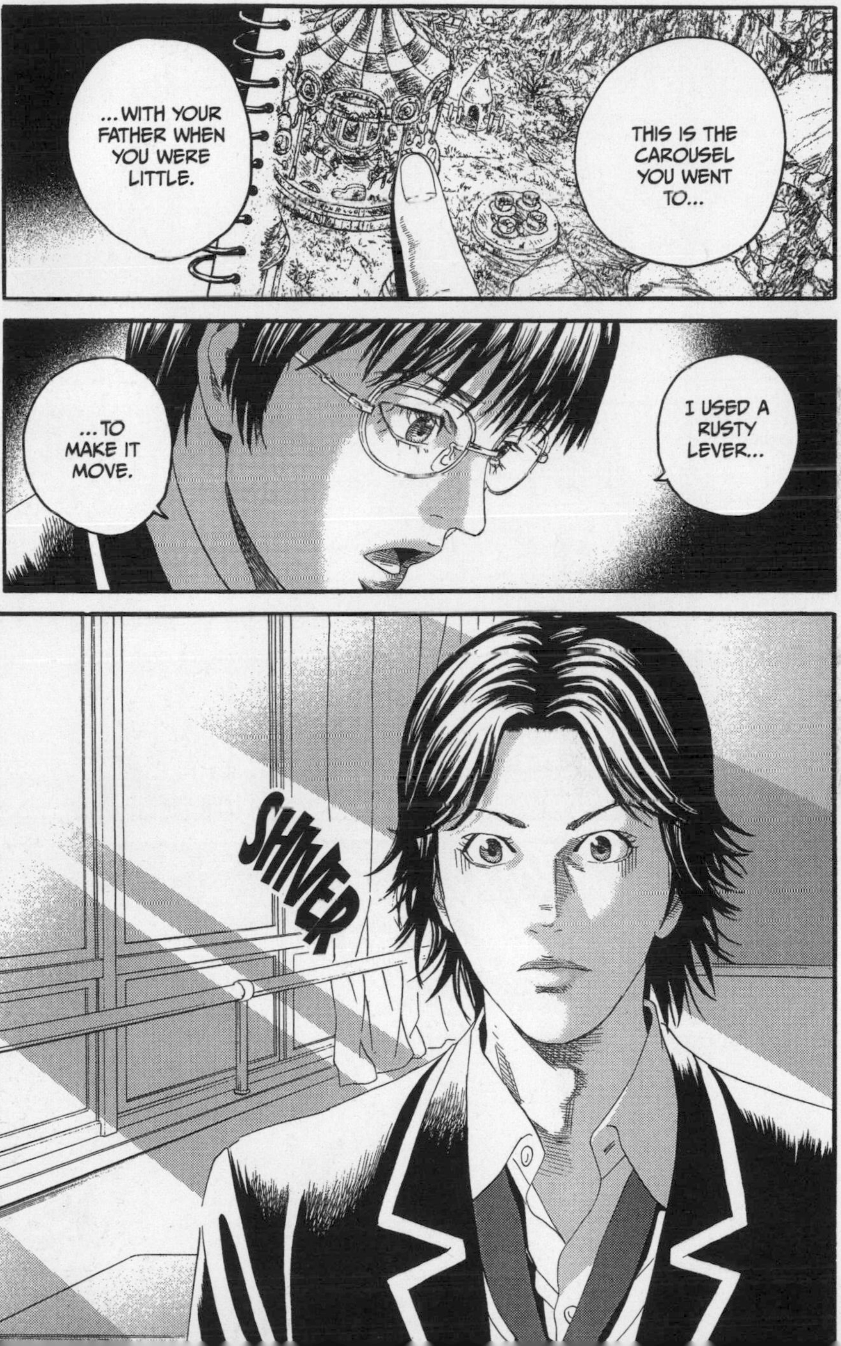
THIS IS THE CAROUSEL YOU WENT TO...
...WITH YOUR FATHER WHEN YOU WERE LITTLE.
I USED A RUSTY LEVER...
...TO MAKE IT MOVE.
SHIVER

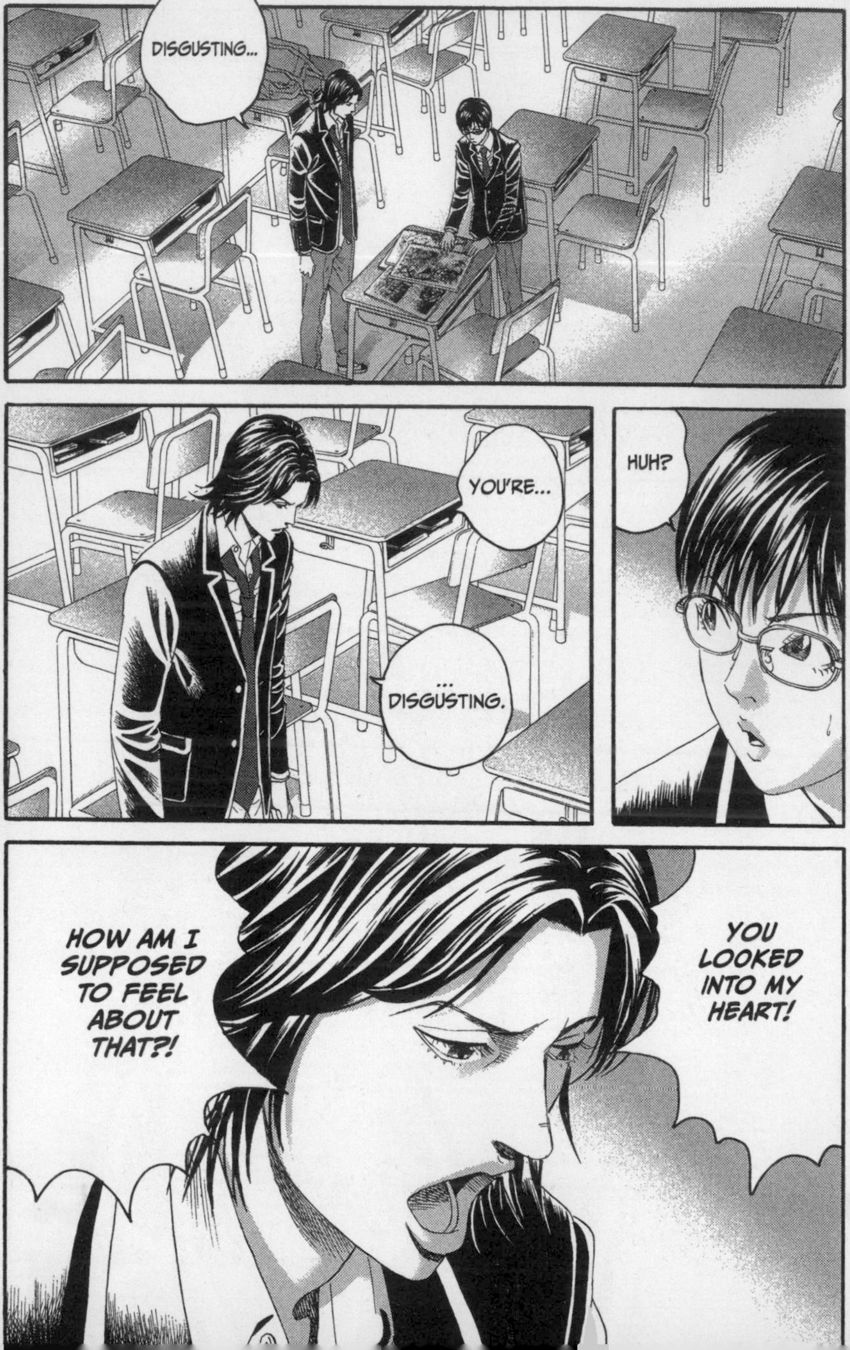
DISGUSTING...
HUH?
YOU'RE...
... DISGUSTING.
YOU LOOKED INTO MY HEART!
HOW AM I SUPPOSED TO FEEL ABOUT THAT?!

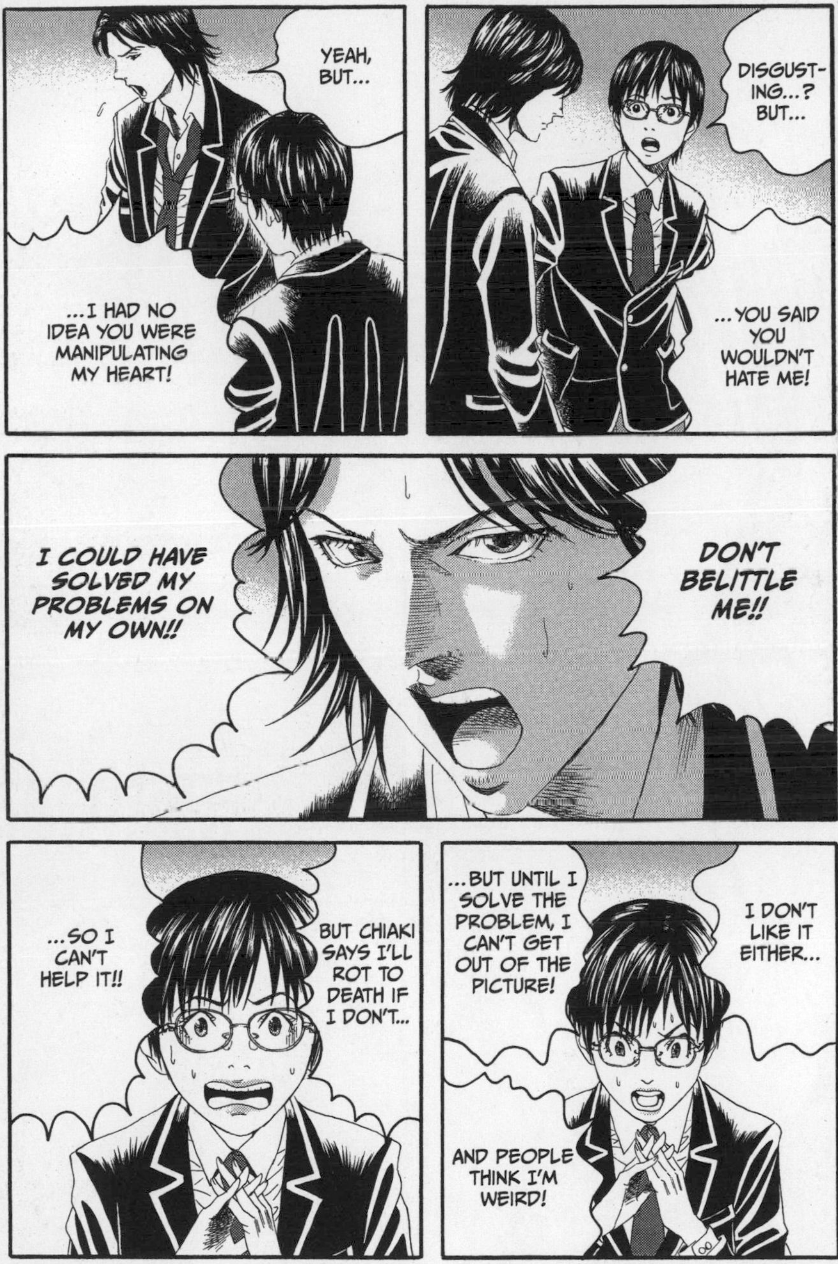
DISGUSTING...? BUT...
...YOU SAID YOU WOULDN'T HATE ME!
YEAH, BUT...
...I HAD NO IDEA YOU WERE MANIPULATING MY HEART!
DON'T BELITTLE ME!!
I COULD HAVE SOLVED MY PROBLEMS ON MY OWN!!
I DON'T LIKE IT EITHER...
...BUT UNTIL I SOLVE THE PROBLEM, I CAN'T GET OUT OF THE PICTURE!
AND PEOPLE THINK I'M WEIRD!
BUT CHIAKI SAYS I'LL ROT TO DEATH IF I DON'T...
...SO I CAN'T HELP IT!!

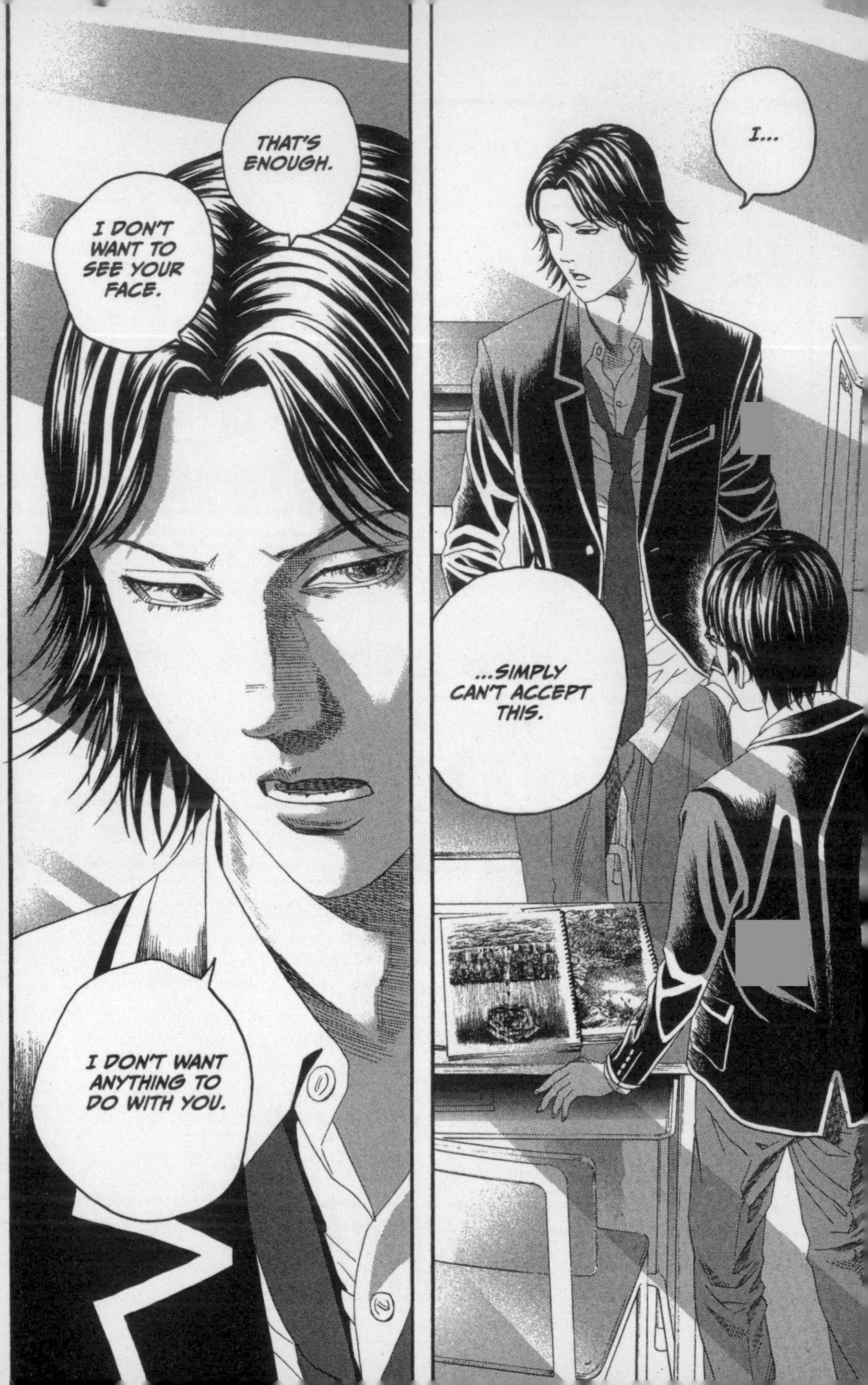
I...
...SIMPLY CAN'T ACCEPT THIS.
THAT'S ENOUGH.
I DON'T WANT TO SEE YOUR FACE.
I DON'T WANT ANYTHING TO DO WITH YOU.

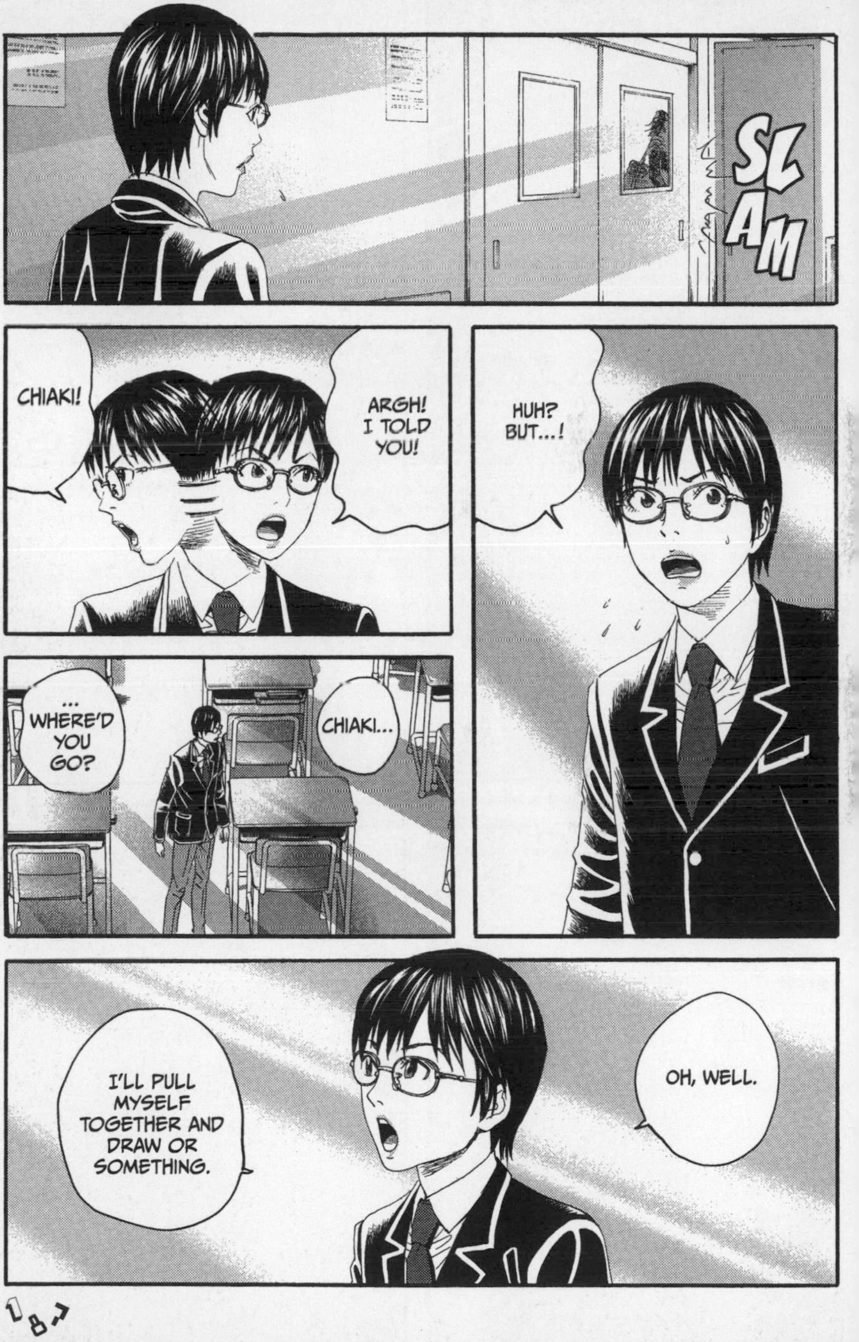
SLAM
HUH? BUT...!
ARGH! I TOLD YOU!
CHIAKI!
CHIAKI...
... WHERE'D YOU GO?
OH, WELL.
I'LL PULL MYSELF TOGETHER AND DRAW OR SOMETHING.

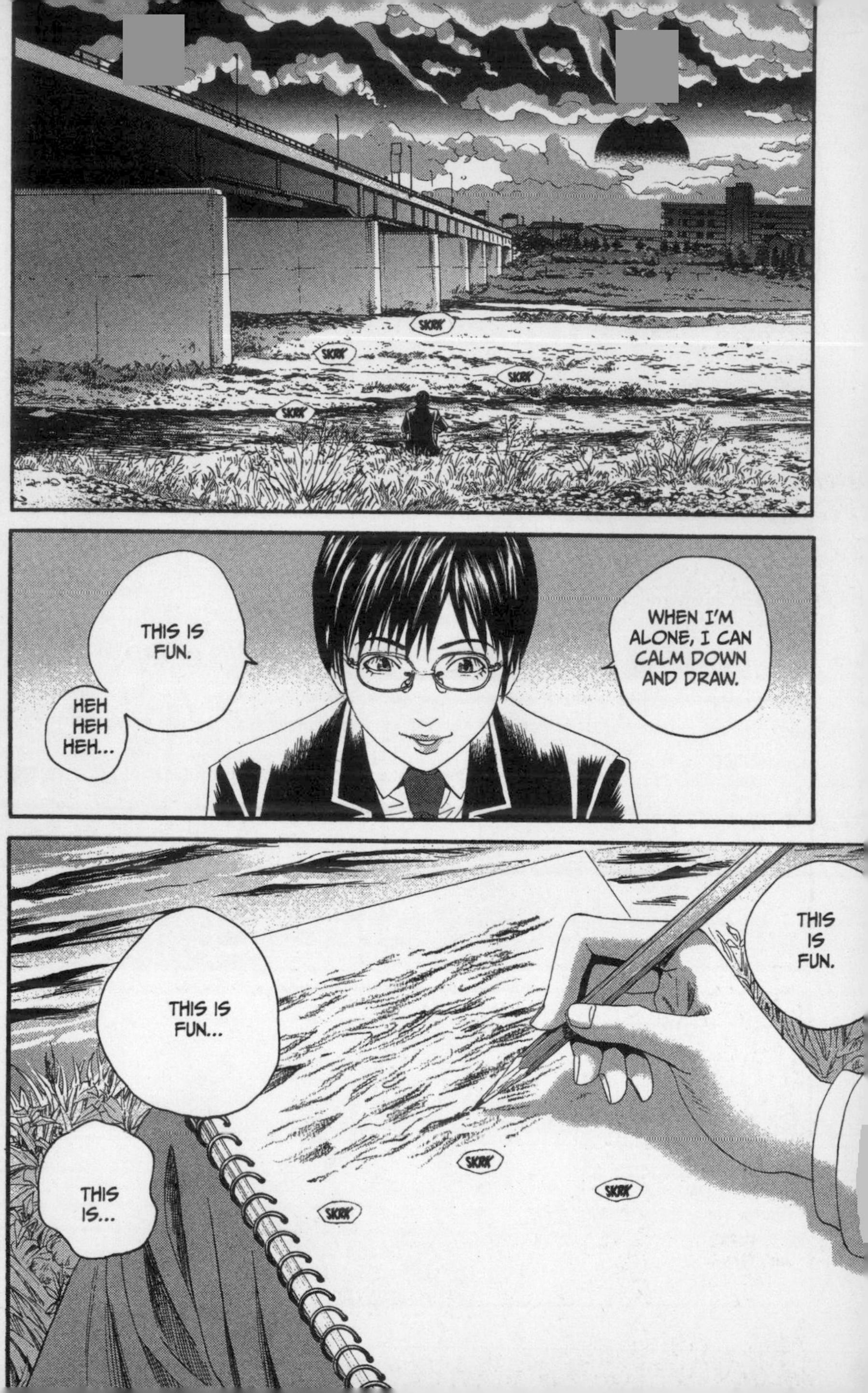
SKRK
SKRK
SKRK
SKRK
WHEN I'M ALONE, I CAN CALM DOWN AND DRAW.
THIS IS FUN.
HEH HEH HEH...
THIS IS FUN.
THIS IS FUN...
THIS IS...
SKRK
SKRK
SKRK

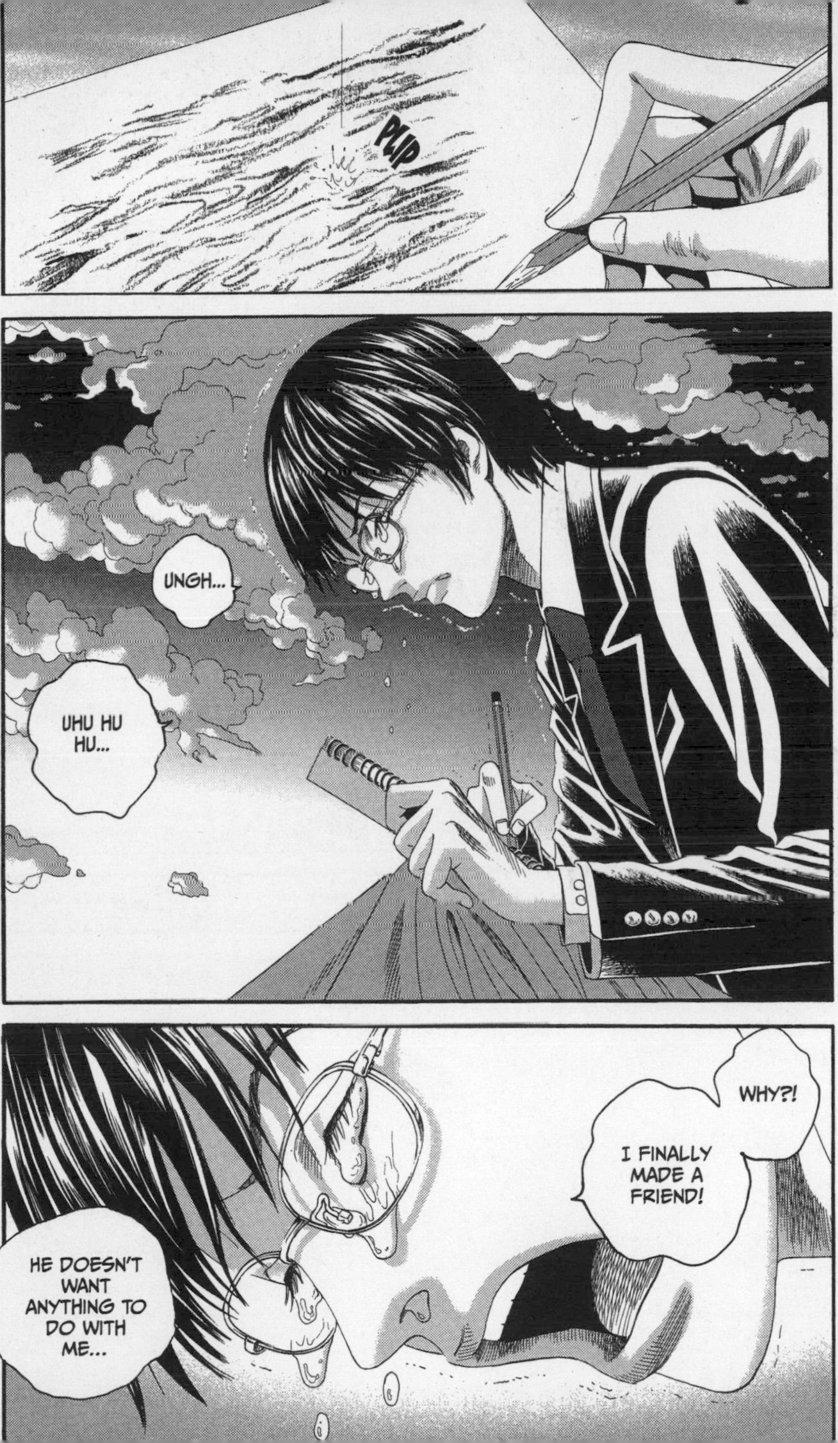
PLIP
UNGH...
UHU HU HU...
WHY?!
I FINALLY MADE A FRIEND!
HE DOESN'T WANT ANYTHING TO DO WITH ME...

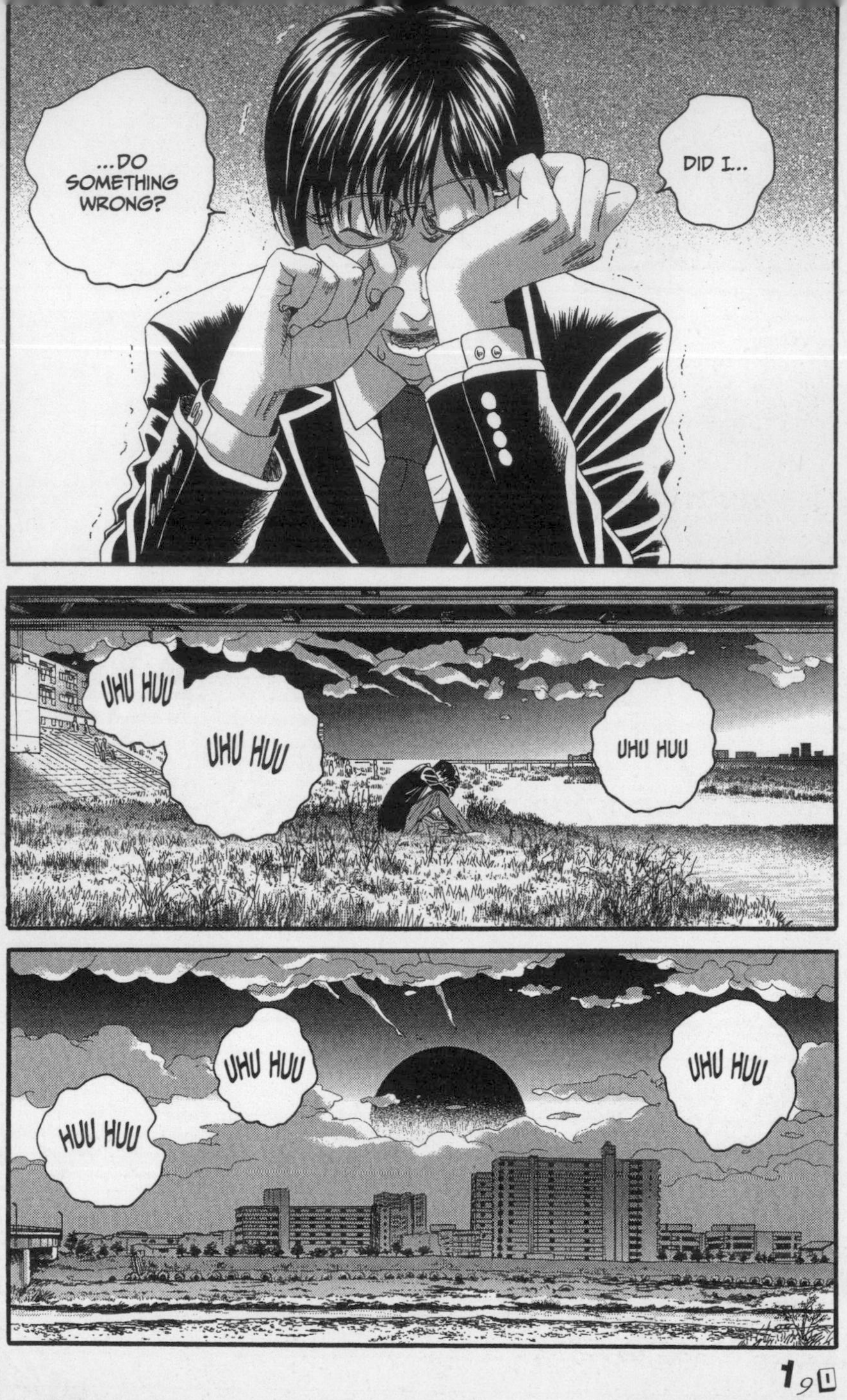
DID I...
...DO SOMETHING WRONG?
UHU HUU
UHU HUU
UHU HUU
UHU HUU
UHU HUU
HUU HUU

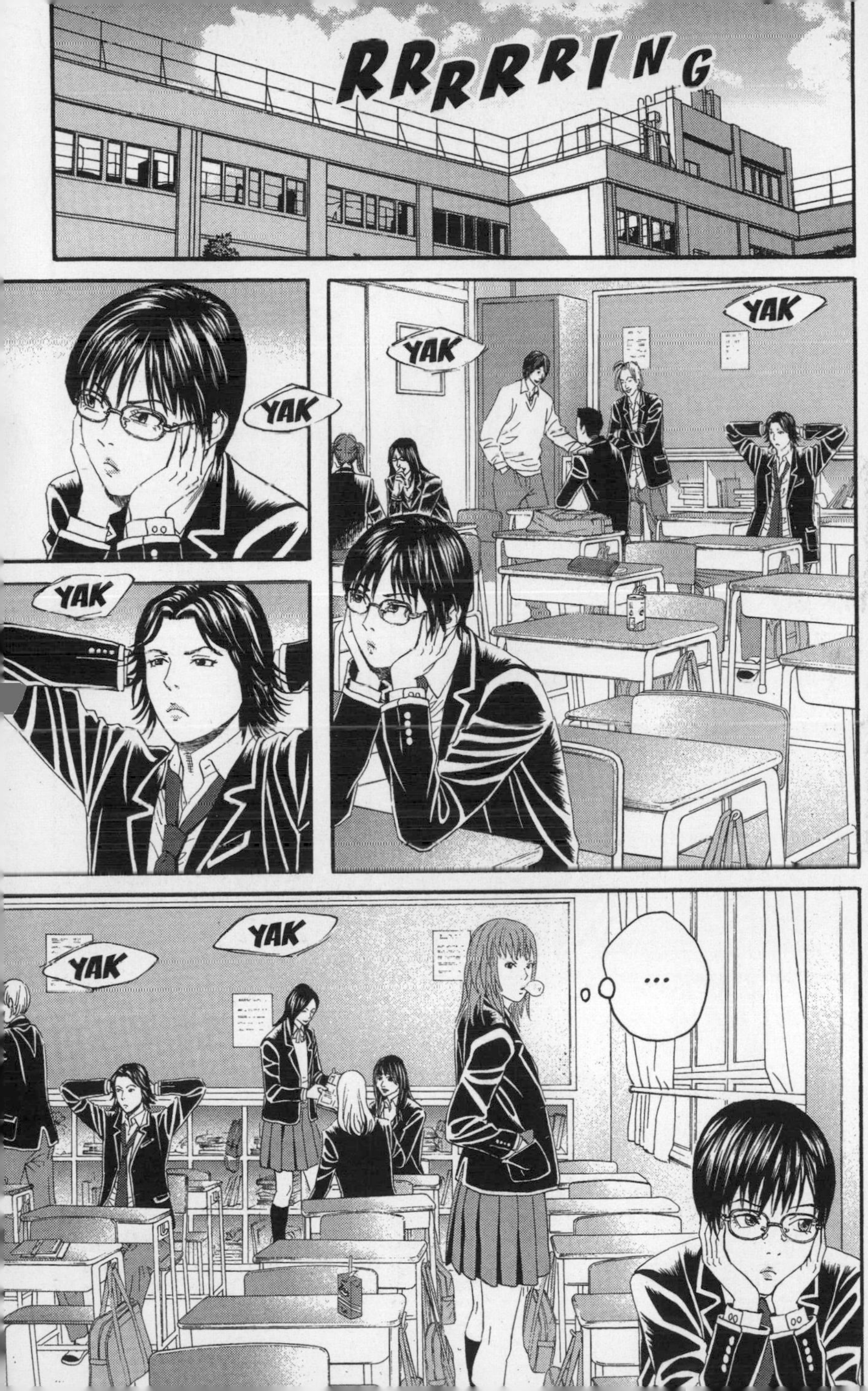
RRRRRING
YAK
YAK
YAK
YAK
...
YAK
YAK

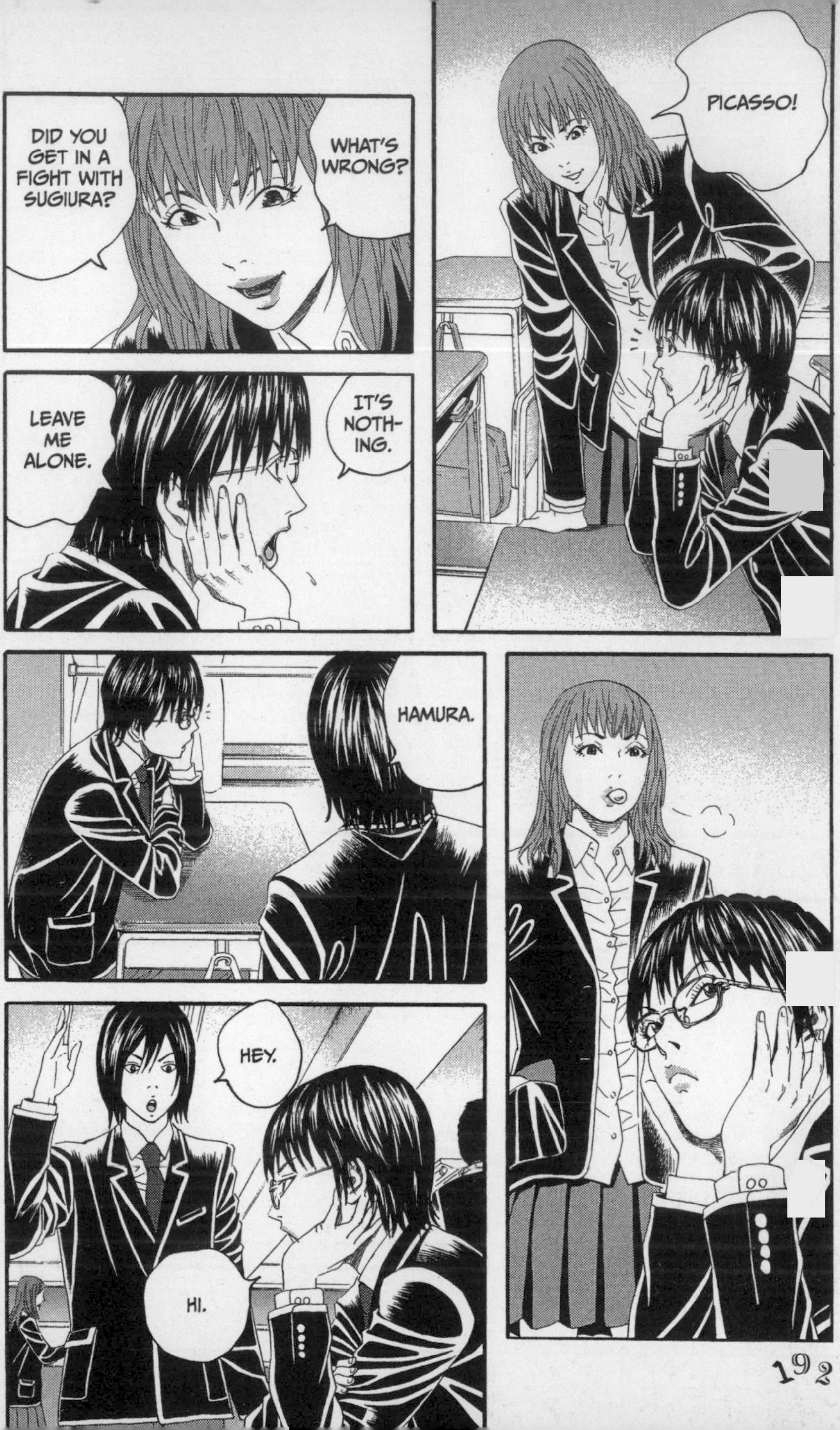
PICASSO!
WHAT'S WRONG?
DID YOU GET IN A FIGHT WITH SUGIURA?
IT'S NOTH-ING.
LEAVE ME ALONE.
HAMURA.
HEY.
HI.

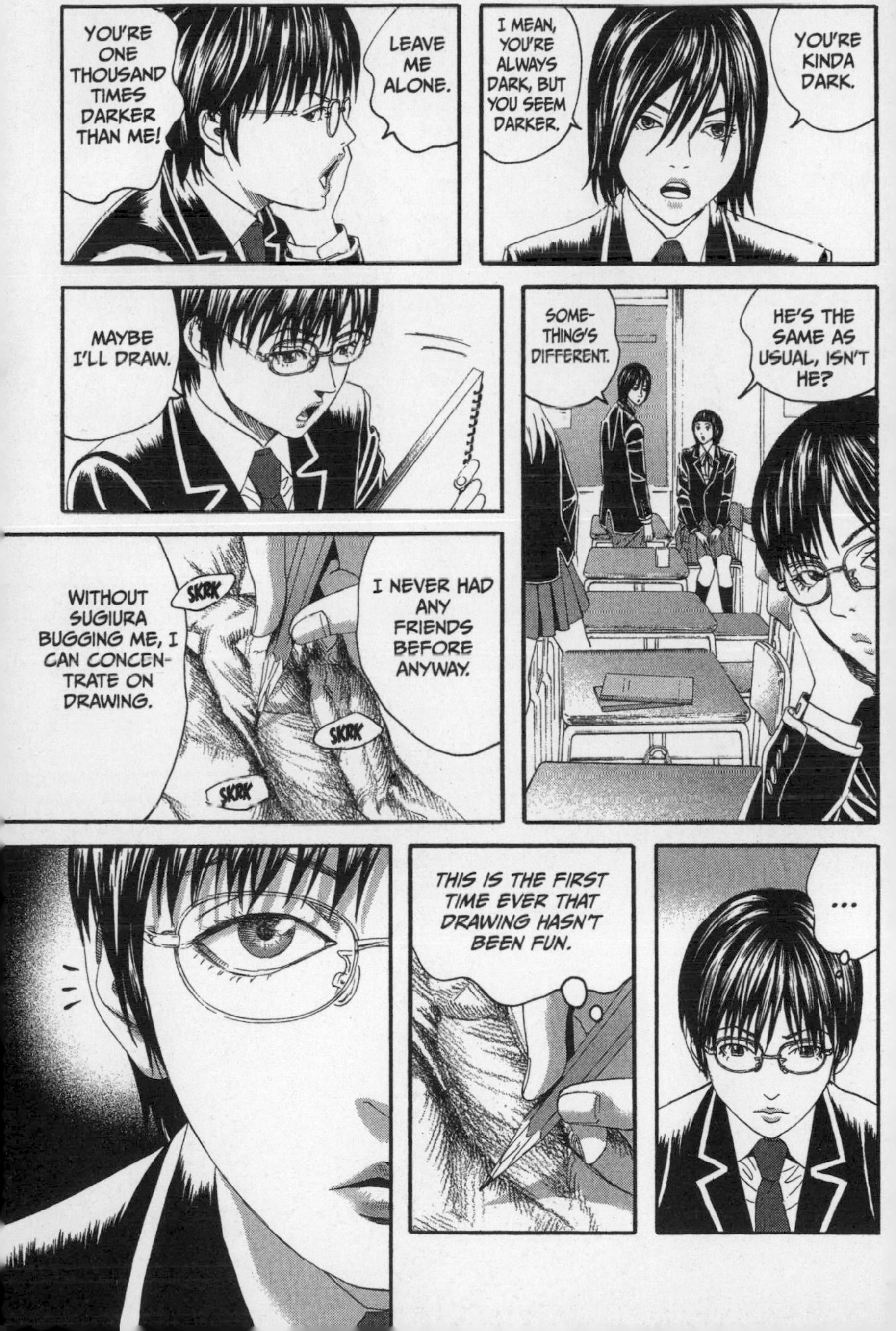
YOU'RE KINDA DARK.
I MEAN, YOU'RE ALWAYS DARK, BUT YOU SEEM DARKER.
LEAVE ME ALONE.
YOU'RE ONE THOUSAND TIMES DARKER THAN ME!
HE'S THE SAME AS USUAL, ISN'T HE?
SOME-THING'S DIFFERENT.
MAYBE I'LL DRAW.
I NEVER HAD ANY FRIENDS BEFORE ANYWAY.
SKRK
WITHOUT SUGIURA BUGGING ME, I CAN CONCEN-TRATE ON DRAWING.
SKRK
SKRK
...
THIS IS THE FIRST TIME EVER THAT DRAWING HASN'T BEEN FUN.

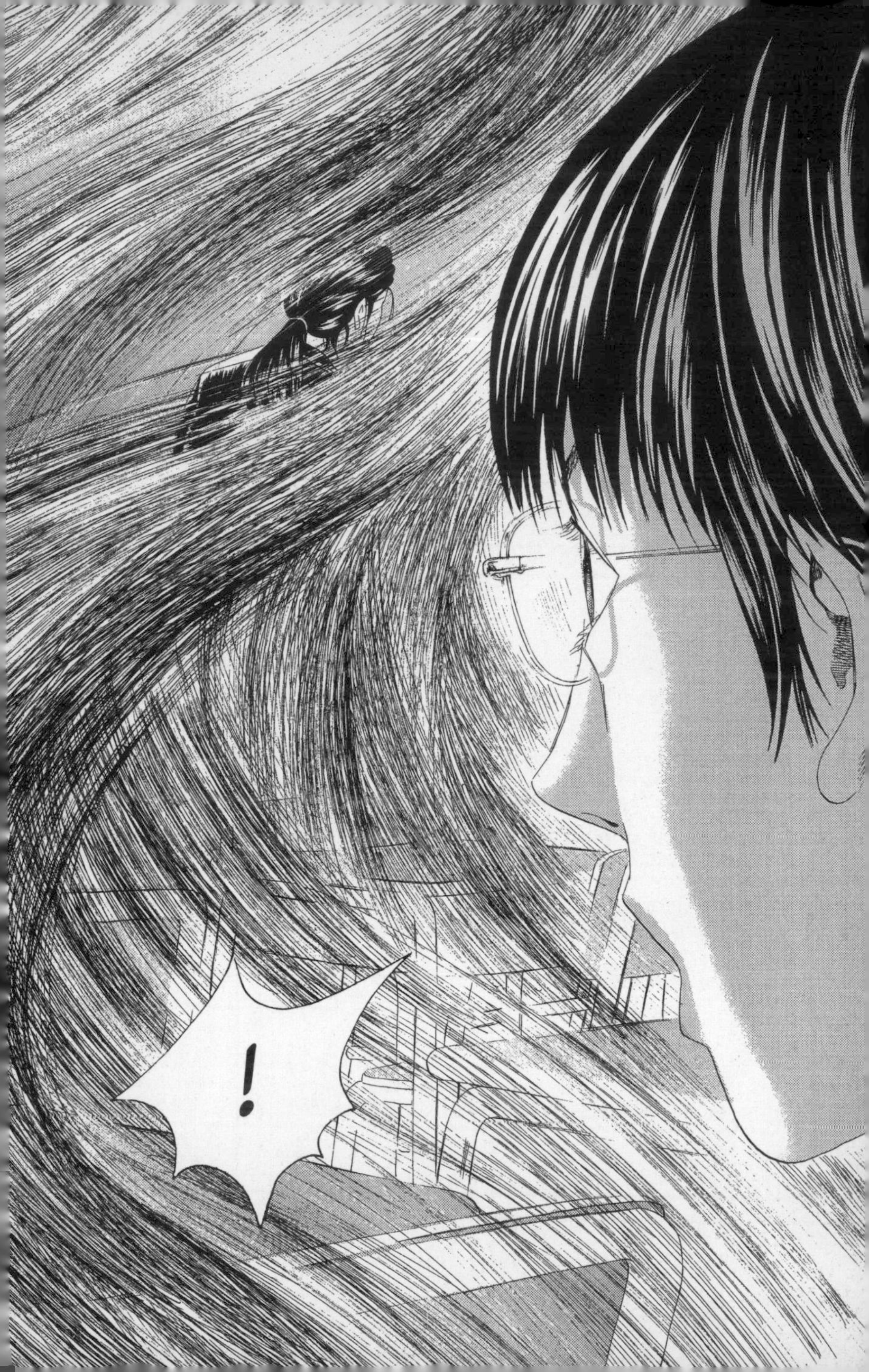
!

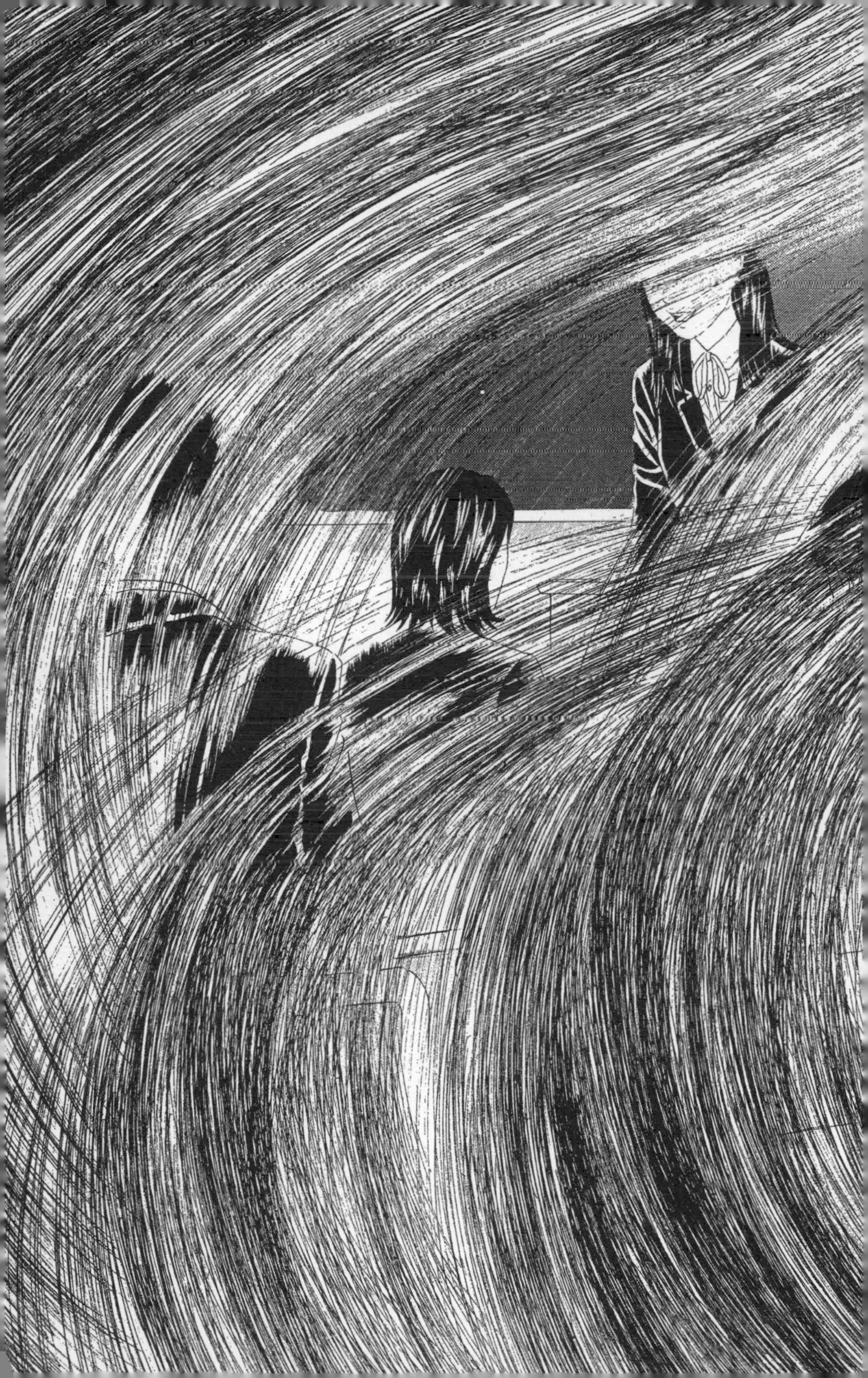

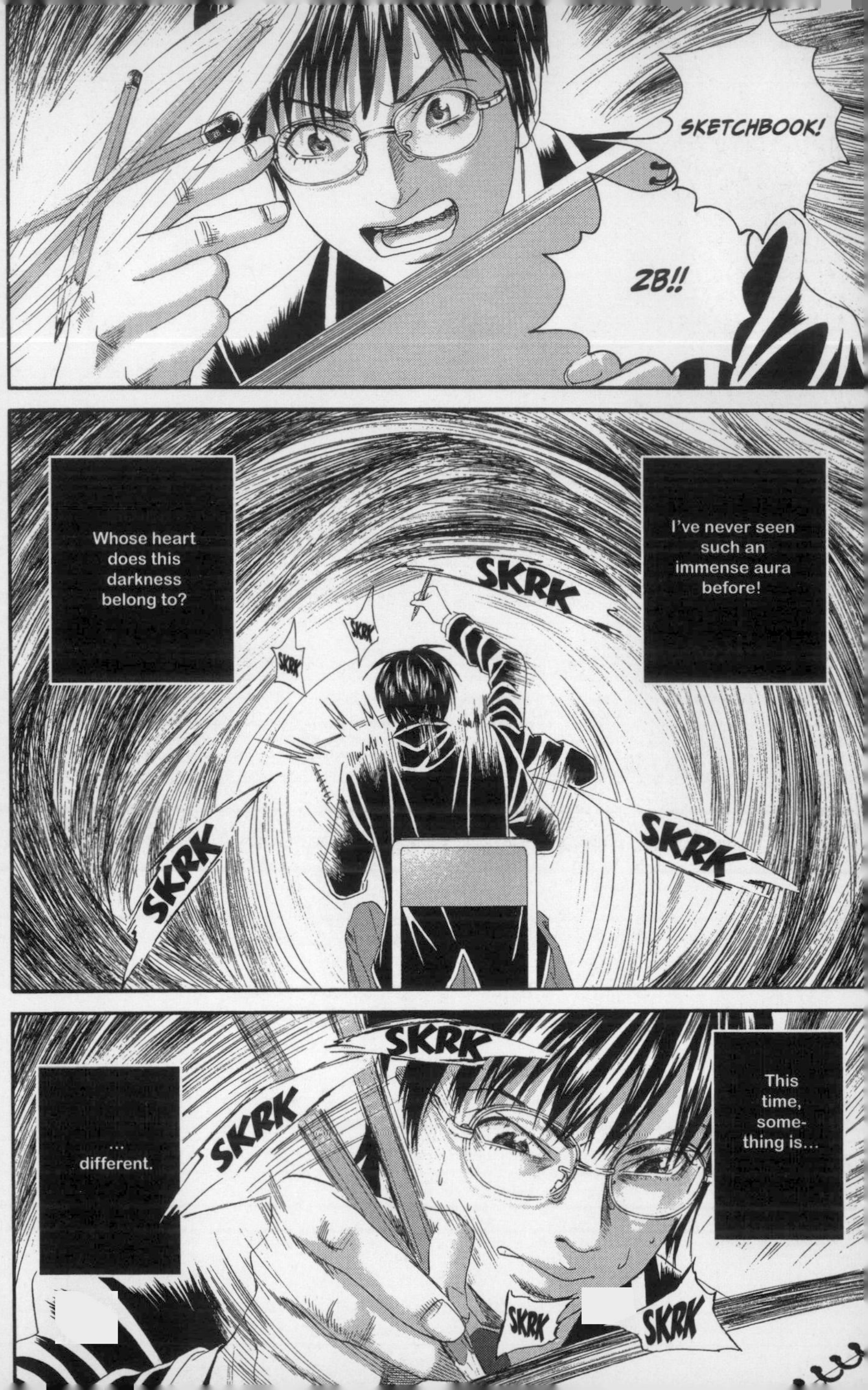
SKETCHBOOK!
2B!!
I've never seen such an immense aura before!
SKRK
SKRK
SKRK
Whose heart does this darkness belong to?
SKRK
SKRK
This time, something is…
SKRK
SKRK
… different.
SKRK
SKRK

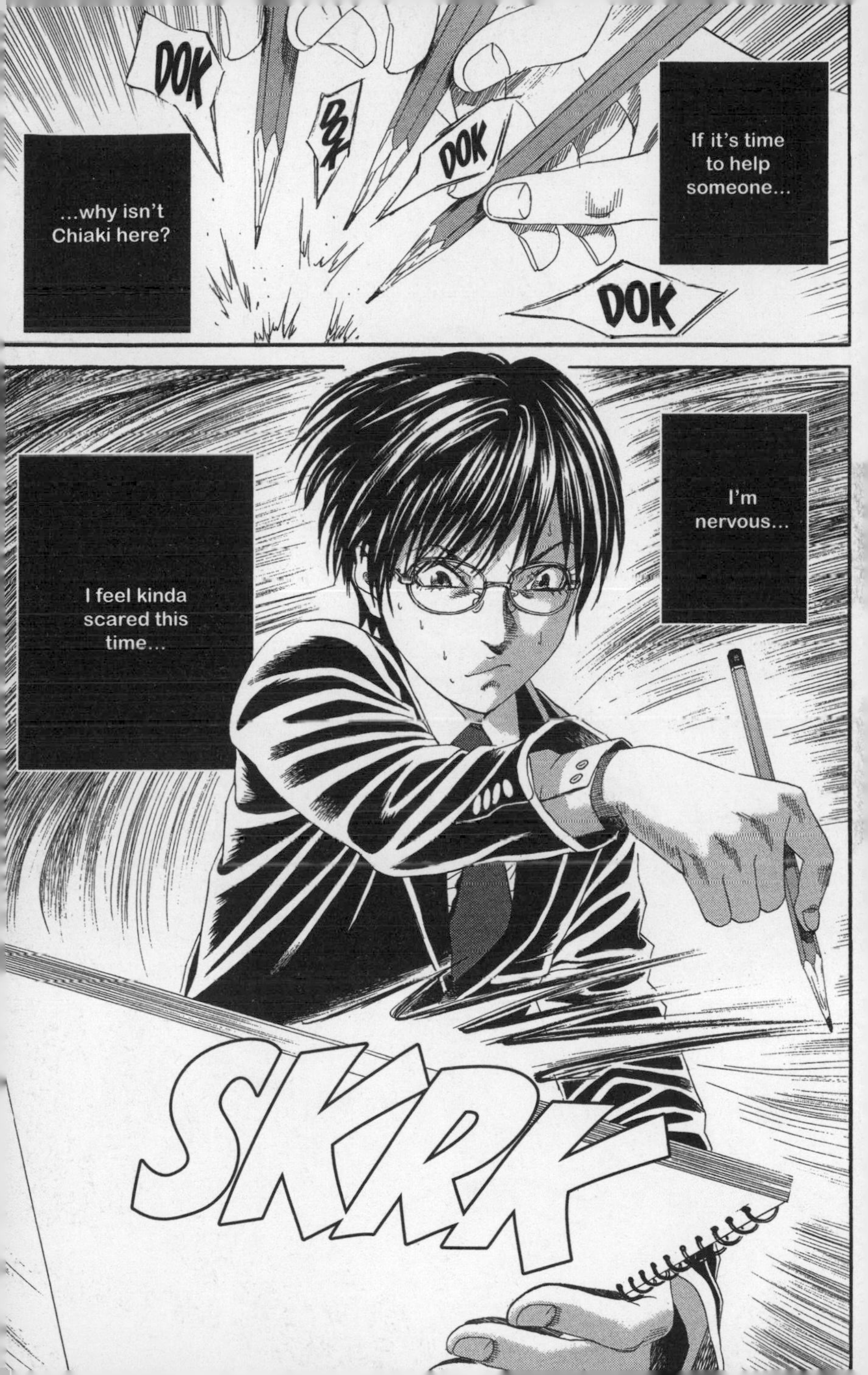
If it's time to help someone...
DOK
DOK
DOK
DOK
...why isn't Chiaki here?
I'm nervous...
I feel kinda scared this time...
SKRK

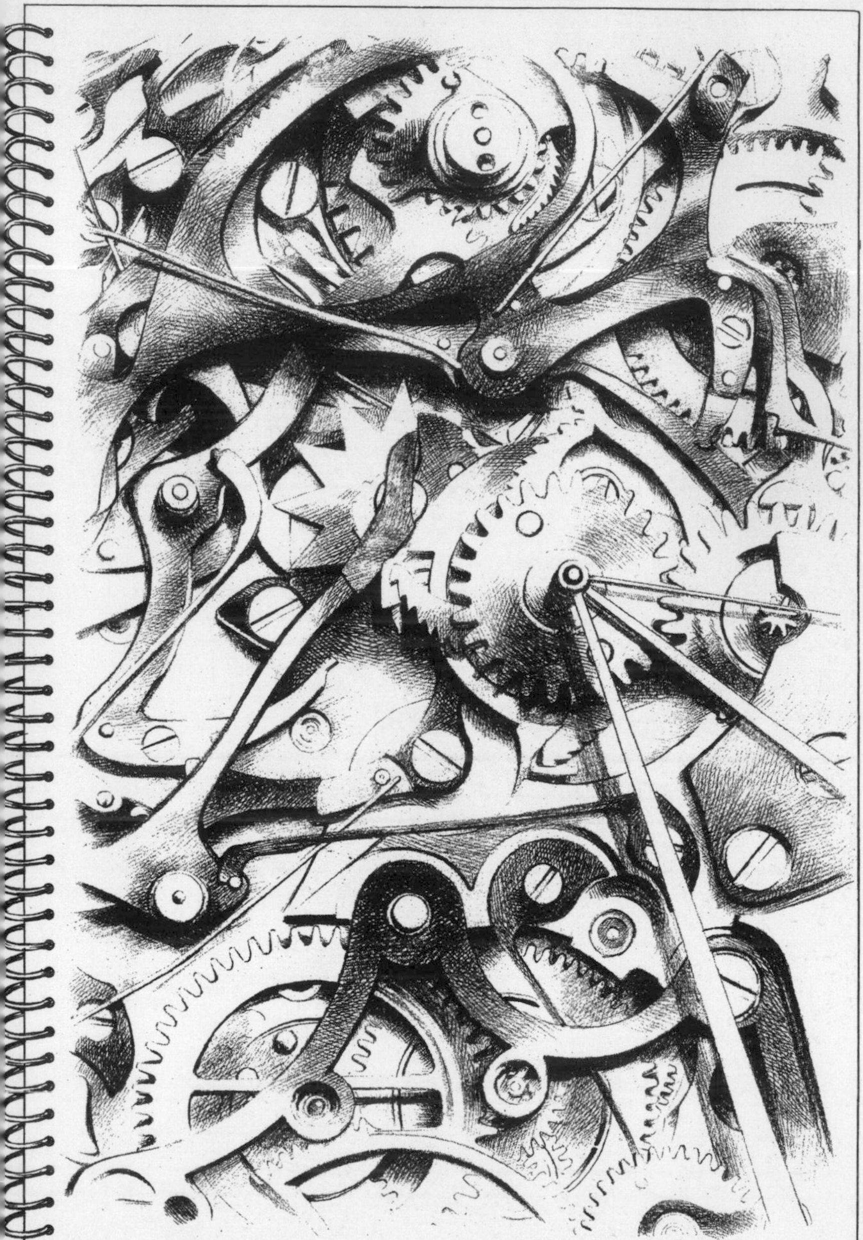

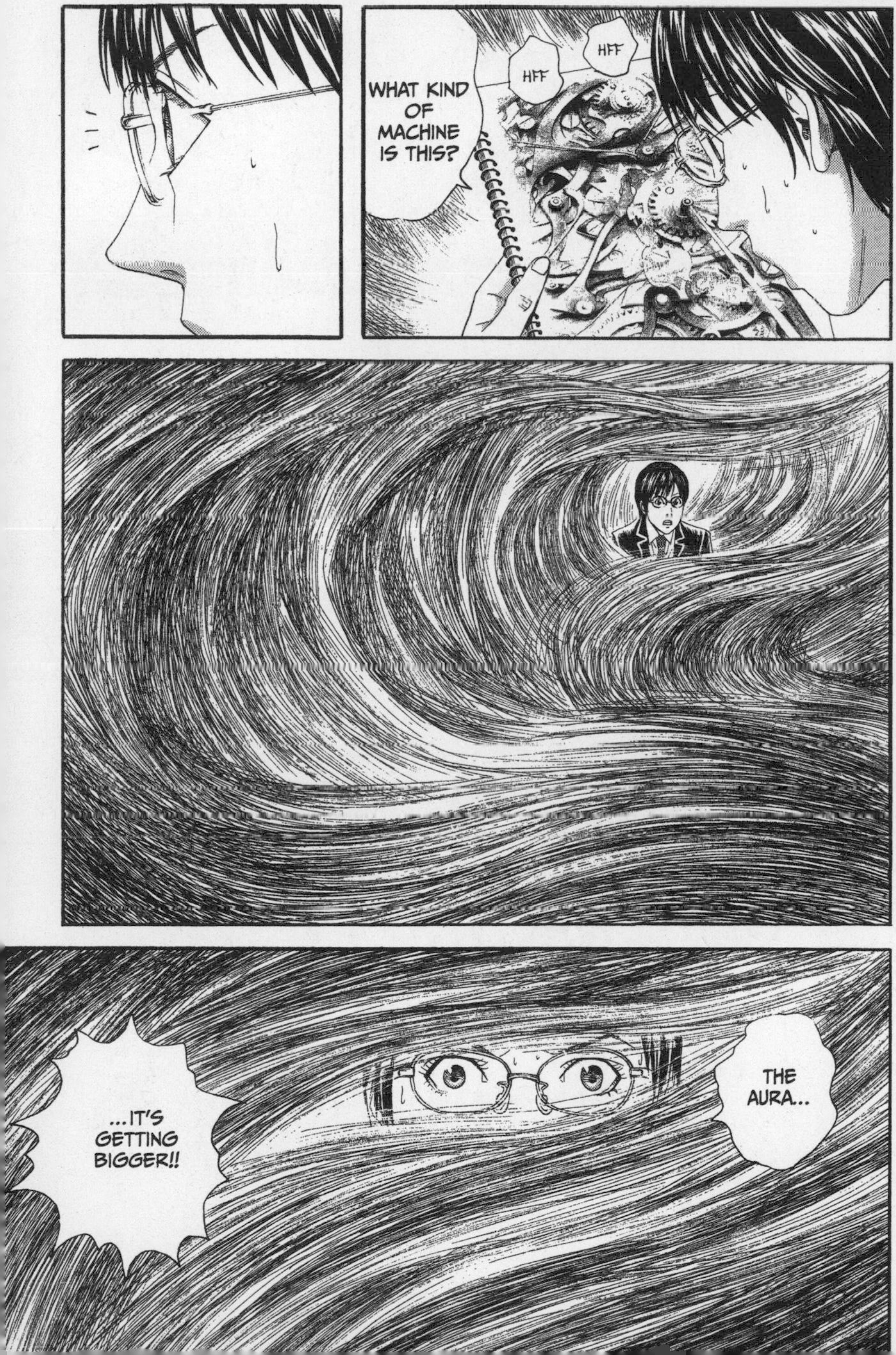
HFF
HFF
WHAT KIND OF MACHINE IS THIS?
THE AURA...
...IT'S GETTING BIGGER!!

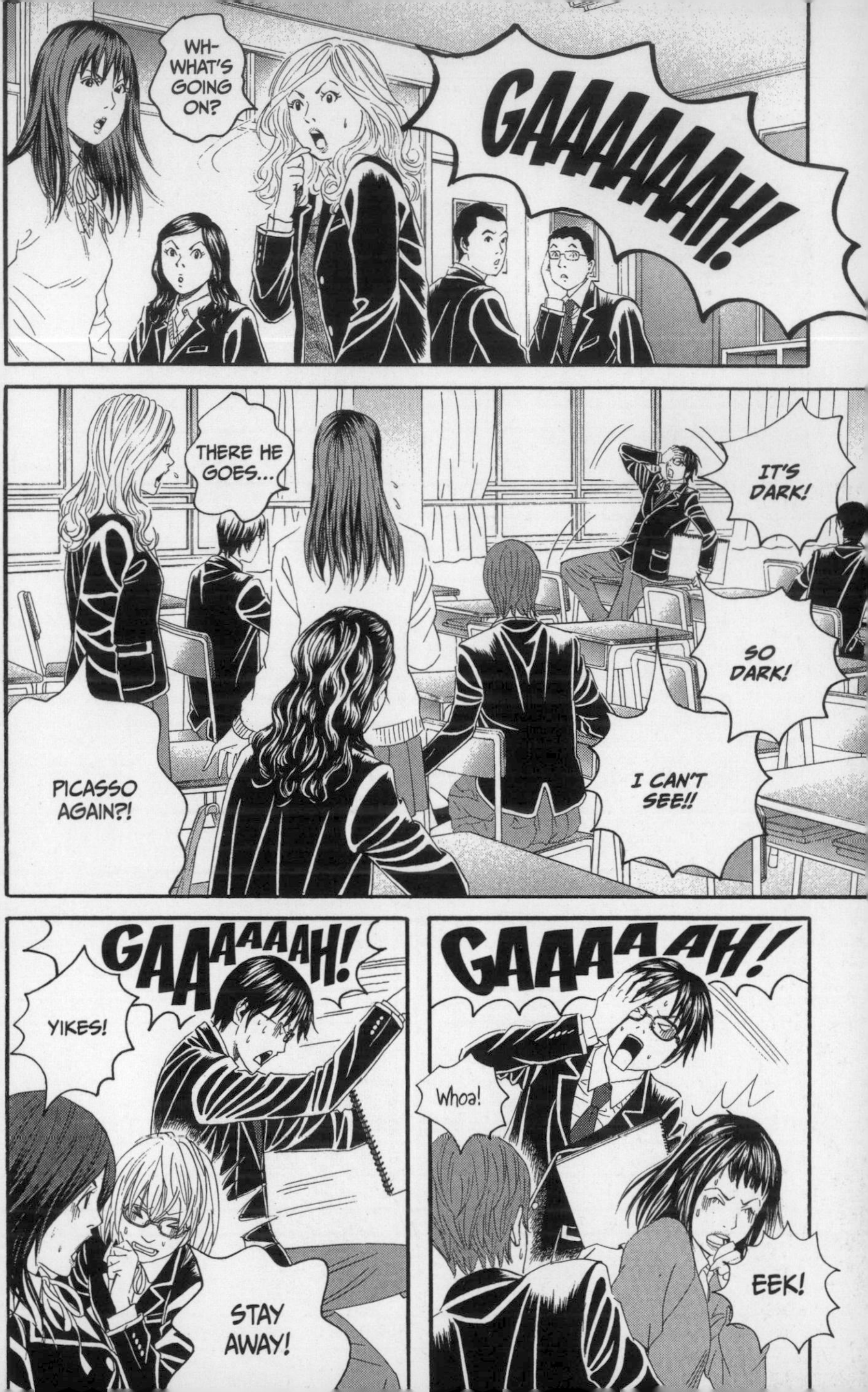
GAAAAAAH!
WH-WHAT'S GOING ON?
IT'S DARK!
SO DARK!
I CAN'T SEE!!
THERE HE GOES...
PICASSO AGAIN?!
GAAAAAH!
Whoa!
EEK!
GAAAAAAH!
YIKES!
STAY AWAY!

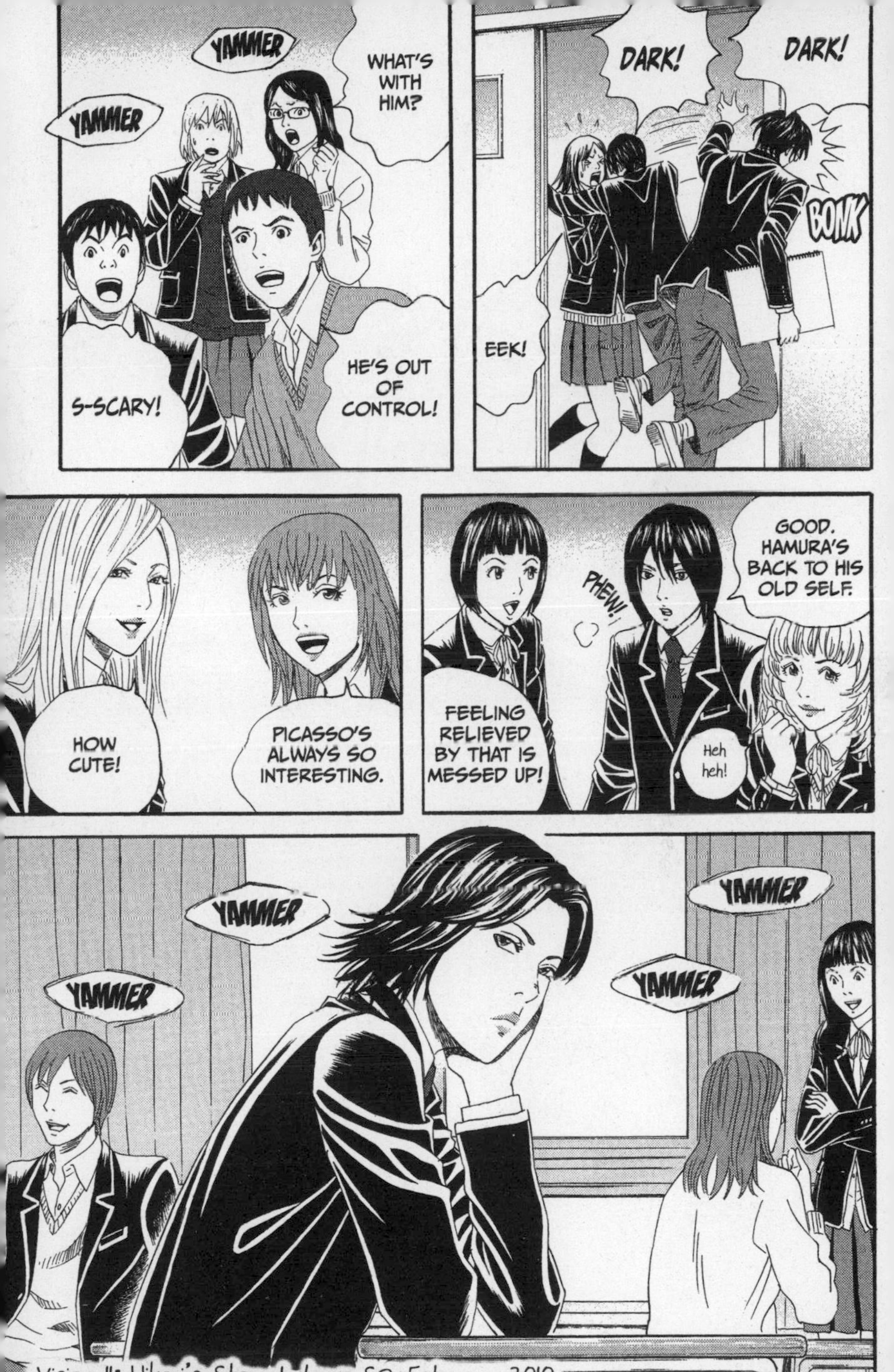
DARK!
DARK!
BONK
EEK!
WHAT'S WITH HIM?
YAMMER
YAMMER
HE'S OUT OF CONTROL!
S-SCARY!
GOOD. HAMURA'S BACK TO HIS OLD SELF.
PHEW!
Heh heh!
FEELING RELIEVED BY THAT IS MESSED UP!
PICASSO'S ALWAYS SO INTERESTING.
HOW CUTE!
YAMMER
YAMMER
YAMMER
YAMMER

Vision 11: Hikari's Story I Jump SQ, February 2010

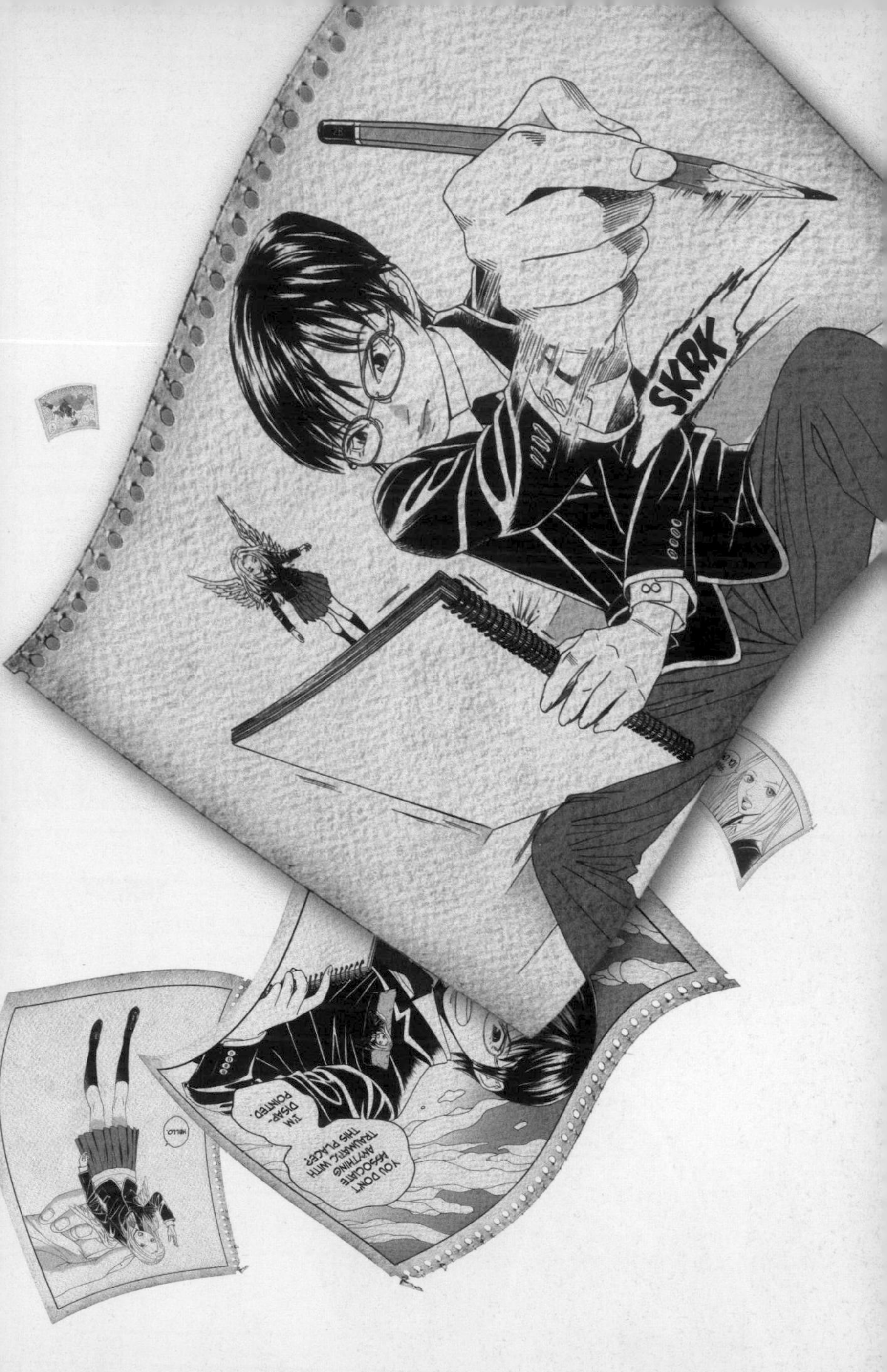
SKRK
YOU DON'T ASSOCIATE ANYTHING TRAUMATIC WITH THIS PLACE?
I'M DISAP-POINTED.
HELLO.

# Vision 11: Hikari's Story ②

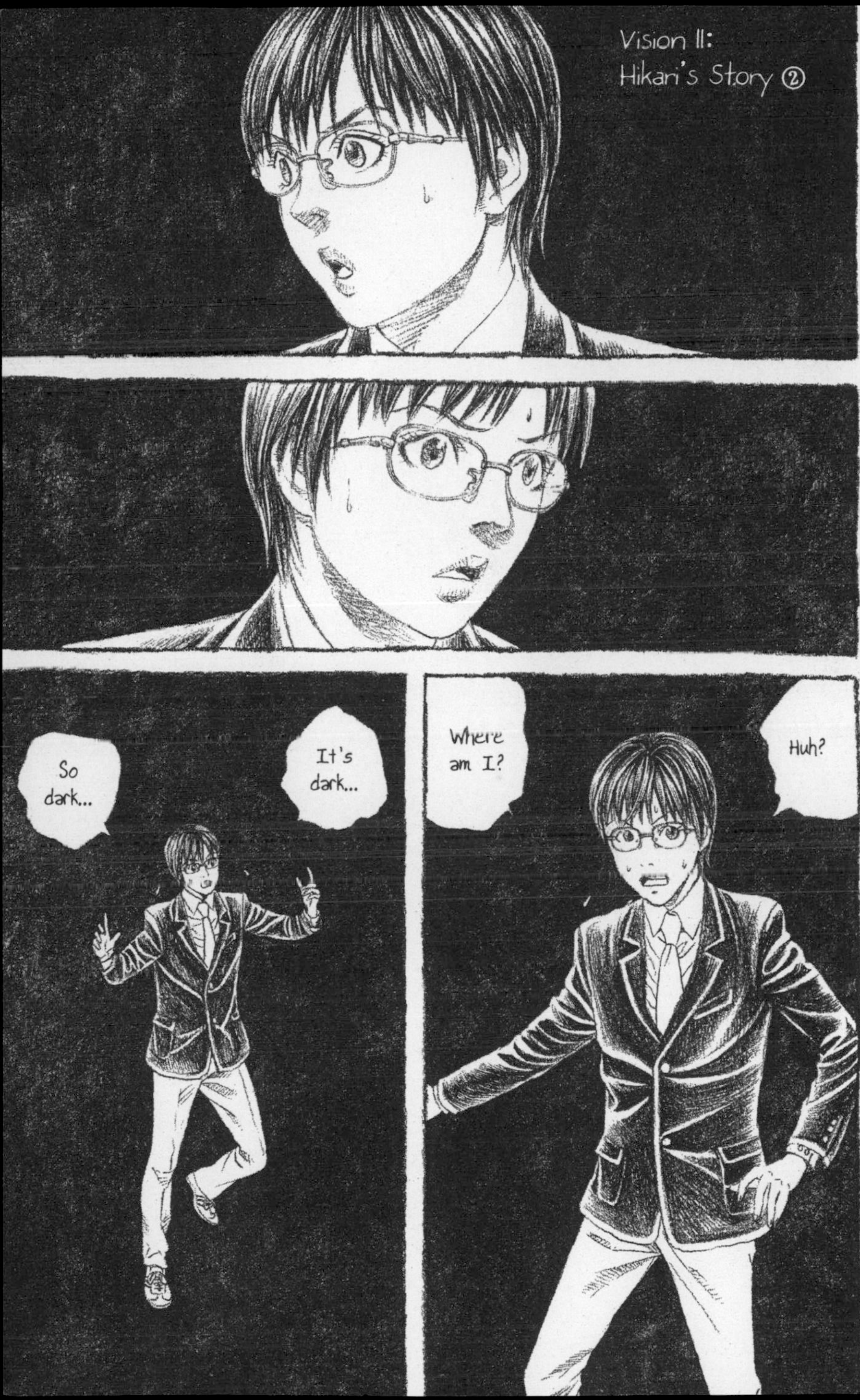
Huh?
Where am I?
It's dark...
So dark...

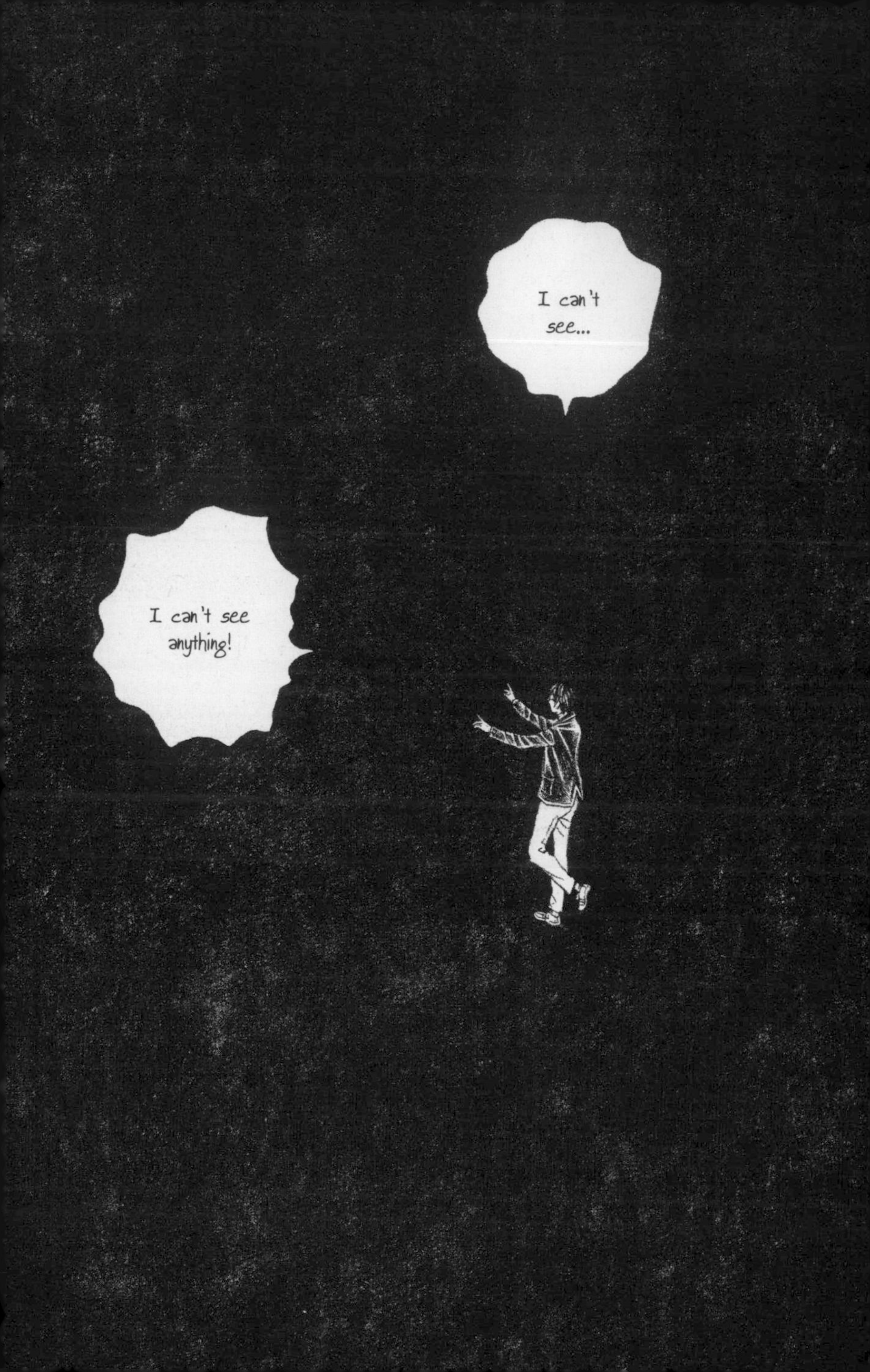
I can't see...
I can't see anything!

Vision 11:
Hikari's Story ②

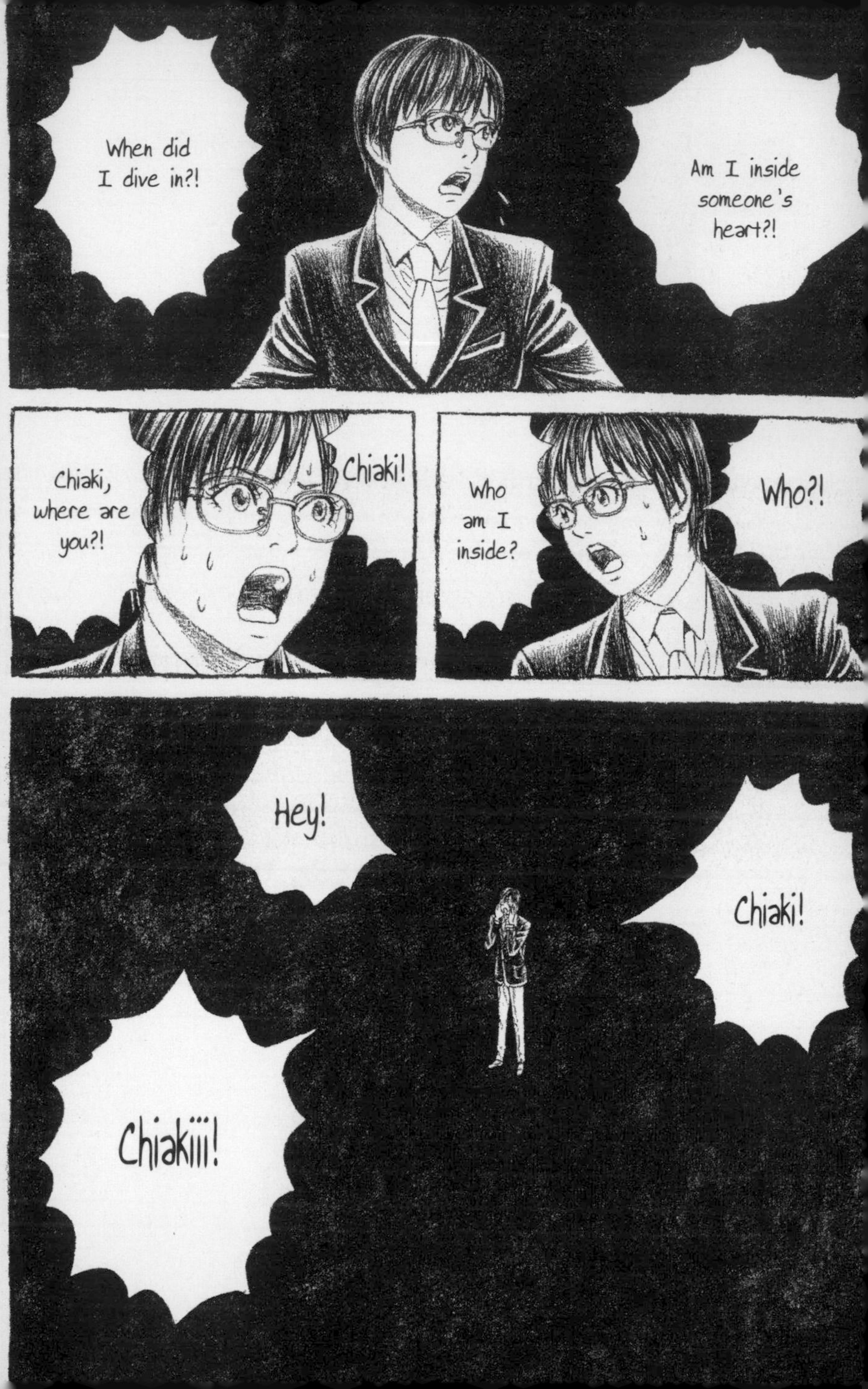
Am I inside someone's heart?!
When did I dive in?!
Who?!
Who am I inside?
Chiaki!
Chiaki, where are you?!
Hey!
Chiaki!
Chiakiii!

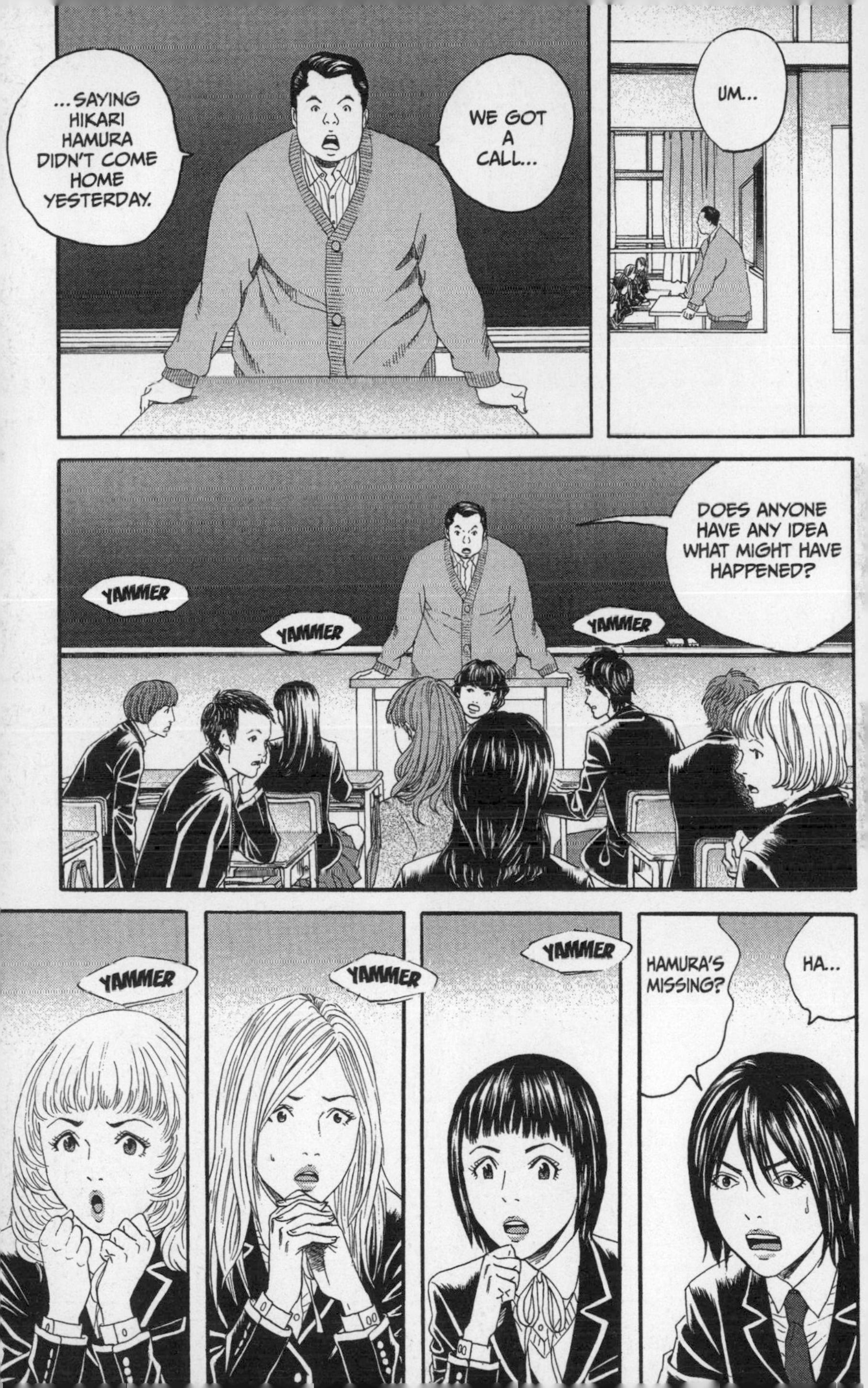
UM...
WE GOT A CALL...
...SAYING HIKARI HAMURA DIDN'T COME HOME YESTERDAY.
DOES ANYONE HAVE ANY IDEA WHAT MIGHT HAVE HAPPENED?
YAMMER
YAMMER
YAMMER
HA...
HAMURA'S MISSING?
YAMMER
YAMMER
YAMMER

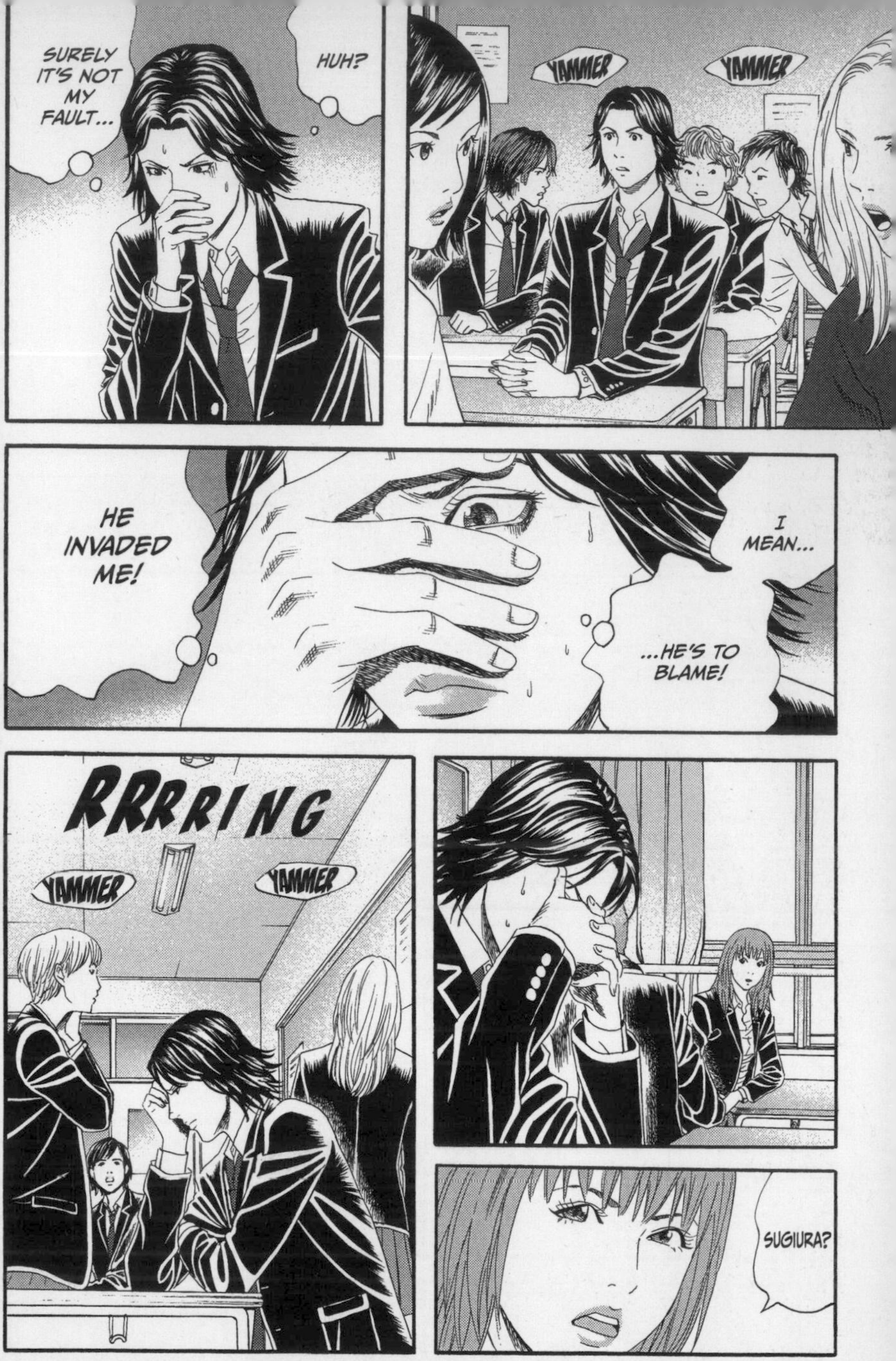
YAMMER
YAMMER
HUH?
SURELY IT'S NOT MY FAULT...
I MEAN...
...HE'S TO BLAME!
HE INVADED ME!
SUGIURA?
RRRRING
YAMMER
YAMMER

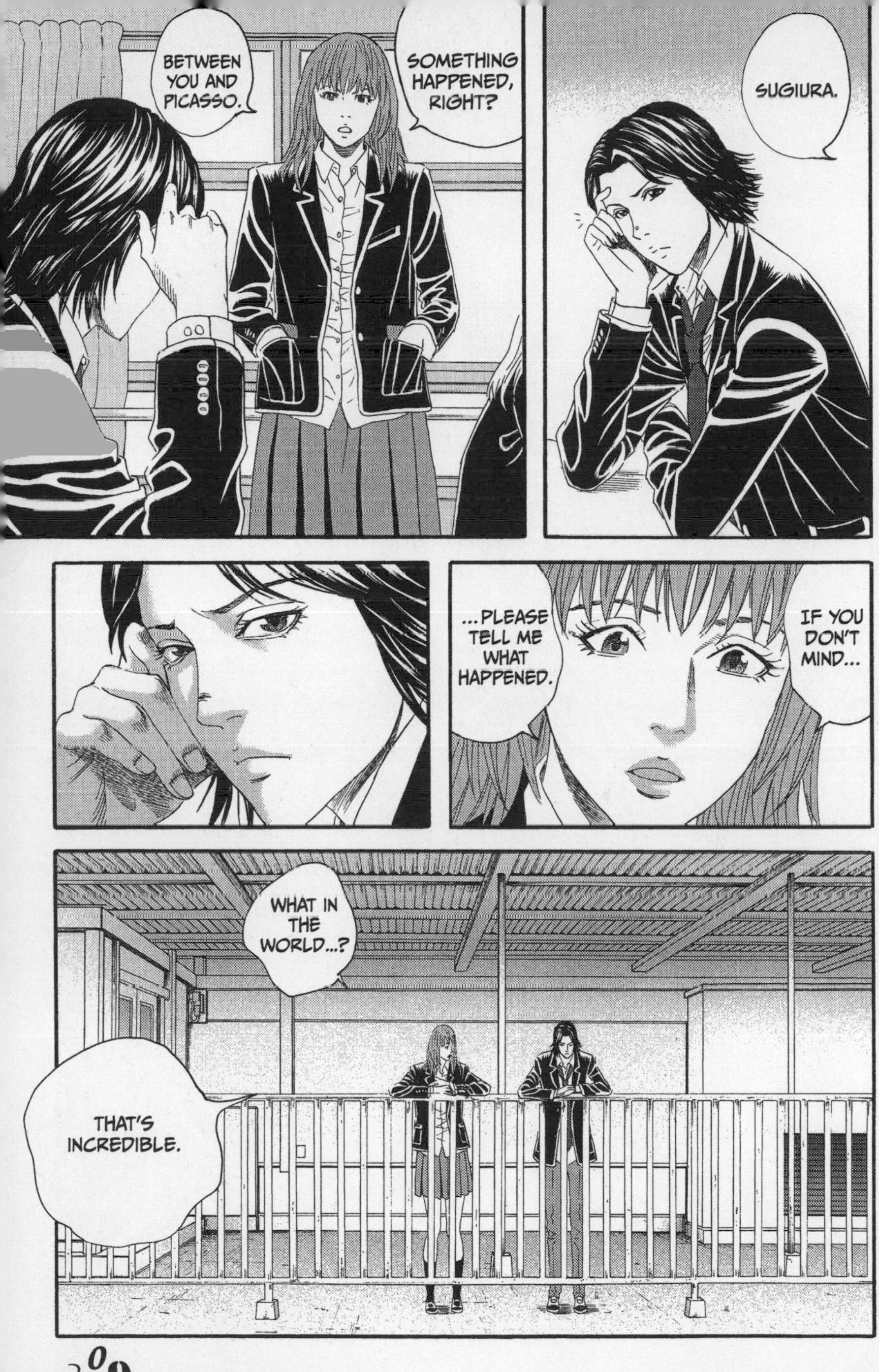
SUGIURA.
SOMETHING HAPPENED, RIGHT?
BETWEEN YOU AND PICASSO.
IF YOU DON'T MIND...
...PLEASE TELL ME WHAT HAPPENED.
WHAT IN THE WORLD...?
THAT'S INCREDIBLE.

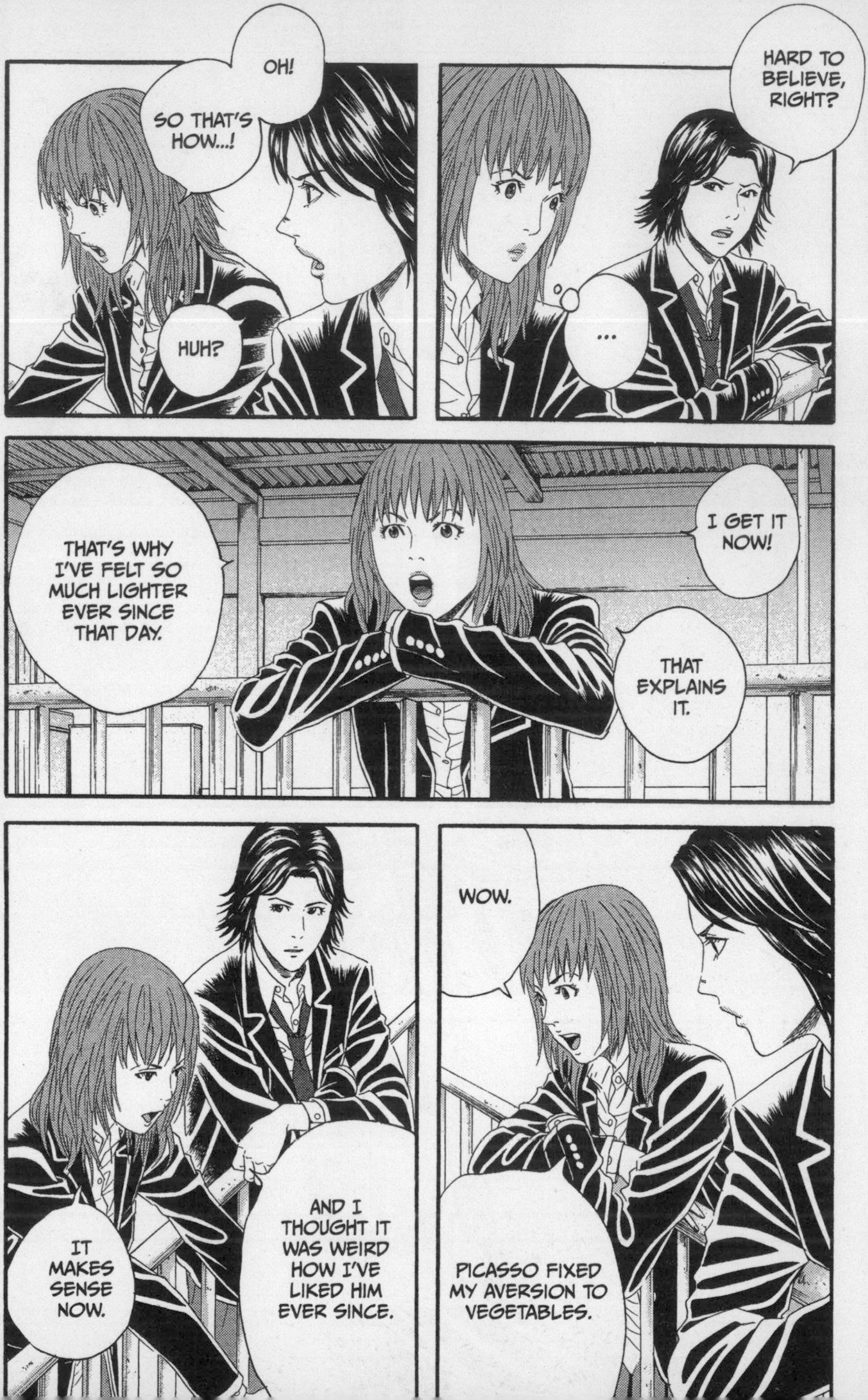
HARD TO BELIEVE, RIGHT?
...
OH!
SO THAT'S HOW...!
HUH?
I GET IT NOW!
THAT EXPLAINS IT.
THAT'S WHY I'VE FELT SO MUCH LIGHTER EVER SINCE THAT DAY.
WOW.
PICASSO FIXED MY AVERSION TO VEGETABLES.
AND I THOUGHT IT WAS WEIRD HOW I'VE LIKED HIM EVER SINCE.
IT MAKES SENSE NOW.

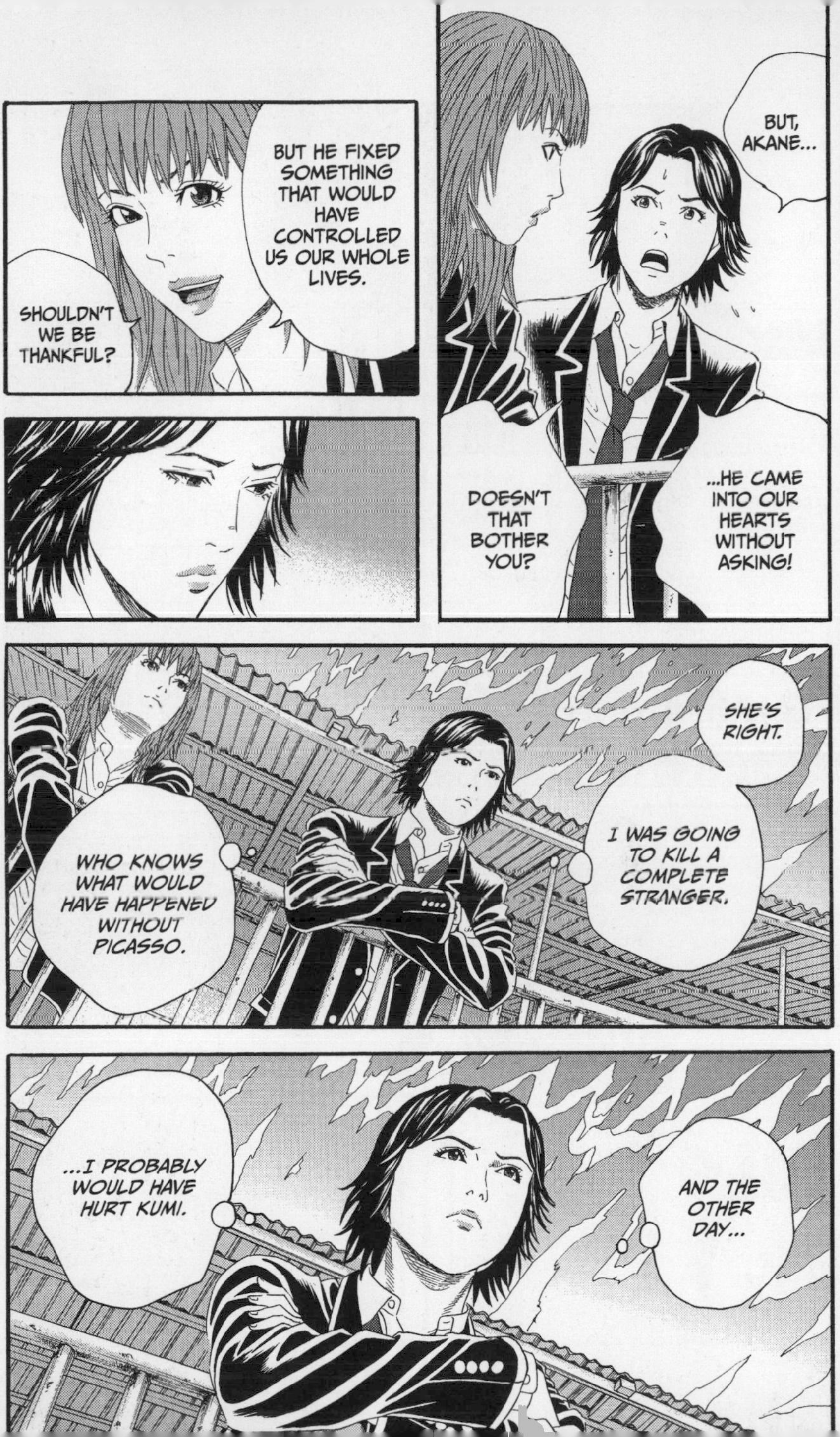
BUT, AKANE...
...HE CAME INTO OUR HEARTS WITHOUT ASKING!
DOESN'T THAT BOTHER YOU?
BUT HE FIXED SOMETHING THAT WOULD HAVE CONTROLLED US OUR WHOLE LIVES.
SHOULDN'T WE BE THANKFUL?
SHE'S RIGHT.
I WAS GOING TO KILL A COMPLETE STRANGER.
WHO KNOWS WHAT WOULD HAVE HAPPENED WITHOUT PICASSO.
AND THE OTHER DAY...
...I PROBABLY WOULD HAVE HURT KUMI.

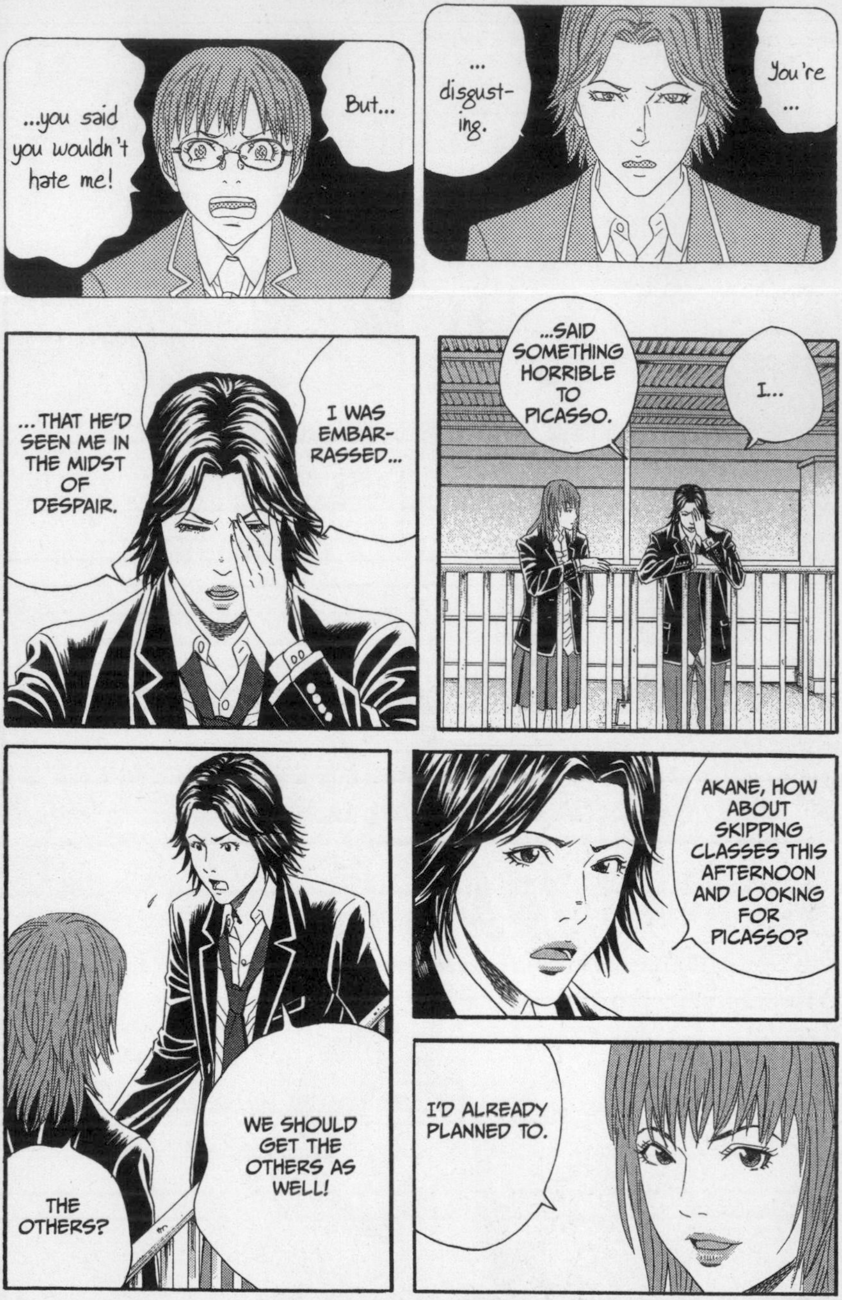
You're ...
... disgust-ing.
But...
...you said you wouldn't hate me!
I...
...SAID SOMETHING HORRIBLE TO PICASSO.
I WAS EMBAR-RASSED...
...THAT HE'D SEEN ME IN THE MIDST OF DESPAIR.
AKANE, HOW ABOUT SKIPPING CLASSES THIS AFTERNOON AND LOOKING FOR PICASSO?
I'D ALREADY PLANNED TO.
WE SHOULD GET THE OTHERS AS WELL!
THE OTHERS?

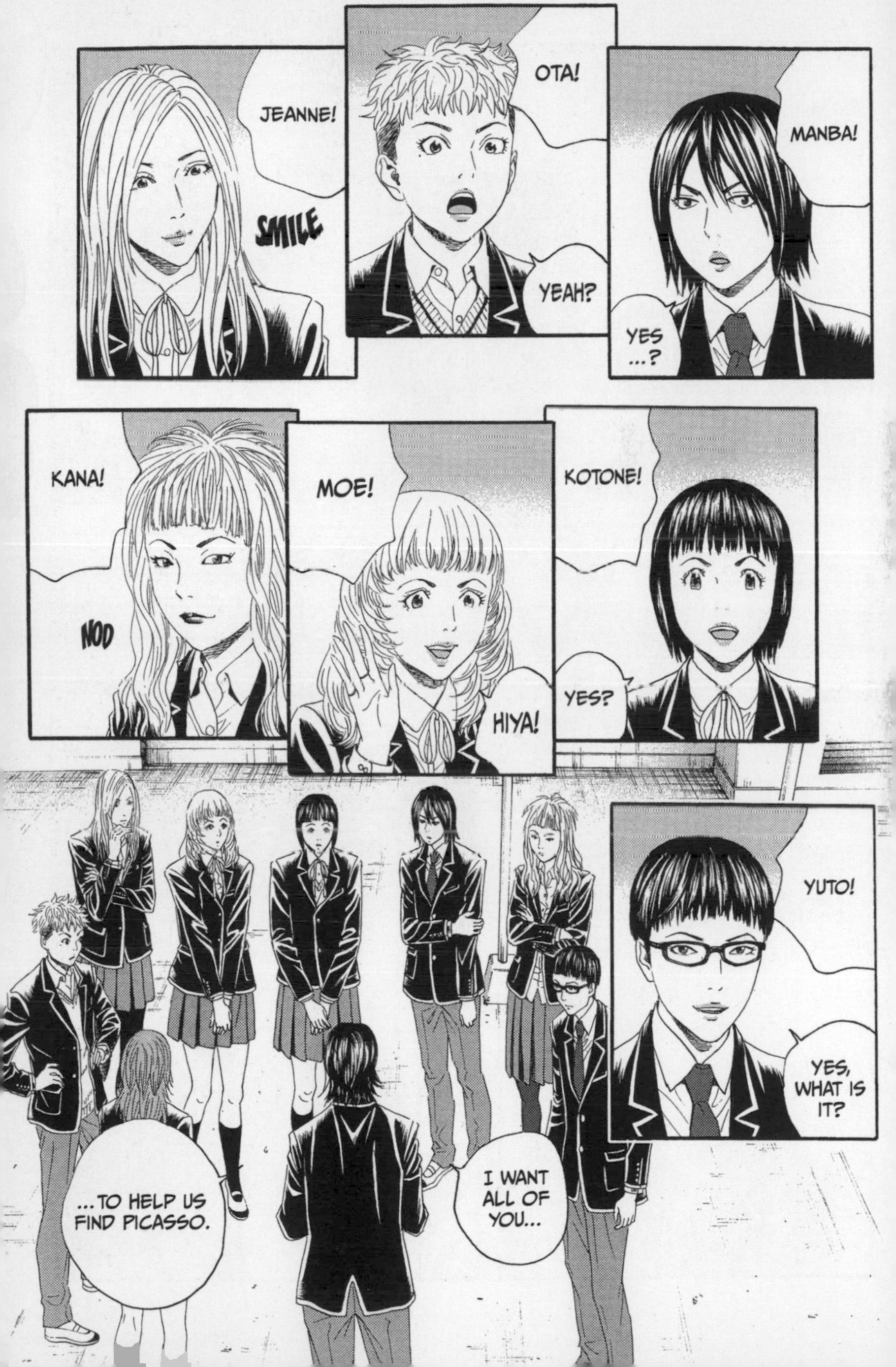
MANBA!
YES ...?
OTA!
YEAH?
JEANNE!
SMILE
KOTONE!
YES?
MOE!
HIYA!
KANA!
NOD
YUTO!
YES, WHAT IS IT?
I WANT ALL OF YOU...
...TO HELP US FIND PICASSO.

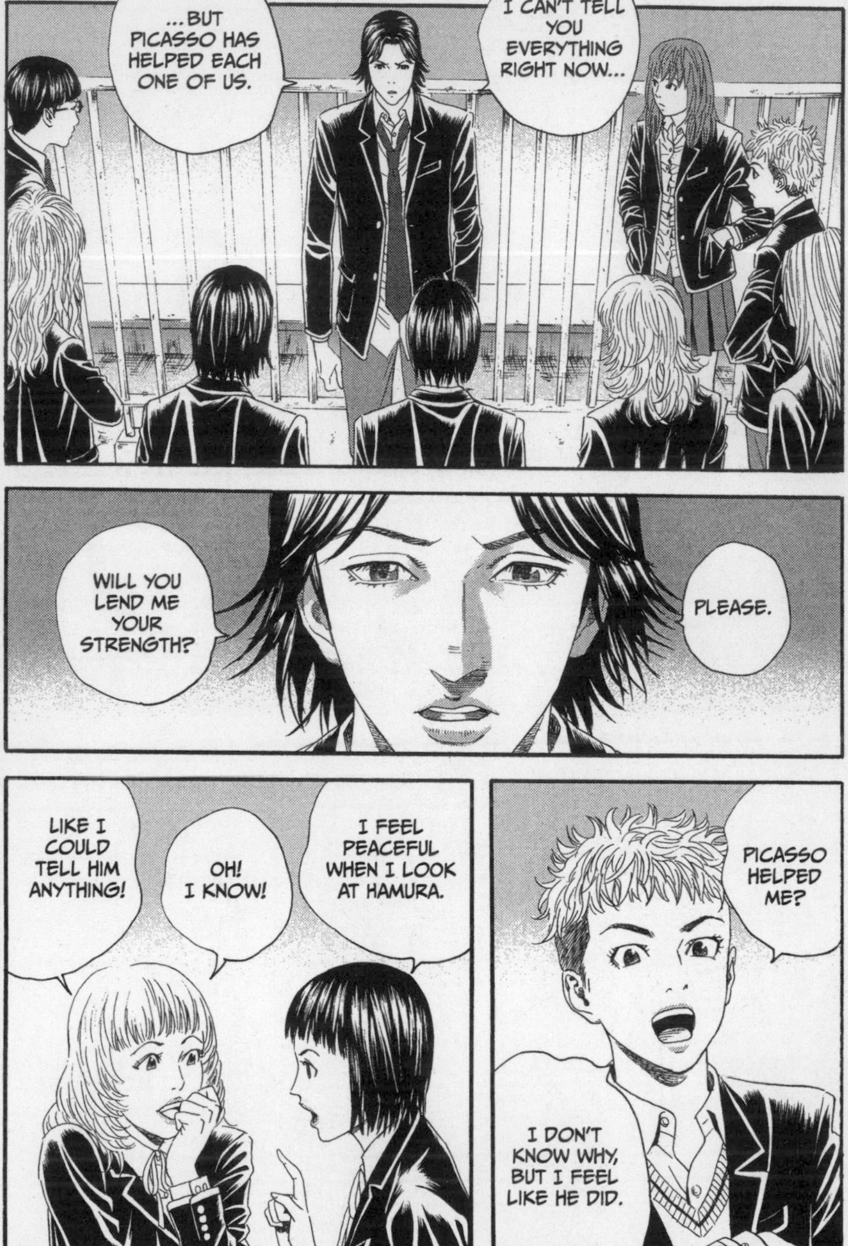
I CAN'T TELL YOU EVERYTHING RIGHT NOW...
...BUT PICASSO HAS HELPED EACH ONE OF US.
PLEASE.
WILL YOU LEND ME YOUR STRENGTH?
PICASSO HELPED ME?
I DON'T KNOW WHY, BUT I FEEL LIKE HE DID.
I FEEL PEACEFUL WHEN I LOOK AT HAMURA.
OH! I KNOW!
LIKE I COULD TELL HIM ANYTHING!

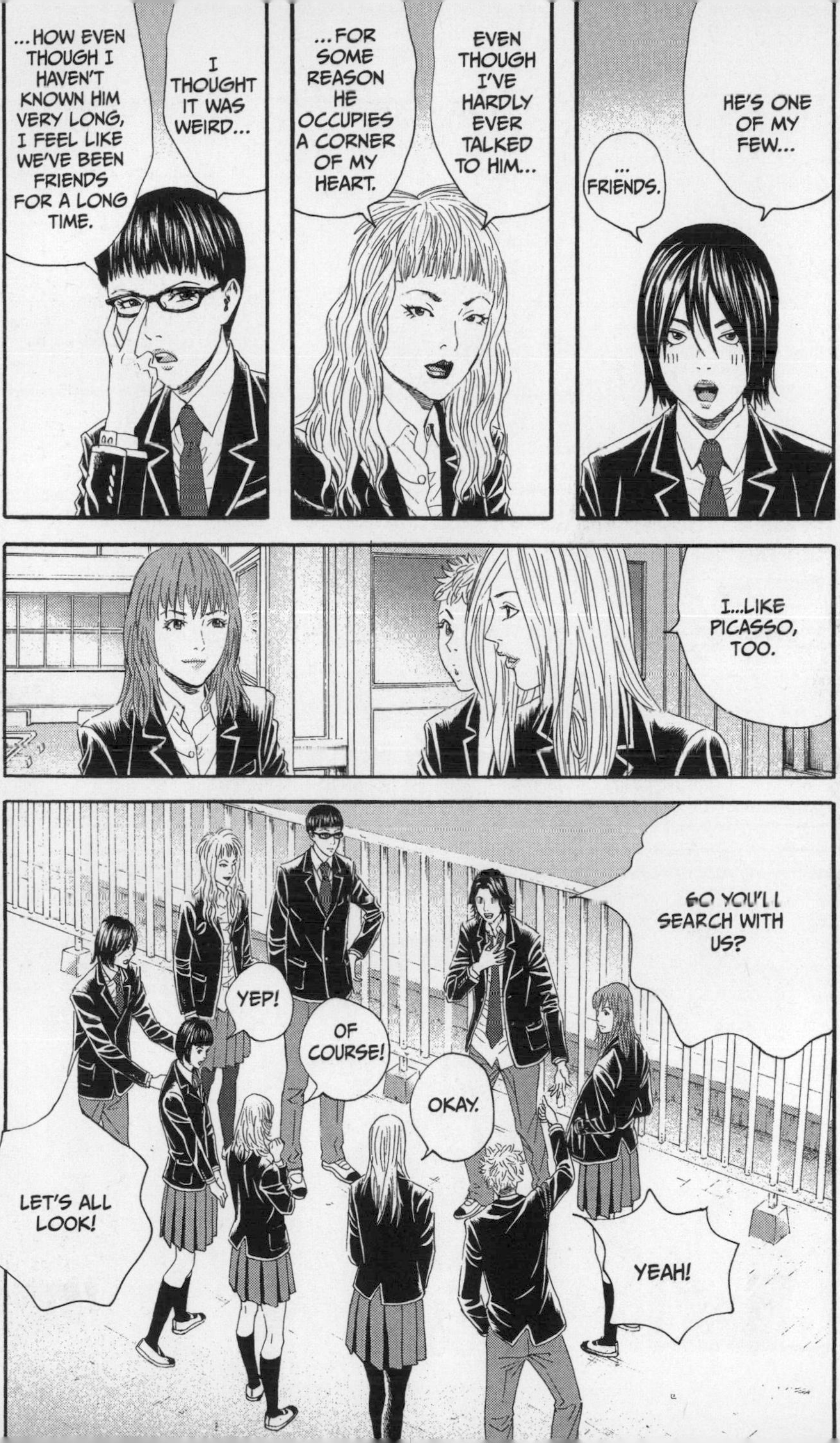
HE'S ONE OF MY FEW...
...FRIENDS.
EVEN THOUGH I'VE HARDLY EVER TALKED TO HIM...
...FOR SOME REASON HE OCCUPIES A CORNER OF MY HEART.
I THOUGHT IT WAS WEIRD...
...HOW EVEN THOUGH I HAVEN'T KNOWN HIM VERY LONG, I FEEL LIKE WE'VE BEEN FRIENDS FOR A LONG TIME.
I...LIKE PICASSO, TOO.
SO YOU'LL SEARCH WITH US?
YEAH!
OKAY.
OF COURSE!
YEP!
LET'S ALL LOOK!

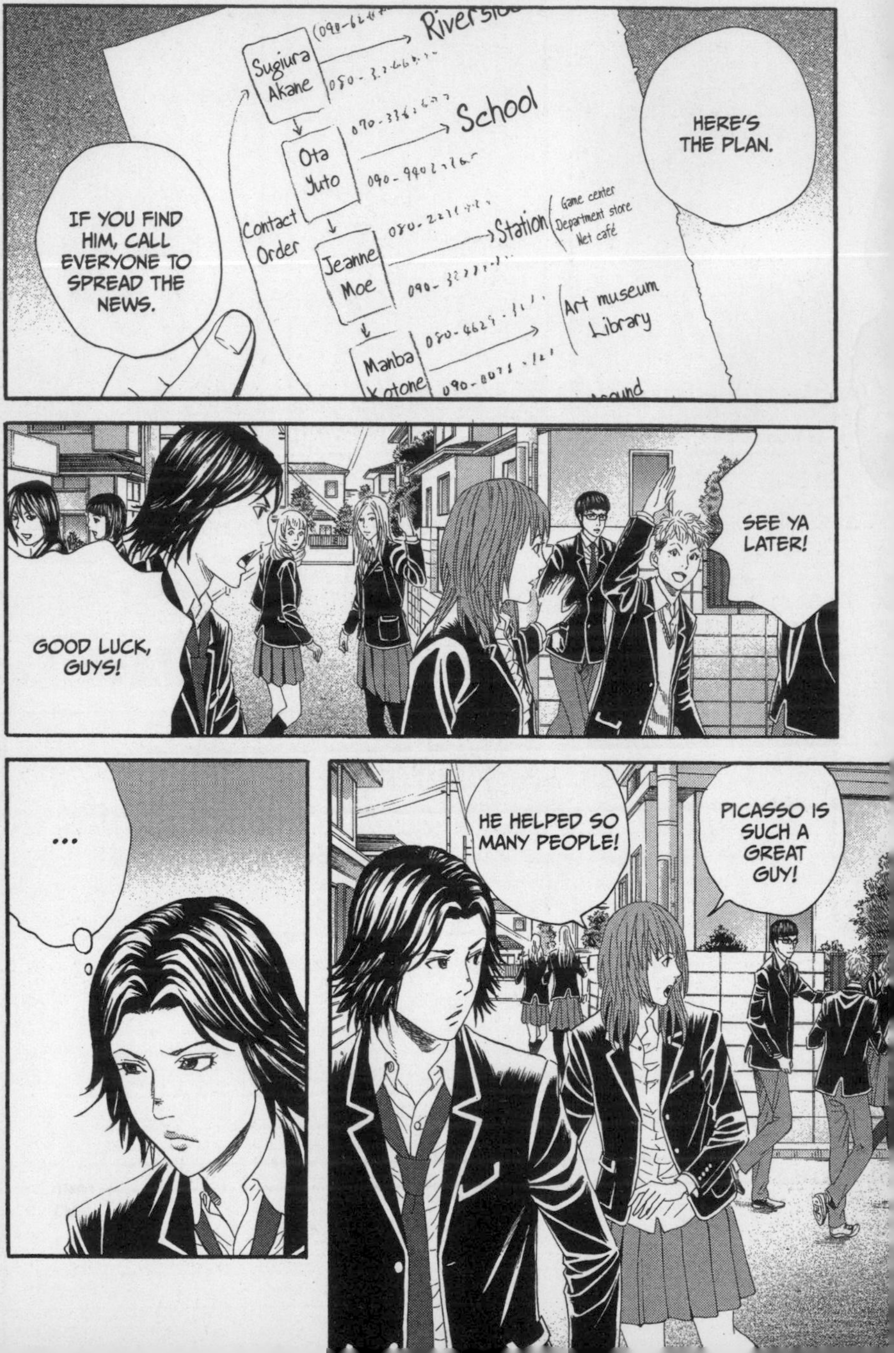
HERE'S THE PLAN.
Sugiura Akane
School
Ota Yuto
Contact Order
Station
Game center
Department store
Net café
Jeanne Moe
Art museum
Library
Manba Kotone
IF YOU FIND HIM, CALL EVERYONE TO SPREAD THE NEWS.
SEE YA LATER!
GOOD LUCK, GUYS!
PICASSO IS SUCH A GREAT GUY!
HE HELPED SO MANY PEOPLE!
...

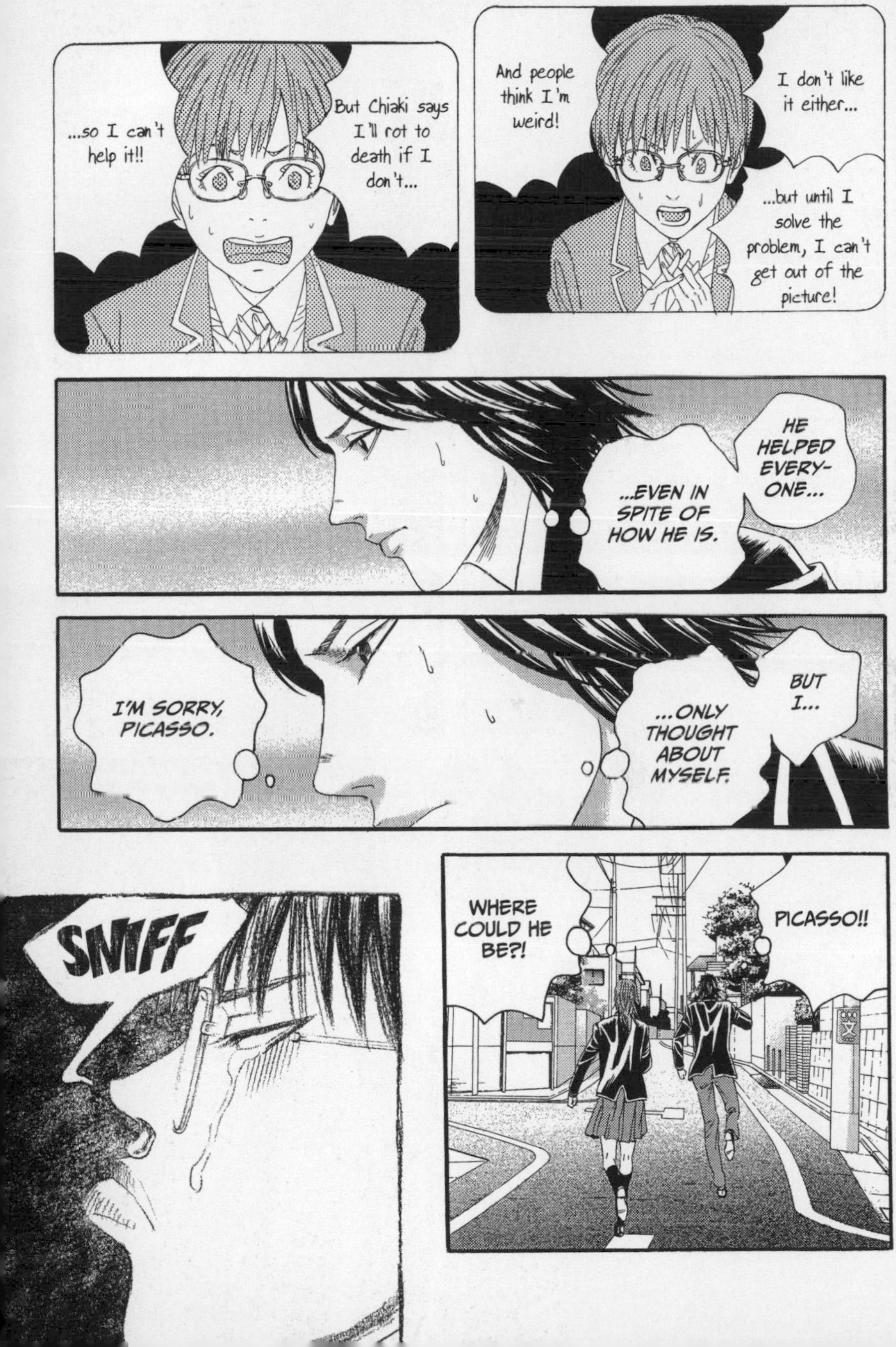
I don't like it either...
...but until I solve the problem, I can't get out of the picture!
And people think I'm weird!
But Chiaki says I'll rot to death if I don't...
...so I can't help it!!
HE HELPED EVERY-ONE...
...EVEN IN SPITE OF HOW HE IS.
BUT I...
...ONLY THOUGHT ABOUT MYSELF.
I'M SORRY, PICASSO.
PICASSO!!
WHERE COULD HE BE?!
SNIFF

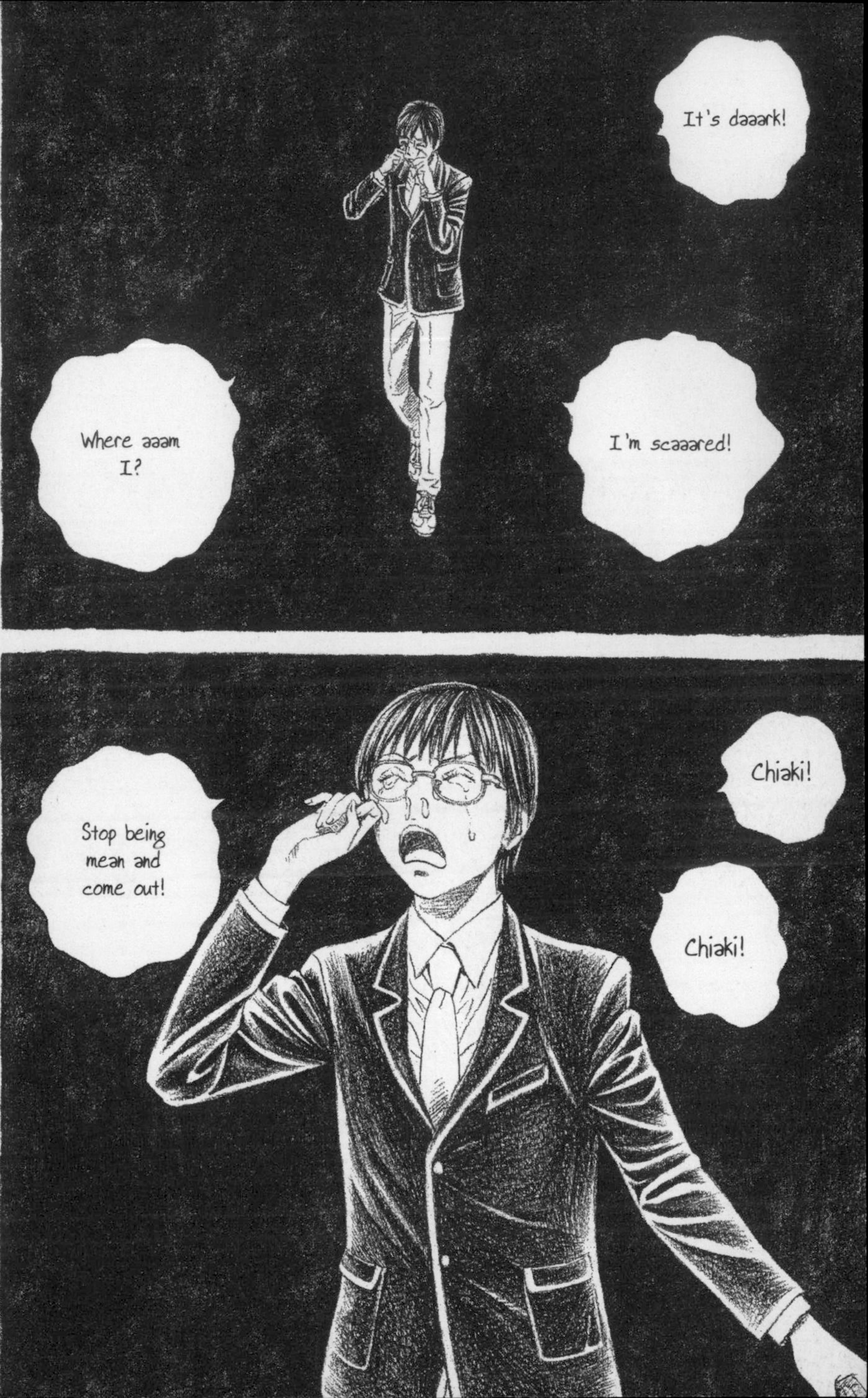
It's daaark!
I'm scaaared!
Where aaam I?
Chiaki!
Chiaki!
Stop being mean and come out!

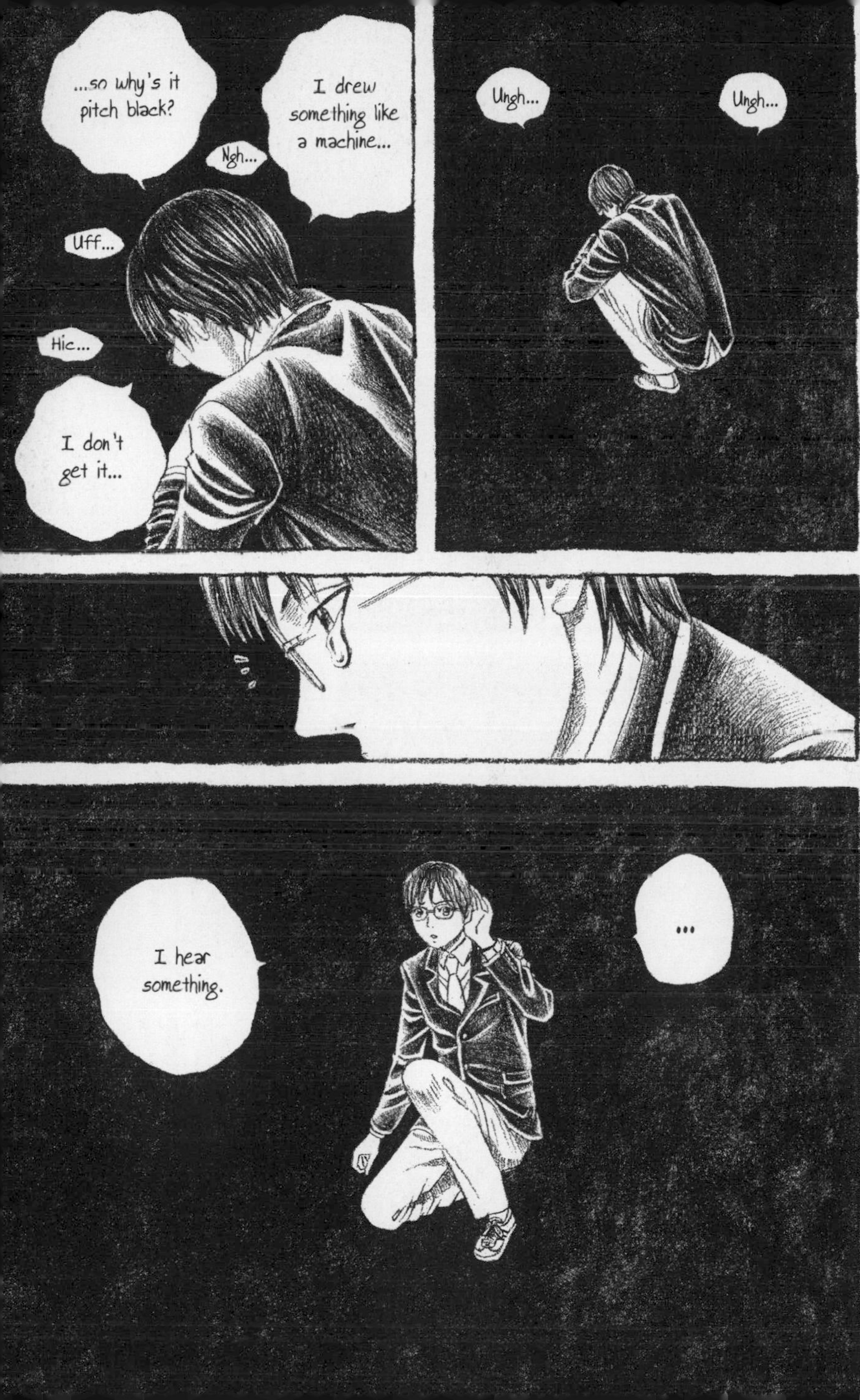
Ungh...
Ungh...
I drew something like a machine...
...so why's it pitch black?
Ngh...
Uff...
Hic...
I don't get it...
...
I hear something.

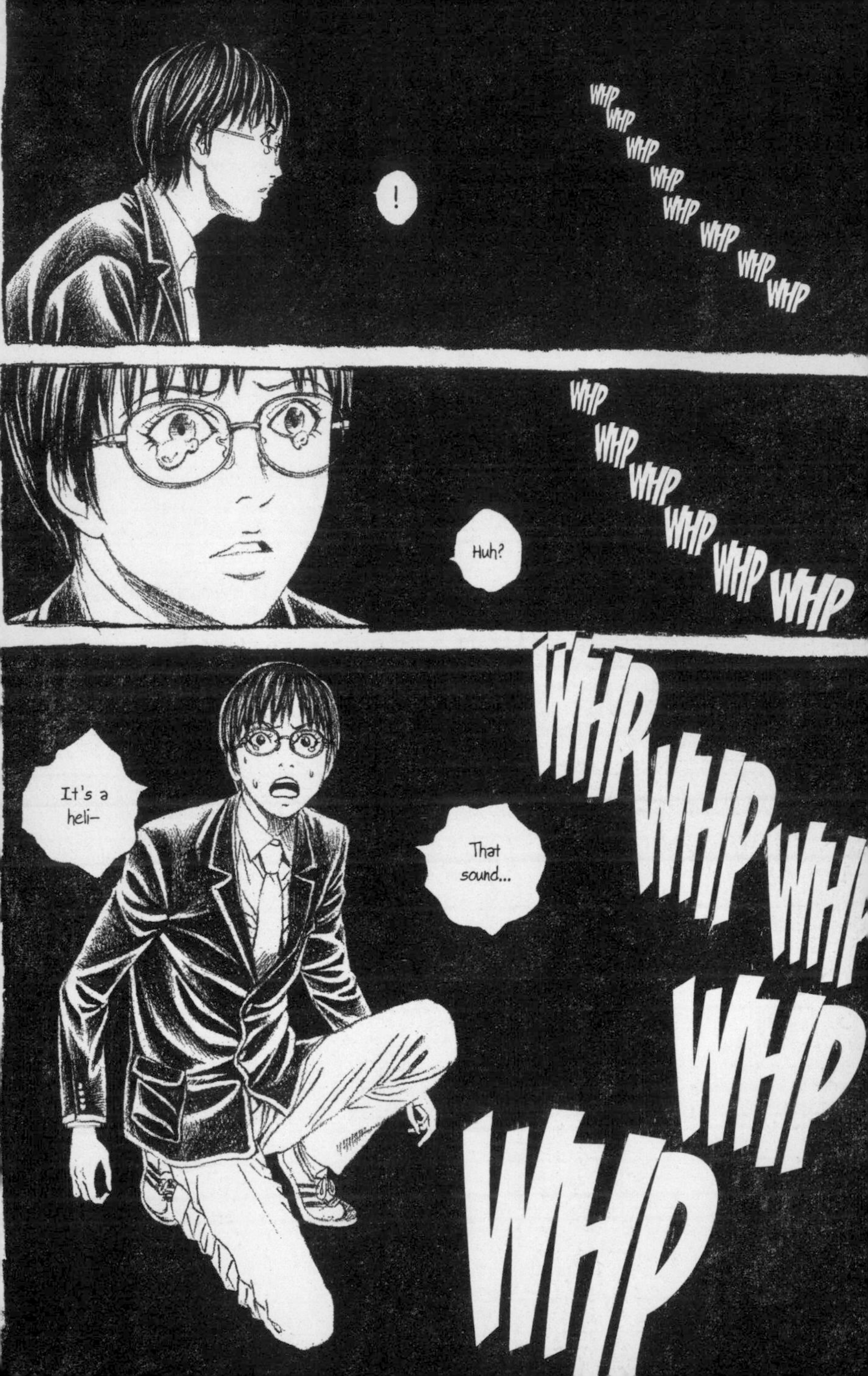
WHP WHP WHP WHP WHP WHP WHP WHP
!
WHP WHP WHP WHP WHP WHP
Huh?
WHP WHP WHP WHP WHP
That sound...
It's a heli–

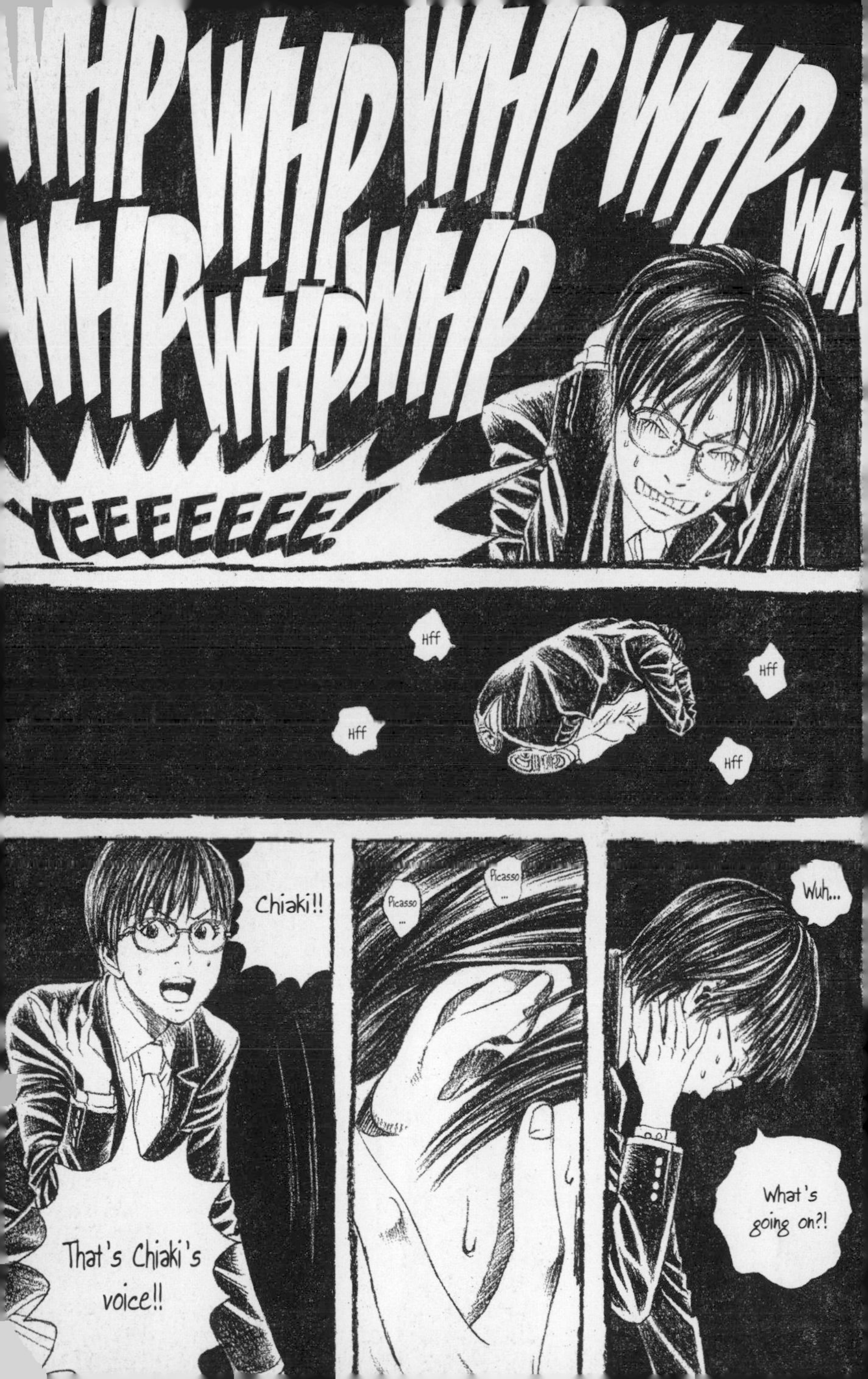
WHIP WHIP WHIP WHIP WHIP WHIP WHIP WHIP wh...
YEEEEEEEE!
Hff
Hff
Hff
Hff
Wuh...
What's going on?!
Picasso...
Picasso...
Chiaki!!
That's Chiaki's voice!!

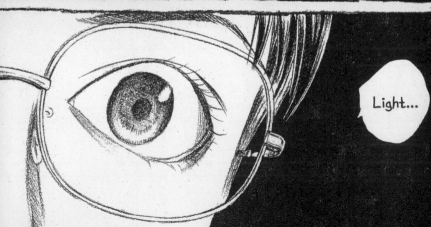

Light...

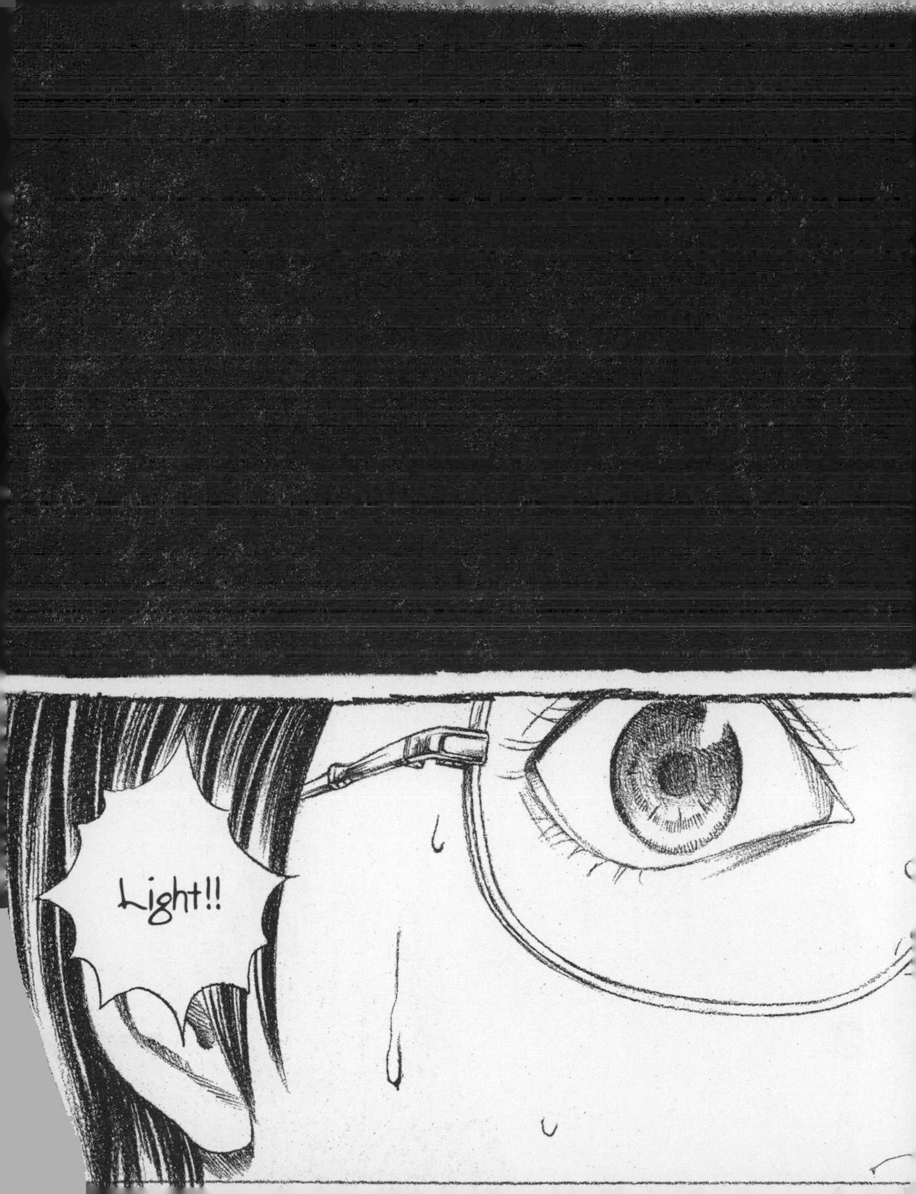
Light!!

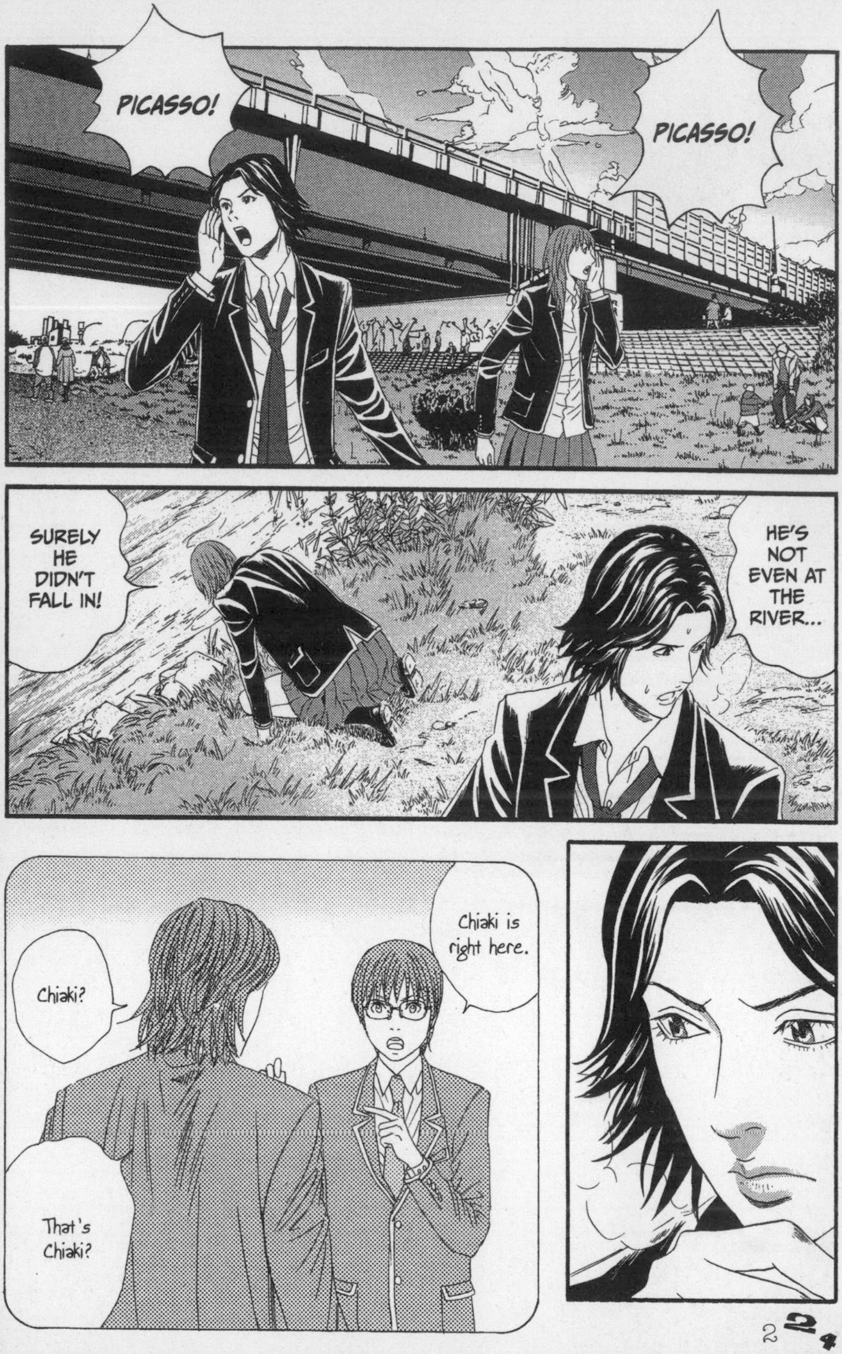
PICASSO!
PICASSO!
HE'S NOT EVEN AT THE RIVER...
SURELY HE DIDN'T FALL IN!
Chiaki is right here.
Chiaki?
That's Chiaki?

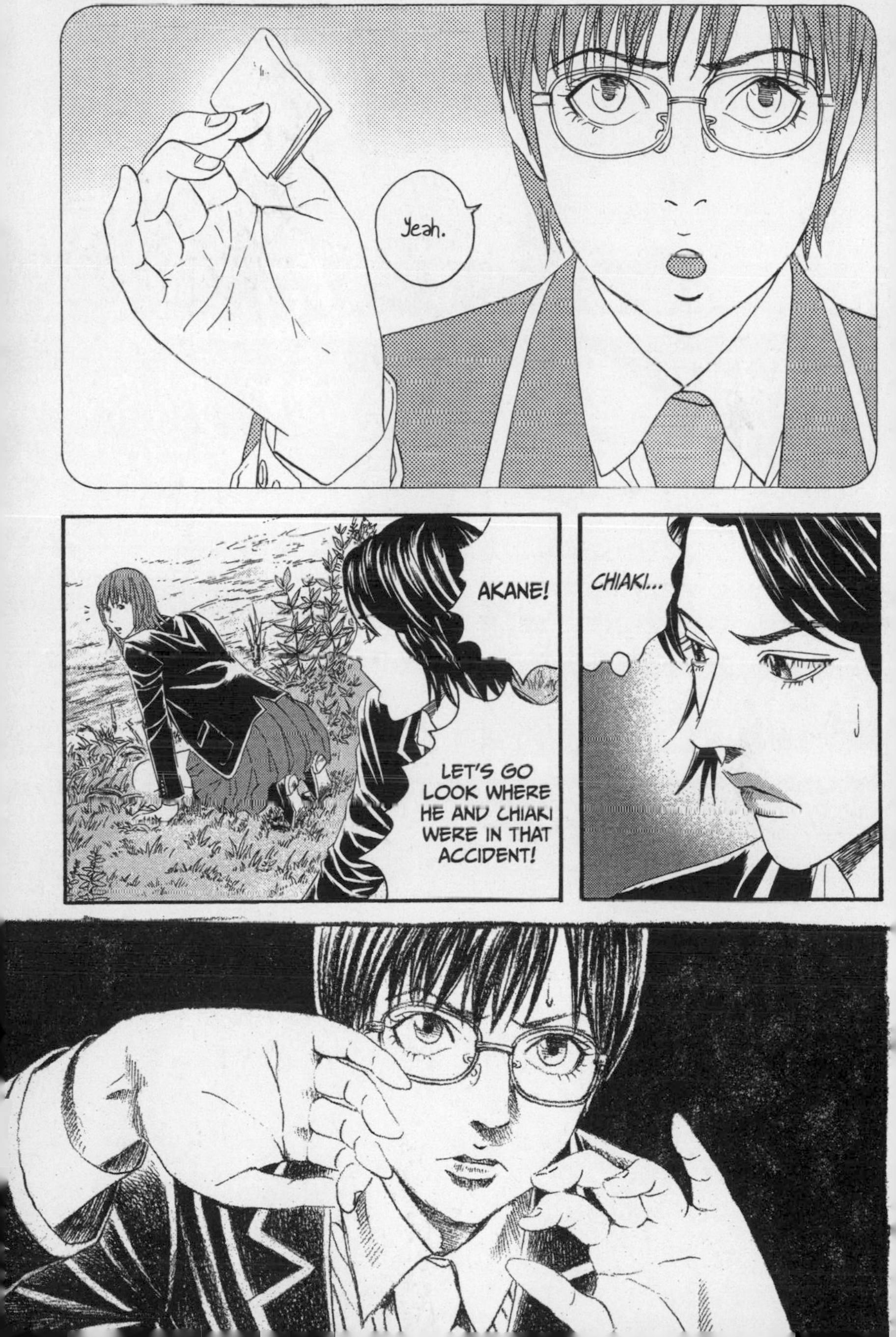
Yeah.
CHIAKI...
AKANE!
LET'S GO LOOK WHERE HE AND CHIAKI WERE IN THAT ACCIDENT!

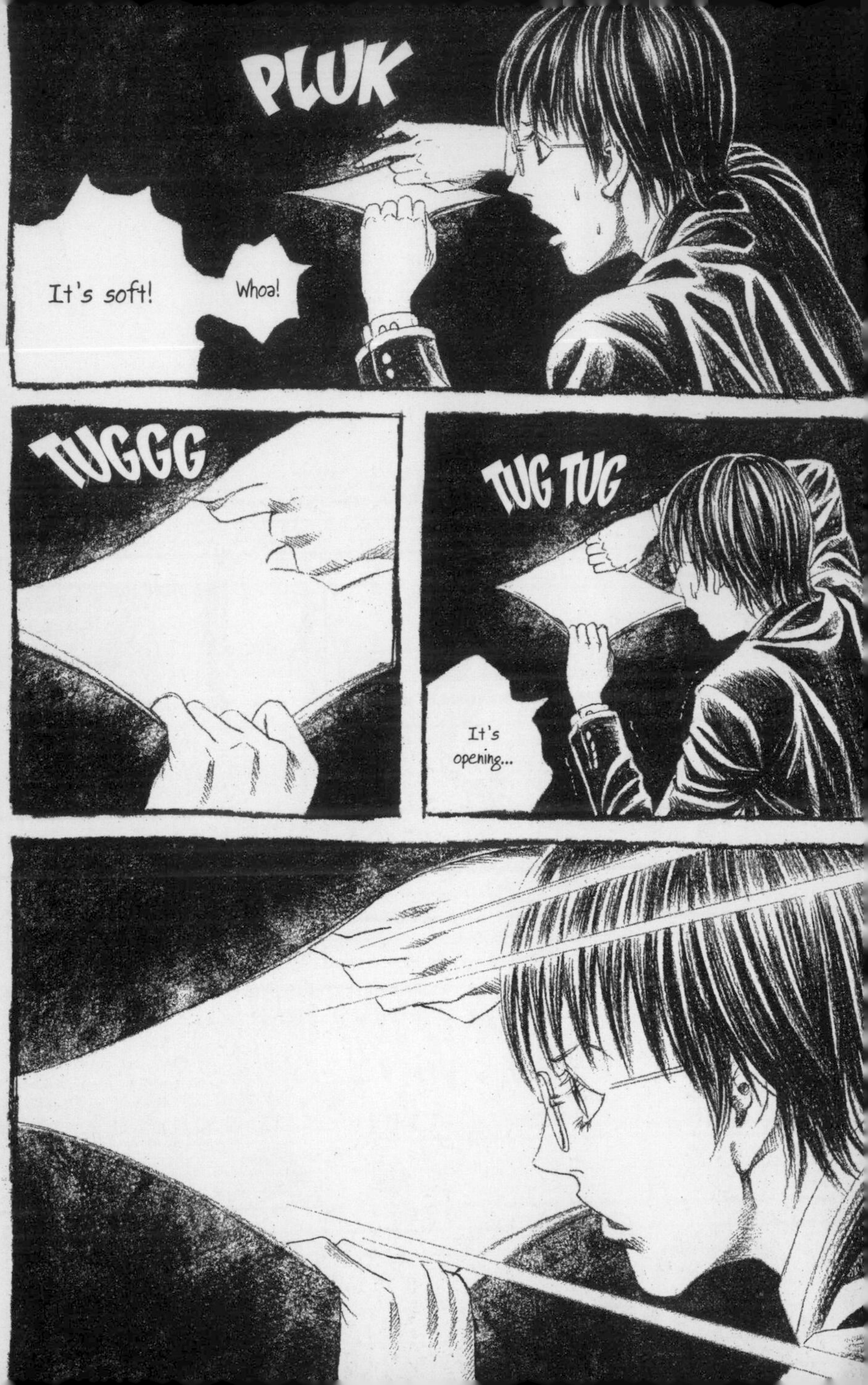
PLUK
Whoa!
It's soft!
TUG TUG
It's opening...
TUGGG

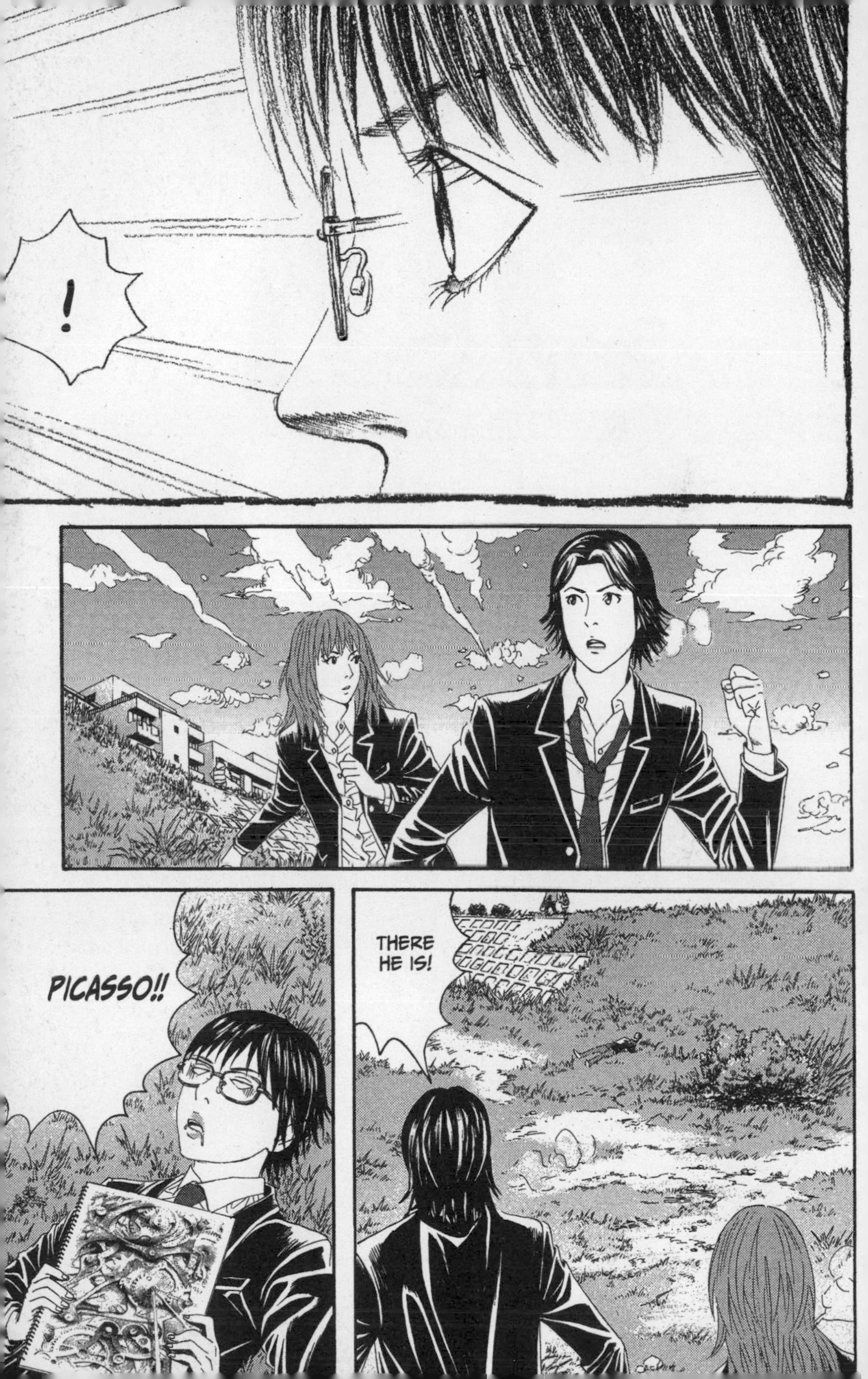
!
THERE HE IS!
PICASSO!!

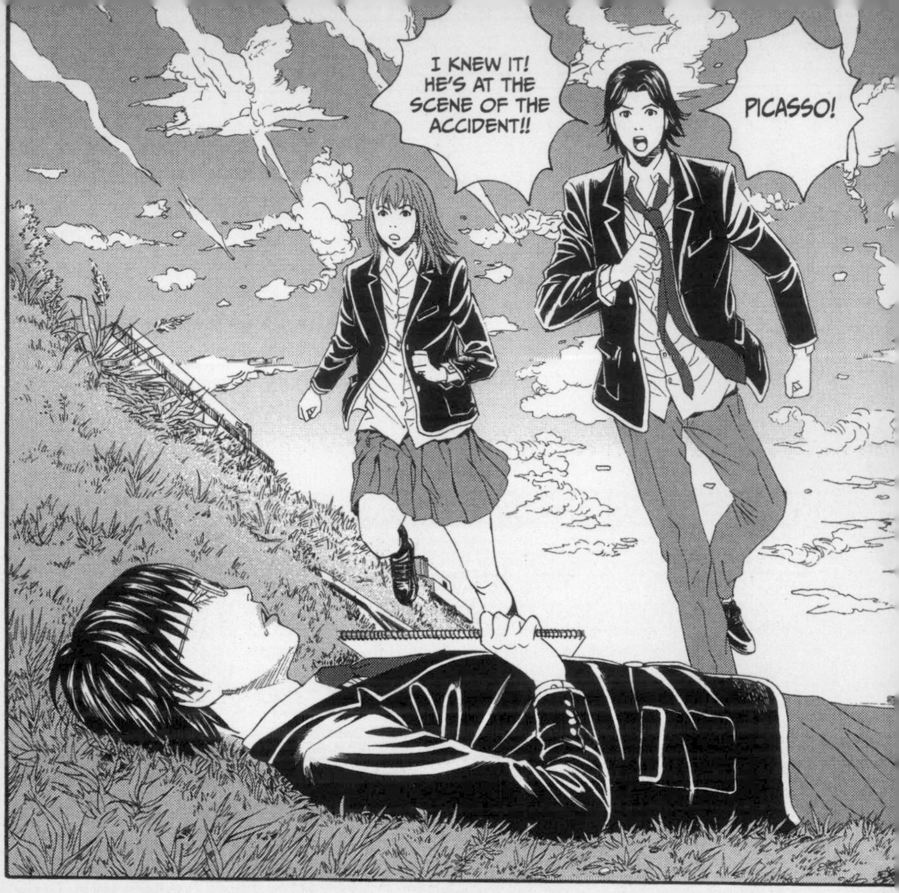
PICASSO!
I KNEW IT! HE'S AT THE SCENE OF THE ACCIDENT!!
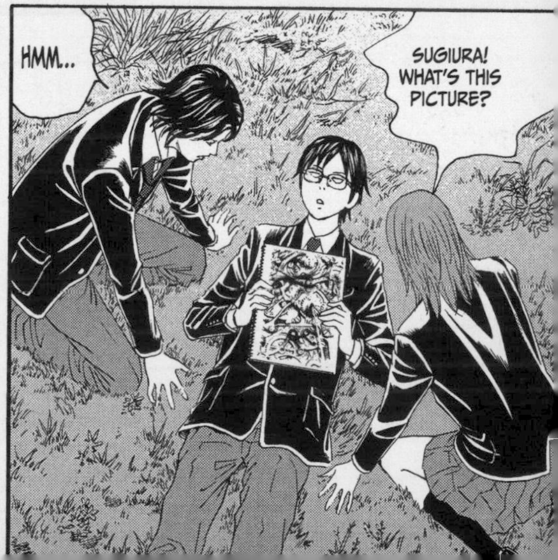
SUGIURA! WHAT'S THIS PICTURE?
HMM...
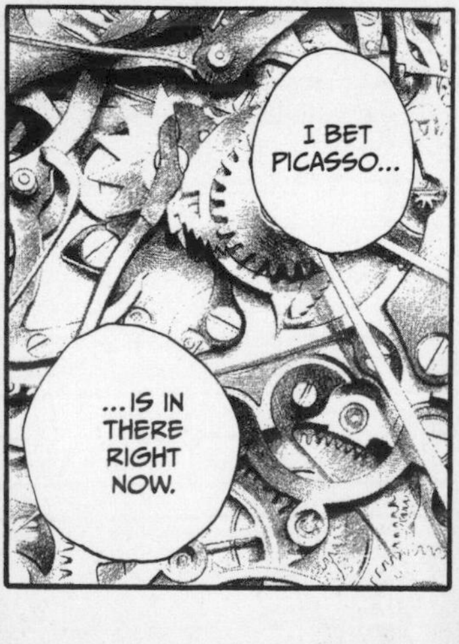
I BET PICASSO...
...IS IN THERE RIGHT NOW.

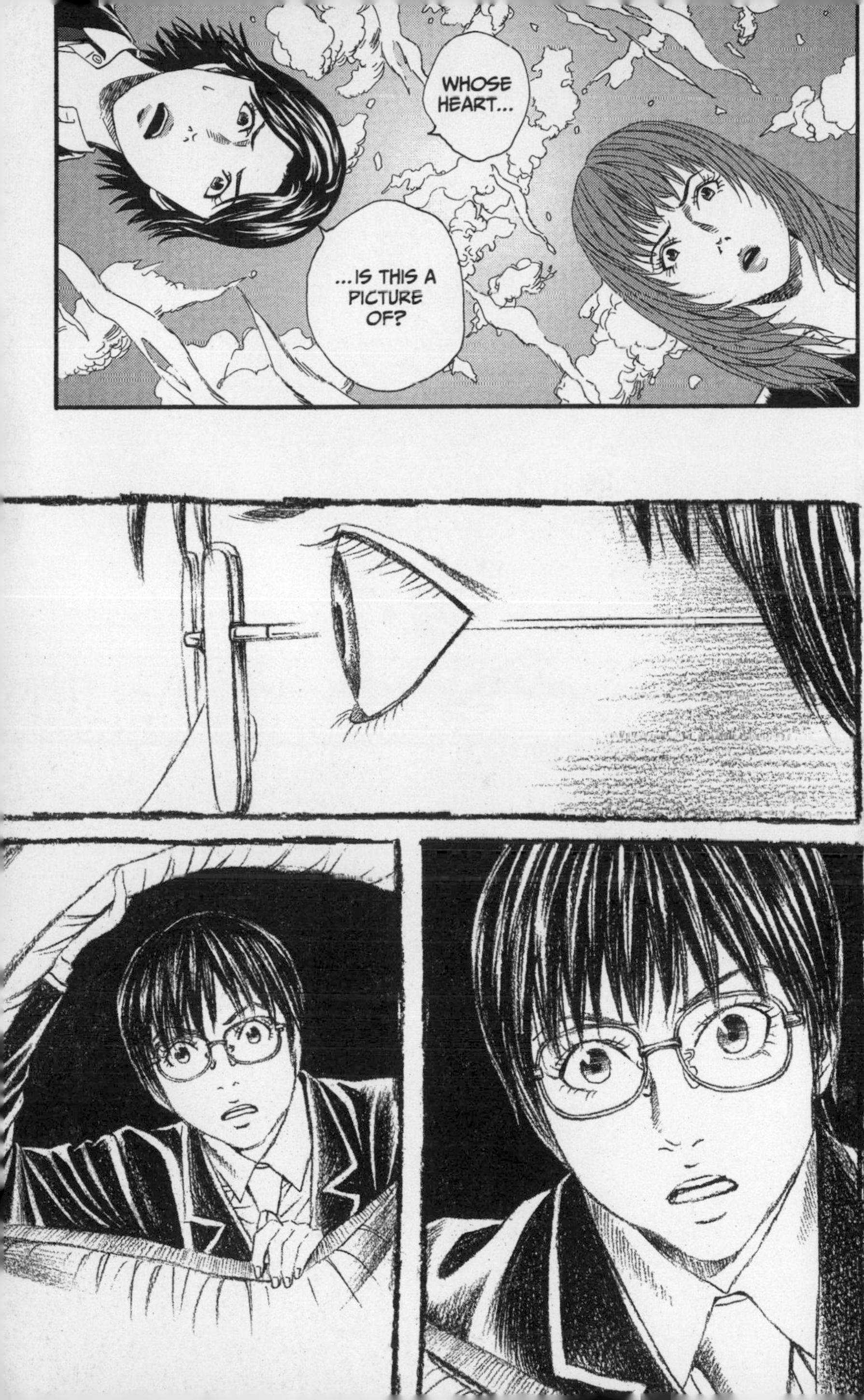
WHOSE HEART...
...IS THIS A PICTURE OF?

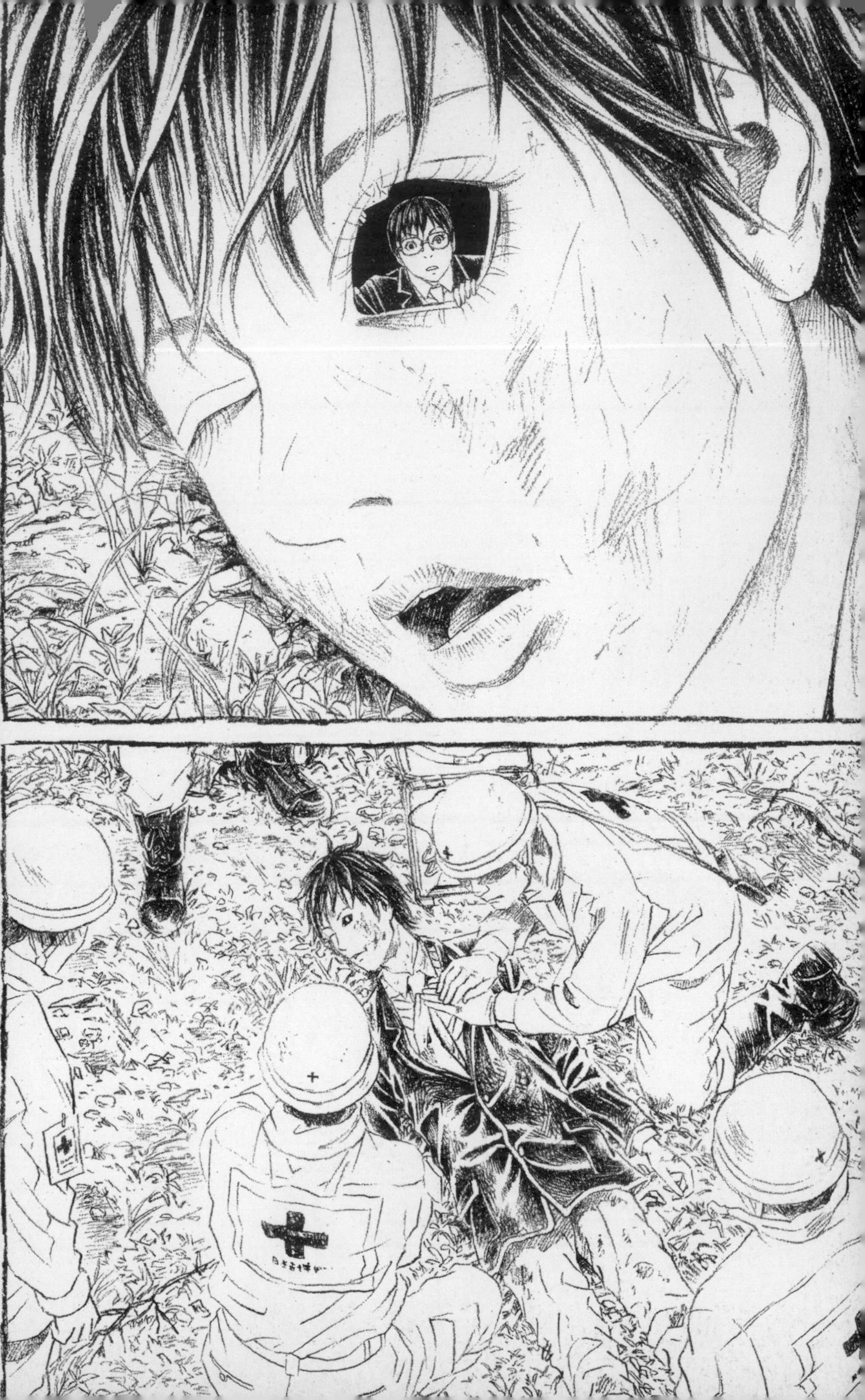

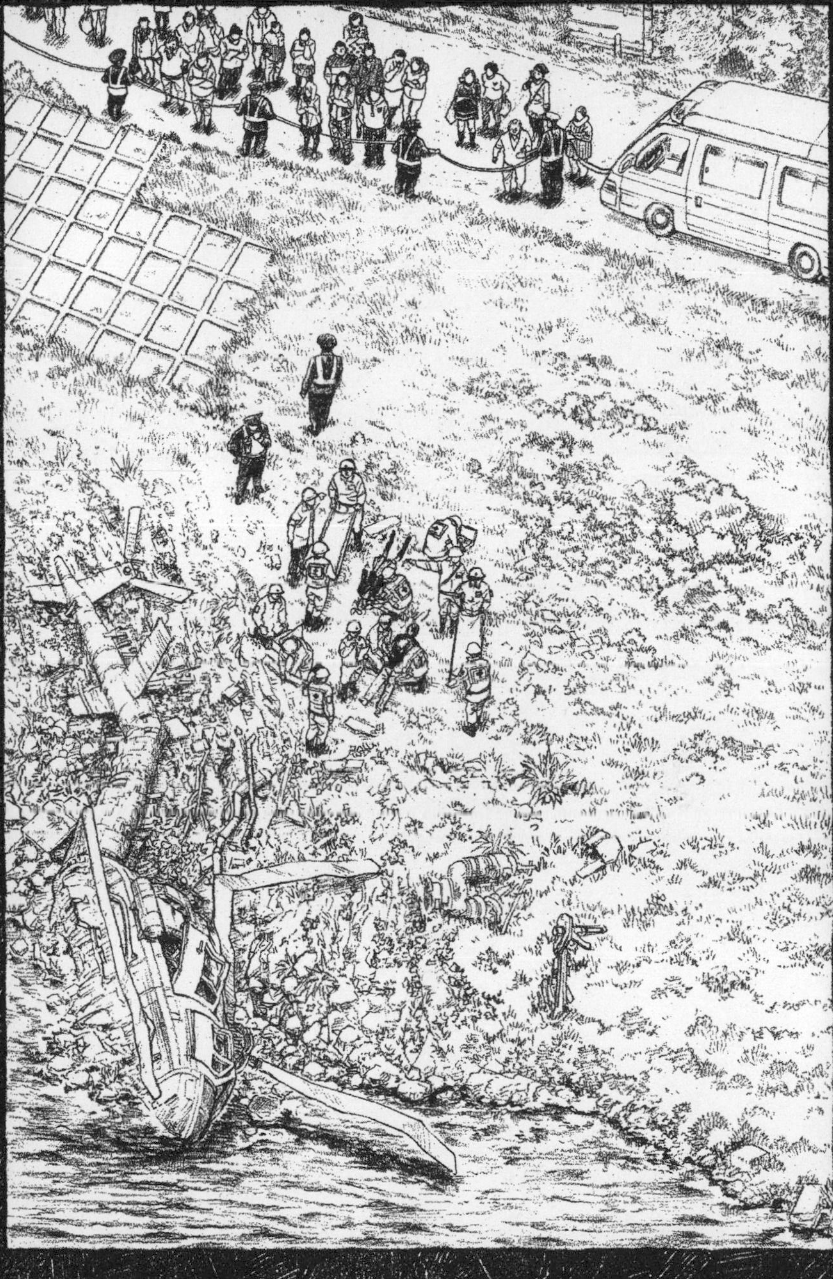

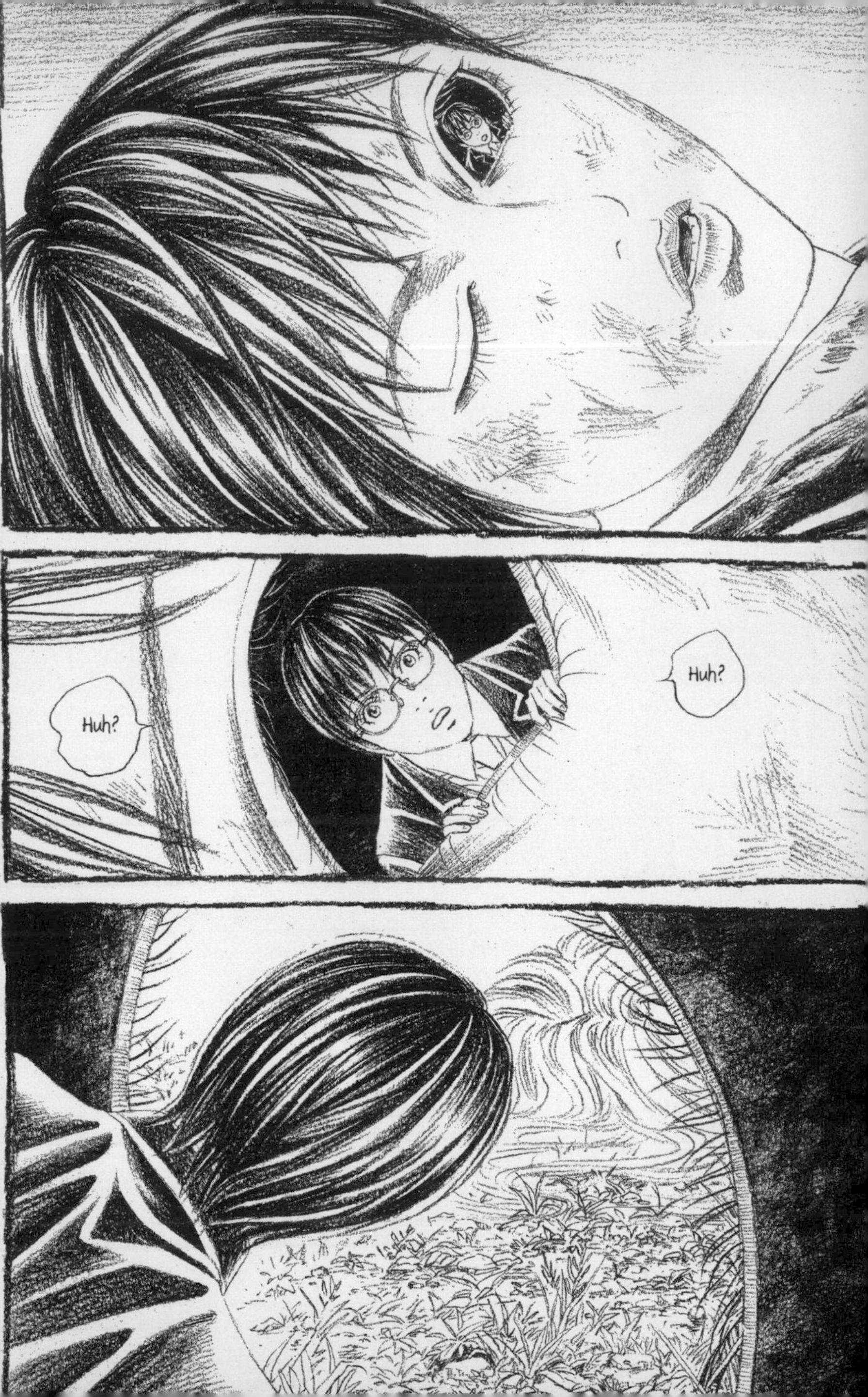
Huh?
Huh?

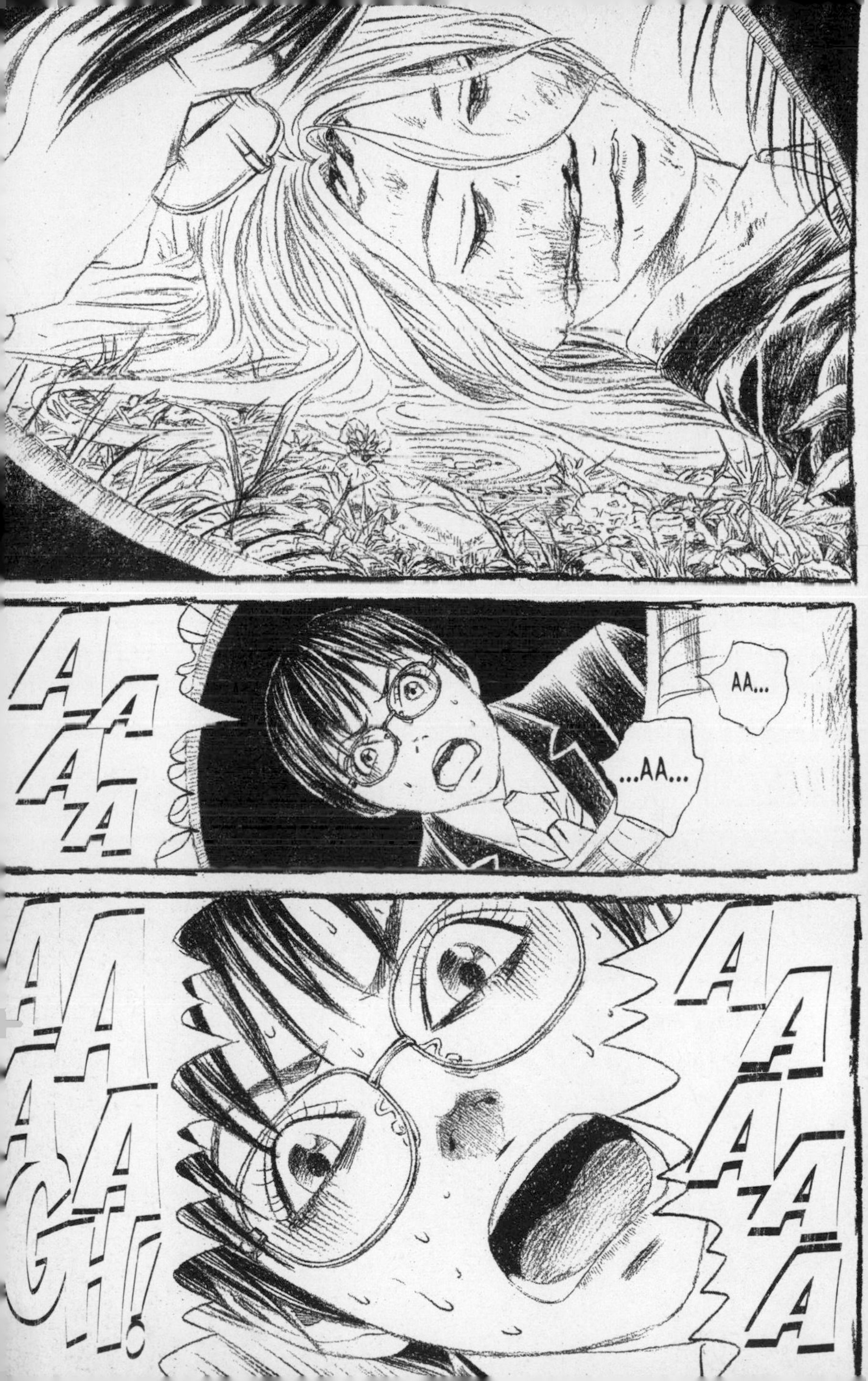
AA...
...AA...
AAAAAA
AAAAAA
AAAAAGH!

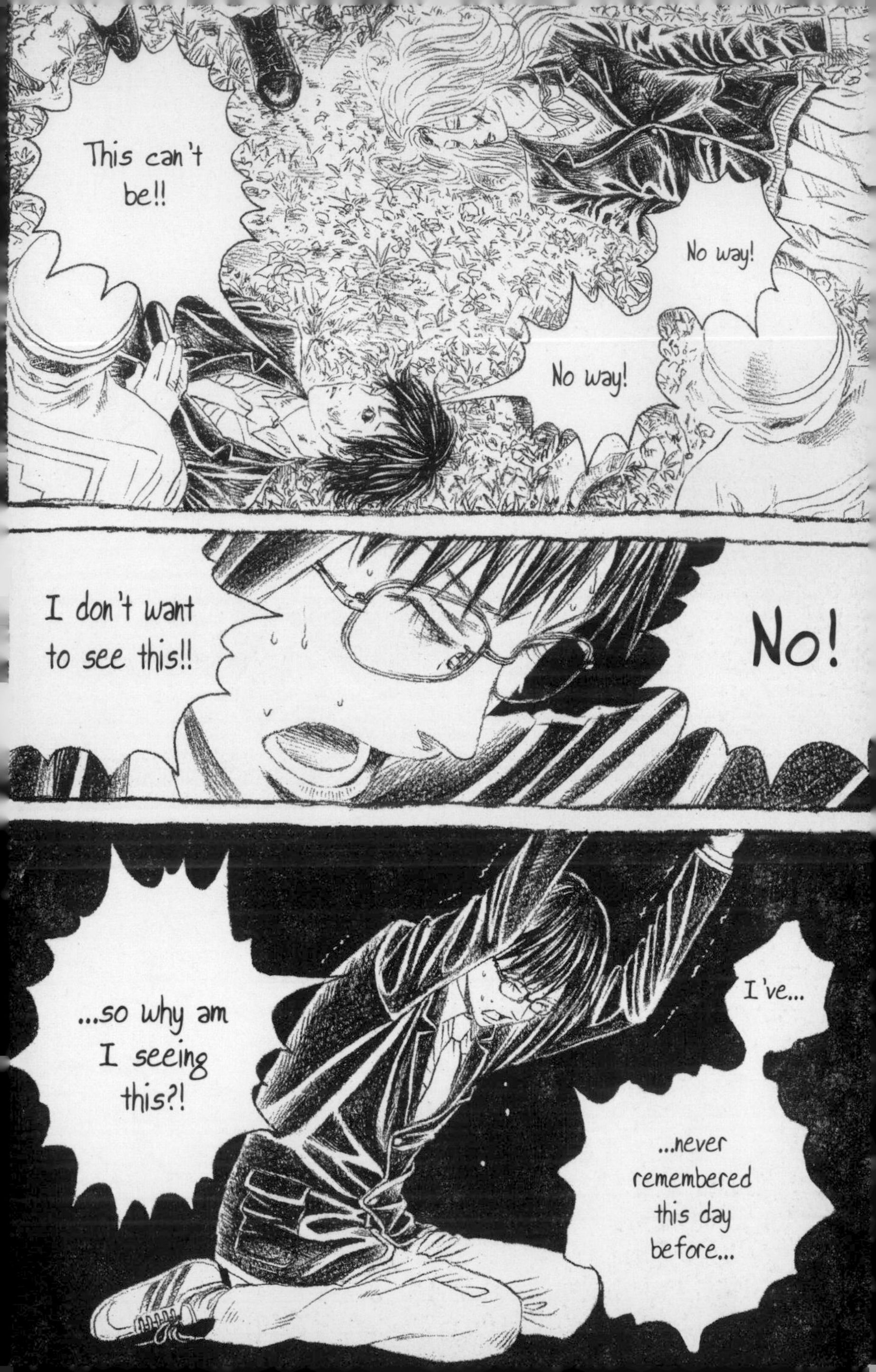
No way!
No way!
This can't be!!
No!
I don't want to see this!!
I've...
...never remembered this day before...
...so why am I seeing this?!

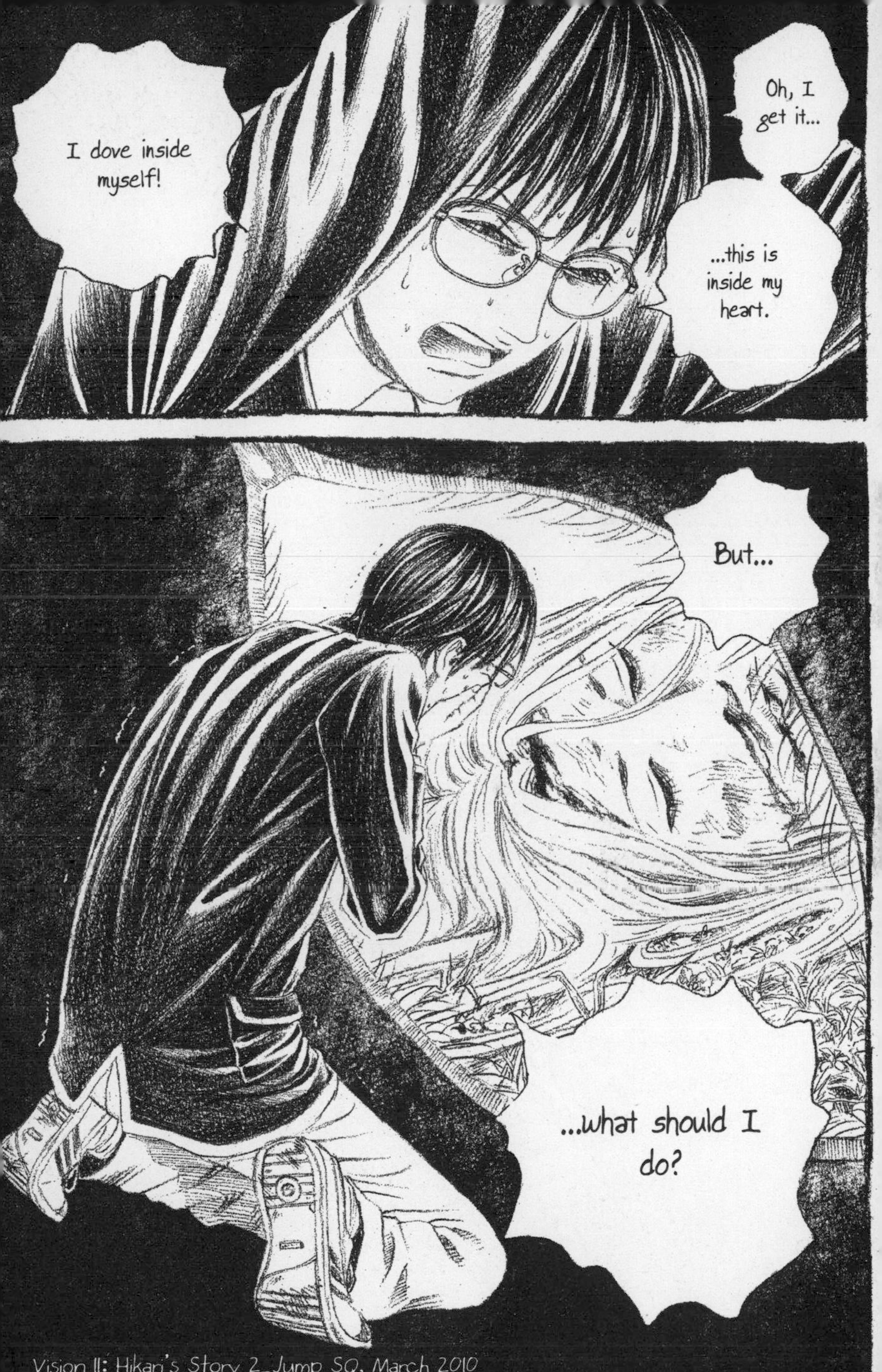
Oh, I get it...
...this is inside my heart.
I dove inside myself!
But...
...what should I do?

Vision II: Hikari's Story 2_Jump SQ, March 2010

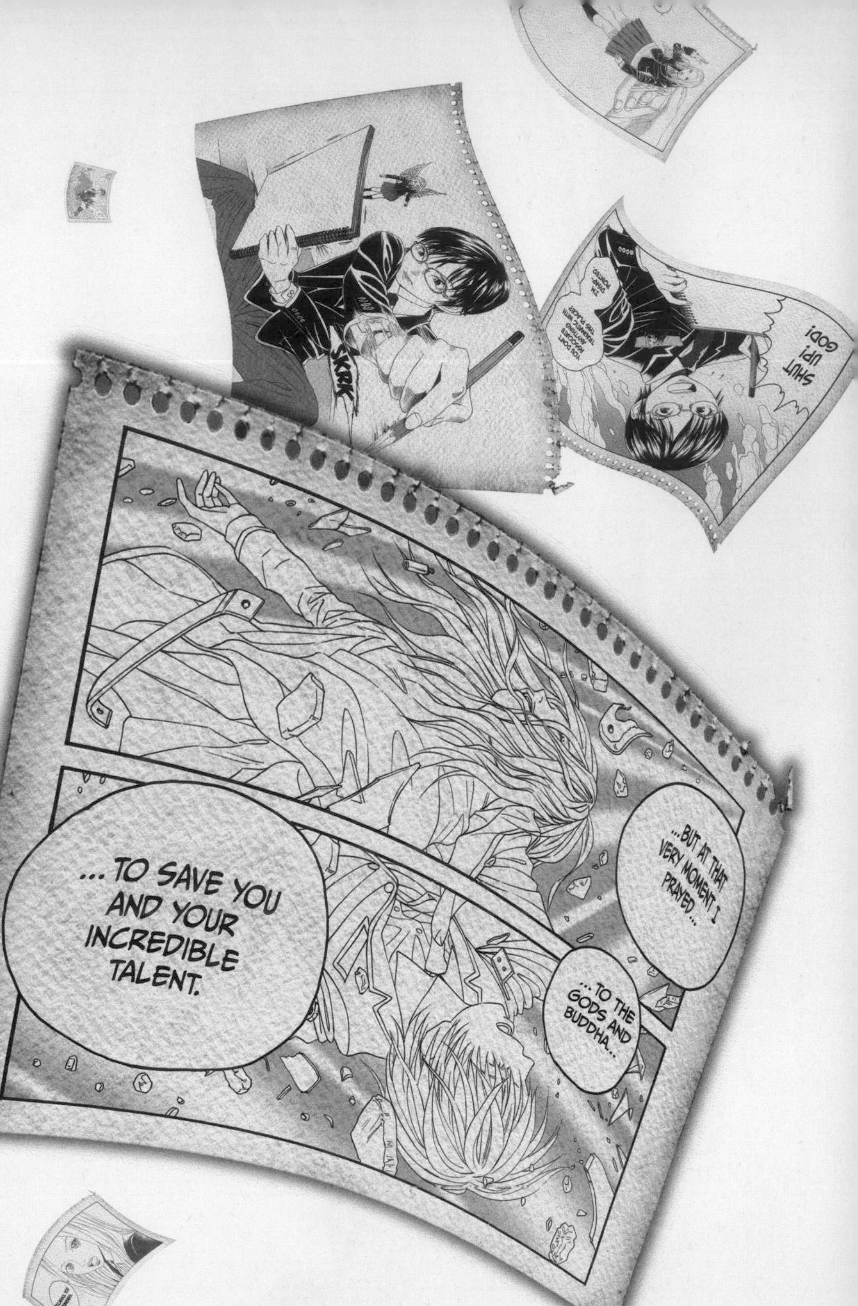
SHUT UP! GOD!
YOU DON'T ASSOCIATE ANYTHING TRAUMATIC WITH THIS PLACE?
I'M DISAP-POINTED.
SKRK
...BUT AT THAT VERY MOMENT I PRAYED...
...TO THE GODS AND BUDDHA...
...TO SAVE YOU AND YOUR INCREDIBLE TALENT.

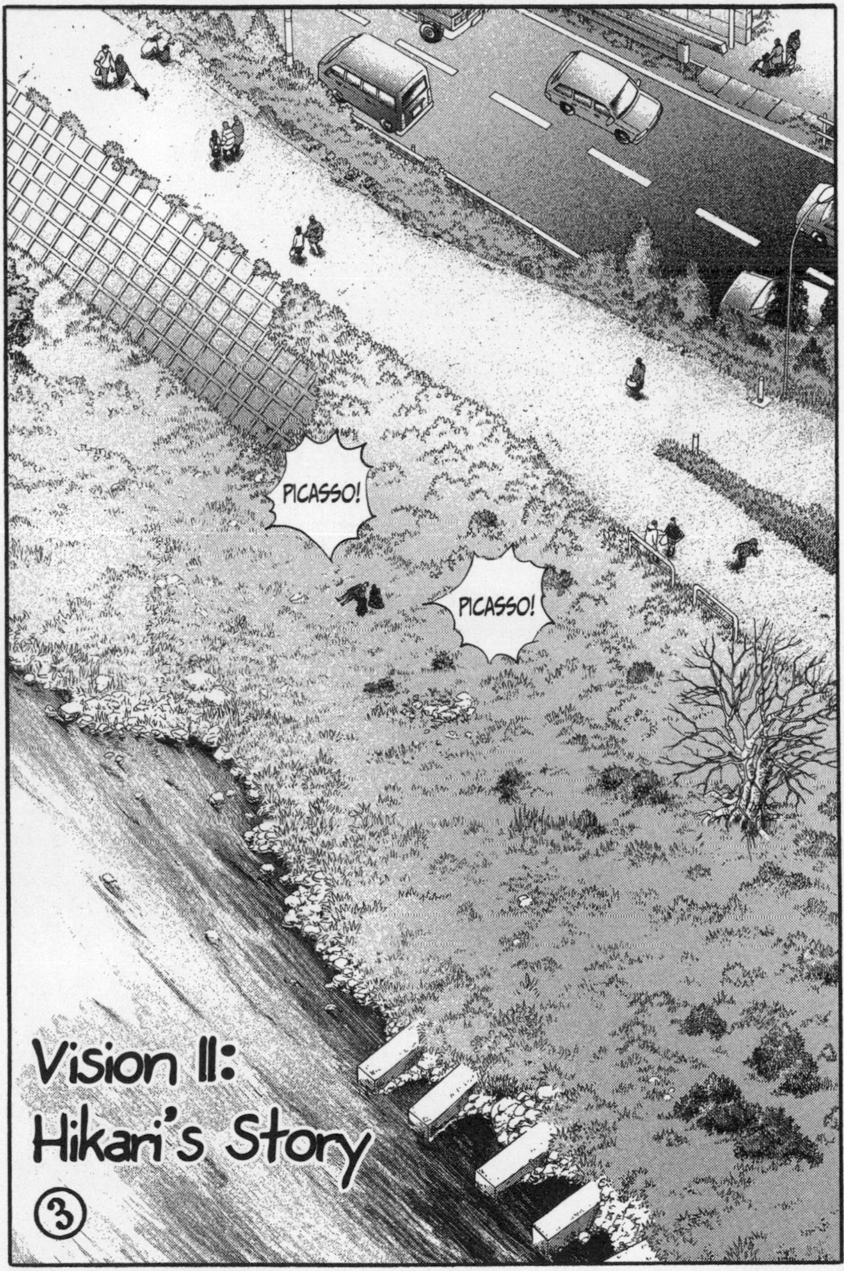
PICASSO!
PICASSO!
Vision 11: Hikari's Story ③

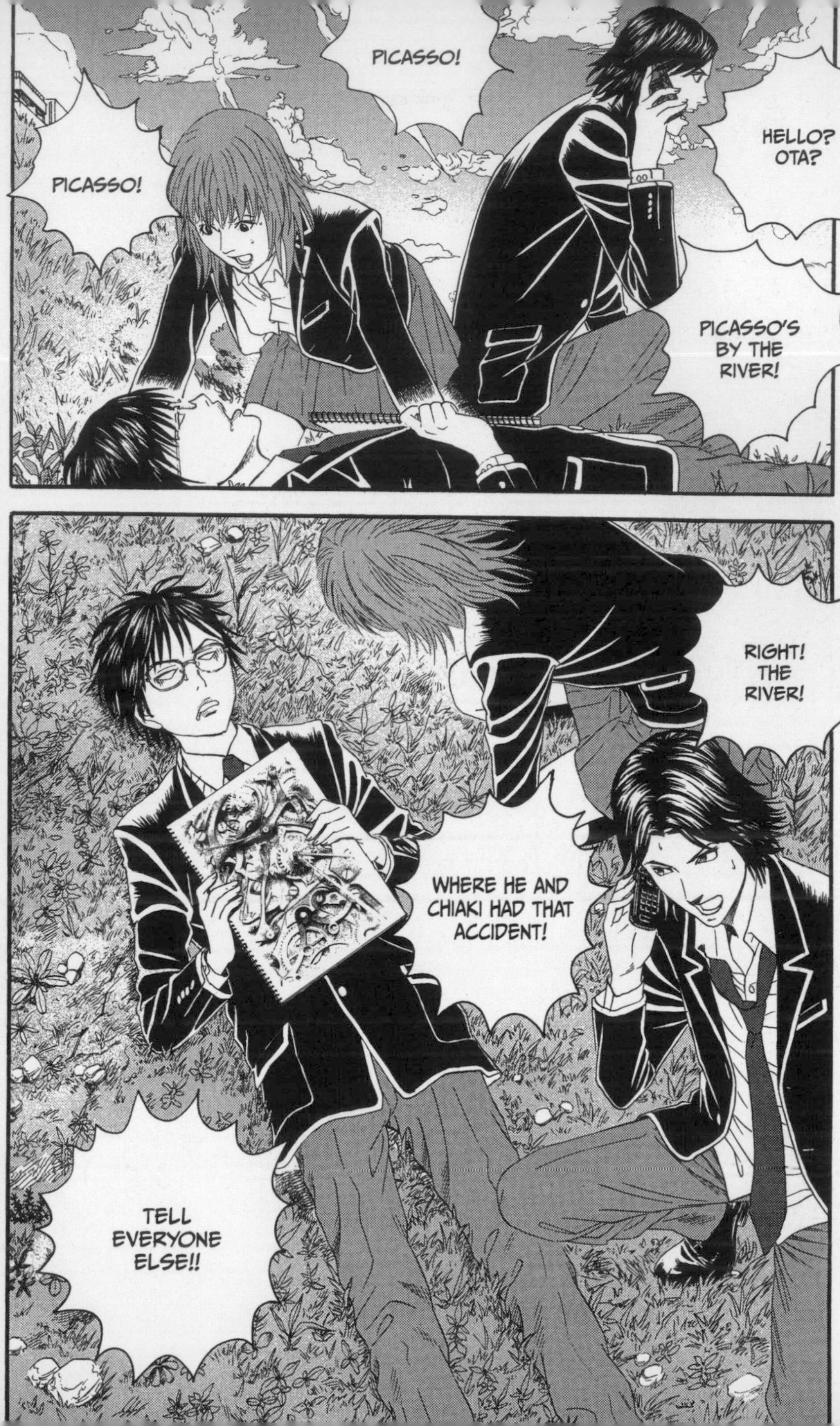
PICASSO!
HELLO? OTA?
PICASSO!
PICASSO'S BY THE RIVER!
RIGHT! THE RIVER!
WHERE HE AND CHIAKI HAD THAT ACCIDENT!
TELL EVERYONE ELSE!!

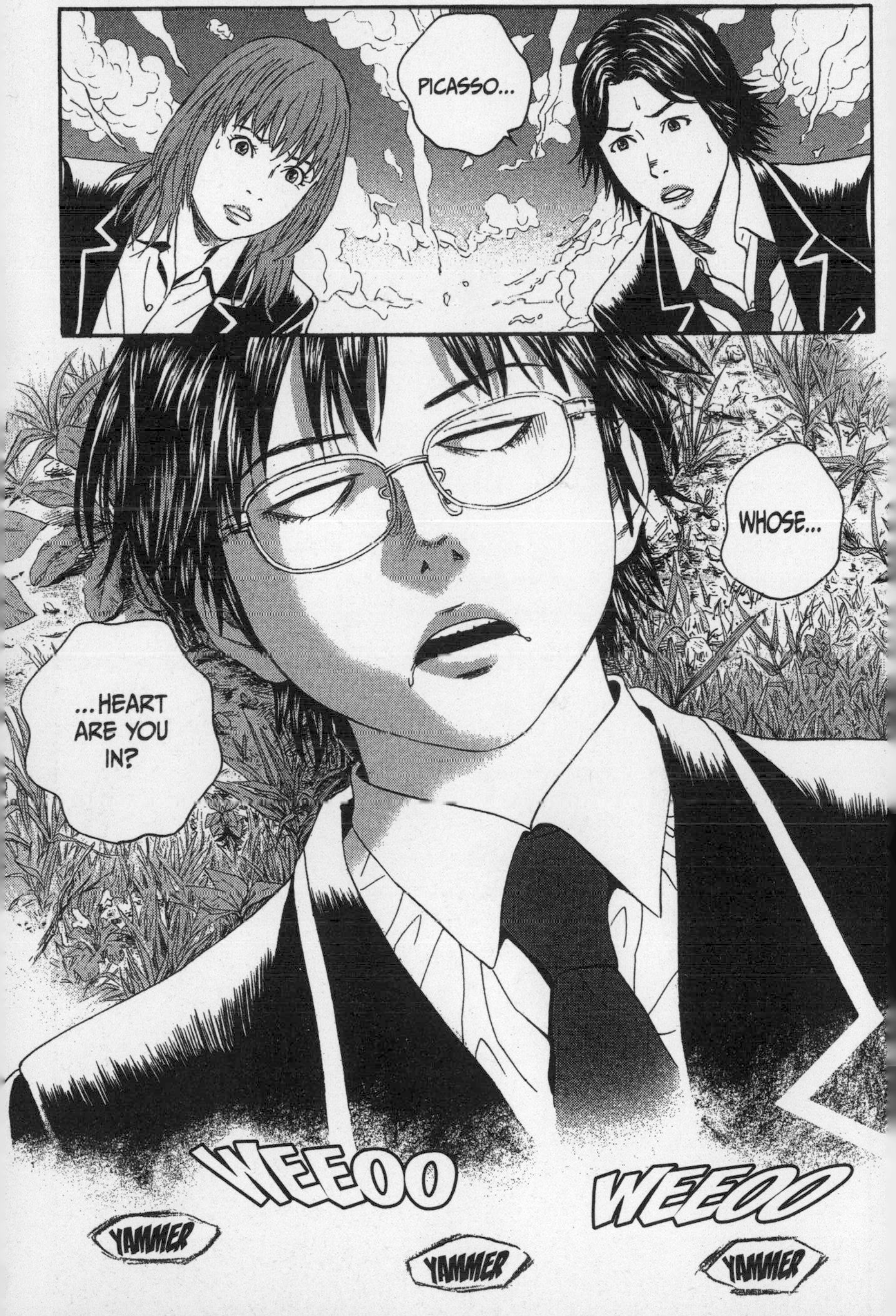
PICASSO...
WHOSE...
...HEART ARE YOU IN?
WEEOO
WEEOO
YAMMER
YAMMER
YAMMER

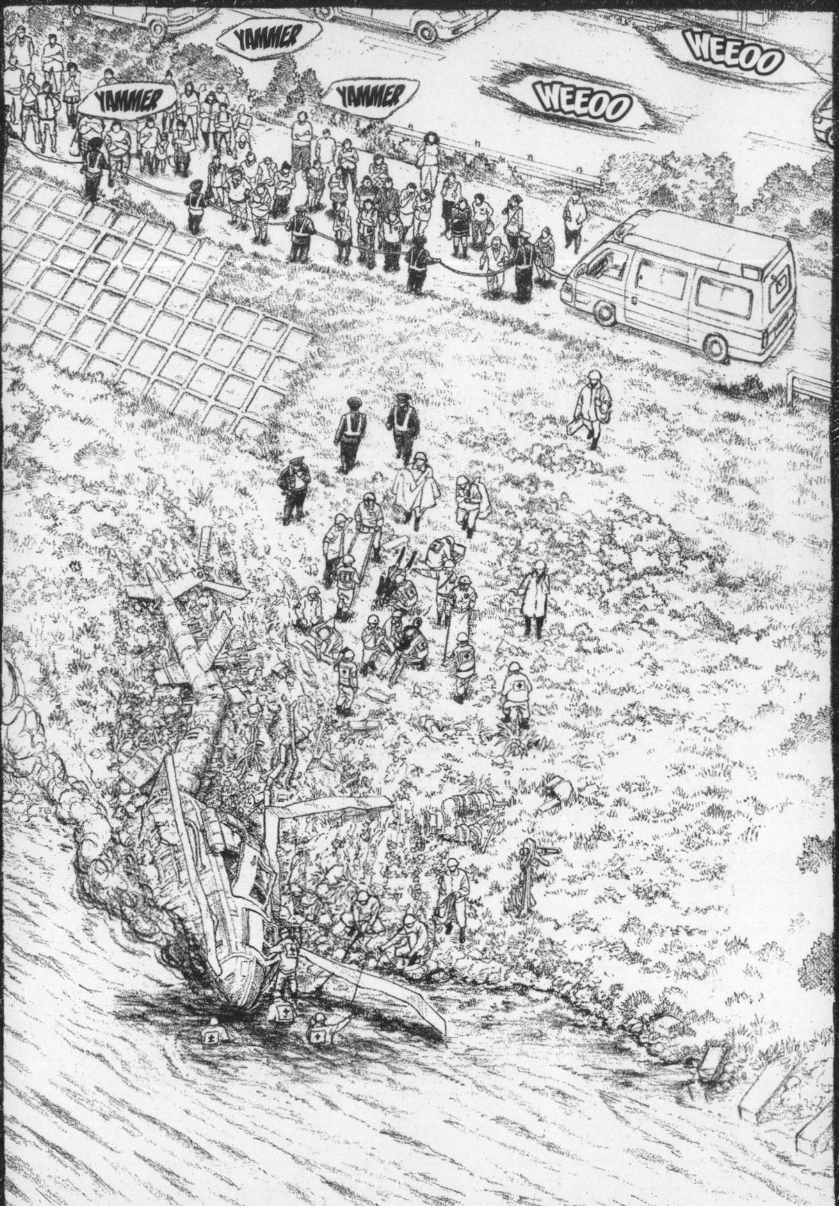
WEEOO
WEEOO
YAMMER
YAMMER
YAMMER

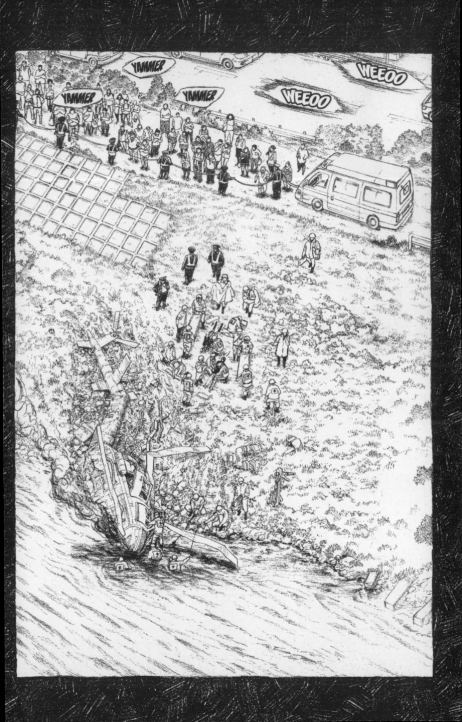

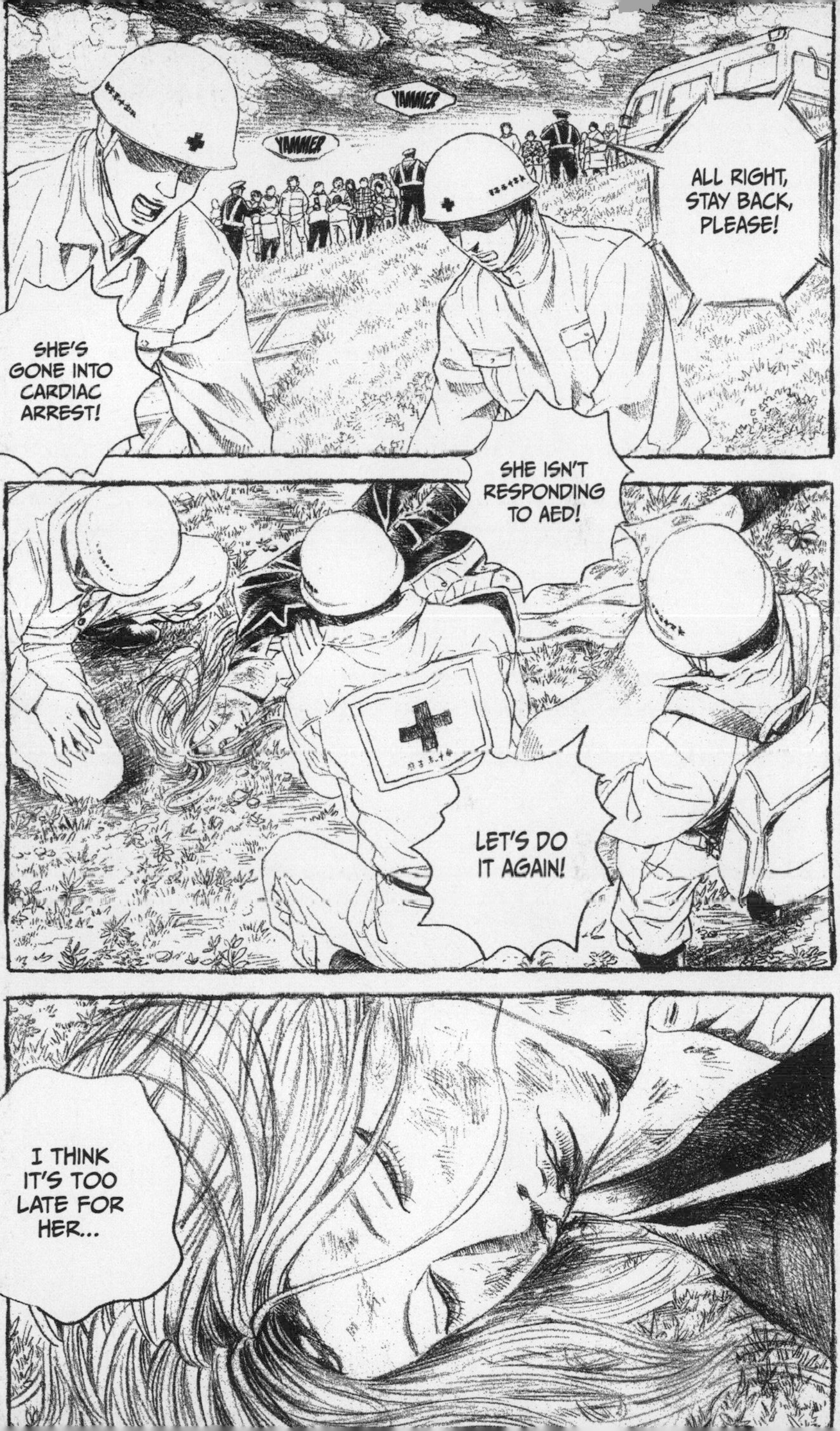
ALL RIGHT, STAY BACK, PLEASE!
YAMMER
YAMMER
SHE'S GONE INTO CARDIAC ARREST!
SHE ISN'T RESPONDING TO AED!
LET'S DO IT AGAIN!
I THINK IT'S TOO LATE FOR HER...

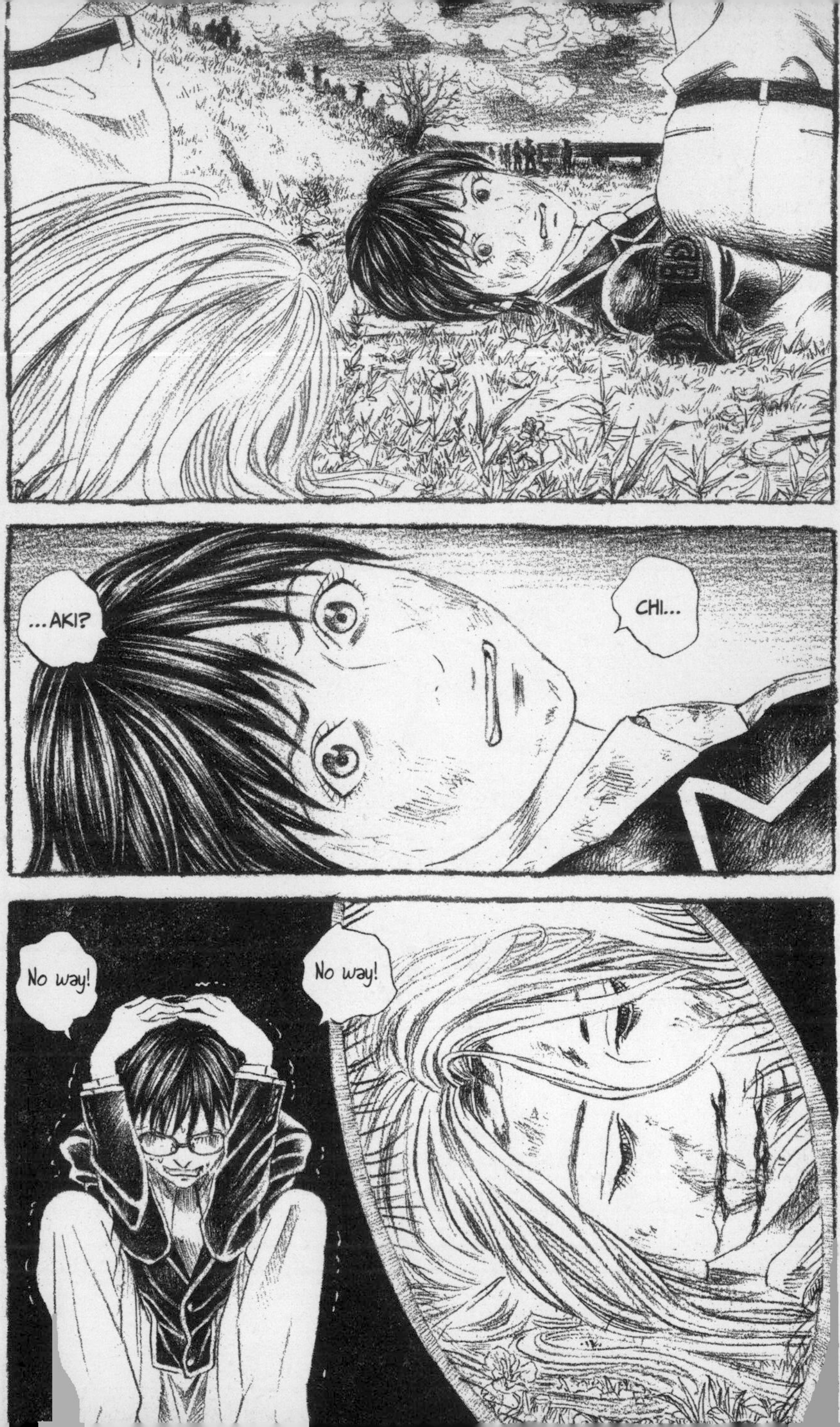
CHI...
...AKI?
No way!
No way!

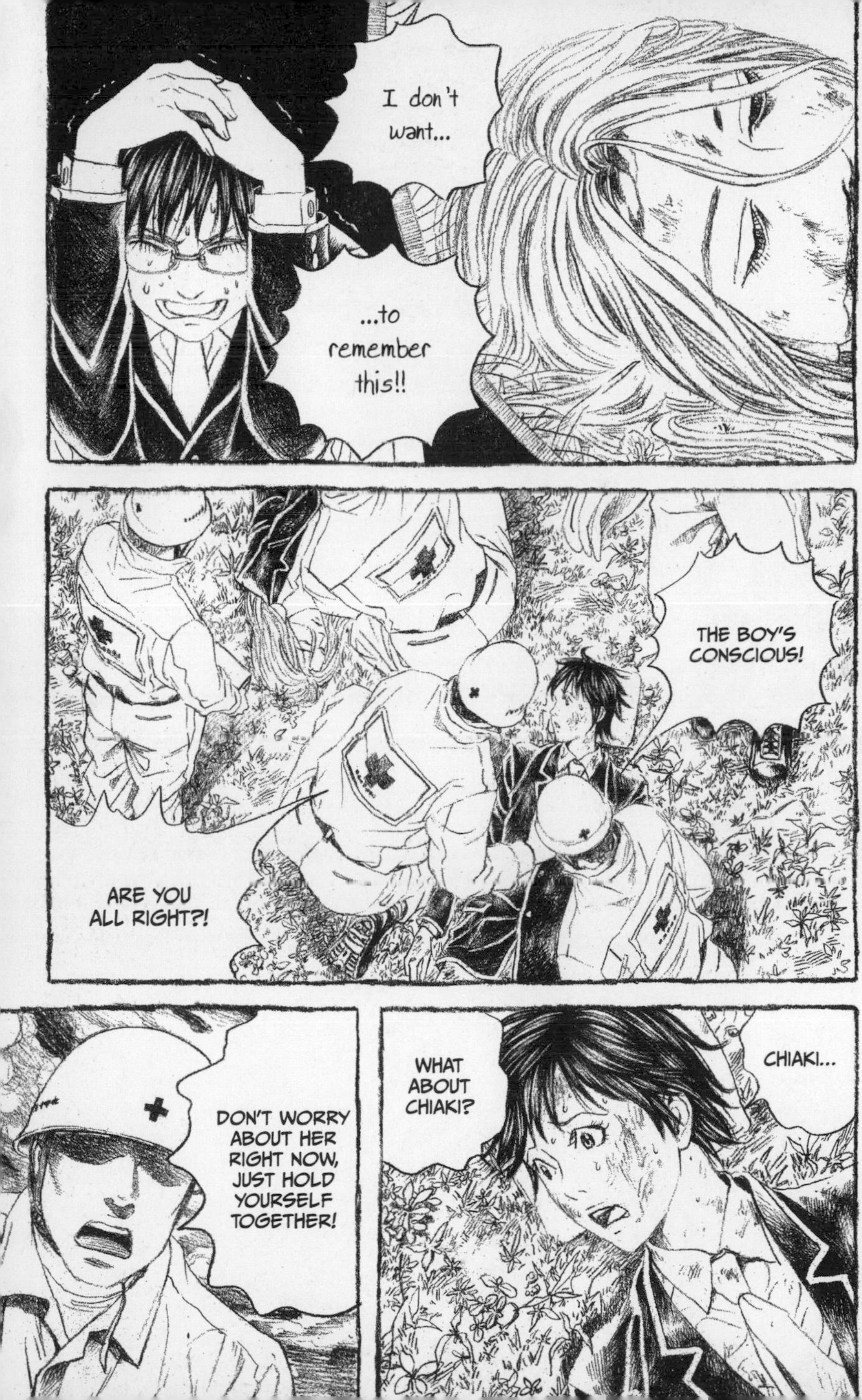
I don't want...
...to remember this!!
THE BOY'S CONSCIOUS!
ARE YOU ALL RIGHT?!
CHIAKI...
WHAT ABOUT CHIAKI?
DON'T WORRY ABOUT HER RIGHT NOW, JUST HOLD YOURSELF TOGETHER!

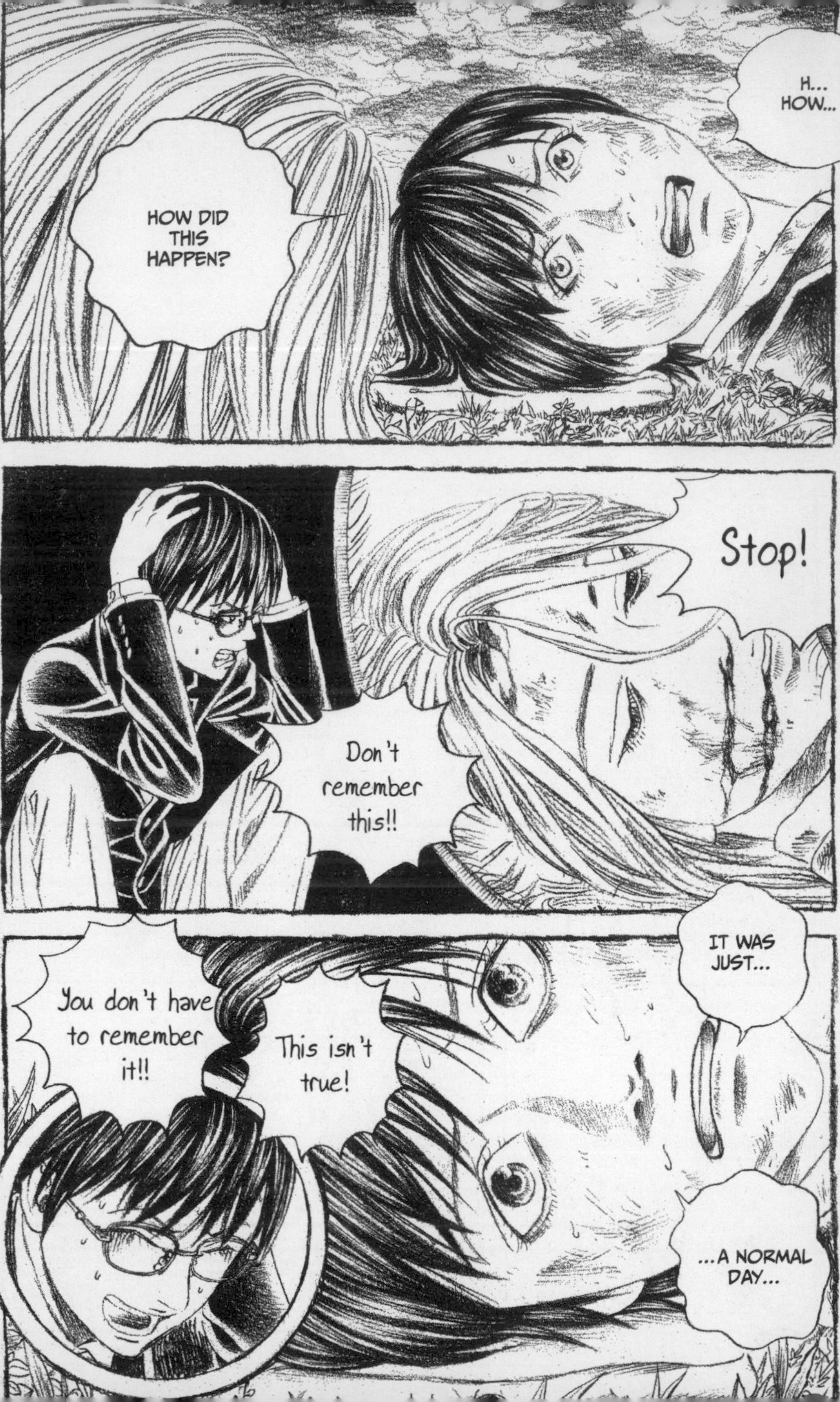
H... HOW...
HOW DID THIS HAPPEN?
Stop!
Don't remember this!!
IT WAS JUST...
...A NORMAL DAY...
This isn't true!
You don't have to remember it!!

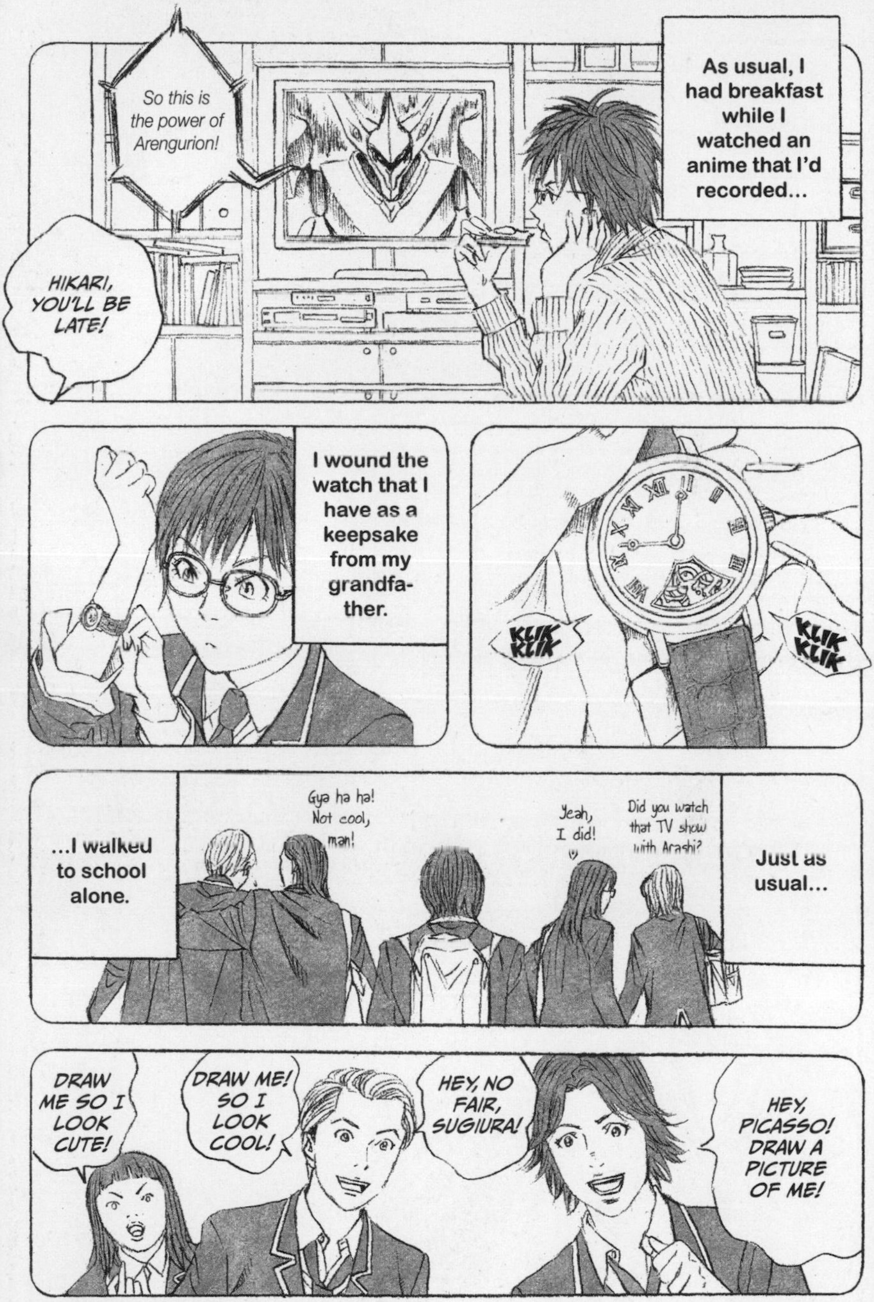
As usual, I had breakfast while I watched an anime that I'd recorded...
So this is the power of Arengurion!
HIKARI, YOU'LL BE LATE!
KLIK KLIK
KLIK KLIK
I wound the watch that I have as a keepsake from my grandfa-ther.
Just as usual...
Did you watch that TV show with Arashi?
Yeah, I did!
Gya ha ha! Not cool, man!
...I walked to school alone.
HEY, PICASSO! DRAW A PICTURE OF ME!
HEY, NO FAIR, SUGIURA!
DRAW ME! SO I LOOK COOL!
DRAW ME SO I LOOK CUTE!

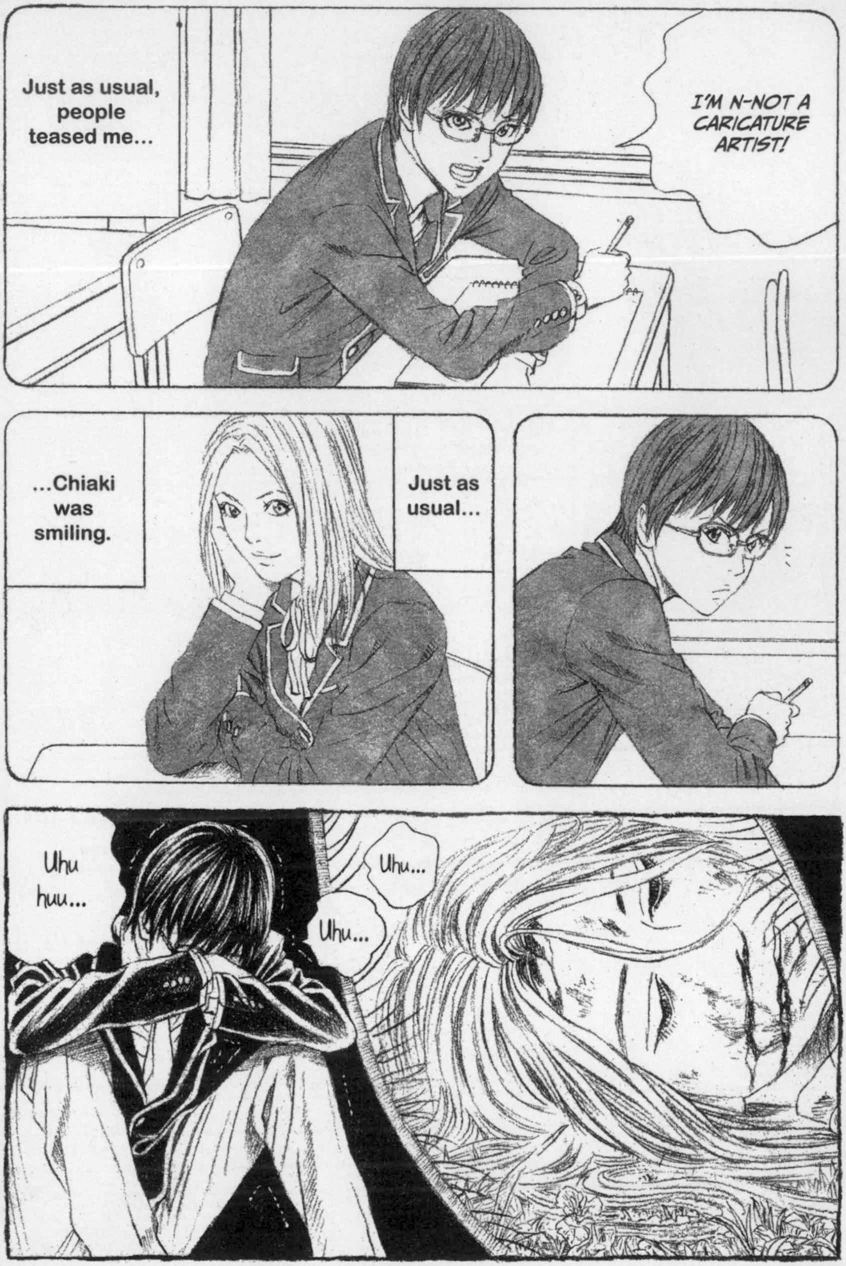
I'M N-NOT A CARICATURE ARTIST!
Just as usual, people teased me...
Just as usual...
...Chiaki was smiling.
Uhu...
Uhu...
Uhu huu...

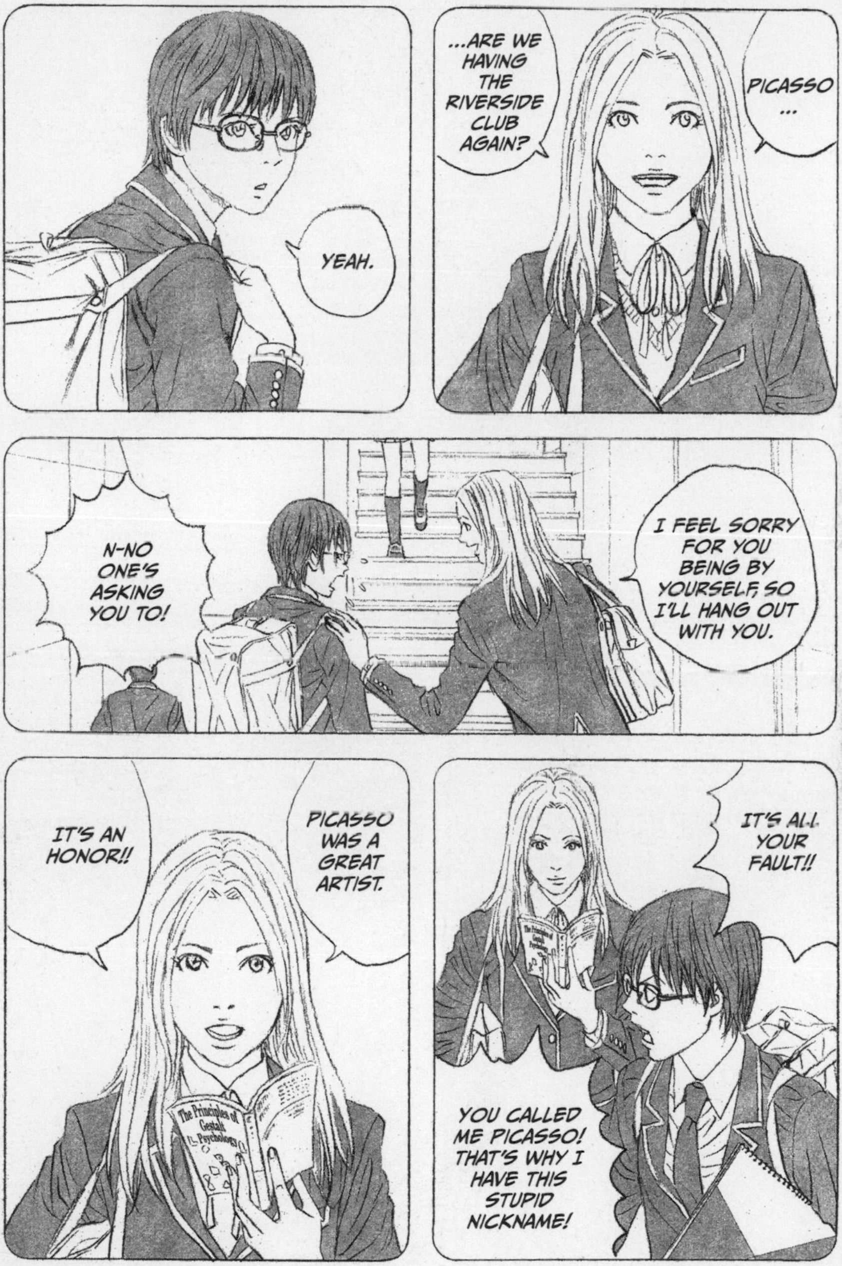
PICASSO ...
...ARE WE HAVING THE RIVERSIDE CLUB AGAIN?
YEAH.
I FEEL SORRY FOR YOU BEING BY YOURSELF, SO I'LL HANG OUT WITH YOU.
N-NO ONE'S ASKING YOU TO!
IT'S ALL YOUR FAULT!!
YOU CALLED ME PICASSO! THAT'S WHY I HAVE THIS STUPID NICKNAME!
PICASSO WAS A GREAT ARTIST.
IT'S AN HONOR!!
The Principles of Gestalt Psychology

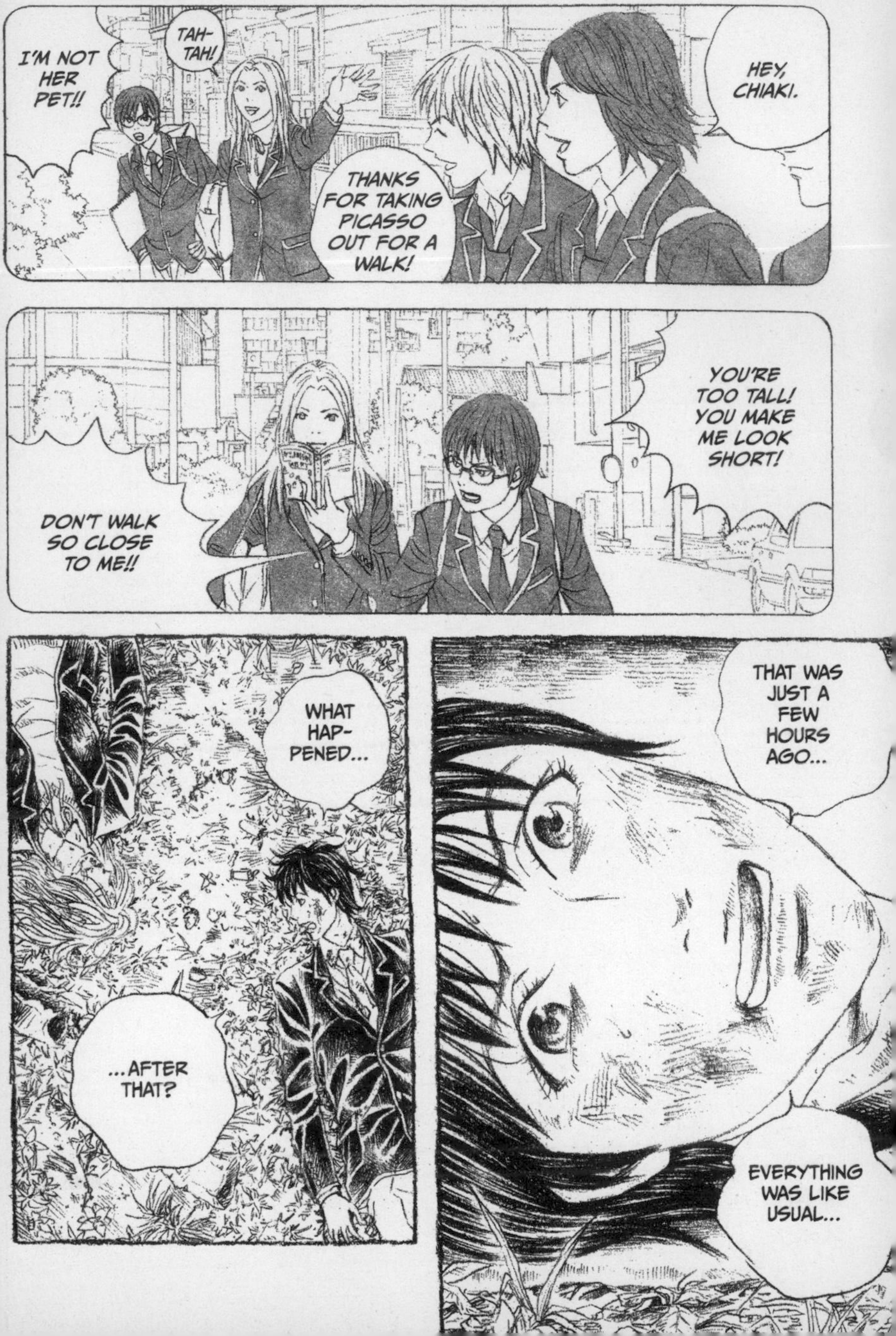
HEY, CHIAKI.
THANKS FOR TAKING PICASSO OUT FOR A WALK!
TAH-TAH!
I'M NOT HER PET!!
YOU'RE TOO TALL! YOU MAKE ME LOOK SHORT!
DON'T WALK SO CLOSE TO ME!!
THAT WAS JUST A FEW HOURS AGO...
EVERYTHING WAS LIKE USUAL...
WHAT HAPPENED...
...AFTER THAT?

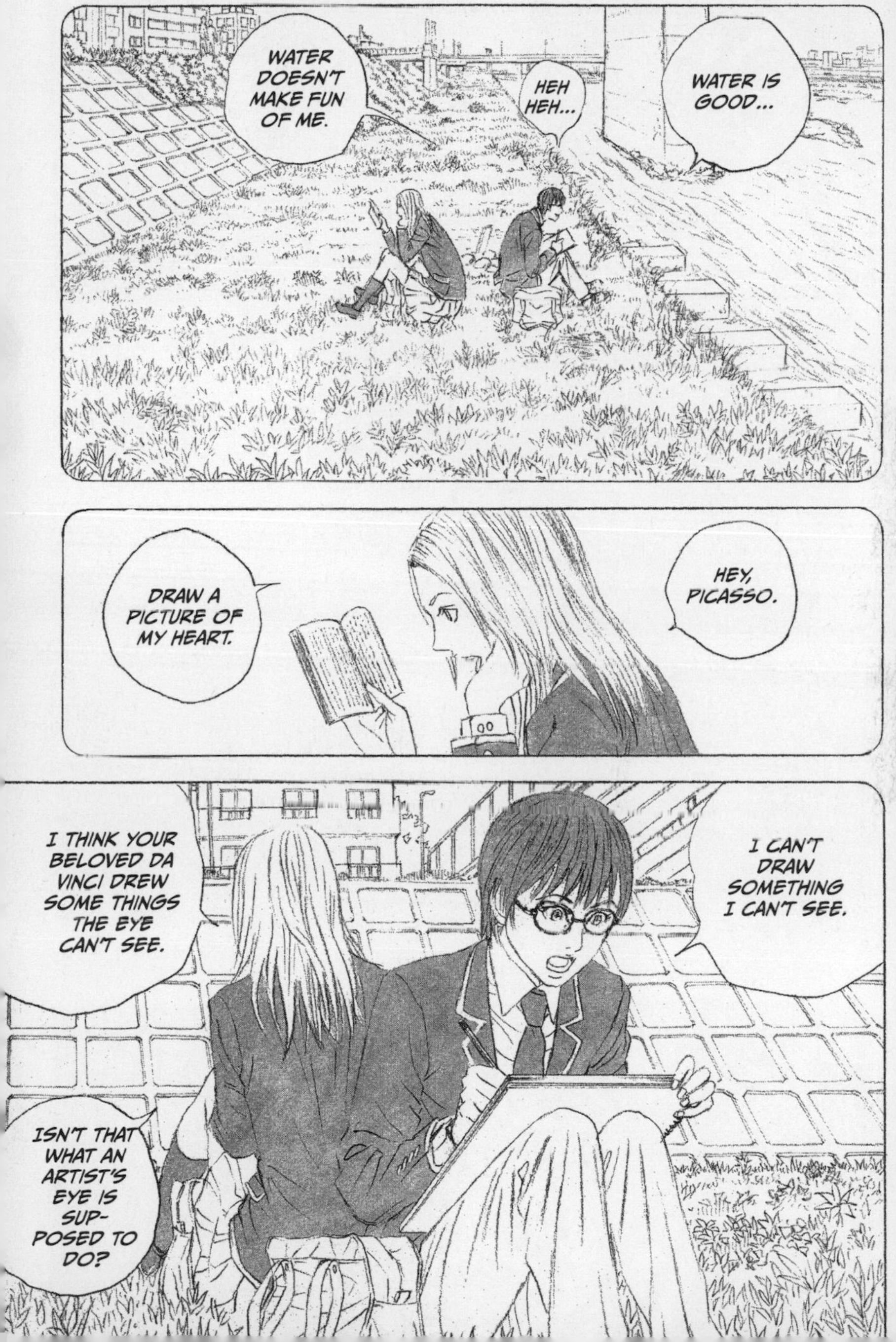
WATER IS GOOD...
HEH HEH...
WATER DOESN'T MAKE FUN OF ME.
HEY, PICASSO.
DRAW A PICTURE OF MY HEART.
I CAN'T DRAW SOMETHING I CAN'T SEE.
I THINK YOUR BELOVED DA VINCI DREW SOME THINGS THE EYE CAN'T SEE.
ISN'T THAT WHAT AN ARTIST'S EYE IS SUPPOSED TO DO?

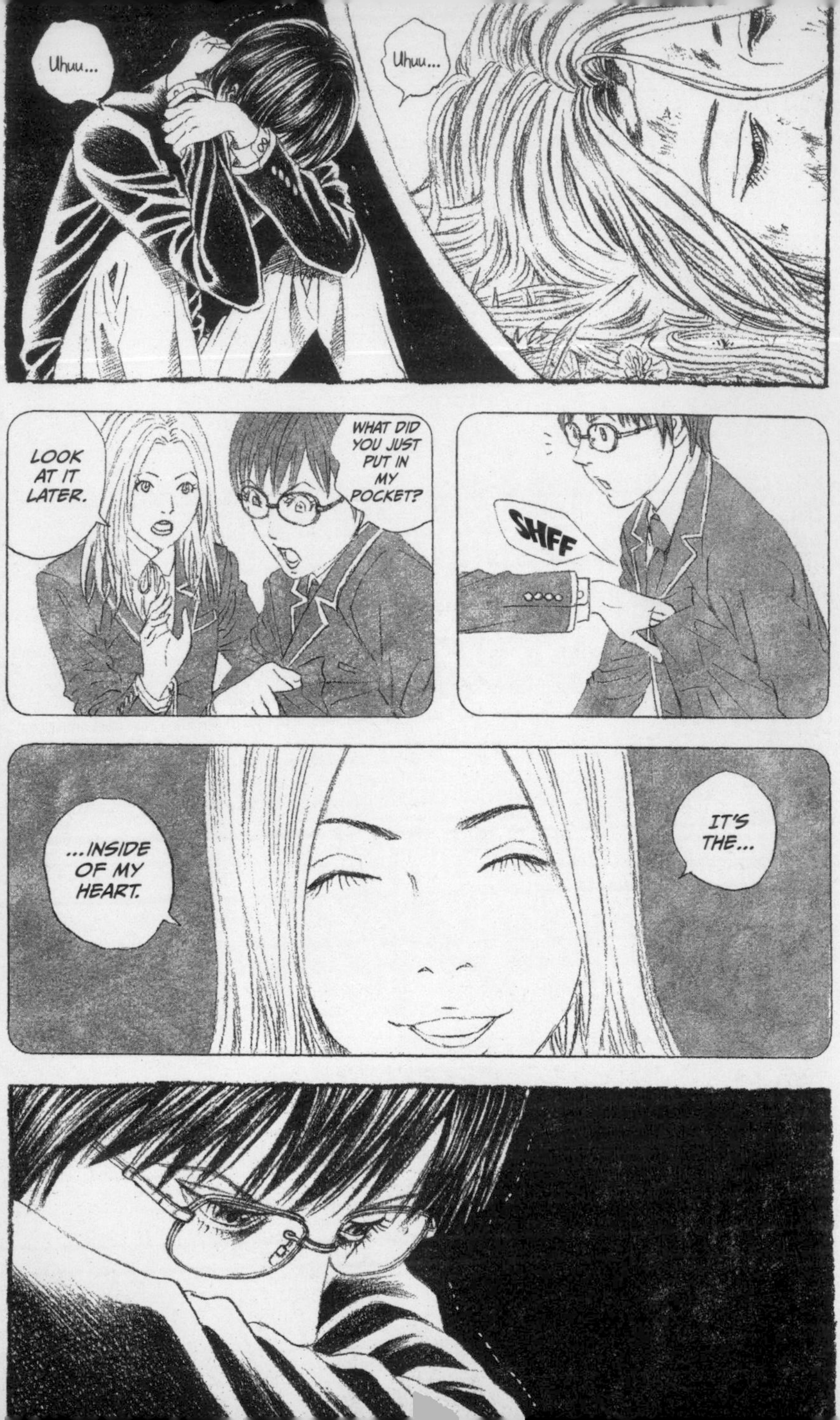
Uhuu...
Uhuu...
SHFF
WHAT DID YOU JUST PUT IN MY POCKET?
LOOK AT IT LATER.
IT'S THE...
...INSIDE OF MY HEART.

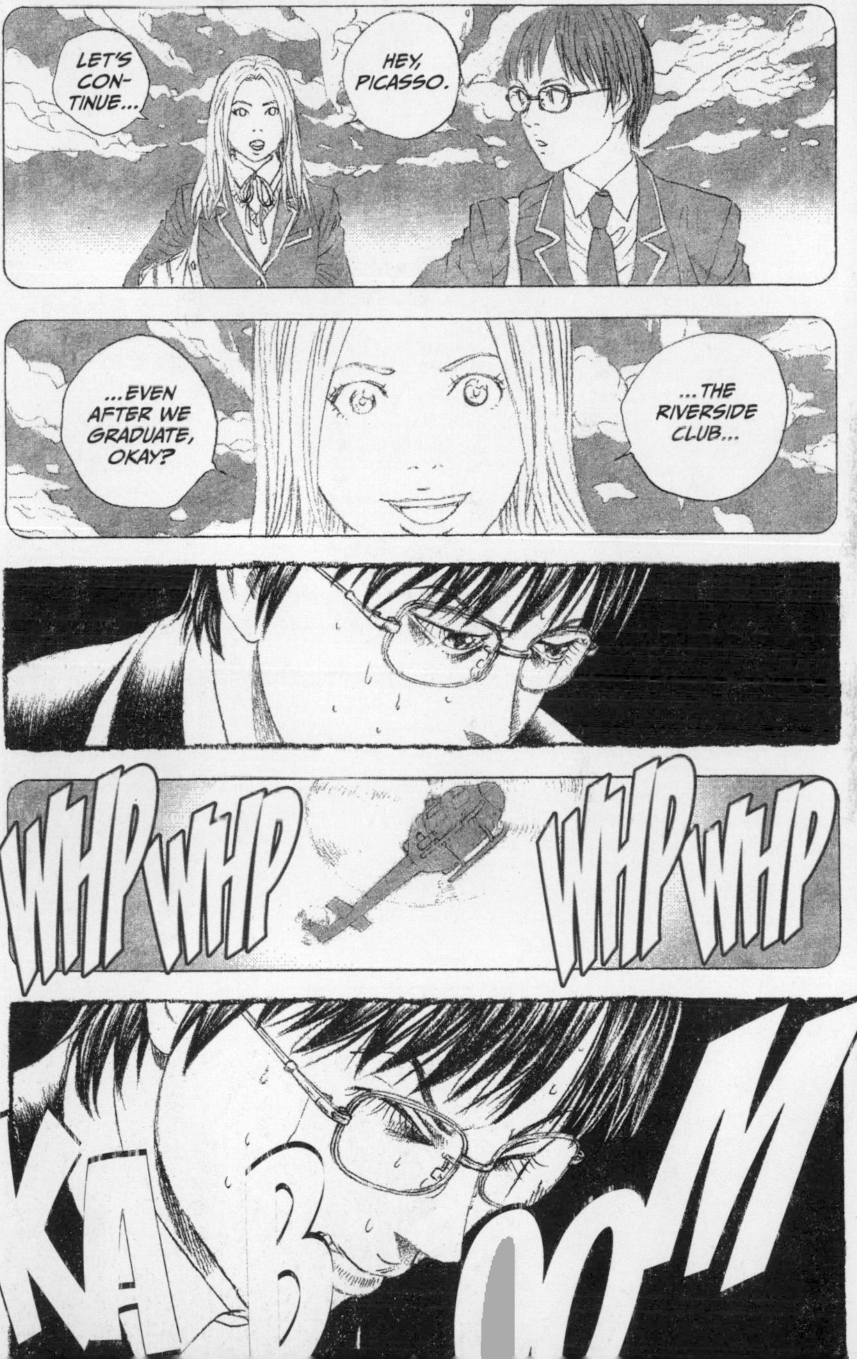
HEY, PICASSO.
LET'S CON-TINUE...
...THE RIVERSIDE CLUB...
...EVEN AFTER WE GRADUATE, OKAY?
WHP WHP
WHP WHP
KABOOM

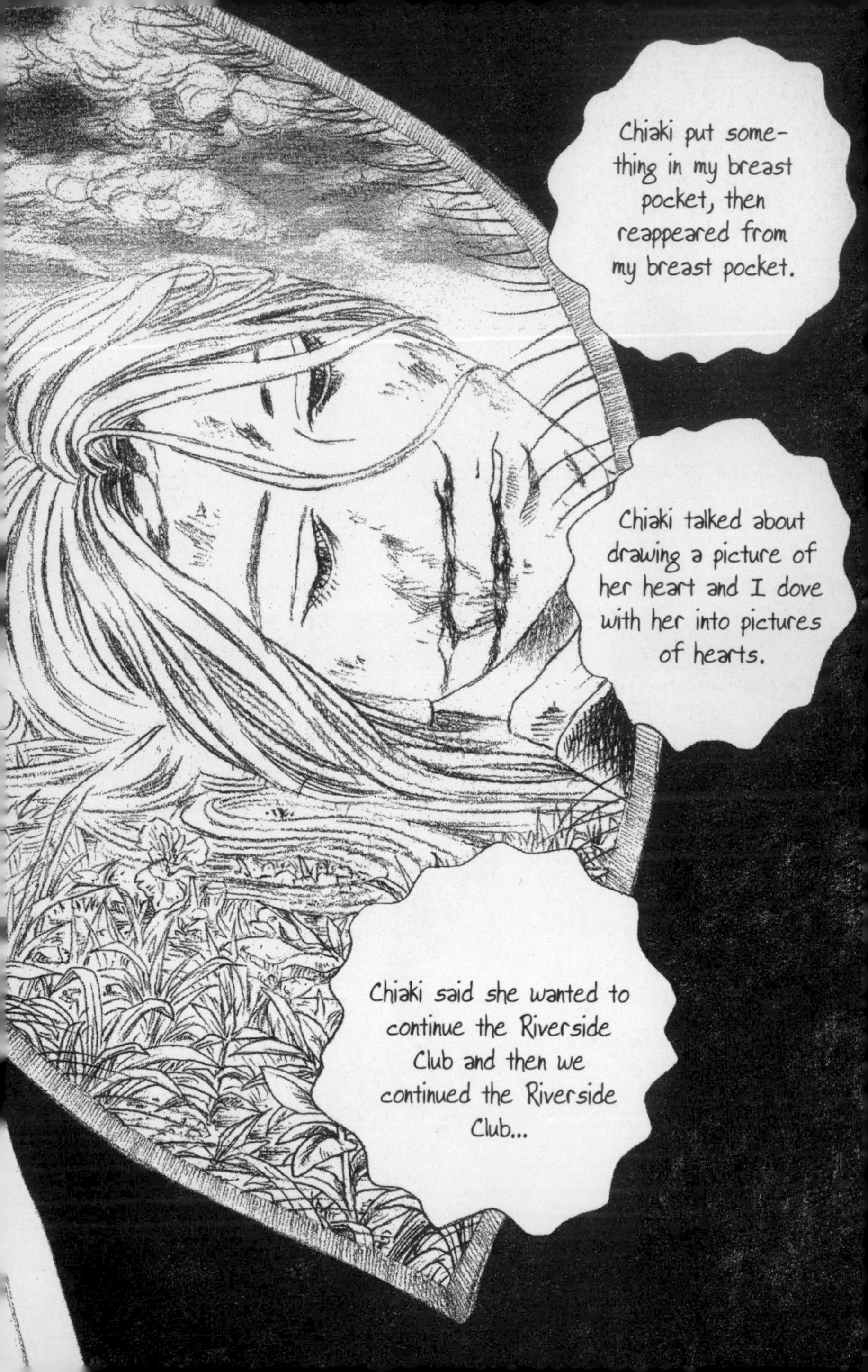
Chiaki put some-thing in my breast pocket, then reappeared from my breast pocket.
Chiaki talked about drawing a picture of her heart and I dove with her into pictures of hearts.
Chiaki said she wanted to continue the Riverside Club and then we continued the Riverside Club...

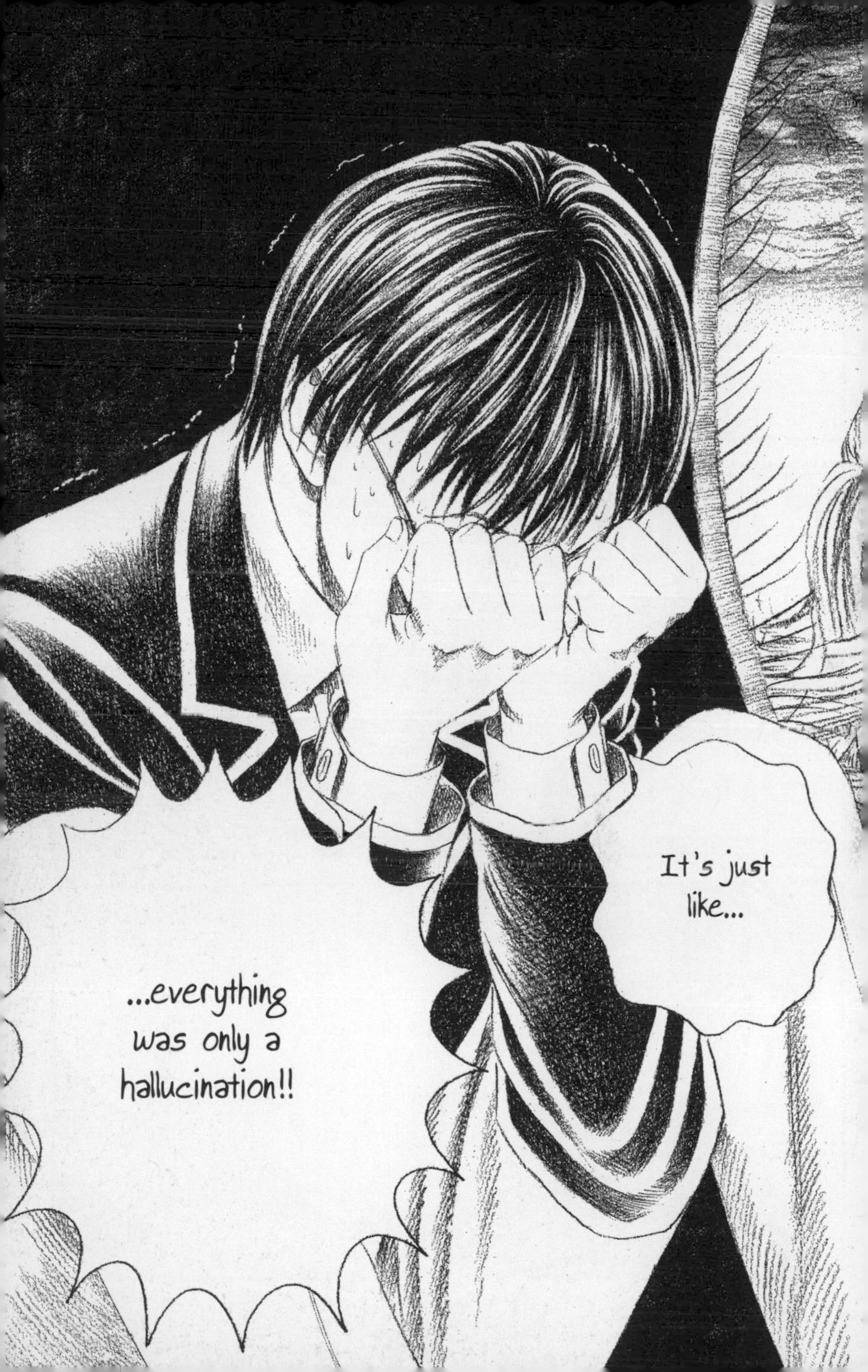
It's just like...
...everything was only a hallucination!!

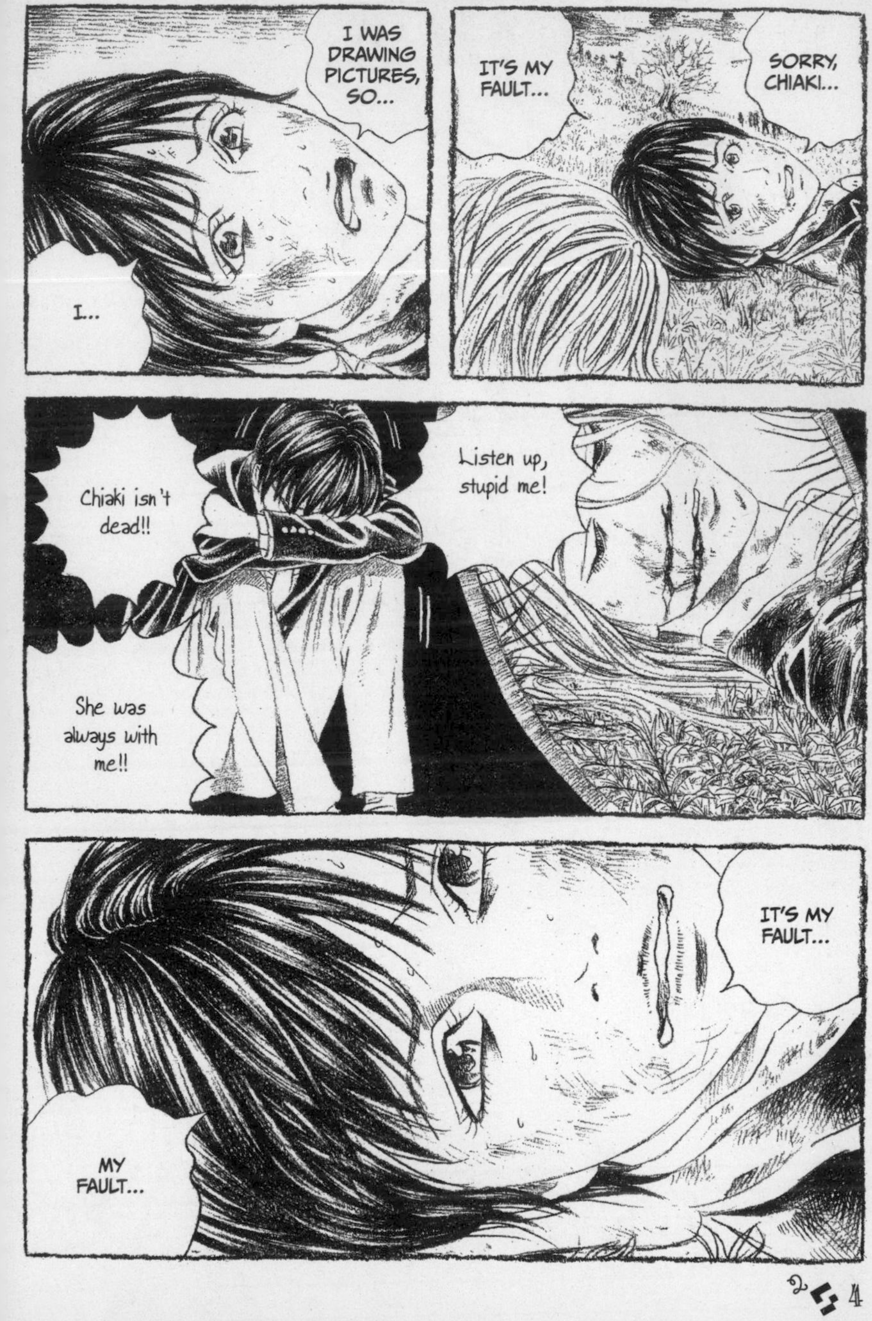
SORRY, CHIAKI...
IT'S MY FAULT...
I WAS DRAWING PICTURES, SO...
I...
Listen up, stupid me!
Chiaki isn't dead!!
She was always with me!!
IT'S MY FAULT...
MY FAULT...

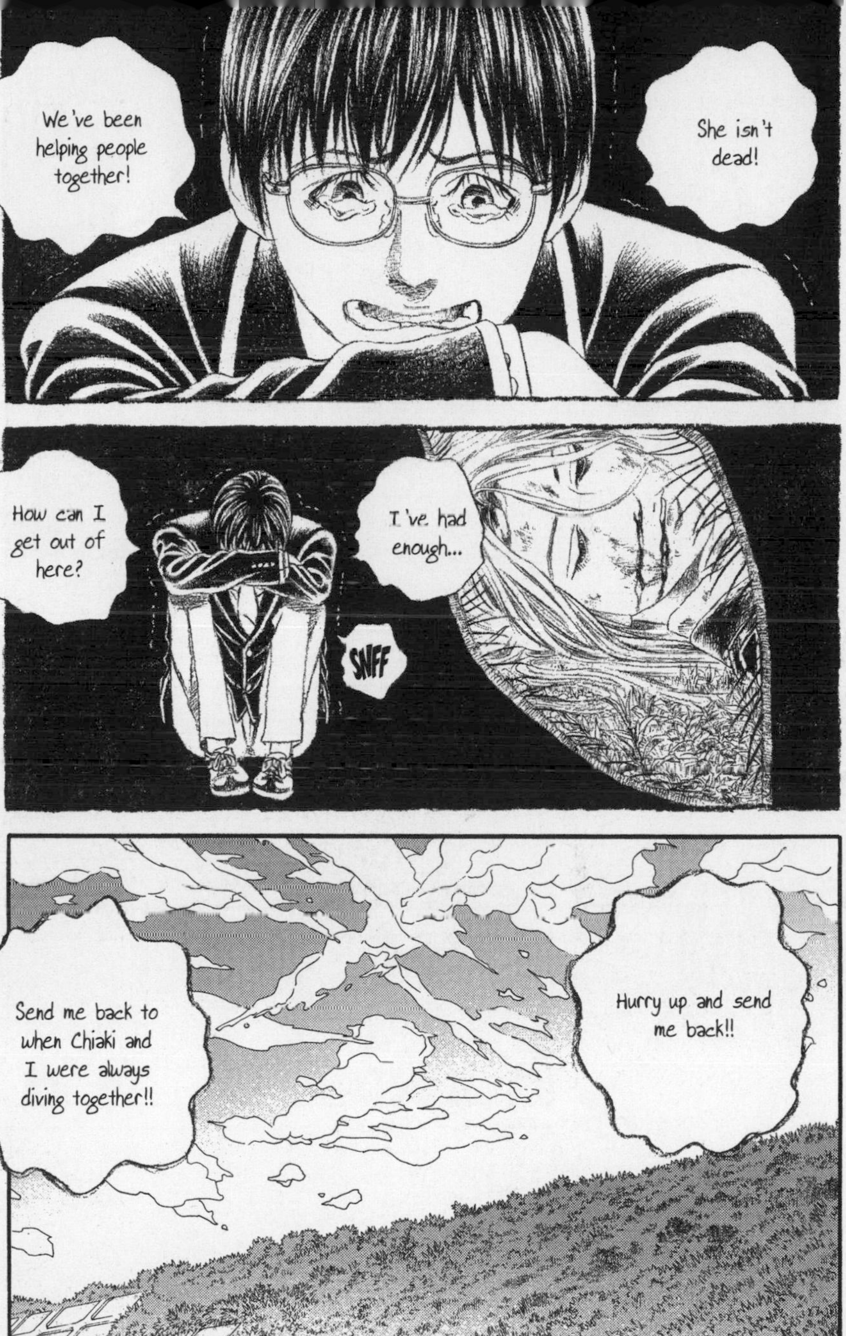
She isn't dead!
We've been helping people together!
I've had enough...
SNFF
How can I get out of here?
Hurry up and send me back!!
Send me back to when Chiaki and I were always diving together!!

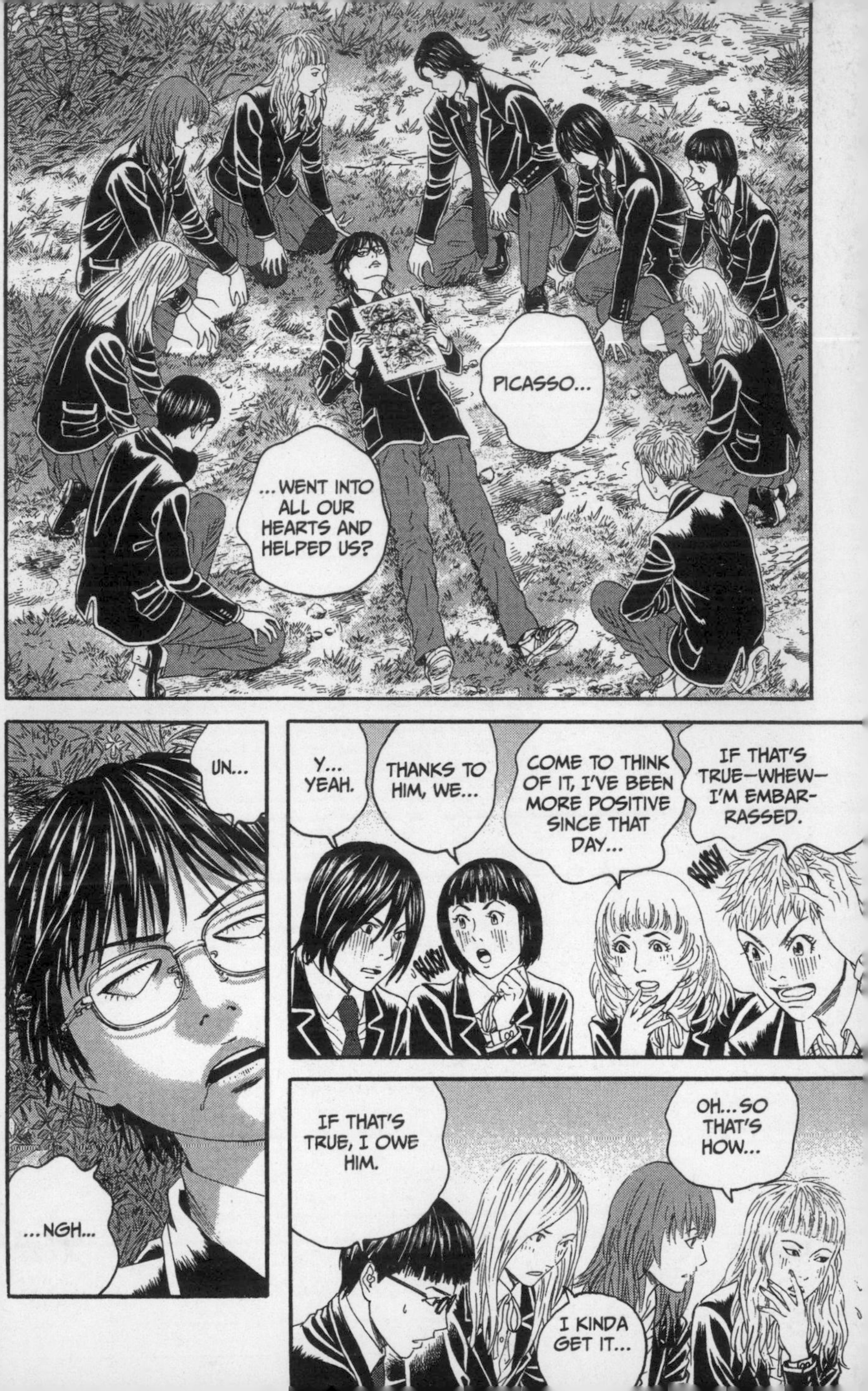
PICASSO...
...WENT INTO ALL OUR HEARTS AND HELPED US?
IF THAT'S TRUE—WHEW—I'M EMBARRASSED.
BLUSH
COME TO THINK OF IT, I'VE BEEN MORE POSITIVE SINCE THAT DAY...
THANKS TO HIM, WE...
BLUSH
Y... YEAH.
OH...SO THAT'S HOW...
IF THAT'S TRUE, I OWE HIM.
I KINDA GET IT...
UN...
...NGH...

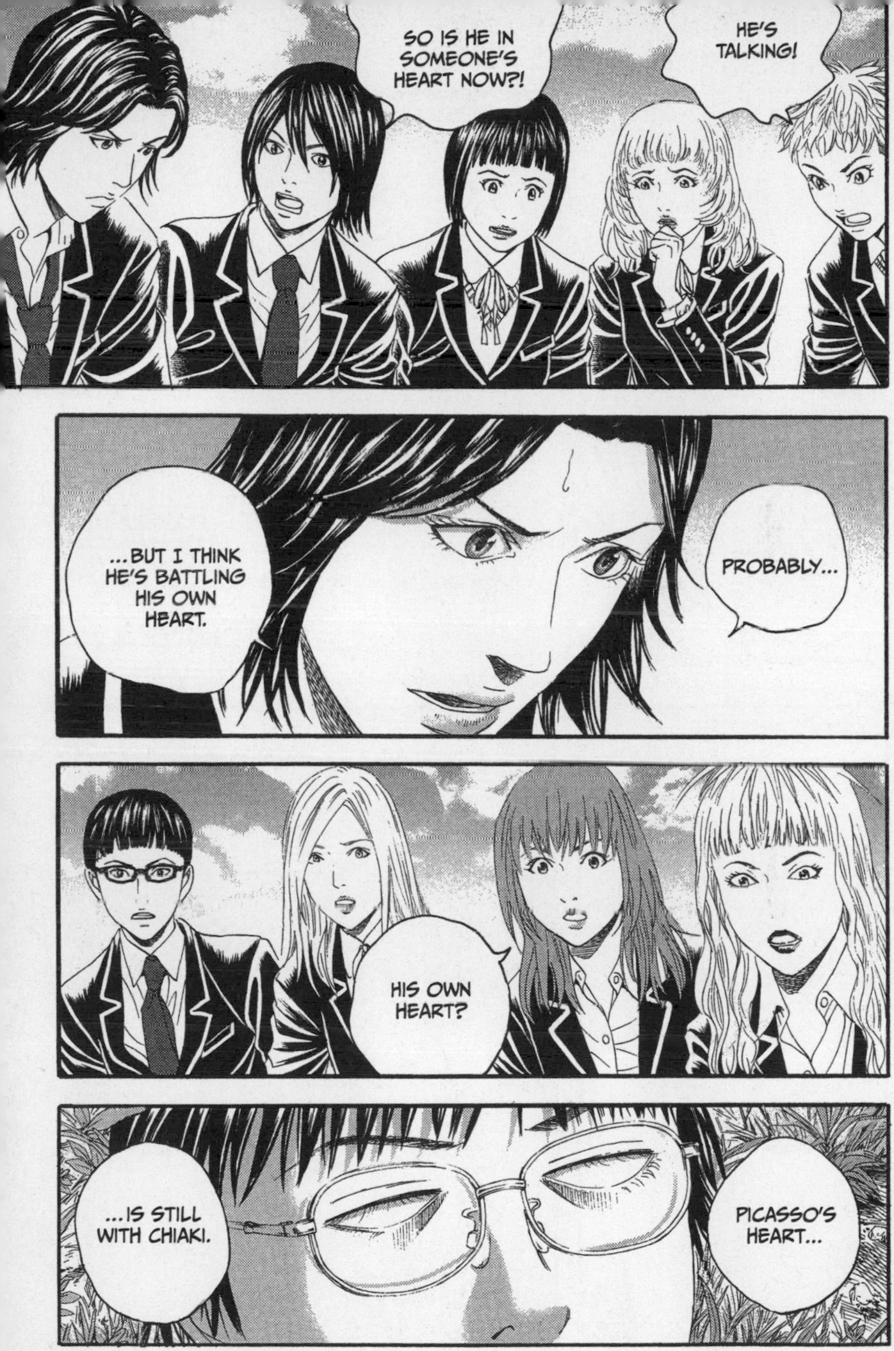
HE'S TALKING!
SO IS HE IN SOMEONE'S HEART NOW?!
PROBABLY...
...BUT I THINK HE'S BATTLING HIS OWN HEART.
HIS OWN HEART?
PICASSO'S HEART...
...IS STILL WITH CHIAKI.

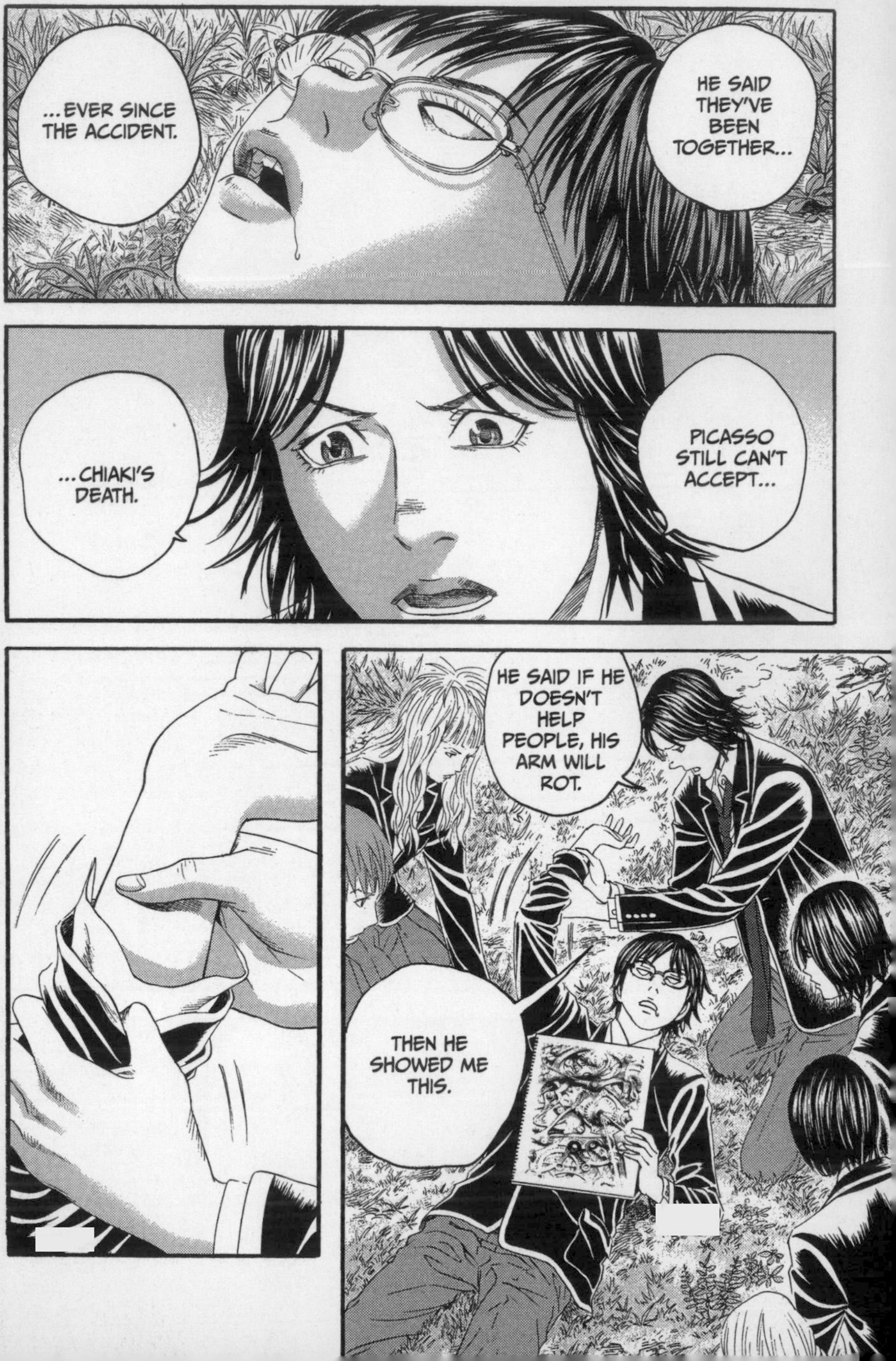
HE SAID THEY'VE BEEN TOGETHER...
...EVER SINCE THE ACCIDENT.
PICASSO STILL CAN'T ACCEPT...
...CHIAKI'S DEATH.
HE SAID IF HE DOESN'T HELP PEOPLE, HIS ARM WILL ROT.
THEN HE SHOWED ME THIS.

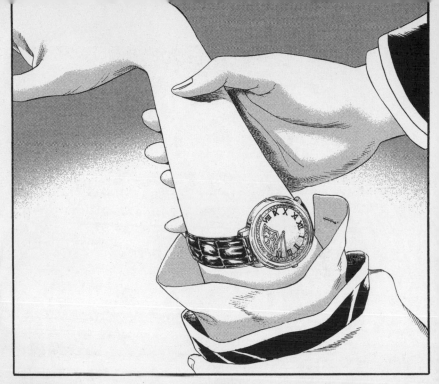

IT'S STOPPED.

A WATCH?

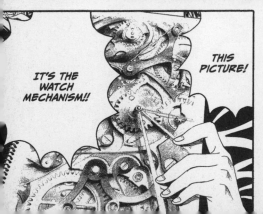

IT'S THE WATCH MECHANISM!!

THIS PICTURE!

!

OH, I GET IT!

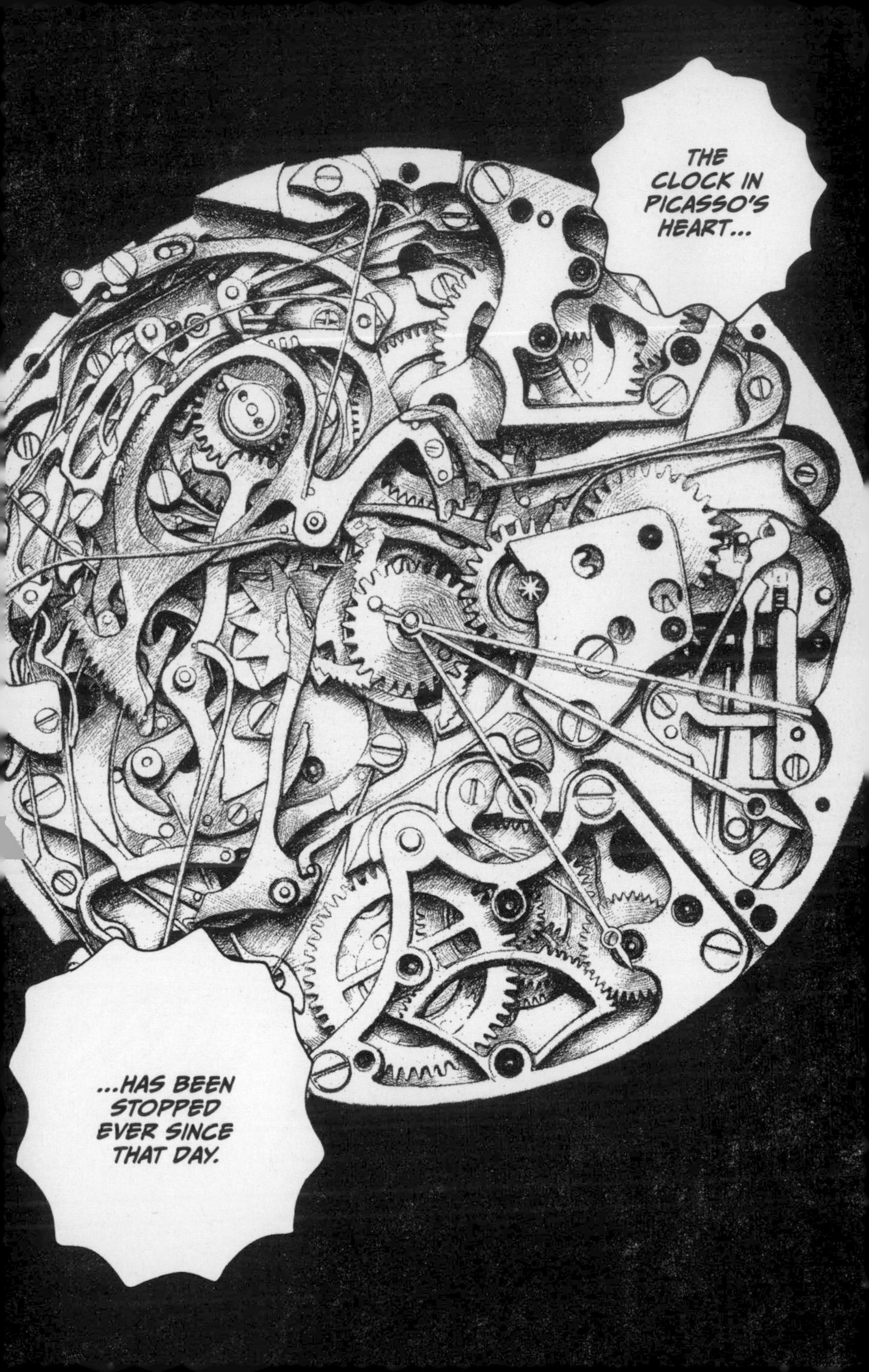
THE CLOCK IN PICASSO'S HEART...
...HAS BEEN STOPPED EVER SINCE THAT DAY.

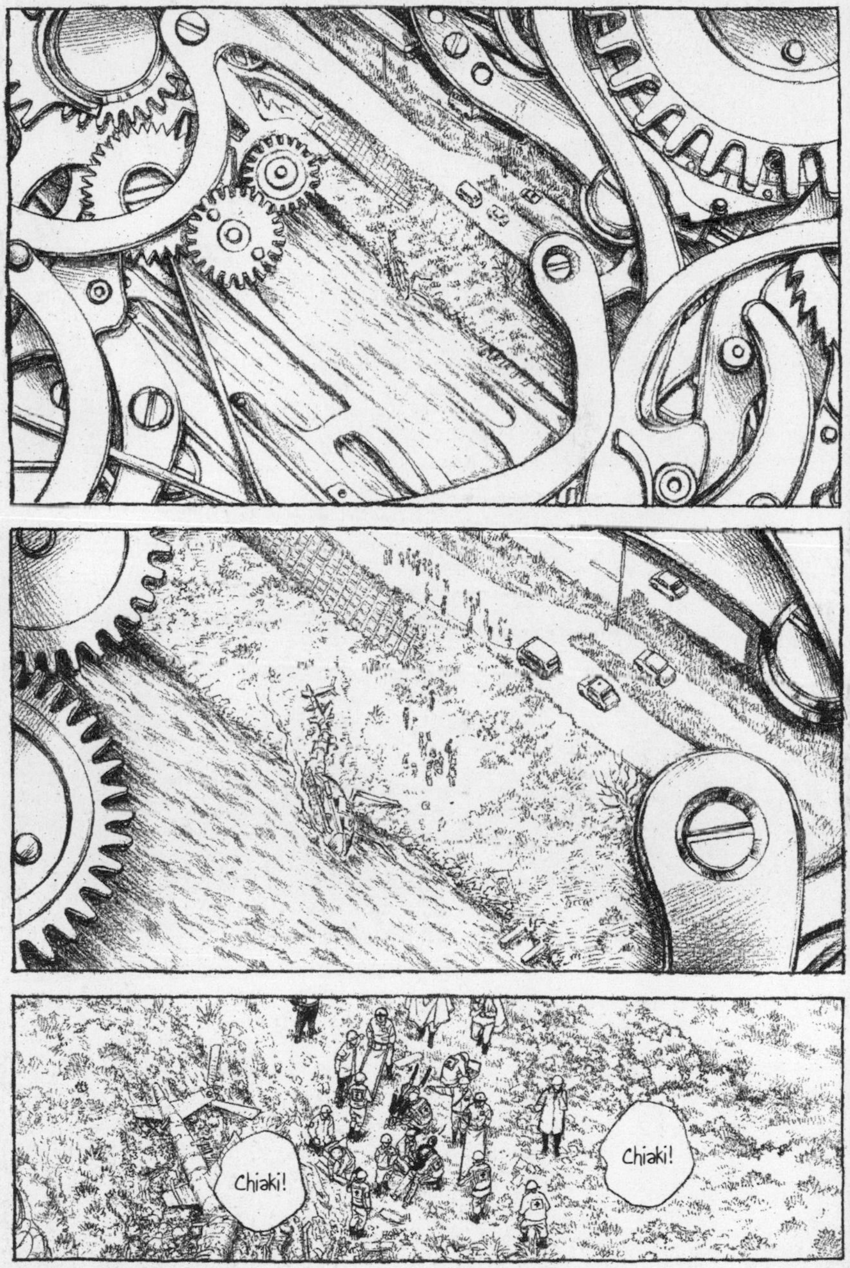
Chiaki!
Chiaki!

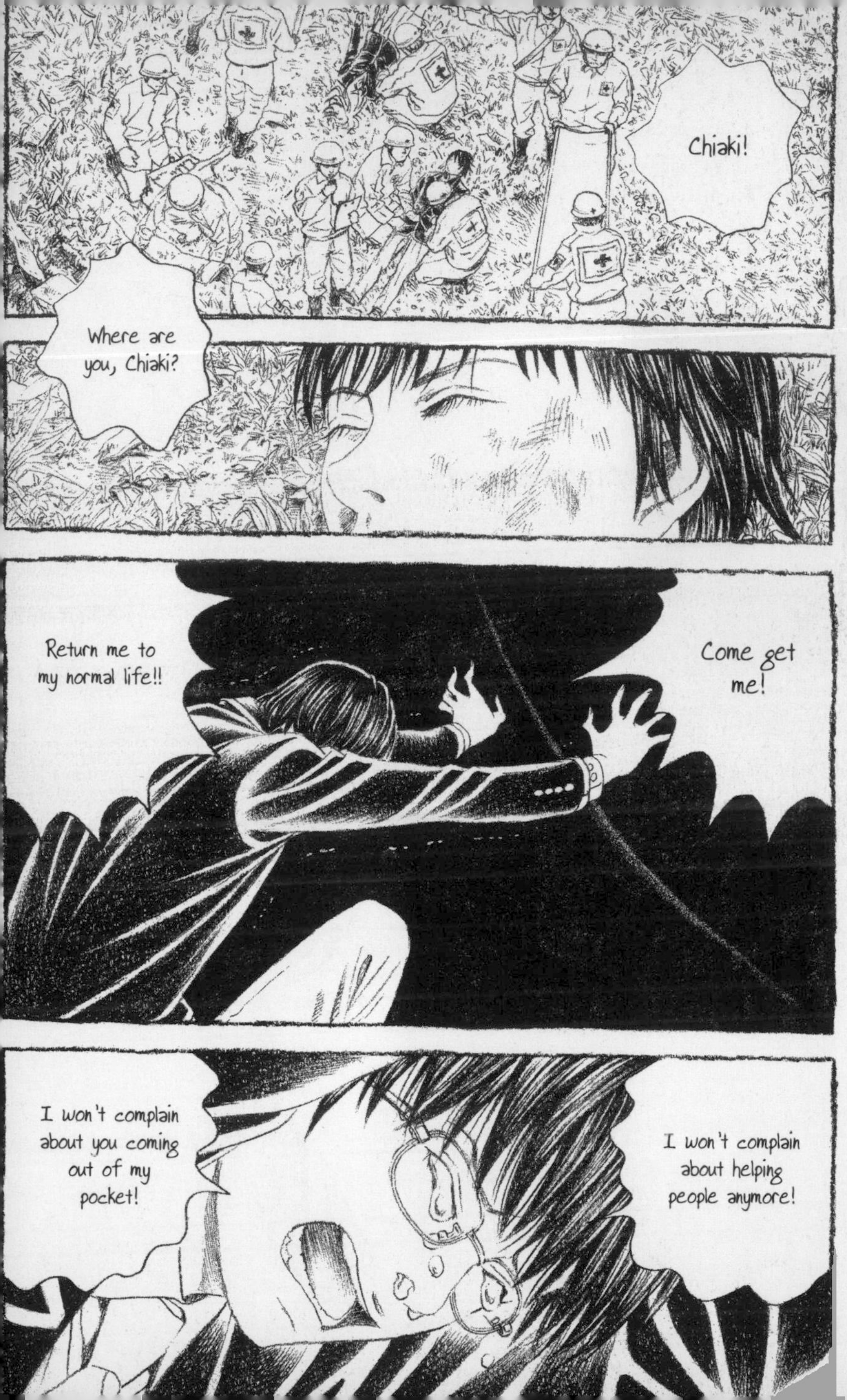
Chiaki!
Where are you, Chiaki?
Come get me!
Return me to my normal life!!
I won't complain about helping people anymore!
I won't complain about you coming out of my pocket!

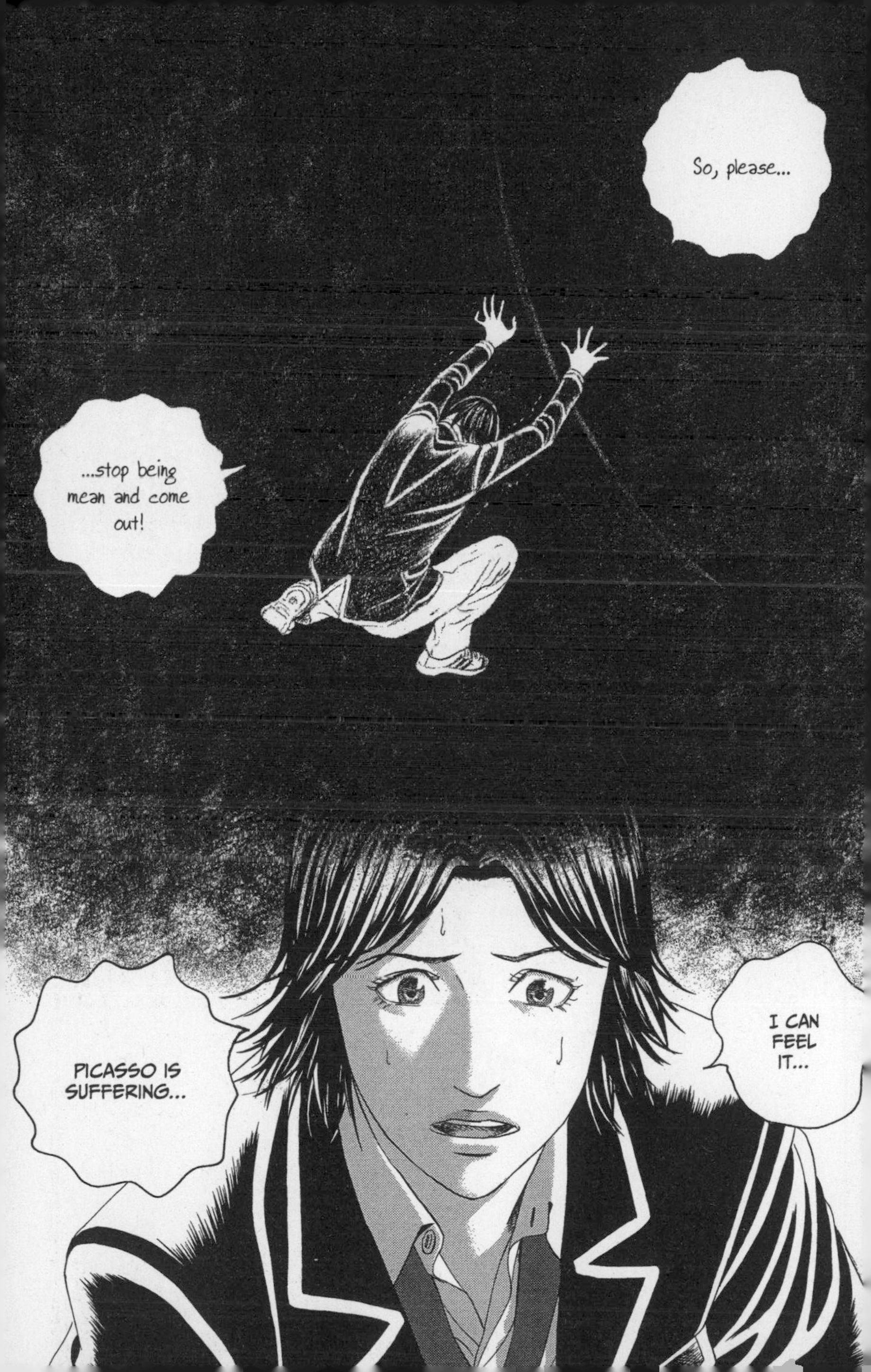
So, please...
...stop being mean and come out!
I CAN FEEL IT...
PICASSO IS SUFFERING...

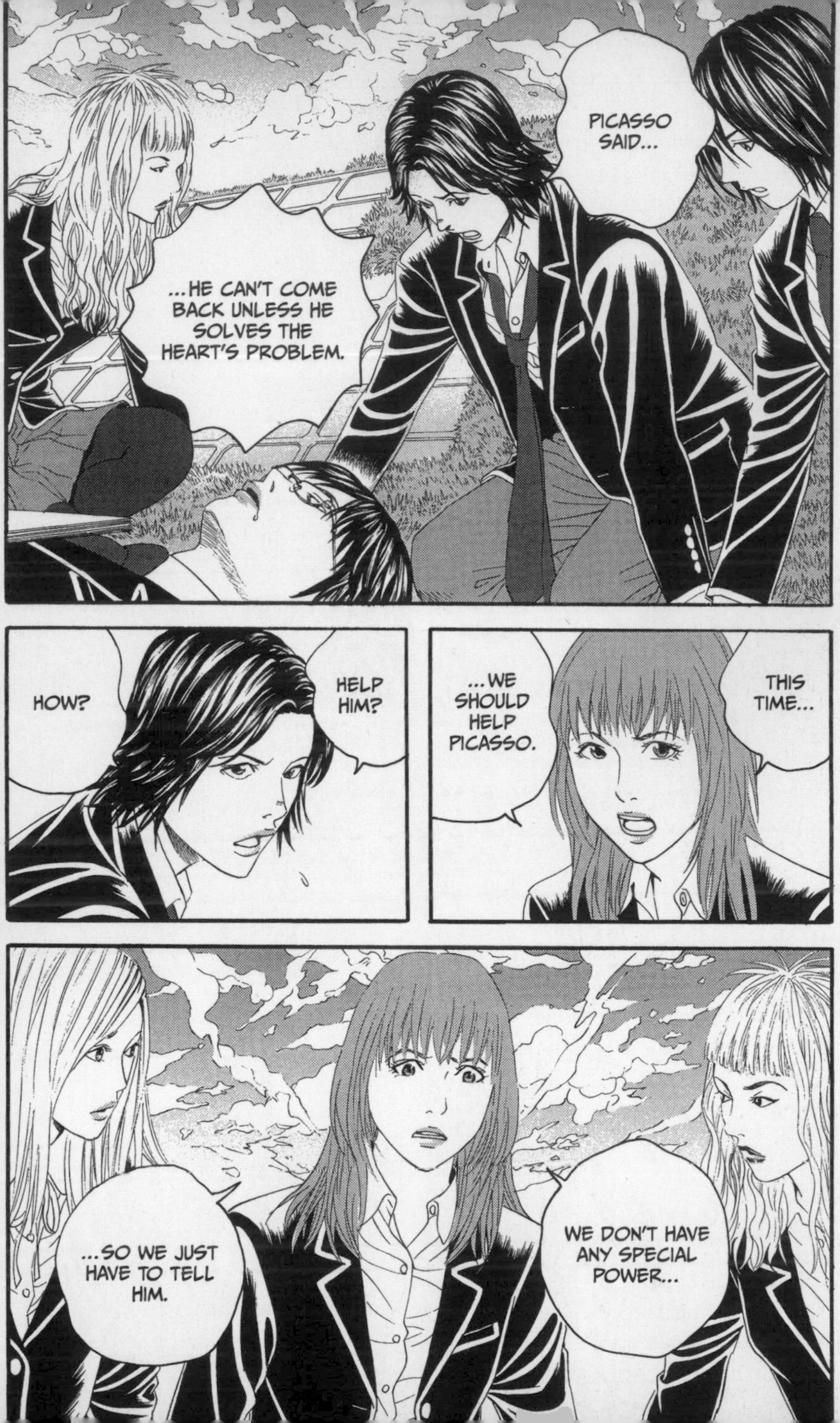
PICASSO SAID...
...HE CAN'T COME BACK UNLESS HE SOLVES THE HEART'S PROBLEM.
THIS TIME...
...WE SHOULD HELP PICASSO.
HELP HIM?
HOW?
WE DON'T HAVE ANY SPECIAL POWER...
...SO WE JUST HAVE TO TELL HIM.

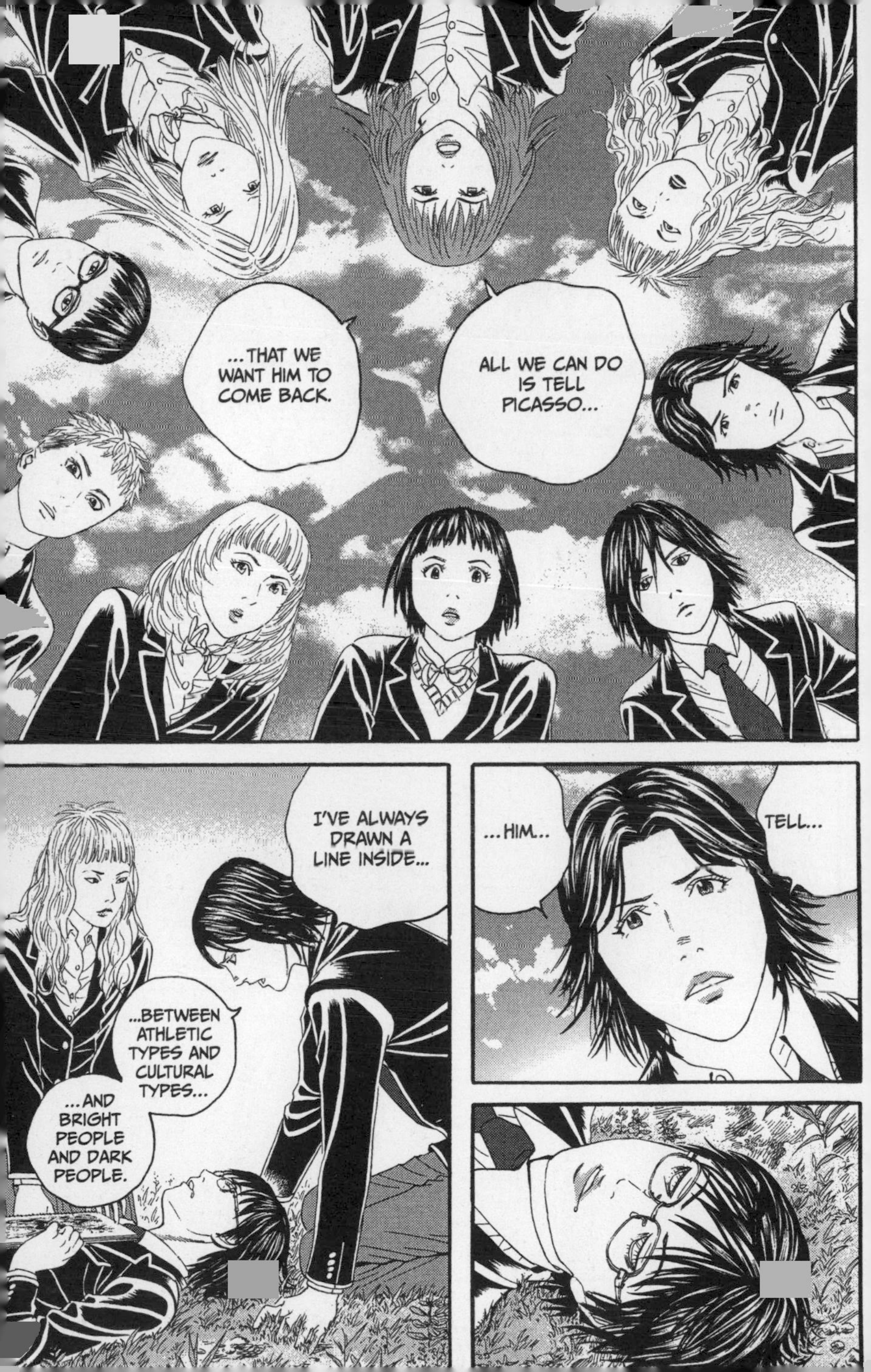
ALL WE CAN DO IS TELL PICASSO...
...THAT WE WANT HIM TO COME BACK.
TELL...
...HIM...
I'VE ALWAYS DRAWN A LINE INSIDE...
...BETWEEN ATHLETIC TYPES AND CULTURAL TYPES...
...AND BRIGHT PEOPLE AND DARK PEOPLE.

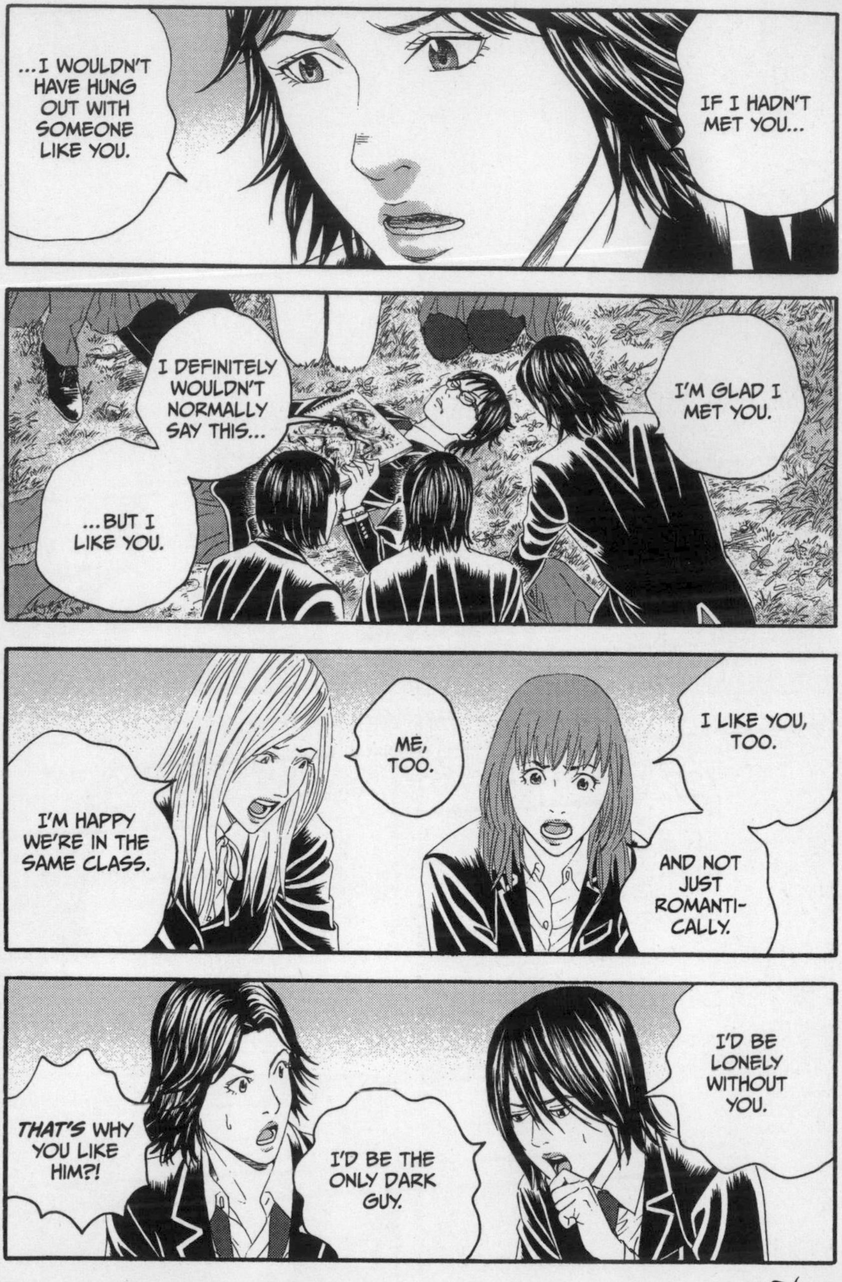
IF I HADN'T MET YOU...
...I WOULDN'T HAVE HUNG OUT WITH SOMEONE LIKE YOU.
I'M GLAD I MET YOU.
I DEFINITELY WOULDN'T NORMALLY SAY THIS...
...BUT I LIKE YOU.
I LIKE YOU, TOO.
AND NOT JUST ROMANTI-CALLY.
ME, TOO.
I'M HAPPY WE'RE IN THE SAME CLASS.
I'D BE LONELY WITHOUT YOU.
I'D BE THE ONLY DARK GUY.
*THAT'S* WHY YOU LIKE HIM?!

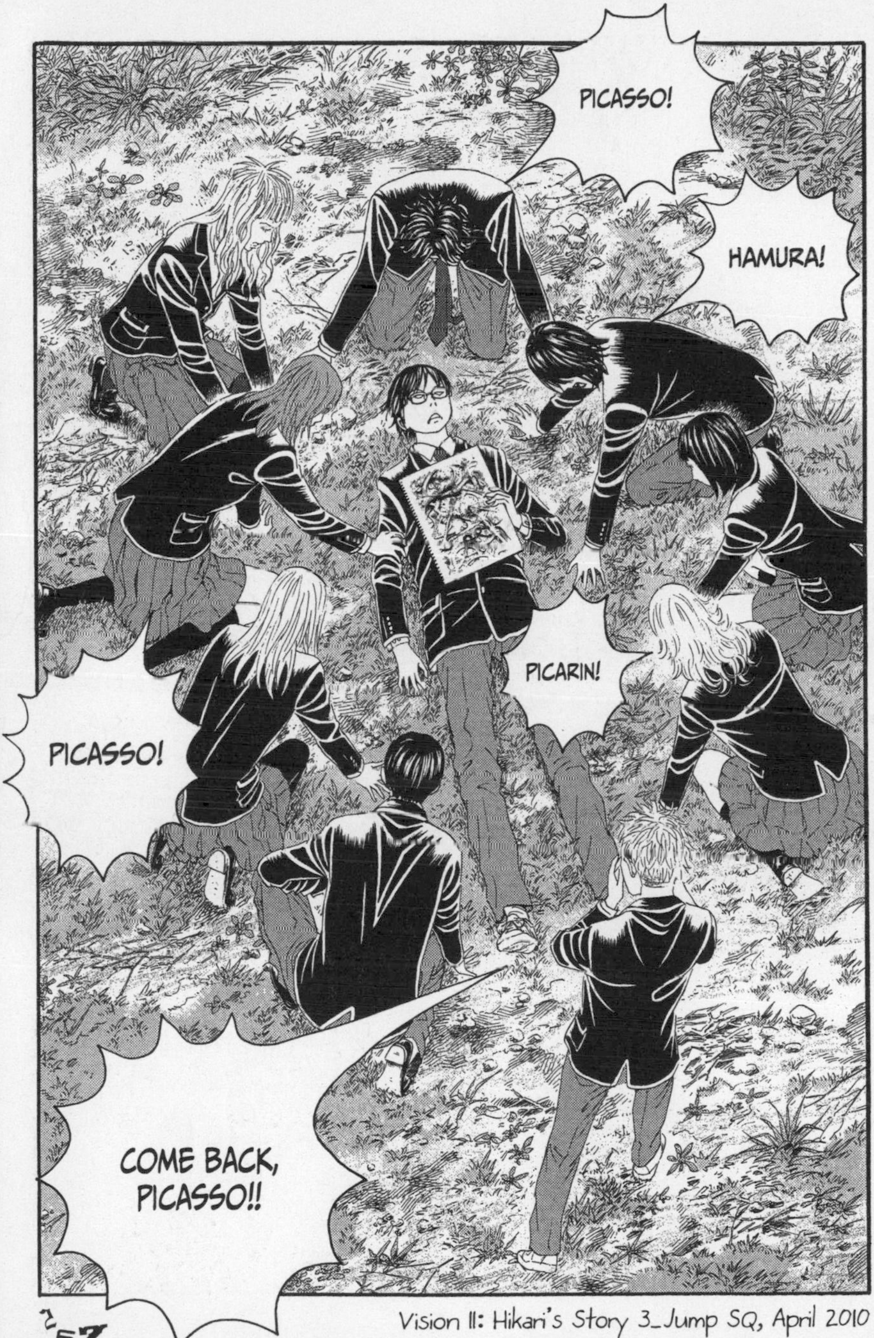
PICASSO!
HAMURA!
PICARIN!
PICASSO!
COME BACK, PICASSO!!

Vision 11: Hikari's Story 3_Jump SQ, April 2010

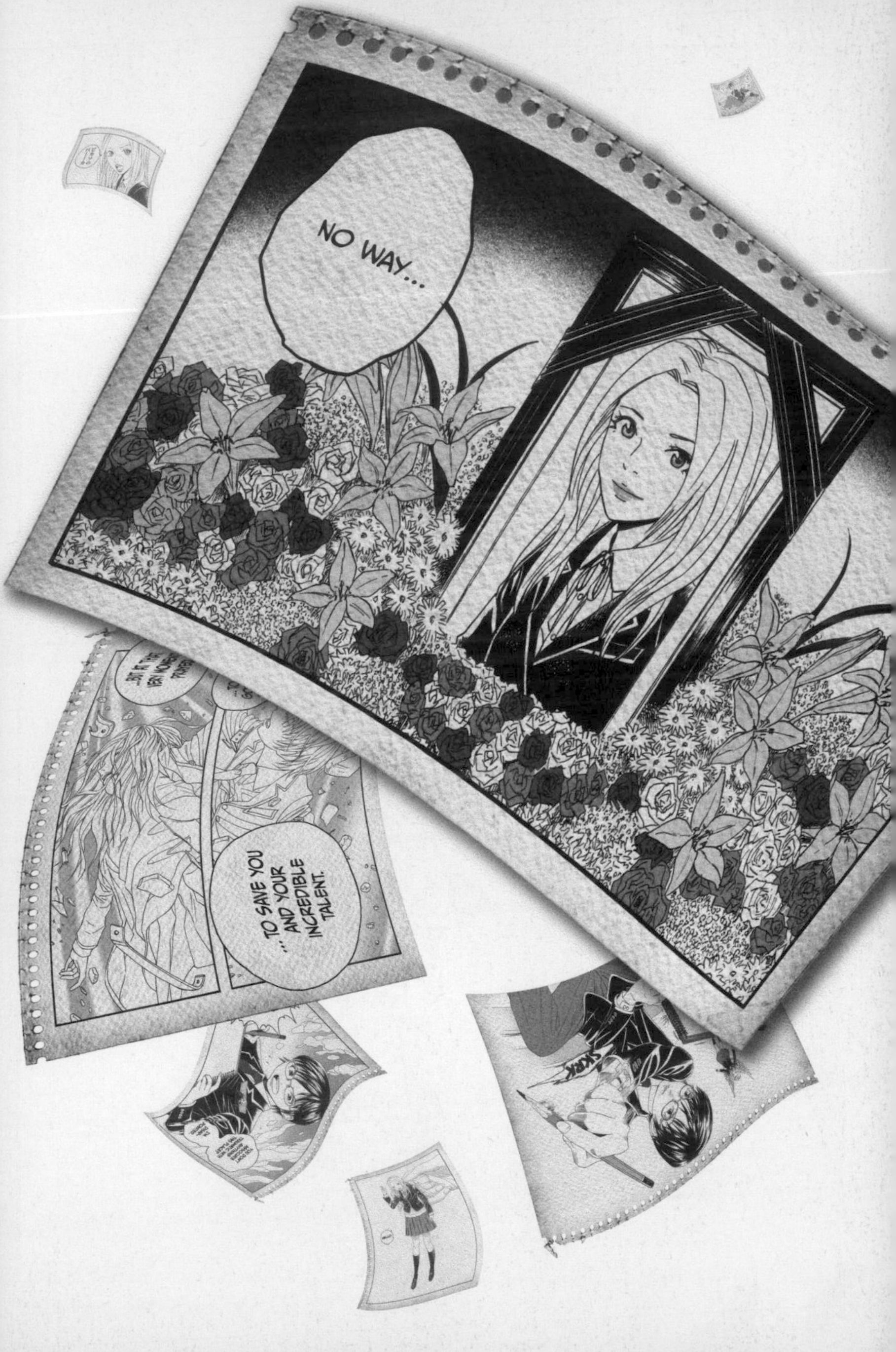
NO WAY...
TO SAVE YOU ... AND YOUR INCREDIBLE TALENT.
SKRK

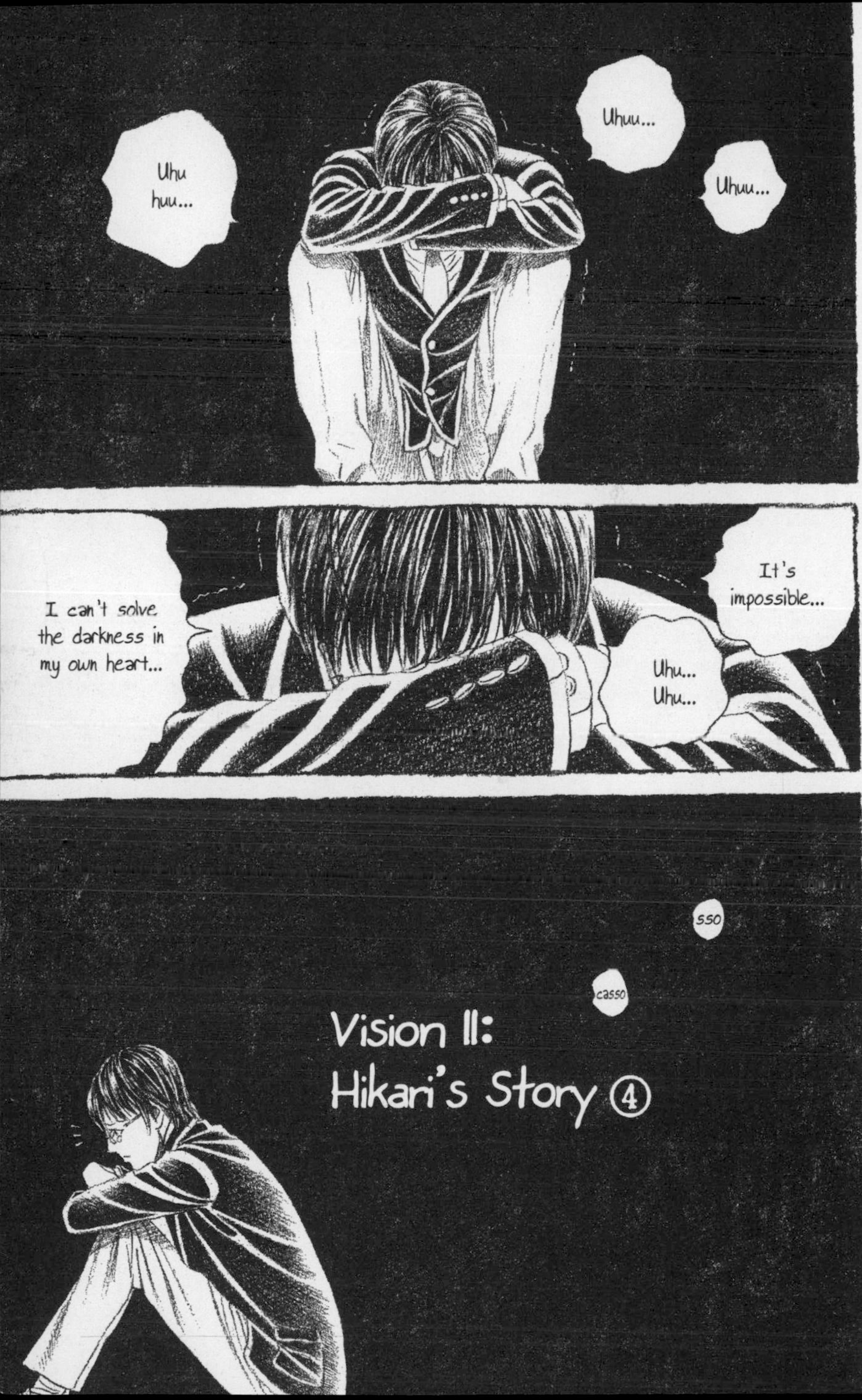
Uhuu...
Uhuu...
Uhu huu...
It's impossible...
Uhu... Uhu...
I can't solve the darkness in my own heart...
sso
casso
Vision 11:
Hikari's Story ④

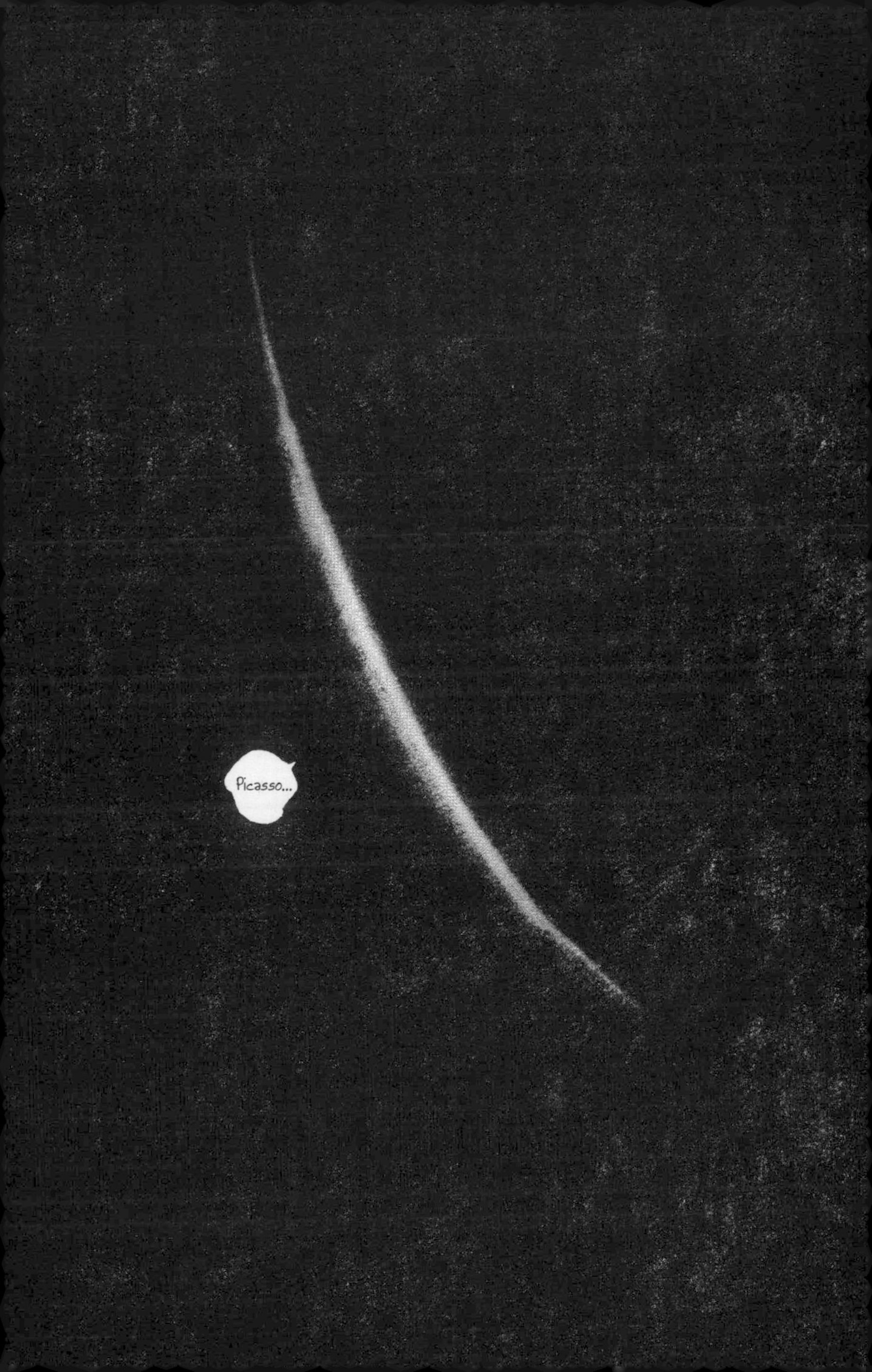
Picasso...

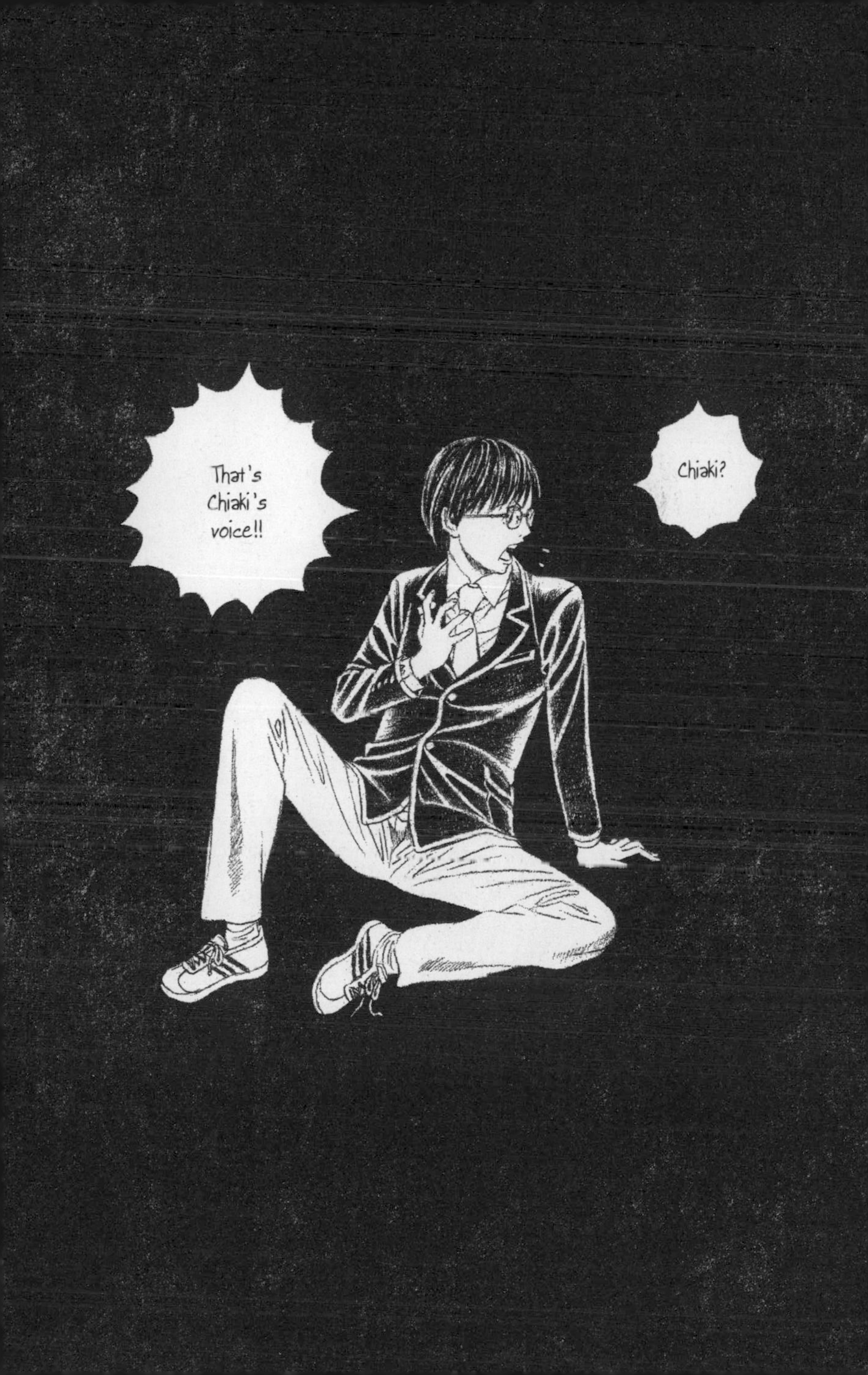
Chiaki?
That's Chiaki's voice!!

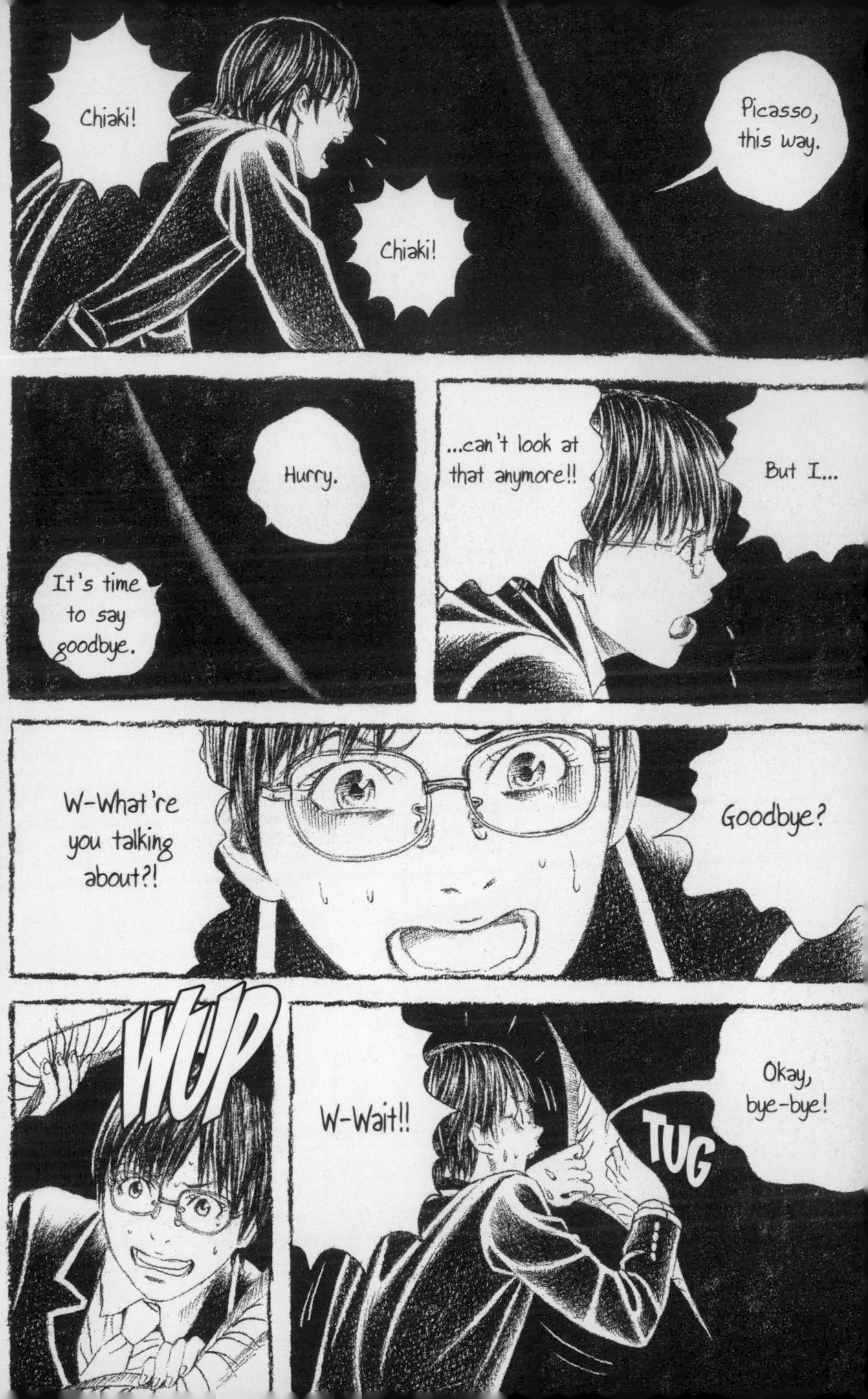
Picasso, this way.
Chiaki!
Chiaki!
But I...
...can't look at that anymore!!
Hurry.
It's time to say goodbye.
Goodbye?
W-What're you talking about?!
Okay, bye-bye!
TUG
W-Wait!!
WUP

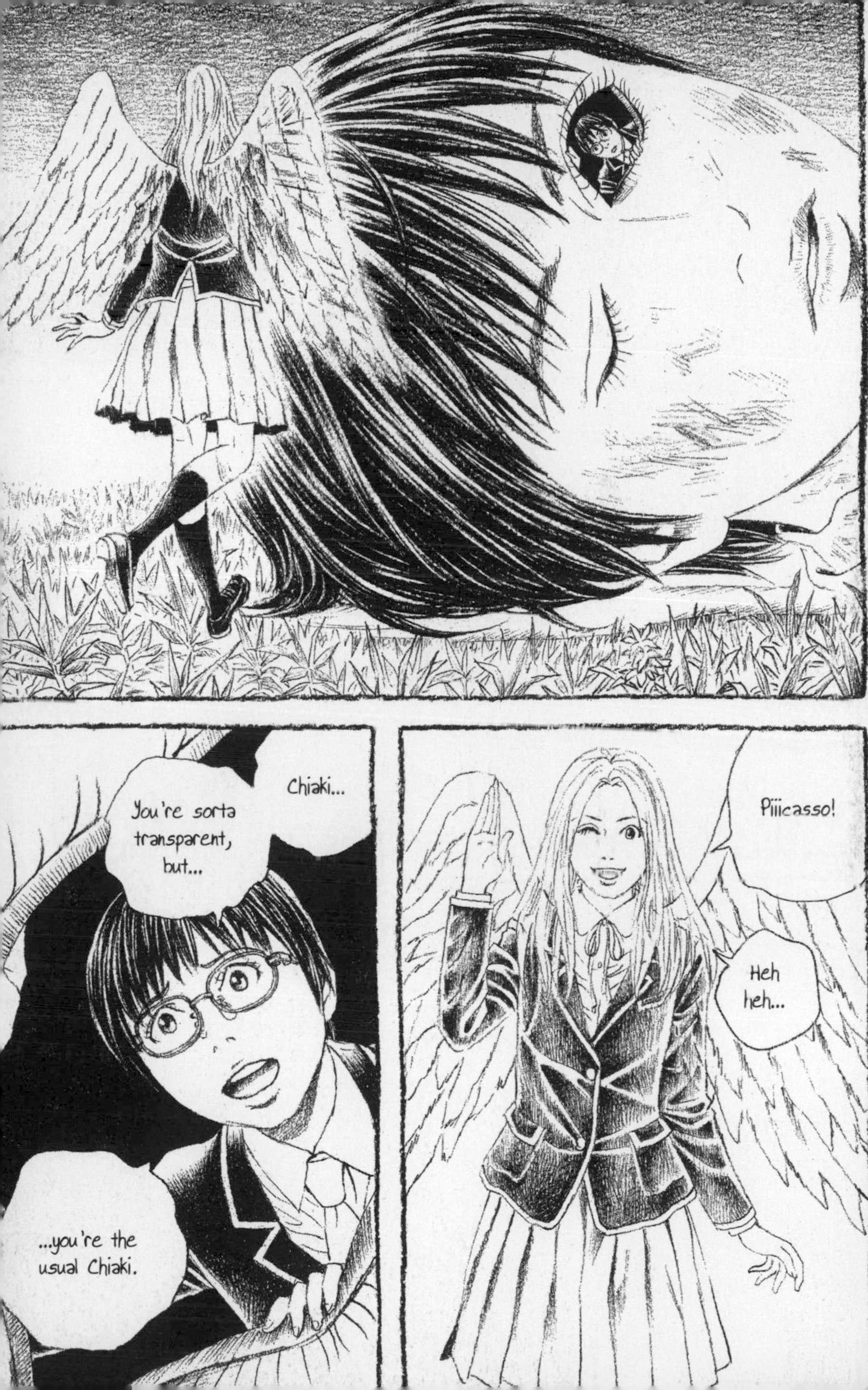
Piiicasso!
Heh heh...
Chiaki...
You're sorta transparent, but...
...you're the usual Chiaki.

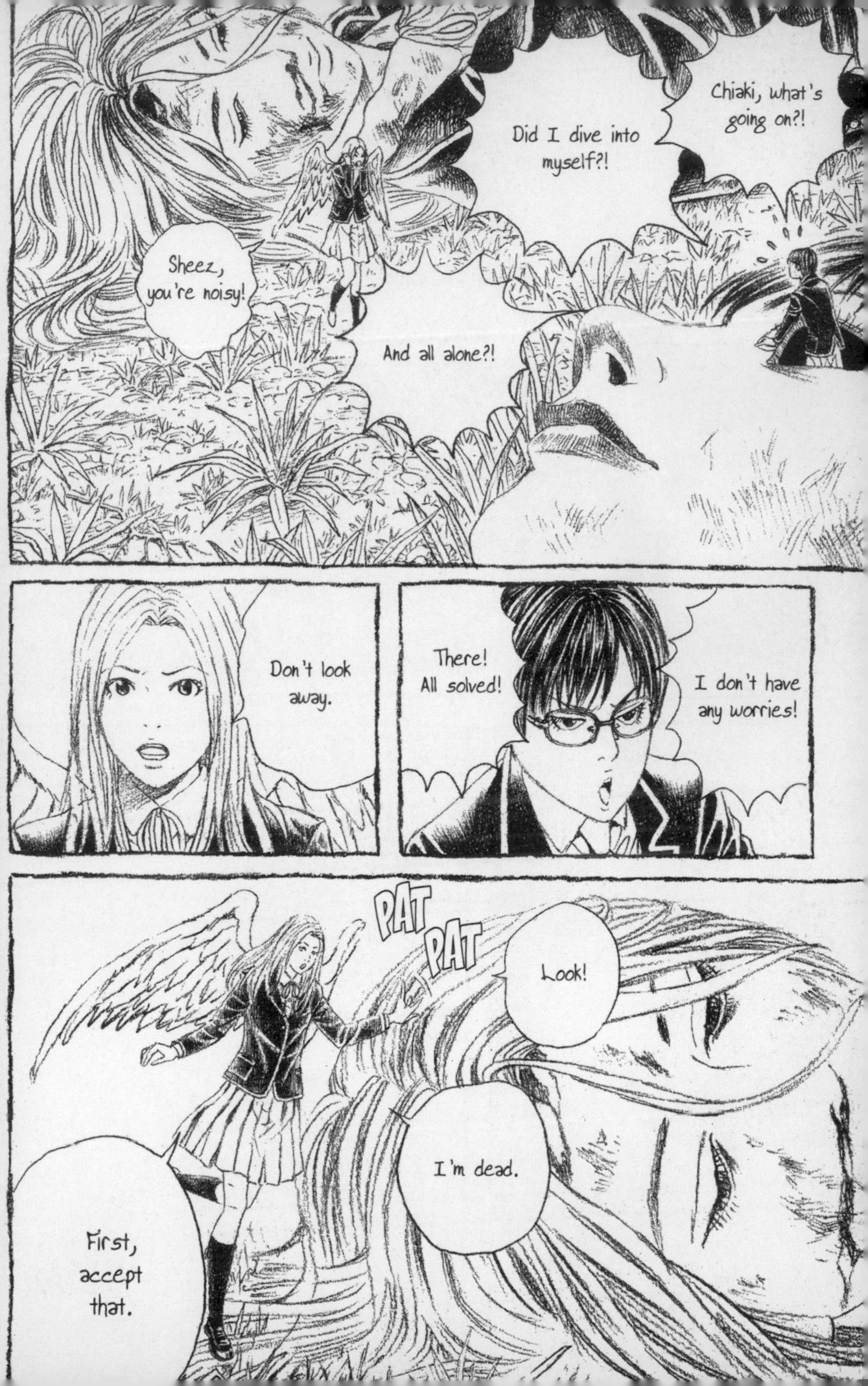
Chiaki, what's going on?!
Did I dive into myself?!
And all alone?!
Sheez, you're noisy!
I don't have any worries!
There! All solved!
Don't look away.
PAT PAT
Look!
I'm dead.
First, accept that.

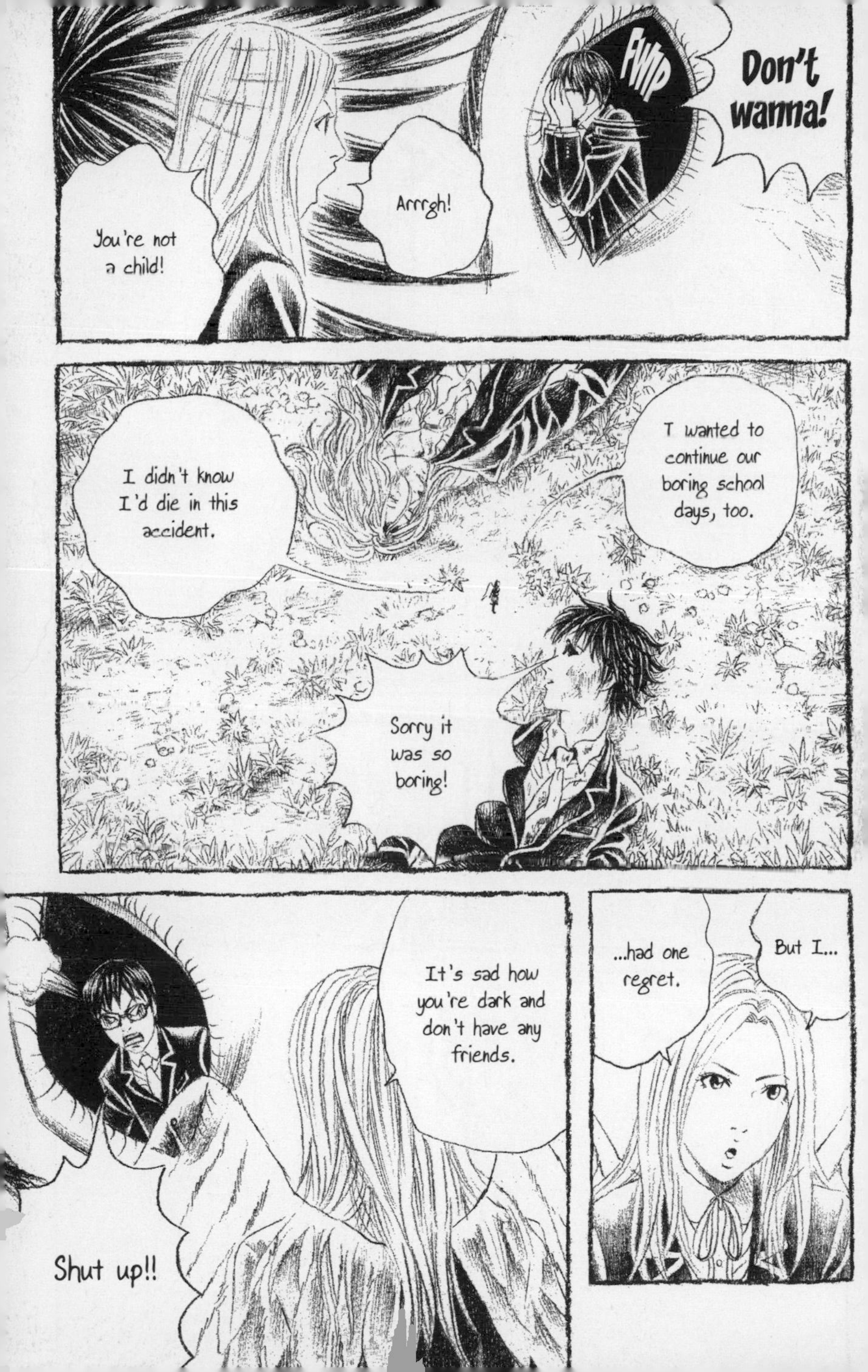
FWP
Don't wanna!
Arrrgh!
You're not a child!
I wanted to continue our boring school days, too.
I didn't know I'd die in this accident.
Sorry it was so boring!
But I...
...had one regret.
It's sad how you're dark and don't have any friends.
Shut up!!

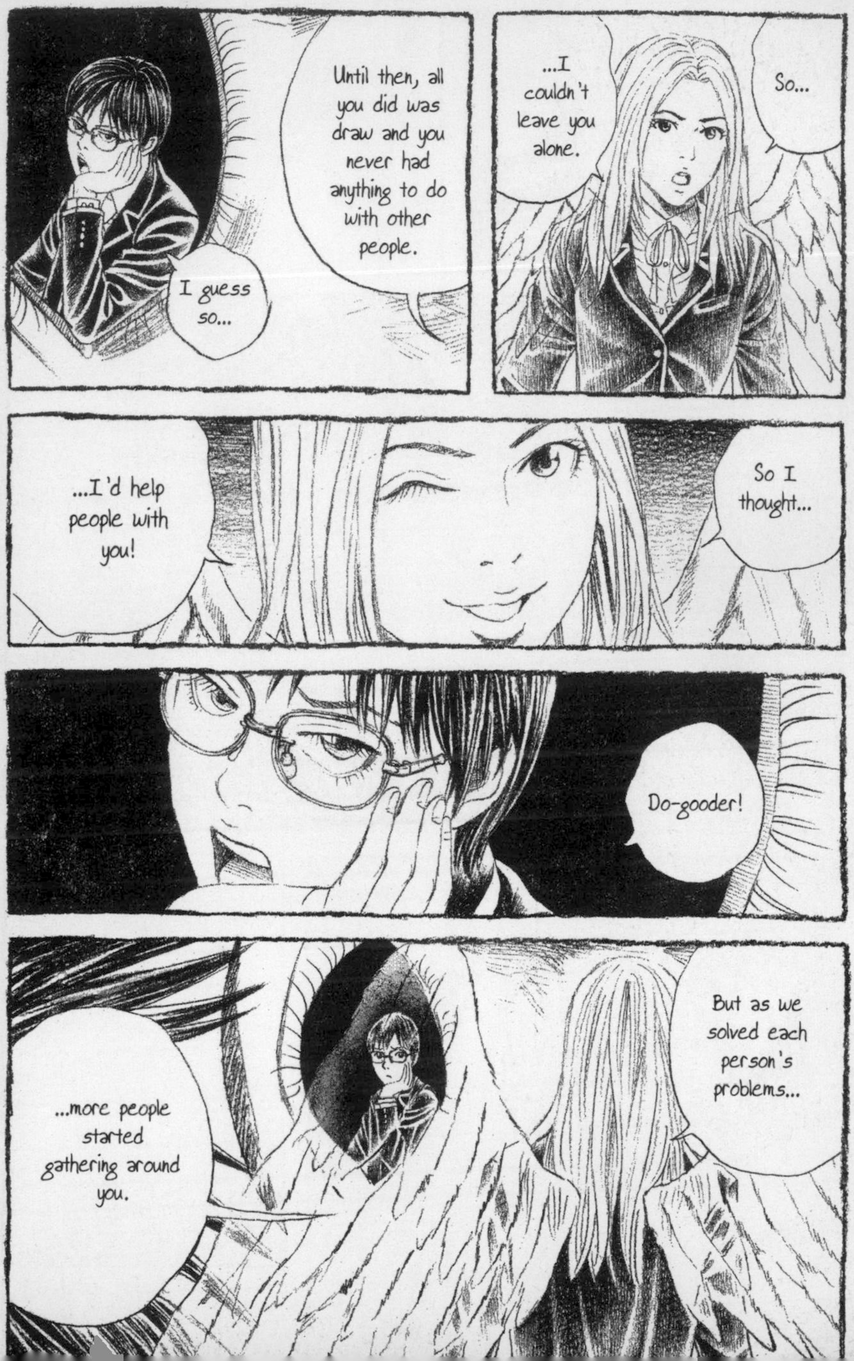

So...
...I couldn't leave you alone.
Until then, all you did was draw and you never had anything to do with other people.
I guess so...
So I thought...
...I'd help people with you!
Do-gooder!
But as we solved each person's problems...
...more people started gathering around you.

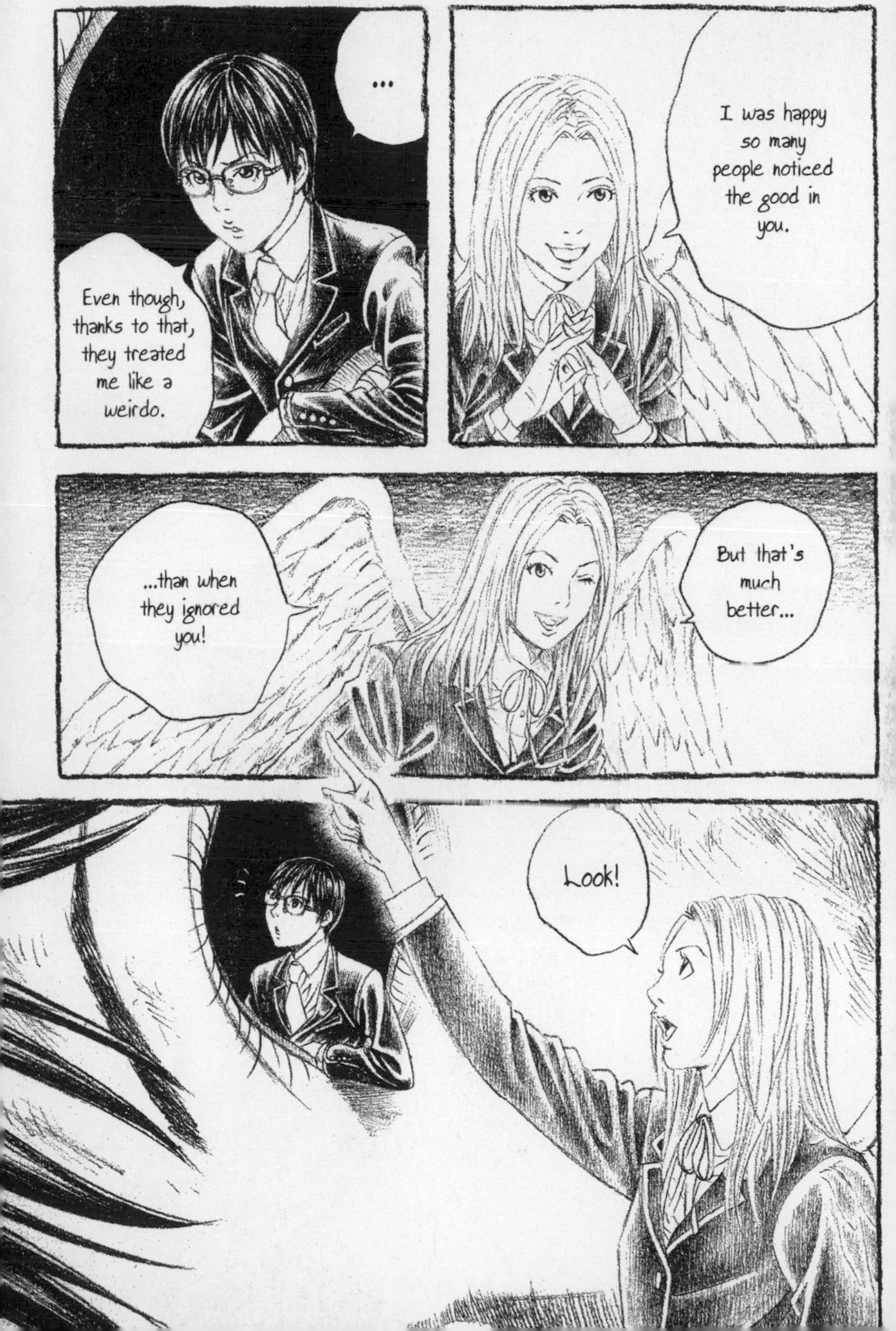
I was happy so many people noticed the good in you.
...
Even though, thanks to that, they treated me like a weirdo.
But that's much better...
...than when they ignored you!
Look!

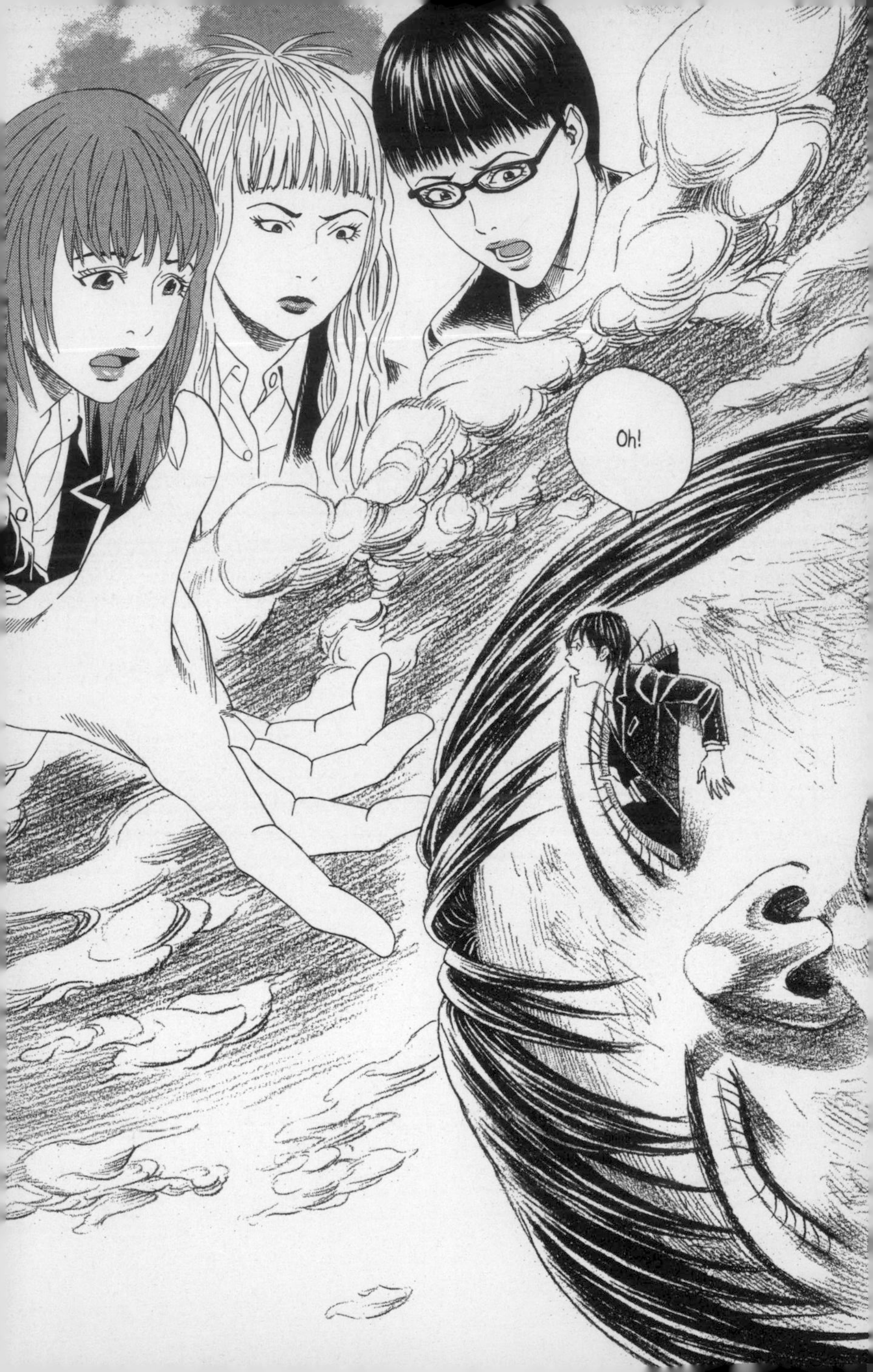
Oh!

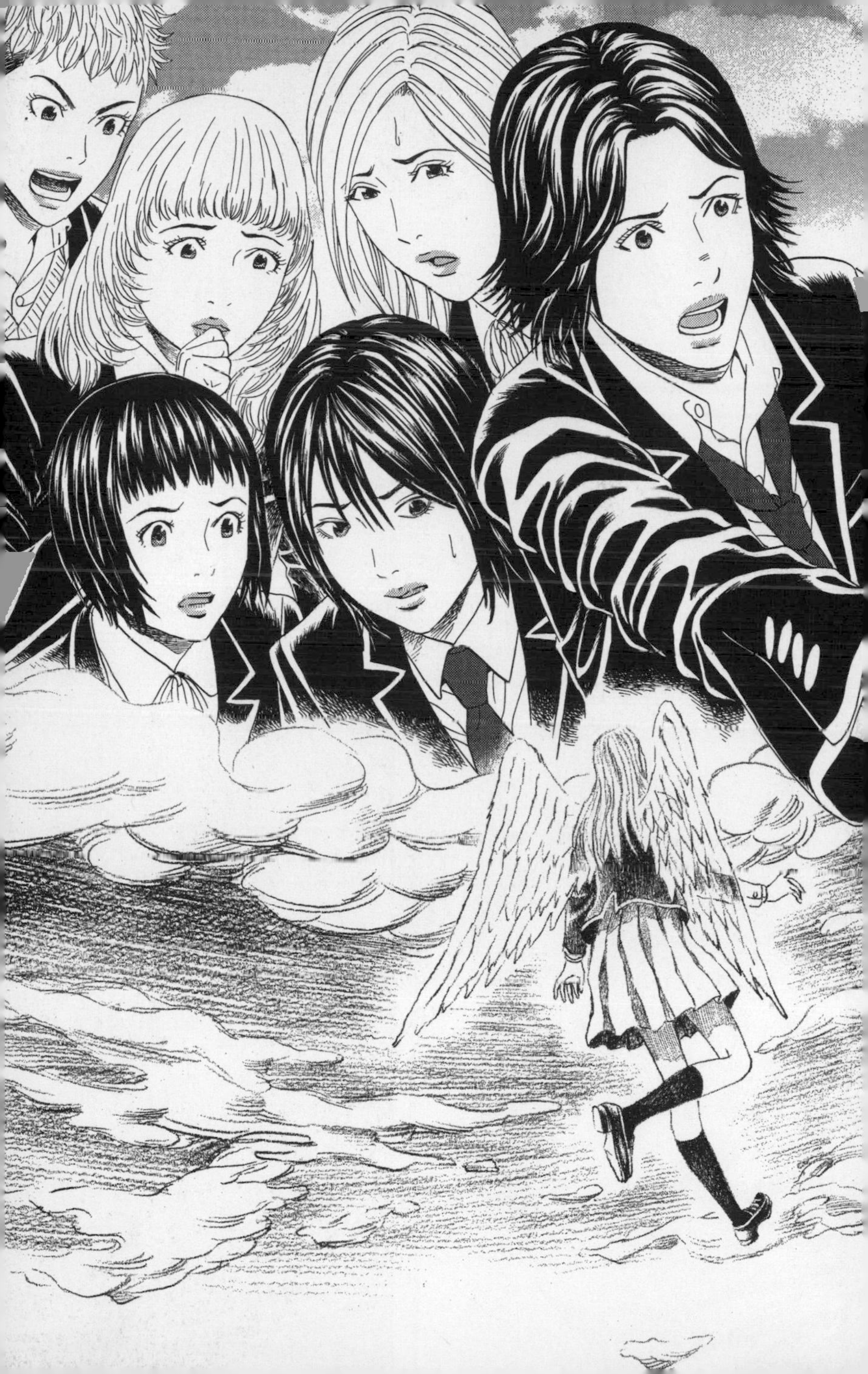

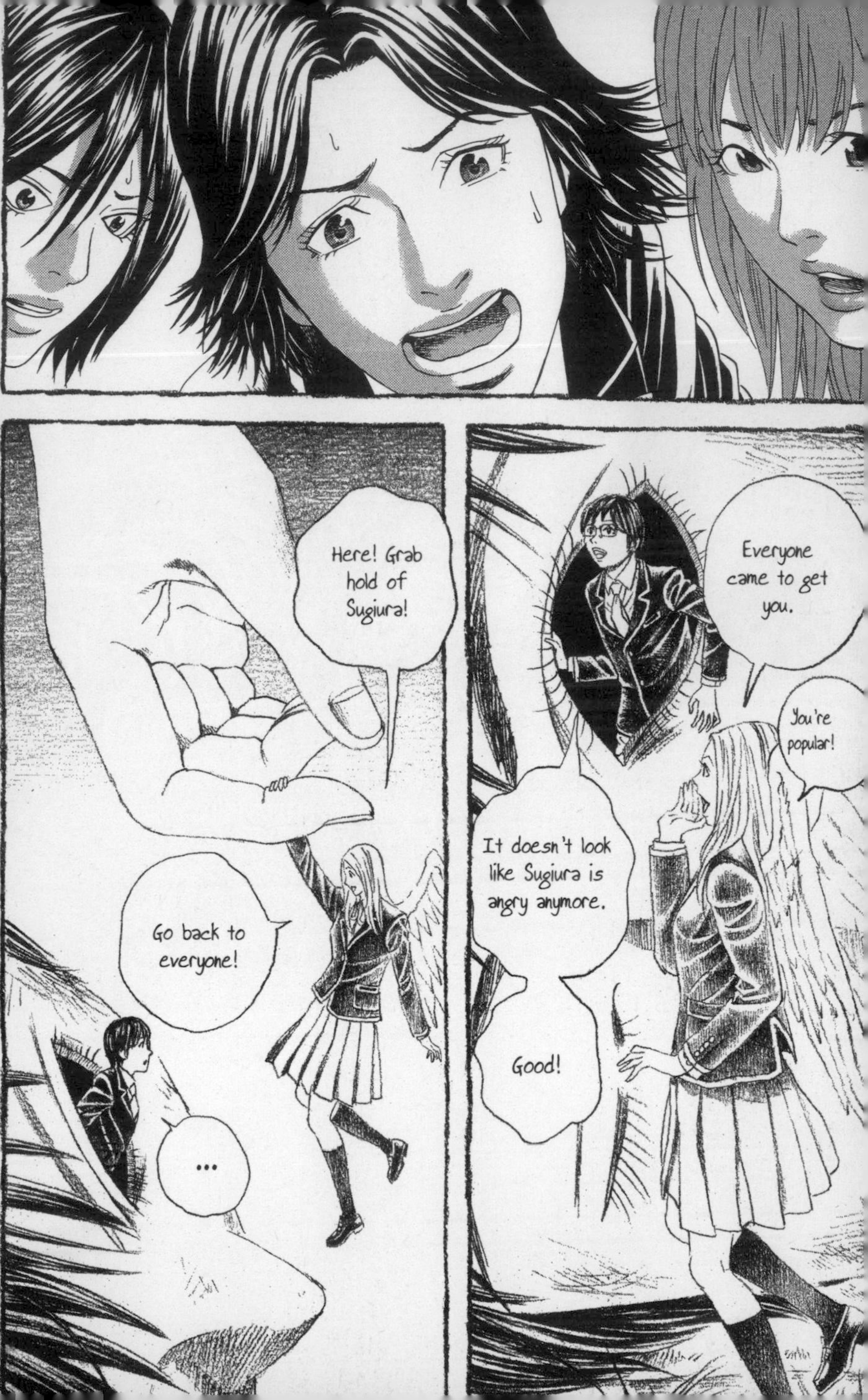
Everyone came to get you.
You're popular!
It doesn't look like Sugiura is angry anymore.
Good!
Here! Grab hold of Sugiura!
Go back to everyone!
...

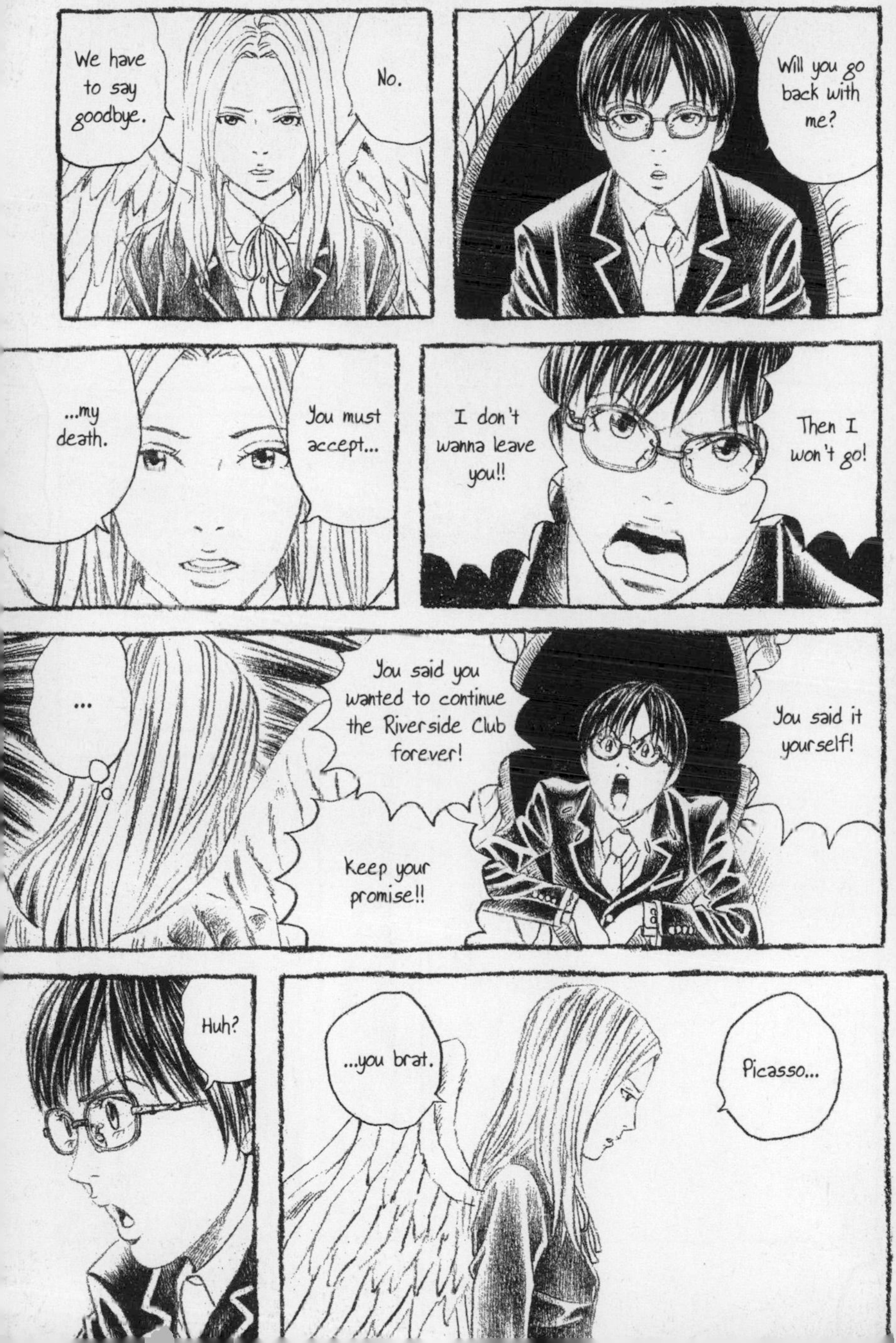
Will you go back with me?
No.
We have to say goodbye.
Then I won't go!
I don't wanna leave you!!
You must accept...
...my death.
You said it yourself!
You said you wanted to continue the Riverside Club forever!
Keep your promise!!
...
Picasso...
...you brat.
Huh?

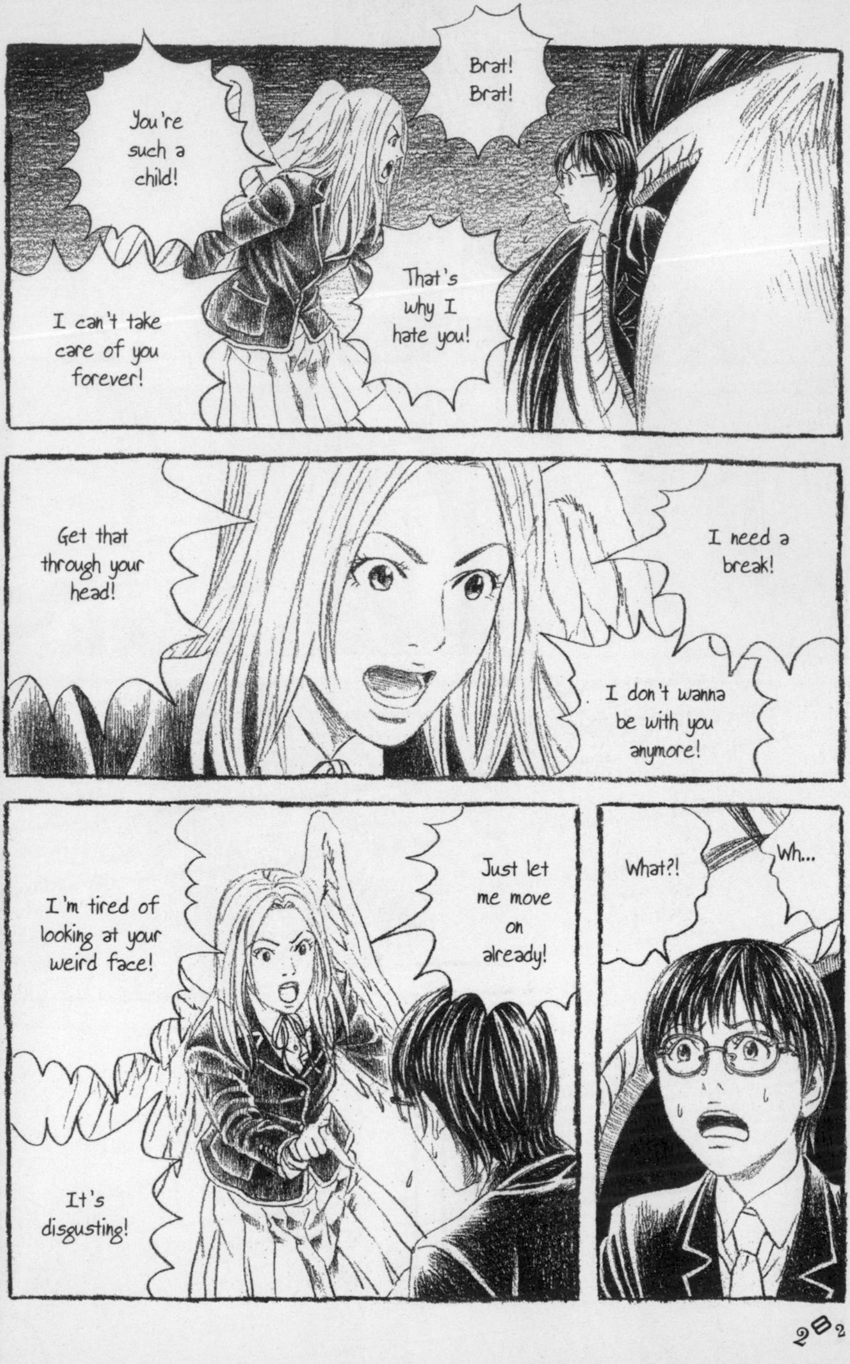
Brat! Brat!
You're such a child!
That's why I hate you!
I can't take care of you forever!
I need a break!
Get that through your head!
I don't wanna be with you anymore!
Wh...
What?!
Just let me move on already!
I'm tired of looking at your weird face!
It's disgusting!

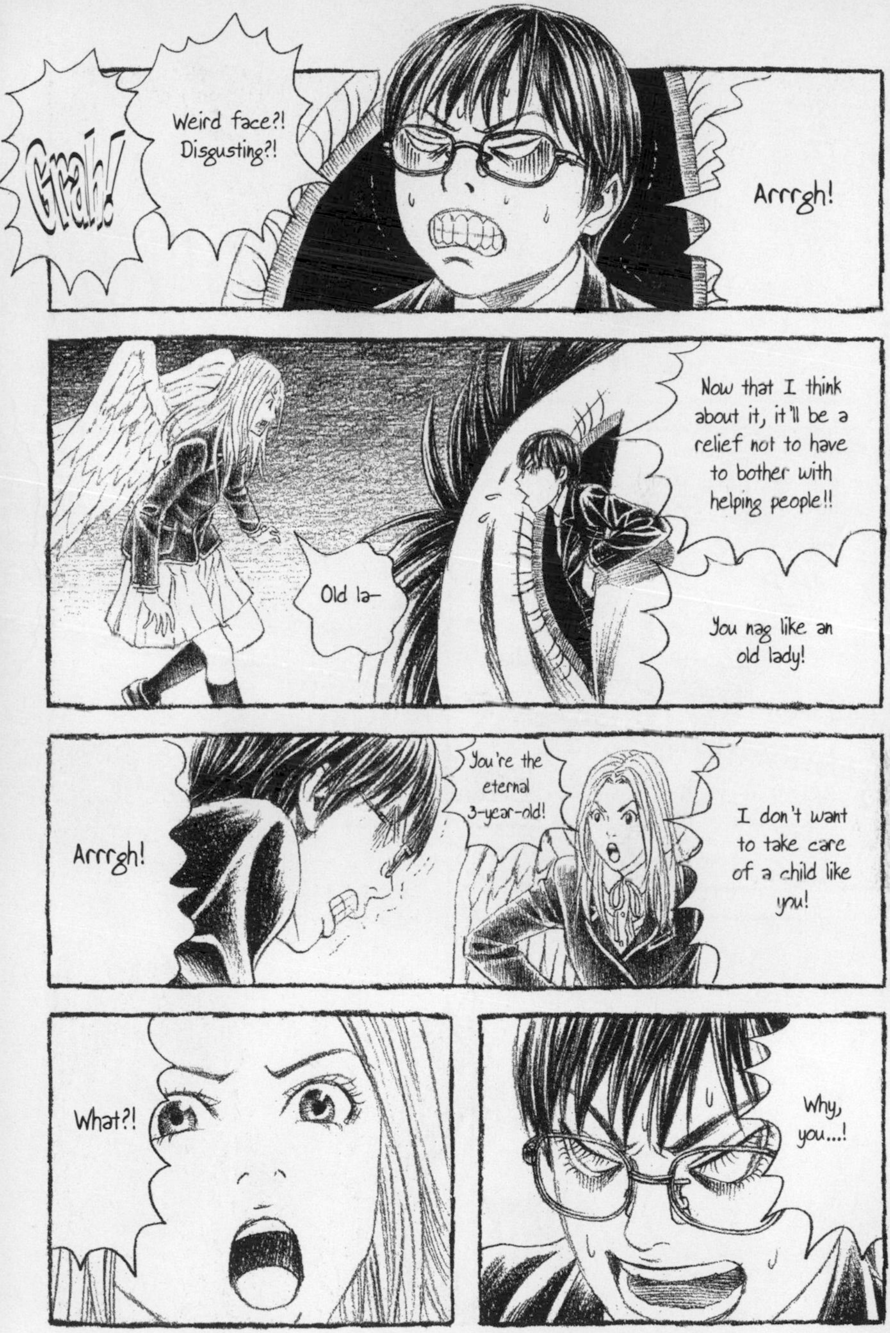
Weird face?! Disgusting?!
Grah!
Arrrgh!
Now that I think about it, it'll be a relief not to have to bother with helping people!!
You nag like an old lady!
Old la–
I don't want to take care of a child like you!
You're the eternal 3-year-old!
Arrrgh!
Why, you...!
What?!

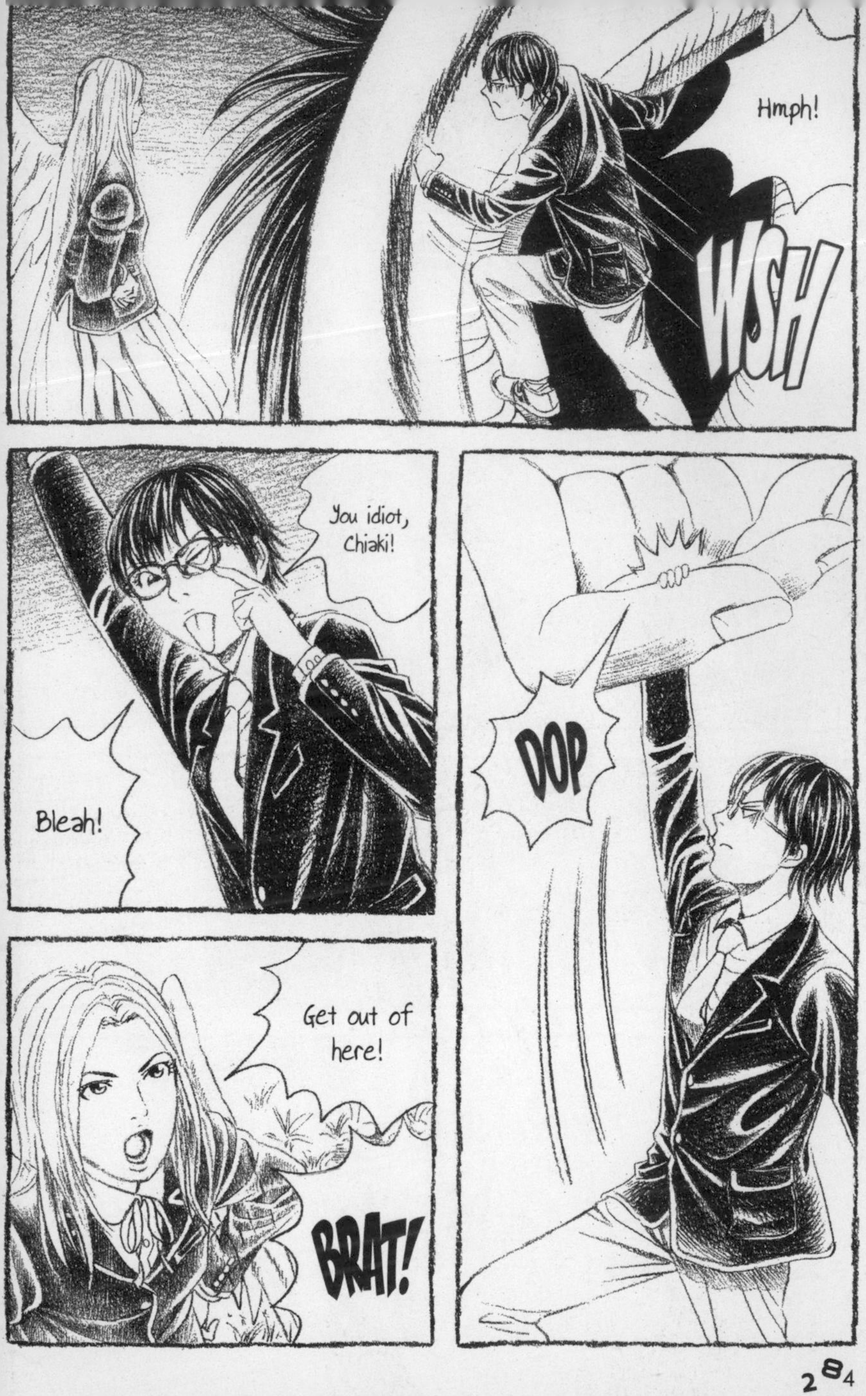
Hmph!
WSH
DOP
You idiot, Chiaki!
Bleah!
Get out of here!
BRAT!

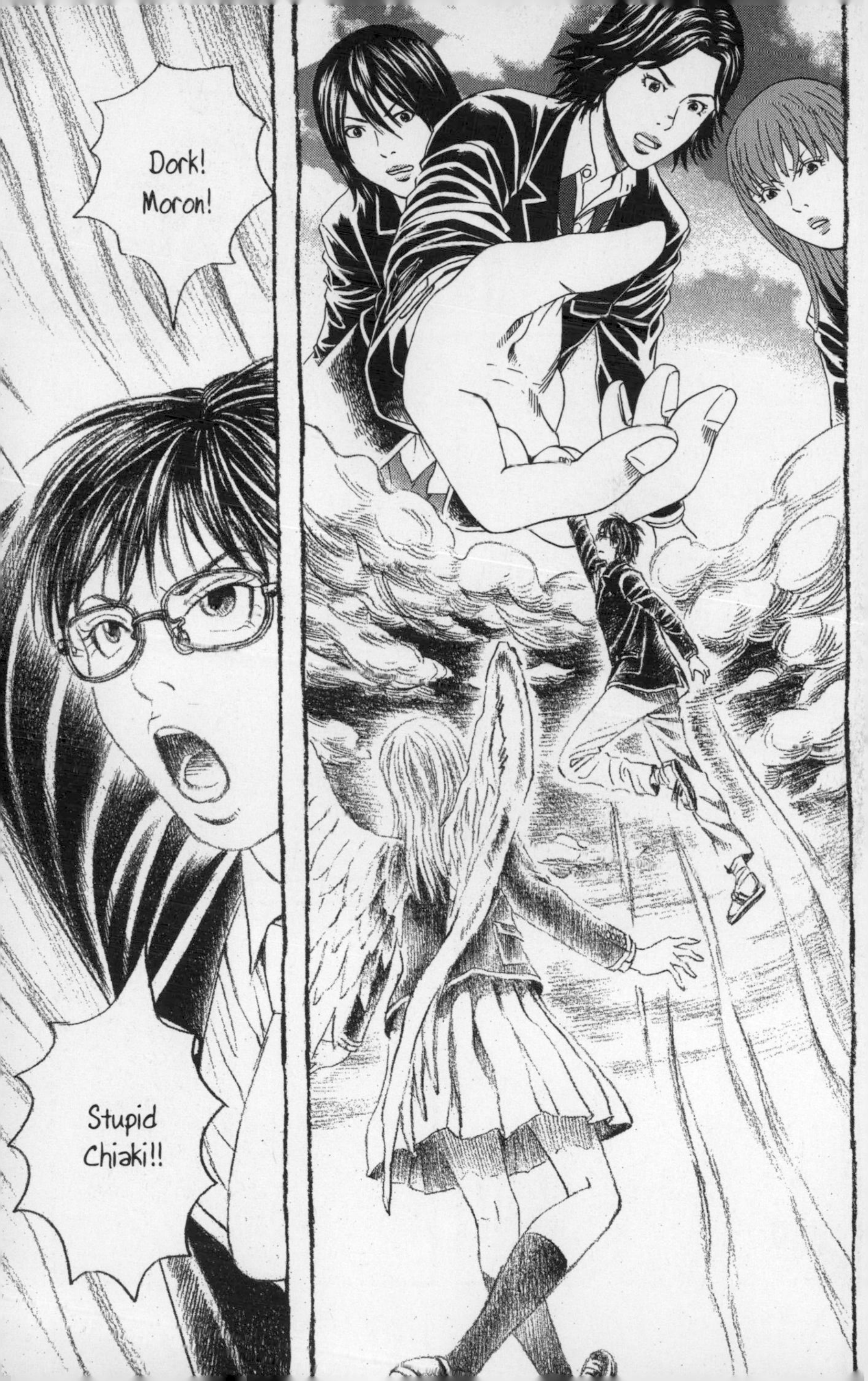
Dork! Moron!
Stupid Chiaki!!

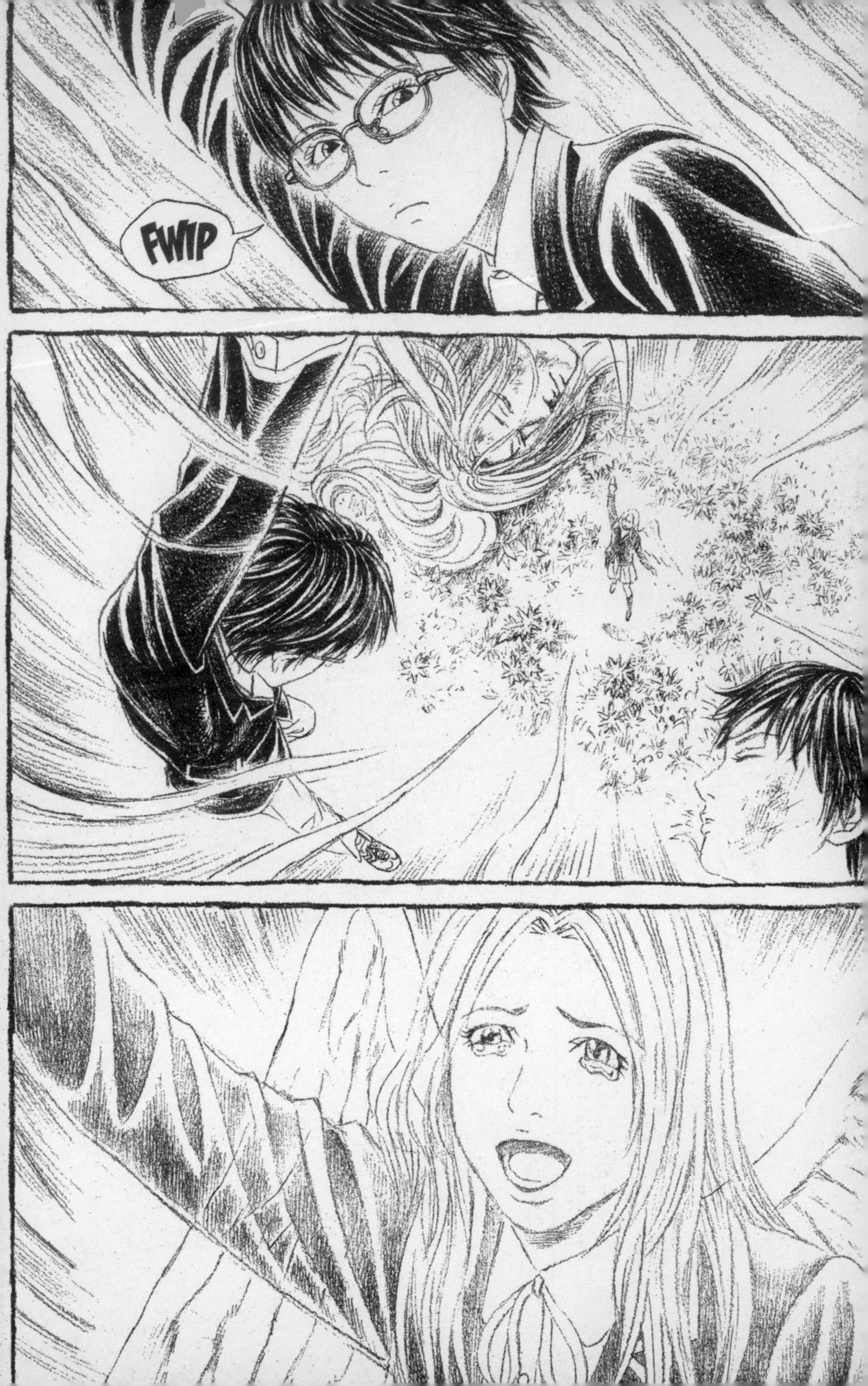
FWIP

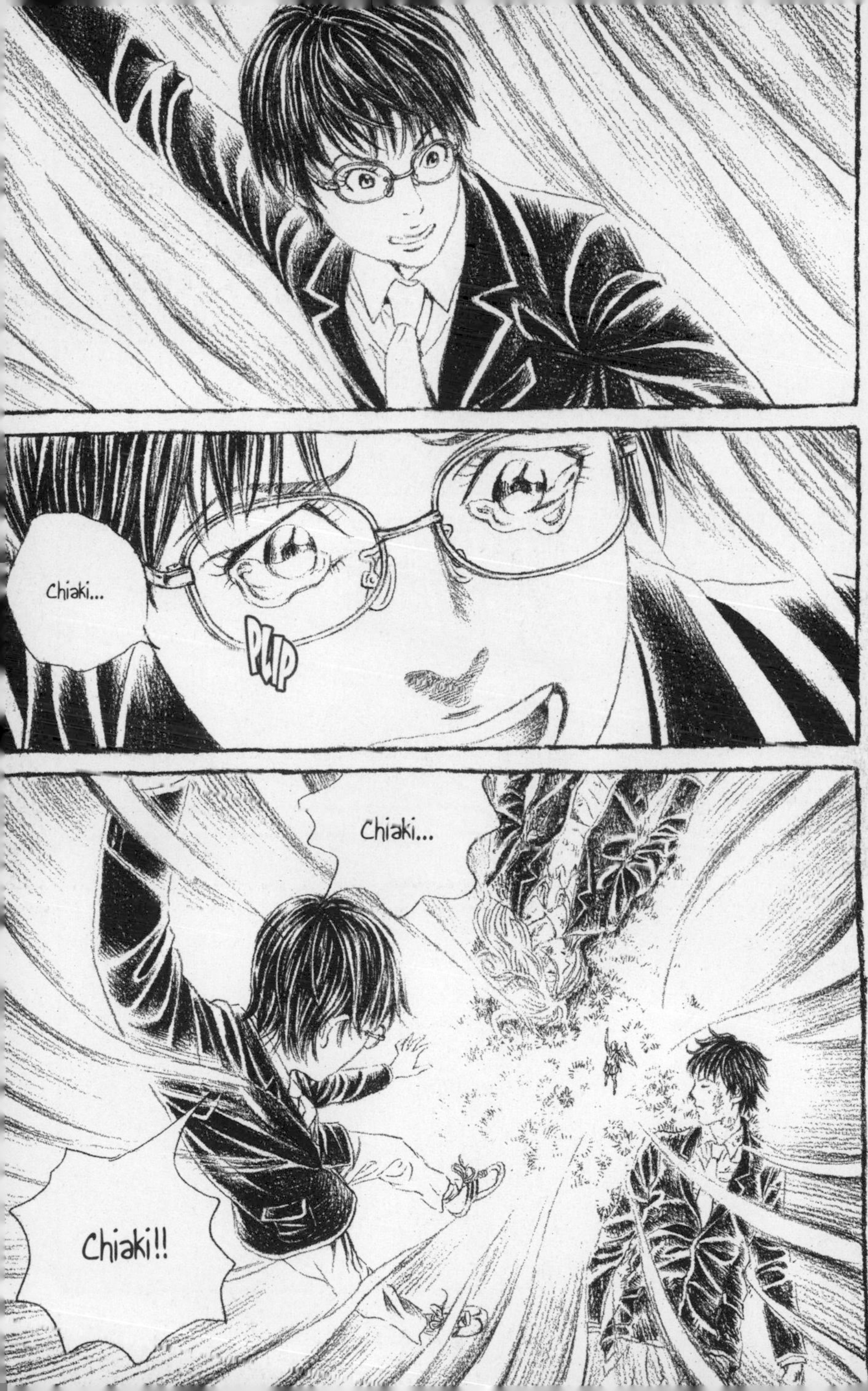
Chiaki...
PLIP
Chiaki...
Chiaki!!

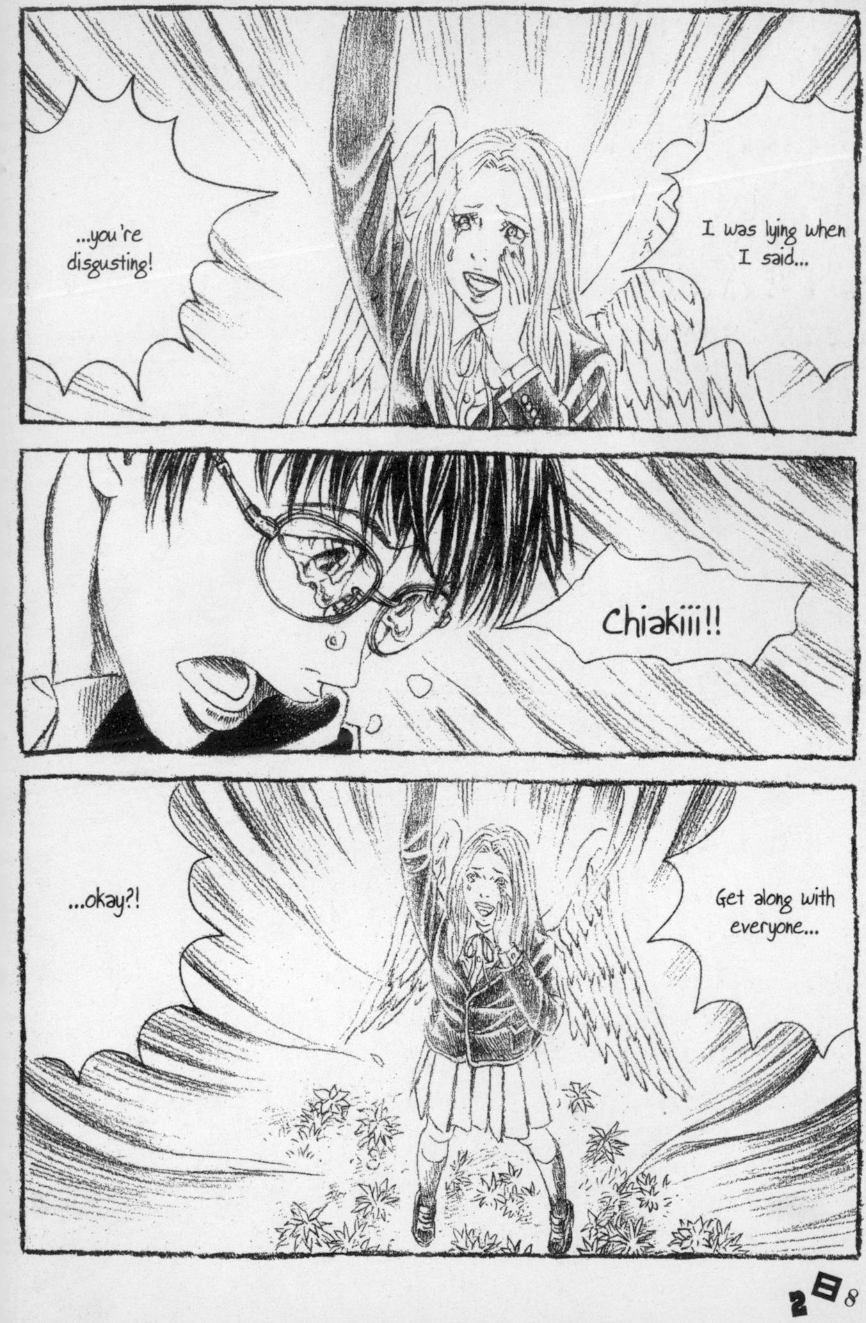
I was lying when I said...
...you're disgusting!
Chiakiii!!
Get along with everyone...
...okay?!

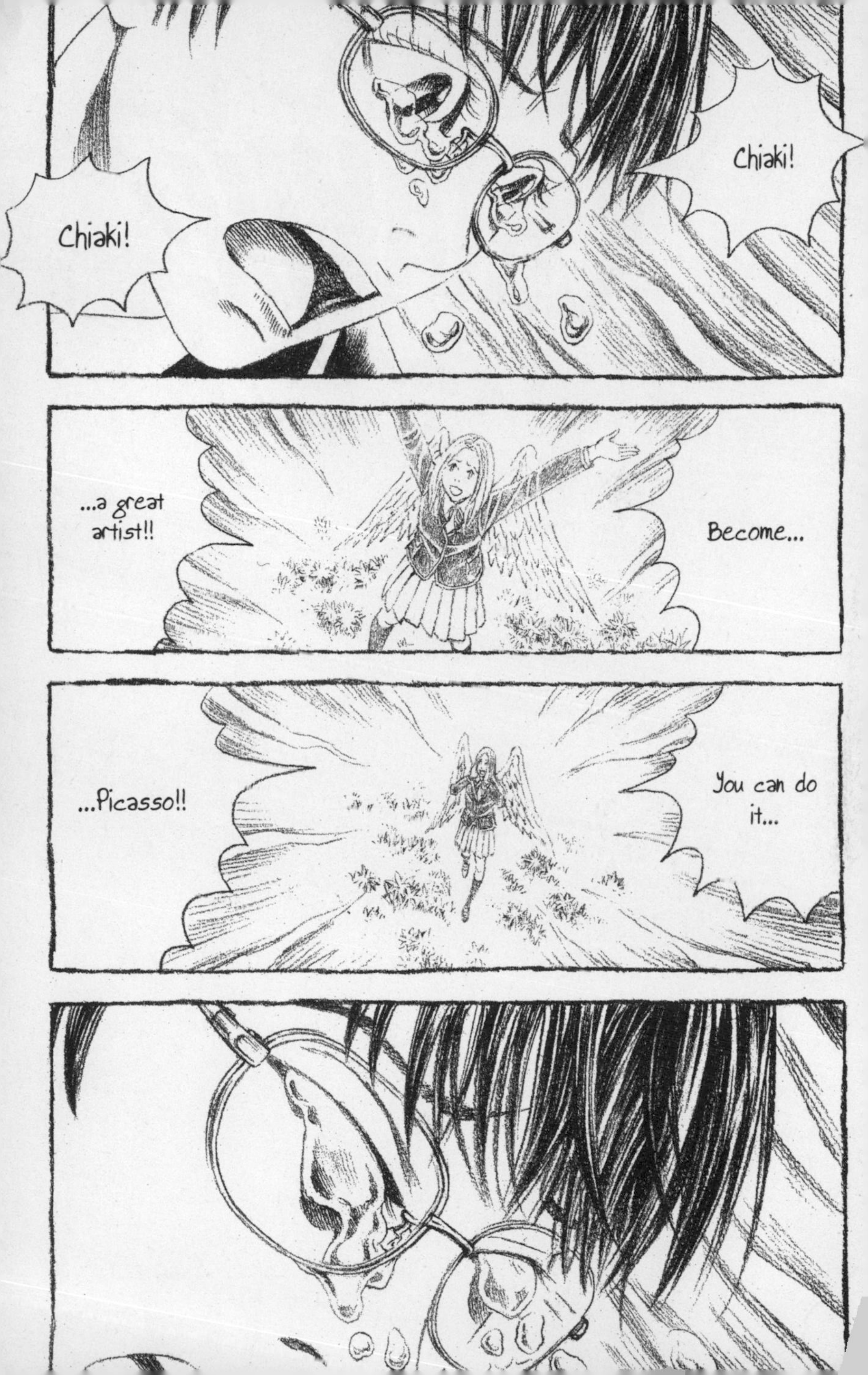
Chiaki!
Chiaki!
Become...
...a great artist!!
You can do it...
...Picasso!!

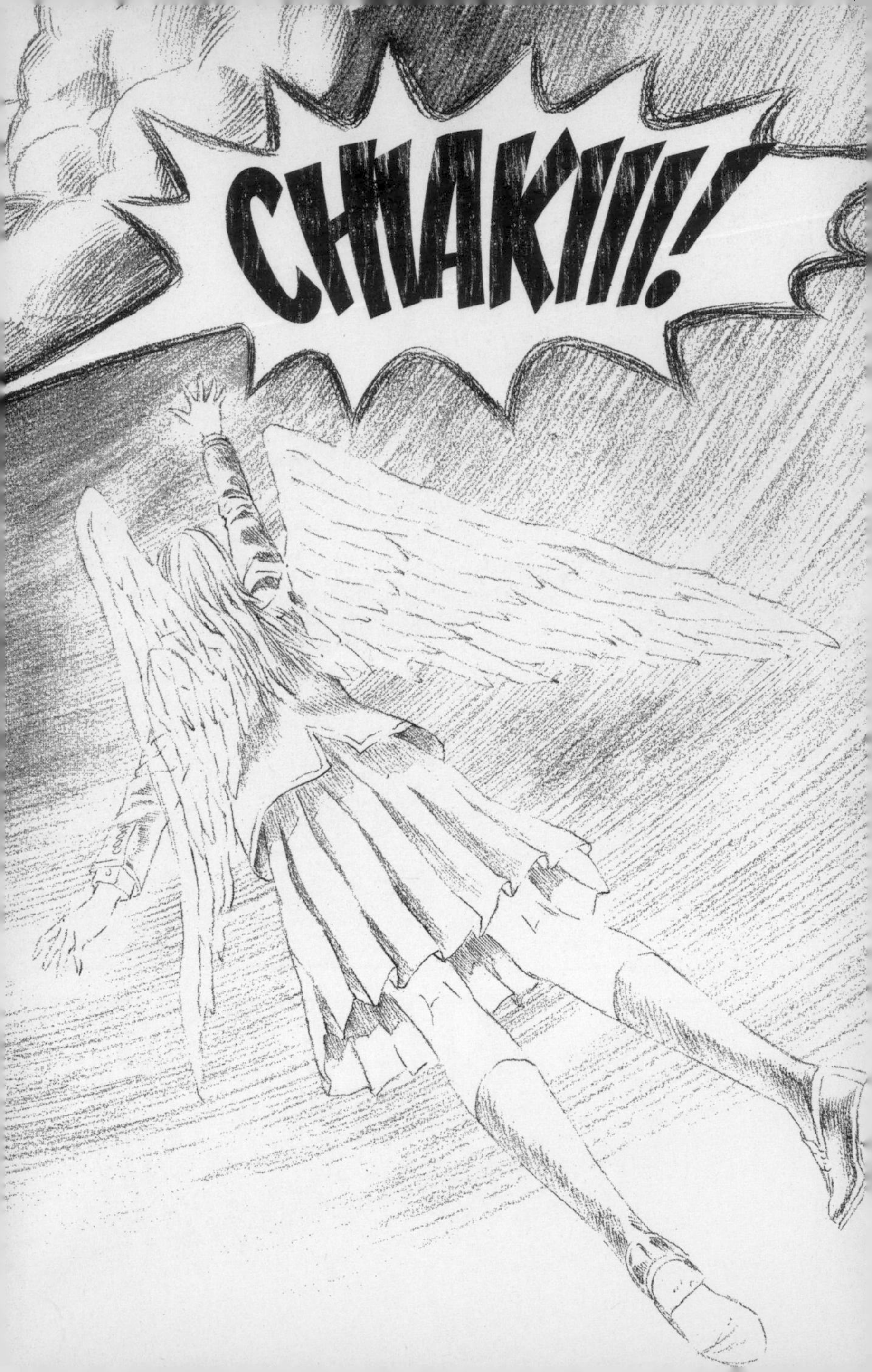
CHAKIII!

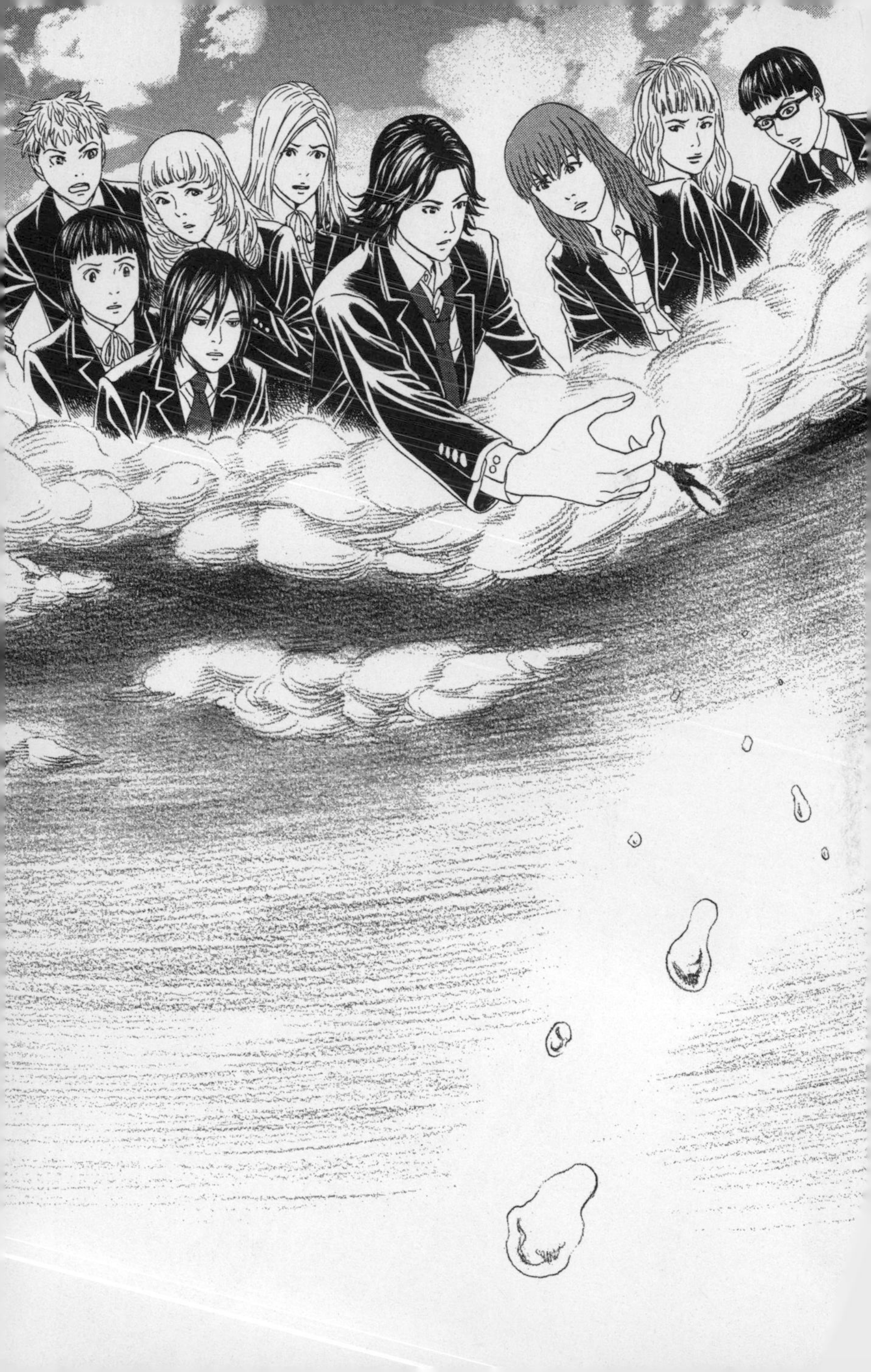

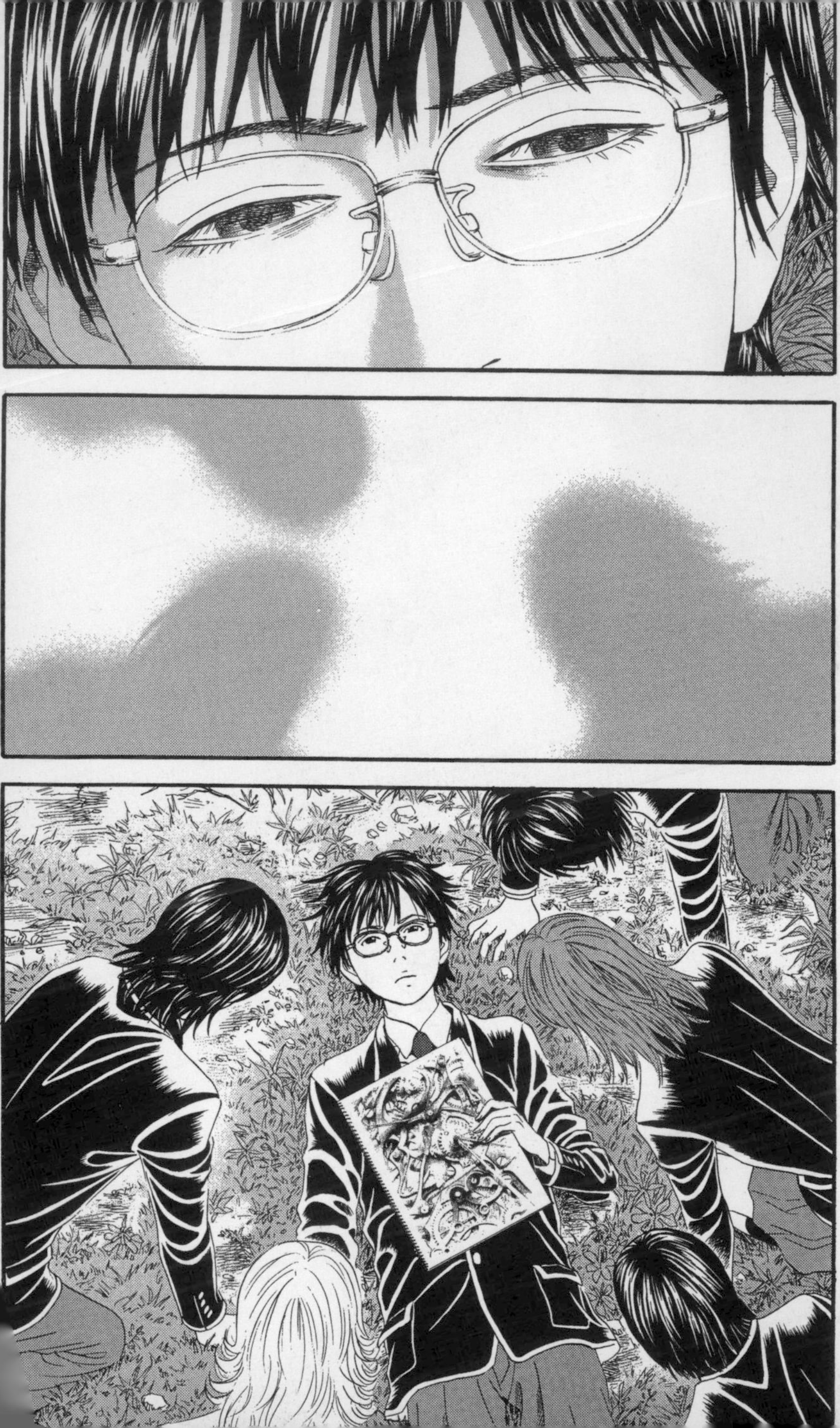

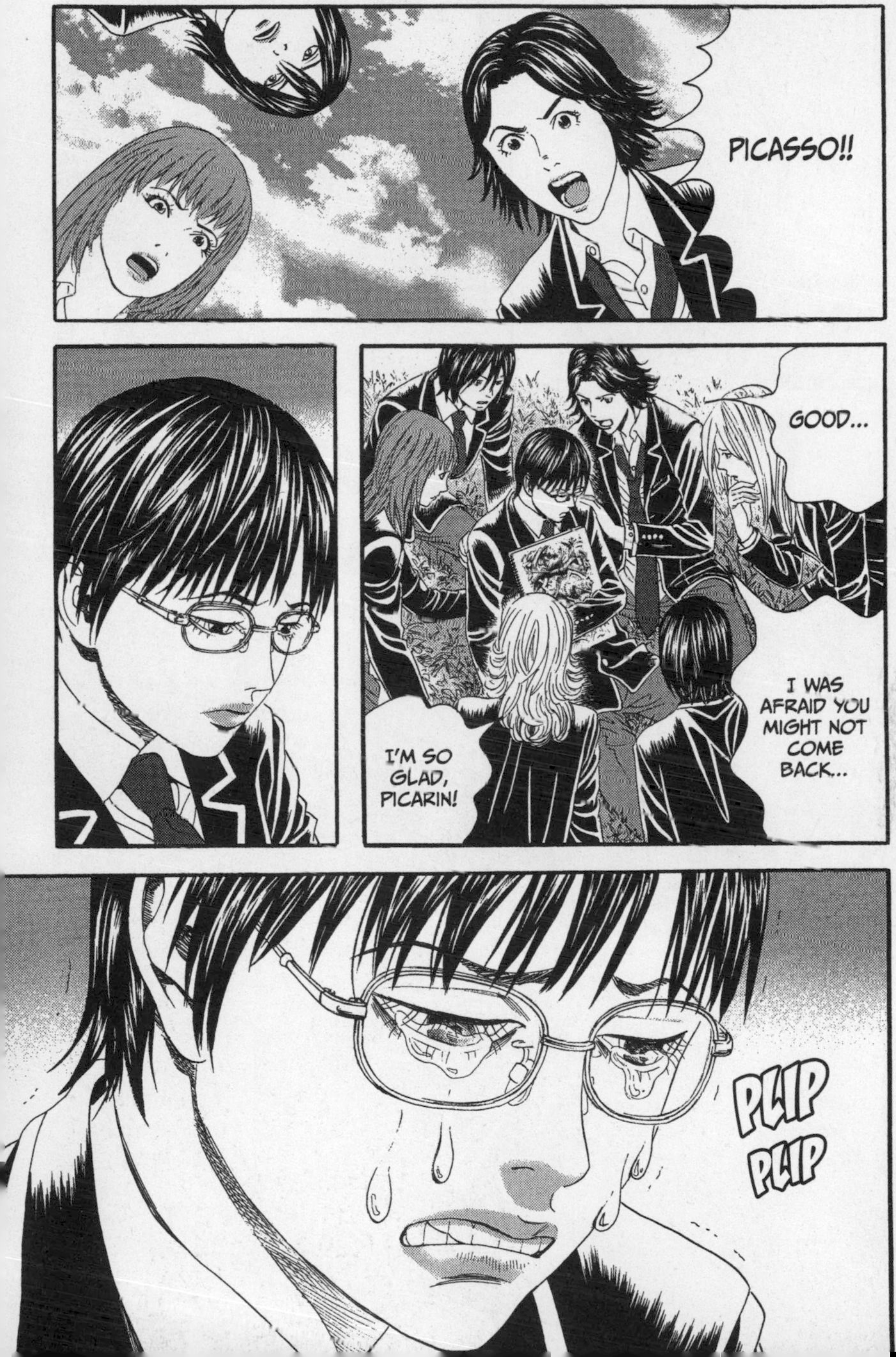
PICASSO!!
GOOD...
I WAS AFRAID YOU MIGHT NOT COME BACK...
I'M SO GLAD, PICARIN!
PLIP
PLIP

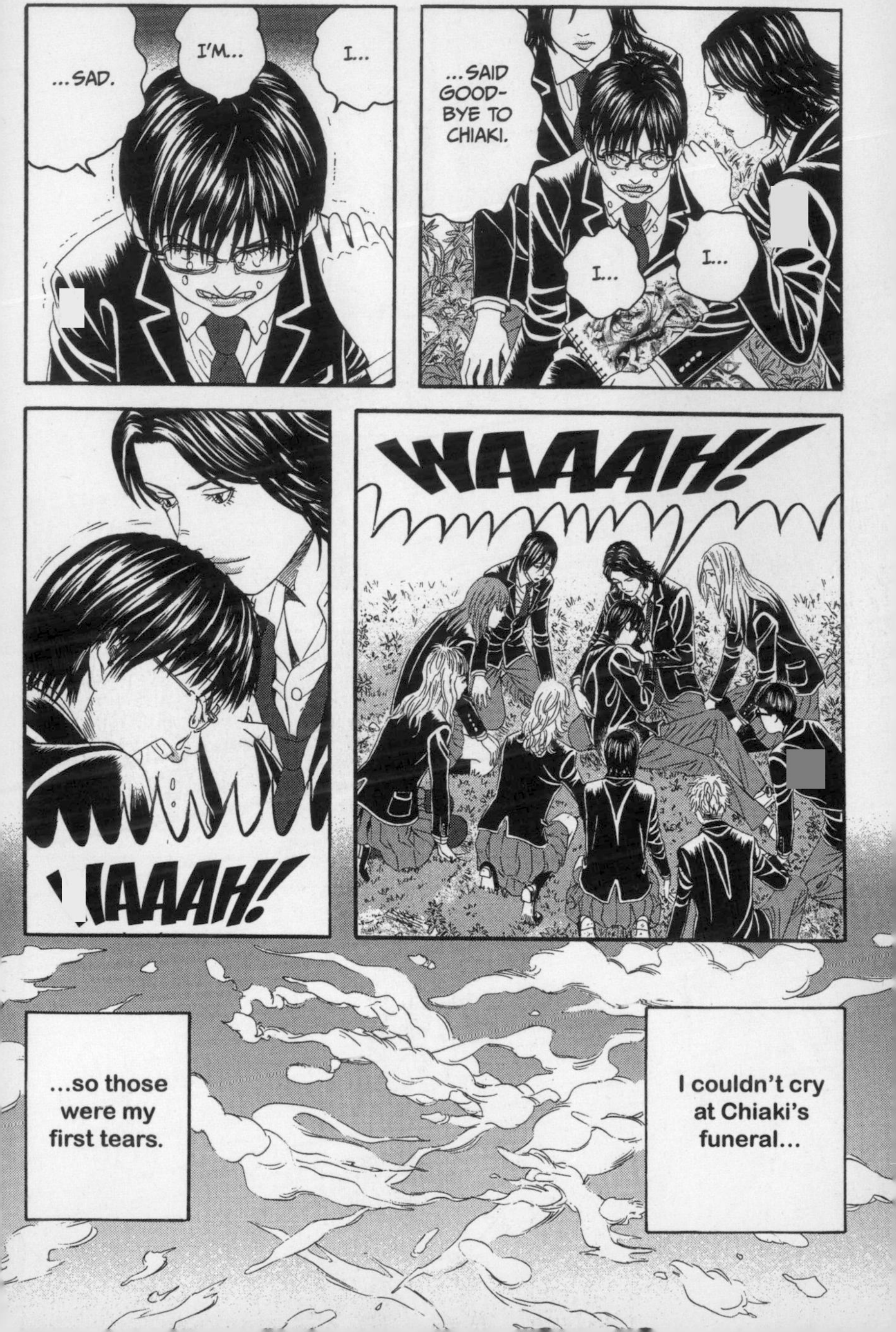
...SAID GOOD-BYE TO CHIAKI.
I...
I...
I...
I'M...
...SAD.
WAAAH!
WAAAH!
I couldn't cry at Chiaki's funeral...
...so those were my first tears.

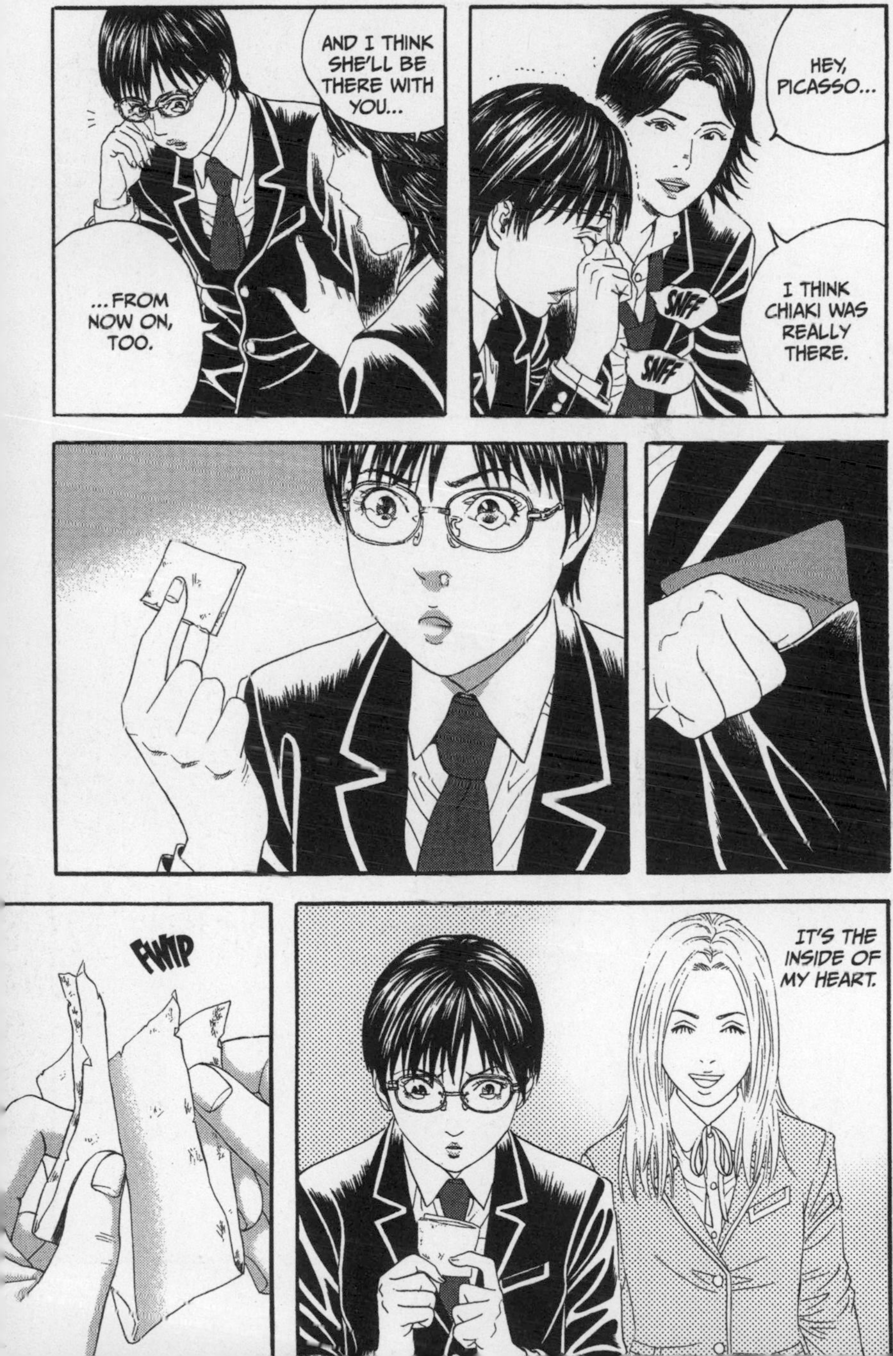
HEY, PICASSO...
I THINK CHIAKI WAS REALLY THERE.
SNFF
SNFF
AND I THINK SHE'LL BE THERE WITH YOU...
...FROM NOW ON, TOO.
IT'S THE INSIDE OF MY HEART.
FWIP

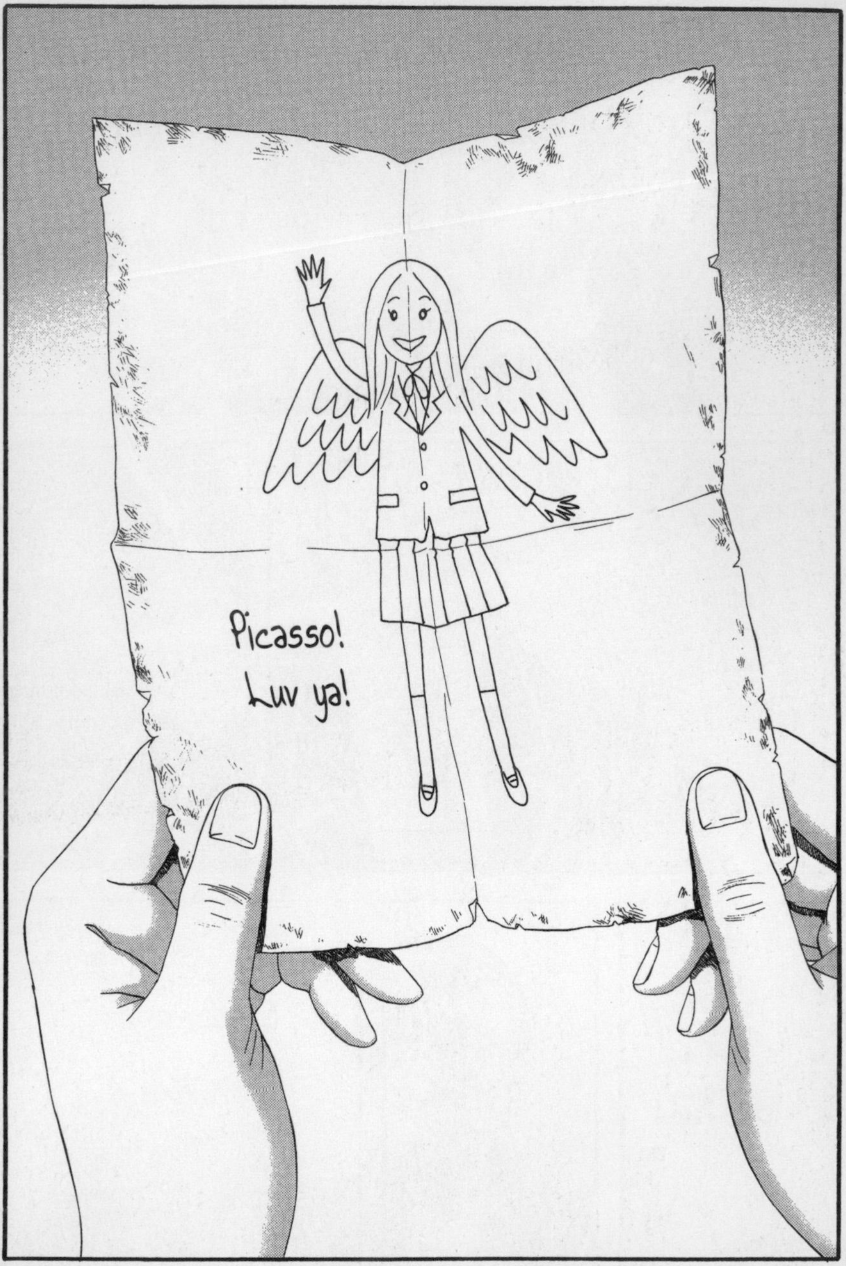
Picasso!
Luv ya!

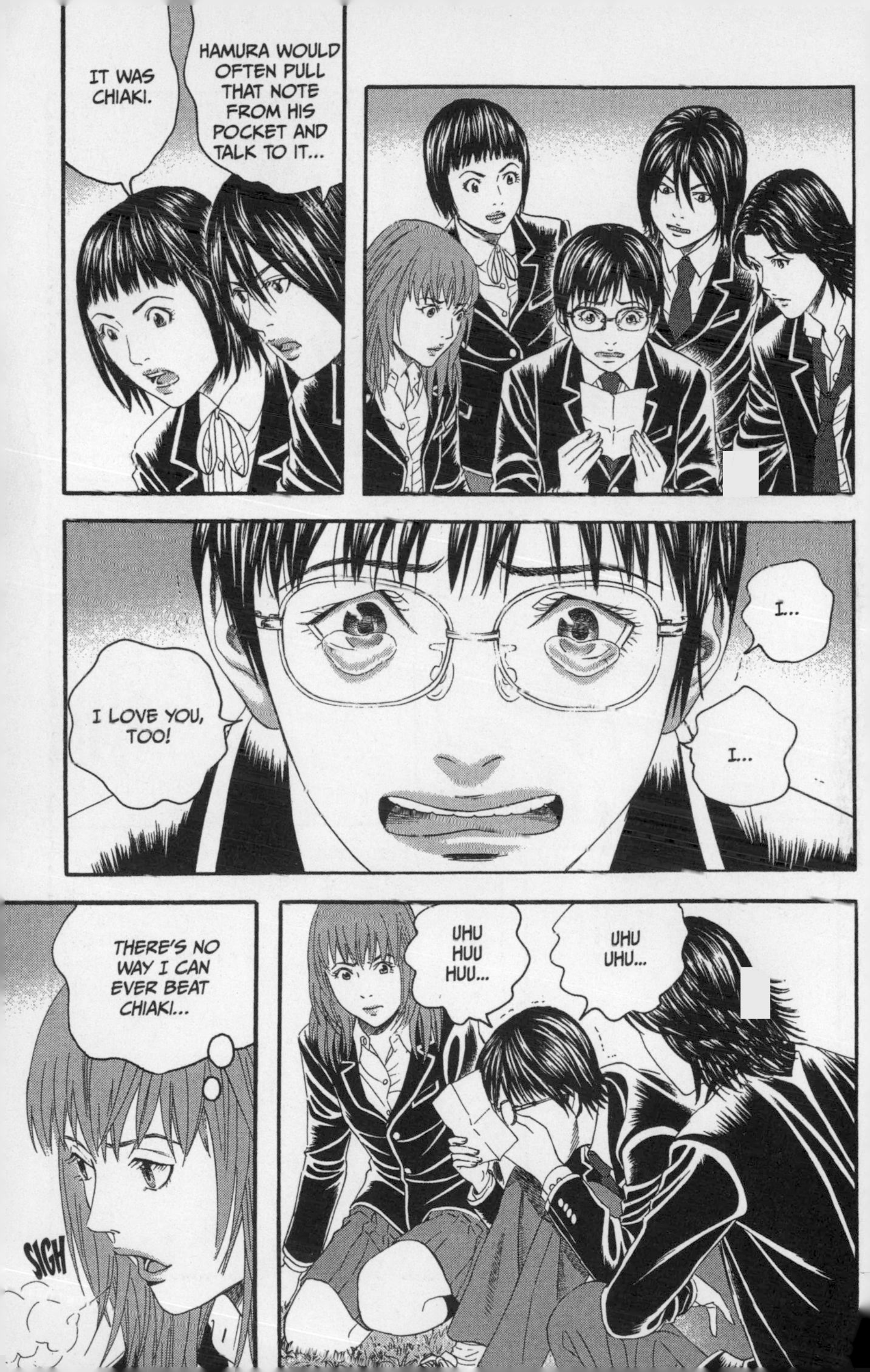
HAMURA WOULD OFTEN PULL THAT NOTE FROM HIS POCKET AND TALK TO IT...
IT WAS CHIAKI.
I...
I...
I LOVE YOU, TOO!
UHU UHU...
UHU HUU HUU...
THERE'S NO WAY I CAN EVER BEAT CHIAKI...
SIGH

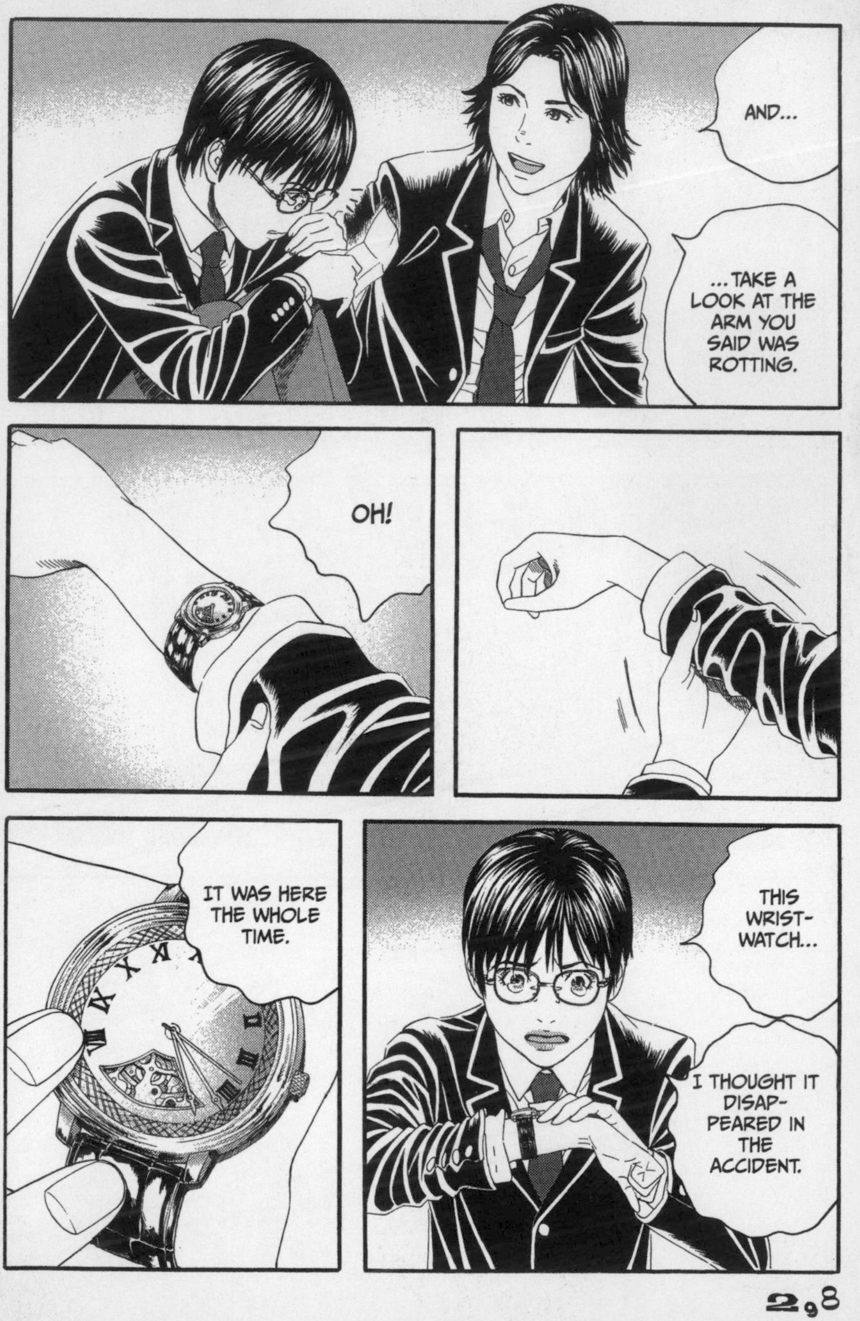
AND...
...TAKE A LOOK AT THE ARM YOU SAID WAS ROTTING.
OH!
THIS WRIST-WATCH...
I THOUGHT IT DISAP-PEARED IN THE ACCIDENT.
IT WAS HERE THE WHOLE TIME.

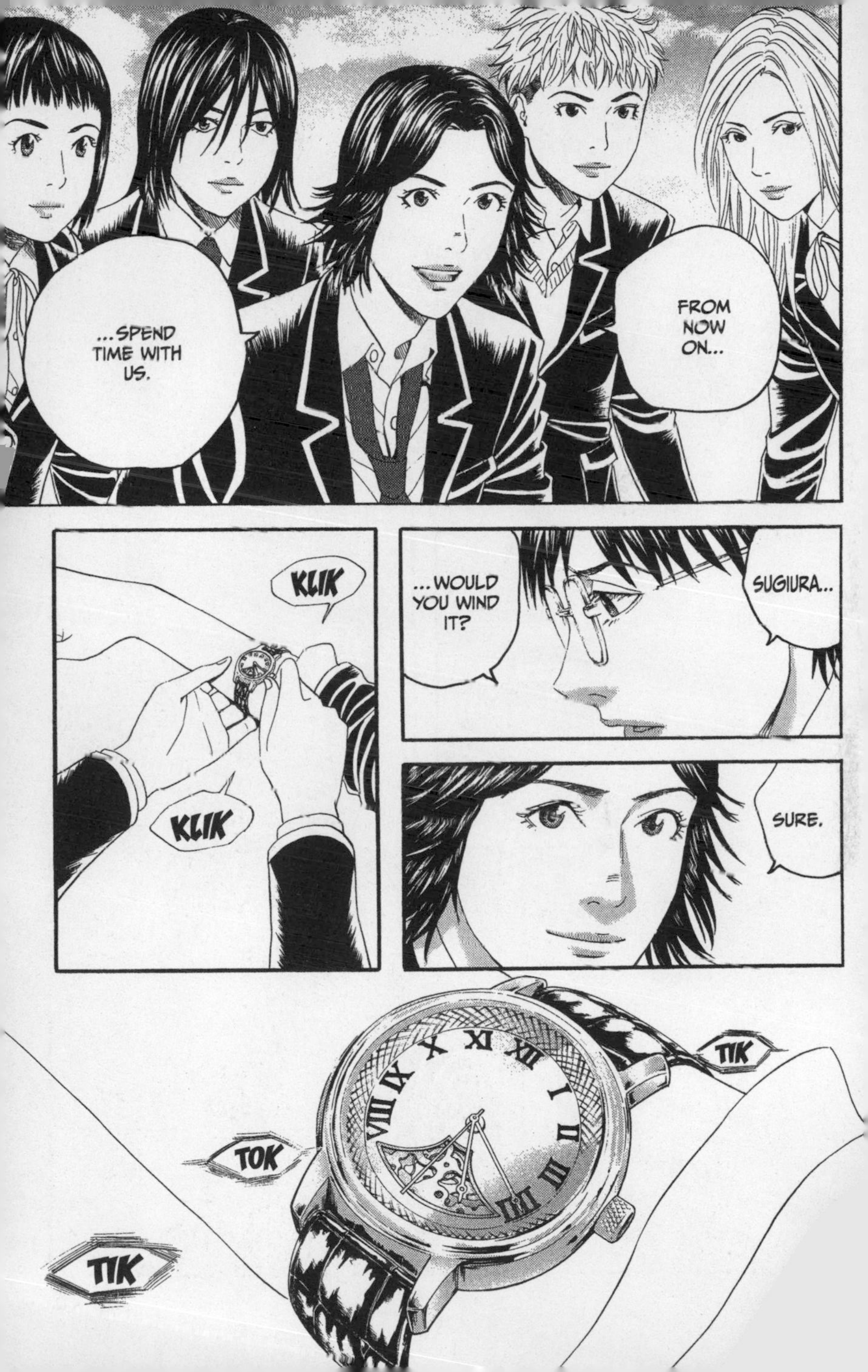
FROM NOW ON...
...SPEND TIME WITH US.
SUGIURA...
...WOULD YOU WIND IT?
SURE.
KLIK
KLIK
TIK
TOK
TIK

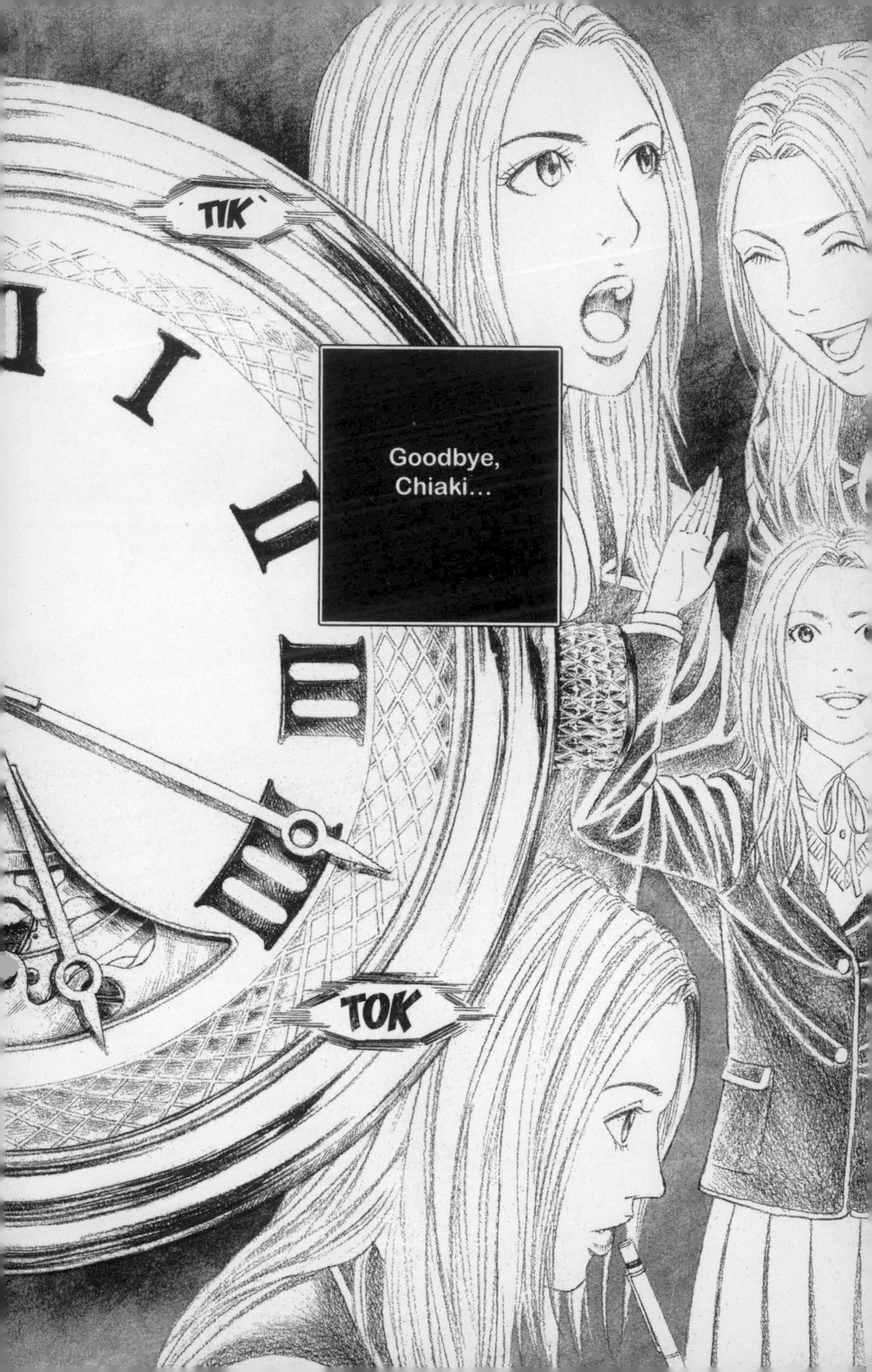
Goodbye, Chiaki...
TIK
TOK

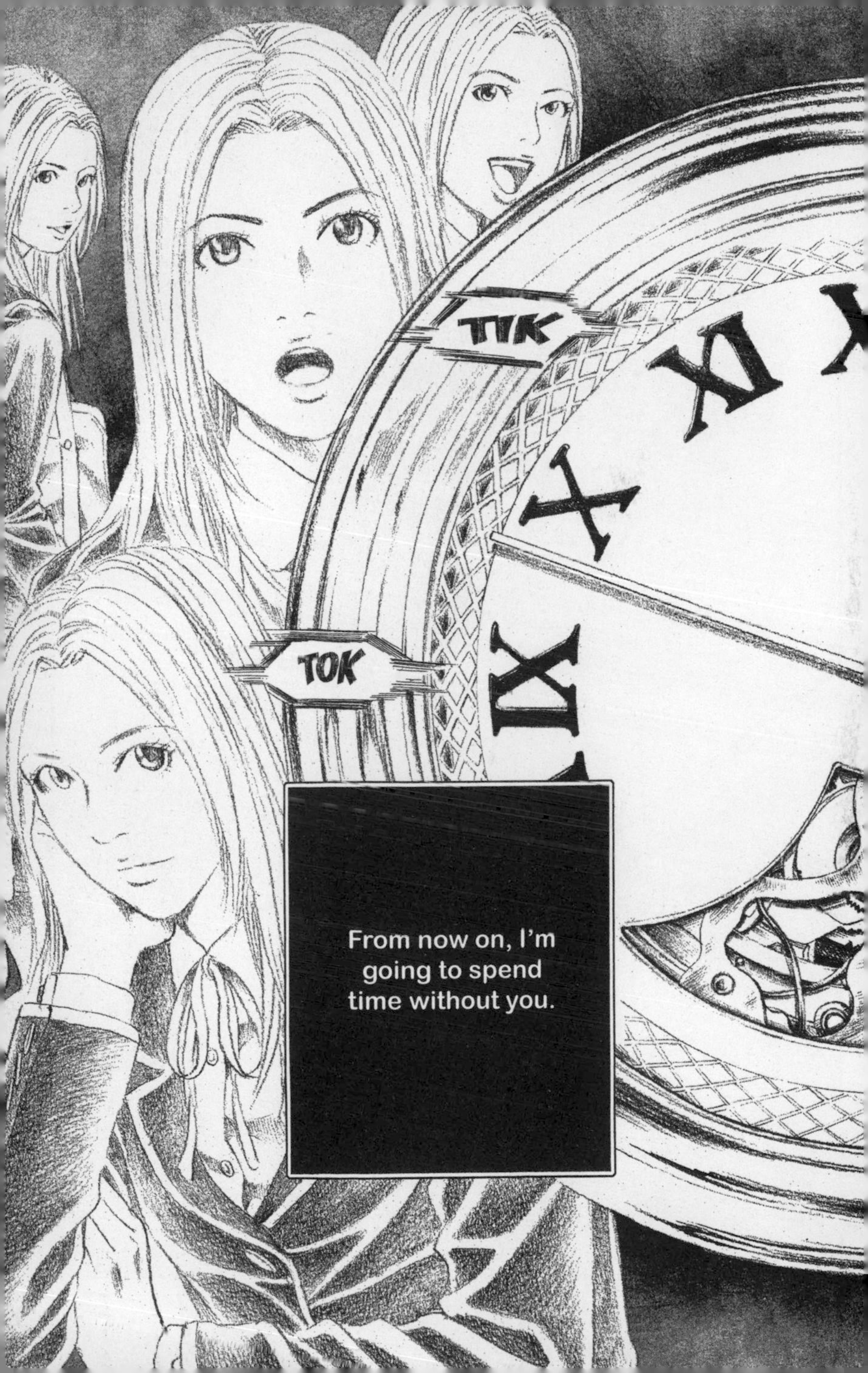
TIK
TOK
From now on, I'm going to spend time without you.

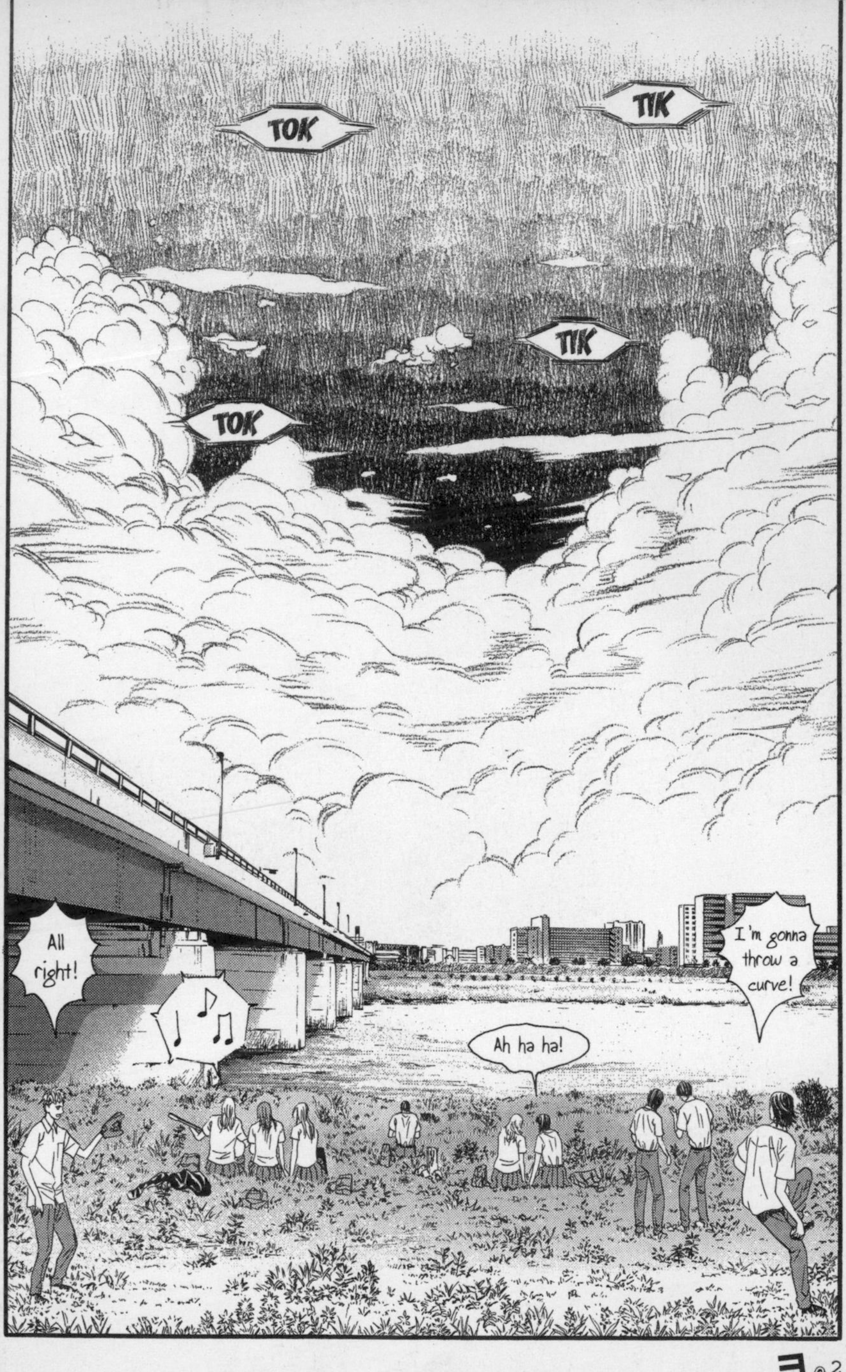
TIK
TOK
TIK
TOK
I'm gonna throw a curve!
Ah ha ha!
All right!

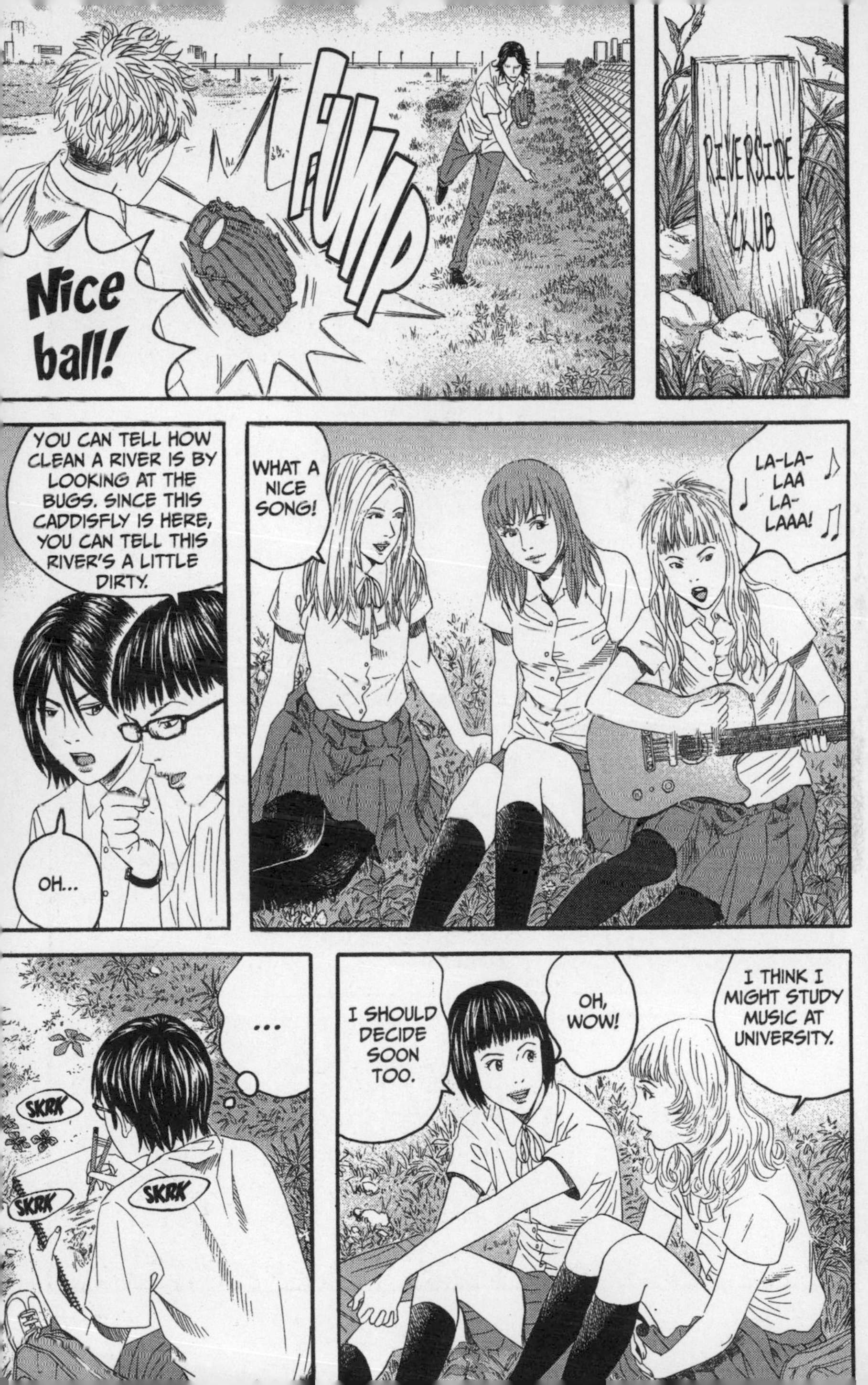
RIVERSIDE CLUB
FUMP
Nice ball!
LA-LA-LAA LA-LAAA!
WHAT A NICE SONG!
YOU CAN TELL HOW CLEAN A RIVER IS BY LOOKING AT THE BUGS. SINCE THIS CADDISFLY IS HERE, YOU CAN TELL THIS RIVER'S A LITTLE DIRTY.
OH...
I THINK I MIGHT STUDY MUSIC AT UNIVERSITY.
OH, WOW!
I SHOULD DECIDE SOON TOO.
...
SKRK
SKRK
SKRK

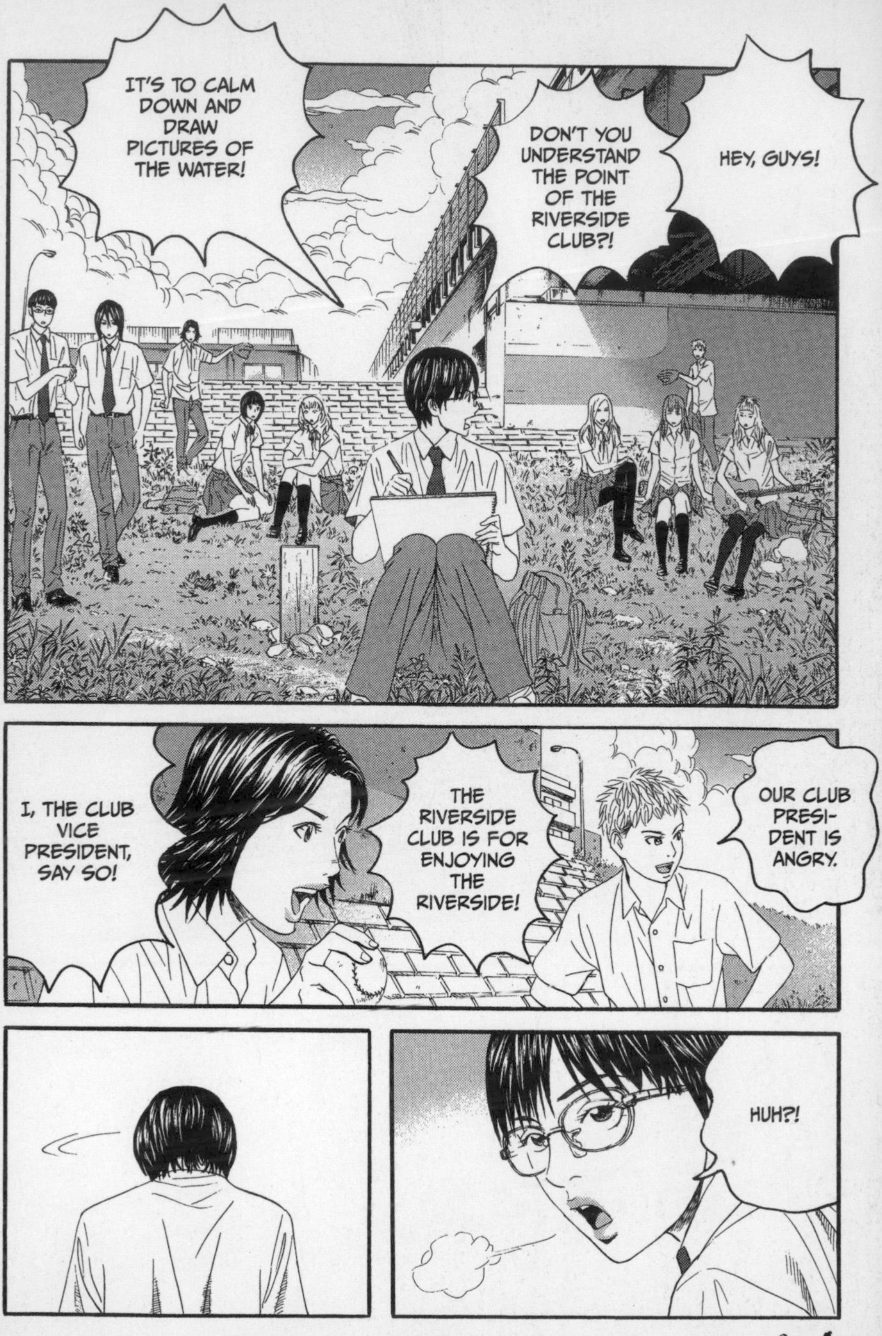
HEY, GUYS!
DON'T YOU UNDERSTAND THE POINT OF THE RIVERSIDE CLUB?!
IT'S TO CALM DOWN AND DRAW PICTURES OF THE WATER!
OUR CLUB PRESI-DENT IS ANGRY.
THE RIVERSIDE CLUB IS FOR ENJOYING THE RIVERSIDE!
I, THE CLUB VICE PRESIDENT, SAY SO!
HUH?!

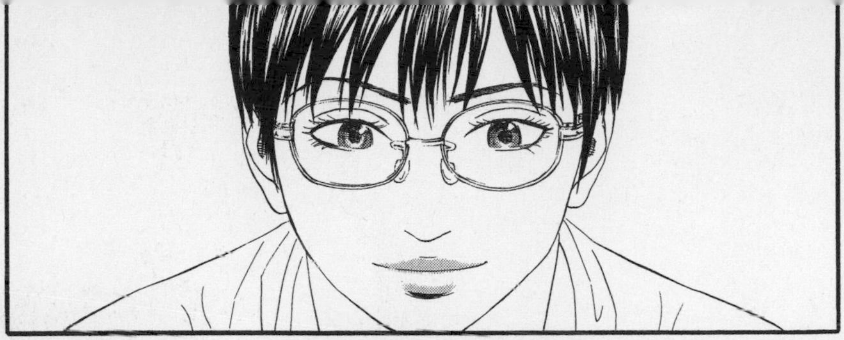

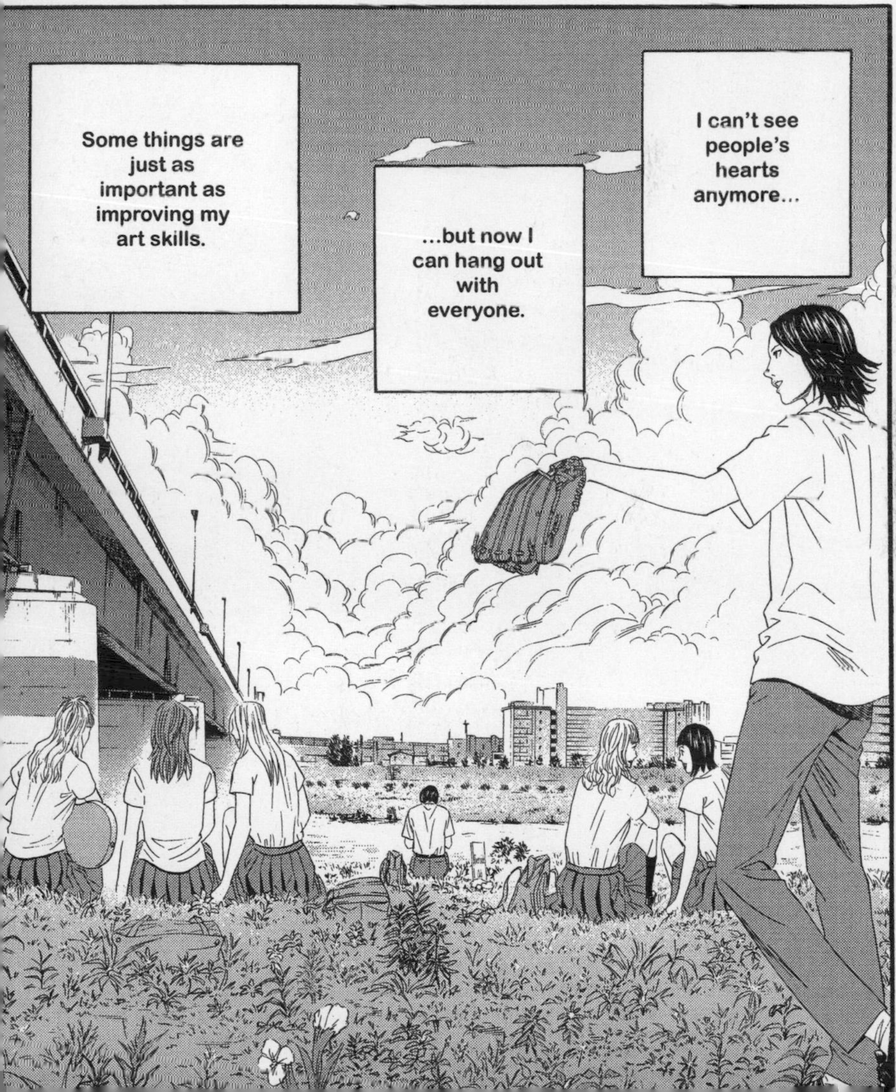
I can't see people's hearts anymore...
...but now I can hang out with everyone.
Some things are just as important as improving my art skills.

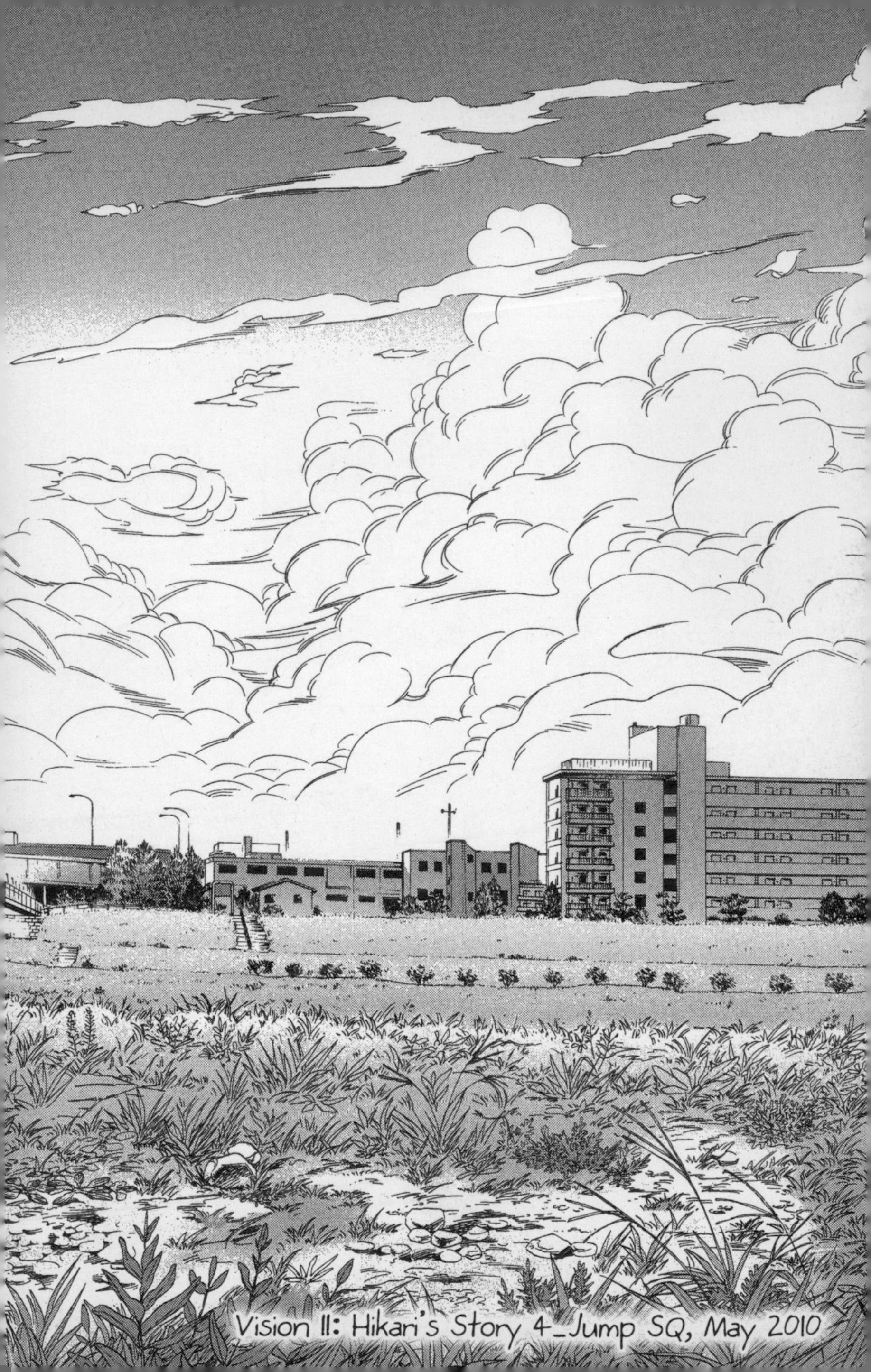

Vision 11: Hikari's Story 4_Jump SQ, May 2010

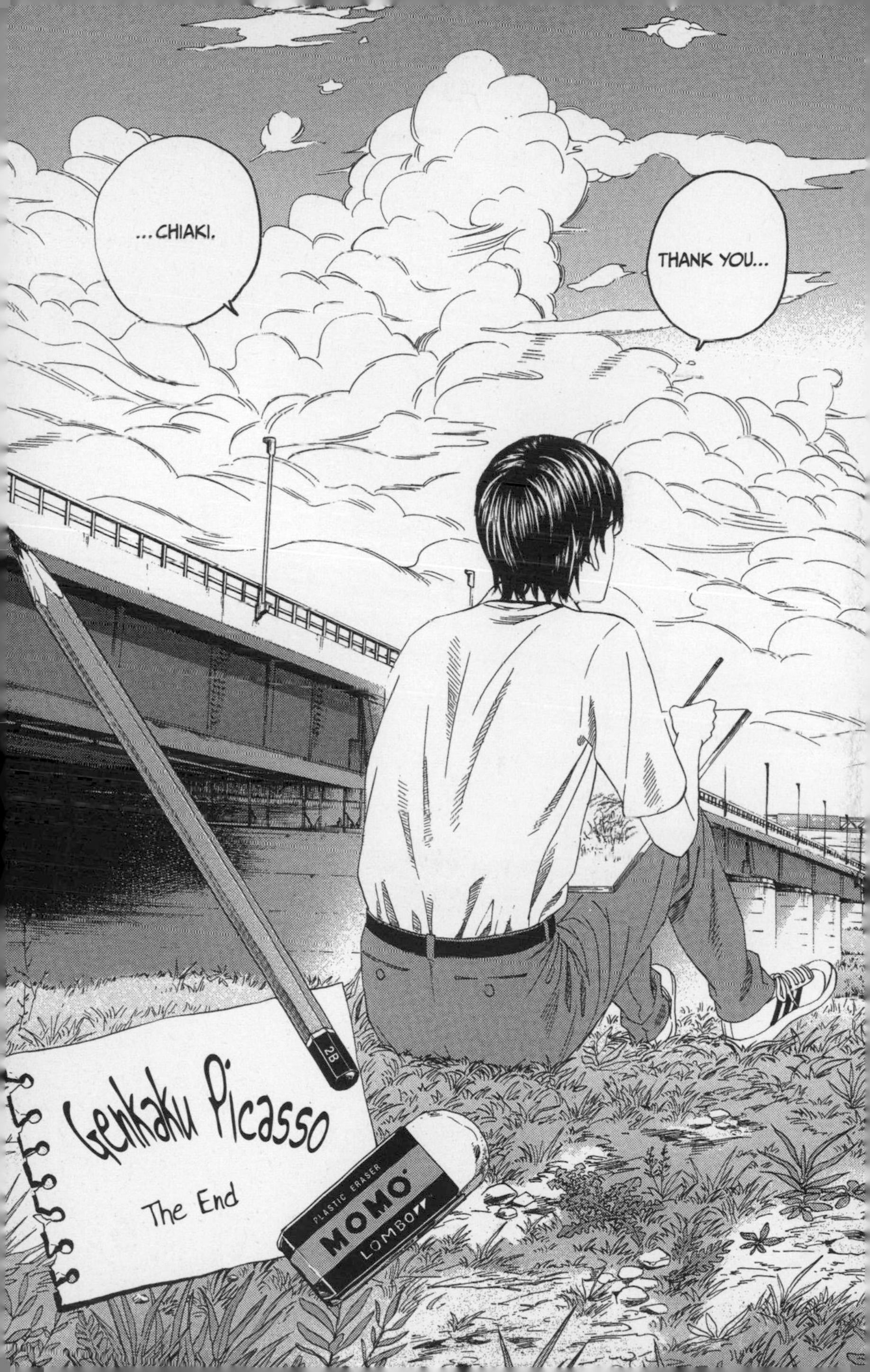
THANK YOU...
...CHIAKI.
2B
Genkaku Picasso
The End
PLASTIC ERASER
MOMO
LOMBO

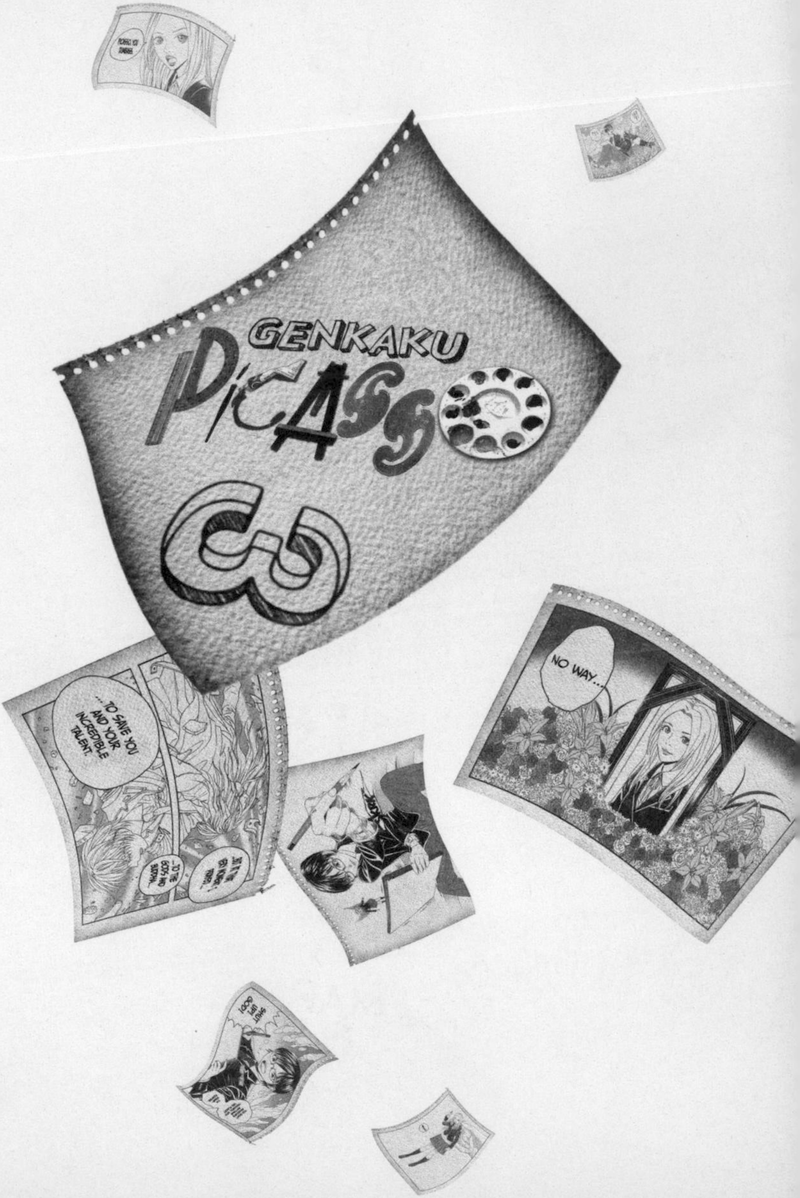
GENKAKU
PICASSO
3
NO WAY...
...TO SAVE YOU AND YOUR INCREDIBLE TALENT.
SHUT UP! GOD!

# AFTERWORD

## USAMARU FURUYA

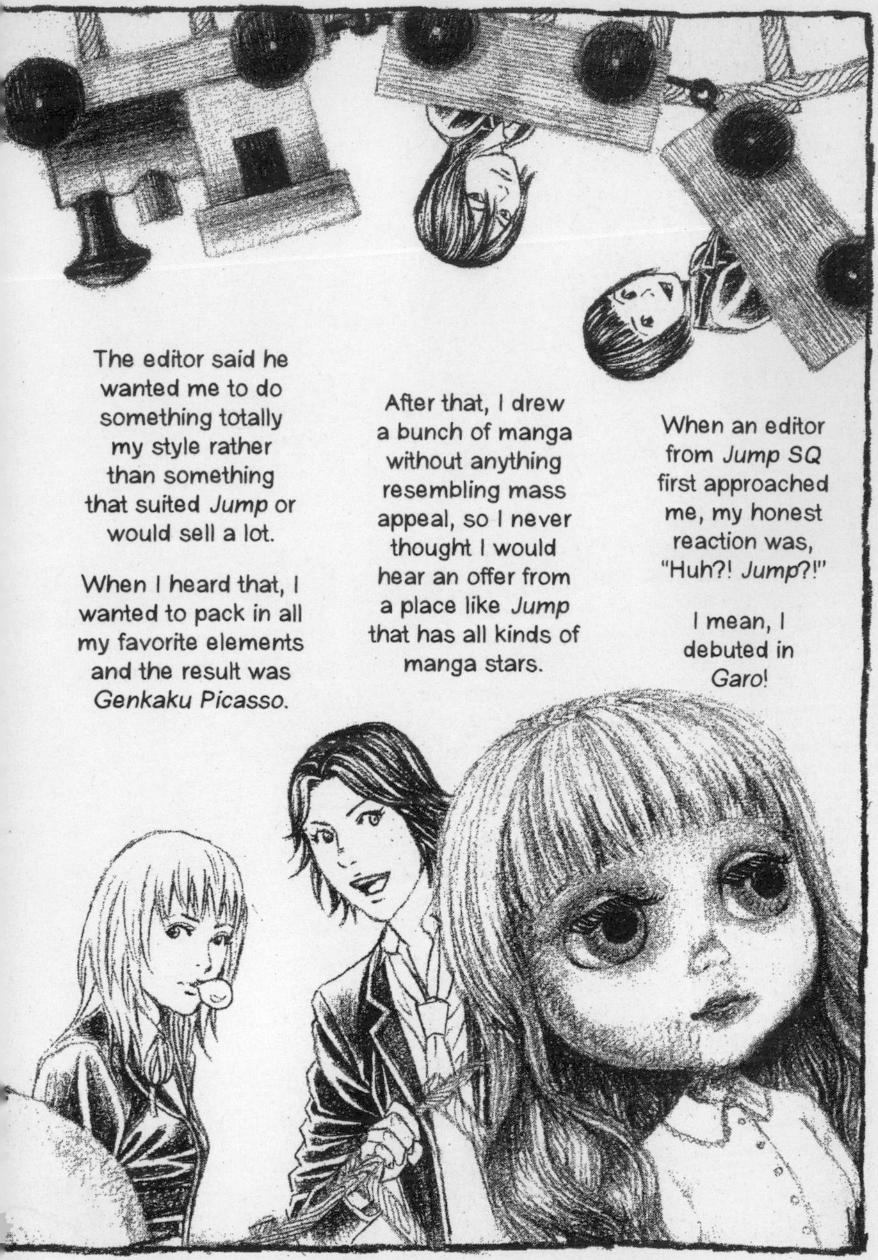
When an editor from *Jump SQ* first approached me, my honest reaction was, "Huh?! *Jump*?!"
I mean, I debuted in *Garo*!
After that, I drew a bunch of manga without anything resembling mass appeal, so I never thought I would hear an offer from a place like *Jump* that has all kinds of manga stars.
The editor said he wanted me to do something totally my style rather than something that suited *Jump* or would sell a lot.
When I heard that, I wanted to pack in all my favorite elements and the result was *Genkaku Picasso*.

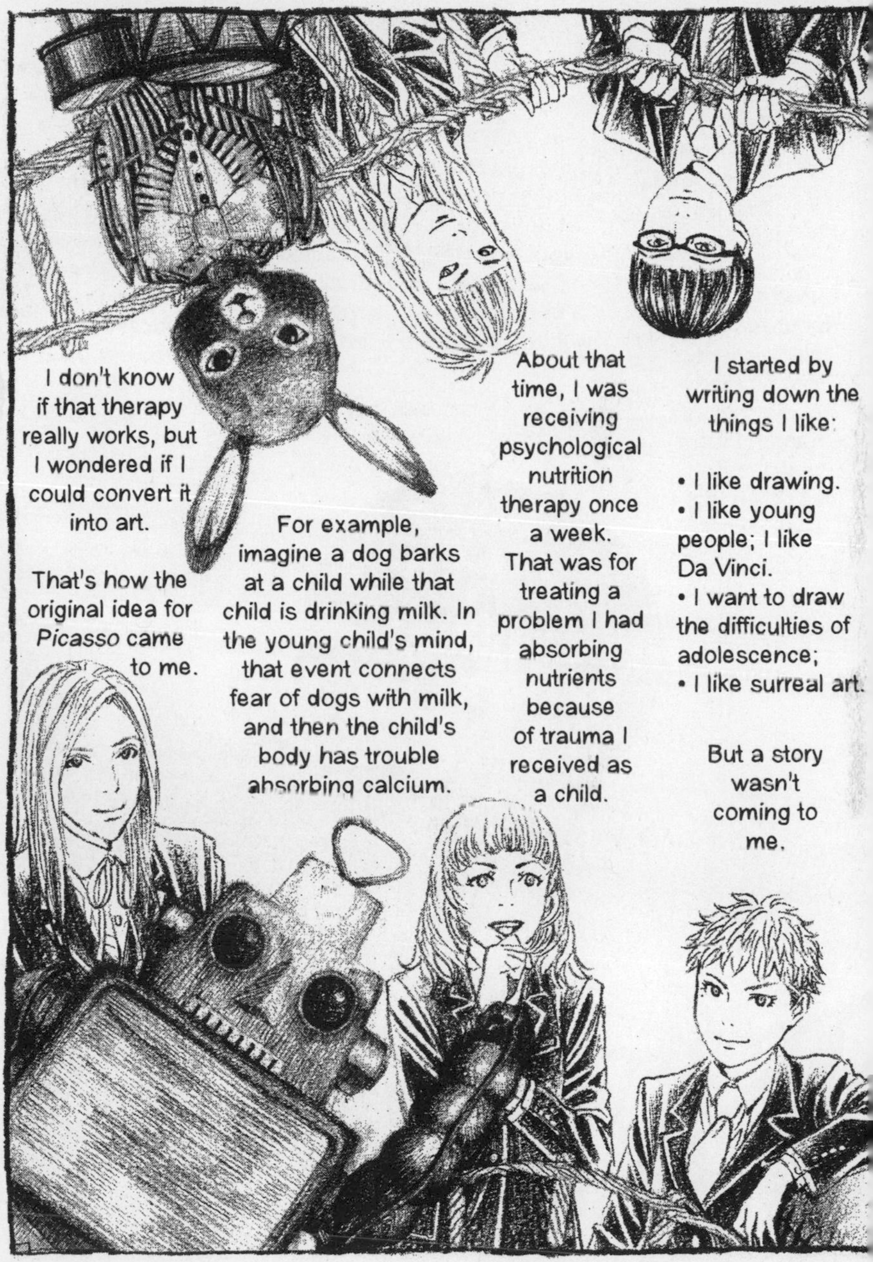
I started by writing down the things I like:
• I like drawing.
• I like young people; I like Da Vinci.
• I want to draw the difficulties of adolescence;
• I like surreal art.
But a story wasn't coming to me.
About that time, I was receiving psychological nutrition therapy once a week. That was for treating a problem I had absorbing nutrients because of trauma I received as a child.
For example, imagine a dog barks at a child while that child is drinking milk. In the young child's mind, that event connects fear of dogs with milk, and then the child's body has trouble absorbing calcium.
I don't know if that therapy really works, but I wondered if I could convert it into art.
That's how the original idea for *Picasso* came to me.

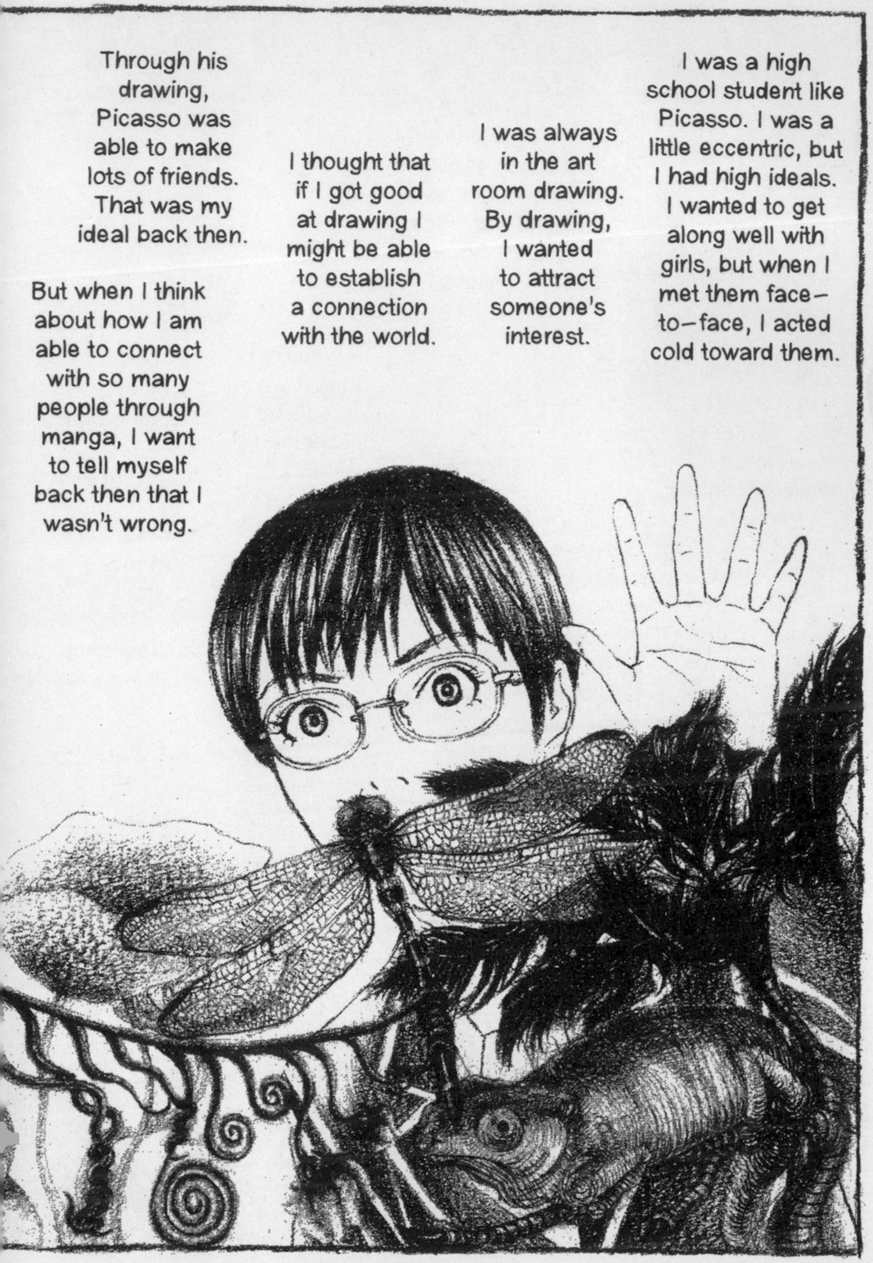
I was a high school student like Picasso. I was a little eccentric, but I had high ideals. I wanted to get along well with girls, but when I met them face-to-face, I acted cold toward them.
I was always in the art room drawing. By drawing, I wanted to attract someone's interest.
I thought that if I got good at drawing I might be able to establish a connection with the world.
Through his drawing, Picasso was able to make lots of friends. That was my ideal back then.
But when I think about how I am able to connect with so many people through manga, I want to tell myself back then that I wasn't wrong.

When a series ends, everyone says it got canceled, but much of the time that's a mistake.

This story was planned to end after eight issues, or two volumes, but I wouldn't have been able to pull it all together that way, so I got to do three volumes. (Each volume is thick, though, so it's more like there are four! Each one's a good value! Ha ha ha!)

Thanks to that, I could bring the series to the conclusion I wanted. *Picasso* is a fortunate manga!

I'd be happy if people think of Picasso and Chiaki and their friends every now and then.

I am grateful from the bottom of my heart to all the fans who cheered this series on! Thank you very much!

—USAMARU FURUYA

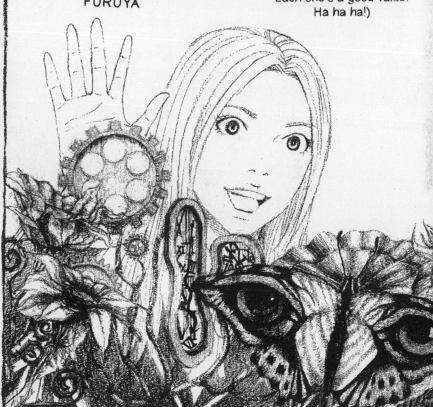

**JAPANESE STAFF**
Tamami Kyo
Ai Kozaki
Yoichiro Hiroki
Momoko Ishii
Naoko Suzuki

**JAPANESE EDITOR**
Juntaro Kosuge

**JAPANESE GRAPHIC
NOVEL EDITOR**
Yuki Design
Jun Kobayashi

**JAPANESE BOOK
DESIGN**
chutte

**THANKS**
neon

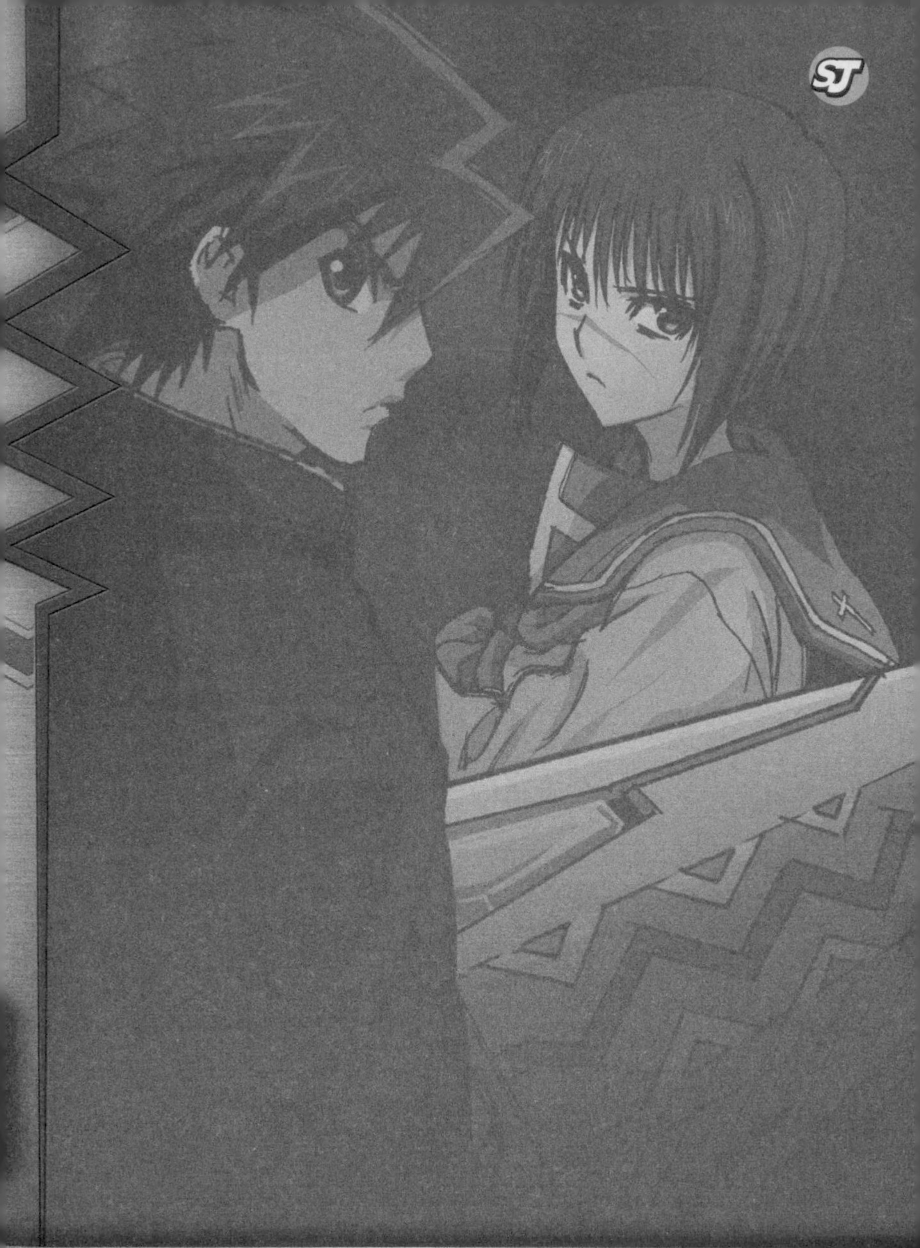

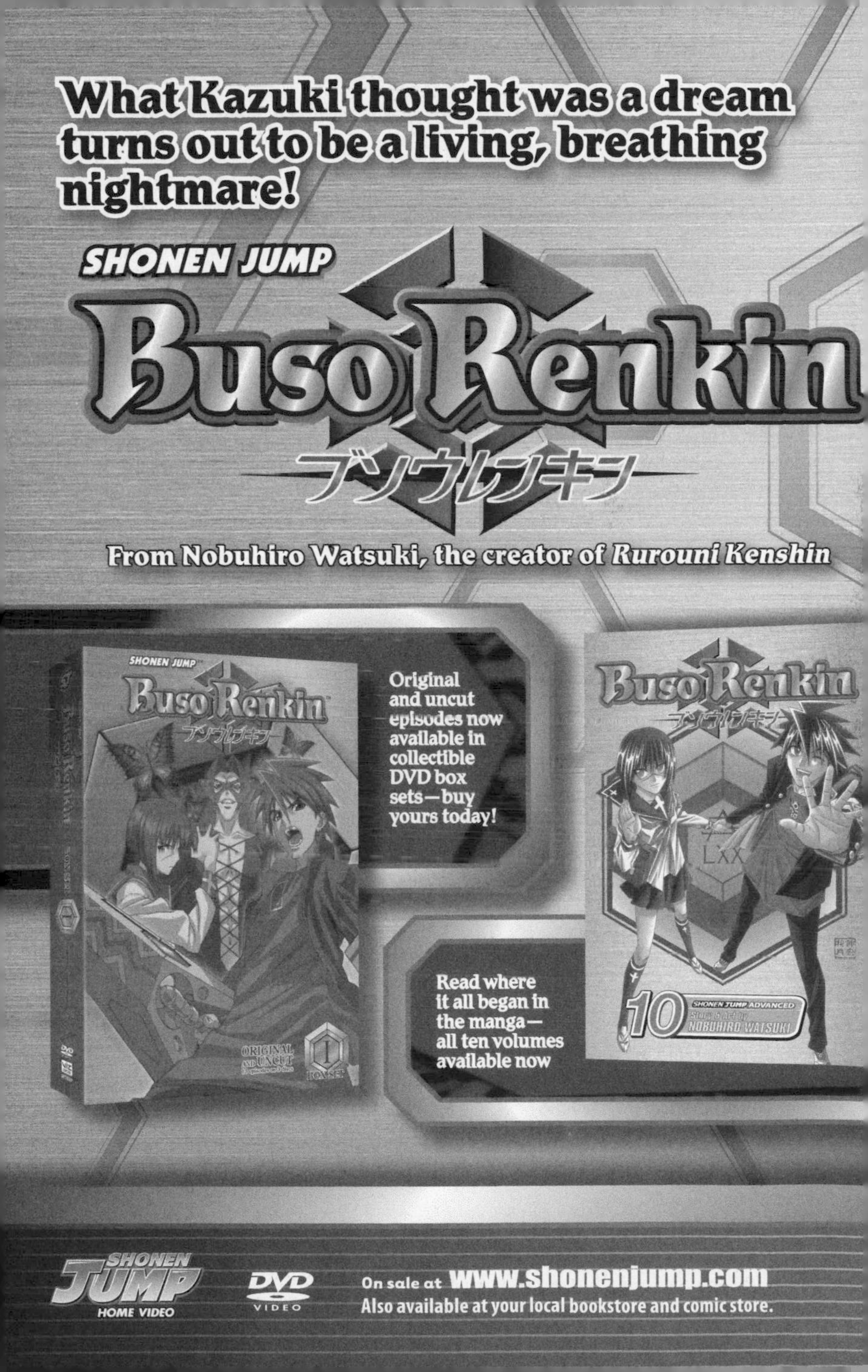

What Kazuki thought was a dream turns out to be a living, breathing nightmare!
SHONEN JUMP
Buso Renkin
ブソウレンキン
From Nobuhiro Watsuki, the creator of Rurouni Kenshin
SHONEN JUMP
Buso Renkin
ブソウレンキン
ORIGINAL AND UNCUT
1
BOX SET
Original and uncut episodes now available in collectible DVD box sets—buy yours today!
Buso Renkin
ブソウレンキン
10
SHONEN JUMP ADVANCED
Story & Art by
NOBUHIRO WATSUKI
Read where it all began in the manga—all ten volumes available now
SHONEN JUMP HOME VIDEO
DVD VIDEO
On sale at www.shonenjump.com
Also available at your local bookstore and comic store.